The Science of Vocal Pedagogy

The Science of Vocal Pedagogy

THEORY AND APPLICATION

D. Ralph Appelman

Professor of Voice
and Director, Institute of Vocal Research
School of Music, Indiana University

BLOOMINGTON *Indiana University Press* LONDON

Library of Congress catalog card number: 67-10107
ISBN 0-253-35110-3

Published in Canada by Fitzhenry & Whiteside Limited, Don Mills, Ontario
Manufactured in the United States of America

4 5 6 7 80 79 78 77 76

To my students

who have taught me

how to teach

Acknowledgments

For their encouragement and advice in assembling much of the material upon which this book is based I express my sincere appreciation to John A. Campbell, chairman, Department of Radiology, Indiana University; Earl D. Schubert, director of postdoctoral linguistics research, Stanford University; Fred W. Householder, research professor of classics and linguistics, Indiana University.

For their reading of the manuscript and for their most valuable suggestions I am indebted to Julius Huehn, chairman, Voice Department, Eastman School of Music, and Harvey Ringle, editor, *NATS Bulletin*.

I am deeply indebted to John W. Ashton, presiding officer, School of Letters, and University professor of English and folklore (formerly Vice-president for graduate development and dean of the Graduate School) and to Lynne L. Merritt, vice-president for research and dean of advanced studies, whose sincere efforts enabled me to carry out sequential research projects under the Grant-in-Aid Fund at the Indiana University Medical Center and at the University of Michigan Department of Linguistics and Communications. This fund also enabled me to secure sophisticated electronic instruments for the analyses and verification of linguistic theories applied to song.

I wish to thank also Phyllis Miller for her excellent drawings of anatomical structures; Flore Wend, soprano; Lila Stuart, soprano; Elizabeth Manion, mezzo soprano; J. Loren Jones, tenor; Ernest Vrenios, tenor; Jorge Gardos, violinist; Carol Jewell, violinist; Manuel Diaz, violinist; and Warner Seige, cellist, for their dedicated service in preparing the recordings which supplement this book.

To the numerous authors in the United States and Europe, particularly those of the Bell Telephone Laboratories whose illustrations have served to edify the chapters of this work, I owe much.

The theories of phonetic standardization and vowel migration and the application of these theories to song are my own and for them I accept full responsibility.

Preface

This book has been written for the student or teacher of voice in the college or private studio, and it has four objectives. The first is to intentionally and directly train the singer's aural awareness of his utterance of the word in song. The second is to describe the scientific theories of vocal pedagogy in a simplified and direct manner. The third is to suggest a phonetic system of teaching voice based upon the International Phonetic Alphabet (IPA). The fourth is to offer an acoustic model of phonemic utterance that may be accepted as a standard of imitation.

The first objective—to intentionally and directly train the singer's aural awarensss of his vocal utterance of the word—is the underlying thought within the chapters of this book. The pedagogy of this aural training is based upon two stable principles: that no disciplined phonation in song can be consummated unless it is aurally controlled and that voice training depends upon sensations developed through imitations of the sung sound aurally conceived.

The aural training is directed toward the development of the singer's "phonemic awareness" and not toward the development of his "vocal timbre." This training is based upon the empirical assumption that if the singer concentrates upon the timbre of the sung sound he frequently impairs and often destroys the integrity of the vowel. If he concentrates upon the phoneme he selects the appropriate timbre to match his intent. (See p. 232.)

The second objective—the description of the scientific theories of vocal pedagogy—is dealt with in the first four chapters of the book.

In this profession it is possible for a person to sing expertly without knowing why or how he does so. Refined physical and mental coordination is an athletic art, and most expert singers possess this coordination naturally. To such singers, the pedagogical theory in Part One, Chapters One through Five, may be less interesting. However, Part Two, Chapters Six through Eleven, is directed toward perfection in vocal performance and is written for everyone who performs publicly.

Courses in vocal pedagogy that are directed toward training teachers of formal disciplined song cannot be built upon the instinctive response of an individual to a singing situation. Therefore, all of the chapters in this book will best serve the student who intends to teach voice, institutionally or privately, by providing for him a physiological and phonetic approach to the act of singing. This scientific information will supply him with a diagnostic tool that, with maturation, will merge with psychological techniques. With the accompanying audio-visual tools, it will provide the experienced teacher with new methods of teaching the difficult processes of phonation, respiration, resonation, and articulation.

It will also serve the teacher or student who faces the arduous task of assembling and interpreting sounds of speech to conform to a similar utterance in song. The person who conducts such research invariably finds that speech sounds and sung sounds are by no means identical and that voice production problems within these two areas are quite different. In the speech act the word is all important, but communication in speech gives a leniency to nuance. In the singing act the word, the musical pitch, and the duration of the sound are synthesized and the singer is subservient to them. Therefore, the basic design of this book is directed toward bridging the gulf between the spoken word, which is familiar to the student as a communication tool, and the sung word, which is unfamiliar to him as a vehicle for aesthetic expression. Such bridging needs scientific implementation and must be presented dramatically if teaching techniques are to be taught properly. Information concerning the sung word and the analysis of many problems pertinent to each subject area are illustrated by both visual and recorded example.

The third objective—to suggest a system of vocal pedagogy based upon the International Phonetic Alphabet—embraces Chapters Six through Eleven. It has been designed to serve as a complete textbook for English diction. When the phonemic principles introduced within this volume are applied to individual performance of songs in a class-audience situation, textual intelligibility is not left to chance, it becomes the result of a logical design.

The singer's only commodity is sound, and the vehicle for sound is the vowel. Therefore, the greater portion of this book is based upon an analysis of each phoneme and its migration within the singer's vocal range of pitch and tonal intensity. A knowledge of phonetics is indispensable for an understanding of this work. Phonetics is a neutral tool in that it is adaptable to any method, be it precise or varied, and it is international in its functional utility.

The IPA provides an objective stability necessary for the analysis of speech sounds used in song, and the development of subject material Part Two is directed toward the establishment of phonemic concepts which are stable, permanent, and demonstrable. Such concepts endow teaching with objective evidence rather than subjective opinion. They also enable the teacher to link theoretical concepts with practical concepts—the scientific with the aesthetic—for, to each student, the word must eventually become beloved.

No attempt has been made in this book to analyze the phonemic character of the vowel aesthetically or to suggest preferred sounds. Quality judgments in song are a studio problem, and within this important dimension, the teacher's directive and preference must be respected.

The fourth objective—establishment of an acoustic model of phonemic utterance that may be accepted as a standard for imitation—is based upon the psychophysical observation that what most teachers of voice hear as a change in vowel color is actually a migration of the phoneme, that the indiscriminate application of phonemic accuracy and misconception of vowel migration* are major causes of poor textual intelligibility by the singer who must perform in a large auditorium or with instrumental masking. Such diction defects may be corrected by developing phonemic accuracy in the sung sound. To develop such accuracy, the model vowels have been designed by the author to serve as a standard sound by which the singer may compare all other vowel sounds at any pitch level or intensity. These acoustic vowels have been named the basic vowel and the quality alternate vowel.

These phonemes have been modeled after the Jones cardinal vowel. They are not intended to be preferred sounds but have been acoustically "placed" by experiment to provide a "home base" from which all vowel migration may occur and to establish phonemic accuracy. The location of these vowels upon a formant chart is the result of many years of research devoted to analyzing the sung phoneme in various pitch areas. Careful consideration was given to the physiological changes accompanying each vowel migration. The results of the research are to be found in the basic and quality alternate vowels, Fig. 101, p. 240, the Vowel Migration Chart, Fig. 103, p. 234, and also in the radiographs that form the kinesiologic analysis of Chapter Ten. Tools of interpretation are needed to fully understand and apply the exact position of these phonemes in their dynamic vocal environment. Such tools are presented visually in the book and as sound on records supplementing the book so that both voice teacher and student may more readily interpret them. They are the vowel formant and its movement within the sung sound; the formant chart; vowel migration and the migration chart; cavity-coupling laws and cavity-coupling; the laws of cavity resonators and their relationship to lip-rounding, lip-spreading, tongue-fronting, and tongue-backing. Such tools have been used by phoneticians for the analysis of vowels for many years, but rarely has the voice teacher used them as they are presented in this book. Here they are used as a means of vowel placement in three pitch levels and as a tool for interpretive vowel migration within the art song. A thorough understanding of these acoustic tools brings to the singer an intelligibility of text that is most rewarding.

Much of the voice science information found in acoustical and anatomical texts is not pertinent to the act of singing. Contemporary writings by biolinguists and bioacousticians are not directed to the voice teacher or the college student, whose scientific vocabulary is inadequate for interpreting complex scientific terminology. Such writing best serves university doctoral candidates in voice science.

Such a work as this should serve all methods of voice culture, implementing all of them with audio-visual tools so that both student and teacher may visualize the physiological act of singing and use such an

* Vowel modification and vowel migration are synonymous in usage but varied in concept. In singing both are controlled by auditory feedback. For a detailed explanation of the differences between vowel modification and phonemic migration, see p. 222.

act as a point of departure for their own methods or tonal preferences.

No text of voice culture or diction would be completely useful without audio-visual materials; therefore, this work has been supplemented with numerous illustrations and with recordings that will serve as guides to clarify various vocal techniques advanced with each chapter. Such audio implements are not available for any of the texts on voice culture or diction presently used by the vocal profession. Within such texts, a gulf separates the written and the spoken or sung word; this gulf has long been the underlying cause of a misinterpretation of the physiological vocal positions that this work purports to establish. Such ambiguity of the written word results from the fact that research evidence (anatomical and acoustical) is unavailable to both author and reader, and vocal misinterpretations often arise from a misunderstanding of a written phrase.

Singing is a demonstrable art, and its pedagogy has long depended upon illustrative sound for interpretation of conceptual problems related to the complex act of singing. An audio-visual text presents both physiological and acoustical evidence of each sound uttered by the singer that is related to phonation (basic tonal production), respiration (breath support in song), resonation (the placement, focus, and point of vocalic sound), and articulation (the physiological analysis of the vocalized sound within a spatial environment).

The proper way to use this book as a teaching tool is to present each chapter in sequence. This method is preferred because concepts are developed progressively from chapter to chapter. For example, suggestions for coordinating respiration (Chapter Two) with phonation (Chapter Three), a most important and difficult phase of voice teaching, are to be found in Chapter Three. Neither student nor teacher will fully understand Chapters Nine and Ten without first having understood the previous chapters. The need for studying the chapters in sequence was demonstrated during use of the manuscript by the author in classes in vocal pedagogy at the doctoral level at Indiana University School of Music.

The Science of Vocal Pedagogy is designed to be used as a textbook. The material in it is used as a two-semester course of study. Part One, "Theory," is used during the first semester for undergraduate as well as graduate courses. Part Two, "Application," is used during the second semester in graduate courses in which studio techniques are developed as each class member teaches a high school student. Part Two also comprises the core of the drill material for a one-semester course of English diction. In this class each student must memorize the two songs in Appendix One, and sing them from a stage. Each song is recorded by two microphones, one placed in front of the singer, the other at midpoint in the auditorium. Evaluations of diction are made from the remote microphone. The criteria of intelligibility is the Evaluation Chart of Appendix One.

Contents

Part II: APPLICATION

TABLES

The following five records are available to supplement the text:

1. Soprano
2. Alto
3. Tenor
4. Bass

(Records 1-4 are identical in content; they include vocal examples of pedagogical principles established throughout the text, and the drill materials in Chapter Ten.)

5. Prosodic elements of interpretation for teaching diction (Verification in song material of the pedagogical principles—includes soprano, alto, tenor, and bass.)

THE SCIENCE OF VOCAL PEDAGOGY

Part I: THEORY

Chapter 1

Vocal Pedagogy and Voice Teaching

> Pedagogy: The art, practice, or profession of teaching; esp., the systemized learning or instruction concerning principles and methods of teaching.—WEBSTER.

In considering this definition of pedagogy in relation to the profession of vocal teaching, most controversies which arise within the profession seem to pivot on the word *systematized*. The respected right of the vocal teacher is, and has been for centuries, complete freedom of thought regarding the choice of teaching philosophy and freedom of utterance regarding interpretation of such a philosophy.

The idea of teaching voice as a standardized system is abhorrent to all who teach the vocal art. The author does not suggest that voice teaching become a system, for the greater part of the singing experience is aesthetic in nature. Although aesthetic experiences and concepts embrace order, they defy the systems of obtaining that order. He does suggest, however, that certain areas of vocal instruction are not aesthetic in nature and that teaching within these areas demands an orderly presentation of fact, rather than opinion.

Vocal pedagogy by necessity is both aesthetic and scientific; its scientific entity is distilled from the pure sciences of mathematics, acoustics, linguistics, and anatomy, so that it may offer immediate utility to an uninformed laity. Within this book, acoustical and physiological evidence has been assembled from the reservoirs of speech and medical research and is so documented.

For its structural stability, vocal pedagogy depends upon scientific evidence scientifically expressed. Singers and teachers who interpret the act of singing as wholly aesthetic find it difficult to accept scientific terminology, for it is hard to abandon the feeling that the unfamiliar is absurd and illogical. Yet science and the art of singing are wholly compatible, for science supplies the vocal art with the stable semantic implement of phonetics, and its use must be perfected through a well-ordered educational process. This view of compatibilty is not yet completely embraced by the institutional or private voice teacher. However, this book is directed toward the realization of that end.

Vocal pedagogy is not an analysis of anatomical and physical phenomena; rather, it is an analysis of a complex psychophysical vocal act. An example of the complexity of such a process is evidenced in the following diagram which represents the firing order or sequence of decisions a singer must make at the precise second at which he utters all sounds within the flowing text of his song. Each of the following subdivisions involves ideas, concepts, images, and feelings necessary to the production of the vocal sound. The singer must first:

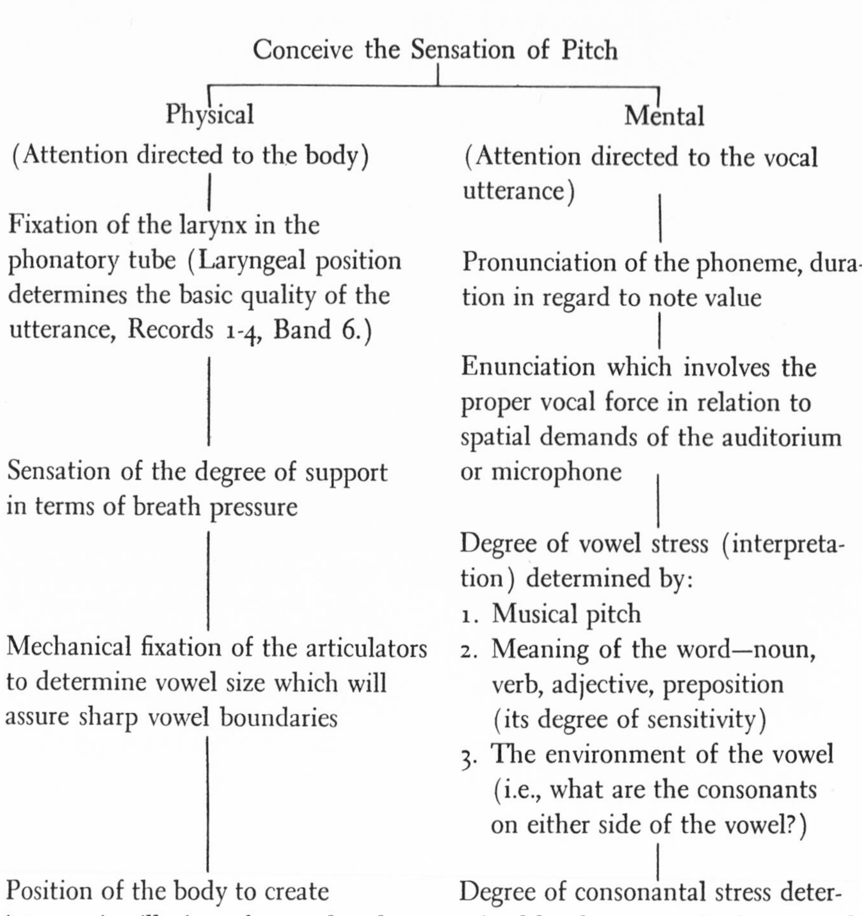

Conceive the Sensation of Pitch
Physical
(Attention directed to the body)
Fixation of the larynx in the phonatory tube (Laryngeal position determines the basic quality of the utterance, Records 1-4, Band 6.)
Sensation of the degree of support in terms of breath pressure
Mechanical fixation of the articulators to determine vowel size which will assure sharp vowel boundaries
Position of the body to create interpretive illusion of textual and musical demands
Mental
(Attention directed to the vocal utterance)
Pronunciation of the phoneme, duration in regard to note value
Enunciation which involves the proper vocal force in relation to spatial demands of the auditorium or microphone
Degree of vowel stress (interpretation) determined by:
1. Musical pitch
2. Meaning of the word—noun, verb, adjective, preposition (its degree of sensitivity)
3. The environment of the vowel (i.e., what are the consonants on either side of the vowel?)
Degree of consonantal stress determined by the same criteria as vowel stress

Collegiate courses of vocal pedagogy have greatly increased in number within schools and departments of music during the past decade. Doctoral degrees in vocal pedagogy are granted currently by four major universities. Most courses of vocal pedagogy are offered at the graduate level in other colleges, but many courses that are basically acoustical and physiological appear in undergraduate curricula. The teacher of these courses is faced with the problem of determining how much science, mathematics, and anatomy to include within a vocal pedagogy course for voice majors seeking a music degree. The answer to this question is to include only such acoustic, linguistic, and physiological facts as will be directly applicable and meaningful as studio tools for vocal diagnosis, or to provide the singer with transferable, factual information that will aid him in his interpretation and performance in song. The author has attempted to stay within the bounds of reality and practicality regarding the scientific and physiological background necessary in the development of the prospective voice teacher and performer. Necessarily, he has reinterpreted contemporary linguistic, acoustic, and anatomical evidence and divided it into practical units directly applicable to the singing act.

Linking Scientific Fact with the Art of Vocalization

Vocal pedagogy cannot survive as an independent educational entity if the physiological and physical facts which comprise its core remain subjects of sciolism (superficial knowledge). Researchers must constantly interpret these scientific facts so that they may become realistic pedagogical tools which may be employed by future teachers of voice.

An implement used to form a bridge between scientific fact and the art of vocalization must be both objective and subjective in nature, it must have stability and permanence, it must be universally employed in the singing act, and it must be adaptable to all conditions of research.

The word is such an implement. It possesses all of the attributes mentioned. It is objective, for it rests upon the solid science of phonetics; subjective, because it conveys the personal intimacy of meaning which is expressed through stress. The word is stable for it can change only as the social order changes; permanent, for life is dependent upon linguistic communication. The word possesses musical universality, for man must express the meaning of his song through the use of meaningful symbols.

Although song is intensified speech, the word as the information bearing element of speech conveys more meaning than the music for which it was written. Words, then, become the logical implement for scientific investigation and aesthetic interpretation.

In song, the word possesses the primary meaning of the utterance. When two settings of the same text by different composers are compared, one composer may have added a greater or lesser stylistic or emotional dimension to the meaning but the information bearing elements of the word remain unchanged.

All sensory illusion is conceived and expressed through words; thus, most cues for the interpretation of the meaning are embodied within the word. The musical structure surrounding that word may or may not exalt its meaning by suggesting a manner in which the word should be sung. When it does, the intent of the word is revealed to the singer through music cues, but most often the intent has to be designed by the singer and the sung text will then reveal the limits of the singer's intellectual and emotional experiences.

An instance in which interpretive cues of meaning are obtained from the text is illustrated in the song, "Widmung" by Robert Schumann, Measures 25 and 26, Record 5, Bands 7, 9, 11, and 13. Directives for the interpretation of the phrase, "Du hebst mich liebend uber mich," are a retardando and a piano. When this passage is sung the voice must possess a tremulous emotional vitality to convey the full intent of the singer's grateful adoration. The music supplies no directive of interpretation. The real cues for intent lie within the words and the singer must search the depth of his emotional experience for the expression of this most personal utterance.

The musical element has a tendency to disturb the structure of the word. For this reason the singer should make every attempt to preserve the word structure within the musical framework. To state this principle another way, to control the vowel is to control the function of the vocal utterance.

VOCAL PEDAGOGY AND THE PREPARATION OF TEACHERS OF SINGING

When the college administrator faces the problem of employing a prospective voice teacher, he uses a music yardstick of evaluation which varies with his need and environment. For this reason academic administrators are divided into two well-defined groups.

One group accepts the professional singer as a standard. Members of this group believe that singing, or the act of singing, should be taught as a terminal skill, that a well-developed singing ability is the complete goal because singing requires public performance and public acceptance of the singer's art. These administrators also believe that successful performers know more about this performing art than anyone else and that they will bring to their students the wealth of vocal knowledge gained through concert experience and private study.

The second group of administrators does not accept the professional singer as a standard. This group believes that the professional singer is apt to be a self-centered individual whose total effort in study has been spent in developing himself within the framework of his vocal problems. They realize that constant effort was necessary to bring his vocal skill to such a high degree of proficiency and that this effort has deprived him of the breadth of social awareness that is gained through the study of academic subjects so necessary in teacher training. They believe that this deprivation of social awareness will prevent him from seeing the "whole picture" when it comes to guiding a student toward a life goal, or in solving complex abstract, social, and personal life problems. They believe that the professional singer is apt to guide the student toward the study of voice as a terminal art with only one goal—the ability to sing well.

At first sight, the two groups seem to be divided on whether to choose teachers who know their subjects or teachers who know how to teach. The real problems are far more complex, and they include disagreement about the purpose and nature of vocal education.

Two facts are obvious. First, every voice teacher should know his subject, but a liberal vocal educator goes far beyond the subject he is to teach. Second, every teacher of voice uses some system or method, but how and where these systems are best learned or acquired is debatable. At best, methods constitute a small part of the professional education of voice teachers.

The qualities that comprise excellence in teaching voice are not well understood. What makes the superb voice teacher? He may well possess qualities which are not easily altered by any college program that leads to an academic degree. Good voice teachers should be used wherever they are found, and voice teaching should be an open rather than a closed profession because, at present, no prescribed college program can assure teaching competence in the studio or in the classroom.

Some superb voice teachers have never been exposed to a professional course of education; others have never seen the interior of a liberal arts college. However, professional courses within educational institutions cannot be built upon such isolated cases. The majority of voice students, both the musical geniuses and those less musical, will benefit from a well-balanced program of preparation for teaching that includes a broad liberal arts education, scholarly knowledge of the subject he intends to teach extended by performance skills, and on-the-job teaching under competent supervision.

Scholarly knowledge means different things in different fields. To a voice teacher, it means the development of vocal proficiency and a thorough knowledge of the physiology of his instrument and its use within a teaching environment. It also means acquiring a liberal education that goes far beyond the task of teaching a person how to sing, for he must see his student clearly and interpret him and his life goals in the light of his endowment, his learning capacity, his sensitivity to text, and his intellect.

In all, scholarly knowledge means more than a collection of facts; it requires a grasp of an intellectual discipline. As an example, the understanding of vocal literature means much more than just a collection of facts about musical literature itself. It involves the complexities of profound texts, as well as the tessitura, vocal proficiency, and the intelligence of the performer.

Although scholarship is essential to good voice teaching, a scholar is not always a good voice teacher even in dealing with mature college students. The scholar is apt to possess less vocal ability than the performer and, because of this deficiency, to demand a lower standard of musical utterance for his student. The scholar may not possess the enthusiastic assurance that the performer radiates—a quality that helps to make him a successful teacher.

No matter how hard one tries to reconcile scholarship and performance, one must admit that the major quest of every voice student is, "How can I learn to sing properly?" This book suggests a positive design for a training procedure that will provide a scholarly, musical climate in which the student may achieve the greatest possible musical accomplishment within the social and cultural domains of Western civilization and, in the process, acquire the tools for teaching such a procedure.

Chapter 2

Respiration

All artful singing is conceptual. A singer cannot possibly sing a pitch knowingly without first conceiving it as sensation. Equally a singer cannot establish a controlled vocal quality or control variations in intensity, without first conceiving these elements as sensations.

SINGING DEFINED

Psychophysically, artful singing is the dynamic (ever changing) act of coordinating instantaneously the physical sensations of respiration (the will to breathe), phonation (the will to utter a sound), resonation (the will to form a particular vowel position), and articulation (the will to communicate by forming both vowel and consonant) into a disciplined utterance.

Such a definition is confined to psychophysical terms because no aesthetic definition of singing is acceptable to everyone. Rightly so, for man interprets his song within the boundary of his own life experience, and the multiplicity of variation within human conduct causes one person to deny the beauty of song, another to embrace it. Yet all men can sing within limits of their own emotional sensations, and for this reason, song has become universal.

Some song is primitive, some has reached the level of an art form. The definition stated above refers only to the rigorous disciplines demanded of the art song as expressed by the contemporary recitalist and the manner in which various conceptual and physical forces are exerted under the organ of sound.

An objective of a singer is to develop an acceptable technique that depends upon a sensation experience learned from an active vocal process which involves the psychophysical acts of respiration, phonation, resonation, and articulation.

In considering the instrument to which such disciplines are applied, one is aware that the total body is involved in the singing process and that each bodily force depends upon the others in the complex act of supporting the laryngeal sound.

BREATHING FOR SINGING

"The mechanics of breathing is a problem requiring, on one hand, the detailed knowledge of the classical anatomist and, on the other, the analytical understanding of an engineer."[1] The profundity of this statement is realized by those who have attempted to analyze, by scholarly research methods, the nature and functions of the respiratory act in song. So complex are the muscular controls of breathing, so minute are their effects when expiration is linked with phonation that a reconciliation of these forces in song has defied accurate physiological description.

Students of voice learn varied processes of the act of breathing that have their origins in the masters of the golden age of song. Teachers speak positively of the breathing process in song, but at best, their directions are more personal than factual because experimental evidence on breath control for singing is not available to them.

The body of knowledge known as voice science has yielded vital information on breathing for speech that provides a firm point of departure for teaching breathing for singing. Yet a variety of social and musical demands separates the speech act and the singing act. Muscle group actions are more varied and complex in singing than in speech because the duration of the sound and changes in frequency and intensity place additional demands upon the antagonist muscles of respiration. (See "Point of Suspension," p. 11.)

The voice student cannot conceivably be compelled to know the anatomy of the respiratory system with the thoroughness of the classical anatomist. The teacher of voice is interested primarily in those muscle group actions that involve expiration during the singing act and secondarily in those which involve inspiration. *The intercostal lift, the abdominal tuck*, and *the feeling of support* are terms that are deeply imbedded in professional terminology and must be investigated during the vocal process of singing.

The physical analysis of muscular action in this book is limited to those activities that are significant in song and to those that will implement the studio experience of explaining the act of breathing by providing a factually correct terminology. For this reason, it concentrates, not on breathing for living, but on breathing for singing.

Some knowledge of anatomy is indispensable for a complete understanding and diagnosis of inspiration and expiration problems in song. The muscles and skeletal structure of the body that provide the necessary leverage for support of and resistance to the breath pressure are the author's only consideration. Within this chapter he hopes to reconcile these physiological concepts and physiological systems.

Support in Singing

Support is the act of constantly sustaining the vocalized sound with the breath pressure. It is realized only when expiration is instantaneously coordinated with phonation. The onset of attack is soft, not hard.

To explain it in other terms used by the profession, it is the sensation of always being "under the tone with a low muscular effort"; it is the sensation of "singing on the breath"; it is the sensation of "establishing an abdominal muscular effort coordinated with the vocalized sound." The inexperienced singer constantly fails to maintain such a connection during intervallic change and more often in diatonic passages where the vowel is altered. In the words of the definition, he fails to sustain the vocalized sound with the breath pressure.

This definition suggests that the objectives of support are as follows:

1. To unify and coordinate the forces of expiration and phonation through action in song by establishing the sensation of a point of suspension through direct action of the abdominal musculature and by using an antagonist musculature in the phonatory effort.
2. To provide the motor activity or driving forces for the production of unwavering sound during phonation by employing the strong muscles of the body.
3. To provide for an ample supply of breath, always allowing for adequate reserve.
4. To relieve all undue tensions of the musculature of the neck and throat.

To understand and apply this definition of support in the singing act, one needs to examine several types of breathing employed by students of singing. Also, one must understand that breathing for singing is always controlled or stabilized expiration; it is not passive as is breathing for living.

The Point of Suspension

The point of suspension is the body sensation created by a balanced pressure of the thoracic muscles of inspiration opposed by the abdominal muscles of expiration.

Such a state of balanced suspension may be illustrated by pressing the palms of the hands together, and increasing the pressure of each hand against the other. The hands do not move because the pressures exerted are equal.

In singing, the driving force of the abdominal musculature often exceeds the resisting force of the thoracic muscles, and controls are lost. Ideally, the entire scale should be sung on the point of suspension where thoracic and abdominal pressures are balanced. Such a condition assures complete control of intensities as well as changes of interval. The Italians, drilling constantly with the messa di voce, attempted to establish this sensation as a basic sensation for all singing. The wise singer will always use the point of suspension as a reference for correctly produced vocal sound.

Clavicular Breathing

This type of breathing is identified by a predominant expansion in the extreme upper chest accompanied by a raising of the shoulders and clavicles during inspiration. This strained physical position creates unsteadiness in the phonated sound and lack of control of pitch and intensity.

A steady descent of the clavicles during expiration is impossible, and unsteadiness within the sung sound is inevitable.

Clavicular breathing creates tensions of the neck and throat that directly affect the vocal resonance. With tension present, the pharynx is less subject to direct control, and the larynx tends to be held at a high position. The singer, lacking an adequate breath supply, is forced to breathe more frequently; thus, he is unable to sustain long phrases, and his general musical utterance suffers.

Thoracic Breathing

Often identified as rib or costal breathing, this type of breathing is characterized by an increase in the transverse dimensions of the thoracic cage, as the singer concentrates on the act of holding the ribs expanded laterally after inspiration. The concept of thoracic breathing depends more upon the singer's thought being directed toward the action of the intercostal muscles and rib-raisers for expiration than upon the action of the lower abdominal musculature. Steadiness of the phonated sound cannot be achieved by this method when it is used as a teaching device. The value of thoracic exhalation is erroneous. "Except for the transverse thoracis [Fig. 15], there is no thoracic musculature of exhalation."[2]

Abdominal Breathing

During expiration the abdominal muscles and strong muscles of the back (Figs. 12-15) act as a sphincter* to thrust the abdominal viscera upward into the domes of the diaphragm, which is in a state of flexible tension during

* A sphincter muscle is one used to close a circle; muscular exertion is applied equally throughout its circumference.

phonation since the muscles of the diaphragm are muscles of inspiration, not expiration. The state of suspended resistance during phonation is provided by the muscles of inspiration, which are now antagonist muscles holding against the force exerted by the abdominal musculature causing the upward thrust of the viscera. "Mechanically speaking, the direct downward pull on the thoracic cage by the antagonist muscles of inspiration firms the skeletal walls of the thorax. The inward pressure of the anterioabdominal musculature forces the viscera and the diaphragm upward."[3] This action applies a steady uninterrupted flow of breath pressure against the vocal folds; this pressure is most efficiently utilized when there is no undue tension in the neck and throat. This state of thoracic and abdominal muscular suspension is sustained during phonation in song and is recognized by the tension of the epigastrium (area below the sternum) and a normal expansion of the thoracic cage. "The anterolateral abdominal muscles are the only indisputable muscles of expiration and should be examined whenever the group behavior of the expiratory muscles is under consideration."[4]

The Dualistic Nature of Support

Support within artful singing demands coordination of the sensation of respiration with the sensations of phonation, resonation, and articulation. This feeling for a suspended, balanced musculature must be synthesized into a single act by the voice teacher who is able to conceive the whole sound as the sum of its parts and to direct the application of such a synthesis to fit the interpretive needs of the art song and aria.

Support in singing is dualistic in concept and performance. To become a successful performer and to achieve self-expression with technical eloquence in passages demanding rapid coloraturas, the singer must employ two remotely related physical sensations, each of which embodies a specific vocal technique.

The first technique of body control and support requires a sensation of abdominal pressure being countered by thoracic resistance in such a manner that the abdominal pressure is always greater than the resisting antagonist forces created by the muscles that comprise the rib-raiser group. (See p. 30.) If the tension of the abdominal and back muscles of expiration is to be increased considerably, the ribs must be held fixed against this abdominal pull so that equilibrium can be maintained. The muscular sensation of effort is felt above the belt line. The singer does not need to concentrate upon low tensions at the pubic arch. Such contractions of the pelvic diaphragm are automatic.

The ability of the singer to increase the abdominal effort at will is assurance that he is always sustaining the sound with the breath pressure. This sensation is one of complete abdominal control of the phonated sound while singing the pulsated scale, melismatic or bravura passages. In creating such an outgoing effort, the singer's attention is directed more toward controlling the sound in its forward movement than in restraining or controlling the breath stream (Records 1-4, Pulsated Drills Applied to Song Literature, Band 4).

The second technique of body control and support is one in which the singer releases the dominating pressure of the abdominal and back musculature and employs a balanced suspension of thoracic and abdominal muscular forces that enable him to sustain the quiet vocalized sound with apparent ease. The sensation of such action is one of resistance[5] or holding back the breath. The point of resistance or the point of suspension may be experienced by inhaling deeply and panting lightly during full inflation. (Notice the high chest and the lateral expansion of the thorax or rib cage.)

Chest Position

When the singer has taken a full breath and holds it in a state of suspension, the chest should be held high (a) to permit lateral expansion to occur in the lower ribs of the thoracic cage and (b) to permit the new breath to be taken instantaneously with very slight movement of the lower thoracic cage. This action makes the breath less noticeable and is the reason why the professional seems to breathe easily because he has developed the proper chest position to provide him with maximum breath and maximum control.

As a drill for sustaining a high chest position and developing a technique for quick inspiration of the breath, sing quietly the following scale pattern—

Exercise No. 10 *Concone*

Copyright by G. Schirmer

Do not interrupt rhythm at the breath point.

If the student is constantly reminded to keep the chest high, he will learn to recognize the physical sensation of resistance associated with body posture during the singing of restrained, quiet passages. In such a system, the resisting antagonist group of muscles becomes more tense and assists in providing an even flow of the breath in the utterance of the quiet sound. When these two muscular forces are in balanced suspension, a condition of equal pressure and resistance prevails, and a correct adjustment of the vocal folds and glottic aperture is the result. When this state of balanced suspension is disturbed, a marked change occurs in vocal quality.[6]

If tension is increased only upon the abdominal musculature, the vocal folds become tense and the glottic aperture becomes smaller. The tone then becomes "pushed" and soft sounds are impossible to achieve. If the tension is increased only upon the antagonist group, the adjustment of the vocal folds becomes more relaxed and the glottic aperture is enlarged. The phonated sound then becomes colorless and uninteresting. Arnold Rose suggests the following four significant concepts for the control of vocal force in song.

> To sing pianissimo, mezzo forte or fortissimo, the singer must realize that the control of the vocal force in singing is accompanied by:
> 1. A conceptual recognition of the amount of vocal force that is to be used.
> 2. An increase or decrease in the amplitude of the vocal fold vibration through an adjustment in the tensions of the respiratory muscles coordinated with the total laryngeal musculature.
> 3. An increase or a decrease in the size of the resonating system (the concept of vowel size).
> 4. By controlling the damping factor in the production of the vowel sound.[7]

When producing a pianissimo sound, the singer must first conceive the amount of vocal force he wishes to use since the pianissimo may be accomplished by varying the amplitude of the vibrator, by making the resonator more efficient, or by controlling the breath pressure.

The amplitude of the vocal fold vibration is controlled by the concept of the singer. All that he needs to do is to conceive a pianissimo sound and the folds will adjust themselves. However, the steady application of breath pressure and the size of the resonator, which affects the quality of the sound, must be deliberately controlled. To control both breath and resonation, a conscious effort must be made to supply additional breath volume without increasing abdominal tensions or disturbing the resistance of the antagonist group of muscles which comprise the rib-raiser group. The sensation is one of excessive abdominal support while holding the rib cage at a high position.

In singing pianissimo sounds, the damping of the high partials of the tonal spectrum is related to the flaccidity of the soft cavity walls and the size of the cavity. The singer finds it therefore, advantageous to relax the jaw, as in the beginning stages of the yawn, thus permitting the cavity walls to become more relaxed because such damping creates a change in vowel color rather than in intensity. This change in vowel color, or quality, creates the illusion of greater differences of volume than actually exist. (See "The Dissipation of Sound Energy—Damping," p. 118.) In applying damping, the experienced singer has an established concept of resonator control which has proven successful for him. Therefore, the position of the mandible, tongue, jaw, and larynx has developed into a familiar concept which has become automatic. Singing a pianissimo with the enlarged resonating system is always difficult for the beginning student, but he eventually must learn to form all words within this larger resonating form.

In singing mezzo forte, the natural, balanced mechanism of expiration and of resonating provides the correct breath pressure for all pitches.

When one is singing fortissimo, more breath is used than when singing pianissimo. The singer must not permit the breath to run freely; rather, he must hold back the breath to permit a proper balance to be created between the breath pressure and the laryngeal control. Again, this control is a conceptual one that involves the vowel and vocal quality.

The Case for Synthesis of Effort

The manner in which support is taught has always been a source of professional controversy. Breathing for singing is best taught when it is coordinated with the sung sound. To teach breathing as an isolated action is to delay the process of synthesis or coordination of phonation and respiration into a single dynamic utterance. Listed below are several physiological reasons why such a synthesis is advantageous:

1. Breathing for living requires complex muscular activity under many different conditions, which are more often passive than forceful; breathing for singing demands a constant uninterrupted flow of breath pressure coordinated with phonation under predetermined conditions.
2. Independent control of the muscles of expiration is impossible. Expiration within the singing act is a synthesized process involving some twenty-five or thirty muscles.
3. The muscular set employed in isolated breathing exercises is quite different from the muscular set used when expiration is coordinated with phonation.
4. Controlled expiration in song is basically conceptual. The singer grasps the idea of linkage of breath pressure and vocalized sound by experiencing the sensation of a particular physical effort; he will miss this experience if breathing is taught as an isolated act.

an ascending and descending five-tone scale as accurately as possible with the same pulsation pattern mastered on a single pitch. The descending five-tone scale will cause some trouble because the singer is constantly thinking in terms of up and down. As he starts the top tone of the scale, he invariably fails to sustain the sound with the breath pressure as he makes the turn into the descending pitch sequence. He fails to sustain a muscular condition of flexible tension that will enable him to control the regular pulsations at all times.

The cause of this failure is basically conceptual and may be remedied by first sustaining the condition of the successful ascending scale over a sloping pattern longer than that required to make the abrupt downward turn demanded by the five-tone ascending-descending scale. The visual imagery that will help the student grasp the problem quickly is this:

This pattern suggests the five-tone scale with an abrupt turn at the top. The pattern which appears below suggests a five-tone scale where the condition and sensation of ascending is sustained through five intervening notes and continued within the descending pattern.

With this concept, the singer reduces the ascending-descending pattern into a level pattern, and pursues the sound in exactly the same manner mastered in the single-pitch drill. Drilling the student on abrupt turns in scale patterns then becomes a simple task. The usual conditions of overexertion and overstressing will be present, but the suggestion of less effort will soon bring about the proper balance or equalization of the forces of expiration and phonation to produce a smooth even scale.

Goal 3 is the application of the same sensation of abdominal support to simple scale patterns with piano accompaniment after the diatonic scale has been mastered. The student should make every attempt to increase the speed and reduce the excessive stressing at each pitch change.

A series of basic exercises that demand the same body control as those described in the basic drills has been presented in *Library of Musical Classics: Thirty Daily Exercises* by Concone, Vol. 555 for low voice, Vol. 294 for high voice (published by G. Schirmer). Exercises 1 through 5 are diatonic and should prove to be no trouble if Goals 1 and 2 are mastered. Exercises 9 and 14 involve the problem of following the sound through pitch skips and alteration of the vocal pattern. Exercises 2, 4, 9, 10, and 14 are recorded on Record 1-4, Band 2.

The drills are based upon the definition of singing that provides the major premise for the writing of this book. Psychophysically, singing is the dynamic act of coordinating instantaneously the physical sensations of respiration, phonation, resonation, and articulation into a disciplined utterance.

Advantages of the Drills

The benefits of a planned muscular discipline are worth consideration:

1. The student cannot sing the drill material unless he is supporting the sound correctly, that is, unless he is coordinating phonation with expiration.
2. Each of the drills consists of a simple act that the student must perform for himself and that enables him to recognize the sensation of coordination.
3. These drills emphasize to the student the need for the developing conscious control of the abdominal musculature to provide a vitalized body action that must be coordinated with phonation in song.
4. Coordination is more quickly accomplished when the vowel sound is ignored. In these drills the neutral vowel [ʌ] as in *up* is used at early stages to encourage coordination. The problem of pointing, focusing, and clarifying the vowel is drilled after the student has coordinated expiration with phonation. Point, projection, and focus are problems of resonation that are basically aesthetic in nature and are based upon teacher preference of sound. Any teacher can bring refinement to a vowel sound provided the respiration problems are solved first.
5. The student is able to recognize the sensation of the pulsated sound when he is practicing away from the teacher's directives. He should have no question in his mind as to whether he is performing the right or wrong action; either he can do it or he cannot.
6. These drills may be omitted for those students who can perform them skillfully. Song materials that embody similar problems of execution may be substituted.

The drills may also be omitted for those students who, for reasons of poor coordination, cannot perform them at all. For such students velocity studies will always be difficult.

In teaching the physical actions associated with the pulsated drills and the concentrated scale exercises (Concone, Marchesi, Abt, etc.), the author has discovered that within a group of twenty voice students, ten are able to execute the drills skillfully when first introduced to them, five find them troublesome and must work on body coordination, and from three to five cannot comprehend the physical action necessary to sing them correctly and find the experience frustrating. Experienced singers with good voices often fall into the last group. Neither chronological age nor experience influences failure to perform the drills accurately, for a very young person who has never had a formal voice lesson may be able to do them perfectly at sight. Coordination of body and sound is an athletic task requiring an ability that varies with each individual singer.

Such a unification of forces involves a discipline of mind and body that many students find difficult to achieve because they do not possess the proper muscular coordination. This lack does not mean that they cannot sing. It does mean that such singers will be limited in their careers, that other vocal faults will emerge within their technique because they lack muscular coordination, and that a vast amount of vocal literature will be denied them because they are technically unable to sing it. The finest singers who attain professional stature usually possess this unification of breath pressure and phonation naturally, but a greater number of voice students must discover this body-voice relationship through thoughtful vocal exercise and guidance, for breathing for singing is a planned muscular discipline which can be learned by those who are dedicated. The full realization of this fact brings to us the thought that expert singing may well be within the reach of only those who, by gift of birth, have an ability to control and coordinate the musculature functions demanded by the singing act.

THE VIBRATO IN SONG

The vocal vibrato may be created by high laryngeal controls which are evident in the vertical movement of the thyroid cartilage. When such controls are employed, the singer is unable to regulate the vibrato rate and the frequency variation tends to exceed one-quarter step as the singer sings piano and one-half step when he sings forte. The vibrato gives the aspect of a tremulo to all sung sounds.

Correctly produced, the vocal vibrato is a vocal ornament that is directly related to the sensation of support. It is physiologically controlled by the muscles of respiration, and is thereby, basically, a respiratory function assisted by coordinated laryngeal controls. It is produced by minute alterations of body pressures which are reflected in undulations of the breath column. This variation in subglottic air pressure causes the pitch to rise and fall as the singer attempts to control the pitch by keeping the mass, length, and tension of the vocal folds constant. The rate at which the pitch fluctuates depends upon the balance of the suspended tension of two muscle groups, (a) the antagonist musculature of inspiration and the abdominal musculature of expiration and (b) the infrahyoid and the suprahyoid muscular groups for laryngeal stabilization. Studies made by the author in radiography and cinefluoroscopy reveal that this undulation is observable throughout the entire phonatory tube and its walls. The singer who does not sing with abdominal support is not able to control the vibrato rate. (An acceptable vibrato rate is between five and seven pulsations each second.) Variation of muscular control to increase or decrease the vibrato rate can be learned. This action is directly related to expiration; the breath pressure must be even and uninterrupted to produce an evenly undulated vibrato. Quick surges of the breath or sudden pressures and relaxations will bring to the sound an unevenness that is most unpleasant to the musically trained ear.

The variation of pitch should not exceed one-quarter of a tone from the center of the sung pitch. If the pitch variation approaches one half-step in the extent of its movement, the sung sound is usually offensive and creates the illusion of insecurity of pitch. Such an effect is usually accompanied by an uneven undulation, with the accent of the sound more pronounced above the center of pitch than below it. The unevenness is caused by excessive pressure of the abdominal musculature at stress points in the natural vibrato rate.

The excessively fast vibrato, which is similar to a bleat and lacks steady undulations, is usually caused by clavicular breathing and a failure to unify respiration with phonation through the use of abdominal musculature. A high laryngeal position is usually present during the singing of such sounds, and the vibrato rate cannot be controlled. A remedy for such a condition is the use of the preceding drills. A wise procedure is to start these drills at the natural vibrato rate, intensify it, and work toward a conscious awareness of the source of muscular exertion and thereby, enable the singer to sustain the sound with the breath. If the vibrato rate is fast and evenly undulated, the scale will be fast, but the pulsation rate can be slowed when need be through a slight relaxation of the abdominal musculature, which is exerting too much force. If the vibrato rate is slow, the scale will be slow, but the pulsation rate can be stepped up by increasing the tension of the supporting musculature.

Many singers and listeners do not hear the vibrato as a separate entity, but rather, they hear it as a total voice quality complex. Such performers do not consider the vibrato rate to be a factor of physical dysfunction in the singing act. The vibrato rates of their voices have been accepted as natural and, therefore, they have reasoned, unchangeable.

The natural vibrato rate and the natural body coordination of the individual have a direct relationship. This relationship is not permanently fixed or set and may be disciplined during the singing act. To assume that the vibrato rate should be constant is to say that the breath pressure should not vary regardless of the drama, intensity, or repose of the musical phrase.

More logically conceived, in the interpretation of emotional musical phrases the vibrato becomes a musical implement which rapidly throbs during the expression of great emotion and tranquilly undulates in the expression of repose. Such use of the vibrato is evident in Records 1-4, Band 3. To reiterate, a perfectly controlled vibrato rate is the result of a balanced musculature conceptually energized by the muscles of respiration (rib-raisers holding against the rib-depressors) assisted by specific laryngeal control, i.e., control of length, tension, and mass of the vocal folds.

THE ANATOMICAL SYSTEM AND MECHANICS OF RESPIRATION

The immediate concern of this chapter is with the respiratory act of breathing for singing. To understand respiration for singing, one must understand the human mechanism by which vocal sounds are produced; also, one must study the functioning of that mechanism in the light of the latest scientific information at hand.[8]

The Lungs

Although they cannot exert any force other than that provided by the elasticity of the tissue itself, the lungs are the primary organs of respiration. Their movement within the respiratory act depends wholly upon the pressures exerted on them by the surrounding musculature.

Each of the two lungs is divided into lobes (Fig. 1). The left lung has two lobes, the right three. In conformation, they follow the outline of the thoracic cage. The base of the lungs follows the conformation of the domes of the diaphragm.

The porous, spongy tissue of the lungs is made up of millions of tiny air sacs, called alveoli, through which oxygen is passed to the blood stream. During expiration the air is passed from the alveoli into larger sacs, the tabules, then to the bronchioles, to the bronchi, the trachea, and the mouth.

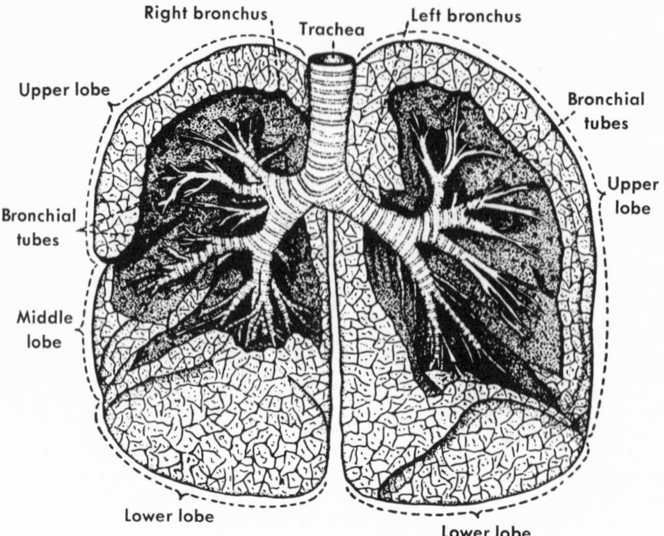

Fig. **1.** The Lungs

Source: Johannes Sobotta and Eduard Uhlenhuth, *Human Anatomy* (7th ed.; New York: Hafner Publishing Co., 1957).

The lungs are enclosed by a delicate membranous sac called the pleura. This enclosure makes the air pressure within the lungs very responsive to forces exerted upon it by the action of the thoracic cage and the abdominal diaphragm. When the pleura is ruptured, the lung collapses. (The pleura is often ruptured deliberately during surgery to repair the lung or to permit diseased areas of lung tissue to heal.)

Vital Capacity

Breathing for singing requires a full inflation of the lungs at each inhalation of breath. The amount of breath that can be taken in at each inspiration varies greatly. For men the average volume is approximately 225 cubic inches; for women the volume is 150 to 175 cubic inches. The amount of air that can be inhaled during maximal inspiration and expiration is called the vital capacity of that individual. Regardless of how hard one tries to expel the last bit of air from the lungs during the expiratory process, a volume of about 100 cubic inches always remains. It is called the residual air.

Despite the fact that some men have a vital capacity of 350 to 400 cubic inches of air and some women 250 to 275, research has proved that no correlation exists between vital capacity and tone quality nor between vocal force or phonation in speech.[9]

The amount of tidal (inhaled) air that passes through the vocal folds during phonation in song during one expiration has not been scientifically determined. Research in phonation for the speech act has revealed that 30 cubic inches of tidal air, or 13 percent of the total vital capacity, is used in a single respiratory cycle.[10] This volume of air is relatively small. The controlled utterance in song is always accomplished under the conditions of forced inspiration and expiration, and the singer is constantly adjusting to variations in pitch, vocal force, duration, and the resonating system for changes in quality or tonal effect. Therefore, the quantity of air used in song during one respiratory cycle may be higher than that required in speech; perhaps it may be as high as 100 cubic inches of tidal air or 54 percent of the vital capacity.

Increased vocal force in singing usually demands a greater expenditure of breath than that required of a sound sung mezzo forte. Increase in loudness, however, is also achieved through an adjustment of the resonating system, alteration of the surface of the cavity walls, and adjustment of the laryngeal musculature in a complex synthesized act. (See "Closed and Open Tones," p. 89.)

Statistics from studies of vital capacity in relation to the speech act[11] reveal that little or no correlation exists between a good or poor speaking voice and the vital capacity of an individual; the person who uses more breath in accomplishing the vocal task is not necessarily a better speaker, nor does he necessarily possess a better voice than that person who uses little breath in expiration. Breathiness of sound excepted, this concept may also be applied to the sung sound. Adequate and accurate research studies are needed to obtain precise information on the respiratory process in song.

The Framework of the Thorax

The thorax (chest cage) is made up of cartilages and bones (Fig. 2); it is covered with a delicate membrane called the pleura:

1. The sternum (breast bone) forms the front of the thoracic cage. Its top supports and articulates with the clavicles. Laterally, it is attached to and articulates with the costal cartilage of ribs one to seven. At the base of the sternum is the xiphoid process, a cartilaginous appendage that serves as a point of attachment for the abdominal musculature.
2. Twelve ribs on each side articulate with the sternum in front by means of the costal cartilages, and articulate at the thoracic vertebra by means of

movable facets that are stabilized by ligaments. The eleventh and twelfth ribs, which are not attached to the sternum, are called "floating" ribs.

3. The thoracic vertebra forms the posterior wall of the thorax.

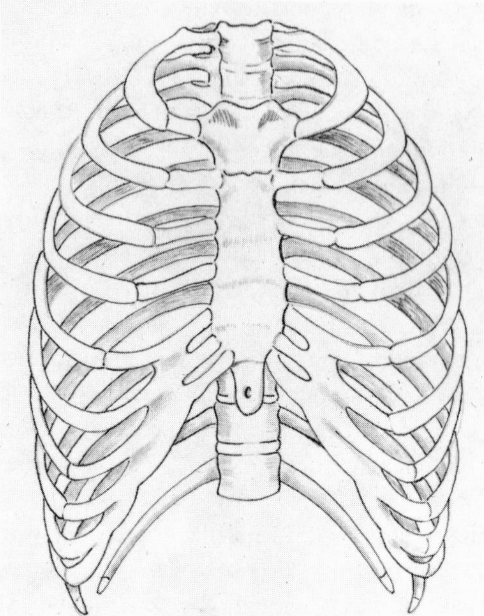

Fig. **2.** The Skeleton of the Thorax

Movement of the Thoracic Cage

Inspiration and expiration for living or for singing are wholly dependent upon the movements of the thoracic cage. During inspiration, the cage moves in three directions simultaneously: vertically, anteroposteriorly, and transversely. Atmospheric pressure of fifteen pounds per square inch at sea level is being exerted constantly upon the body. Differences between the outside air and the air within the respiratory system are constantly being adjusted by the cage movement. Any movement of the thoracic cage is followed by a corresponding movement of the lungs. If the thoracic cavity is enlarged by movement of the ribs, cartilages, and the diaphragm, the capacity of the pleural cavity increases. This act lowers the pressure within the lungs, and air rushes in from outside the body. As the capacity of the thoracic cage is decreased, the pleural cavity is put under pressure and the air is expelled.

The ribs are articulated to the vertebra by their facets and to the sternum by the costal cartilages in such a manner that, when they are lifted upward, the lateral dimension between the ribs on either side increases. This movement, which causes an increase in the transverse dimension of the thorax, is very much like that of raising a bucket handle. The anterior-posterior dimension between the sternum and the spinal column (Fig. 3) also increases. The increase in the vertical dimension of the thorax is caused by the descent of the diaphragm, which forms the floor of the thoracic cage.

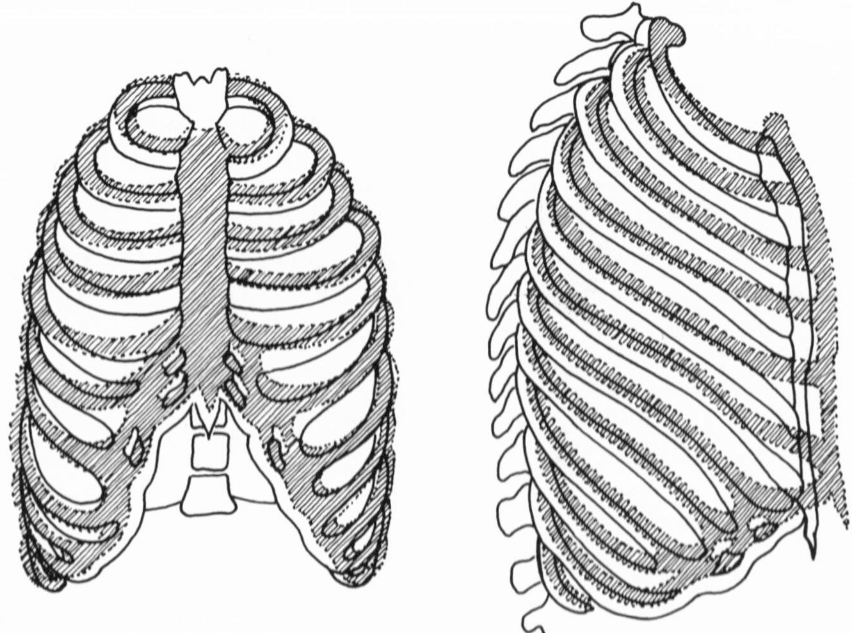

Fig. 3. Movement of the Thoracic Cage

Muscles are either striated (striped, skeletal, voluntary), e.g., pectoralis, or unstriated (smooth, organic, or involuntary), e.g., trachealis. The muscles of respiration are striated muscles. Every muscle is paired, each one has a mirrored homologue on the opposite side of the midline of the body. The only exception to this is the diaphragm. All striated muscle has an origin and an insertion. The origin is the fixed end, the insertion the movable end. Action will occur at the point of insertion of each muscle. The direction of pull is always toward the origin.

Every muscle, agonist, has its antagonist. When the agonist relaxes, the antagonist contracts and vice versa.

THE MUSCLES OF INSPIRATION

Inhalation can occur only when the air pressure within the lungs is less than the atmospheric pressure outside the body. The air then rushes into the lungs. To permit the air to enter, the pleural space within the thorax must be increased.

In addition to the muscles governing the descent of the diaphragm, other muscles of the thorax increase the pleural space and cause the air to enter the lungs. These muscles may be divided into rib-raisers and rib-depressors.

The action of each of the rib-raisers is to lift the ribs during the process of inspiration and to suspend this condition during the process of forced expiration of the breath in song. The rib-depressors serve as guying muscles and exert a downward pull on the ribs when the vertical fibers of the diaphragm contract, thus moving the lower border of the rib cage outward and upward during forced inspiration.

Rib-Raisers	*Rib-Depressors*
pelvic diaphragm	serratus posterior inferior
abdominal diaphragm	quadratus lumborum
pectoralis major	
pectoralis minor	
latissimus dorsi	
levatores costarum	

The Pelvic Diaphragm[12]

Two diaphragms are necessary to produce controlled inspiration and expiration in song. The pelvic and the abdominal diaphragm each have different functions. The pelvic diaphragm serves as a sling to support the compressed viscera during forced inhalation. Although it is somewhat stabilized during inspiration, it is more firmly stabilized during expiration (Fig. 4).

The pelvic diaphragm is formed by the paired muscles levator ani. Together they form a funnel-shaped muscular floor to the pelvic cavity and so support the visceral contents of the pelvis.

Origin—Each muscle originates along a line beginning in front of the inner side of the pubic arch. These most important fibers extend along the side wall of the pelvis as far back as the ischial spine.

Action—Each muscle acts as a fulcrum to support the viscera during respiration. The pelvic diaphragm need not be consciously controlled during the forced expiration in singing, for the will to expire forcefully causes it to become fixed simultaneously with the contraction of the abdominal muscles of expiration.

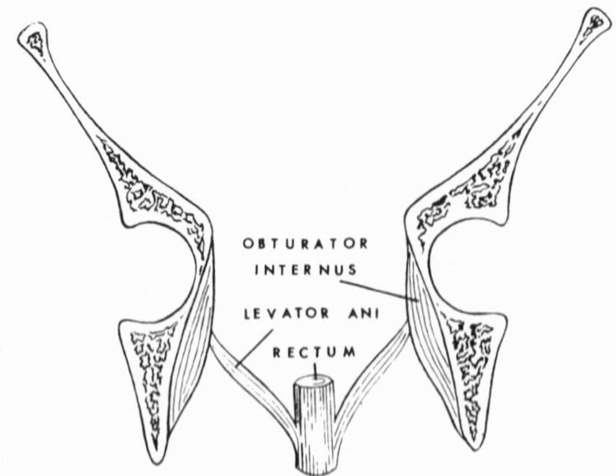

Fig. **4.** Pelvic Diaphragm
(after Cates-Basmajian)

The Abdominal Diaphragm[13]

Origin—The muscular fibers in the abdominal diaphragm are divided into three parts:

1. The vertebral, which arise as crura from the lumbar vertebra. Figs. 5A and 5B).
2. The costal, which arise from the costal margin.
3. The sternal, which arise from the xiphoid process (tip of the sternum).

Insertion—They all pass upward and converge on the central tendon.

Action—Contraction of all of the muscular fibers of the diaphragm draws the posterior part of the central tendon downward and forward, compressing the abdominal viscera. This action of lowering the floor of the thorax causes an increase in the vertical dimension of the pleural cavity and a sudden decrease in atmospheric pressure within the lungs; outside air then rushes in.

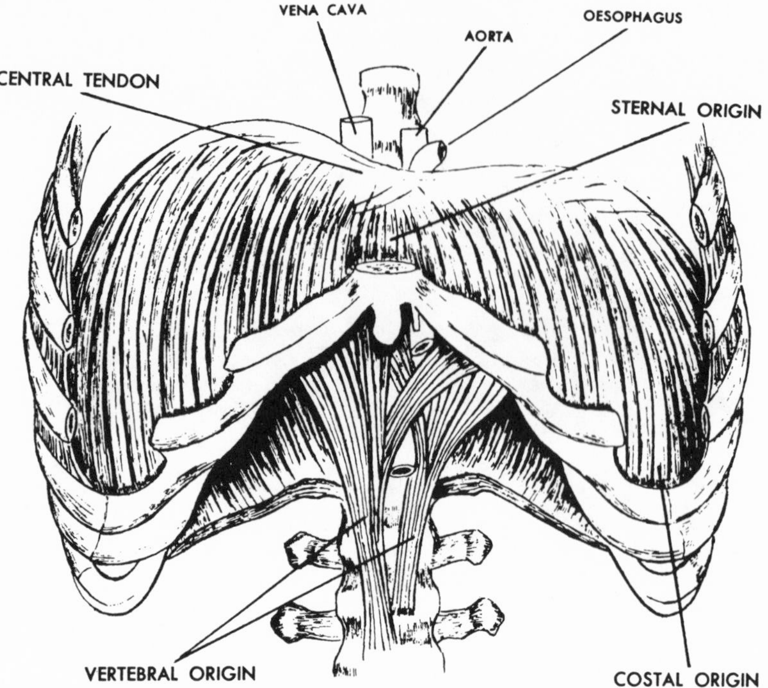

Fig. **5A.** Abdominal Diaphragm, Front View
Source: H. A. Cates and J. V. Basmajian, *Primary Anatomy* (Baltimore: Williams & Wilkins Co., 1955).

Contraction of the vertical muscular fibers of the diaphragm, that is, those fibers inserted into the costal margins, moves the lower border of the rib cage outward and upward. This action increases the transverse diameter of the thorax (Fig. 6).

The diaphragm serves as the floor of the thorax and the roof of the abdomen. It is double-domed with the right dome slightly higher than the left (Fig. 5A).

At the apex and center of the diaphragm is the "central tendon," a solid cartilaginous sheet almost elliptical in shape to which all of the muscle fibers of the diaphragm are attached. Through the central tendon pass the aorta (the large artery carrying blood from the heart), the vena cava (the great vein returning blood to the heart from the lower part of the body), and the esophagus (the foodway to the stomach).

If the ribs are held fixed in any way, contraction and relaxation will result

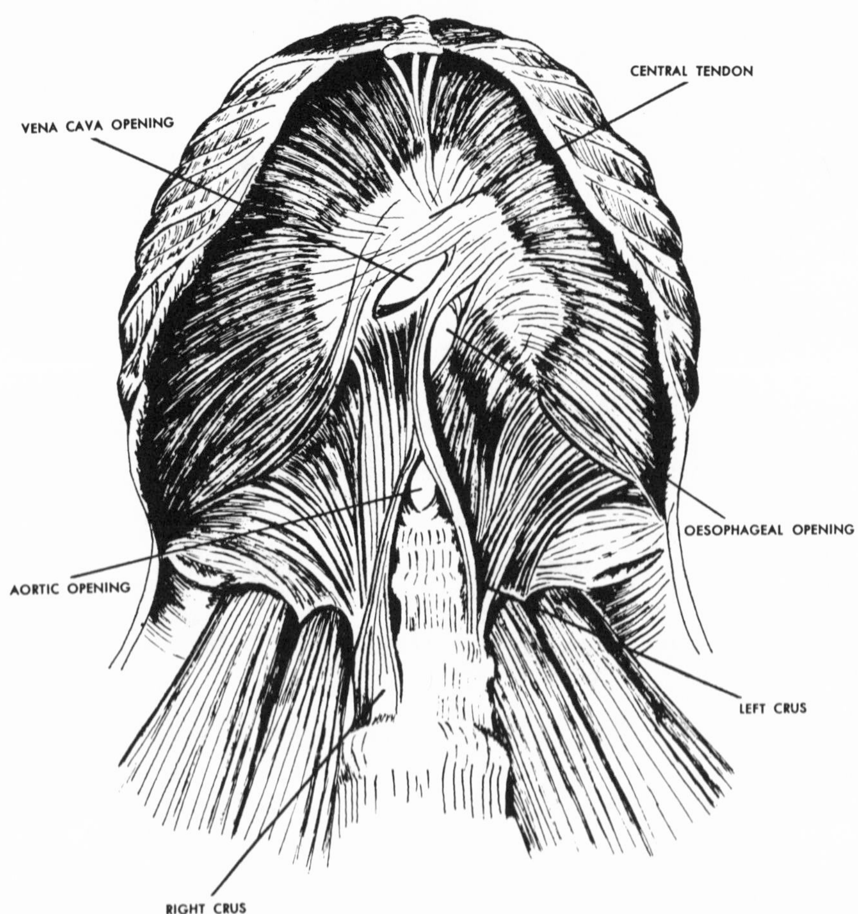

Fig. **5B.** Abdominal Diaphragm, View from Below
Source: Wilber D. Bowen and Henry A. Stone, *Applied Anatomy and Kinesiology* (6th ed.; Philadelphia: Lea & Febiger, 1949).

only in the upward or downward movement of the dome. There are no muscles capable of raising the diaphragm. Ascent of the diaphragm results from the upward thrust of the abdominal viscera by the action of the abdominal musculature as the rib cage is held in the state of suspension by the antagonist muscles of inspiration.

The diaphragm descends one and five-tenths centimeters during quiet breathing. During forced inspiration the excursion is from six to seven centimeters.[14]

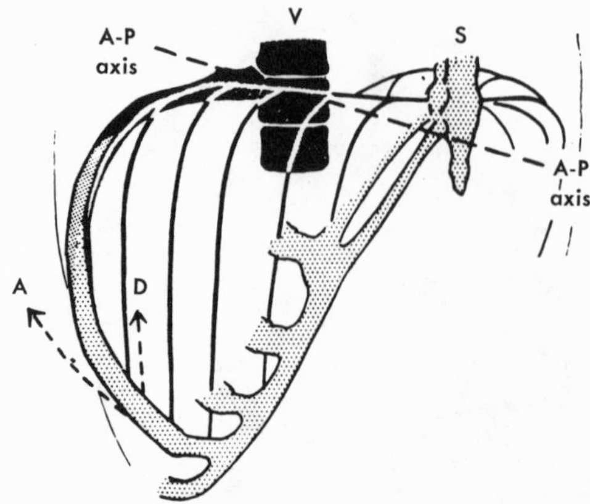

Fig. **6.** The Action of the Diaphragm on the Costal Margin

The ninth rib and costal cartilage are shown passing from the vertebral column (*V*) posteriorly to the sternum (*S*) anteriorly. *A* is the arc of movement of the rib about the vertebro-sternal (*A-P*) axis. *D* is the direction of the costal fibres of the diaphragm at their origin. Contraction of these fibres causes an upward and outward movement of the rib. Reproduced by kind permission from *The Respiratory Muscles and the Mechanics of Breathing* by E. J. Moran Campbell (London: Lloyd-Luke [Medical Books], 1958).

Pectoralis Major (Fig. 7)

Origin—Bicipital groove of the humerus.
Insertion—Collar bone (clavicle), sternum, and upper five or six ribs.

Pectoralis Minor (Fig. 8)

Origin—Coracoid process of the shoulder blade.
Insertion—Lower four or five ribs.

Levatores Costarum (Fig. 9)

Origin—Spinal process of each vertebra.
Insertion—First and second ribs below the point of origin.

Latissimus Dorsi (Fig. 10)

Origin—Bicipital groove of the humerus.

Muscles of Inspiration

(after Sobotta)

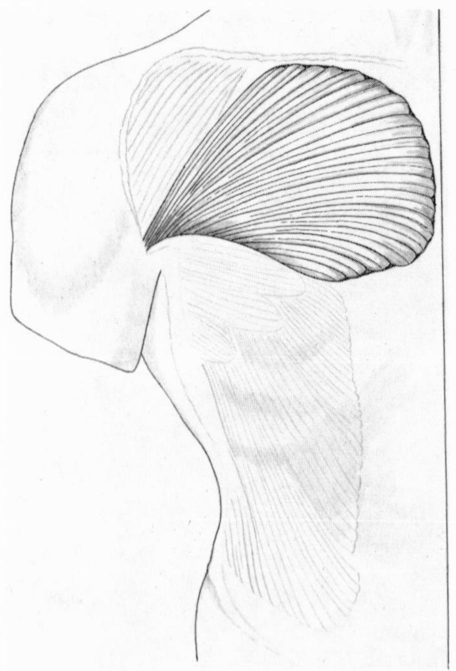

Fig. **7.** Pectoralis Major

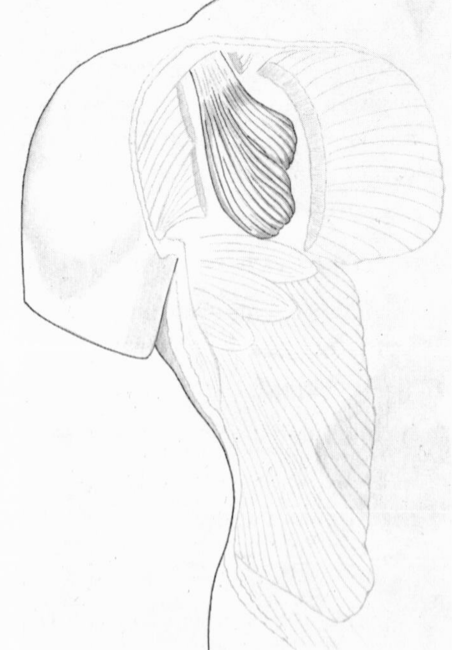

Fig. **8.** Pectoralis Minor

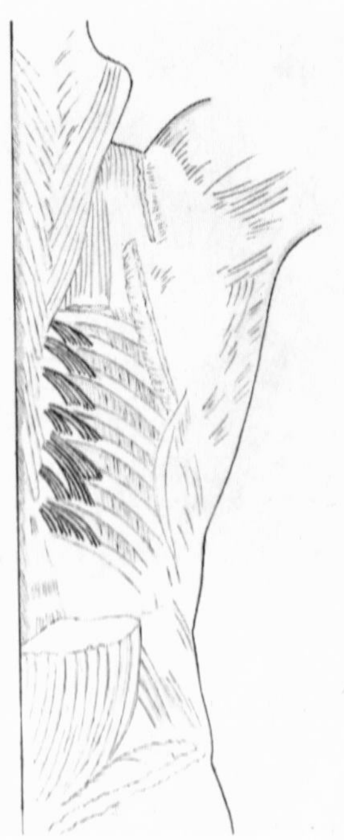

Fig. **9.** Levatores Costarum

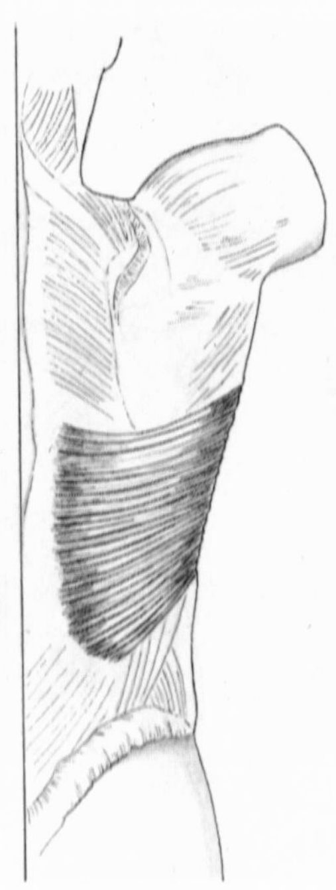

Fig. **10.** Latissimus Dorsi

Insertion—Spinal process of the lower six thoracic vertebra, lumbar and sacral vertebra, crest of the pelvis, and lower four ribs.

Action—The rib-depressors serve as antagonist muscles during the process of inspiration by pulling downward against the upward force exerted by the rib-raisers and to aid indirectly in controlling the expulsion of air during the process of exhalation.

Serratus Posterior Inferior (Fig. 11A)

Origin—Thoracic and lumbar vertebra.
Insertion—Lower four ribs.

Quadratus Lumborum (Fig. 11B)

Origin—Crest of the ilium (pelvis).
Insertion—Twelfth rib.

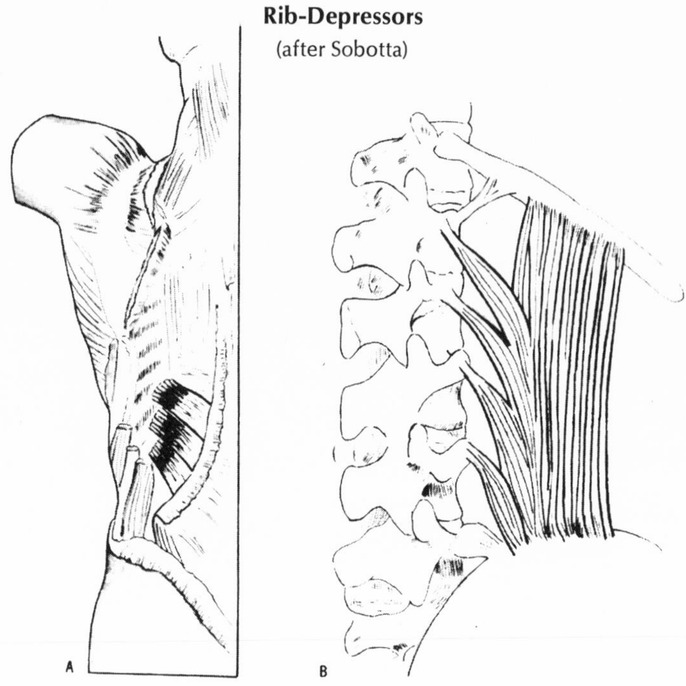

Fig. **11A,** Serratus Posterior Inferior **B,** Quadratus Lumborum

THE MUSCLES OF EXPIRATION

Expiration occurs when the abdominal musculature and muscles of the thoracic cage exert a force against the pleural cavity, thereby, creating stronger pressure within the lungs than that of the outside air. The singing act demands controlled expulsion of the breath stream. Therefore, the singer must conceive of the act of expiration in song as one of balanced suspension with the muscles of inspiration, the rib-raisers, acting as antagonists, and the muscles of expiration acting as the control muscles which supply an even pressure in the expulsion of the breath.

The most important muscles in the expulsion of the breath are the following abdominal muscles: rectus abdominus, transverse abdominus, external oblique, internal oblique, transverse thoracis, and latissimus dorsi.

Rectus Abdominus (Fig. 12)

Origin—Sternum and lower four ribs.

Insertion—Pubic arch.

Action—This large muscle, extending vertically up to the front of the abdominal wall, is one of the strongest muscles of the body. It is enclosed within a fibrous sheath. Its action is to compress the abdominal viscera, forcing them inward. The great length of the muscle is interrupted by cartilaginous sections called tendenous inscriptions, which permit pressure to be concentrated at various points on the abdominal wall.

Transverse Abdominus (Fig. 12)

Origin—This muscle runs horizontally across the body; posteriorly, the lumbar facia; inferiorly, the inguinal ligament and crest of the pelvis; superiorly, the lower six costal cartilages.

Insertion—It interdigitates with the rectus abdominus and is attached inferiorly to the crest of the pubic arch.

Action—To compress the viscera and contract the thorax.

External Oblique (Fig. 13)

Origin—Lower eight ribs.

Insertion—Crest of the pelvis, crest of the pubic inguinal ligament.

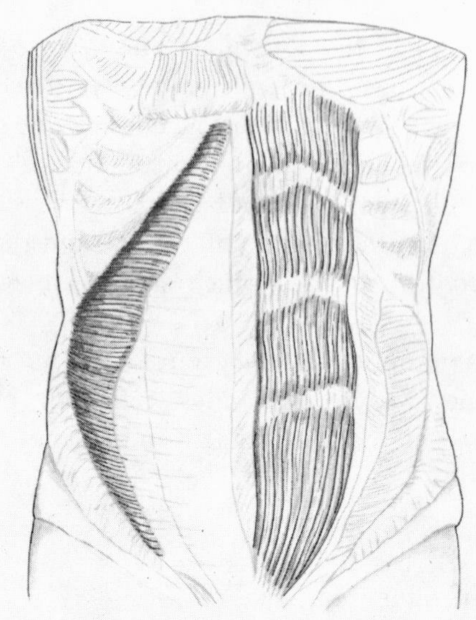

Fig. **12.** Rectus Abdominus and Transverse Abdominus

Action—Compresses the abdomen and depresses the thorax. This muscle extends downward and forward from its point of origin to the crest of the pelvis, forming a long wide wall that greatly aids in controlling the breath during expiration.

Internal Oblique (Fig. 14)

Origin—Crest of the pelvis inguinal ligament and the lumbar fascia.

Insertion—Lower six costal cartilages.

Action—Depresses thorax. This muscle extends upward and forward from its point of origin. The muscle fibers run upward, crossing in an opposite direction the fibers of the external oblique.

Transverse Thoracis (Fig. 15)

Origin—Lower portion of the sternum.

Insertion—Second to sixth ribs.

Action—Depresses the ribs during exhalation.

Muscles of Expiration
(after Sobotta)

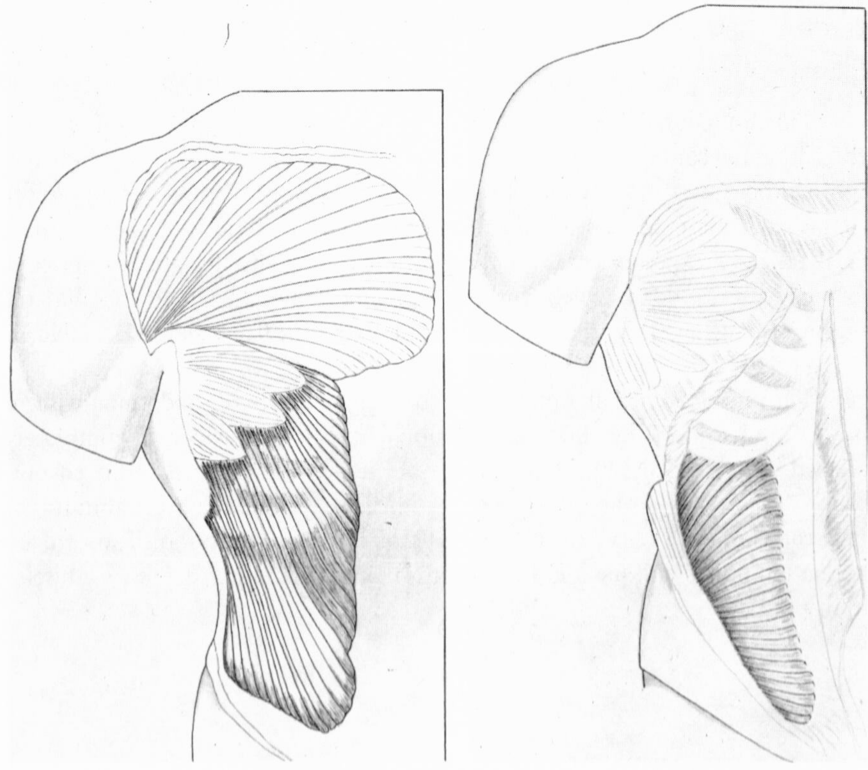

Fig. **13.** External Oblique

Fig. **14.** Internal Oblique

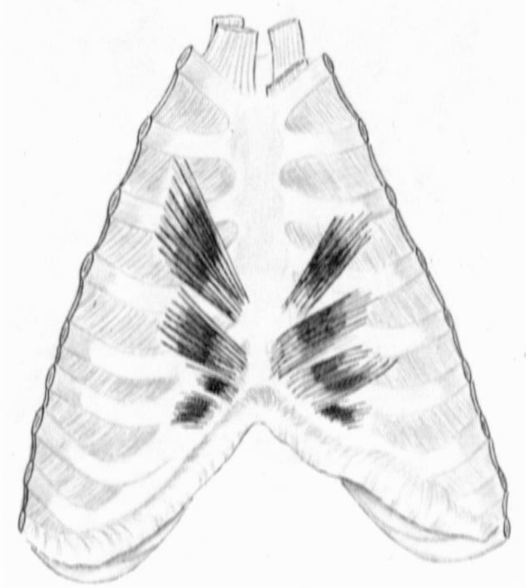

Fig. **15.** Transverse Thoracis

Latissimus Dorsi (Fig. 10)

This muscle has been described as a rib-raiser facilitating inspiration, for the latissimus contains muscle fibers that are able to elevate the ribs. Contraction of the muscle as a whole during forced expiration compresses the lower thorax and, therefore, assists expiration. During long periods of singing, muscular fatigue is experienced in the lumbar-thoracic region; this fatigue originates in the latissimus dorsi, which, with the abdominal muscles, creates a sphincter during expiration. It is the only large muscle of the back that is capable of doing this.

The muscles of exhalation in the preceding list force the abdominal viscera inward and upward against the abdominal diaphragm, which is completely relaxed during exhalation. The volume of air within the lungs is forced outward in a steady even breath stream as the domes of the diaphragm are thrust into the thoracic cavity and as the walls of the thorax are forced inward by the action of the oblique and transverse abdominus and the depressor muscles of inspiration.

Chapter 3

Phonation: The Larynx as a Biological-Biosocial Organ

Few singers know the laryngeal mechanism intimately; many mispronounce its name for the greater part of their lives. Many singers become expert with no instruction or knowledge of the instrument. Yet to those who pause and consider it, the larynx becomes an object of wonder.

Science identifies the larynx primarily as a vegetative organ to aid man in breathing, eating, and working, but when a singer is performing he never thinks that man was not supposed to sing; rather, he is deeply engrossed in the act of singing. He is controlling his sound. During his years of preparation as a singer, he has attained many goals that lead to a refinement of his vocal technique in mastering this sound, and even today he is urged to undertake more difficult tasks as evidenced by the public demand for near perfection of vocal utterance in concerts and on recordings.

What is this instrument within the throat of man that is capable of creating such sounds as are heard in song? Basically, the human larynx is made up of a cartilaginous framework consisting of five cartilages and a dozen muscles, each with its own special function. For the present let us consider how this vocal organ became what it is today.

Such a consideration may lead to the realization that many musical goals that singers hope to attain are impossible because of the variation of muscular and structural imbalances within the laryngeal mechanism of each individual. Singers who can produce all of the attributes of song—beauty of sound, flawless technique, fine intellect, sensitivity to text—have, indeed, a rare gift of nature.

According to Negus, speech is an "overlaid function"[1]—that is, the mechanism used for communication (vocal fold, epiglottis, and the laryngeal framework) was designed primarily to aid man in survival. The vestibule, the area immediately above the larynx, cannot tolerate foreign particles of food for even a brief second. The larynx performs such acts as swallowing, keeping sediment from entering the respiratory tract, and aiding man in lifting, climb-

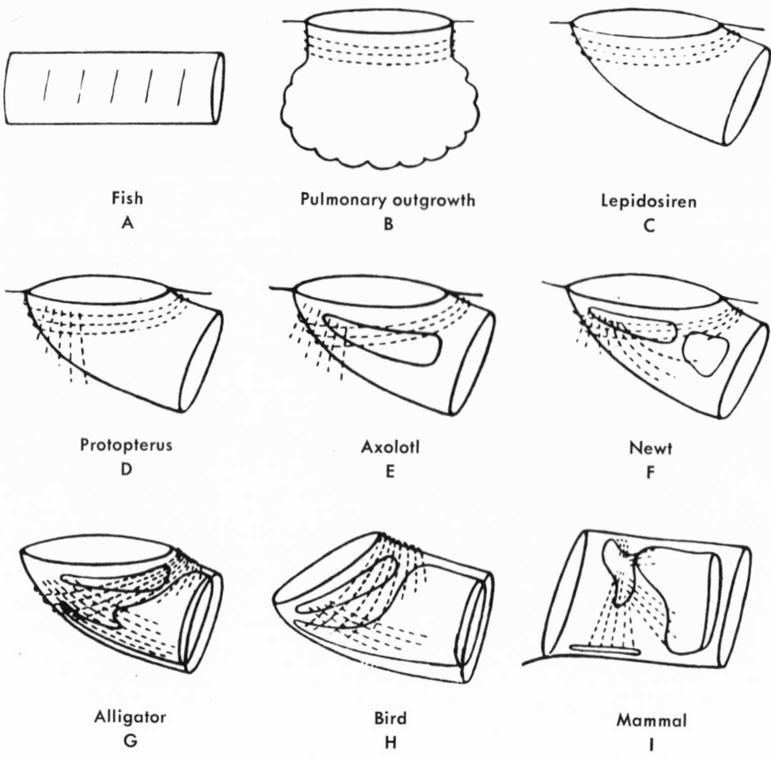

Fig. **16.** Evolution of the Larynx

Biological science has provided evidence that during embryonic states the human larynx passes through stages similar to those through which man has passed to arrive at his present civilized state. Negus[3] traces the development of the larynx in man as he evolved from an aqueous state to that of a terrestrial being as follows: **A,** Fish—The gills of the fish are used to exchange carbon dioxide in the water. **B,** The Climbing Perch—This fish can stay out of water longer than other fish because it has a pulmonary air sac with a slit valve to exchange carbon dioxide and oxygen from air. **C,** The Australian Lung Fish—The elongated trachea turns off toward the thorax, the slit and the valve are still present. **D,** The Uganda Mud Fish—The valvular mechanism is provided with side musculature. **E,** Salamanders—Two lateral cartilages appear to stabilize the laryngeal framework. They correspond to the arytenoid cartilages of higher animals. **F,** Newts—The two cartilages separate, forming arytenoid and half cricoid cartilage. **G** and **H,** Reptiles and Birds—The cricoid cartilages forms a complete ring and the thyroid elements are fused with the cricoid to provide more support. **I,** Apes and Higher Mammals—There is a separation of the thyroid and cricoid cartilages, a shortening of the arytenoid cartilages and a tilting of the laryngeal aperature. The sphincteric muscles are divided into components. The larynx assumes characteristics similar to that in man, except that the velum touches the epiglottis to permit a keen sense of smell. In man, the larynx lies lower between the fourth, fifth, and sixth vertical vertebrae and the velum and larynx are separated by a three-inch space. The larynx in man assumes a lower position because of his erect posture and the muscular problems inherent within the speech act. Reprinted from *The Lancet,* May 27, 1924.

ing, and fulfilling tasks involving physical effort. A man cannot lift a heavy object without laryngeal closure, and he can become quite hoarse in the prolonged performance of this act.

This fact reveals that these primary laryngeal functions in man are still in their primitive state. However, in his rise toward civilization, man was confronted with problems of communication. His hand gestures being limited, he used voice (laryngeal vibration plus resonance) for his communicative purposes. As life became more complex, he added more and more sounds until speech was formed (purposive voice[2]). However his laryngeal organs were still used for survival and remained the same throughout the evolutionary process. Thus, these laryngeal organs have passed from a primary biological state to a biosocial state and have served both purposes in the life of man.

If speech is an overlaid function, singing surely is also. An art form has been superimposed upon a primarily primitive mechanism which varies markedly with each individual in size and musculature. This art form demands infinite controls and imposes all aspects of intensity, pitch, and duration. All forms of singing are now regarded as expressions of emotion; they have become beautiful to man's ear and quite essential for his well-being.

Any singer may be reeducated to conform to a standard of utterance. This fact is apparent in that each individual has learned speech sounds as he hears them used within his environment. Man alone has the ability to originate and use any complicated set of symbols for communication purposes. Consideration of this fact is important in training for new speech skills: reeducation and control of dialectal habits, singing in a foreign language, and the learning of speech forms in song.

THE LARYNX OF MAN TODAY

The Structure

As explained by Johannes Sobotta,[4] the laryngeal framework consists of three cartilages—the epiglottis, the thyroid cartilage, and the cricoid cartilage (Fig. 17)—held together by ligaments, muscles, and joints. The thin, leaf-shaped cartilage, the epiglottis (Fig. 17), is attached to the thyroid cartilage by means of the thyroepiglottic ligament (Fig. 19). It is attached to the inferior surface of the anterior part of the thyroid cartilage just above the origin of the vocal folds (Figs. 17 and 19). The thyroid cartilage (Figs. 17-19) is shield-shaped and is the most prominent of the laryngeal framework. Support-

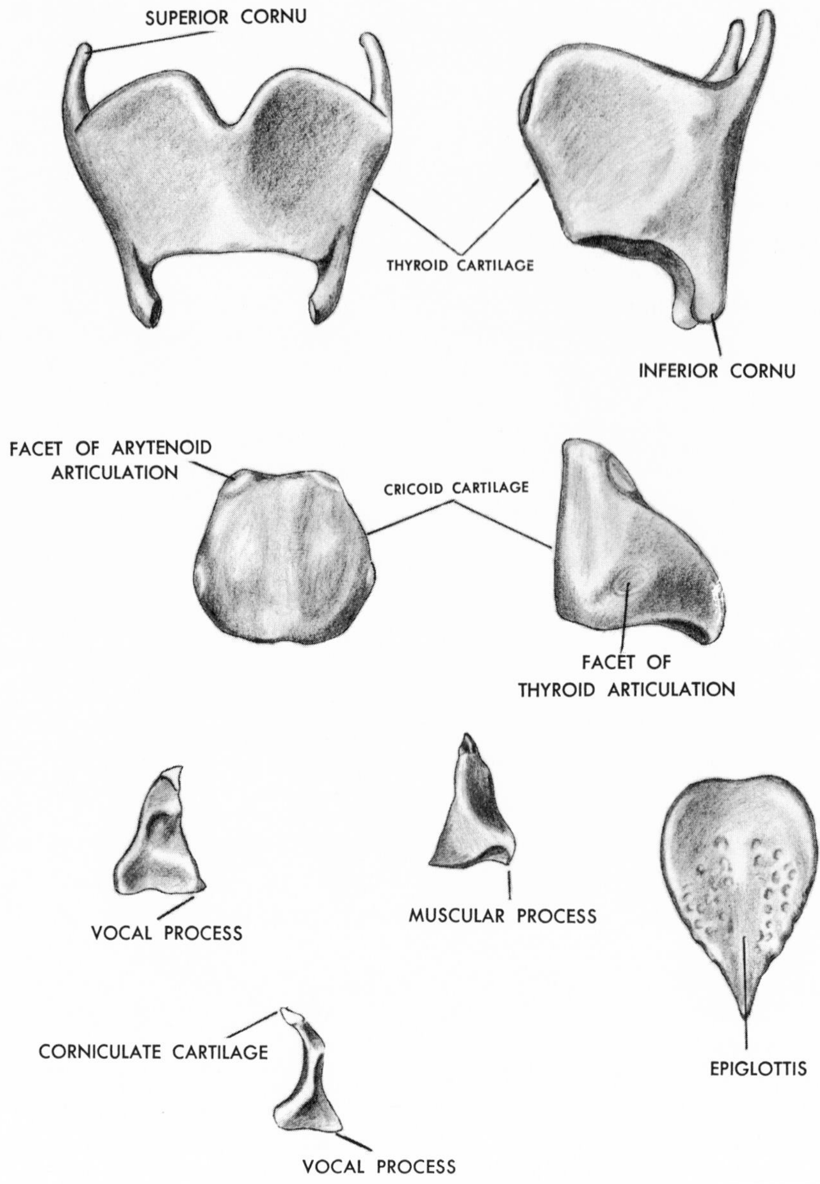

Fig. **17.** Cartilages of the Larynx
(after Sobotta)

ing the thyroid is the cricoid cartilage (Figs. 17 and 18), which is ring-shaped and higher in the back than in the front. The cricoid and the thyroid are articulated with a movable joint at the point of the inferior cornu and the arch of the cricoid (Figs. 17-19). The arytenoids (Figs. 17 and 19), two tiny pyramid-shaped cartilages with triangular bases, are seated on the posterior prominence of the cricoid cartilage and furnish the posterior attachment for the vocal folds (Fig. 19).

Ligaments and Membranes

The ligaments and membranes of the larynx in man today are as follows:

1. Hyothyroid ligament—Connects the hyoid bone and the thyroid cartilage, and extends from cornu of hyoid downward to cornu of thyroid (Fig. 18).

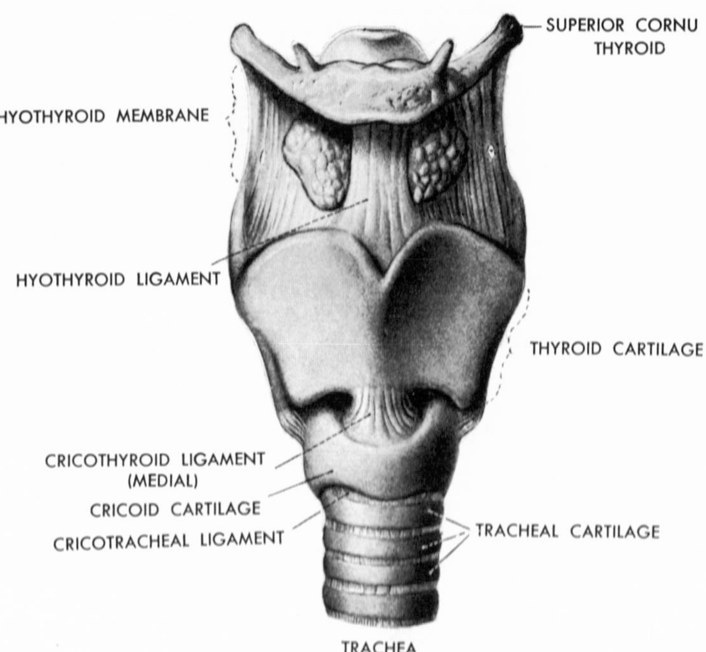

Fig. **18.** Ligaments and Membranes, Anterior

Source: Johannes Sobotta and Eduard Uhlenhuth, *Human Anatomy* (7th ed.; New York: Hafner Publishing Co., 1957).

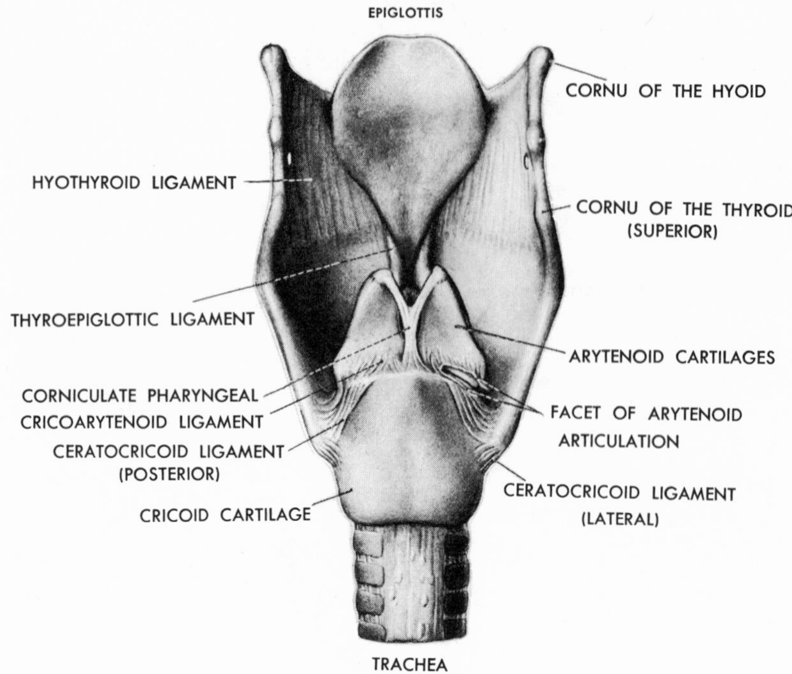

Fig. **19.** Ligaments and Membranes, Posterior

Source: Johannes Sobotta and Eduard Uhlenhuth, *Human Anatomy* (7th ed.; New York: Hafner Publishing Co., 1957).

2. Cricotracheal ligament—Connects the cricoid cartilage and the trachea (Fig. 18).
3. Thyroepiglottic ligament—Connects the epiglottis and the thyroid cartilage (Fig. 19).
4. Cricothyroid ligament (medial)—Connects the cricoid and the thyroid cartilage at their anterior position (Fig. 18).
5. Ceratocricoid ligament (lateral)—Connects the cricoid and the thyroid cartilage at the inferior cornu and the posterior surface of the cricoid (Figs. 18-19).
6. Ceratocricoid ligament (posterior)—Connects the cricoid and the thyroid cartilage at the inferior cornu and the posterior surface of the cricoid (Fig. 19).

7. Cricoarytenoid ligament—Connects the arytenoids and the cricoid cartilage (Fig. 19).
8. Corniculate pharyngeal ligament—Connects corniculate cartilage with the cricoid cartilage at the pharyngeal wall (Fig. 19).
9. Vocal ligaments—Paired thickened stripes of elastic cone that originate at the inner surface of the angle of the thyroid cartilage and extend posteriorly to the vocal process of each arytenoid cartilage (Fig. 20).
10. Aryepiglottic fold—These membranes follow, even to the individual folds, the contour of the skeleton of the larynx and its ligaments (Figs. 21-22). From the epiglottis (Figs. 21-22), the two aryepiglottic folds pass backward to the tips of the corniculate cartilages and forms the lateral boundaries of the vestibule. In addition, the corniculate cartilages and the cuneiform cartilages (Figs. 21-22) are contained within the posterior-superior surface of the fold. They are identified as knob-like elevations in the surface of the membrane. Their function is to draw the opening of the vestibule together.
11. Conus elasticus and cricothyroid membrane—The conus elasticus (Fig. 20) is a short cone-shaped tube which hangs like a tough curtain between the thyroid and the arytenoid cartilages. It is the framework upon which the muscular function of the vocal folds is based. The cone form leans forward so that the tip of the cone is attached to the lower border of the thyroid cartilage at its median raphe. As the sides of the cone drape downward they spread and form a circle at the base of the cone; this circle is attached to the upper surface of the cricoid cartilage (Fig. 20). The

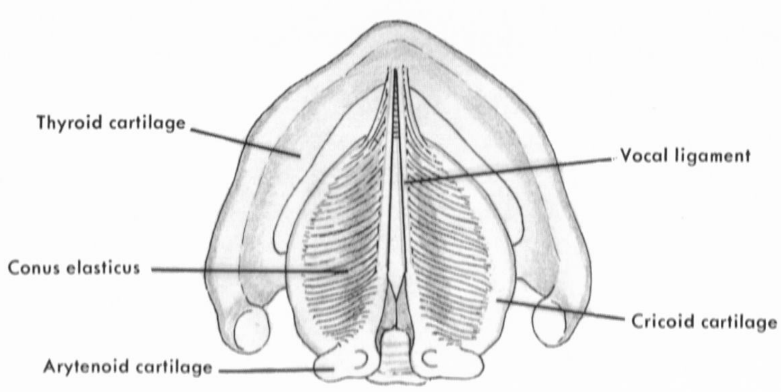

Fig. **20.** Conus Elasticus

conus is slit along its upper edge, and the upper borders of the slit form the vocal ligament (Fig. 20). The posterior and superior portion of the slits are attached to the base of the vocal process of each arytenoid. The arytenoids in their gliding articulations open and close the slit (the glottis). The anterior portion of the cone forms the cricothyroid membrane. The conus elasticus is covered with muscle and tissue, which are loosely attached to it. As the thyroarytenoid muscle contracts the conus becomes firm. It has three points of attachment. The lower border of the thyroid cartilage, the upper surface of the cricoid cartilage, and the inferior surface of the vocal process of each arytenoid.

Above the vocal fold is the laryngopharynx or the vestibule (Fig. 21). It is bordered anteriorly by the epiglottis, posteriorly by the arytenoid cartilages

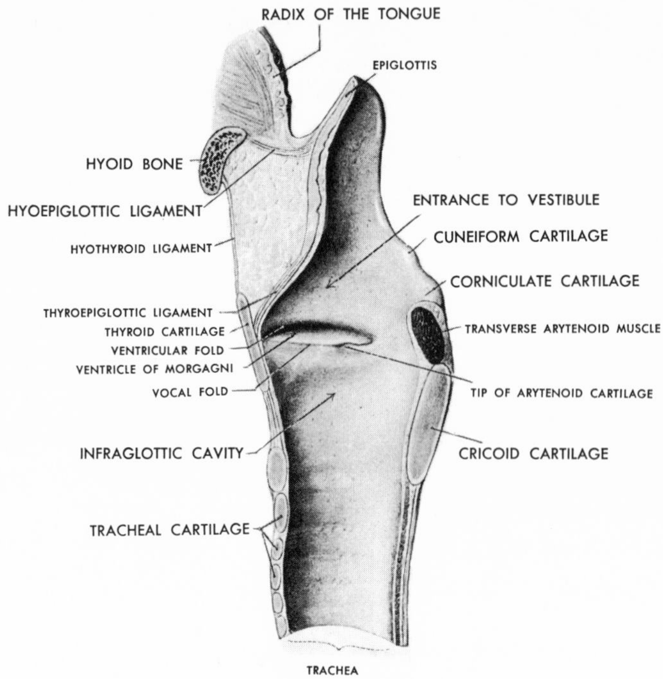

Fig. **21A.** Laryngopharynx (Vestibule), Section, Lateral View

Source: Johannes Sobotta and Eduard Uhlenhuth, *Human Anatomy* (7th ed.; New York: Hafner Publishing Co., 1957).

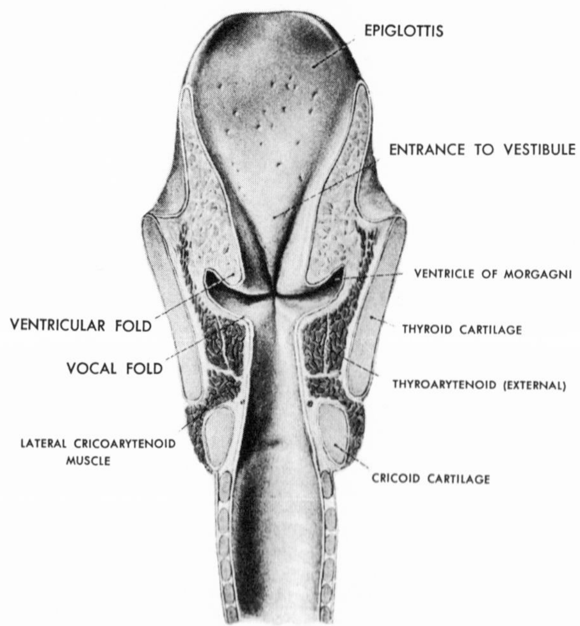

Fig. **21B.** Laryngopharynx, Section,
Posterior View

Source: Johannes Sobotta and Eduard Uhlenhuth, *Human Anatomy* (7th ed.; New York: Hafner Publishing Co., 1957).

and laterally by a membrane (the aryepiglottic folds), which forms a wall between the epiglottis and the arytenoids (Figs. 21A–21C). The false vocal folds or ventricular folds are formed from the lower part of this membrane (Figs. 21A and 21B). These folds are part muscle and part ligament, and they spread out above and parallel to the vocal folds. The space between the vocal and the false vocal folds is called the ventricle of Morgagni (Figs. 21A and 21B). Fig. 21C displays the laryngopharynx and its position in the foodway. Since the cartilaginous framework of the larynx is completely covered by membranous tissue from the tip of the epiglottis to its continuation with the trachea, the laryngopharynx is a closed resonating system. The lower pharyngeal area (piriform sinus) is part of the foodway which surrounds the laryngopharynx, laterally and posteriorly, permitting it to be suspended, almost freely, in the foodway during phonation. The contour of the laryngopharynx is altered during

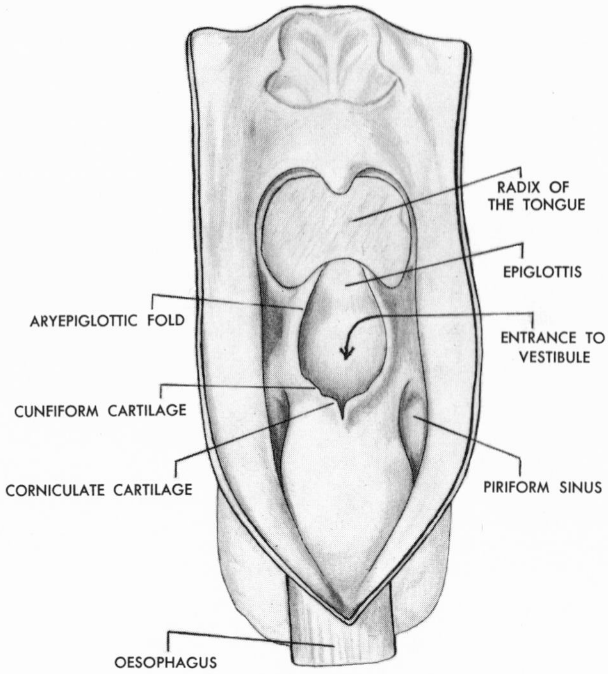

Fig. **21C.** Position of the Laryngopharynx in the Foodway (after Sobotta)

the production of vowels. (See Fig. 41.) Not only is the orifice altered, but its transverse and vertical aspects also are altered.

MUSCULATURE AND MECHANICS OF PHONATION

A method of instruction which relates a specific muscle structure to a specific respiratory or phonatory act is bound to be seriously defective and oversimplified. All disciplined vocal utterance in song is derived through the unification of numerous muscle complexes that are interrelated and form a huge gestalt. The performer recognizes these unified actions as a single sensation.

However, one must realize that specific laryngeal muscles cause the arytenoid cartilages to slide or revolve, which in turn approximate the vocal folds

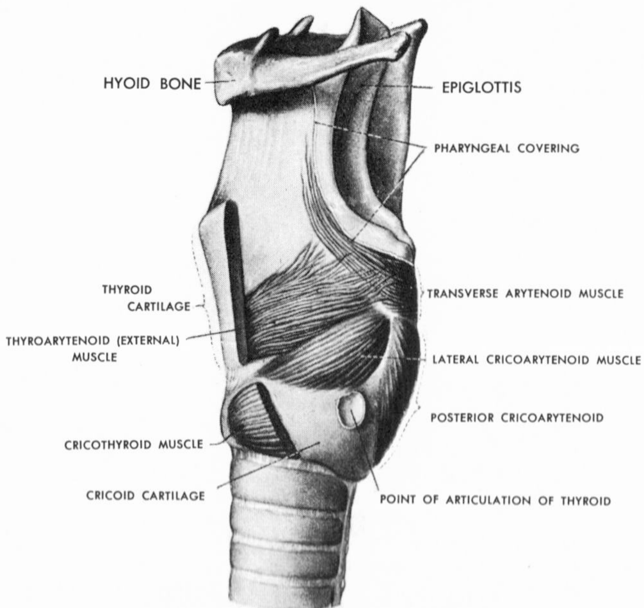

Fig. **22A.** Muscles of the Larynx, Lateral View

Source: Johannes Sobotta and Eduard Uhlenhuth, *Human Anatomy* (7th ed.; New York: Hafner Publishing Co., 1957).

and close the glottis in preparation for the act of phonation. Six of these muscles, three of them paired, are prime movers and can be used to explain the mechanics of phonation. They are known as the intraarytenoid muscles. They consist of the transverse, oblique, posterior, lateral cricoarytenoid, cricothyroid, and thyroarytenoid.

Transverse Arytenoids

Origin—Posterior surface and outer border of each arytenoid (Figs. 23A and 23B).

Insertion—Outer border of each arytenoid.

Action—Draws together the arytenoid cartilages, closes glottis respiratoria (between arytenoids).

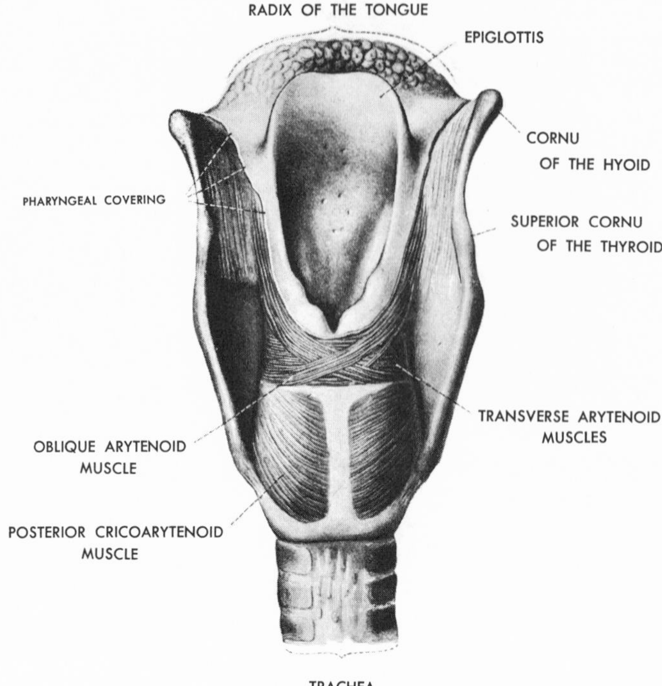

Fig. **22B.** Muscles of the Larynx, Posterior View

Source: Johannes Sobotta and Eduard Uhlenhuth, *Human Anatomy* (7th ed.; New York: Hafner Publishing Co., 1957).

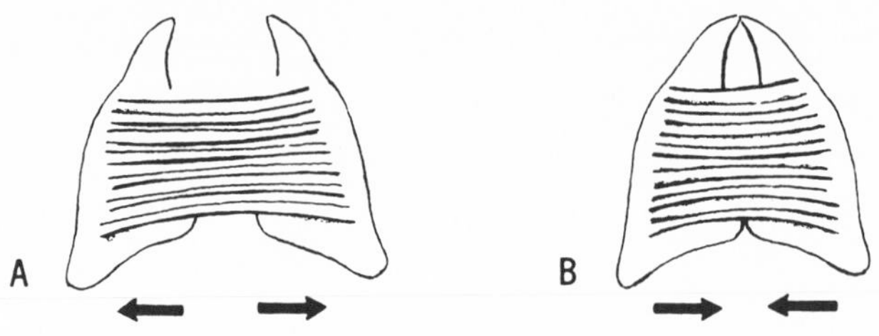

Fig. **23A,** Transverse Arytenoids, Origin and Insertion
B, Transverse Arytenoids, Action

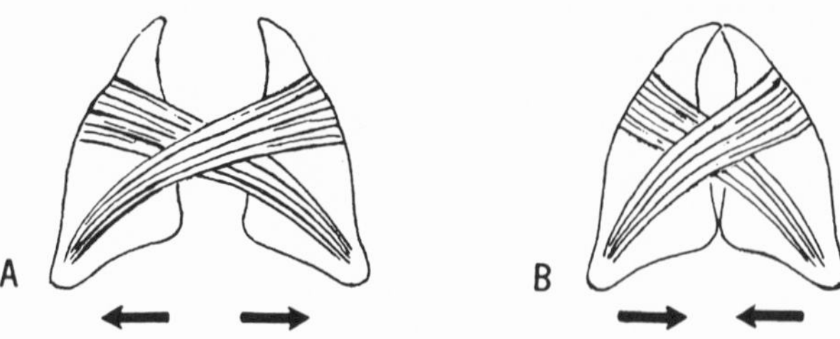

Fig. **24A,** Oblique Arytenoids, Origin and Insertion
B, Oblique Arytenoids, Action

Oblique Arytenoids (Figs. 24A and 24B)

Origin—Base of posterior surface of one arytenoid.

Insertion-Apex of posterior surface of opposite cartilage. Fibers of each muscle cross to form an X.

Action—Stabilizes the arytenoids by drawing tips of arytenoids together and aids in closing the glottis.

Posterior Cricoarytenoids (Figs. 25A and 25B)

Origin—Posterior surface of the cricoid cartilage.

Insertion—Muscular process of each arytenoid.

Action—Rotates vocal process of arytenoid cartilage outward so that the vocal processes are drawn away from the midline. Opens the glottis vocalis.

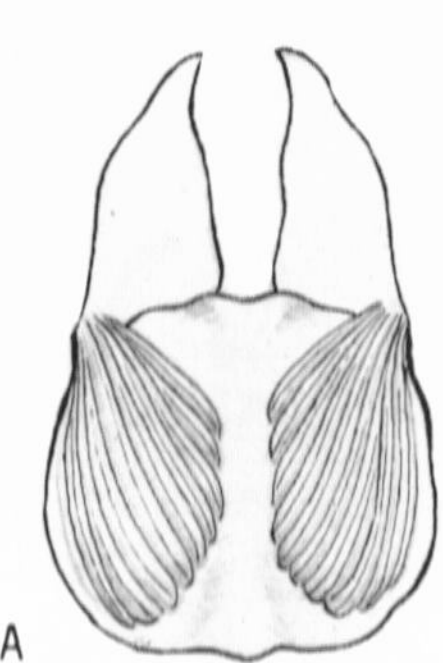

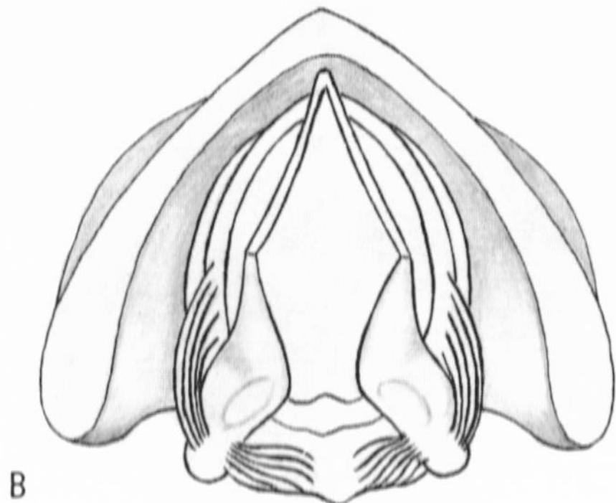

Fig. **25A,** Posterior Cricoarytenoids, Origin and Insertion
B, Posterior Cricoarytenoids, Action

These muscles tilt the arytenoid backward with consequent rise of the vocal process and the tensing of the vocal ligament.

Lateral Cricoarytenoids (Figs. 26A and 26B)

Origin—Upper border and side of each cricoid cartilage.

Insertion—Muscular process of each arytenoid.

Action—Pulls the arytenoid cartilage forward, and when opposed by the action of the posterior cricoarytenoids, creates a state of suspended tension in the vocal ligament. This action rotates the arytenoids and moves the vocal processes inward, and thus closes the glottis vocalis.

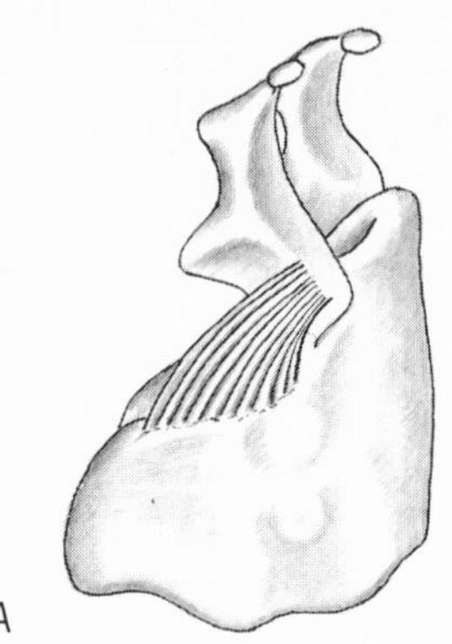

A

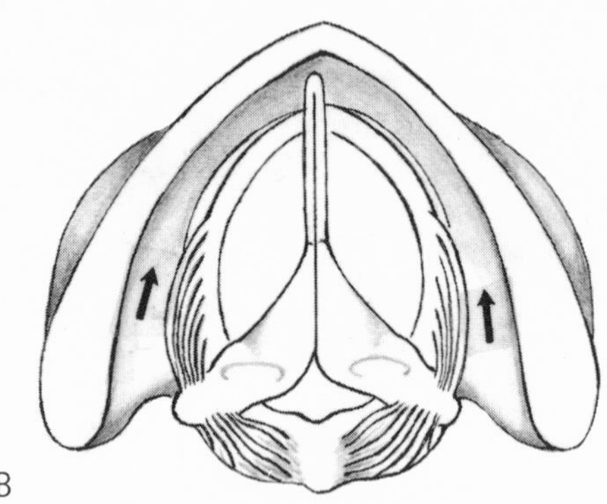

B

Cricothyroid (Fig. 27A)

Origin—Oblique fibers, anterior border of the cricoid cartilage.

Insertion—Lower lamina and inferior cornu of the thyroid.

Action—By drawing the inferior cornu forward these fibers tilt the cricoid cartilage upward. This action approximates and lengthens the vocal folds rendering them tense in preparation for phonation (Fig. 27B).

Origin—Anterior fibers. Front and superior superior surface of the cricoid cartilage.

Insertion—Anterior border and lower lamina of the thyroid cartilage (Fig. 27A).

Action—Depresses the thyroid cartilage and elevates the arch of the cricoid cartilage, or draws the thyroid forward and downward. This combined action increases the distance between the vocal processes of the arytenoid and the lamina of the thyroid. It elongates the vocal folds and renders them tense, provided the arytenoids remain fixed. This downward tilt is effected by the singer to give stability to the phonated sound and to permit him to increase intensity as the pitch is maintained. The pitch is also raised by stretching the vocal folds. The degree of the thyroid tilt affects pitch, intensity, and quality of the vocal sound (Fig. 27C).

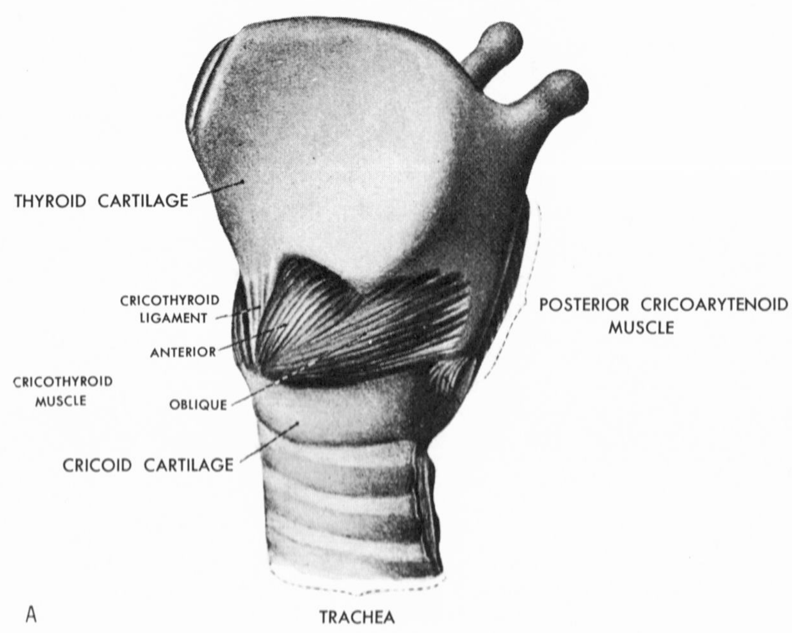

Fig. **27A.** Cricothyroid, Origin and Insertion

Source: Johannes Sobotta and Eduard Uhlenhuth, *Human Anatomy* (7th ed.; New York: Hafner Publishing Co., 1957).

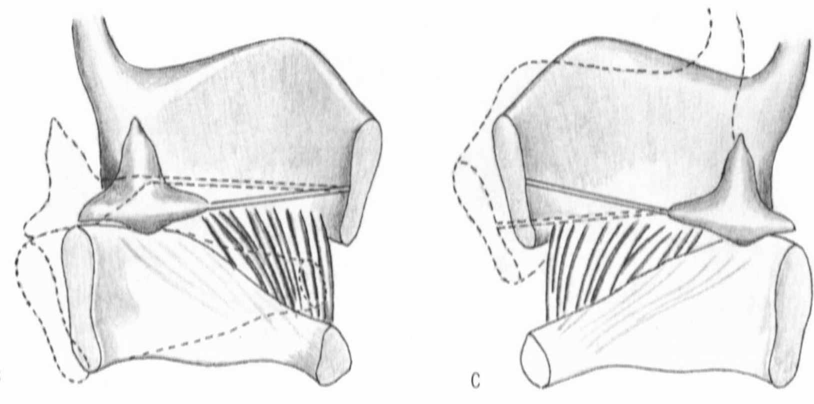

Fig. **27B.** Cricothyroid, Action

Fig. **27C.** Cricothyroid, Action

Thyroarytenoid

This muscle is divided into two parts, the vocalis muscle and the external thyroarytenoid.

Vocalis Muscle. (Figs. 28A and 28B)

Origin—The angle of the thyroid cartilage.

Insertion—The vocal process of the arytenoid cartilage.

External Thyroarytenoid. (Figs. 28A and 28B)

Origin—The angle of the thyroid cartilage.

Insertion—The base and anterior surface of the arytenoid cartilage. Laterally, it is attached to the wall of the thyroid cartilage.

Fibers of the vocalis muscle are nearest the vocal ligament and are attached to its inferior and lateral surface. Fibers of the external thyroarytenoid interdigitate with the fibers of the vocalis muscle and are attached laterally and anteriorly to the inner wall of the thyroid cartilage.

These two segments of muscle run parallel to each other with points of insertion indicated above. However, some of the fibers of the vocalis muscle are short and do not extend to the vocal process of each arytenoid cartilage. These fibers, attached to the vocal ligament and conus elasticus (Fig. 20), perform the refined tasks of controlling the conformation of the vocal fold in its various states of thickness and thinness during changes of pitch.

When the vocal folds are not approximated, as in the absence of phona-

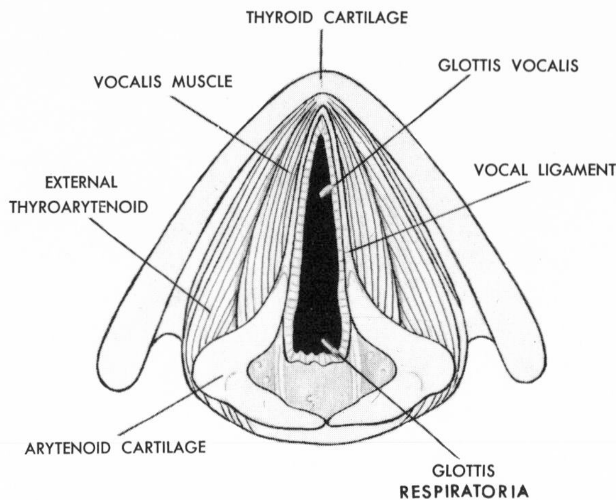

Fig. **28A.** Thyroarytenoid, Origin and Insertion, Superior View (after Sobotta)

tion, a space is created between them called the rima glottidis or glottis. During passive breathing the glottic opening extends from the thyroid cartilage to the posterior border of the arytenoids. Its anterior-posterior length in the male is approximately twenty-four millimeters, and in the female approximately fifteen millimeters.

That portion of the glottis extending from the thyroid cartilage to the tip of the vocal process of the arytenoid is known as the glottis vocalis. That portion of the glottis which lies between the arytenoid cartilages is known as the glottis respiratoria (Fig. 28A). Chronic breathiness in the vocalized sound is sometimes caused by a failure of the arytenoids to approximate, thereby permitting the glottis respiratoria to remain open.

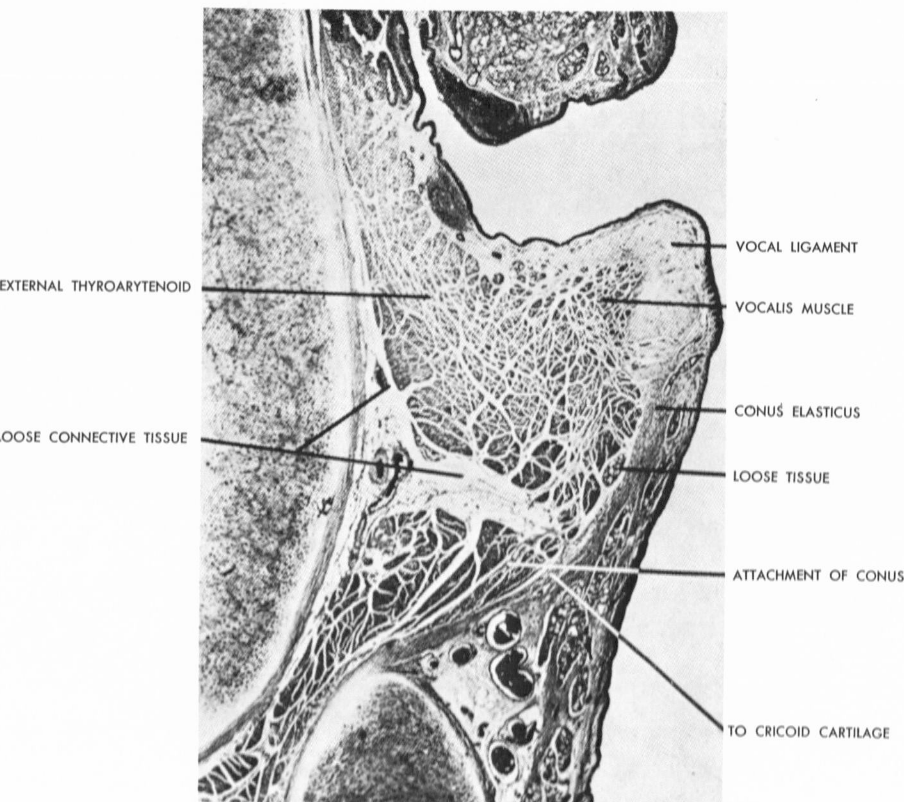

Fig. **28B.** Thyroarytenoid, Posterior Section of the Left Fold

Source: Reproduced from A. Mayet, "Bau und funktion des musculus vocalis und seine Beziehungen zer lig. vocale und conus elasticus," *Acta Anatomica,* Vol. 24 (1955), 15-25. Hamalaun-Eosin, illustrator. Basel (Switz.), and New York: S. Karger.

Action—The independent action of these thyroarytenoid muscles may:

1. Relax and shorten the vocal ligament by drawing the arytenoids towards the thyroid cartilage for the singing of low pitches (Fig. 29A).
2. Draw the vocal processes of the arytenoids downward and inward, approximating the vocal folds (Fig. 29B).

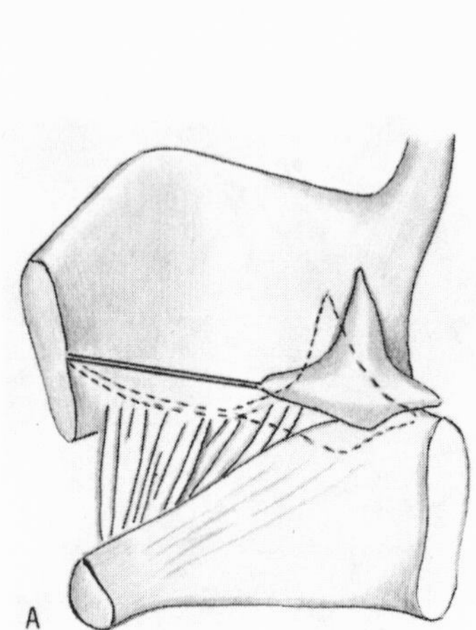

Fig. **29A.** Thyroarytenoid, Action, Lateral View

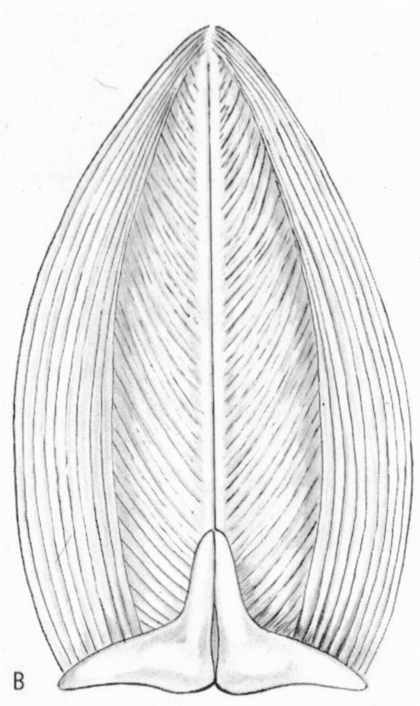

Fig. **29B.** Thyroarytenoid, Action, Superior View

3. Pull the vocal folds apart by their lateral contraction.
4. Become stabilized throughout their entire length and, thereby, aid in raising the pitch of the phonated sound.
5. Vary both the length and thickness of the vibrating segment.
6. Render a portion of the vocal fold tense while the remainder is relaxed. Thus, an elliptical opening between the vocal folds is maintained for the production of higher pitches.

Such control of the glottic opening results from the action of certain fibers of the vocalis muscle that are fastened to the border of the vocal ligament. They are able to pull apart against the tension of a portion of or the entire length of each fold, in order to establish the final pattern in which the vibration will take place. Pressman suggests physiological reasons for such an elliptical opening based upon the arrangement of fibers in the vocalis muscle described by Piersol.[5]

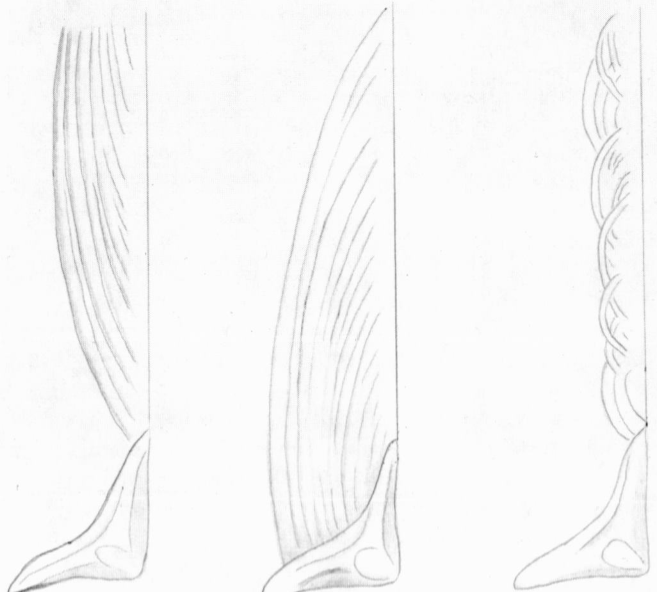

Fig. **30.** Suggested Arrangement of Fibers in the Vocalis Muscle

Source: Joel J. Pressman, "Physiology of the Vocal Cords in Phonation and Respiration," *Archives of Otolaryngology*, Vol. 35 (1942).

1. Fibers arising anteriorly in the thyroid cartilage and passing posteriorly more or less parallel to the general direction of the cords,* to terminate at different levels [Fig. 30 A]. The innermost fibers are very short and terminate in the anterior portion of the cords. The more lateral fibers are longer, inserting farther and farther posteriorly until the most lateral ones extend from the anterior point of origin on the thyroid cartilage to the posterior extremity of the cords near the arytenoids or into the vocal processes themselves.
2. Fibers arising at various points within the substance of the vocal cord and conus elasticus (of which the former is a part) and passing backward to insert on the body and vocal process of the arytenoid cartilages [Fig. 30 B].
3. Fibers arising here and there in the substance of the cords and extending backward for varied distances to insert on the same cord at a more posterior point [Fig. 30 C].

* The use of *vocal folds* instead of *vocal cords* in this work preserves the concept of the fold as a functional wedge of flesh whose inner fibers are altered in length, mass, tension, and elasticity mentally by the singer. *Vocal cords* is suggestive of the segmental vibration of a string in which mass, tension, and elasticity are unalterable.

None of these three groups can be recognized as an entity, since a great deal of intertwining of the fibers of each group with those of the others takes place.

The action of these groups of fibers is on the cord and is probably as varied as the arrangement of the fibers is complex. Their most important action in phonation seems to take place after the cords have been strongly and completely approximated and tensed by the adductor group. When this tension and adduction have been accomplished, it then becomes necessary to reopen the cords by some means which permits them to retain their relatively rigid elasticity. The action of these internal fibers of the thyroarytenoideus muscle is admirably suited for the purpose. Starting with the arytenoids tightly closed and the vocal bands on stretch and closely adherent, those internal fibers of the thyroarytenoidei which arise on the thyroid cartilage and insert into the cordal structure contract. They thus pull apart, against the tension of the adductors, those portions of the vocal cords into which they insert [Fig. 31]. This action takes place in much the manner that an archer draws back the tense bowstring of his bow, the arm of the archer representing the muscle fibers of the thyroarytenoideus muscle and the taut bowstring representing the tensed vocal cord. When the pull of these fibers is released, the

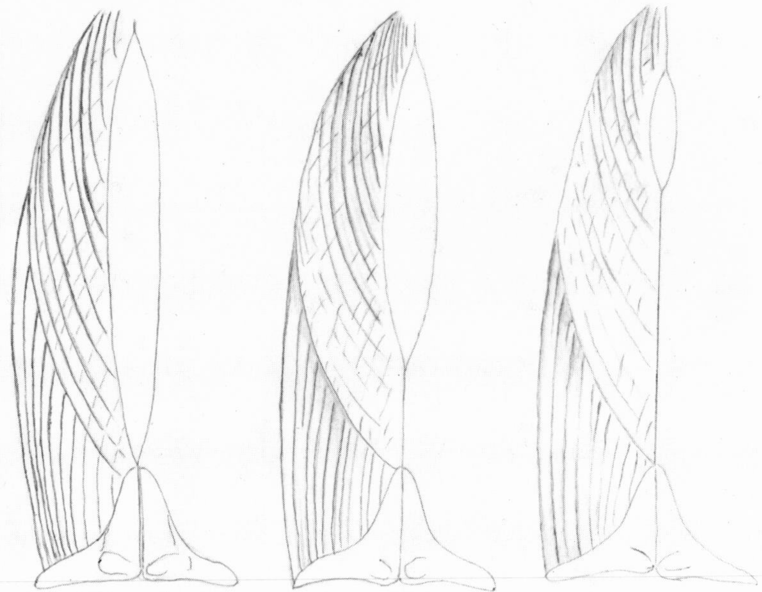

Fig. **31.** Adduction of the Vocal Folds Causes a Rise in Pitch by Contraction of the Fibers of Vocalis Muscle

Source: Joel J. Pressman, "Physiology of the Vocal Cords in Phonation and Respiration," *Archives of Otolaryngology*, Vol. 35 (1942).

> cord returns sharply to the midline, corresponding to the release of the bowstring by the archer. The length of the cord pulled apart is determined by the number of fibers of this portion of the thyroarytenoideus muscle which are called into play. The variation in the length of cord pulled apart is important from the standpoint of variations in pitch.
>
> Those fibers of the thyroarytenoideus muscle arising in the vocal process of the arytenoid and extending forwward to be inserted into the cord at different points have the same action, supplementing that just described, except that the pull comes from a posterior instead of an anterior point. The chief reason for believing that there are such fibers is that if a segment of the cord is to be bowed laterally, as actually occurs, instead of anterolaterally, a compensatory group of fibers must exert a posterior pull against the action of any group that might arise anteriorly.
>
> The fibers arising in one portion of a cord and inserting in another further supplement this action and give the margins of the glottis increased elasticity and rigidity.[6]

The numerous possibilities of action of the thyroarytenoids depend upon the action of the other laryngeal muscles (posterior cricoarytenoids, lateral cricoarytenoids, and the cricothyroid) which act as guying muscles during the complex act of phonation. If these muscles are not balanced correctly one with the other as antagonists, an imbalance occurs within the system, and this imbalance is evident in the vocal utterance in such effects as breathiness caused by improper closure of the glottic aperture or faulty pitch caused by an imbalance between the actions of the posterior cricoarytenoids and the thyroarytenoids. When the posterior cricoarytenoids are weak, the thyroarytenoids become much too tense in attempting to hold the pitch constant. Lack of range often results from insufficient tension within the thyroarytenoid. Tension within the vocal folds is coordinated with the contraction of the cricothyroid muscle (Fig. 27B); the resulting tilt of the thyroid tenses the vocalis muscle for thoracic fixation or phonation.

THEORIES OF LARYNGEAL VIBRATION

In considering the physical principles of laryngeal vibration, the scientist is faced with several basic facts that are either physiological or physical in nature. All theorists have accepted these facts; however, they differ in their analyses of the mechanism which controls the refined movements of the thyroarytenoid muscles in the production of pitch and of various tone qualities.

Husson[7] and his coworkers have produced the neurochronaxic theory that motor impulses from the central nervous system cause rhythmic contractions of the thyroarytenoid muscles producing the vibrations requisite for any given tone. However, as pointed out by Negus and others,[8] tones as high as 2,048 cycles per second have been recorded by the human voice, but tonic contractions of the thyroarytenoid muscle may occur with stimuli only to 110 cycles per second. Therefore, the thyroarytenoid cannot function clonically on all pitches.

Because of these objections, contemporary researchers favor an aerodynamic theory in which air flow and cavity resonances seem to affect frequency and intensity rather than direct muscular and neural controls.

Two theories will be considered, the reed theory and the vibrating string theory.

Contemporary vocal theorists accept the following as facts:

1. That all vocalized sound is the result of expiration of air through the cone-shaped narrowing of the phonatory tube at the apex of the trachea (Fig. 21B).
2. That further constriction is applied by the vocal folds which are capable of completely or partially interrupting the expired air.
3. That both the vocal folds and walls of the airway are elastic and yield under pressure (Figs. 44–46).
4. That the vocal folds are capable of varying in length, tension, and contour—thereby regulating the size, shape, and the position of the glottic aperture—as well as undergoing vibrating movements.
5. That the laryngeal muscles do not produce the vocal sound. Rather, phonation is an aerodynamic phenomenon in which the muscles merely adjust and hold the folds in a certain position, tension, and shape. The modulation of the expired air stream, caused by the movement of the vibrating vocal folds, makes the sound. The resulting pressure variations create the multiple sine waves which comprise the complex vocal spectrum.

The Larynx as an Air-Column Instrument— The Reed Theory

For many years teachers have described the action of the vocal folds as analogous to the vibrating reeds of the oboe. According to the reed theory, changes in pitch are caused (a) by changing the contour of the glottic aperture, (b) by altering the elasticity of the margins of the folds, and (c) by varying the contour of the total resonating system.

According to Jackson and Schatz,[9] tone production and pitch variation at the larynx are analogous to a mechanism in which the reeds come together momentarily and more or less close off the expired air. They then open and allow the air to escape in puffs. This process repeated rapidly represents the vibration of the already approximated vocal folds; it is not to be confused with simple abduction (separation) or adduction (bringing together). In this manner the air stream is cut off periodically by the approximation of the folds. This rapid escape of air is what produces the sound. At this point the reed theory seems to be sound, for the expanded air does escape in puffs. Evidence that rapid escape of air in puffs will produce sound is found in the function of a siren which consists of a circular metal plate perforated around its margin. A jet of air directed toward the holes while the plate rotates rapidly will produce an intense sound. The intervals between the small apertures represent the opening and the closing of the reed or vocal fold. An increase in the velocity of the wheel's rotation causes a rise in pitch.

According to the reed theory, the vocal folds vary the pitch in much the same way that pitch is changed by the lips of a bugler, that is, by enlarging or diminishing the size of the orifice, by varying its firmness and shape, and by changing the force of the expired air. Jackson[10] says that the total resonating system is involved in pitch change, an area extending from the labial orifice to the bifurcation of the trachea into the two bronchi; that with each rise in pitch, both supraglottic and infraglottic air columns are decreased, vertically and transversely, two to three millimeters.

Because this action does occur, at first it seems to support the reed theory for it involves the principle of forced vibration. (See p. 117, No. 1.) Those who advance this theory assume that the vibrator is dominated by the resonator which causes the vibrator, or reed, to vibrate in the period of the system as the system changes its contour and dimension in the production of vocalized sound. The defenders of this theory believe that a total system or gestalt is involved in which both laryngeal musculature and phonatory airway contribute to changes in pitch and vocal quality.

A closer examination of the laws of forced vibration reveal the fallacy of the reed theory: The conception of a reed or air-column instrument fails because the principle of instrumental design is to make the frequency of the instrument dependent, not upon the natural frequency of the reed, but upon the natural frequency of the air column to which it is coupled.

When making lip slurs on the trumpet, the reverse of this principle is true, the vibrator dominates the resonator and the slur is accomplished by moving a perfect fifth upward or downward by lip tension and increased breath pressure alone. Slurs on reed instruments are accomplished in a similar manner. The clarinet has a natural interval of the twelfth, but in both cases it is the domination of the vibrator over the resonator that effects the smooth transition from one frequency to another.

Changes of pitch in singing arise, at least in part, from the variation in length, tension, and mass of the vocal folds. In this case, the vibrator dominates the resonator, compelling the resonator to respond to a frequency related to the vibrator regardless of the natural frequency of the resonator.

The Vibrating-String Theory

Each string of a stringed instrument is tuned to specific pitches, which are determined by the tension, length, mass, and elasticity of the string. The greater the tension the higher the pitch of the resulting sound when the string is plucked or bowed. If the tension is doubled, the pitch will rise one octave. A short string will produce a higher pitch than a long string; the pitch will rise one octave if the string length is halved.

The thickness or mass of a string affects both pitch and timbre. If the mass of the string is decreased the pitch rises, and if the mass is increased, the pitch lowers because of greater inertia created by the additional mass.

The mass of a string depends upon its elasticity. In a flexible elastic material, less inertia is produced and a greater mass may be employed before the limit of its tension is reached.

Therefore, a note of the same pitch can be produced with string of varying length, tension, mass, and elasticity provided the ratios between these elements are correct. The tone quality will vary in each case; this variation accounts for the differences between instruments of the same type, particularly between two different makes of violins.

This principle of vibrating strings also confirms the variation between singers of the same tessitura, type, or class in that each will vary his application of amplitude, mass, length, and tension while producing the same pitch.

The vibrating-string theory precludes that the vocal folds are able to produce tones just as they are produced upon the violin, the force of expired air provides the energy by which the tone is made at the larynx.

This theory also includes the concept that pitch may be varied in the larynx by increasing the tension of the vocal folds just as pitch is elevated by tightening the violin string.

The tension of any vibrating string is controlled by its elasticity. Elevation of the pitch can be carried to a limited point by this process of elongation or tightening.

The action of the thyroarytenoid in singing an ascending scale is illustrated in the Bell Telephone pictures. They show that in the production of the lowest note of the scale the glottis is open widest in its posterior part, nearest the arytenoid cartilages, and that the vocal folds are short and thick. As this pitch

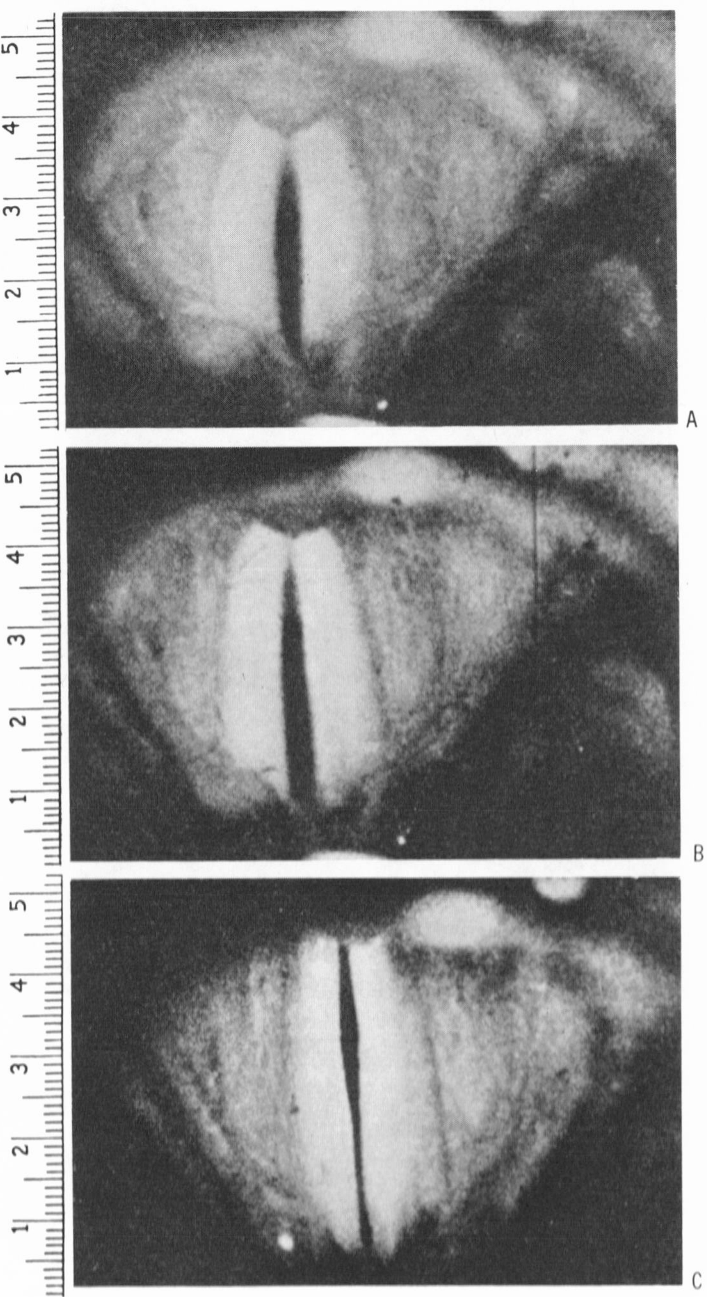

Fig. **32.** Pitch Change

Action of the vocal folds during changes of pitch in the middle voice shows alterations of mass, length, and tension of the folds. *A* is at b, 123; *B* at b, 246; and *C* at e, 329. Source: Bell Telephone Laboratories, Inc.

is sung, the laryngeal muscles are under the least tension and the amplitude of the vibrations are most extreme. The lateral movement of the folds extend through the entire thyroarytenoid. The folds are loose and flaccid (Fig. 32).

As the pitch rises, the cricothyroid muscles tense and tilt the thyroid cartilage so that the vocal folds gradually become longer, thinner, and more tense. Here the amplitude of the vibration decreases as the tension of the fold increases. This increase in tension is created by the action of the inner fibers of the vocalis muscle, the lateral cricoarytenoid, the posterior arytenoids, and the cricothyroid muscles. This added tension causes the amplitude of the vibrations to decrease and the glottic aperture to narrow gradually until the opening becomes linear in shape (Fig. 33). At this point the vocal folds are vibrating at their full length. This mode of vibration is characteristic of the middle register before adduction.

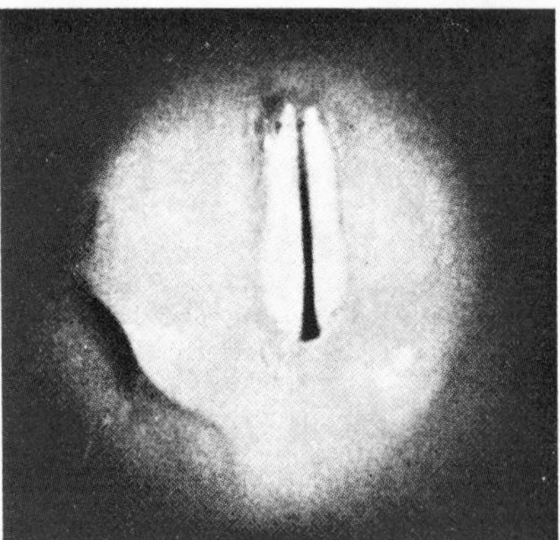

Fig. **33.** Position of the Vocal Folds in the Production of Middle Tones

The enlarged posterior hiatus has disappeared, the margins of the vocal folds now parallel one another. Variations in the length and tension of the folds and in their degree of approximation produce with this same pattern variations of pitch within reasonable limits. Source: Joel J. Pressman, "Physiology of the Vocal Cords in Phonation and Respiration," *Archives of Otolaryngology,* Vol. 35 (1942).

The tension upon the thyroarytenoid muscle continues to increase, but the elasticity of the folds is not sufficient to permit further stretching. At this point further elevation of the pitch is achieved in a manner similar to fingering a violin. In singing, this functional foreshortening is achieved by the approximation of a portion of the vocal folds against each other, beginning posteriorly (Fig. 34). The segments in contact with each other are not able to vibrate so

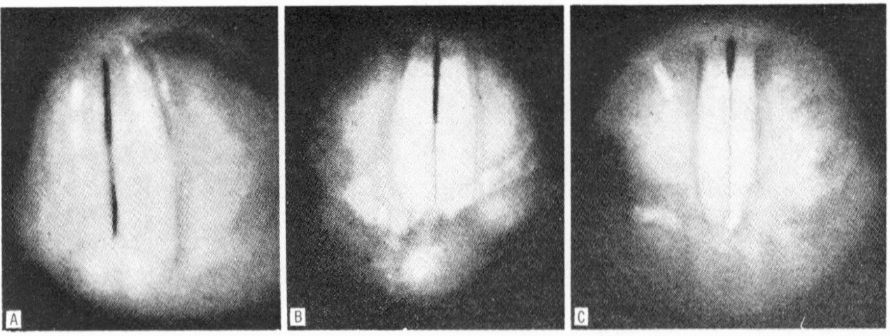

Fig. **34.** Position of Vocal Folds in the Production of Higher Tones
In *A* the folds are in the first stage of adduction. In *B* adduction of the folds has shortened the length of each fold which is free to vibrate, raising the pitch of the sung sound. In C the segments free to vibrate are very short, and the tone produced is very high. Source: Joel J. Pressman, "Physiology of the Vocal Cords in Phonation and Respiration," *Archives of Otolaryngology*, Vol. 35 (1942).

that each contacting segment is said to be in the state of adduction. This pressing together of the posterior portion of the vocal folds permits the remaining shorter segment to vibrate, and a corresponding elevation of the pitch is produced. As greater lengths of the vocal folds come in contact with each other, the glottic aperture becomes smaller. The reduction in the size of the glottis further tends to elevate the pitch according to the acoustic principles of air passing through a smaller orifice. This elliptically shaped glottis is achieved by the contraction of the inner fibers of the vocalis muscle and by the strong guying action of the total laryngeal musculature. (Fig. 31). To reiterate, vocal sound starts with the modulation of tracheal air flow resulting from the vibrations of the glottic margins. The frequency (and the resulting pitch) of the sound is varied by changes in the elasticity of the glottal margins and the length which is free to vibrate, these changes are controlled by the thyroarytenoid and associated musculature.

This act conforms with the law of vibrating strings except that the vocal folds grow longer from the lower to the middle tones instead of shorter. However, at this point the mass of the folds decreases (They become thinner as the pitch rises.); further elevation of the pitch is brought about by an increase of tension and refined controls of the total laryngeal musculature.

The larynx of man as a biosocial organ has no exact functional counterpart in man-made instruments, and teaching techniques must be built around conceptual differences in tonal control but with complete insight and an awareness of the physiological and the psychological phenomena involved in each vocal act.

SYNTHESIS OF ACTION IN PHONATION FOR SINGING

Action of Body Musculature

Phonation for singing is produced by the laryngeal generator. The body's muscular action begins with inspiration:*

1. The thoracic musculature is set.
2. The pelvic diaphragm contracts, supporting the viscera (coccygeus levatores ani).
3. Abdominal diaphragm contracts, lowering the floor of the thorax and compressing the viscera. Other muscles involved are serratus superior, serratus inferior, quadratus lumborum, pectoralis major, pectoralis minor, and latissimus dorsi.
4. These actions increase the anterior-posterior vertical diameter of the thorax and the upper part of the abdomen, widen the intercostal spaces, and thus permit air to rush in.

The muscular action of expiration is sphincteric (closing a circle). Compression of the viscera is instantaneous and equal from all musculature.

1. The muscles of the abdominal wall contract: transverse thoracic, rectus abdominus, transverse abdominus, internal oblique, and external oblique.
2. The pelvic diaphragm contracts. Active contraction of these muscles dominates the holding action of the diaphragm and thereby elevates the abdominal viscera, pushes the domes of the diaphragm into the thoracic cavity, and decreases the volume of the cavity and also of the lung.

Action of Laryngeal Musculature

1. Arytenoids are approximated, closing the glottis respiratoria; the muscles involved are the posterior, oblique, and transverse arytenoids.
2. Vocal processes are rotated and meet at midline closing the glottis vocalis; the muscle involved is the lateral cricoarytenoid.
3. Arytenoid cartilages are fixed on their facets; muscles involved are the cricoarytenoid, posterior, and lateral.
4. Elasticity of the fold is increased. Muscular action involves cricothyroid, cricoarytenoids, and thyroarytenoids.
5. As the elasticity of the folds increases, breath pressure forces the vocal folds to rise and separate in a rippled wave that begins deep in the laryngeal fibers of the thyroarytenoids. This wave moves upward[11] as well as anteriorly from the arytenoids to the epiglottis; as the breath passes through the conical

* For specific action of this musculature, see Chap. 2, "Respiration."

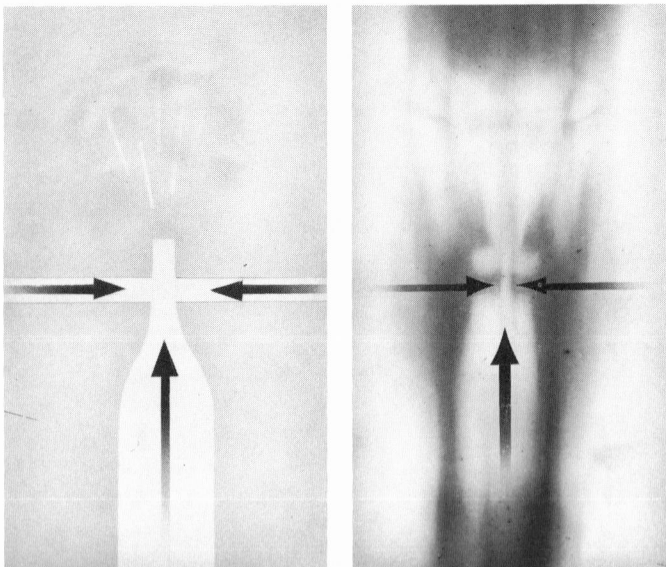

Fig. **35.** Bernoulli Effect in Singing

trachea and expands into the broader vestibule, it causes reduced lateral pressure upon the vocal folds. This reduced pressure creates a sucking effect (Bernoulli effect, Fig. 35), which, with the elasticity of the vocal folds, draws them together and the entire process is repeated.

The modulation of the respiratory air stream creates the audible laryngeal "buzz" as it passes through the glottis. The complex sound waves (not sinusoidal—see p. 121) thus emitted are the result of pressure variations of the escaping bursts or puffs of air and not the result of the mechanical vibration of the folds themselves.

Pitch changes, then, are not directly attributed to a single act of lengthening, thinning, tightening, or loosening of the vocal folds. Rather, the pitch change is caused by the modulation of tracheal air pressure resulting from the changes in the elasticity of the glottal margins. It is thus assumed that the changes in the elasticity are caused by changes in mass, length, and tension of the thyroarytenoid in a synchronized act, a most complicated process. In summary, three wave-like movements of the vocal lips occur during phonation:

1. A horizontal displacement along the glottis takes place during the opening phase as noted in the Bell Telephone high-speed motion pictures of the human vocal cords. The glottis opens anterior-posteriorly and closes posterior-anteriorly (Fig. 36A). Svend Smith describes the variation between the Bell subject and his own subject as follows (Fig. 36B):

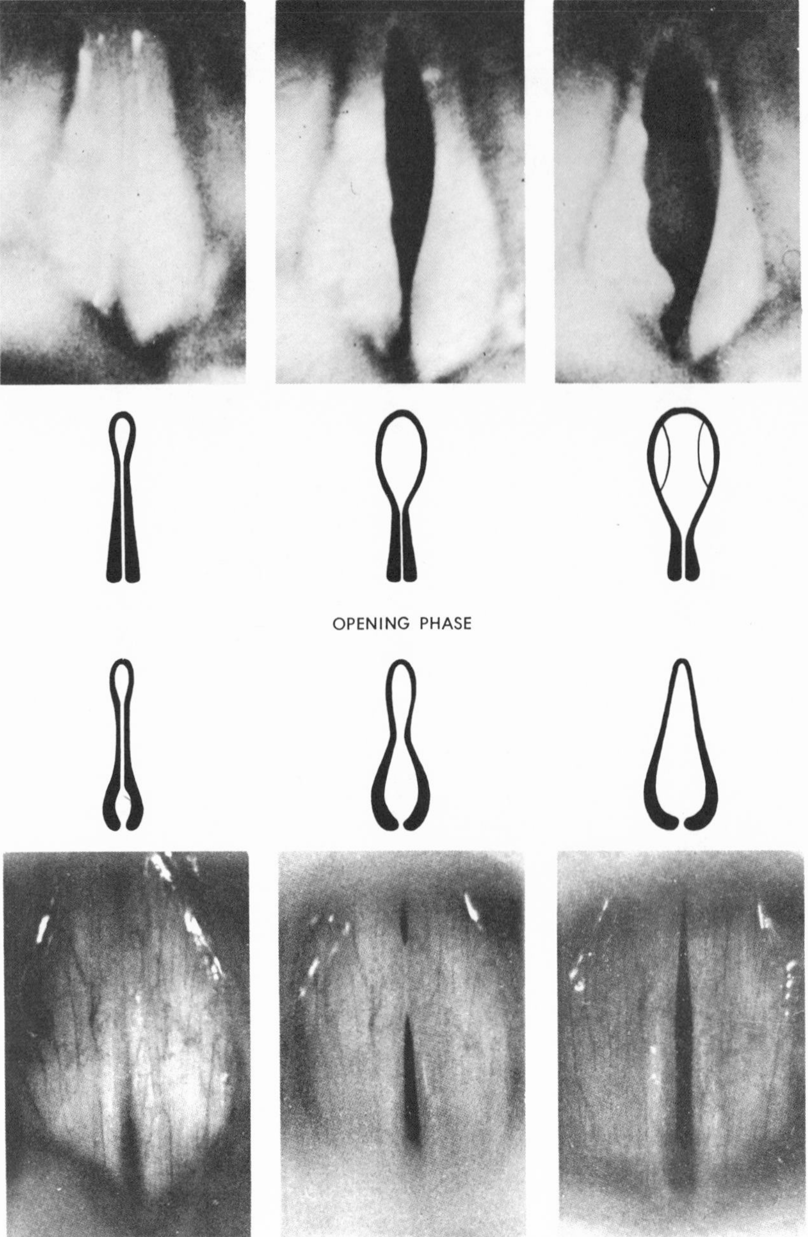

Fig. **36A.** A Comparison of Vocal Fold Vibration

Source: upper photographs, Bell Telephone Laboratories, Inc.; lower photographs, Svend Smith, "Remarks on the Physiology of the Vibration of the Vocal Cords," *Folio Phoniatrica,* 6 (1954), 196–271. Published by S. Karger, Basel (Switz.) and New York.

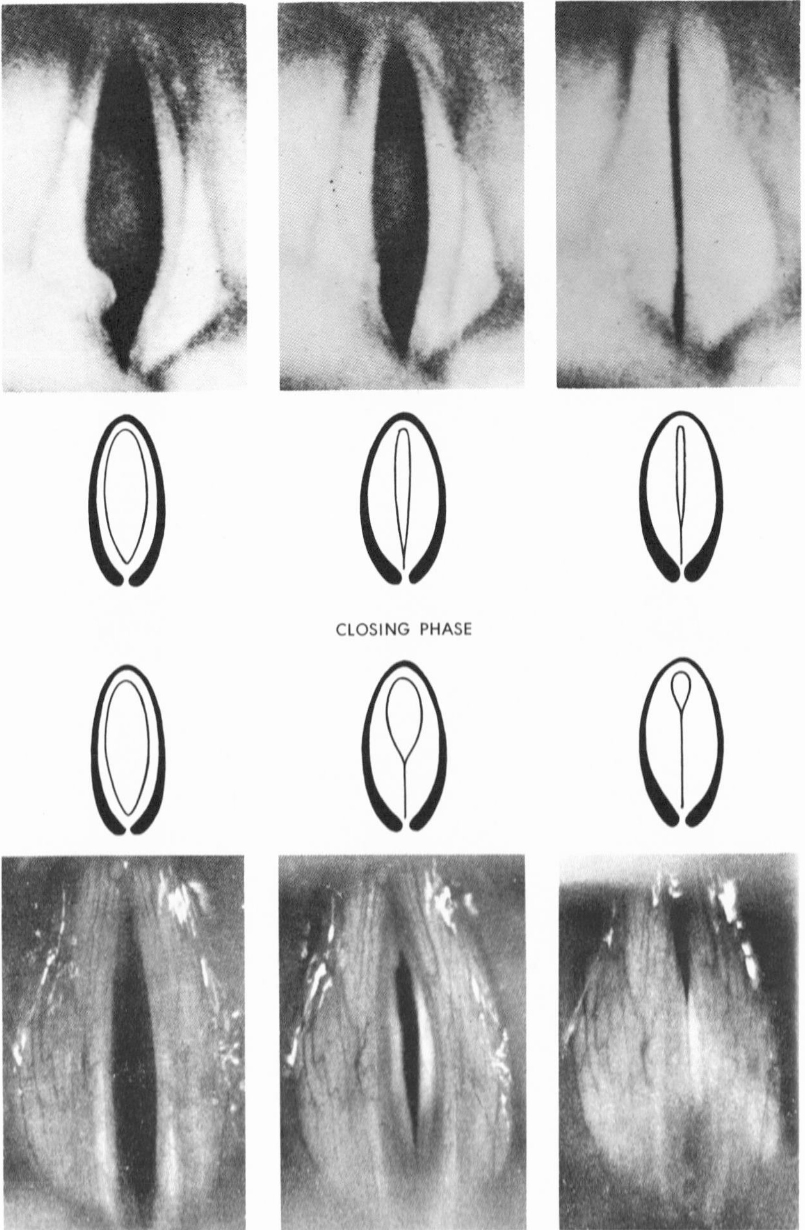

Fig. **36B.** A Comparison of Vocal Fold Vibration

Source: upper photographs, Bell Telephone Laboratories, Inc.; lower photographs, Svend Smith.

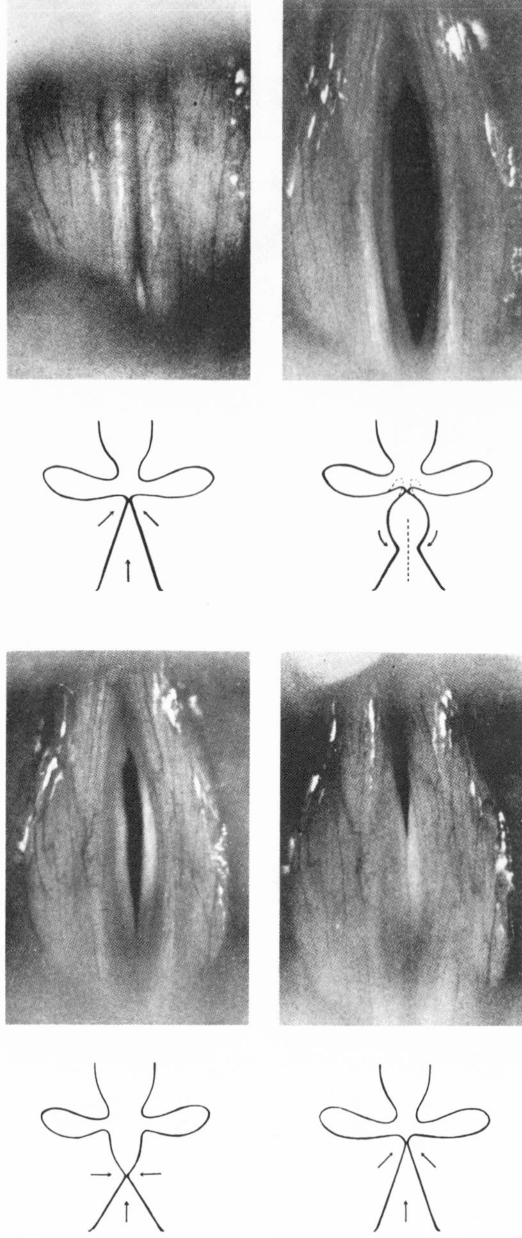

Fig. **37.** Vertical and Lateral Movement of the Folds

Source: Svend Smith, "Remarks on the Physiology of the Vibration of the Vocal Cords," *Folio Phoniatrica,* Vol. 6 (1954), 196-271. Published by S. Karger, Basel (Switz.) and New York.

> Several pictures in the Bell film reveal a bottle-like opening as the next phase after the initial front explosion. This means that the arytenoid region is the last to be opened. Of course this is only the case when the interarytenoid and lateral muscles work in a fully normal manner. In the case of a slight insufficiency [of breath]—as could most often be expected in a subject during laryngoscopy—both the front and rear part of the glottis may open simultaneously [my subject]. This would presumably cause a less violent explosion of air giving in its turn fewer overtones in the voice production [less glottic shock].[12]

The vocal folds can open anterior-posteriorly as well as posterior-anteriorly depending upon the nature of the attack and upon the coordination between the total laryngeal musculature and the breath pressure.

2. A vertical movement of the cords begins from underneath the opening and progresses upward and outward.
3. The third wave-like movement is a movement of the medial planes surrounding an air bubble. In viewing the schema, one must remember that the vocal folds are in a rolling motion, moving in these pictures posterior-anteriorly, from the bottom of each picture to the top (Fig. 37).

Smith describes the action in the following manner:

> After the explosion (i.e., release of pressure) a stream of air follows. The velocity of air—together with some lateral pressure of the [external thyroarytenoid] vocal muscles—tends to suck the two medial planes against one another. The edges would not be the first portion of the vocal lips to be sucked, because they are in an excursion phase, being thrown out laterally and upwards. But the subglottic parts of the vocal lips are free to be sucked. According to the law of Bernoulli the planes now meet, not in their whole length at the same time, but gradually and well down in the subglottic region. The descending movement of the lips would support this subglottic phase of adduction.[13]

THE ANATOMY OF THE HUMAN RESONATING SYSTEM

A consideration of the laws of resonance within hard-walled Helmholtz resonators reveals the applicability of these same laws to the human resonating system.

Resonance in song depends upon four cavities that are stable resonators and upon the characteristics of these cavities to vary greatly in their ability to change in size, shape, aperture, and length of neck of the aperture. They are listed below with their respective volumes:

1. The nasal cavity (75 cubic centimeters).
2. The oral cavity (100 cubic centimeters).
3. The pharyngeal cavity and its subdivisions, the nasopharynx, the oropharynx and the laryngopharynx (80 cubic centimeters).
4. The trachea (35 cubic centimeters).[14]

The nasal cavity (Fig. 38) extends from the floor of the cranium to the roof of the oral cavity. The septum divides this large cavity into two separate cavities called fossae, which act as resonators in the production of nasal sounds. The nasal fossae are not amenable to change, and their conformation cannot be changed during phonation at any pitch or intensity. The nose has no other significant resonating cavities. This nasal cavity has two orifices, the anterior nares at the front of the nose and the posterior nares at the opening into the oropharynx. Neither of these orifices is subject to control.

The oral cavity (Fig. 38), the narrow passage from the mouth to the pharynx, extends from the pillars of the fauces to the labial orifice and is the most amenable to change. The shape and size of the oral cavity may be varied by the movement of the mandible, the tongue, and the lips. Too often the labial orifice is ignored as an important articulator in singing; many teachers seek a minimum of lip movement during the production of all vowel sounds. The professional singer, however, has learned that lip-rounding and lip protrusion when singing the rounded frontal vowels provide a stability and comfort not available when he fails to utilize the wide variety of shapes and sizes which this most flexible orifice is capable of forming.

The pharynx (Figs. 38 and 39), approximately four and one-half inches in length, extends from the base of the skull to the level of the sixth cervical vertebra. It is subdivided into three separate cavities; each contributes a quality component to the tonal spectrum by being a part of a tightly coupled system during the production of all sounds. As a resonating cavity the pharynx is relatively undamped.

The nasopharynx (Figs. 38 and 39) extends vertically from the base of the skull to the velum anterior-posteriorly from the posterior nares to the pharyngeal wall. It is a closed resonator and does not serve a primary function during the production of most vowels and consonants because the uvula is pressed firmly against the pharyngeal wall, thus closing the entrance to the nasopharynx.

The soft palate is raised and the velum is pressed against the pharyngeal wall by the action of the levator veli palatini, a muscle originating at the base of the cranium and extending to the palate and uvula.

The muscles which pull the palate away from the posterior wall of the

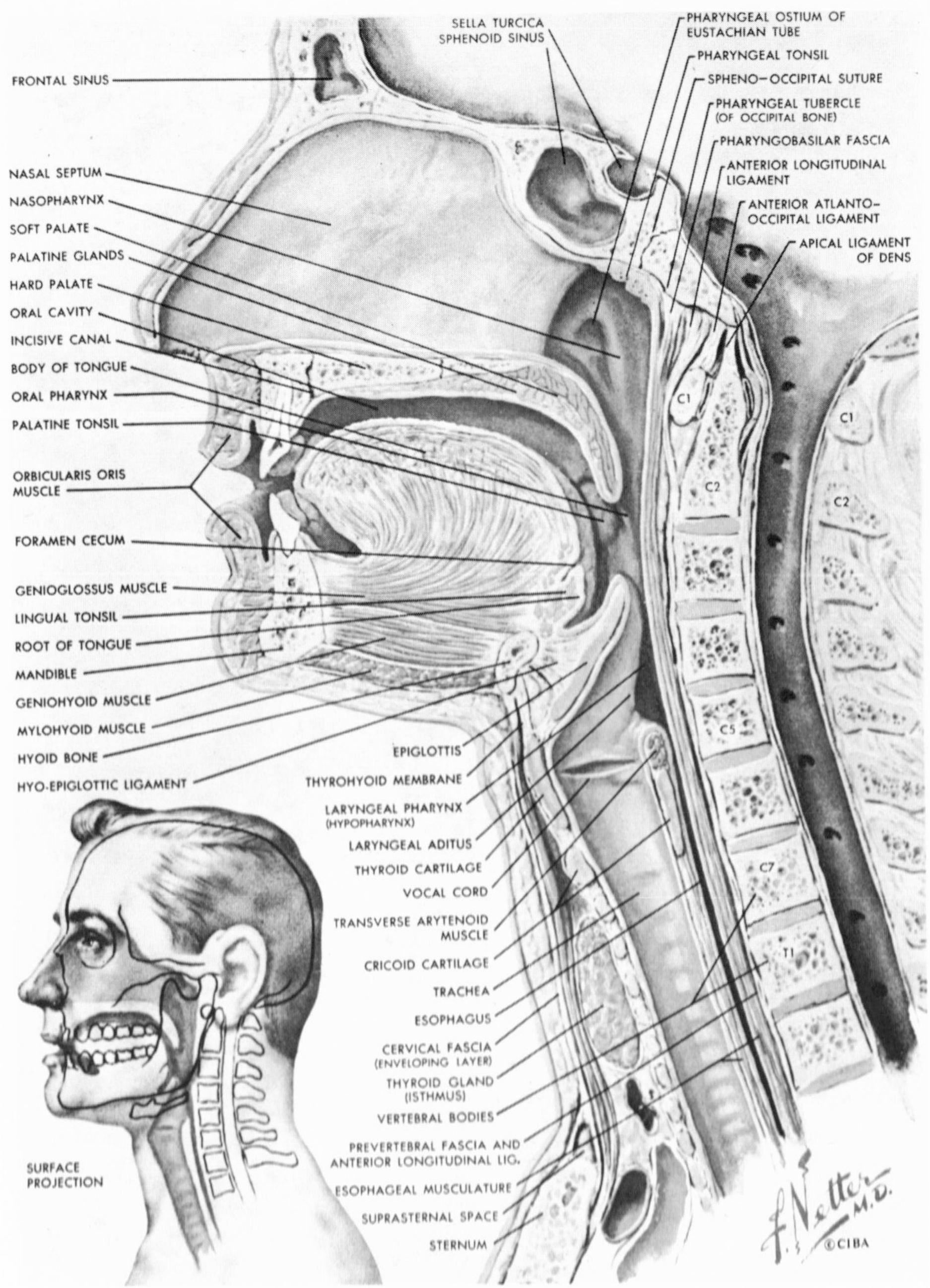

Fig. **38.** The Human Resonation System, Lateral View

From *The Ciba Collection of Medical Illustrations* by Frank H. Netter, M.D. Copyright Ciba.

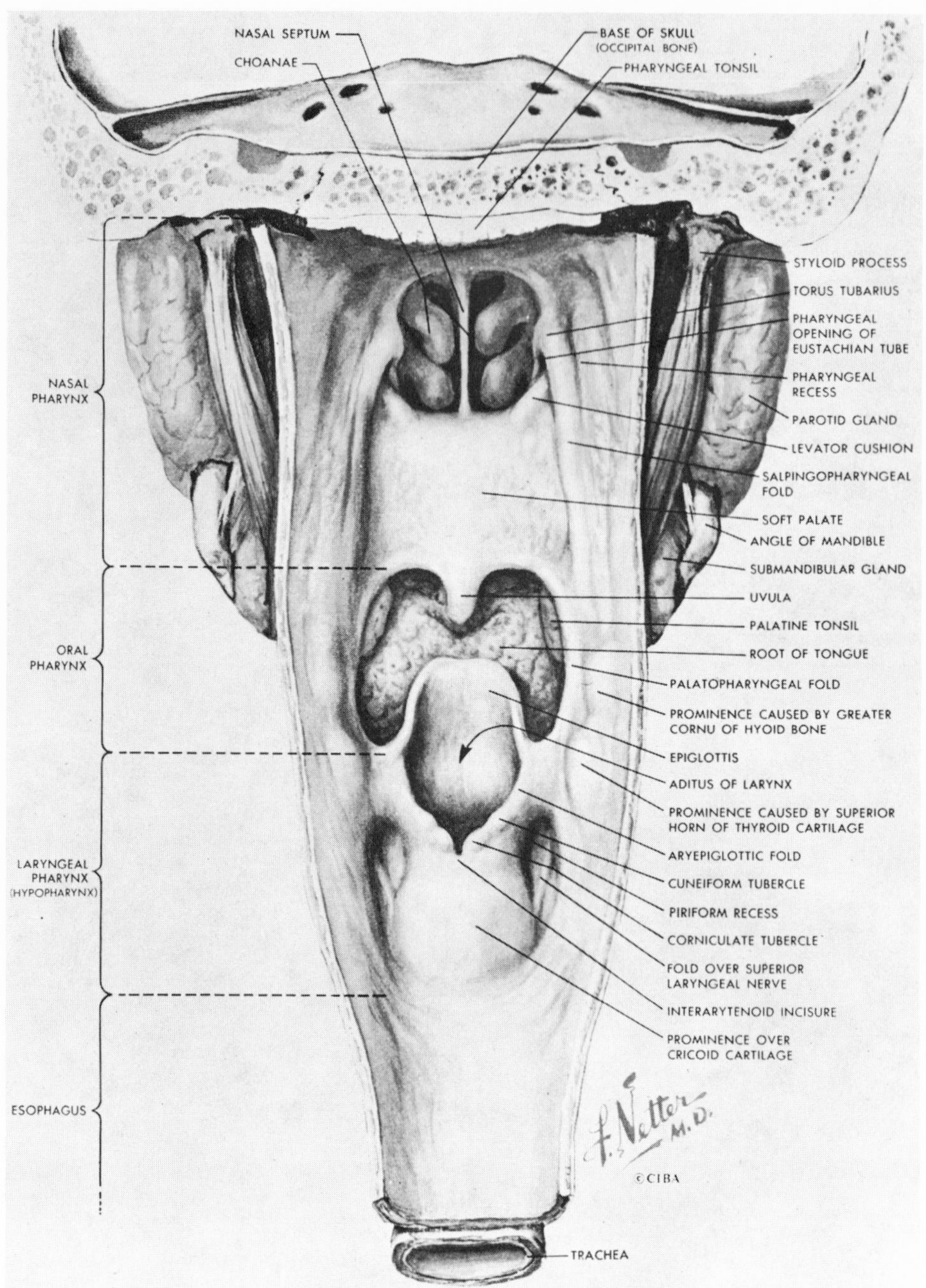

Fig. **39.** The Pharyngeal Cavity and Vestibule

From *The Ciba Collection of Medical Illustrations* by Frank H. Netter, M.D. Copyright Ciba.

pharynx are the palato-pharyngeus, the palato-glossus, and the tensor palati, which is antagonist to the levator veli palatini.

This movement permits the pharyngeal isthmus to remain open during the act of breathing and closed during the act of swallowing in order to prevent the passage of food into the nasal cavity.

As the uvula and soft palate are raised, they become tense and present a taut, hard surface for the reflection of sound. As the uvula and soft palate are loose and pendant, damping increases. This characteristic affects vowel quality and phonemic migration. The nasopharynx serves as a resonator in the production of the nasal continuants [n], [m], [ŋ], and when the velum is deliberately removed from the pharyngeal wall during the production of vowels.

The oropharynx (Fig. 39) extends vertically from the velum and uvula to the tip of the epiglottis. The anterior boundary is the postdorsum and the root of the tongue; the posterior border is the pharyngeal wall. The oropharynx is most amenable to change through the movement of the larynx. Its transverse dimension is altered by the action of the pharyngeal constrictor muscles and muscles of articulation.

The laryngopharynx (vestibule Fig. 39) is an important resonator in the coupled phonatory system, which will be described in this chapter. It extends from the tip of the epiglottis to the superior surface of the vocal folds, its lateral boundaries are the aryepiglottic folds which completely enfold it. Its superior orifice is the epiglottis, which covers it as a lid during the act of swallowing. The inferior orifice is the glottis. The laryngopharynx has within its musculature the ventricular folds (false vocal folds), which rise and nearly approximate during phonation. In rising they create beneath them, another potential resonating system, the ventricles of the larynx (Fig. 40). The formant contribution of the ventricles to the tonal spectrum is somewhat in doubt at this time.

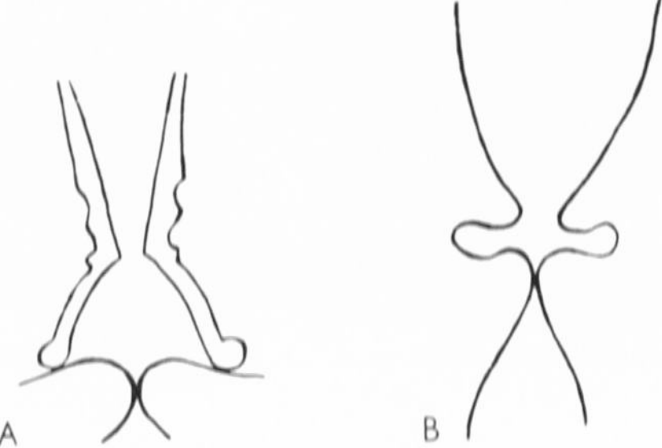

Fig. **40A,** Trumpet Mouthpiece and Player's Lips
B, Vocal Fold and Laryngeal Ventricles

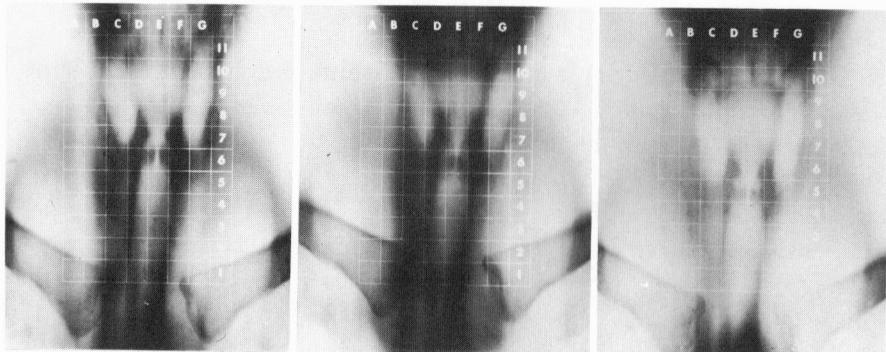

Fig. **41.** Movement of the Vestibule, Anterior View
Source: D. Ralph Appelman, "Study by Means of Planigraph, Radiograph, and Spectograph of Physiological Changes During Register Transition in Vocal Tones" (Ph.D. dissertation, School of Music, Indiana University, 1953).

Musehold suggests that the ventricles and ventricular folds form a cup-shaped cavity with a point of constriction at the ventricular fold approximation much the same as the fixed cavity within a trumpet mouthpiece (Fig. 40).[15] This assumption is a logical one, but further research is needed for its substantiation.

Tomograms made by the author at Indiana University in 1953[16] reveal the changes in the vertical and transverse conformation of the vestibule and the ventricles during the singing three vowels [i], [a], and [u], pitch f, 349 cycles per second (Fig. 41). Changes in the laryngeal position are also evident at the level of the vocal folds. The white air spaces at each side of the vestibule are the piriform sinuses, part of the foodway. They serve as an open area permitting the lateral expansion of the vestibule during phonation.

A most primary vestibular movement is evident in the variation of the position of the epiglottis during the phonation of the front and the back vowels when they are sung within the stable vowel pitch range. This anterior-posterior movement reveals changes in the vestibular opening, which alters the conformation and dimension of the vestibule during the production of each vowel (Figs. 41 and 42). During phonation this movement is controlled by movements of the tongue root anteriorly and the holding action of the thyro-epiglottic and the aryepiglottic muscles.

The Trachea

The trachea (Fig. 43) is a cartilaginous membranous tube extending from the subglottic larynx to the division of the bronchi. It is approximately eleven

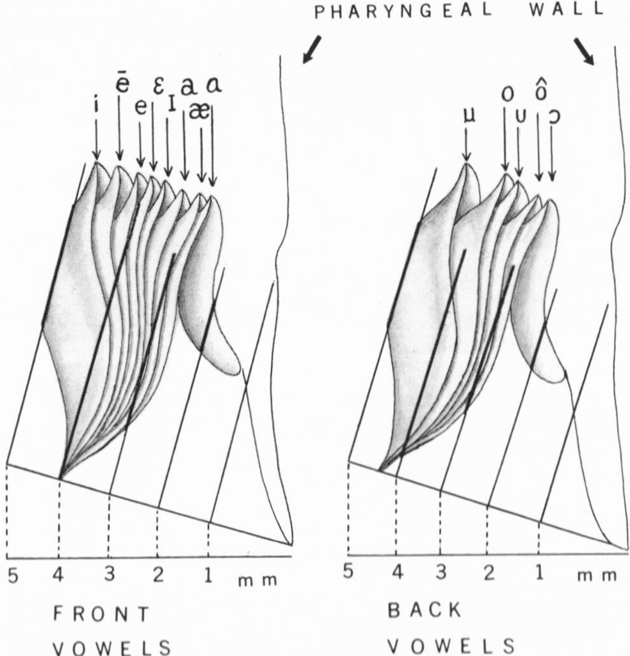

Fig. **42.** Anterior-Posterior Movement of the Epiglottis,* Lateral View

Variation in the position of the epiglottis during the phonation of vowels in the stable vowel pitch range, reveals changes in the vestibular opening which alters the conformation and dimension of the vestibule during the production of each vowel. (See also Fig. 41.)

centimeters long in men and ten centimeters long in women. The trachea has eighteen cartilages, each of which forms two-thirds of a ring. The posterior third of the circumference is made up of transverse fibers called the trachealis muscle. This muscle contracts the tracheal ring and, thereby, decreases its diameter. Relaxation of the trachealis enlarges the ring and permits the passage of large volumes of air during forced respiration.

The trachea is an important resonator in the phonatory tube, but little empirical evidence pertains to its specific function as an infraglottic resonator in singing.

Tomograms[17] reveal a tracheal alteration—a bulbous enlargement below the base of the cricoid cartilage—during the production of high pitches and increased vocal force. This condition appears in all voices. The lateral expansion

* This movement is evident in X-ray photographs which appear in Chap. 10.

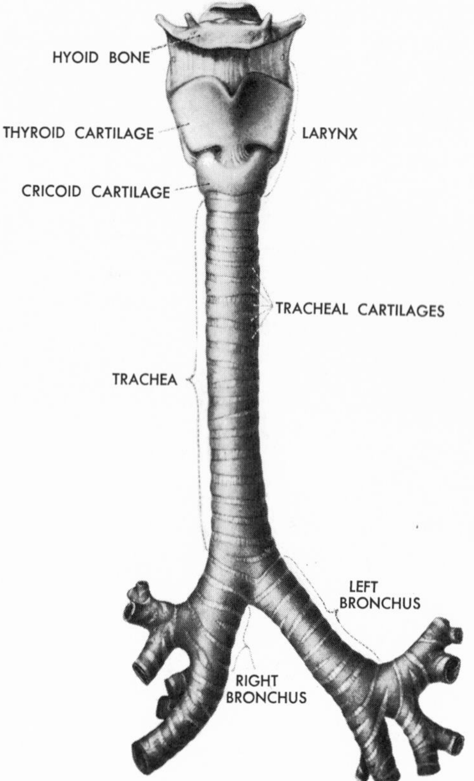

Fig. **43.** The Trachea
Source: Johannes Sobotta and Eduard Uhlenhuth, *Human Anatomy* (7th ed.; New York: Hafner Publishing Co., 1957).

is caused by infraglottic pressure, since the contraction of the trachealis muscle permits only an increase in the anterior-posterior expansion of the tracheal ring (Figs. 44–46).

The Open Throat in Singing

The open throat used in singing is the result of increasing the anterior-posterior, transverse, and vertical dimension of the oral and pharyngeal cavities from their normal positions used in the production of speech sounds. Although the movements of the postdorsum and root of the tongue are responsible for altering the size and shape of the pharyngeal cavity (See kinesiologic analysis

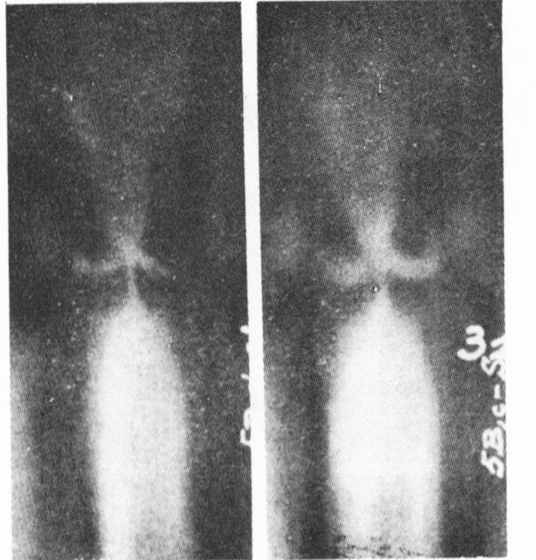

Fig. **44.** Light Soprano Singing F Sharp, 672 cps, Vowel [i]
Left, piano; right, forte.

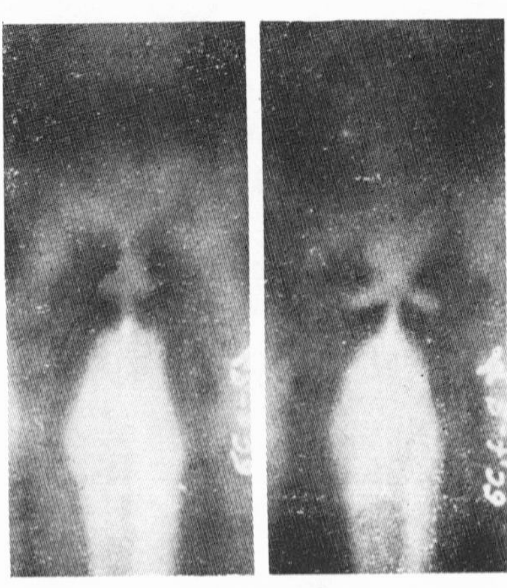

Fig. **45.** Dramatic Soprano Singing Middle C, 246 cps, Vowel [a]
Left, chest register, forte; right middle register, piano.

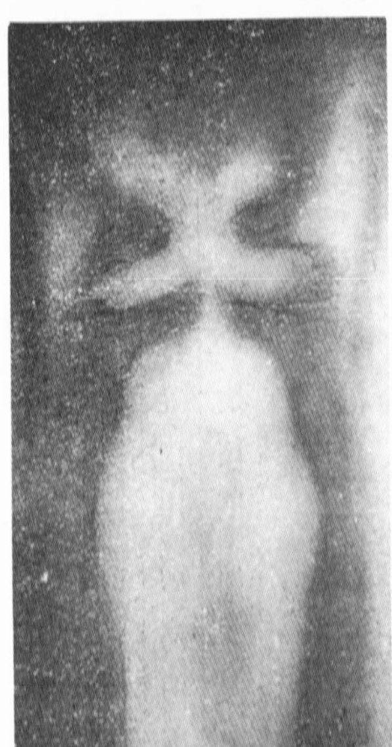

Fig. **46.** Bass, Spoken Sound, Vowel [a]

Source: Guiseppe Bellussi and Allesio Visendaz, "Il Problema Dei Registri Vocali Alla Luce della Technia Roentgenstratigrafica," *Archivo Italiano di Otologia Rinologia e Laringologia,* March-April 1949.

of vowels, Chap. 10), the suprahyoid and the infrahyoid muscles of the throat and neck create a state of muscular suspension through their action as antagonists, which firms the pharyngeal walls and stabilizes the larynx in the phonatory tube at any chosen position during singing (Figs. 47–48).

The hyoid bone serves as a central ring to which these two groups of muscles are fastened, and each group pulls in the opposite direction. Thus firmed, the hyoid bone provides a fulcrum for the quick, violent actions of the tongue during articulation in singing. Since the hyoid and the thyroid cartilage are connected by membrane and muscle, the larynx closely follows the movement of the hyoid bone in its ascending and descending movements.

Proper positioning of the larynx in the phonatory tube is a primary factor in the establishment of a sound vocal technique, for the domination of either muscle group will affect the length, tension, mass, and elasticity of the vocal fold and determine the volume of the pharynx. Each laryngeal position will affect the timbre and character of the voice and determine its function.

The singer's problem is to select the laryngeal position which is most

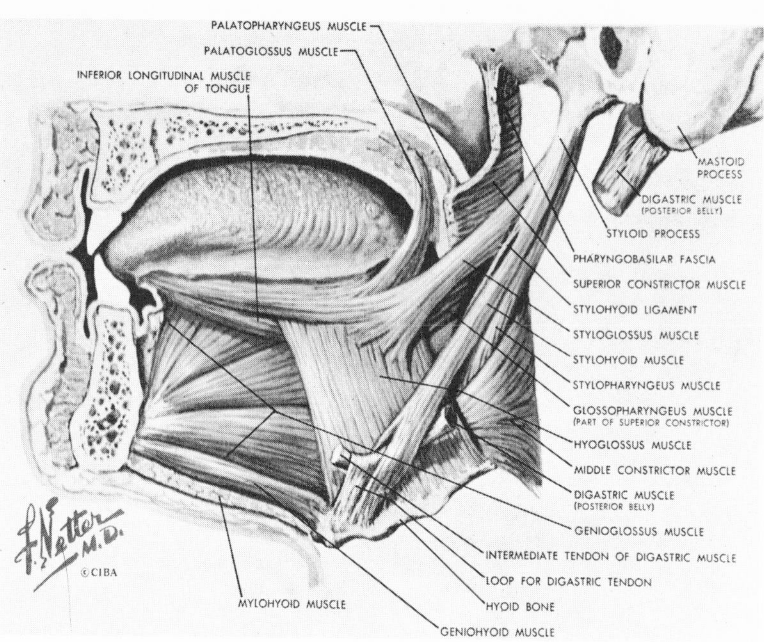

Fig. **47A.** Suprahyoid Muscles
From *Clinical Symposia* by Frank H. Netter, M.D. Copyright Ciba.

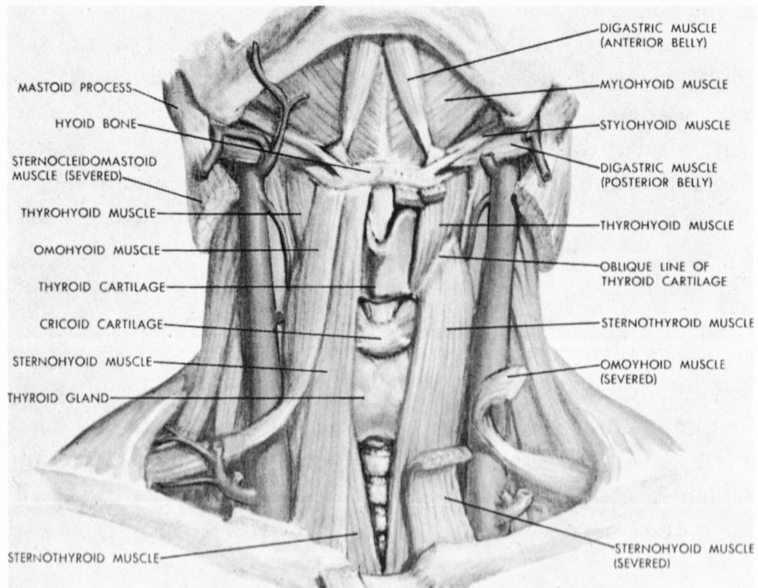

Fig. **47B.** Infrahyoid Muscles
From *Clinical Symposia* by Frank H. Netter, M.D. Copyright Ciba.

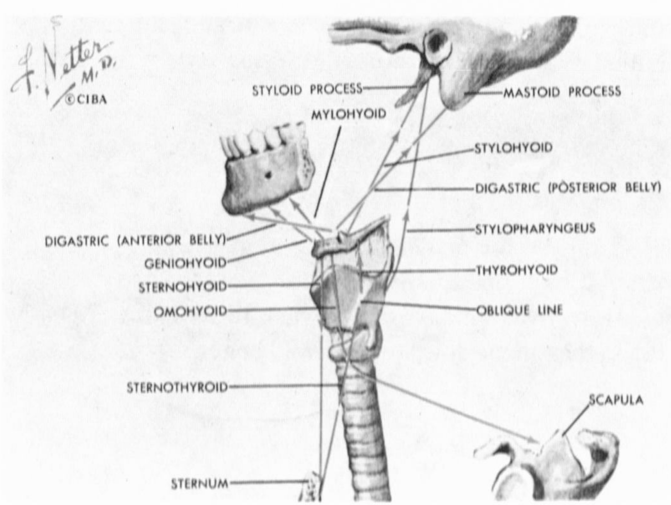

Fig. **48.** Suprahyoid and Infrahyoid Muscles, Action
From *Clinical Symposia* by Frank H. Netter, M.D. Copyright Ciba.

natural for him. Each voice has its own dimension and compatible laryngeal position for singing (Records 1-4, Band 6). If the larynx is depressed too far through the action of the infrahyoid muscles and sustained in such a position by the balanced muscular system described above, the resulting large pharyngeal space causes a dark, highly damped sound that is difficult to sustain and it also causes each phoneme to lose its integrity because of the extreme alteration of the coupled system. (See "Point, Projection, and Focus," p. 236.) If the larynx is held too high, the uttered sound becomes blatant and colorless.

The sensation of finding the proper open throat and laryngeal position in the middle voice is that of the first stage of a yawn. A yawn at the point of maximum muscular contraction is far too extreme for a good singing position, however, the expanded throat sensation must always be accentuated as the pitch is raised. The singer and the teacher must remember that the suprahyoid and infrahyoid muscle groups always act as a unit in their antagonism and never as independent muscles. (See migration levels, Fig. 103, p. 234, all of the vowel sounds recorded within this work are sung with an open-throat position.)

The Suprahyoid Muscles

The suprahyoid muscles raise the hyoid bone and the larynx. They also firm the walls of the pharynx during singing. These muscles are responsible for tense and lax conditions of a phoneme. Place the fingers under the chin and pronounce [i], [ɪ], and [ē] in sequence; notice the alternation of tense, lax, tense conditions. These muscles are genioglossus, stylohyoid, mylohyoid, geniohyoid, and digastric.

Genioglossus

Origin—Front of the mandible.
Insertion—Lower fibers to hyoid bone.
Action—Lifts hyoid and larynx, or when the hyoid is firmed by the infrahyoid, it draws the tongue down to the hyoid bone.

Stylohyoid

Origin—Cranium.
Insertion—Hyoid bone.
Action—Raises hyoid bone and larynx.

Mylohyoid

Origin—Mandible.
Insertion—Hyoid bone.
Action—Raises hyoid bone and larynx.

Digastric

Origin—Fore part of lower jaw. It forms a V shape as it passes through a tendonous loop to its point of insertion.
Insertion—Mastoid process.
Action—Raises the hyoid bone upward and back.

Geniohyoid

Origin—Mandible.
Insertion—Hyoid bone.
Action—Raises the hyoid bone and the larynx.

The Infrahyoid Muscles

The infrahyoid muscles lower the hyoid bone and depress the larynx. They also firm the pharyngeal walls during phonation. They are sternohyoid, sternothyroid, thyrohyoid, and omohyoid.

Sternohyoid

Origin—Sternum and clavicle.
Insertion—Hyoid bone.
Action—Depresses the hyoid and the larynx.

Sternothyroid

Origin—Sternum.
Insertion—Side of thyroid.
Action—Depresses the larynx, draws the thyroid cartilage downward, or assists the cricothyroid in tilting the thyroid cartilage forward and downward.

Thyrohyoid

Origin—Side of thyroid cartilage.
Insertion—Front of hyoid bone.
Action—Draws hyoid bone downward and depresses the larynx.

Omohyoid

Origin—Clavicle.
Insertion—Hyoid bone.
Action—Depresses the larynx and hyoid bone.

THEORIES OF REGISTRATION

Vocal Registers

The exact cause of registration in the singing voice is unknown. For those who seek specific information to perfect a teaching technique, the confusion of principle and terminology in voice teaching is indeed disappointing.

Professional singers more than teachers tend to believe that vocal registers do not exist. Most professionals are natural singers who have perfect body coordination and have never really confronted a register problem, or perhaps register breaks which did occur have disappeared with maturation. The average singer conceives of the vocal scale as one long extended register. His artistic goal is to pass from one register to another diatonically or intervallically without a noticeable change in quality, but the single register is more often an objective in teaching than a reality in the student voice. Many teachers believe that the head and the chest are the only registers. However, just as many believe that three registers exist (the head, middle, and chest). Despite the confusion in terminology, singers continue to sing an even scale and teachers continue to theorize.

In the human voice, registration is a physiological and an acoustical fact. Years of research by European teams[18] have contributed evidence of its existence and have verified that all voices have three registers that may be utilized in singing, but this research has contributed little information on their function. They define the vocal register as follows:

> A register within the human vocal scale is a series of sounds of equal quality. The musical ear distinguishes them from another series of sound also of equal quality. The limits of each series are marked

> by "points" of passage sometimes called "lifts." The timbre of each series, or register, is the result of a constant rapport of harmony. To the male singer the primary register change at the upper part of the scale gives a certain vibrating sensation perceptible to the head. To the female the primary register change at the lower part of the scale gives a certain vibratory sensation to the chest. Each area of identical quality depends upon the adjustment of the resonating cavities.
>
> Registers are produced by a mechanism that functions in the production of sound. The principal characteristic of this mechanism is the manner in which a particular laryngeal vibration is coupled with the supraglottic (area above the vocal folds) and the infraglottic (area below the vocal folds) resonators.[19]

Since one octave separates the masculine and feminine voices, the point of transition from the chest register to the head register for women occurs at the same height in the scale. Therefore, the point of transition occurs by acoustical law and through an adaptation of the total resonating space, always on the level of the same frequencies, E flat, 311 Hz and F 350 Hz.

All pitch skips that involve moving from one register to another demand a conscious adjustment of the coupled resonating system and the phonatory mechanism in one synchronous act. Enlargement of the resonators is no more important than controlling the vocal folds. Each act must complement the other.

At the moment of passing (transition between registers), the position of the larynx in the phonatory tube changes much more in the trained voice than it does in an untrained voice. The greater change results from the trained singer's attempt to enlarge the pharyngeal resonators by yawning and simultaneously stabilizing and tilting the thyroid cartilage forward, thereby tensing the vocal folds (Fig. 27).

The single-register voice is not altogether a matter of vocal education. Some voices, through practice, may become homogeneous and uniform in quality and emission, but such an achievement is hardly within reach of all voices. A beautiful voice that fulfills the ideals of Western vocal culture is a gift of birth, and methodical teaching is not the principal element in its production.

Manuel Garcia's Theory of Registration

The theory of registers advanced by Manuel Garcia, frequently quoted by teachers of singing, should be considered. Garcia achieved fame as a teacher and for his invention, the laryngoscope, which is widely used. He said:

> Every voice is formed of three distinct portions, or registers, namely, chest (lowest), medium (middle), and head (highest). [These names are incorrect but accepted.]
>
> A register is a series of consecutive homogeneous sounds produced by one mechanism differing from another series of sounds equally homogeneous, produced by another mechanism, whatever modifications of timbre or strength they may offer. Each of the three registers has its own extent and sonority which vary according to the sex of the individual and the nature of the organ.[20]

The chest voice in women was considered by Garcia to be strong and energetic; however, he believed that it should not be used above the notes e flat and e natural, for to do so would abuse it. He also believed that the middle register is of equal extent in all female voices, that it differed only in strength and quality, but that it too frequently was veiled and weak.

Garcia believed that the head voice (Fig. 49) is the highest and most sonorous and that it possesses the power of penetration. He observed that in robust voices the medium register blends easily with the head register, but that in weak voices the union is unstable and often broken.

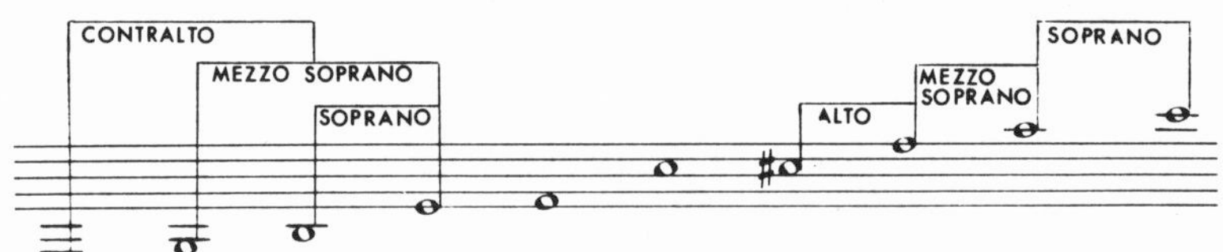

Registers in the Female Voice
(After Garcia)

Garcia believed the middle and upper registers in male voices were remnants of the adolescent voice, and considered the entire singing range of the male voice to be predominantly chest voice. The tenor has greater skill in using the falsetto or head register, but he blends the top notes by using the closed or dark timbre (Fig. 49).

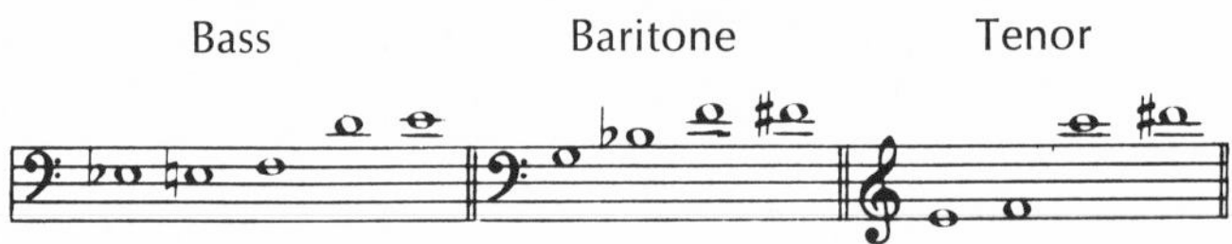

Registers in the Male Voice
(After Garcia)

Closed and Open Tones

The terms *closed tones* and *open tones* are synonymous with *closed vowels* and *open vowels* (Figs. 74A and 74B, p. 229). They are used interchangeably with the terms *covered tones* and *uncovered tones*. These terms are rooted deeply in the traditions of voice teaching and generally have been accepted by phoneticians and voice scientists. Luchsinger[21] has stated that the term *cover* or the use of the darkened vocal timbre as a device for bridging into the upper voice was first exploited about 1830 by French singers, notably Duprez. Up to that time the *voix blanche* or the white tone was preferred. Diday and Petrequin[22] described the new technique as "voix sombrés, couverte, ou en dedans" (dark voice covered within the larynx). The physiological descriptions are similar to our present understandings of low, stable laryngeal positioning and an enlarged resonating system.

However, most phoneticians describe such vowels as being tense (closed) or lax (open). These descriptive words indicate the degree of muscular tension present in the uttered sound. The bright, ringing quality present in the open vowels and the veiled, softer sounds of the closed vowels are not caused entirely by an alteration of the coupled system (Fig. 74). Gordon Peterson* of the Bell Telephone Laboratories has explained the change in vocalic quality in these words:

> The walls of the mouth and pharynx can be changed in texture by changing the tension of the musculature of the lips, tongue, and pharyngeal walls. As a result, the reflection of selected overtones is modified, so that the timbre of the vowel tone being uttered is itself modified, or even shifted in the direction of a different vowel. The difference between [i] and [ɪ], for example, and between [u] and [ʊ] are apparently achieved partly by a change of muscular tension in the tongue, though typically there is also change in the size of the mouth cavity. This change of lingual tension can easily be detected by placing the thumb and forefinger under the lower jaw and pressing firmly against the tissue below the tongue while pronouncing [i]-[ɪ] and [u]-[ʊ]. It may be concluded that when the inner surface of the mouth cavity, especially the floor, is firm, the cavity selects from the tone complex the proper combination of fundamental and overtones to produce [i], while the musculature is soft, the cavity selects the

* In Claude Merton Wise, *Applied Phonetics*, 1957. Reprinted by permission of Prentice-Hall, Inc., Englewood Cliffs, New Jersey.

> combination appropriate for [ɪ]. In similar fashion, firm cavity surface helps to produce [u], soft surface to produce [ʊ]. Accordingly, [i], [u], and the like are called tense vowels, and [ɪ], [ʊ], and the like, lax vowels.[23]

These terms identify changes in tone that may be detected by the ear, and as such, they also identify the vocal adjustment that enables a singer to pass evenly from the middle register to the upper register. The "covering" mechanism of transition from the chest voice to the upper voice is used primarily in male voices. It is always effected with the closed vowel—the reason for "covering" is to avoid the open vowel sound. The contralto and the dramatic soprano may sometimes use it, but the soprano and coloratura soprano do not use it at all because the point of primary transition occurs on the low pitches of the female voice (Fig. 51). This adjustment in the male voice commonly is taught by imitation or by trial and error, since the exact nature of the action is unknown.

The terms *open* and *closed* have been used extensively by teachers of bel canto, the vocal techniques of the eighteenth century, which placed emphasis upon beauty of sound and brilliance of performance rather than on dramatic expression or romantic emotion.

One of the objectives of the singers of bel canto was the development of a vocal scale that was pure, unbroken, and uninterrupted. The transition of registers—either up or down the scale—demanded a modification in the tonal color of the topmost notes to prevent them from becoming disagreeable and harsh and to preserve the quality of the vowel sound as well as an even tonal line. The bel canto expression, "All vowels must be modified in the head voice for the sake of beauty," has caused teachers to use the modifications of vowels as a means for transition into the upper voice.

The voice of a man or woman of college age is a voice in transition, and the vocal problems confronted by such a person are numerous and varied. Seldom is such a voice stable and mature. The problems of range and register are a concern of the teacher, but they are doubly important to the impatient student. Therefore, the attempt to develop range in itself is not wise, for to do so makes the problem a primary objective of both teacher and student; in many instances, such an objective has become a studio fetish.

The basic phonatory position of the closed vowel or covered tone and its transition into the upper voice may be taught to any male student after he has acquired a knowledge of phonetics and after he is able to reproduce vowels in both open and closed position in both speech and song.

The most important factor in the selection of the proper phoneme (vowel position) by a singer is his awareness of the manner in which the resonators are coupled to produce a particular vowel sound (Fig. 75).

Transition for the Male Voice

Teachers of singing realize and research verifies that all voices have three registers that may be utilized in singing. Each register is separated by a point of transition; these points are indicated upon the diagram in Fig. 51. The pitches upon which these points are found depend upon the character of each individual voice and its tessitura. Thus, the point of passage may vary a major second above or below the pitch suggested.

In male voices the transition most likely to be evident to the performer and the listener is the transition from the middle register to the top register

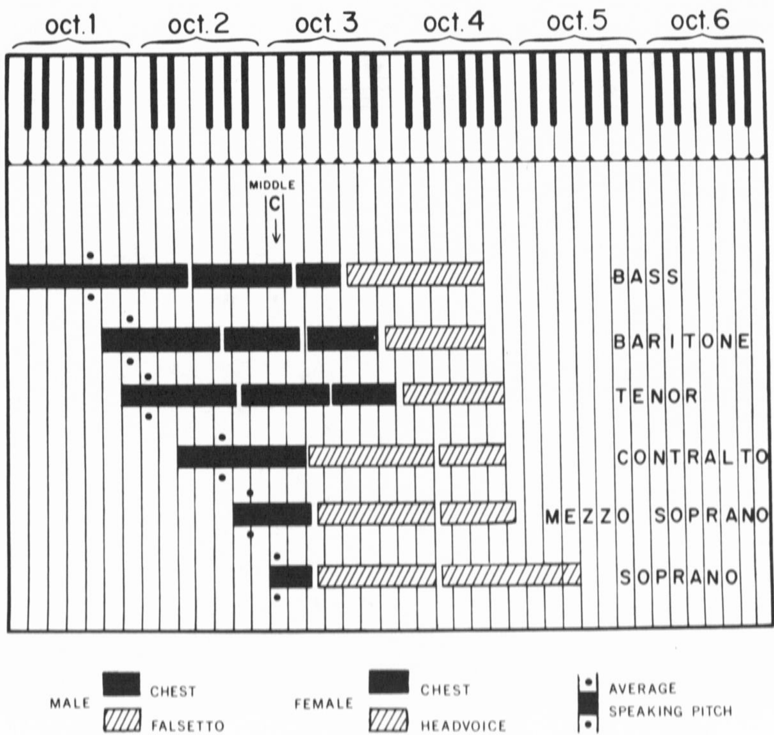

Fig. **49.** Registration Chart
(After Tarneau)

because the change is effected by alteration of the phonatory mechanism as well as a change in the resonating system. However, in many voices this transition point is not evident to the listener, nor does it pose a problem to the singer. The lower points of transition are as follows:

for bass for baritone for tenor.

They are evident only in the beginning singer's scale and do not need special pedagogical technique.

In making the transition into the upper voice, an instantaneous coordination of respiration (breath support), phonation (unrestricted vocal sound), and resonation (forming the proper vowel) must occur; otherwise, the transition will seem awkward to the listener, and uncomfortable and unstable to the performer. The upper points of transition are as follows:

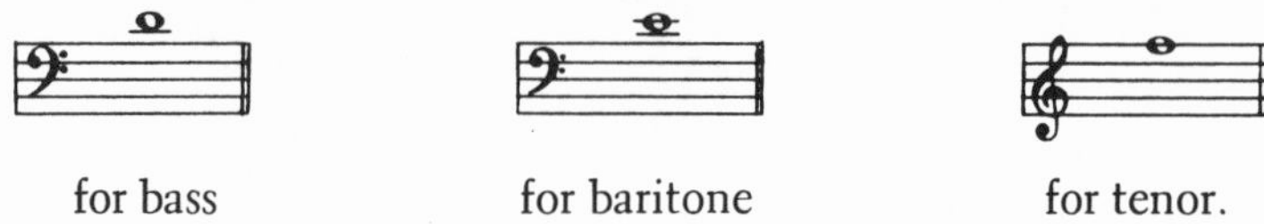

for bass for baritone for tenor.

The student eventually will discover the ideal coordination of these four forces by directives from his teacher. Here he needs to examine visually only the position of the resonators and articulators during such a transition. (See the kinesiologic analysis, Chap. 10; the student may examine the same transitions aurally on Records 1-4, Band 5.)

All transitions into the upper voice by the male singer are made with a closed vowel. The back vowels [u] and [o] and the central [ʌ] are vowels that make this transition automatic. All covered vowels are closed sounds. The [ʌ] as in *up* is considered neutral and more "singly resonant" than other phonemes and, although it is an open vowel within the staff, from top space E it becomes a closed neutral sound. Teaching this transition by using an open vowel sound is not possible because, when the male sings notes above top space E, treble clef, the sound becomes disagreeable and harsh.

The student has more difficulty learning the transition into the upper voice by using the central vowel [ɑ] or any of the frontal vowels. The easiest procedure is to start with [u] as in *food* and progress clockwise around the vowel triangle until the frontals are reached and mastered. (Consult Chap. 9, for complete register changes and the recordings for performance of such changes.)

Transition for the Female

In the female voice the transition from the middle to the lower chest register—

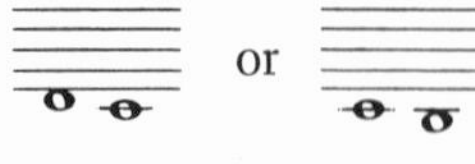

for the contralto

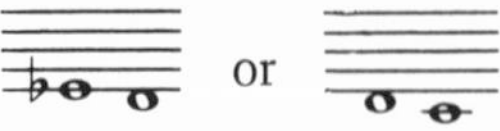

for the soprano or mezzo soprano

is most evident to both singer and listener because the transition is effected by an adjustment of the phonatory mechanism. A woman may have a strong muscular adjustment of the larynx and throat, which permits her to make this transition downward and upward into the chest voice with no evidence of a change in quality. However, such singers are the exception and not the rule. The chest voice is a necessary part of the female singer's vocal range and should be so conceived and developed.

The female problem of bridging occurs while making the transition downward from the middle voice into the chest voice (black area, Fig. 49) or upward from the chest voice to the middle voice.

Most experienced female singers tend to extend the chest quality to—

G or A

in formal singing. They should never carry the chest quality or mechanism above—

E flat.

The higher this quality is carried, the more difficult and obvious the transition becomes, and the more strident the voice sounds.

In making the transition from middle register to chest register descending, a female singer usually "feels" a change in mechanism, she decreases vocal force by using less energy and by slightly lowering the jaw. She attempts to "ease" her voice into the lower registration mechanism. The basic vowel is always maintained through this pitch change—ascending or descending without modification.

The quality of the middle voice, that pitch area from—

E flat to B flat,

should become the model quality for notes below—

C.

The female singer should avoid excessive vocal force while singing in the chest area.

The secondary point of transition for the female voice occurring on the suggested pitch—

is not evident to the listener, but it is evident by its instability to many singers as they attempt to pass into the top register by pitch skip or by diatonic scale. Descending scales sung on the neutral vowel [ʌ] help to strengthen this point of transition.

The Adduction of the Vocal Folds

Pressman attributes the primary change in register, or the "break" in the voice, to the moment of adduction of the posterior portion of the thyroarytenoid evident in the production of pitches which lie above the point of transition in the male voice. (See p. 92.) Such a premise assumes that an identical change in mechanism will occur in the female voice at the primary register change into the chest voice. (See p. 93.) It assumes that the female can sing all of the tones above chest voice with a portion of the vocal folds in adduction, that is, with the posterior portion of the folds in adduction, as in Fig. 34 never as in Fig. 33. This theory is most plausible and could be the answer to changes in sensation experienced by the male or female singer at such points of transition. However, adduction may or may not take place in all voices. Variation of laryngeal function as well as breath pressure may be employed. (The detailed synthesis of damping and register change is described on pp. 89, 92, and 119.)

Physiological Changes. Studies at Indiana University, using tomography and cineradiology (X-ray motion pictures)[24] as a means of analysis, reveal that, during the transition from a low pitch on which an open vowel is sung to a higher pitch above the register change on which a closed vowel is sung, the larynx is lowered an average of three to five millimeters in forming the front vowels and five to eight millimeters in forming the central and back vowels. This act of lowering the vibrator (vocal fold) causes the entire phonatory tube, extending from the oral cavity to the bifurcation of the trachea, to increase its basic dimension, this increases the coupled system so that the pharynx becomes the primary resonator.

The physiological changes which occur at the point of passage at the primary register change in both male and female are illustrated in Figs. 50A and 50B. (The sound resulting from these changes may be heard on Records 1-4, Band 5.) The laryngeal alterations sound bilabial.

The anatomical alterations shown in Fig. 50A and 50B are most dramatically displayed as the singer sings the open and closed positions upon the same pitch, E natural for the bass voice and C-256 for the mezzo soprano. The singer must remember that, when he is moving through the point of passage, ascending or descending, muscular control of the laryngeal position and alterations of the dimension of the resonating system will cause this change to occur gradually.

This enlargement of the resonating system is necessary to accommodate the alterations in the laryngeal function which occur at the point of passage of the vowel sound. Perhaps the most significant physical alteration to be sensed by the male singer as he "passes" or "bridges" into the upper voice or by the female singer as she passes downward into the lower voice is the lowering of the larynx and the narrowing of the vestibule which determines the phonemic characteristics of the uttered sound.

As the larynx is lowered, it imparts to the laryngeal organs a stability they could not attain with the vibrator at a higher point and with the phonatory tube altered in width and length. The physical sensation experienced by the singer during the adjustment is primarily that of a yawn. The physiological action consists of lowering and fixing the larynx through the action of the antagonist musculature, described on page 84. The increased laryngeal tension also secures the adducted portion of the vocal folds and permits the margins of the reduced glottal aperture to become stable and to vibrate freely (Fig. 31B). These muscles act to depress the floor of the mouth, the base of the tongue and the larynx. The broadening of the supraglottic space results from the action of this muscular set, which, when combined with the firming action of the suprahyoid muscles, adds stability to the pharyngeal area through an opposing action.

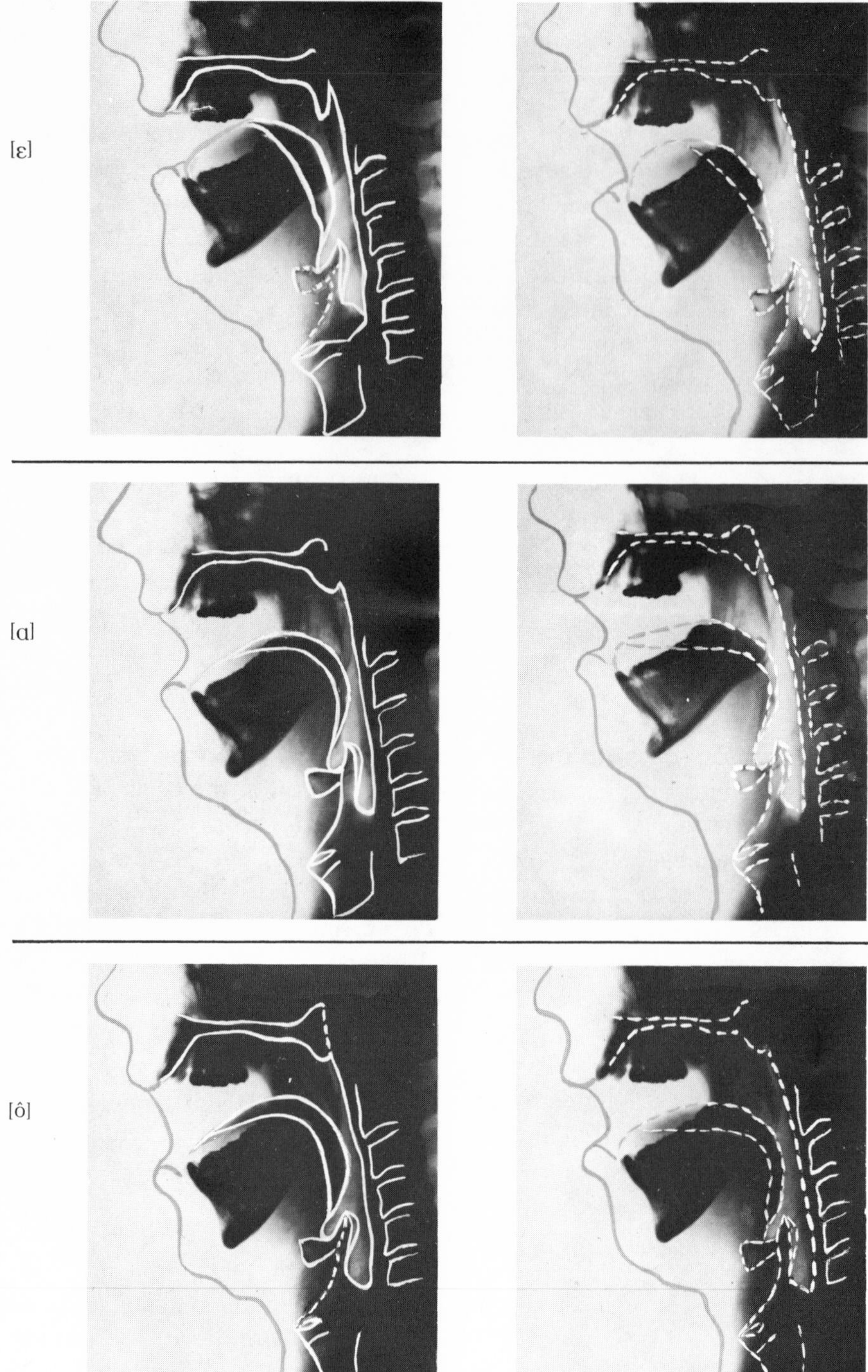

Fig. **50A.** Radiographs of Male Voice at the Primary Register Change

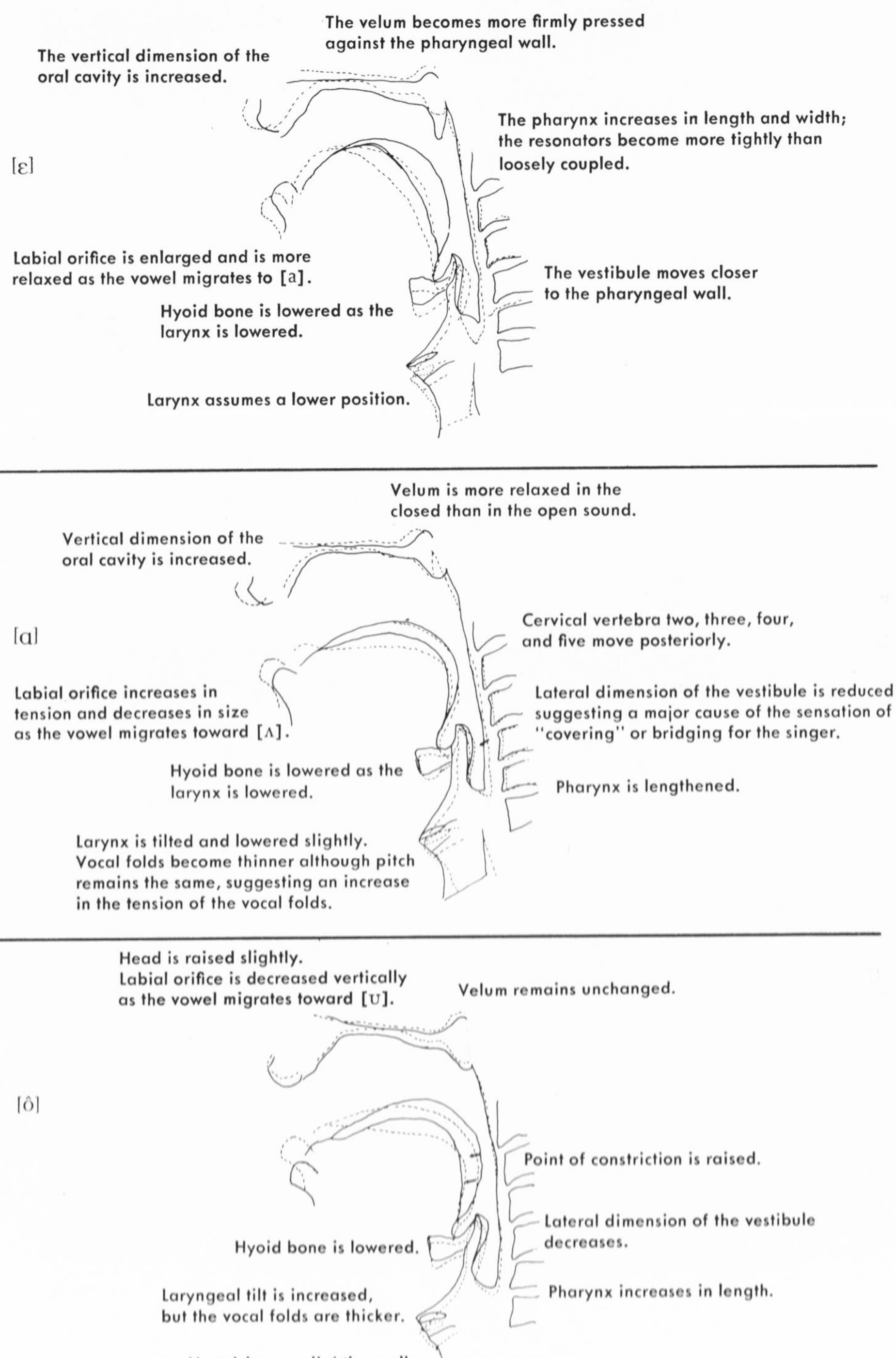
The velum becomes more firmly pressed against the pharyngeal wall.
The vertical dimension of the oral cavity is increased.
The pharynx increases in length and width; the resonators become more tightly than loosely coupled.
[ɛ]
Labial orifice is enlarged and is more relaxed as the vowel migrates to [a].
The vestibule moves closer to the pharyngeal wall.
Hyoid bone is lowered as the larynx is lowered.
Larynx assumes a lower position.
Velum is more relaxed in the closed than in the open sound.
Vertical dimension of the oral cavity is increased.
[ɑ]
Cervical vertebra two, three, four, and five move posteriorly.
Labial orifice increases in tension and decreases in size as the vowel migrates toward [ʌ].
Lateral dimension of the vestibule is reduced suggesting a major cause of the sensation of "covering" or bridging for the singer.
Hyoid bone is lowered as the larynx is lowered.
Pharynx is lengthened.
Larynx is tilted and lowered slightly. Vocal folds become thinner although pitch remains the same, suggesting an increase in the tension of the vocal folds.
Head is raised slightly. Labial orifice is decreased vertically as the vowel migrates toward [ʊ].
Velum remains unchanged.
[ô]
Point of constriction is raised.
Lateral dimension of the vestibule decreases.
Hyoid bone is lowered.
Laryngeal tilt is increased, but the vocal folds are thicker.
Pharynx increases in length.
Ventricles are slightly smaller.

Superimposition of negatives display anatomical movement.
Solid line——open vowel Dotted line . . . . . closed or covered vowel

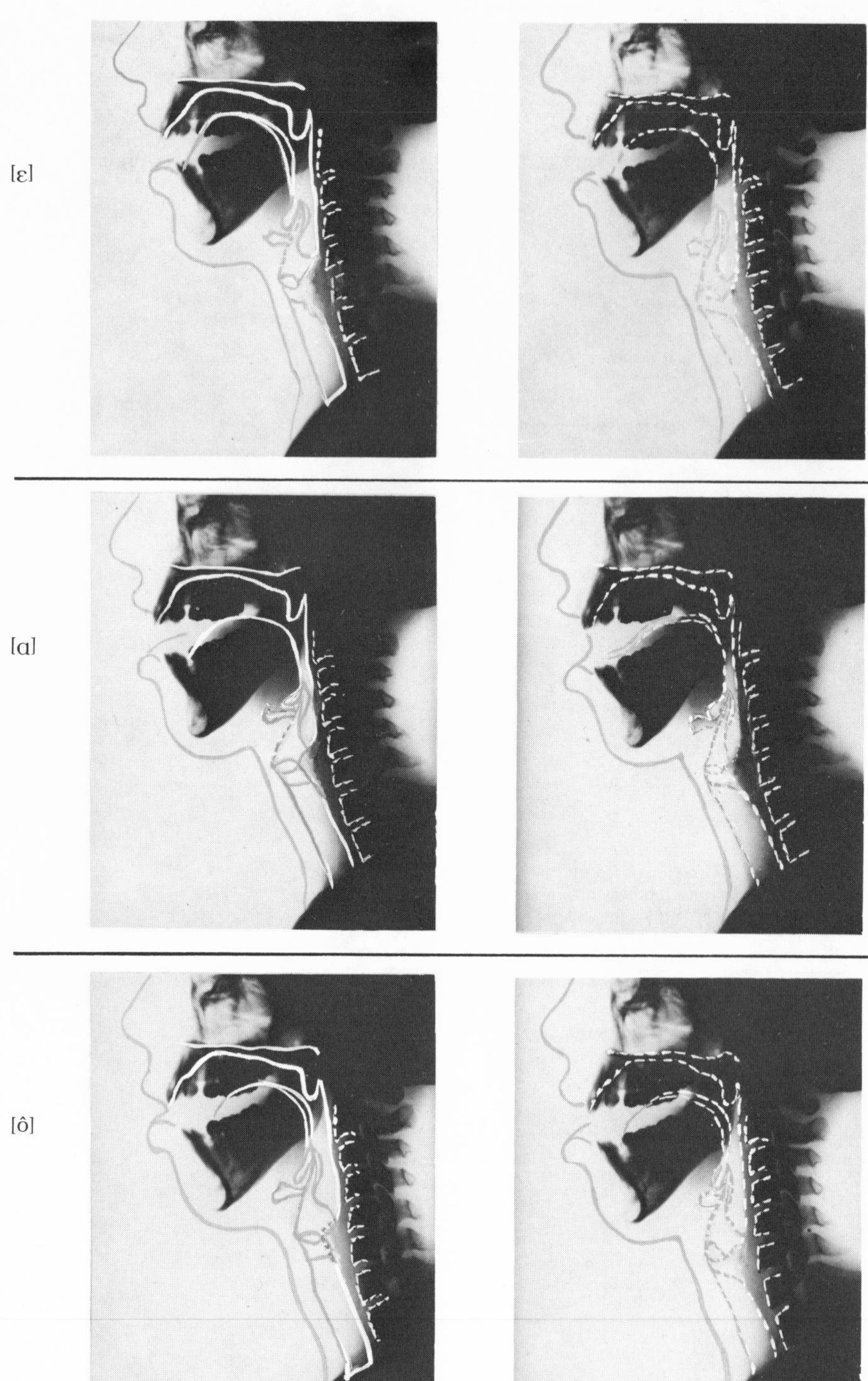

 Fig. **50B.** Radiographs of Female Voice at the Primary Register Change

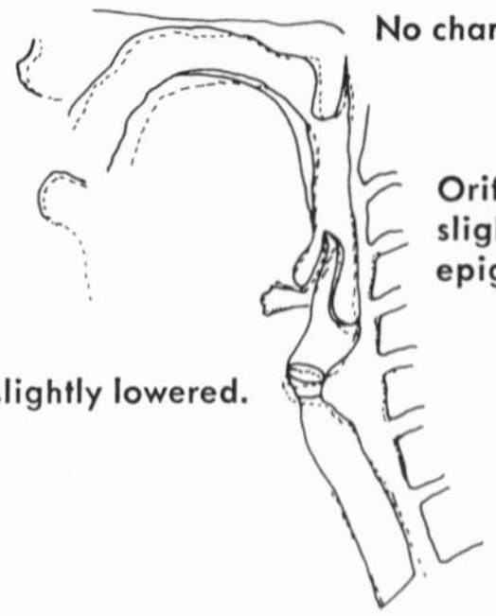

[ɛ]

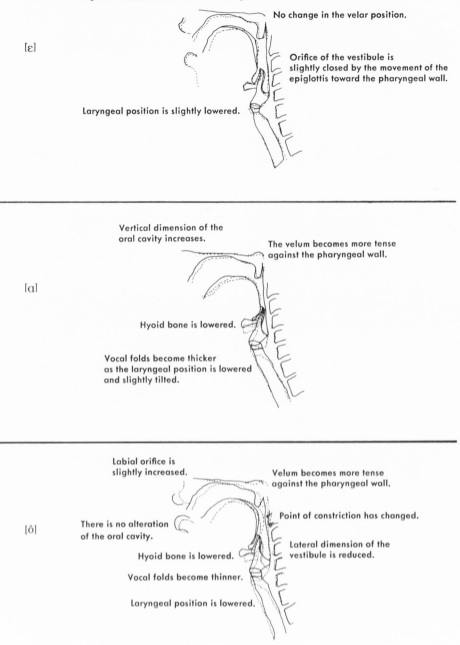

No change in the dimension of the oral cavity.

No change in the velar position.

Orifice of the vestibule is slightly closed by the movement of the epiglottis toward the pharyngeal wall.

Laryngeal position is slightly lowered.

[ɑ]

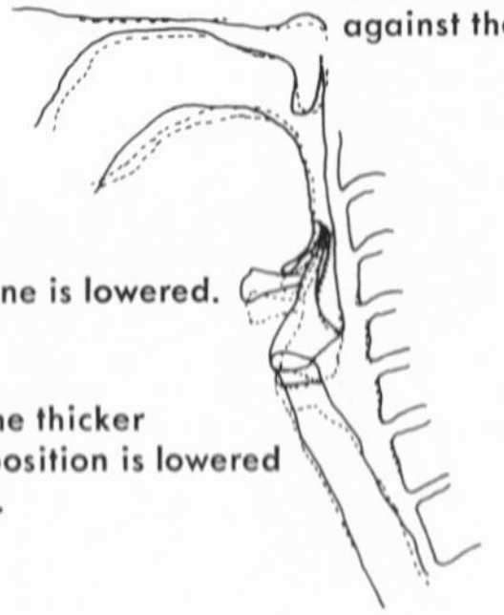

Vertical dimension of the oral cavity increases.

The velum becomes more tense against the pharyngeal wall.

Hyoid bone is lowered.

Vocal folds become thicker as the laryngeal position is lowered and slightly tilted.

[ô]

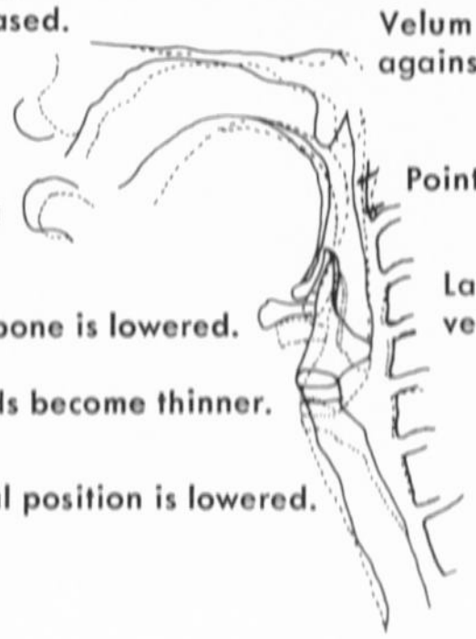

Labial orifice is slightly increased.

Velum becomes more tense against the pharyngeal wall.

Point of constriction has changed.

There is no alteration of the oral cavity.

Lateral dimension of the vestibule is reduced.

Hyoid bone is lowered.

Vocal folds become thinner.

Laryngeal position is lowered.

Superimposition of negatives display anatomical movement.
Solid line ——— middle voice Dotted line . . . . . chest voice

PEDAGOGICAL PRINCIPLES

Intensity, Laryngeal Function, and Registration

Constant singing within a proper pitch range and within controlled intensity limits will result in vocal growth, but the use of excessive range and excessive intensities may permanently impair the human voice. A proper pitch range is one which is suitable for a specific voice and not a class of voices; i.e., all sopranos do not possess the same tessitura, and what would be easy for one may be difficult for another. The same rule would apply to voices regarding the use of proper intensities. Too many singers sing pitches that are above their natural tessitura and sing them much too loudly, too constantly. Many authors have described the physical process by which the proper balance between pressure and resistance may be attained,[25] i.e., the balance between the driving force of the abdominal musculature, the resistance of the thoracic musculature, and the laryngeal controls necessary to produce a vocalized sound that will not result in a deterioration of the voice. Such pedagogy may only be taught by psychological systems, and to the singer, the residual concept of such a proper balance is always a sensation. He remembers how he felt when such a physical state was attained. (See "Support," p. 11.)

The coordinate relationship of mental concepts of tone to respiratory and phonatory disciplines of the body in song has long been a most disturbing problem for the voice teacher. Contemporary scientific research of Pressman, Sonnonin, Rose, Van Den Berg,[26] and others has contributed a logical interpretation of this phenomenon which tends to support the vibrating-string theory.

A change in intensity always should be effected gradually by a disciplined coordination of the laryngeal muscles and the muscles of expiration. Such a change involves a gradual alteration of the length, mass, and tension of the vocal folds and a constantly increasing or decreasing breath pressure. Singers often effect this change by conceptual means, i.e., by attempting to avoid a change in quality (timbre) or by attempting to maintain a particular vowel color. Regardless of the pedagogy involved, the residual rule is that the change must be made gradually and smoothly.

The gradual change of intensity on a single pitch at the point of register transition, rather than diatonic drills which involve high tessitura, is the basis of the bel canto technique as reported by Mancini, Bernacchi, and Issac Nathan by Reid.[27] Such statements as those which follow give evidence of the importance of the coordinate control of the laryngeal action and the breath pressure in developing a firm singing technique:

> The excessive use of the messa di voce, or swelled tone by early Italians was a persistent attempt to join the two registers.[28]

> As the early Italians always considered the art of singing to mean an absolute control over dynamics and an ability to swell and to diminish the intensity of the tone, the inference is plain that the registers are to be joined by swelling from piano to forte.[29]

> In the advanced stages of training, the performance of the messa di voce must be practiced continuously until there is an exact matching of both quality and intensity at each point of transition. After this technique has been mastered the break disappears. . . . This is the singing style known as Bel Canto.[30]

Singing the Messa di Voce

An increase in breath pressure will elevate the pitch of a sung sound. Therefore, to sing messa di voce the pitch must be maintained while the breath pressure is varied. Such an act directly changes the amplitude of the vibrations of the vocal folds through the alterations of their length, tension, mass, and elasticity. This change in amplitude must be in direct ratio to the alterations of the abdominal and the thoracic pressure and must be accompanied by a fixation of the volume of the resonating space for each vowel that is sung.

In effecting the transition from a forte to a piano sound, the amplitude of vocal fold vibration will decrease. The decreasing abdominal pressure will result in less breath flow. The thoracic, or diaphragmatic, pressure will increase and cause a sensation of holding back the breath. The resonating space must remain open and expanded to the jaw position assumed during the production of the forte sound to preserve the integrity of the phoneme.

In effecting the transition from a piano to a forte sound the reverse is true. The amplitude of the vocal fold vibration and the abdominal pressure will increase. The thoracic pressure will decrease. To preserve the integrity of the phoneme and to accommodate the increased intensity, the volume of the total phonatory tract will increase.

Laryngeal Action and Pitch Change*

To sing a scale evenly, the same ratios of breath pressure to laryngeal control are employed as those employed in singing the messa di voce, for the ratio between pitch change and the increase of intensity in a sung scale passage should be constant.

The thoracic and diaphragmatic pressure should be increased gradually

* See also p. 69.

as the pitch is raised to give the singer the sensation of holding back the breath. If this control is not achieved, the scale becomes much louder as the pitch rises. Drills must be devised to teach the voice student how to develop these controls lest he learn a process of singing in which he cannot vary intensity throughout the scale and in which he depends upon the same intensity for the production of all song.

VOCAL PEDAGOGY AND LARYNGEAL CONTROLS

The following statements by Pressman are a summation of the application of the foregoing theories of respiratory and laryngeal functions as they may be applied to a teaching process.

Because of variations among persons in the length, breadth, general outline, and tension of the vocal folds, as well as in habits concerning the degree of the expiratory force utilized in producing tones, production of any given tone in different subjects by exactly the same mode or method of laryngeal action is impossible. Even two persons with strikingly similar voices of exactly the same range are not likely to produce a particular tone in exactly the same way. Each singer will vary in concept of tone quality, vowel postures, and breath support. If, for example, one singer uses slightly less expiratory force than the other in producing an exactly equivalent tone, the diminished air pressure must be compensated for by an increased approximation or by tension of the vocal folds. For instance, one singer may even need to bring the posterior tips of the folds into contact for adduction, whereas this would not be necessary for the singer who utilizes a greater force of expired air. Thus, two singers can produce the same sound in two different ways. Yet, these differences in expired air pressure and laryngeal configuration may result not only in the production of the same tone, but the volume of the sound thus produced may also be exactly the same. Differences in the resonating system of the two persons and other indeterminate characteristics account for production of the same tone even though the expiratory pressures and the contour of the vocal folds remain the same.

Therefore, one can never ascribe a particular laryngeal picture to the production of any given tone. However, certain broad general principles do apply, and with respect to any larynx, one can predict within certain limits what changes will take place in that larynx as one begins at the lowest note which the particular larynx can produce and ascends the scale to reach its highest possible note.

Chapter 4

Laws That Govern Vocal Sound

THE PROCESS OF SOUND ANALYSIS*

An analysis of sound demands an interpretation of the laws that govern the propagation of sound through material media. Sound may be defined as "any vibratory disturbance in a material medium which is capable of producing an auditory sensation in the normal ear."[1] The vibratory motion of any sounding body is transmitted to the ear through any medium, such as air, solids, and liquids. Such a motion creates energy, which is conveyed from particle to particle until it reaches the ear or is dissipated within the medium. In the propagation of sound, all particles within the medium are disturbed in the direction in which the sound is propagated. Such a disturbance is called a longitudinal wave (Fig. 51).

One must remember that air as a gaseous medium possesses elasticity. Each particle has the ability to return to its original position after imparting the energy within the sound wave to its neighboring air particle within the medium. The prong of the tuning fork, as it moves to the right (Fig. 51), compresses the air particles. This compression wave travels through the medium longitudinally. As the prong of the fork swings to the left, pressure is decreased behind the surrounding particles, and they are drawn back in a rarefaction phase. Thus, all sound depends upon the magnitude of the pressure changes emitted by a vibrating body. The rate at which a vibrator oscillates is controlled by its mass, weight, and length and the force exerted upon it. The number of oscillations during each second determines the number of com-

* Some teachers and singers who seek answers to vocal problems may consider the physical area a subject of erudition. Those who regard it thus do so only because they fail to realize that every physical law herein presented may be interpreted demonstrably as a function within the singing act.

A singer's only product is sound and his thorough understanding of the laws of sound will permit him to form more meaningful concepts that are directly related to the adjustment of his resonating system as he sings. For the teacher, such understanding will provide a diagnostic implement that will lend his judgment stability. Both singer and teacher must ultimately translate these laws of sound into the psychophysical area of disciplined sensation.

pressions and rarefactions each second. This movement is expressed in terms of frequency, that is A 440 equals 440 compressions and rarefactions per second or 440 cycles per second (cps).

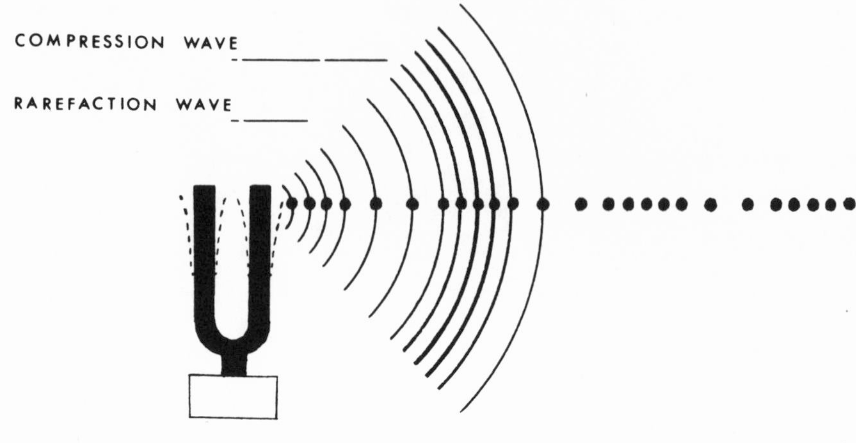

Fig. **51**

Simple Sounds

The wave forms which follow show graphically the periodic disturbances occurring in the medium through which the wave motion is propagated. These curves do not constitute a picture of the actual to and fro motions of particles; they provide a convenient means of displaying the properties of sound wave components in terms of time and air pressure.

Fig. 52 illustrates the variation in air pressure (14.2 pounds per square inch) created by two complete oscillations of a tuning fork. Air pressure is indicated at the left of the diagram. Amplitude, is indicated by the range of pressure variation above and below the zero line; time is indicated in centiseconds on the bottom line.

A sinusoid is a graphic representation of the pressure and displacement characteristics in time within a uniform vibration. It is usually used to portray sine waves, simple wave forms without overtones that are emitted by a vibrator exhibiting uniform periodic oscillation, such as a tuning fork, a pendulum, or a wheel (Fig. 53).

The graphic representations of these vibrating bodies are called sinusoids

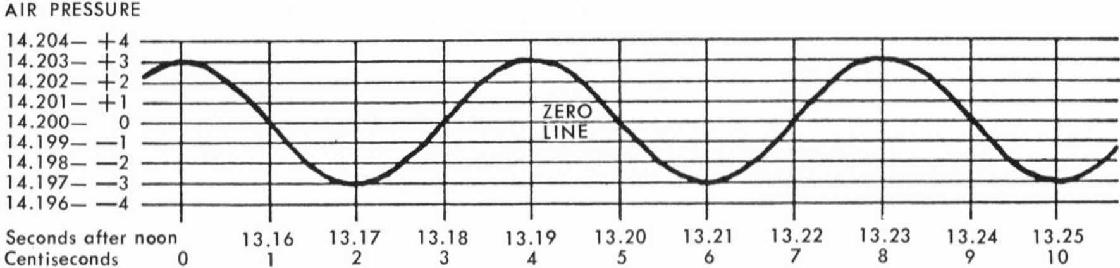

Fig. **52.** Sound Waves from a Perfect Tuning Fork

Although the pressure changes in this illustration appear to be quite small, they represent an extremely loud sound. Source: Martin Joos, *Acoustic Phonetics*, Monograph No. 23, *Language* suppl. Linguistic Society of America, 24, 2 (April-June 1948).

or sine waves because they are trigonometric functions of right angles and are identical to the movement of a point on the circumference of a uniformly revolving circle when that movement is projected on the diameter of the circle by means of perpendiculars.[2]

Observe in Fig. 54 that as the point *b* moves steadily around the circle *AA′ BB′* the point *C* oscillates back and forth upon the diameter *AB* in a uniform, exactly repetitive motion. This motion is identical to the movement of the pendulum and tuning fork. It is called simple harmonic motion.

The mathematical derivation of the word *sine* or *sinusoidal* is as follows: The sine of an angle of a right triangle is defined as the ratio between the side opposite that angle and the hypotenuse. Since the radius of the circle forms the hypotenuse of each of the triangles that have been formed and is, therefore, the same in all of them, the value of the respective sines of the successive angles

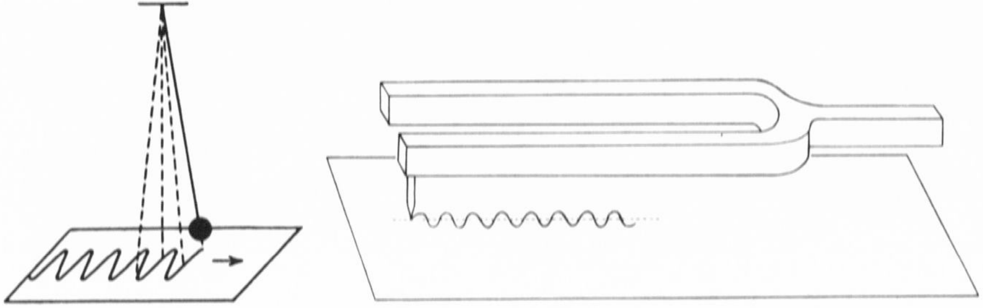

Fig. **53.** Examples of Simple Wave Forms

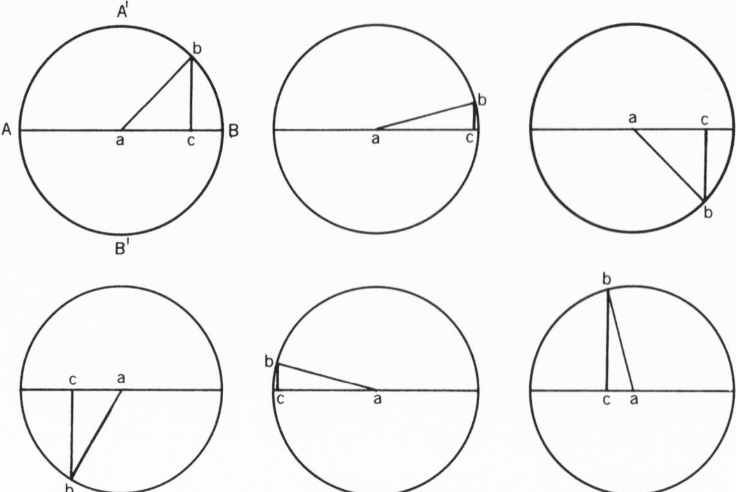

Fig. **54.** Examples of the Movement of the Perpendicular (Sine) Along the Diameter

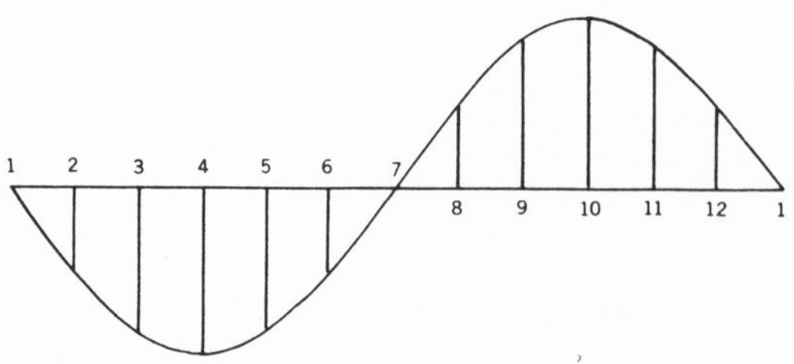

Fig. **55A.** Example of a Sine Wave

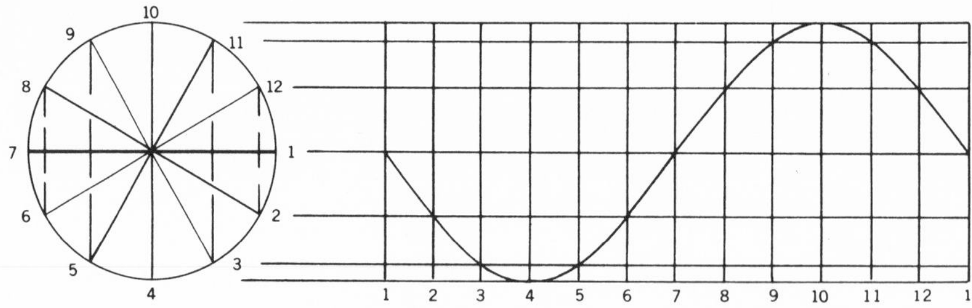

Fig. **55B.** Example of a Sine Wave

about the center may be expressed by the lengths of the side opposite those angles, or of the perpendiculars themselves. Therefore, the sine is the perpendicular.

To graphically display the sine waves formed by the simple harmonic motion of a wheel, the length of each perpendicular *bc* of Fig. 54 and the velocity of the moving wheel must be considered. Each perpendicular is arranged equidistant upon a horizontal axis to represent time in centiseconds, perpendiculars above the line represent the compression phase, and those below the line represent the rarefaction phase (Fig. 55A).

In Fig. 55B the height of each perpendicular, or sine, of the points of rotation of C spaced at intervals of thirty degrees are extended laterally for display. The vertical lines suggest time in centiseconds.

The employment of the mechanics of simple harmonic motion by transferring the motion of C in Fig. 56 to a source outside of the circle is illustrated in Fig. 56. The motion of the piston–cam shaft relationship within the modern gasoline motor or the piston–drive wheel relationship of the steam locomotive are examples of such mechanical transfer of simple harmonic motion.

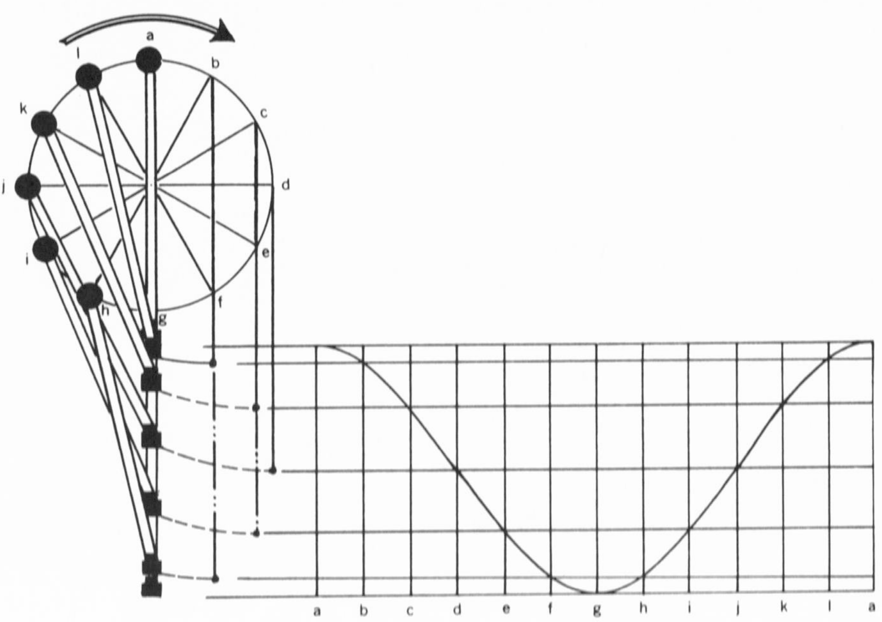

Fig. **56.** Example of Mechanics of Simple Harmonic Motion

Complex Sounds

Any complex sound wave is the sum of its sinusoids, or to state it differently, any complex sound with a repetitive wave form is usefully described as a series of pure tones. This fact is based upon a mathematical theorem named for its discoverer, J. B. J. Fourier (1768-1830): Every wave form, no matter what its nature may be, can be reproduced by superimposing a sufficient number of simple harmonic waves; that is, every complex wave can be built by piling up pure tone waves.

The components of a complex sound structure are called partials and harmonics. A partial is defined as:

> A component of sound sensation which may be distinguished as a simple tone that cannot be further analyzed by the ear and which contributes to the timbre of the complex sound. The frequency of a partial may be either higher or lower than the basic frequency, and it may or may not be an integral multiple or submultiple of the basic frequency. If the frequency is not a multiple or submultiple, the partial is inharmonic. . . . [An harmonic is defined as] a partial whose frequency is an integral multiple of the fundamental, i.e., fundamental A, 110 cps; second harmonic, 220 cps; third harmonic, 330 cps, etc.[3]

The Spectrum of Complex Sounds. The spectrum of sound is analogous to the spectrum of optics. When white light passes through a prism, the light breaks up into many colors. In acoustics, the term spectrum is used to describe the many simple sounds—the sinusoids—that make up a complex sound.

Fig. 57 shows the fundamentals and upper partials of the tones emitted by three different instruments. Such charts are known as sound spectra, and the length of the vertical lines indicates the relative strength of the several harmonics.

> Timbre is that attitude of auditory sensation in terms of which a listener can judge that two sounds similarly presented and having the same loudness and pitch are dissimilar. Timbre depends primarily upon the spectrum of the stimulus, but it also depends upon the wave form, the sound pressure, the frequency location of the spectrum and the temporal characteristics of the stimulus.[4]

Not only is the ear able to detect the difference in sound characteristics, but the visual representation of the wave forms of each sound source reveal differ-

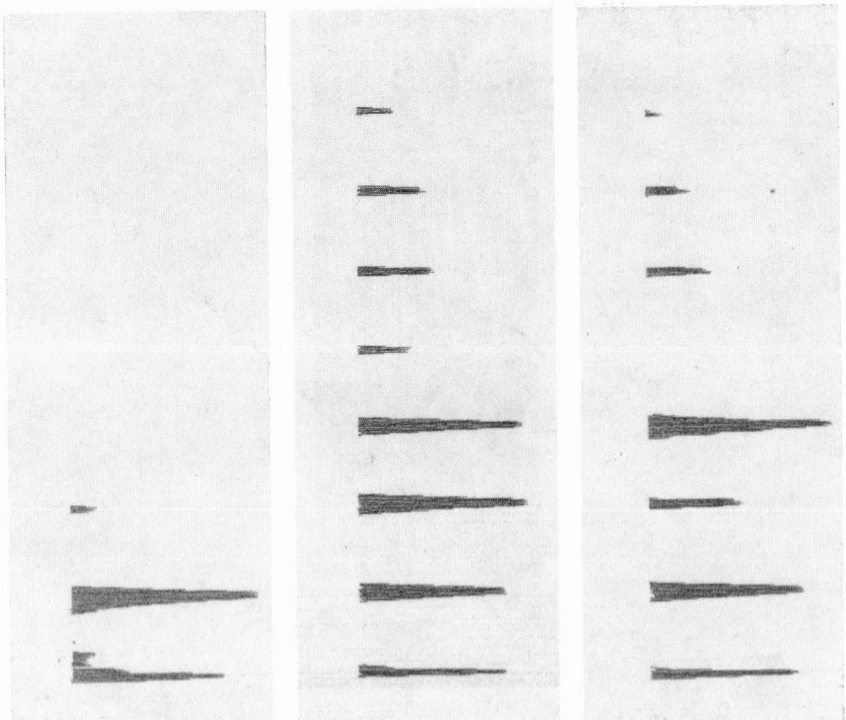

Fig. **57.** Spectogram of Tuning Fork (left), Clarinet, and Cornet

ent sound characteristics. In Fig. 58 recorded wave forms of three musical sources have the same frequency and amplitude. The differences among the examples result from changes in the wave form which are determined by the number, frequency, and distribution of the partials within it.

Any given frequency has its harmonic series. "A harmonic series of sounds is one in which each basic frequency in the series is an integral multiple of the fundamental frequency."[5]

The first sixteen harmonics, based upon C-65.4 as a fundamental are shown in Fig. 59; a corresponding harmonic series may be set up on a fundamental of any frequency. The hundreds of partials in the complete spectra extend into the ultra-audio region. The spectra of complex sounds consists of simple multiples of the fundamental frequencies as shown in the figure below.

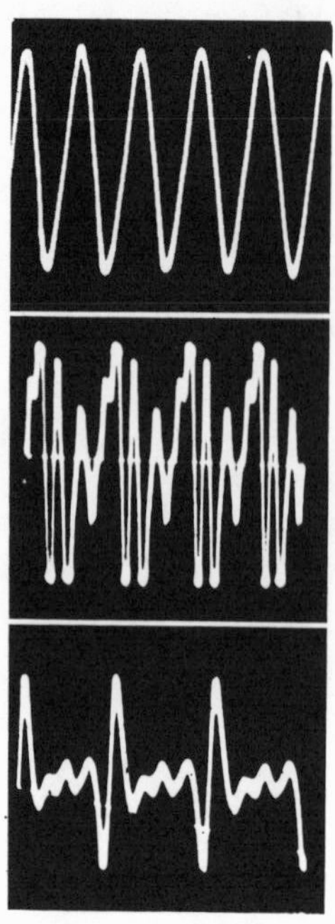

Fig. **58.** Wave Forms of Tuning Fork (top), Clarinet, and Cornet

Each vibrates at a frequency of 440 and at approximately the same intensity. From *Musical Acoustics* by Charles A. Culver, Copyright 1956, McGraw-Hill Book Co. Used by permission.

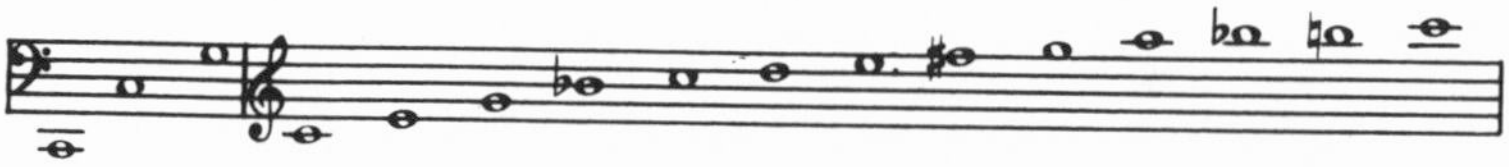

Pitch	C	C	G	C	E	G	B♭	C	D	E	F♯	G	A	B♭	B	C
Partial No.	1	2	3	4	5	6	7	8	9	10	11	12	13	14	15	16
Natural Spectrum of "C"	65.4	130.8	196.2	261.6	327	392.4	457.8	523.2	588.6	654	719.4	784.8	850.2	915.6	981	1046.4
Tempered Spectrum of "C"	65.4	130.8	196.0	261.6	329.6	392	466.1	523.2	587.4	659.2	698.4	783.9	880	932.4	987.8	1046.4
Beats per second					2		10		1	5	9		30	17	6	

Fig. **59.** The Harmonic Series

The inharmonic partials of the tempered scale shown above (5, 7, 9, 10, 11, 13, 15) are not exact multiples of the fundamental, and when sounded with the natural scale, they give the effect of roughness. The beats caused by the difference in frequency gives a vibrato effect to the sound rather than smoothness. Inharmonic partials are usually among the higher partials and may be small or large in amplitude.

PHASE, REENFORCEMENT, AND INTERFERENCE

When two or more sinusoidal waves moving in the same direction cross the zero line at exactly the same point in time, they are exactly repetitious and are in phase with each other.

The phase of a periodic quantity, for a particular value of the independent variable,* is the fractional part of a period through which the independent variable has last advanced through zero from a negative to a positive direction.[6]

In Fig. 60, A represents the superimposition of two simple harmonic motions of equal period but of different amplitudes. Here the vibratory motions, *W1* and *W2*, are in the same phase, crest over crest, trough over trough. The vibrations now *reenforce* one another, and the resultant (indicated by the solid line *W*) has an amplitude that is equal to the sum of the amplitudes of waves *b* and *d*. This characteristic of a wave crest in concurrence with another wave crest is known as reinforcement.

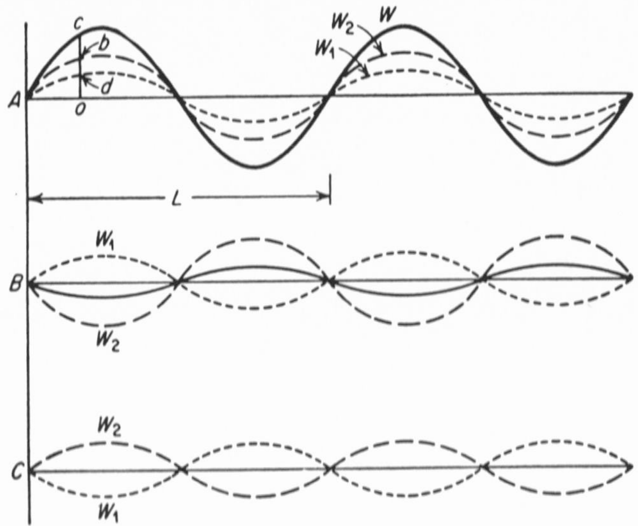

Fig. **60.** Superimposition of Two Simple Harmonic Motions
From Musical Acoustics by Charles A. Culver, Copyright 1956, McGraw-Hill Book Co. Used by permission.

* Since *phase* is a consideration of comparison only when more than one wave is present, the term *independent variable* represents the "reference" wave of energy with which all other waves are compared.

B represents the superimposition of two simple harmonic motions (dotted lines) of equal period, which vary in amplitude but are in opposite phase, crest over trough and trough over crest. The constituent vibrations now pull in opposite directions and so partially neutralize one another, the amplitude of the resultant (represented by the solid line) is equal to the difference of the amplitudes of *W1* and *W2*. This characteristic of a wave trough in opposition to a wave crest is known as interference. *C* indicates the superimposition of two wave systems of equal amplitude but of opposite phase. *W1* subtracted from *W2* is zero, an example of complete interference.

Fig. 61 illustrates the manner in which complex waves are formed by the superimposition of two or more sine waves of unequal period that are in phase at every half centisecond.[7] Each point in the resultant wave *C* may be easily determined by using dividers; *ab* plus *cd* equals *ef*; likewise, *gh* minus *jk* equals

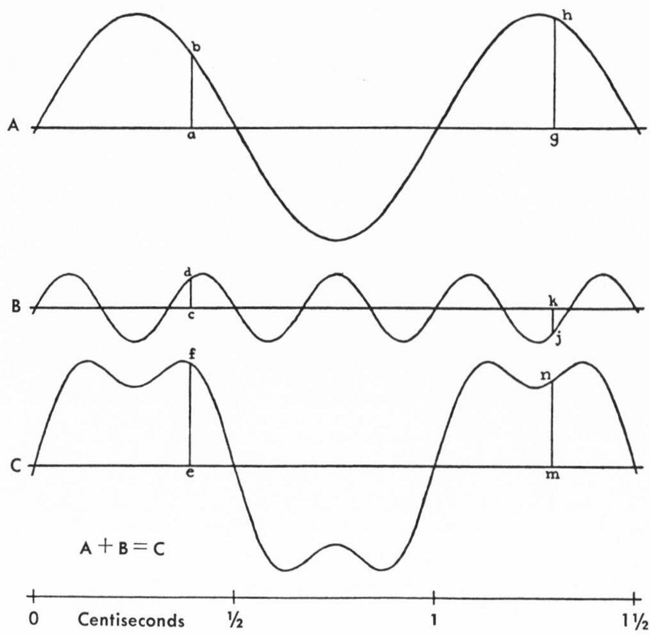

Fig. **61.** A Complex Wave as a Sum of Sinusoids

Here *A* represents a 100~ sinusoid, *B* represents a 300~ sinusoid, and *C* represents their sum, a complex or nonsinusodial wave.
Source: Martin Joos, *Acoustic Phonetics*, Monograph No. 23, *Language* suppl., Linguistic Society of America, 24, 2 (April-June 1948).

mn. (*jk* is subtracted because it lies below the zero line.) This point-by-point relationship can be summarized: *C* is the sum of *A* and *B*.

Joos further illustrates that a complex wave does not necessarily contain any fundamental component. In Fig. 62, *D* contains a fourth, a third, and a second harmonic but no fundamental. The fundamental, however, can be easily determined as the point of exact repetition or the point of greatest reinforcement of A, *B*, and C. In this illustration all three waves cross the median line while moving in the same direction. At one centisecond, A is 200 cps, *B* is 300 cps, and *C* is 400 cps. The fundamental is 100 cps at zero amplitude.

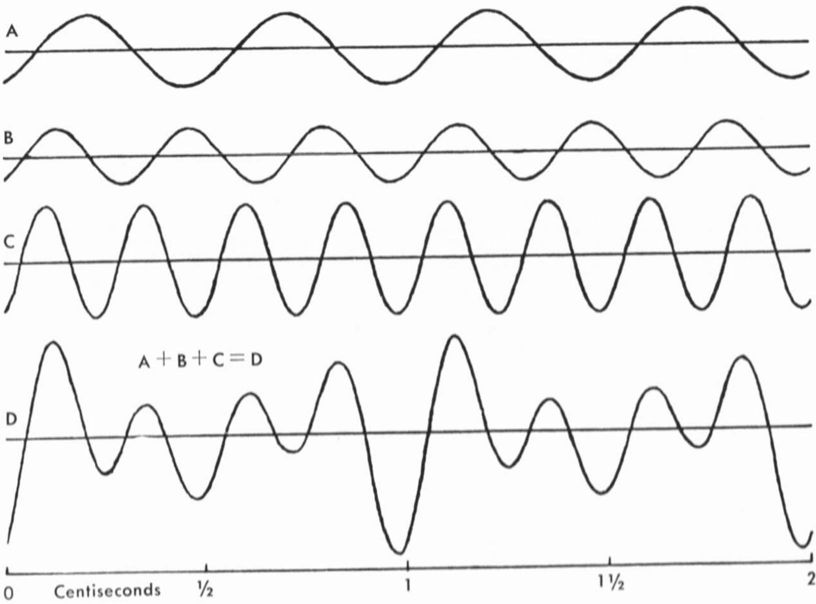

Fig. **62.** A Complex Wave May Have No Fundamental Component

Source: Martin Joos, *Acoustic Phonetics*, Monograph No. 23, *Language* suppl., Linguistic Society of America, 24, 2 (April-June 1948).

Even a square wave (Fig. 63) may be analyzed as consisting of sinusoids, but an infinite series of them is needed to create a square wave. Only the first four are shown here (*A*, *B*, *C*, and *D*). They are the fundamental and odd harmonics three, five, and seven. If more than four harmonics had been used, the resemblance of *T* and *S* would have been still closer.

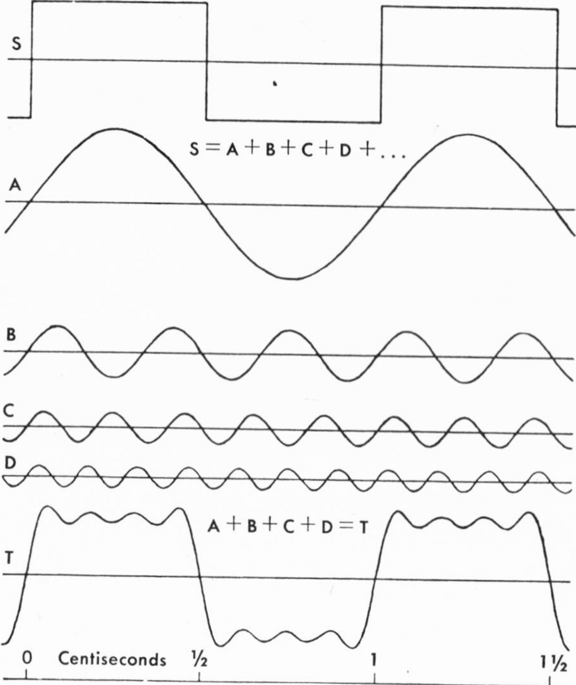

Fig. **63.** Even a Square Wave Is a Sum of Sinusoids

But it takes an infinite set (series) of sinusoids to add up to a square wave. Four of the components are shown here as *A, B, C, D*. By themselves these four add up to form the wave *T*; if more than four had been used, the resemblance of *T* to *S* would have been still closer. Source: Martin Joos, *Acoustic Phonetics,* Monograph No. 23, *Language* suppl., Linguistic Society of America, 24, 2 (April-June 1948).

Joos holds that the rectangular wave of Fig. 64 crudely resembles the glottal tone, "especially of the soprano voice."[8] This wave is shown here to illustrate that it also can be analyzed into sinusoids. Fig. 64 shows a rectangular wave with the positive part (compression) lasting one-tenth of the period, the negative part (rarefaction) nine-tenths. Its components have the amplitude shown in Fig. 64.

For comparison with the wave displayed in Fig. 64 the glottal wave form in Fig. 67 of this chapter illustrates the latest contemporary theory of laryngeal vibrations advanced by the Swedish acoustician Gunnar Fant.[9] (Note that the conformation of this wave form is different from that of Fig. 64. The variation is the result of the length of time the glottis is open.)

Fig. **64.** A Rectangular Wave and Its Components

A Rectangular wave can also be analyzed into sinusoids, but the analysis is not shown here as it was in Fig. 63. Instead it is represented by the table printed below. This rectangular wave resembles the glottal tone, especially of a soprano voice. Source: Martin Joos, *Acoustic Phonetics,* Monograph No. 23, *Language* suppl., Linguistic Society of America, 24, 2 (April-June 1948).

Harmonic	*Amplitude*	*Harmonic*	*Amplitude*
Fund.	1.000	16	0.192
2	0.951	17	0.154
3	0.873	18	0.106
4	0.770	19	0.053
5	0.647	20	0.000
6	0.513	21	0.048
7	0.374	22	0.086
8	0.238	23	0.114
9	0.111	24	0.128
10	0.000	25	0.129
11	0.091	26	0.118
12	0.159	27	0.097
13	0.201	28	0.068
14	0.220	29	0.034
15	0.216	etc.	etc.

TYPES OF VIBRATION

Free Vibration

"Free vibration is the vibration of a freely elastic system in its own natural period after all driving forces have been removed from the system."[10] A weight fastened to the end of a spring when displaced from its position of rest and then released will oscillate vertically, and because of its elasticity the spring will overshoot its position of rest on both the ascent and descent. Such oscillations will continue until the energy, created by the weight's displacement, has been dissipated by the friction of the spring and the force of gravity. All motion will stop at the weight's original point of rest.

When the system is undisturbed by outside forces the number of up and down oscillations of the weight per second is called the natural period. The frequency depends upon the mass of the weight and the tension of the spring.

A pendulum that is raised from its point of rest and permitted to swing will pass its point of rest in each oscillation for some time and will swing in its own free period without the aid of additional driving force. But eventually the force of gravity and friction of the air will bring it to its point of rest. The frequency (number of swings per second) depends only upon the length of the pendulum.

A tuning fork will vibrate for several seconds but will soon stop. Every elastic system has its own natural period of vibration. If it is set into motion and no other force is applied, it will vibrate only in its particular frequency.

Maintained Vibration

Maintained vibration may be defined as that type in which repeated impulses are given to the vibrator so that it continues to vibrate in its own natural frequency. The pendulum swinging in free vibration may be made to swing indefinitely when a small force is added to it precisely as it changes direction. This additional force exerted by the escape mechanism balances the factors which normally would cause the pendulum to cease swinging.

Leaping upon a springboard will force it to vibrate in the natural frequency and the movement will build up until it reaches great amplitude. If the application of the force is not properly timed, little movement will result.

If this principle of timing the applied force is translated into the realm of sound and a pulsating force is applied to an elastic system, the period of the pulsating force corresponds to the natural frequency of the system and the sound is amplified considerably. When one blows over the lip of a bottle, the hiss resulting has many overtones within it. One overtone just matches the natural frequency of the bottle cavity and causes the air within the bottle to oscillate in and out with regularity and the bottle note sounds loud and clear practically without hiss. A resonator which improves the efficiency of the generated sound at its own frequency is reinforcing the vibrated sound; the phenomenon is called reinforcement. The tone from the bottle will continue to sound so long as the air within it is activated.

Forced Vibration

If the frequencies of the vibration and that of the resonance system do not coincide, one of two things may happen, depending upon the relationship of the vibrator to the resonator, the materials used, and the size of the resonator and vibrator.

1. The vibrating source may change its natural frequency so that it vibrates more or less in the period of the system. Most wind instruments fall into this group, the pitch of the note depending not on the natural frequency of the reed but upon the natural frequency of the air column to which it is coupled. The vibrator serves to agitate the air column within the resonating tube. The resonator alone determines the pitch of the note. This means that the natural frequency of the resonating tube must be varied for every note. In most wind instruments this change is made by lengthening the tube by depressing valves or closing finger holes which alter the natural frequency of the tube.
2. The vibrating source may compel the system to vibrate at a frequency related to its own, regardless of the natural frequency of the resonator. If the stem of a vibrating tuning fork is held on a flat surface, that surface will vibrate as long as the fork is held there, and it will vibrate in the frequency of the fork. The diaphragm of a loudspeaker is forced to vibrate with the frequency of the electric current. As soon as the current is stopped the vibration will cease. All methods of recording and reproducing sound depend upon forced vibration. The ear drum is forced into vibration by the propagated sound wave. When a stringed instrument is played, the sound comes mainly from the body of the instrument and partly from the contained air. The strings of these vibrating instruments of a particular mass, length, and tension give the pitch of the note and are then forced to vibrate.

The resonance of the human voice is representative of forced vibration; to understand it, one must know something about the selectivity of resonance and how the partials of the tone are affected.

THE PHENOMENON OF RESONANCE

Resonance occurs when a resonator is in tune with its vibrator—when compression from the sound source coincides with compression from the resonator and when the rarefaction from the sound source coincides with rarefaction of the resonator. The characteristic tendency of a resonator is to amplify or reinforce those tones with which it is compatible and to dampen or eliminate those tones with which it is not compatible. Thus, the quality of a vocalized tone depends upon those partials passed (reinforced) by the resonating system.

> The resonator itself is usually a cavity or a sounding board; both respond well to certain frequencies. Such a resonator makes possible a more effective transfer of energy from the vibrator, producing the

> sound to the surrounding air with greater energy than if the resonator were not present. [However, resonators do not add energy, they make a more efficient transfer of vibrations from the vibrating source. The efficiency of transfer gives the illusion of amplification of the sound.]
>
> The selectivity of a sounding board is fixed. Its size, mass and surface determine the amplification of sound. The selectivity of cavities, however, varies as the orifice, cavity area and surface vary.[11]

Cavity Resonators

A single resonator is able to respond to either sympathetic or forced vibration.

A resonator vibrating in tune with the frequency of its generator is in sympathetic vibration. If the generated sound is withdrawn, the resonator will continue to vibrate in its own natural free period.

A resonator that is not in tune with its generator but is forced to vibrate by the generated sound is in forced vibration. When the generated sound has been removed the resonator continues to vibrate for a very short period, which is determined by the damping factor. (This period represents the time rate of amplitude decay.)

When a resonator is compelled to vibrate, forced vibration affects both the resonator and the generator. The resultant frequency is somewhere between the natural frequencies of both resonator and generator. The influence of the generator is stronger than that of the resonator upon the generator.

Resonators of brass and other metals may be sharply tuned to respond to only a few frequencies. A Helmholtz resonator—spherical and of brass—is such a resonator. Soft-walled resonators, which are fibrous or flesh, can respond to many different frequencies and are able to reproduce many different gradations of tone quality.

THE DISSIPATION OF SOUND ENERGY—DAMPING

When a vibrator imparts its energy to an elastic medium the energy appears in the vibration of that medium. A loss of energy will steadily decrease the amplitude of the vibrations. Some energy is expended in overcoming the resistance of the air to the vibrating material, and some is dissipated into the air as sound waves. As the energy is lost, the vibrations cease to be heard. The time rate at which the energy is dissipated in a vibrating body is known as damping. This time rate varies considerably.

When a tuning fork is struck and held in the air it will vibrate for a long time. The vibrating fork loses its energy slowly and therefore is lightly damped. If it is placed against a solid object, the energy of the vibrating body is dissipated rapidly in setting the solid object in motion, and it is heavily damped. A heavily damped vibrator will amplify the original vibrations to a greater extent than will a lightly damped vibrator.

Damping and Cavity Resonance

A sharply tuned resonator is selective; that is, it will respond only to a few frequencies within the complex tone emitted by the vibrator. A sharply tuned resonator is lightly damped and requires a longer period for its vibrations to build up and die away, but the sharply tuned resonator will amplify the vibrations emitted by the generator to a greater extent than will the heavily damped resonator.

A resonator that is not sharply tuned is not selective and responds to many frequencies emitted by the vibrator with little or no amplification of them. Such a resonator permits the vibrations to build up and dissipate rapidly and is heavily damped. When the resonator is so heavily damped that the sound ceases the moment that it is energized the resonator is said to be critically damped. For this reason an acoustic system can be sharply tuned only by reducing the damping, and light damping can be obtained only at the expense of selectivity.[12] The human resonance cavities are almost critically damped. That is, vibrations of air cease immediately and also start vibrating with equal promptness. The cavities of the vocal tract are responsive to a very wide range of frequencies.

In the human resonating system damping depends upon the size of the cavity. As the oral and pharyngeal cavities are enlarged, walls of soft flesh become more taut, damping decreases and vowels become brighter. The veiled-tone effect used for singing piano passages is accomplished by enlarging the cavity and relaxing the walls to permit them to become soft and flaccid, thus causing the cavity to become less responsive to the high partials within the laryngeal and cavity tones. (See "Closed and Open Tones," p. 89.)

In considering the variability of cavity resonators, one should remember that the effects obtained with the spherical brass Helmholtz resonator (Fig. 65) are analogous to those obtained with the head, mouth, pharynx, and nasal cavities. These cavities are selective according to the following laws:

1. The larger the cavity of the resonator, the lower the frequency to which it will resonate, provided the dimensions of the aperture and the neck remain constant.

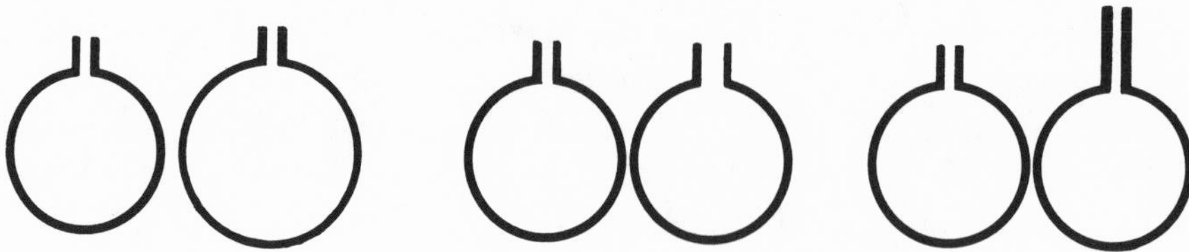

Fig. **65.** Helmholtz Resonators

The pair of resonators on the left have the same size aperture and length of neck. The size of the cavity varies. The resonators in the middle have the same size cavity and length of neck, but the caliber of the aperture varies. The resonators on the right have the same size cavity and caliber of aperture. The variation is in the length of neck.

2. The larger the aperture of the cavity, the higher the frequency to which it will resonate, provided the cavity and length of neck remain constant.
3. The longer the neck of the aperture, the lower the frequency to which it will resonate, provided the dimensions of the aperture and cavity remain constant.
4. The softer the texture of the cavity walls, the more the cavity emphasizes low overtones.

Generally, the longer and narrower the neck of a cavity resonator, the lower the pitch to which it will respond, and because damping is reduced to a minimum, the more selective its tuning will be. Such a resonator will respond at its maximum effect to a very small deviation in frequency. Conversely, the shorter and wider the neck, the higher the frequency to which it will respond, and because damping is heavy, the wider the range of frequencies to which the resonator will respond significantly.

The significance of these laws involves lip-rounding in singing; the presence or absence of neck (lips) and aperture (mouth opening) directly affect the accurate reproduction of any of the basic vowels in singing.

ANALYSIS OF SPEECH IN SONG

The quality or timbre of a vocalized sound is determined by the number, intensity, and distribution of the partials which compose it. Such a relationship depends upon the following:

1. The nature of the laryngeal vibration.
2. The changes made in that sound as it passes through the resonating system.

The combination of these two factors causes some partials to be reinforced, others to be weakened. Awareness of instrumental differences and ability to identify the voice of an individual depends upon the constant fluctuation of the overtone structure within either sound.

Speech forms in song are produced by constantly shifting the cavities through articulation, thereby causing variations in the overtone structure which are recognized as vowels.

Nature of Laryngeal Vibrations

Every vocalized tone is a complex one in which the high frequencies (harmonics) are simple multiples of the lowest or fundamental frequency. If the fundamental is 440 cps, its second harmonic will be 440 multiplied by two or 880 cps; the third harmonic will be 440 multiplied by three or 1,320 cps, and so on. Since a complex sound is composed of many simple sounds, the vocal spectrum can become quite involved, as it is in the examples of vocal acoustic spectra in Figs. 66 and 67.

Fant's theory of laryngeal vibrations is the one most frequently accepted by leading voice scientists and phoneticians. His statement regarding "the voice source" follows:

> The primary source of energy for the production of voiced sounds is the contraction of the respiratory muscles resulting in an over pressure in the lungs and thus in an air flow that is periodically varied in magnitude owing to the opening and closing of the valve folds over

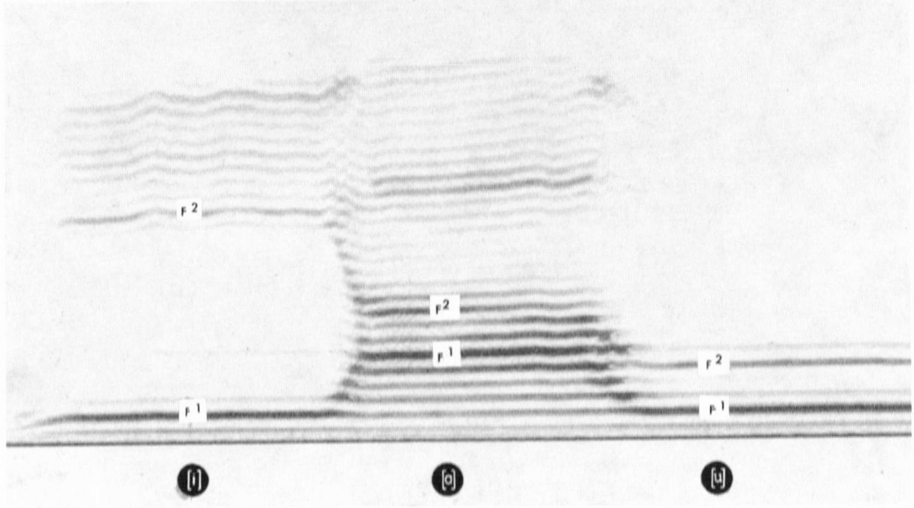

Fig. **66.** Harmonic Analysis of Sung Sounds Showing the Vowel Spectra [i], [ɑ], [u].

> each fundamental voice period. The acoustic function of these folds should not be regarded as an analogy to vibrating membranes.
>
> All sound waves are pressure variations, and the varying pressures resulting from bursts of air escaping through the glottis are the glottal sound waves, not the vibration of the mechanical folds themselves. Actually, pressure variations cause a modulation of the respiratory air stream but do not generate sound oscillations of a significant magnitude by a direct conversion of mechanical vibration to sound.[13]

The wave forms in Fig. 67 are calculated wave forms and spectrum envelopes of the voice source. Curves I and II have been derived from area measures taken from the Bell Telephone Laboratory film of the vocal cord. Curve III has been derived from the glottis area versus time pictures given by Chiba and Kajiyama. The wave marked *o* is a wave adapted by Gunnar Fant.

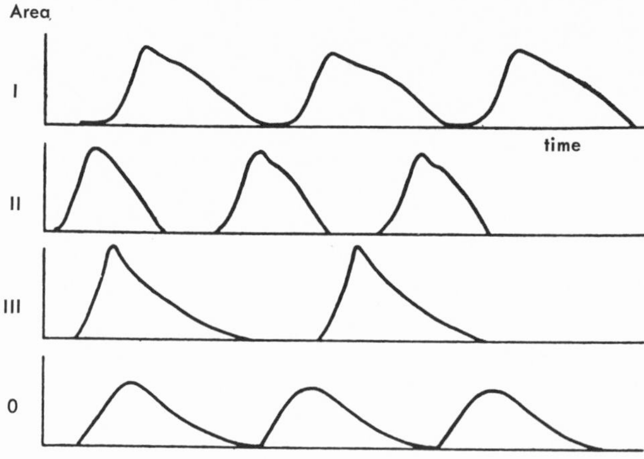

Fig. **67.** Glottal Wave Form Suggested by Fant
Source: Gunnar M. C. Fant, *Acoustic Theory of Speech Production* (The Hague: Netherlands: Mouton & Co., 1960)

The wave forms in Fig. 69 are photographs taken from a dual beam oscilloscope of laryngeal sounds recorded by two microphones.[14] The first, a probe microphone, was placed within the vestibule near the level of the vocal folds (top wave). The second, a condenser microphone, was placed at a position six inches in front of the mouth (bottom wave). The probe microphone tube was cut at one-centimeter intervals, and six vowels were recorded and photographed at each interval (Fig. 69).

These wave conformations at the laryngeal level within the vestibule, greatly resemble the glottal wave forms in Fig. 67. Note the complexity of

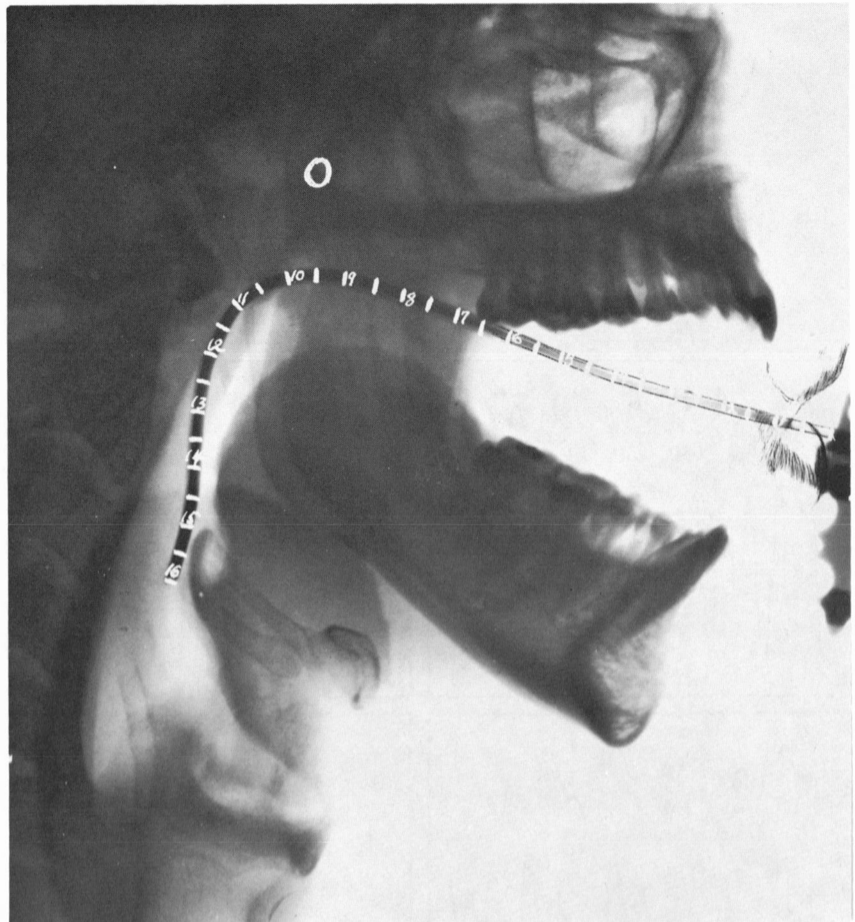

Fig. **68.** A Study of the Function of the Primary Resonating Area

Source: Kenneth L. Davis, Jr., "A Study of the Function of the Primary Resonating Areas and Their Relation to the Third Formant in the Singing Tone"(Mus. D. dissertation, School of Music, Indiana University, 1964).

the phonated sound after it has passed through the resonating cavities of the pharynx and oral cavities. Note also that each of these waves seems to be a compression wave with no rarefaction phase. This wave form can be described as an addition of sine waves, each of lesser amplitude, emitted by the air stream of the glottis. Since these glottal wave forms are the sum of their sinusoids, apparently each of these sine waves has contributed to the glottal wave conformation by reinforcement, interference, and phase.

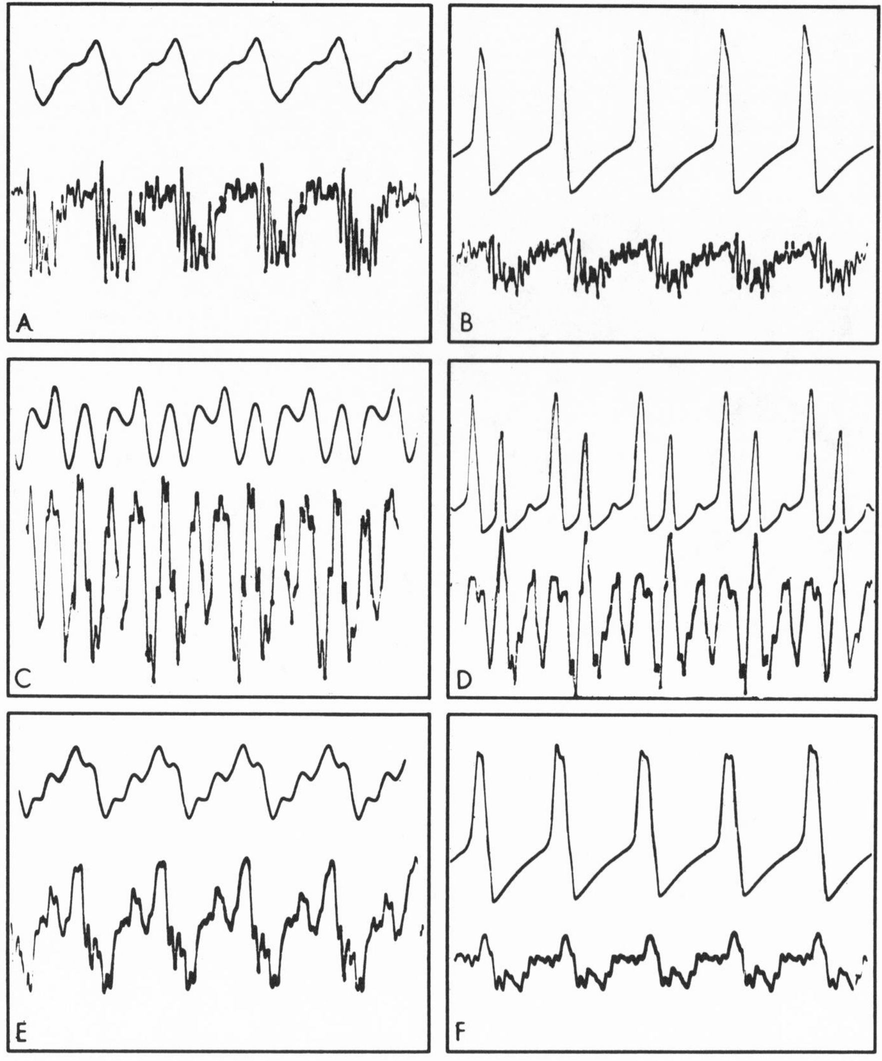

Fig. **69.** Wave Forms of Glottal Sounds

A, Vowel [i], Probe Microphone—16 cm; **B,** Vowel [e], Probe Microphone—10 cm; **C,** Vowel [ɑ], Probe Microphone—16 cm; **D,** Vowel [ɑ], Probe Microphone—10 cm; **E,** Vowel [u], Probe Microphone—10 cm; **F,** Vowel [u], Probe Microphone—10 cm. Source: Kenneth L. Davis, Jr., "A Study of the Function of the Primary Resonating Areas and Their Relation to the Third Formant in the Singing Tone" (Mus. D. dissertation, School of Music, Indiana University, 1964).

Such a glottal tone can be described by its spectrum which may be schematized as in Fig. 70. This laryngeal spectrum does not conform to any particular sound; the ear would interpret it as some kind of buzz. The length of each vertical line indicates the strength of each overtone.

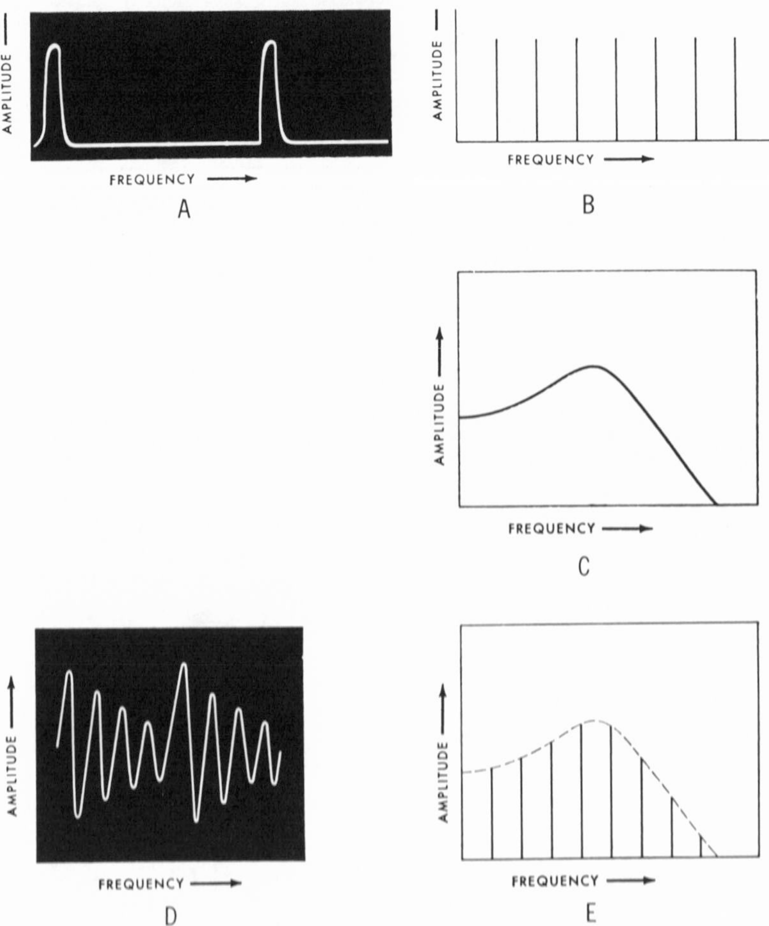

Fig. **70.** An Explanation of Formants

A, the wave shape of a pulse train; *B*, a spectrum of a train of short pulses; *C*, the frequency response of a simple resonator; *D* and *E*, the wave shape and the spectrum, respectively, of a sound wave produced when a series of pulses, like those in *A*, are applied to a resonator whose frequency response is shown in *C*. Source: *The Speech Chain* by P. B. Denes and E. N. Pinson, published by Bell Telephone Laboratories, Inc. (1963).

FORMANTS AND THE HUMAN RESONATING SYSTEM

The Creation of Vowel Formants

The human resonating system, described physiologically on page 73, is a series of air-filled cavities which act as resonators. Each cavity has its own natural period of vibration which will respond as a sinusoidal tone when it is excited by the same frequency emitted by the vibrator.

As the sound passes through the resonating cavities of the throat and mouth, the profile of the spectrum changes, since each cavity resonates to some of the tones in the spectrum more readily than to others and each adds its own characteristics to such tones. This reinforcement gives the partials greater energy at the point of cavity resonance. These points of greater energy are called formants.

In passing through the resonating system of the throat and mouth, the partials in the harmonic sequence do not change from their original location in

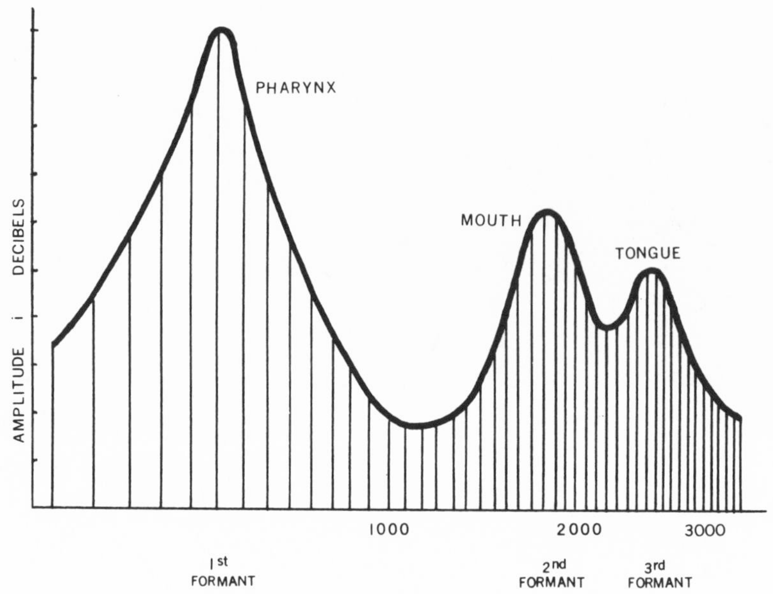

Fig. **71.** Vowel Sound [i]

The laryngeal tonal spectrum is altered by cavity resonances creating formants.

the tonal spectrum; rather, some are strengthened and reinforced by cavity resonance, while others are weakened or damped out (Fig. 71).

The values of the natural frequencies of the resonating cavities within the vocal tract are determined by their shape; as a result, as the shape of the tract is altered the amplitudes of the partials within the spectrum will be greater at different frequencies. Thus, every configuration of the total vocal tract has its own set of characteristic formant frequencies which gives to the laryngeal sound a particular vowel quality.

The resonance frequency of any cavity is not necessarily equal to the frequency of any partial of the spectrum. The frequencies of the formants need not be the same as those of the partials, but they may coincide. The formant frequencies are determined by the configuration of the total vocal tract as a series of resonators while the partials within the spectrum are determined by the vocal folds. The vocal tract and the vocal folds can change independently of each other.

When the cavities of the throat and mouth remain fixed, a laryngeal sound of lower pitch may be passed through the system, and the vowel characteristic will remain the same because the energy within each formant has not varied. Only the fundamental will be lower since it is determined by the frequency of the vibration of the vocal folds (Fig. 72).

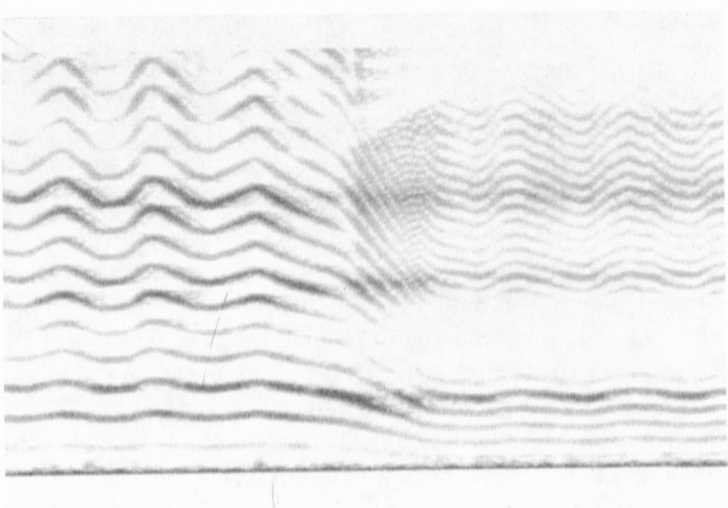

Fig. **72.** Octave Drop, Bass Voice Singing [ɛ] on Two Pitches, C-523 to C-251

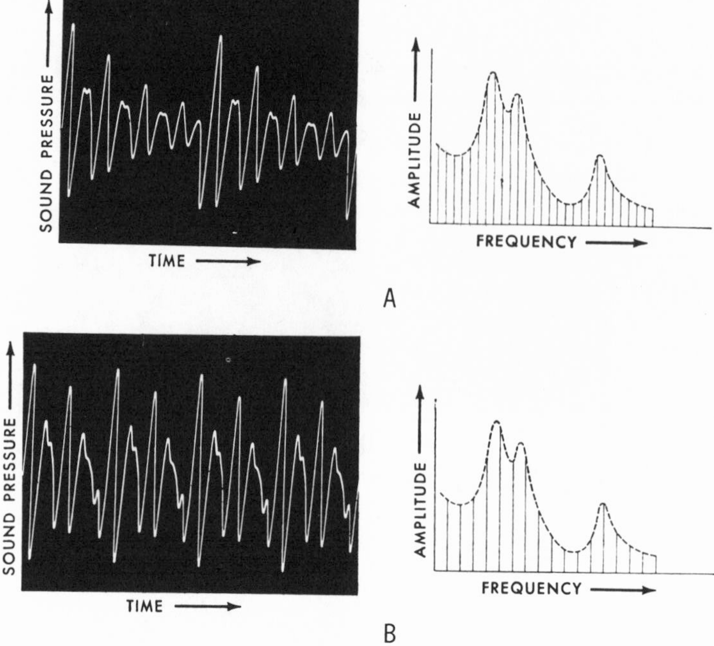

Fig. **73.** The Wave Shape and Corresponding Spectra of the Vowel [ɑ]

A, Pronounced at a Vocal Fold Frequency of 90 cps; **B,** pronounced at a Vocal Fold Frequency of 150 cps. Source: *The Speech Chain* by P. B. Denes and E. N. Pinson, published by Bell Telephone Laboratories, Inc. (1963).

Cavity-Coupling Defined

A coupled system is composed of a generator and any number of resonators that could vibrate independently if they were not joined together. If any part of the coupled system is set into vibration, another part of the system will be forced to vibrate. This second resonator modifies the vibration of the first. If a third resonator is added, it will exert a periodic force upon the other two, thus modifying the total system.[15]

Whether a system is tightly coupled or loosely coupled depends upon the degree of constriction at the orifices which join such a system.

A loosely coupled system is one in which the influence exerted by one part of the system upon another is small. In such a system each resonator tends to vibrate near its own natural frequency. Such a condition is evidenced

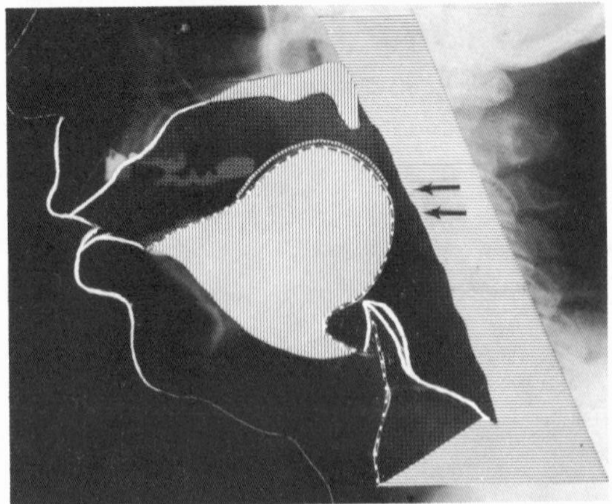

Fig. **74A.** A Closed Vowel, [u], Loosely Coupled

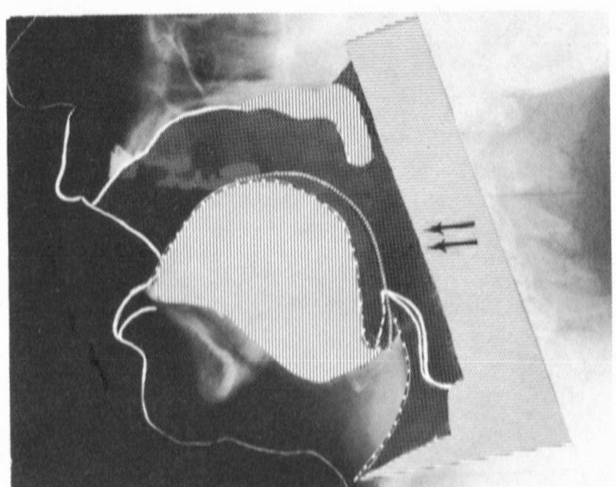

Fig. **74B.** An Open Vowel, [a], Tightly Coupled

in the tense vowels [i], [ē], [o], and [u]. When both back and front orifices are small, and the cavities are divided into clearly defined resonating areas (Fig. 74A).

A tightly coupled system is one in which a strong influence is exerted upon one part of the system by another. This system, displaying the characteristics of a single resonating system, is observable in all vowels except the high frontals as they migrate from closed to open position in both crescendo and pitch change. As the back orifice is enlarged, the cavity-coupling tends to become a single or tightly coupled system rather than a loosely coupled system;

[a] is the most tightly coupled of all phonemes since it is made with little or no tongue stricture (central orifice) and an almost neutral lip position (front orifice) (Fig. 74B). The physiological analysis of each vowel sound is given in Chapter Ten.

Origin of the Formant in a Coupled System

The experiments of Paget and Russell[16] have suggested that the mouth and the pharynx must be considered a double resonator. This concept, first called multiple resonance by Wheatstone in 1834, was investigated further by Helmholtz[17] when he concluded that the vowels [ɑ] as in *calm,* [ɔ] as in *more,* [u] as in *who,* and [ɒ] as in *not* resulted from single resonances but that the vowels [æ] as in *hat,* [ɛ] as in *men,* and [i] as in *eat* resulted from double resonances—that is, from two separate notes. One is produced in the cavity behind the tongue, and the other is caused by a constriction at the mid-point of the tongue and the hard palate as in a bottle with a narrow neck.

In 1890 and 1930 Paget recorded the fact that R. J. Lloyd suggested that every vowel derives one chief resonance from the anterior part of its articulation and another from the posterior or pharyngeal part. Paget made many models of double resonance cavities to determine the nature of cavity coupling and finally concluded:

> By this time the principle of vowel formation was becoming clear, that there must be, in effect, two resonating cavities, each producing a separate resonance; provided these resonances are correct, neither the exact shape, cross section or length of the cavities are material. The two cavities behave like two Helmholtz resonators joined together in series.[18]

D. C. Miller in 1916 confirmed Helmholtz's views that some of the vowels are the result of double resonance.[19] G. O. Russell made a radiographic study in 1928 of the physiological causes of vowel quality differences.[20] This study revealed that, as the tongue moves into position to form a vowel sound, the pharynx and the oral cavity are altered. In this manner, the vocal tract may be regarded as a coupled resonator joined by a resistance point or neck.

Dunn's statement, "The vocal tract may be thought of as a series of cylindrical sections, with acoustical mass and compliance uniformly distributed along each section,"[21] is illustrated in Fig. 75 in which the oral and pharyngeal cavities, with their connecting passage, are compared with joined cylindrical sections. Each change in the size and shape of the vocal tract corresponds to a change in the acoustical system. Spectrograms reveal cavity resonances of three formants for each vowel.

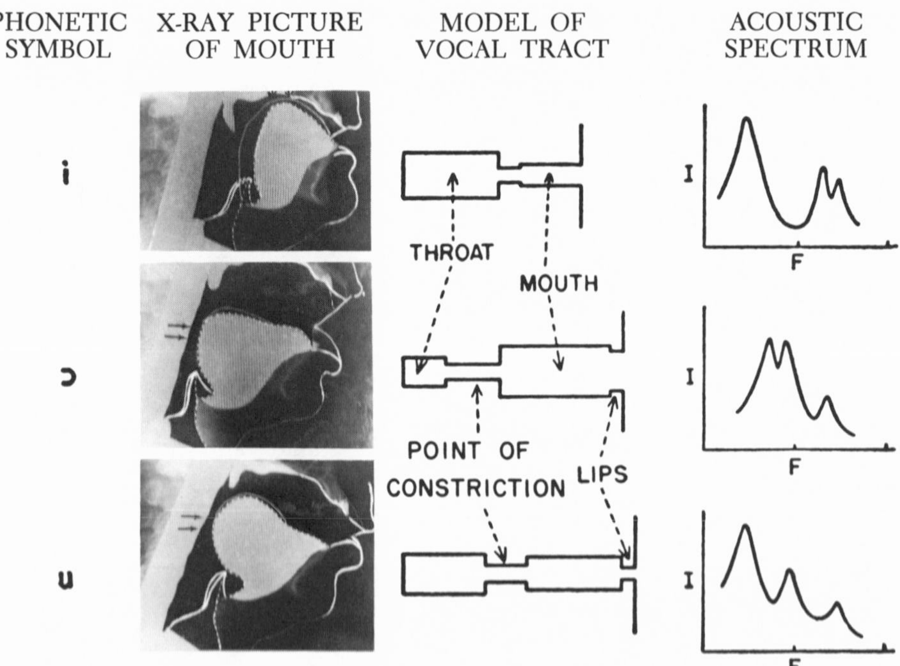

Fig. 75. Vocal Tract Configurations Showing Cavity Relationships and Spectra for the Vowels [i], [ɔ], and [ʊ]

Many scholars have regarded the vocal cavities as double resonators, but Crandall[22] is probably the first to explain theoretically the relationships between the two characteristic frequencies of a vowel and the shape and size of the vocal cavity on the basis of the double resonator theory.

According to Crandall, each sung vocal tone has ten to fifteen prominent formants; only the first two are needed to analyze the vowel sound. In just which area of the phonatory system these formants originate has long been a question among physicists. Most of them have assumed that the lowest (first) formant developed in the larger pharyngeal area, and the higher (second) formant, in the smaller oral cavity.

Most voice scientists tend to oversimplify the function of the coupled resonating system in the human voice. Studies by Fant [23] have substantiated Dunn's earlier conclusion[24] that for the frontal vowels the first formant originates in the pharynx and the second formant originates in the oral cavity.

For the vowel [ɑ], the first formant depends equally upon the front and back cavity, while the second formant depends more upon the front than upon the back cavity.

For the vowels [o] and [u], the first formant depends more upon the lip section of the front cavity than on the tongue section. The second formants of these two vowels are more dependent upon the front cavity than the back. The third formant of all the vowels depends upon the area in front of the tongue constriction or medial orifice.

> In the case of the very open vowels a division of the cavity system above the larynx into separate parts loses some of its significance. The more open a vowel is, the less well the separate parts of the vocal cavities act as separate resonators.[25]

In studying complex sounds, one needs to know the intensity and frequency of each component or partial within a given sound at a specific point of time.

The spectrograph or sonograph[26] is an analyzing instrument that (a) provides an instantaneous record of the composition of any selected sound at any certain instant and (b) isolates and records only those frequencies that are essential to the recognition and understanding of the sung sound.

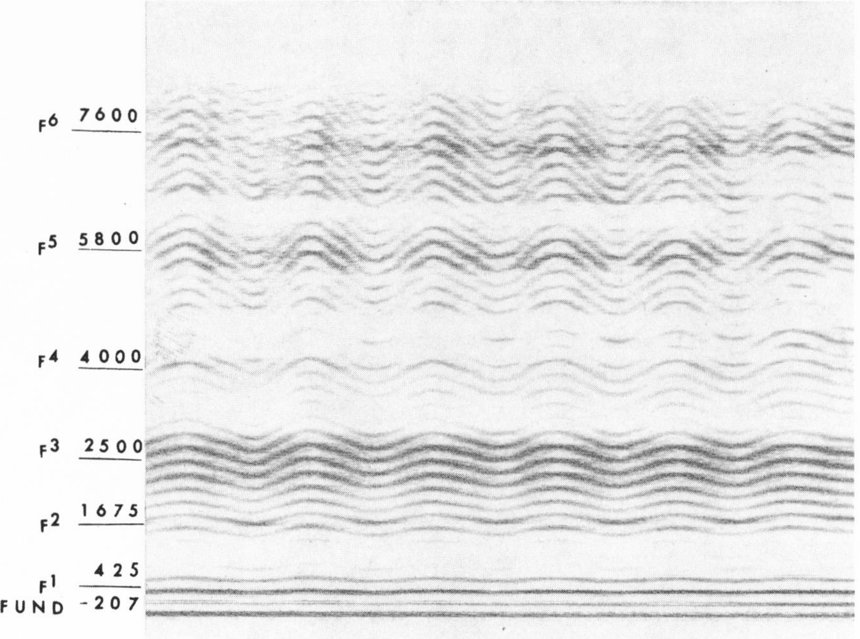

Fig. **76.** Spectogram Displaying Harmonic Analysis from 0 to 8,000 cps of the Vowel [e]

The six formants are caused by various cavity formations in the phonatory tract. The undulated pattern is caused by the vibrato.

When using narrow pass-band filtering the resulting spectrograph, consists of a series of parallel lines, and each line represents an overtone or partial. Analysis can be made of complex tones up to 8,000 cps (Fig. 76).

When a complex vocalized sound is passed through a sonograph and broad-band filtering is used, the parallel lines burned by the stylus upon the paper are much broader and will reveal a concentration of energy among certain groups of partials in the tonal spectrum (Figs. 77-80).

PHYSIOLOGICAL CHANGE AND FORMANT MOVEMENT

The formants of women have a higher frequency than those of men, and the formants of children are higher than those of both men and women. However, the ratio of frequency change between each phoneme is the same for men, women, and children.

When a phoneme is altered during the singing of a single pitch, the physiological cause for formant movement is indicated on the formant charts (Figs. 77-80).

First Formant Movement

In singing the high frontal vowels [i], [ē], and [ɪ] the first formant is lowered by forming a firm tongue occlusion which creates a secure inner orifice. If this inner orifice disintegrates, the first formant is raised (Fig. 77).

To sing the vowel [i] near the basic vowel position, within the stable vowel pitch range (high voice F^1 350, F^2 2,500; low voice F^1 300, F^2 2,100), a singer needs to establish a firm occlusion of the tongue blade to the alveolar ridge. In controlling the position of the first formant for the vowel [i], the firmness of the inner orifice is more important than spreading the lips or increasing the size of the pharyngeal cavity.

In the middle and low frontal vowels the first formant movement depends upon the volume of the pharyngeal cavity and lip-spreading.

To sing the vowels [e], [ɛ], [æ], [a], [ɑ], within the suggested frequency areas, the first formant is raised by progressively lowering the tongue and jaw positions as indicated in Chapter Nine. This action creates a change in the coupled system by decreasing the volume of the pharyngeal cavity and increasing the volume of the oral cavity (Fig. 78).

In the back vowels the first formant movement depends upon lip-rounding. To sing the vowels [ɔ], [o], [ʊ], and [u] within the suggested frequency areas, the first formant is lowered by progressively increasing the lip-rounding (Fig. 78).

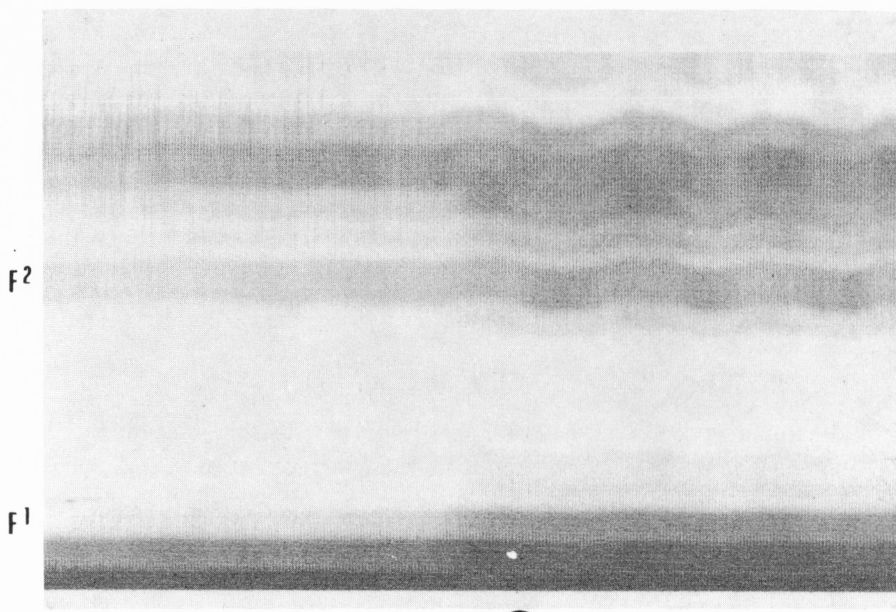

Fig. 77A. Spectrogram Showing Rise in Frequency of Formant One

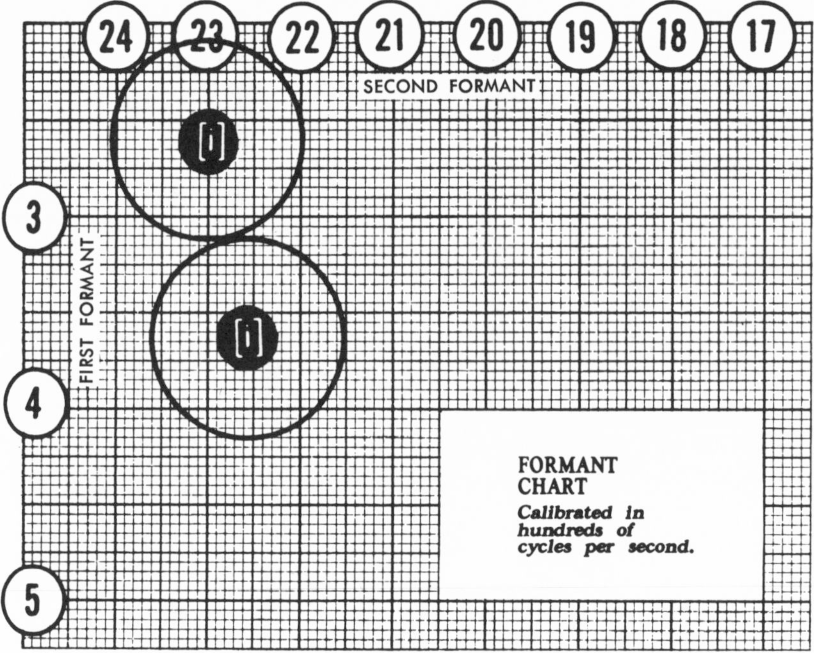

Fig. 77B. Formant Chart Showing Rise in Frequency of Formant One

When tongue occlusion is lessened in passing from a closed tense to a less tense [i], positions on the formant chart indicate vowel [i] migration caused by this action.

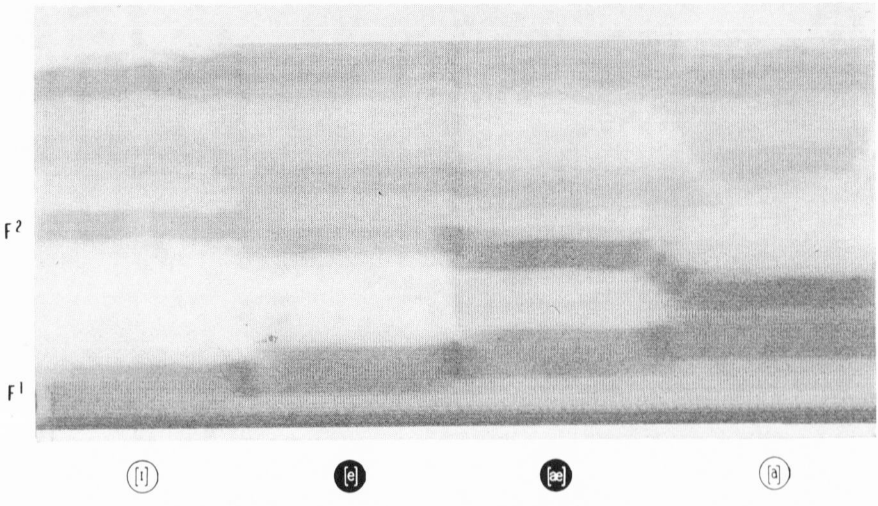

Fig. **78A.** Spectrogram Showing Formant Movements of Frontal Vowels

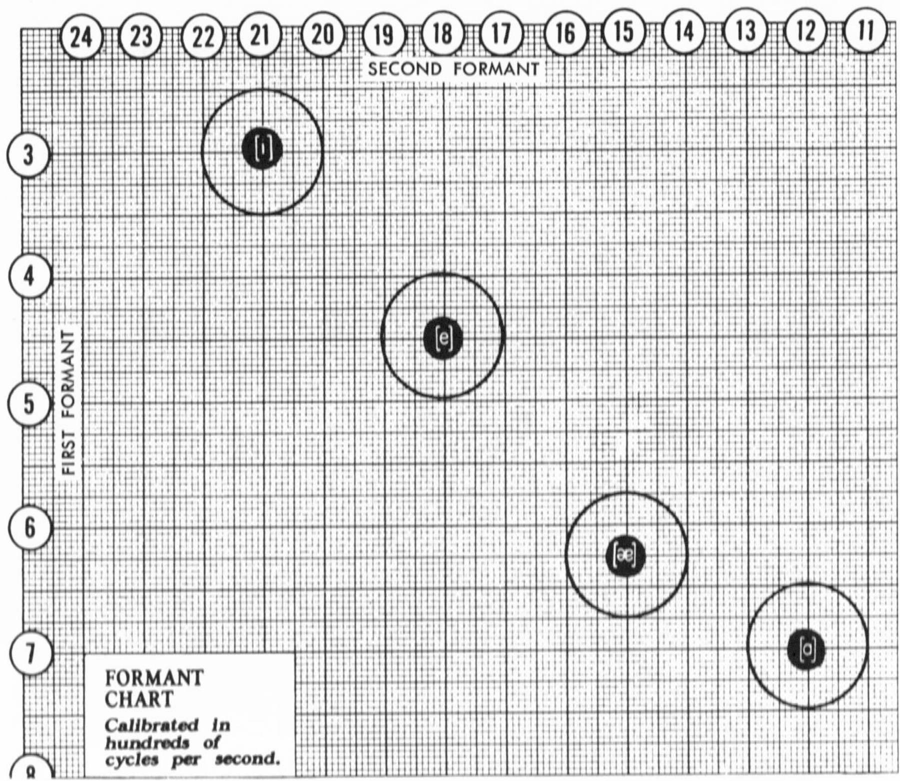

Fig. **78B.** Formant Chart Showing Formant Movements of Frontal Vowels

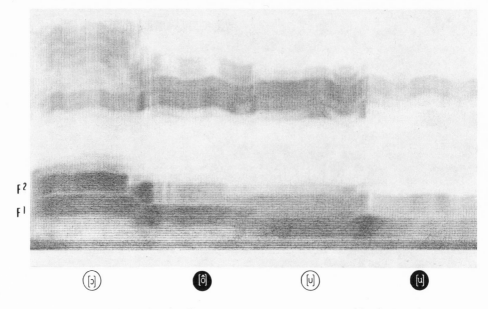

Fig. **78C.** Spectrogram Showing Formant Movements of Back Vowels

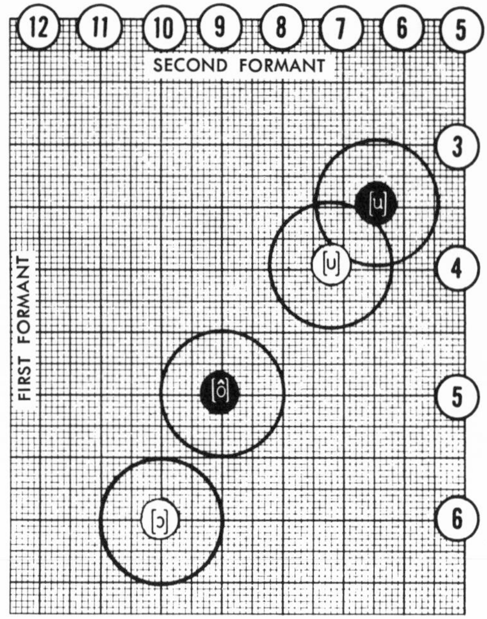

Fig. **78D.** Formant Chart Showing Formant Movements of Back Vowels

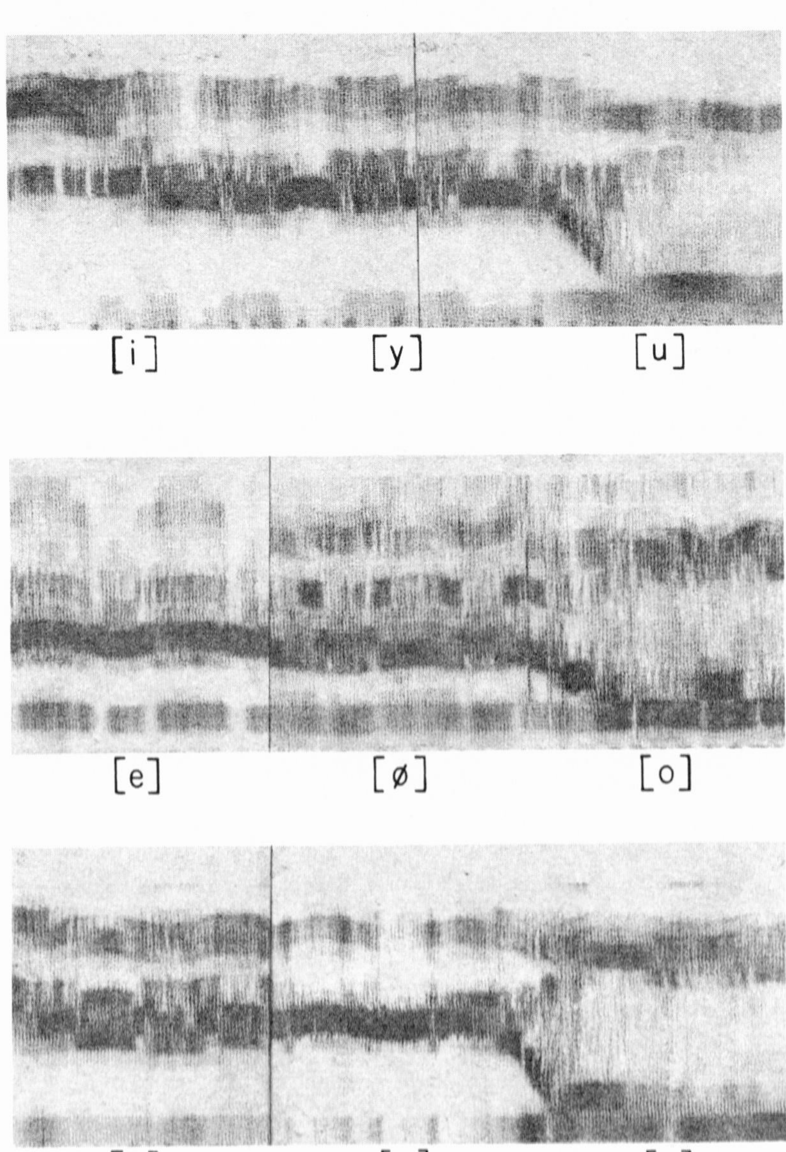

Fig. **79A.** Spectrogram Showing the Effect of Lip-Rounding and Tongue-Backing upon the Frontal Vowels

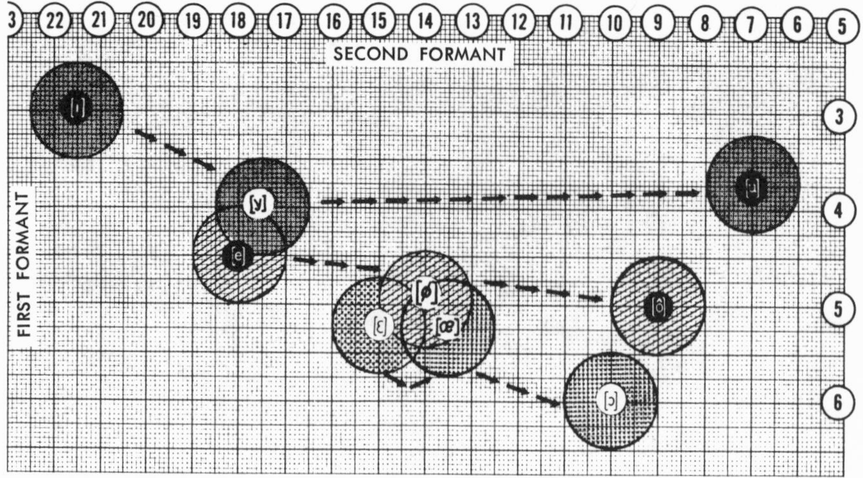

Fig. **79B.** Formant Chart Showing the Effect of Lip-Rounding and Tongue-Backing upon the Frontal Vowels

The Second Formant Movement

Increasing the volume of the oral cavity lowers the second formant, and decreasing it raises the second formant. To increase the volume, the singer lowers either the tongue or the jaw. The basic vowel and quality alternate positions established in this book are formed by moving both tongue and jaw to attain maximum sonority of a particular cavity adjustment for singing (Fig. 78A).

Lip-rounding lowers the second formant, and lip-spreading raises it. Tongue-backing lowers the second formant, and tongue-fronting raises it.

The obvious formant movement when the vowel [i] migrates to the French vowel [y] is caused by a change from lip-spreading for [i] to lip-rounding for [y]. As the vowel [y] migrates to the vowel [u], the formant alterations are achieved by tongue-backing and lip-rounding. The same lip and tongue movements cause the formant alterations of [e] to [ø] to [ô]; [ɛ] to [œ] to [ɔ] (Figs. 77A, 77B, 79A, and 79B). "A direct relation exists between the second formant lowering and the front cavity lengthening."[27]

Pitch Change and Vowel Formant Movement

Vowel formants, characteristic concentrations of energy within the tonal spectrum, are found in limited regions of frequency within which they must

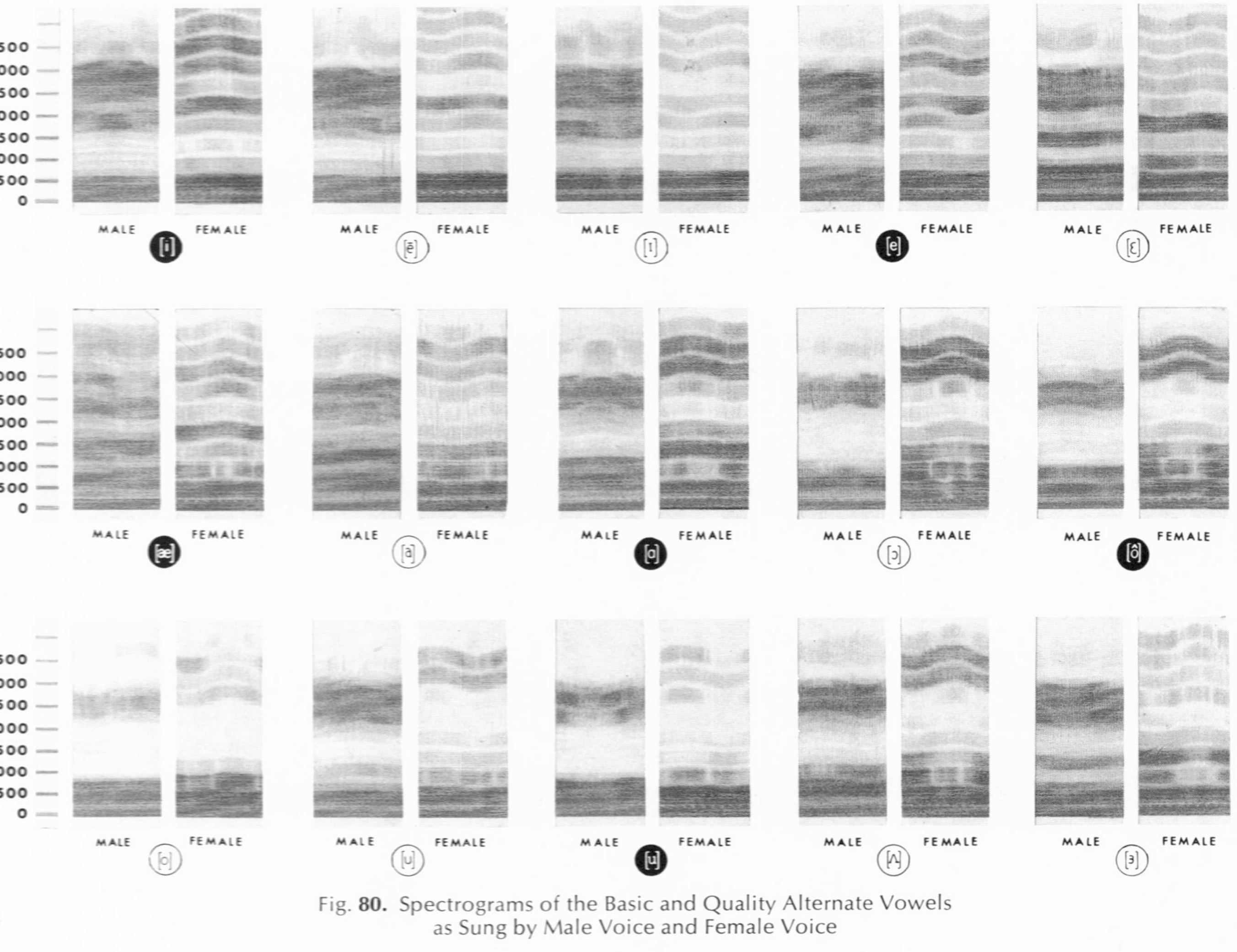

Fig. **80.** Spectrograms of the Basic and Quality Alternate Vowels as Sung by Male Voice and Female Voice

remain. If the pitch to be sung is changed so much as to go above the regions of formant recognition, the resultant sound will be heard as some other vowel.[28] The alteration of the coupled system which accompanies such a change is described in the kinesiologic analysis of each phoneme in Chapter Ten. (The areas for vowel stability are shown in Fig. 102, p. 230.)

Intensity and Vowel Formant Movement

All frontal vowels may be sung with more extreme lip-spreading and with an extreme frontal tongue position at pianissimo and piano levels when they are sung within their limited pitch areas (Fig. 102, p. 230). As intensity is increased above the mezzo piano level, so must the size of the cavity and orifice increase. The cavity coupling is changed somewhat by moving the point of constriction of the tongue and palate slightly downward and backward, thereby creating a larger frontal cavity and less constriction at the inner orifice. This action causes the first formant to rise and the second formant to lower, and the ear hears this cavity alteration as a migration of each frontal vowel to or toward a phoneme directly below it, depending upon the increase of intensity and the lowering of the mandible (Fig. 22 and Records 1-4, [i] Band 7, [a] Band 13).

This same action occurs with the singing of the back vowels. An increase in the volume of the cavities and the separation of the point of constriction at the inner orifice causes these vowels to migrate toward the neutral vowel [ʌ] and [ʊ] (Fig. 103 and Records 1-4, [ɔ] Band 14, [u] 19).

Chapter 5

Sound as Sensation

Vocal utterance as a means of musical communication depends upon hearing. Without auditory feedback* the art song could not exist, for the singer could not master the numerous variations in pitch dynamics demanded by a sophisticated musical culture. Without the sense of hearing the listener would be unable to detect melody, nuance, quality, volume, and phrasing within a musical sound and thereby would be deprived of the aesthetic value music offers. Only when a person loses this faculty does he realize how truly remarkable it is and how difficult life can be without it.

THE DUALISTIC NATURE OF SOUND

To hear is to interpret sound.

To the physicist, sound is a form of energy, an organized movement of particles within any medium. The physicist's sound can be measured and controlled to do work, or it can alter the position of objects and generate heat.

To the psychologist, sound is a sensation, something that exists only within ourselves. Such sensations create emotions and change our conduct. Sound is real but intangible. One cannot weigh it or see it; one can only feel the effects of it.

Where the physicist's sound can be controlled, measured, and organized, the psychologist's sound is conceptual. It may be high or low, loud or soft, pleasant or unpleasant. The psychologist who wishes to relate the sensation of sound to objects and events in the physical world is forced to compare the pitch, loudness, or timbre, as reported by a subject, with the intensity (in decibles), frequency (in cycles per second), and the complex wave form (or analysis of the sound spectra).

* To demonstrate the singer's dependence upon auditory feedback a simple experiment may be performed. Attach a speaker system to a tape recorder through output jacks on the recorder. Record as usual, but turn on the speaker system while recording. The sound will emerge from the speaker a fraction of a second later than the sung word, causing the singer considerable confusion. Such an experiment will reveal just how much the singer relies upon auditory feedback rather than upon proprioceptive feedback for sensing the desired position for the resonators and the articulators.

The physiologist interprets for both the physicist and psychologist how the sound waves are received and passed through the outer and middle ears into the cochlea; there the sound is transformed into nerve impulses to be received by the brain. The physiologist interprets for the physicist how such neural impulses correspond in patterns of time to the original pattern of the physicist's sound wave, and for the psychologist, how such nerve impulses generate our subjective sensations. Such a study, a blending of objective and subjective data, is known as psychophysics.

The physical properties of a sound are inherent in the sound waves and can always be measured independent of any human observer. The subjective properties of a sound are characteristic of the sensations experienced by a human listener and cannot be measured without him.

Hearing must be discussed in psychophysical terms, for such terms will always indicate a relationship between the objective and subjective aspects of sound and their impact upon human conduct.

THE SENSITIVITY OF THE EAR

Man has not been able to create a mechanical implement that is able to transfer motion from one point to another as effectively and efficiently as do the ossicles of the middle ear when they transfer pressure variations from the outer ear to the hydraulic system of the inner ear. The manner in which such a transfer of motion is accomplished never fails to bring to the thoughtful observer a sense of awe and leads him to a new respect for his ability to hear and interpret the sounds of life about him.

The sensitivity of the ear is remarkable. Judson and Weaver[1] hold that at the most favorable pitch (3,000 cps) the ear will detect periodic pressure changes of less than one one-thousandth of a dyne per square centimeter. Such a pressure is equivalent to the weight of a human hair one-third as long as its diameter. Since the normal weight of the air is about one million dynes per square centimeter, the ear responds to a periodic change of one-billionth part of the value of this pressure. Hallowell Davis states:

> The human ear is so sensitive that at its best it can almost hear the individual air molecules bump against the ear drum in their random thermal flight. The distance that the eardrum moves in and out with each wave when we hear just the faintest audible tone at the most favorable frequency is less than one-tenth of the diameter of a single hydrogen molecule. This distance is, of course, far less than we can see under the best microscope. We cannot think of it in terms of inches for it is less than a hundred millionth of an inch. If the capital

'I' at the beginning of this sentence were enlarged to the height of the Empire State Building a hundred millionth of an inch would correspond to about the thickness of a piece of cigarette paper.[2]

Animals have an even more efficient means of collecting sound energy. Their outer ears are much larger and are able to gather in more of the sound signal. But the inner ear of man is as sensitive as it can usefully be. If the inner ear were more acute, the sound of molecular motion would create a continuous hiss that would mask the meaningful faint sounds around us, and the threshold of hearing would be raised.

To interpret properly the listening process, one must define the constituents of audible sound in physical and psychophysical terms.

THE PHYSICAL ASPECTS OF FREQUENCY

Frequency is the measure of the number of times per second that a vibrating particle executes a complete cycle. As illustrated by Fig. 50. Frequency is measured in cycles per second (cps).[3]

Frequency is not synonymous with pitch. Frequency is an observation of an aspect of sound which is determined by assistance of instruments; whereas pitch is determined by a direct observation of an aspect of sound as it affects the ear and is entirely subjective.

The Measurement of Frequency

The musical scale is a scale of frequency. Fig. 81 shows the frequency of notes of the musical scale which are mathematically constructed in order to provide for all possible changes of key. The system of intervals is based upon an equally tempered scale in which each octave consists of twelve equal intervals.[4] The frequency of a note is determined by multiplying the frequency of any note by one of the following factors:

Equally Tempered Scale

Unison	1.000	Diminished fifth	1.4146
Minor second	1.0591	Perfect fifth	1.4987
Major second	1.1222	Minor sixth	1.5878
Minor third	1.1893	Minor seventh	1.7821
Major third	1.2604	Major seventh	1.8881
Perfect fourth	1.3355	Octave	2.0000

Each octave thus attained will be the exact multiple of another octave.

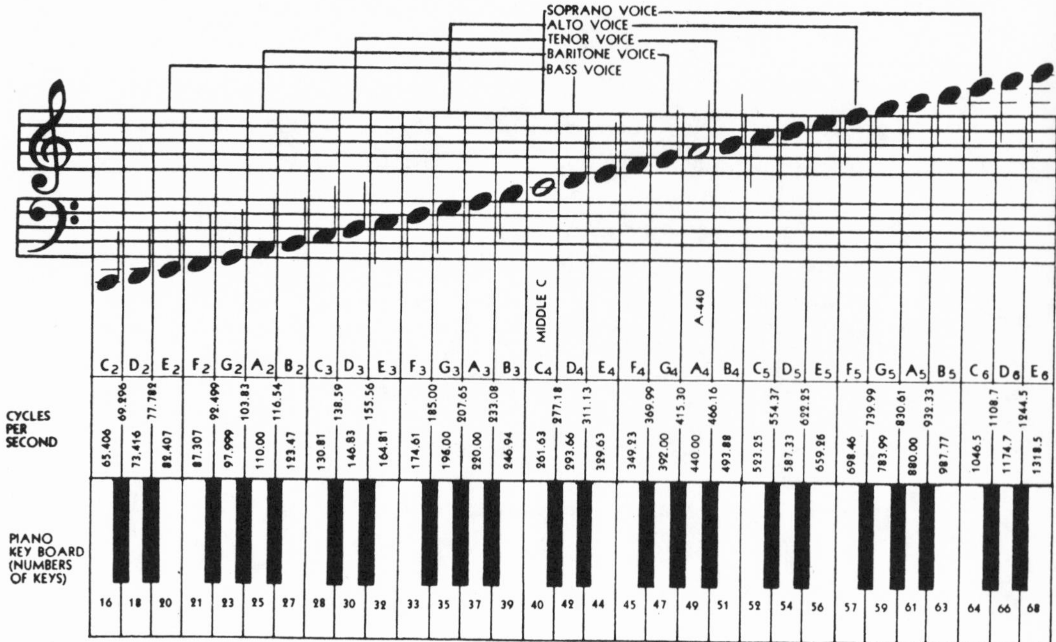

Fig. **81.** Frequency of Notes of the Musical Scale

Chart courtesy of Conn Corporation, Elkhart, Indiana, world's largest manufacturer of band instruments.

Frequency Limits of Audible Sound[5]

The range of audible frequencies extends from about 20 to 20,000 cps. For the ear the most sensitive range is from 500 to 4,000 cps; this range is shown in Fig. 82 to be almost the same range as that which is important in understanding speech. Above 4,000 and below 500 cps, the sensitivity of the ear declines more and more rapidly with the increase in age. Young people are able to distinguish sounds well between 18,000 and 20,000 cps where a man or woman of forty has difficulty hearing frequencies above 11,000 or 12,000 cps. In Fig. 82 the lowest line divides the audible tones from the inaudible and shows how both low frequency and high frequency sounds must be made more intense to be heard.

The low threshold curve of hearing[6] suggests hearing sounds under ideal conditions: Young adults with healthy ears, extremely quiet environment, and a subject who is skilled in the process of listening to faint sounds.

The average threshold curve of hearing is represented by the broken line in Fig. 82. This line is not fixed. Hearing acuity can vary fifteen decibels above

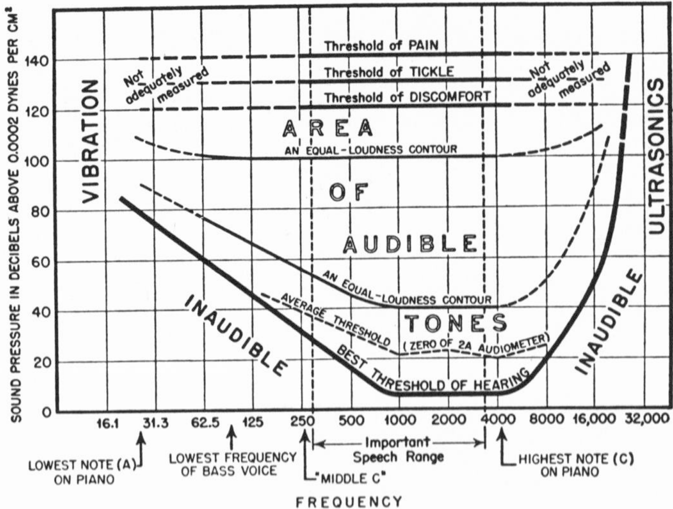

Fig. **82.** Thresholds of Hearing
Source: Hallowell Davis, *Hearing and Deafness* (4th ed.; New York: Rinehart Books, Inc., 1951).

and below this line and still be normal; the threshold depends upon the frequency and the person who is being tested.

The best threshold of hearing curve bounds the area of audibility. Below the line sounds are not heard. Above the line sounds are heard with varying degrees of acuity that depend upon frequency and intensity. As an example, the average best acuity of hearing occurs between 1,000 and 4,000 cps at an intensity level of 20 decibels. For tones above 4,000 cps and below 1,000 cps the intensity of each tone has to be raised to be perceived aurally. The area of audible speech is bounded above by thresholds of discomfort (tickling and pain); such thresholds are sensed only when the intensity level is 120 decibels or greater.

THE PSYCHOPHYSICAL ASPECTS OF PITCH

> Pitch is that aspect of auditory sensation which the listener organizes upon a scale running from low to high. Pitch is chiefly a function of the frequency of the sound, but it is also dependent upon the intensity and the timbre of the sound.[7]

Pitch is used for a relative subjective comparison between musical sounds; one depends upon the timbre of the sound to detect the difference between two notes of the same pitch produced by different instruments such as a piano or a violin, an oboe or a clarinet.

For the singer, pitch depends upon intensity to a profound degree. Stevens quotes Miles[8] in describing an experiment in which the singer is required to reproduce vocally the pitch of a tuning fork (middle C). When the fork is

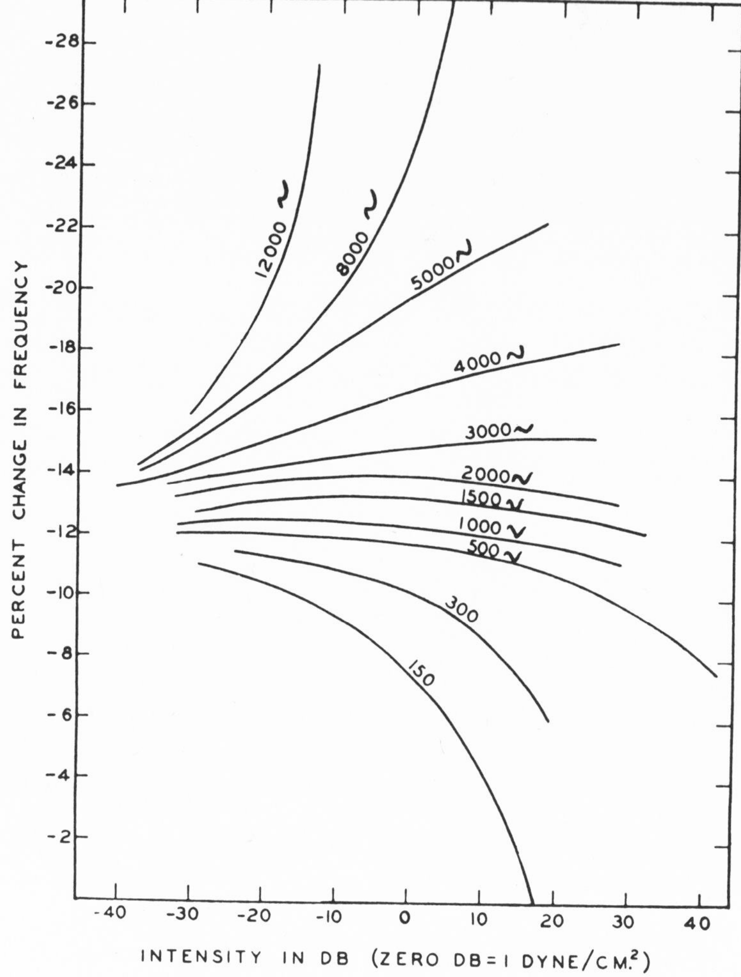

Fig. **83.** Contours Showing How Pitch Changes with Intensity
The percentage change in frequency necessary to keep the pitch of a tone constant in the face of a given change in intensity can be taken as a measure of the effect of intensity upon pitch. Source: Stanley Smith Stevens and Hallowell Davis, *Hearing* (New York: John Wiley & Sons, Inc., 1963).

held close to the ear, in his attempt to match the pitch, the singer sings a lower pitch. He actually hears the louder tone as lower.

In an experiment conducted by Stevens[9] tones ranging from 150 cps to 1,200 cps were tested to determine the effects of intensity upon the audible range of hearing. Two tones of slightly different frequencies were presented alternately to an observer. He was allowed to adjust the intensity of one tone until the pitch of the two tones appeared equal. Although the frequency of the vibrator was not altered, the observer psychophysically compensated for the difference in intensity, thereby making the two tones sound equal in pitch.

One should note that this phenomenon does not occur when complex tones are used. The pitch is held constant because one or more of the partials are stable and do not change with changes of intensity.

Fig. 83 illustrates the relationship between pitch and intensity which must be maintained in order to keep a tone at a constant level of pitch. It also shows what happens to the pitch of tones of various frequencies when the intensities are altered. For low tones the pitch lowers with intensity. For high tones the pitch raises with intensity.

The Measurement of Pitch

The relation of pitch to frequency is not one to one. In 1937 Harvard University psychophysicists devised an electronic piano with knob adjustments on the keys which permitted a wide range of frequency variation for each key. Subjects faced the task of tuning the piano to equal appearing pitch intervals evenly spaced along the scale. The frequency of each tone was then measured. Stevens describes the research experiment as follows:

> The subjects did not tune the piano to equal steps of the physicist, nor . . . to that of musical intervals. A new scale of pitch measurement was devised. To measure the intervals of the new pitch scale, units called "mels" from the word "melody" were created. A 1,000 mel tone was determined to be a sound with a frequency of 1,000 cycles and an intensity of 40 db.[10]

An examination of the graph in Fig. 84, will show that in the lower parts of the scale an equally spaced octave determined by the mel scale will vary 100 mels when compared with the frequency scale, but at the upper end of the piano (2,000 to 3,000 cycles) the octave represents a 700 mel variation when compared with the frequency scale. "These measurements confirm the feeling often expressed by pianists that the higher musical octaves sound larger than the lower ones.[11]

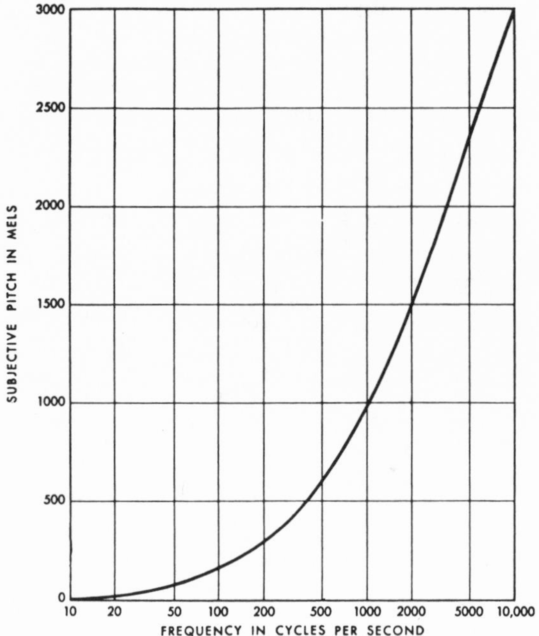

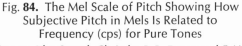

Fig. **84.** The Mel Scale of Pitch Showing How Subjective Pitch in Mels Is Related to Frequency (cps) for Pure Tones

Source: The *Speech Chain* by P. B. Denes and E. N. Pinson, published by Bell Telephone Laboratories, Inc. (1963).

S. S. Stevens describes the research effort as follows:

> Was there a physical explanation of this? To account for the form of the mel scale the researchers studied the structure of the human ear. Asking: Where are the points at which different frequencies stimulate the basilar membrane of the inner ear? Comparing the mel scale with a sort of anatomical map showing the membrane where each frequency sets up its maximum vibration, they found an amazing coincidence. In tuning the electronic piano, the listeners had adjusted the tones so that the points of stimulation on the basilar membrane were equally separated. Equal pitch extent, therefore, meant equal separation along the membrane.
>
> The Organ of Corti behaves like a specialized piece of skin. Just as a touch anywhere on the skin produces a sensation that seems to be localized in a particular place, so a "touch" on the sensitive cells of the inner ear produces a sensation localized in a kind of subjective

space that we call pitch. The "mel" scale of pitch provides an accurate map of the cochlea, in which a distance of one millimeter on the basilar membrane corresponds to 100 mels.

When musicians are asked to set a pure tone precisely one octave above another pure tone, they tend to set the upper tone a little sharp. Many musical egos are shaken when the musician discovers he is unable to produce a perfect octave by ear.[12]

THE PHYSICAL ASPECTS OF INTENSITY

Intensity refers to a dimension of a stimulus. It is a measure of the strength or magnitude of the stimulating agent. In plane progressive sound waves, intensity is measured in terms of pressure or energy flow (power).[13] "Sound pressure, therefore, in a specified direction at a point, is the average rate of sound energy transmitted in the specified direction through a unit area normal to this direction at the point considered."[14]

Intensity is not synonymous with loudness. Intensity, like frequency, is a physical aspect of sound which must be observed with the aid of instruments; loudness, like pitch, is a subjective aspect of sound which may be observed directly.

Intensity is difficult to define because the values of a sinusoidal (See definition on p. 104.) sound wave must be specified in order to completely determine the sound wave. Sound is two dimensional and intensity is one of its dimensions,[15] frequency is the other.

The propagation of sound involves the rapid oscillation of air particles in an elastic medium.

This oscillation involves a transfer of energy through the medium, and it ends by exerting a minute force against any surface which the wave strikes. Since this force or pressure varies during each to-and-fro oscillation, the term *intensity* derives from the amplitude or amount of increase or decrease in pressure in each oscillation of the particle.

The Measurement of Amplitude or Pressure of Intensity

In considering the movement of air particles one also must consider the force which disturbs them from their positions of rest. Such a force is called pressure. It is measured by a force unit called the dyne. "The dyne is a force which will produce a change in velocity of one centimeter per second in a gram mass in one second."[16] The force of gravity exerts a pressure of 1,000 dynes upon one square centimeter mass. Normal atmospheric pressure is equal to about one million dynes per square centimeter.

Pressures within sound waves are very small. The smallest pressures sufficient to produce an audible sound within the human threshold of hearing is .0002 dynes per square centimeter.

The Measurement of Power of Intensity

As an air particle is disturbed it transfers its energy to an increasing number of particles which tend to dissipate the energy and particle velocity. To measure the energy available at a point away from the sound source, one must use a measure of power which will indicate the sound's intensity, or particle velocity, in very small quantities.

When the application force results in the displacement of a particle, work is done. Power is the amount of work accomplished in a given time. Its unit is the erg per second. Since the erg per second is too small for practical use the power or intensity of a sound wave is measured in watts per square centimeter. A just audible sound within the human threshold of hearing has a sound intensity of 10^{-16} watts or ten billionths of a watt.[17]

The Decibel Scale of Intensity

The human ear is extremely sensitive to variations in the amplitude of sound waves, which are interpreted here as variations in air pressure.

Variations in air pressure may cause the amplitude to increase while the frequency remains constant. In this case, the movement of the point of the pendulum is analogous to the oscillation of an air particle. Variation in amplitude of an oscillating body may be illustrated by hanging two pendulums, each of the same length, and starting them swinging, one in a long arc, the other in a short arc. Both will cross the point of rest at the center at the same moment; i.e., frequency is constant while the amplitudes are different.

Likewise, variation in air pressure may cause the frequency to change while the amplitude remains constant. The oscillations of the air particle may be illustrated by shortening the string of one pendulum by one half. The number of complete oscillations, cps, will be doubled in the shorter pendulum, but the amplitude will be the same, provided each weight is released at the same point. (Fig. 86).

Since the ear responds to an extremely wide range of intensities from a just audible sound to one with an intensity ten billion times more powerful,

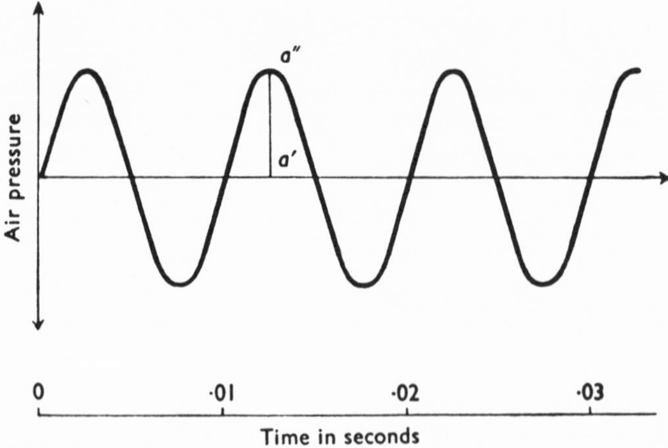

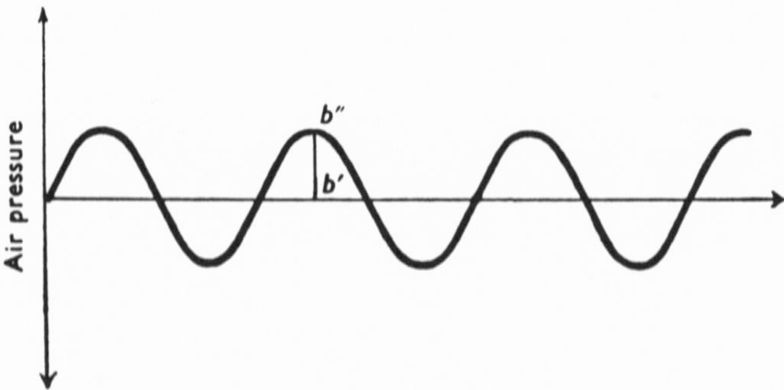

Fig. **85.** Two Sounds, One with Twice the Amplitude of the Other

Source: Peter Ladefoged, *Elements of Acoustic Phonetics* (Chicago: University of Chicago Press, 1962).

acoustic engineers have found it convenient to use a logarythmic system that will compare the relative value of one sound to another. First, they had to establish a reference level of intensity with which all other sounds could be compared.

Such a reference sound was determined by listening to a 1,000-cycle tone at an intensity level where the sound first becomes audible. Such a sound has the acoustic power of 10^{-16} watts per square centimeter and the acoustic pressure of .0002 dynes per square centimeter. This point of just audible sound was called zero decibels. Once such a reference level was established, considering the amplitude or power of any sound as being so much more or less than that of the reference sound was a simple task.

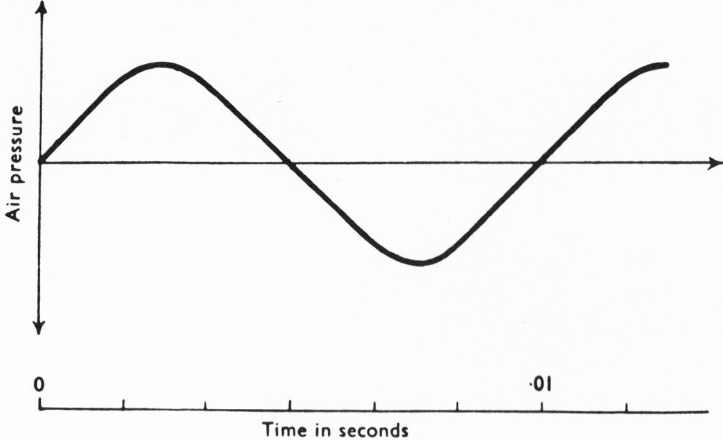

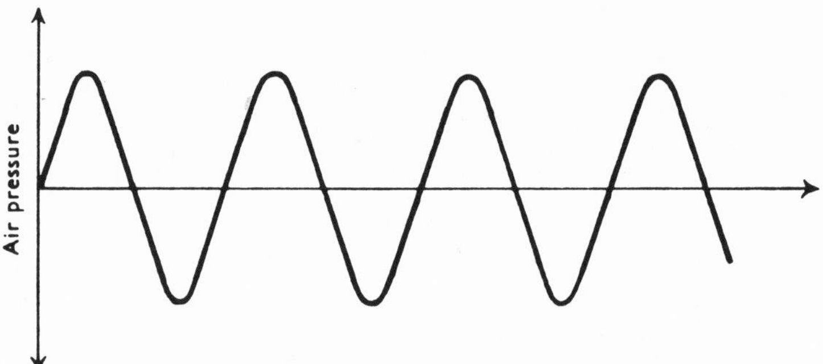

Fig. **86.** Two Sounds with Equal Amplitudes, But One with a Frequency of 100 cps, and the Other with a Frequency of 300 cps
Source: Peter Ladefoged, *Elements of Acoustic Phonetics* (Chicago: University of Chicago Press, 1962).

The following graph by Ladefoged (Fig. 87) shows approximately thirteen equal steps to intensity, starting from the reference pressure of .0002 dynes per square centimeter, and the intensity power level of 10^{-16} watts per square centimeter to the threshold of pain. One can see that the difference in power (in actual watts per square centimeter) is far greater between steps twelve and thirteen than it is between steps one and two; but the power ratio between any two adjacent steps remains the same.

One logarithmic unit to the base of ten, of the ratio of one acoustic power to another is known as a bel. Since the bel is a rather large unit, in practice a

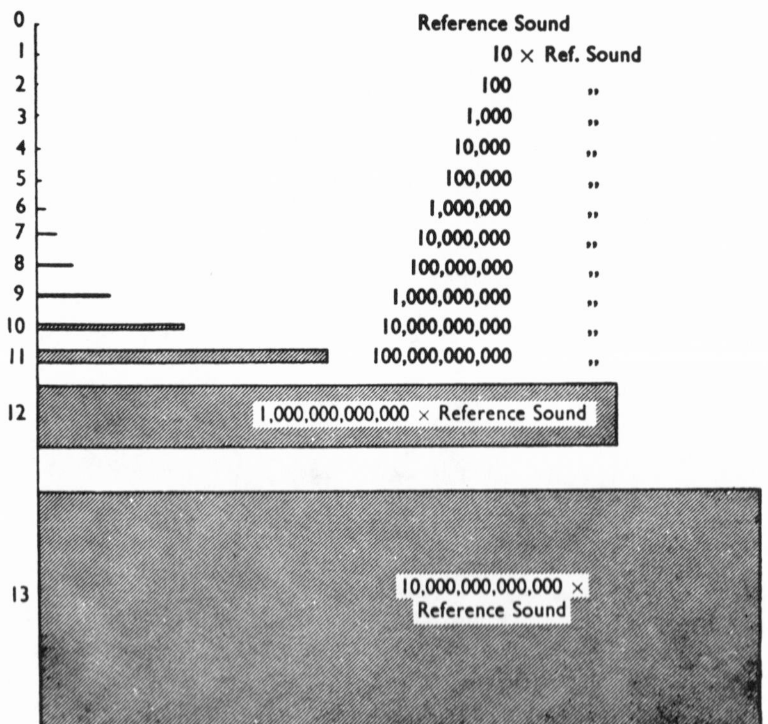

Fig. **87.** The Powers of Sounds Constituting Thirteen Approximately Equal Steps of Loudness

The power of each sound in watts per square centimeter is proportionate to the area of each block. Source: Peter Ladefoged, *Elements of Acoustic Phonetics* (Chicago: University of Chicago Press, 1962).

unit whose value is one-tenth of a bel is used. It is called the decibel. The following table explains this statement:

Power Ratio Between Sounds	*Common Logarithm of the Power Ratio*	*Difference in Bels*	*Difference in Decibels*
10 to 1	1	1	10
100 to 1	2	2	20
1,000 to 1	3	3	30
10,000 to 1	4	4	40

All that one has to do to find the common logarithm of the power ratios shown in the above table is to count the number of zeros. The difference in decibels between the two sounds can then be found by multiplying this number by ten.

When this system is applied to the power ratios in Fig. 87, the common logarithm of the sound at the threshold of pain and the reference level is 13 because the number has 13 zeros in it. The difference between the two sounds is 10 multiplied by 13 or 130 decibels. The difference between step three and step five is 20 db since the power at step five is 100 times greater than at step three and the common logarithm of 100 is 2.

When the power ratio between two sounds is some intermediate value such as 47 to 1, logarithm tables are used to find the proper differences between the sounds.

THE PSYCHOPHYSICAL ASPECTS OF LOUDNESS

> Loudness is the intensive attribute of an auditory sensation, in terms of which sounds may be ordered on a scale extending from soft to loud. Loudness depends primarily upon the sound pressure of the stimulus, but it also depends upon the frequency and wave form of the stimulus.[18]

Loudness depends upon the amplitude of a sound wave. Fig. 87 shows a loud sound in which the pressure variations are large and a softer sound in which they are much smaller.

The Measurement of Loudness

Gustav Theodore Fechner of Leipzig, Germany, published *Elements of Psychophysics* in 1860. In this work the author set forth a law known as the Weber-Fechner law which expressed the relation between stimulus and sensation by a simple rule:

> As stimuli are *multiplied* to greater magnitude sensations increase by *addition;* i.e., each time the intensity of the sound is doubled, one step is *added* to the sensation of loudness. This is a logarithmic process and Fechner's law states that sensation grows as the logarithm of the stimulus.[19]

Since the law applied to a stimulus of any kind—light, vision, taste, touch, and smell—the "just noticeable differences" between stimulus and the sensation could be measured and experimental psychology was established as a science.

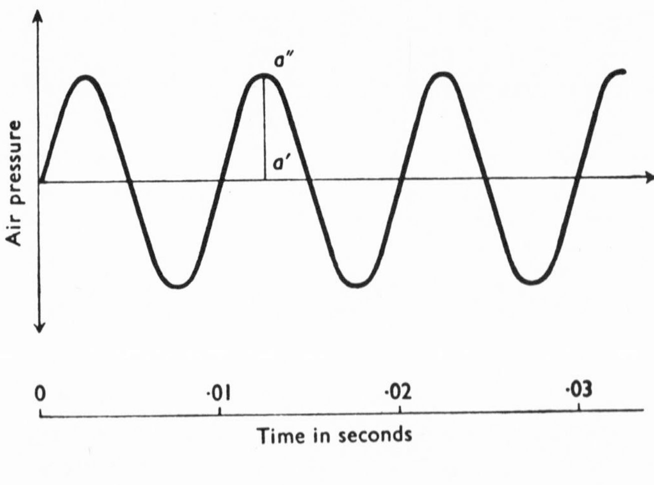

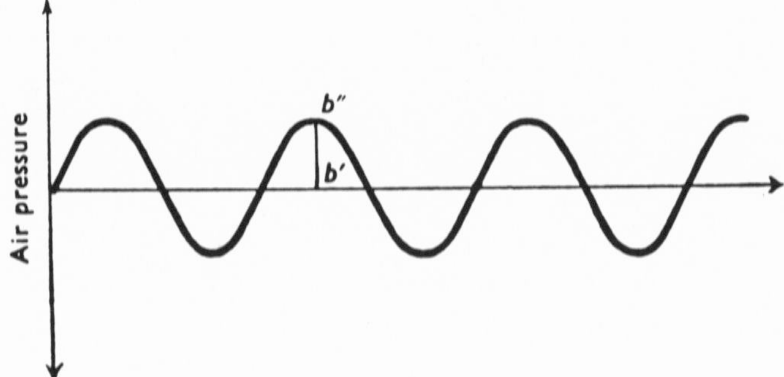

Fig. **88.** Two Sounds, One Twice as Loud as the Other and One with Twice the Amplitude of the Other

Source: Peter Ladefoged, *Elements of Acoustic Phonetics* (Chicago: University of Chicago Press, 1962).

Loudness Level Scale

To determine the psychophysical relationship between loudness and intensity levels, it was necessary to create a new scale of measurement that would be wholly compatible with the loudness level and the intensity level as shown in Fig. 89. The empirical choice for such a unit of measurement was the phon.

To establish a sound level scale, many listeners with headphones, heard a 1,000 cycle tone at 40 db. A second tone was fed into the earphones, at say 200 cps. By turning a dial the listener could adjust the 200 cps tone until the two tones were equally as loud. Other tones of various frequencies were matched in loudness with the 1,000 cps–40 db sound, and their positions were recorded. For example, all points on the 60 phon contour were rated equal in loudness to a 1,000 cps sound at 4 db. The loudness level of a given tone was defined as the intensity (measured in decibels) of a 1,000 cps tone that sounded equal in loudness to a given tone. The unit of loudness level was named the phon. The numbers on each of the contours in Fig. 89 are the number of phons corresponding to that particular contour.

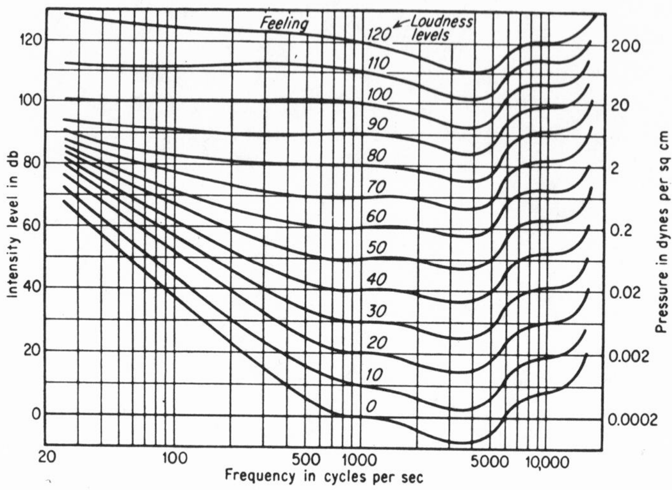

Fig. **89.** Loudness Level Contours Adopted by the American Standards Association, 1936

Loudness levels in phons are indicated in the center of the chart. Source: *The Speech Chain* by P. B. Denes and E. N. Pinson, published by Bell Telephone Laboratories, Inc. (1963).

Thus a 100 cps tone must have an intensity of about 62 db to have a loudness level of 40 phons, while a 30 cps tone will have to have an intensity of about 80 db of 40 phons.

Loudness level becomes apparent when one listens to present day high-fidelity music. If the volume decreases both bass and treble seem to fade; accordingly, the volume of the bass and treble portions of the spectrum are raised to bring the total sound into balance. The reason is that the threshold of hearing is lowest between 1,000 and 4,000 cps (Fig. 82, p. 147) and when the loudness of the music is reduced the musical sounds reproduced within this range are heard where frequencies below 1,000 cps and above 4,000 cps are not heard.

The Numerical Loudness Scale

The phon scale of loudness level (Fig. 89) is used to arrange sensations in order of increasing magnitude. It cannot tell the scientist how much greater in magnitude one tone is than another; it can only tell him that one is greater than another.

The Weber-Fechner[20] law was disproved in the nineteen-thirties by acoustic engineers who required a means of measuring loudness. The decibel measured sound energy in logarithmic units, but it did not prove to be the proper scale for listening comparisons. "It was apparent to anyone who listened that a loudness of 50 decibels was not one-half the loudness of 100 decibels; 50 db is defined as the quiet buzz of a normal room, and 100 db is equivalent to the din of a boiler factory."[21]

A scale was needed which would express numerical relations between magnitudes of sensations measured. In the case of loudness the numerical scale devised by the psychoacoustic laboratory at Harvard University was identified by the word *sone* (Latin for *sound*) as its unit of loudness measurement. It is known as the sone scale. By definition one sone is the loudness of a 1,000 cps tone at 40 db.

Researchers[22] found that each increase of 10 db in the intensity of a sound stimulus doubles the sensation of loudness. The experiments showed that the sensation of loudness grows by multiplication and not by addition, as was claimed by Fechner.

To evaluate the loudness relationship a listener is asked to compare two tones and to adjust the intensity of one of them until it is twice as loud (or half as loud as the other). Experimenters[22] have found that the perceived loudness is not proportional to the loudness level (Fig. 90). To increase the loudness from 0.1 sones to 10 sones one must increase the loudness level from 20 to 66 db Stevens now believes[23] that the relation of loudness to the intensity of a 1,000-cps tone can be expressed by the rule: An intensity increase of 10 db corresponds to a loudness ratio of two to one, and to a typical listener, loudness is a power function of sound pressure. The power exponent or multiplying factor for loudness is about .03 power of its sound energy. An increase of 10 db (between 40 and 50 cps) at the intensity of a 1,000 cps tone at 40 db increases the sone level six times from the original base of 40 db. A second 10 db increase (between 80 and 90 db) increases the sone level by twenty sones (25 to 45) (Fig. 89).

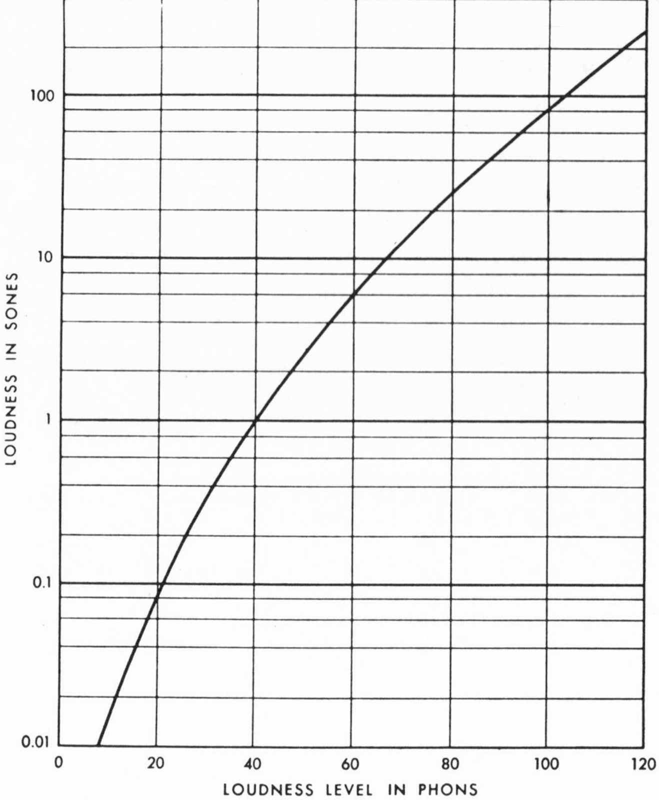

Fig. **90.** The Loudness Function

Perceived loudness in sones depends upon the loudness level of the stimulus in db. Calibration on the ordinate is in logarithmic division of fifths. Source: *The Speech Chain* by P. B. Denes and E. N. Pinson, published by Bell Telephone Laboratories, Inc. (1963).

THE ANATOMY AND PHYSIOLOGY OF THE EAR

The Outer Ear

The external ear, the pinna, is mainly an ornament. Man has never developed it to use as a focusing device as do most animals. The human ear canal is irregularly oval in cross-section and varies from man to man in size and shape. It is approximately twenty-five centimeters in length. Acoustic waves falling on the external ear funnel down the ear canal and set the eardrum into vibration. Denes and Pinson state:

> Because the ear canal is an acoustic resonator it amplifies frequencies near its own frequency. Thus the pressure at the ear drum for tones near this resonance (from 3,000 to 4,000 cps) may be two to four times greater than the pressure at the entrance to the canal. This effect permits us to detect many sounds that would be imperceptive if the drum were located at the surface of the head.[24]

The tympanic membrane, the eardrum, lies at the end of the auditory canal. It is a pearl gray wall composed of a thin, tough fibrous membrane that is fastened to the bony wall of the canal by a ring of tough fibrous tissue (Fig. 91).

The membrane is cone-shaped inward toward the middle cavity. The handle of the hammer (the malleus), the first of the three ossicles that transmit the vibrations of the drum to the middle ear, is attached to the inner surface of the drum. It keeps the membrane stretched tightly and cone-shaped. This tension is increased by the aid of the tensor tympani muscle (Fig. 92).

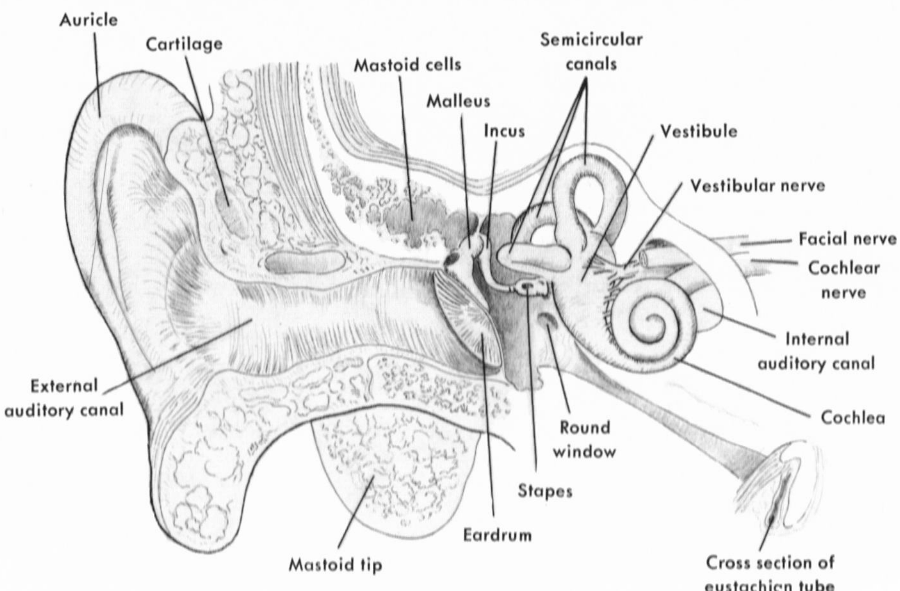

Fig. **91.** The Outer, Middle, and Inner Ears
After Hallowell Davis.

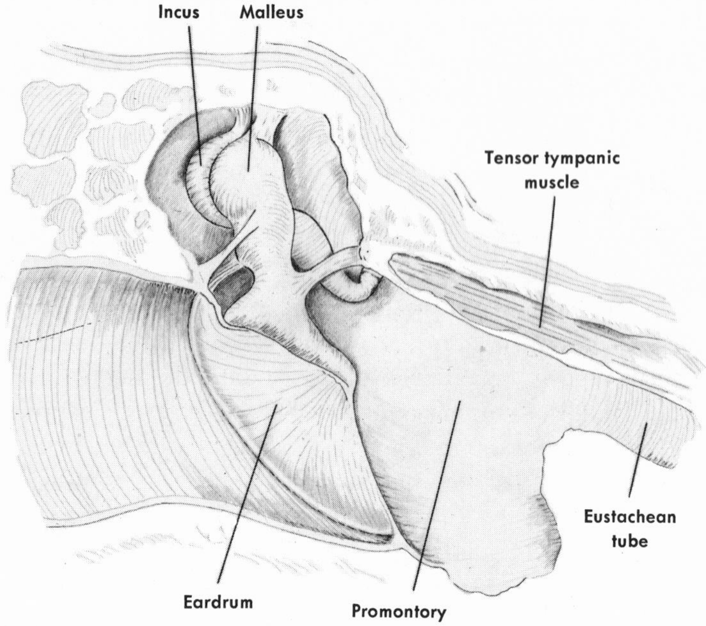

Fig. **92.** The Middle Ear
After Hallowell Davis.

The Middle Ear

The middle ear is a cavity in the bony structure of the skull. This cavity contains three small bones called the auditory ossicles—the malleus, the incus, and the stapes. These ossicles, which form the mechanical linkage between the eardrum and the inner ear, are suspended from the cavity walls by ligaments (Fig. 92).

Motions of the eardrum are transmitted through the malleus, which is attached to the eardrum, to the incus (anvil), the second of the ossicles. The incus ends in a long curved tip and is connected to the head of the stapes (stirrup), the last of the three ossicles.

The stapes is shaped like a stirrup, and its oval base fits into the oval window of the inner ear. The variation of air pressure causes the tympanic membrane to move back and forth, a motion transmitted through the first two ossicles to the stapes. It rocks back and forth in the oval window and compresses the fluid of the inner ear. The stapedius muscle attached to the neck of stapes pulls the stapes outward and backward; it thus acts as an antagonist muscle to the tensor tympani muscle, which pulls in the opposite direction. The combined action of these two muscles tends to suspend the ossicles and hold them steady during their rapid movement of complex vibrations.

The round window is located beneath the oval window. It is covered with an elastic membrane stretched flat. Its function as a resilient shock absorber will be explained later.

The eustachian tube running between the middle ear and the mouth cavity effectively links the middle ear with the outside air, equalizing the pressures in the middle ear and permitting the ossicles to work freely. Swallowing normally causes the eustachian tube to open momentarily, allowing the pressures to equalize.

Denes and Pinson[25] have revealed that the mechanics of the middle ear accomplish amplification of the outside sound. Their studies have led to the following conclusions, briefly stated. The middle ear increases the amount of acoustic energy entering the fluid-filled inner ear by increasing the amplitude of the pressure variations at the oval window. The ossicles behave like a lever, producing greater force at the footplate of stapes than the force applied at the malleus. This pressure amplification in the middle ear enables us to hear sounds whose energies are about one thousand times weaker than could otherwise be heard (Fig. 93).

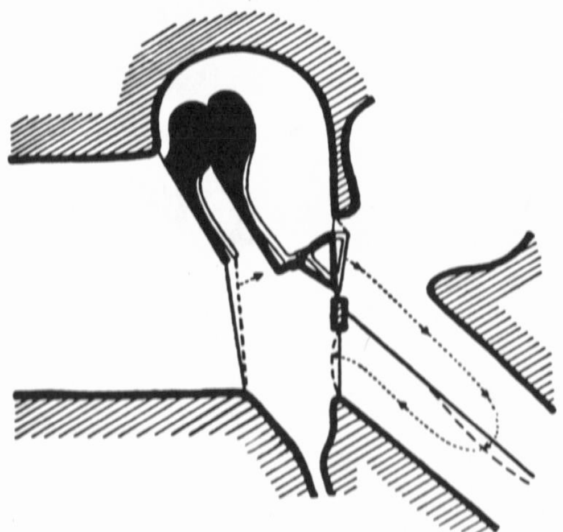

Fig. **93.** Mechanics of the Middle Ear
Source: Stanley Smith Stevens and Hallowell Davis, *Hearing* (New York: John Wiley & Sons, Inc., 1963).

The Inner Ear[26]

The inner ear is contained within the temporal bone, the hardest bone structure of the body. It is a series of channels filled with a clear watery fluid containing delicate membranous sacs, which are themselves filled with a watery fluid and contain sensory cells, each having its own function. The vestibule is a central portion that lies immediately behind the oval window. On one side it joins the cochlea, which is the organ of hearing, and on another side, the loops of three semicircular canals that form the sense organs of balance and turning (Figs. 91 and 94A).

The cochlea is coiled like a snail shell in a flat spiral of two and one-half turns. The canal within the cochlea is slightly over one inch in length (thirty-five millimeters) and ends at the apex of the spiral. The canal is partly divided into two galleries by a spiral shelf of bone protruding from the inner wall of the canal. This shelf is called the spiral lamina. The division is completed by a fibrous, flexible basilar membrane, which stretches from the edge of the bony shelf to the spiral ligament. This ligament attaches it to the outer wall of the canal. The upper gallery is called scala vestibuli, the lower, scala tympani. Both galleries are filled with watery fluid called perlymph, which makes both galleries an incompressible hydraulic system (Fig. 95A and 95B). The oval

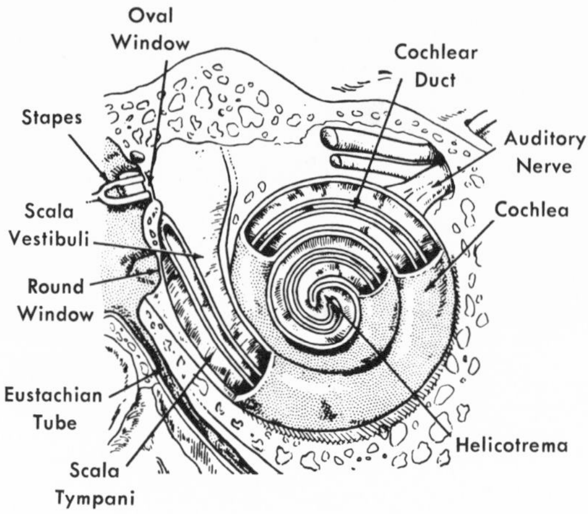

Fig. **94A.** The Cochlear Portion of the Inner Ear
Source: *The Speech Chain* by P. B. Denes and E. N. Pinson, published by Bell Telephone Laboratories, Inc. (1963).

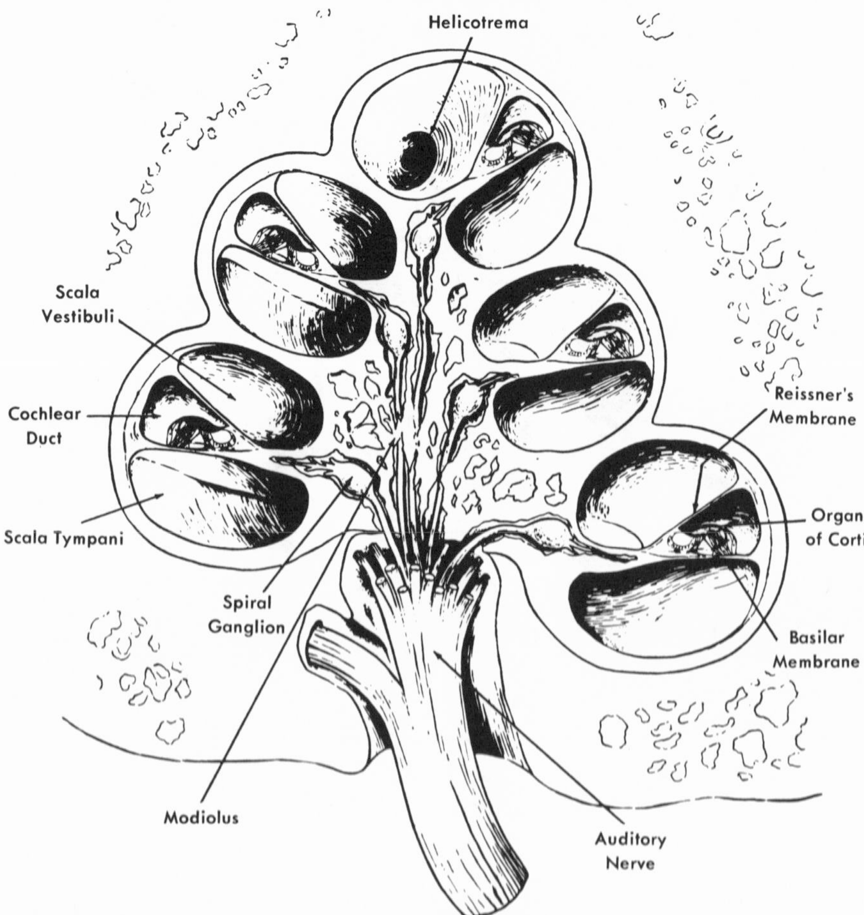

Fig. **94B.** Diagram of a Section Through the Core of the Cochlea
Source: *The Speech Chain* by P. B. Denes and E. N. Pinson, published by Bell Telephone Laboratories, Inc. (1963).

opening provides a window into the vestibule, which is continuous with the scala vestibuli, and the round window is the termination of the scala tympani.

The basilar membrane and the bony shelf terminate before the end of the spiral canal is reached, so that both galleries are continuous and permit the fluids to pass freely between them. This opening at the apex of the canals is called the helicotrema (Fig. 95A and 95B). The basilar membrane is thirty-two millimeters in length, it is broadest at the apex of the spiral canal (one-half millimeter) and narrowest at the base of the canal near the oval window (one-

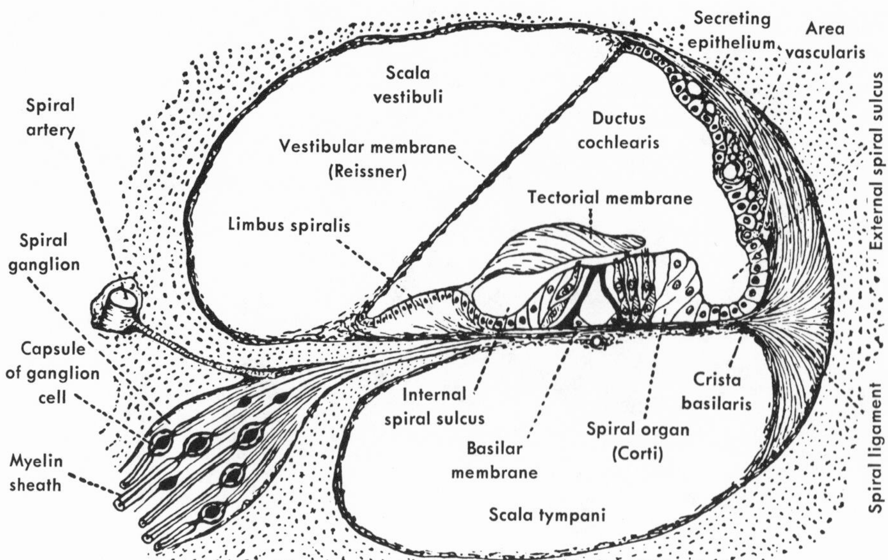

Fig. **95A.** Cross Section of Cochlear Canal
After Hallowell Davis.

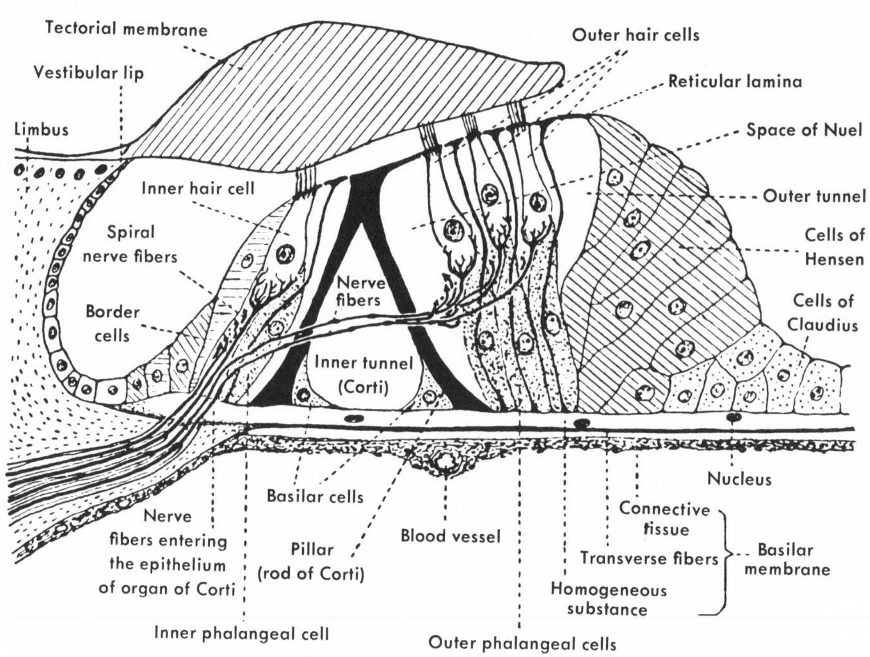

Fig. **95B.** Cross Section of Spiral Organ (Papilla) or Organ of Corti
Source: Andrew Theodore Rasmussen, *Outlines of Neuro-Anatomy* (Dubuque, Iowa: Wm. C. Brown Co., Pub., 1947).

twentieth of a millimeter). The membrane is thin and taut at its base near the stirrup and thick and loose near the helicotrema.

Upon the surface of the basilar membrane within the scala vestibuli lie the sensory cells of hearing known as the organ of Corti (Fig. 95A). Separating the organ of Corti from the fluid of the scala vestibuli is a thin resilient membrane called Reissner's membrane (Fig. 95A). The area within the organ of Corti is filled with a heavy thick fluid called endolymph.

The sensory cells are hair cells, each with dozens of microscopic protruding hairs arranged in four parallel rows that run the full length of the basilar membrane in its spiral ascent to the helicotrema. About 3,500 hair cells stand side by side in an inner row, and approximately 20,000 slightly smaller hair cells are evenly spaced in orderly arrangement in three outer rows.[27] The rods of Corti form a triangle to supply support and stiffness to the organ (Fig. 95B).

Stretching out above the hair cells is the tectorial membrane, soft, gelatinous, and yielding. The tiny hairs of each cell are imbedded in this soft membrane. Any bending or movement of the hair cells sets off nerve impulses in the nerve fibers attached to the lower end of each hair cell (Fig. 95B).

The nerve fibers run from the hair cells to the central core of the cochlea, where they join like strands of rope to form the auditory nerve and pass to the brain.

Each nerve fiber connects with more than one hair cell, and each hair cell connects with several nerve fibers in adjacent but overlapping zones. Thus no hair cell is responsible for a single frequency. Several cells and fibers send impulses to the brain simultaneously, even if the sound is sinusoidal.

ANALYSES OF SOUNDS BY THE EAR

The experiments of George Von Békésy[28] have revealed that when a sound pressure impulse causes the footplate of stapes to rock in the oval window the fluid within the cochlea is suddenly compressed causing the basilar membrane at the vestibule to bulge into the scala tympani. This sudden downward thrust creates an undulating wave which sweeps along the basilar membrane. The wave turns at the helicotrema, traverses the fluid of the tympani gallery where the shock of the wave is absorbed by the bulging of the round window.

As the wave moves along the basilar membrane its amplitude increases until it reaches a maximum then falls off sharply as the wave dies out. The frequency of sound is detected by the ear (Fig. 96) at the point that this wave reaches its greatest amplitude upon the basilar membrane. For high frequencies, the wave height is greatest at the oval window where the basilar membrane is

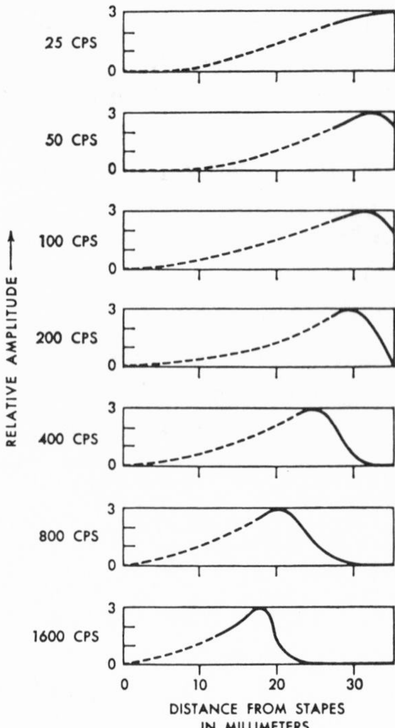

Fig. **96.** The Envelopes Indicate the Extent of Basilar Membrane Displacement for Different Frequencies of Sinusoidal Excitation Applied at the Stapes
Source: *The Speech Chain* by P. B. Denes and E. N. Pinson, published by Bell Telephone Laboratories, Inc. (1963).

lightest and stiffest. For the lower frequencies, the wave height is greatest at the upper end where the membrane is broader and more elastic.

The action which creates the energy necessary for the transmission of a signal to the brain is a shearing action between the organ of Corti (Fig. 97), which rests upon the basilar membrane, and the tectorial membrane, which is suspended over it. Each moves in the opposite direction. This shearing action causes the hairs to bend and their cells generate electrochemical impulses for transmission by the auditory nerves to the brain.[29]

When a complex wave strikes the eardrum, the motion of stapes responds to each sinusoid within the waves tonal spectrum and the undulation of the basilar membrane becomes as complex as the spectrum. The energy of each partial then creates a certain wave height which determines the number of nerve cells that will fire at that particular point of the wave crest. If the signal is weak, one or two nerve cells will fire. If it is strong many will be affected.

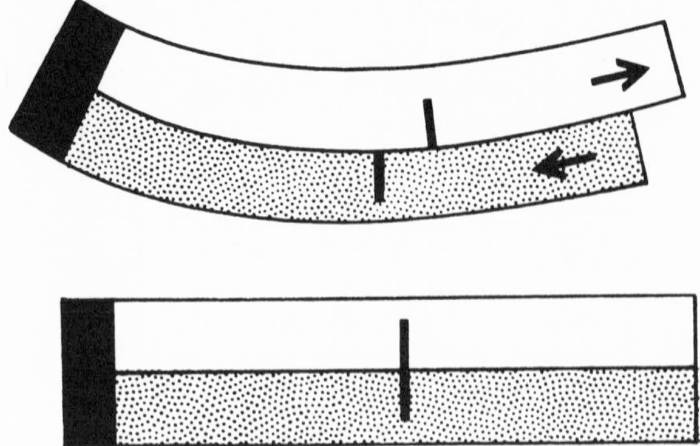

Fig. **97.** Shearing Actions of Membranes

Denes and Pinson[30] state that the sensation of loudness may be determined by the number of pulses reaching the brain's auditory areas each second. The fact that different fibers have different thresholds may play an important role in determining such a sensation; however, only further research will provide factual evidence of this subtle aspect of hearing.

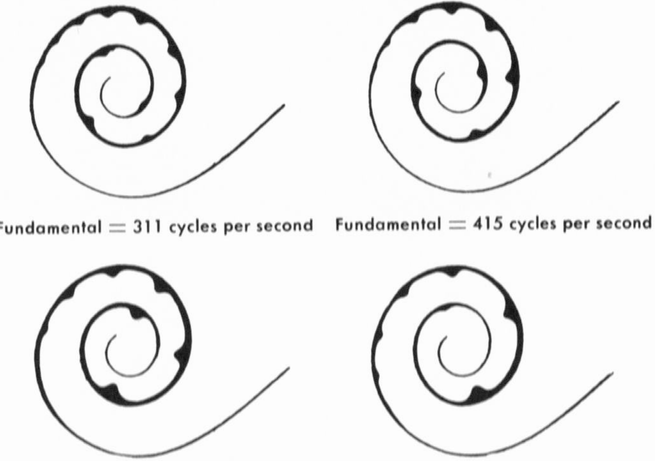

Fig. **98.** Auditory Patterns for Four Notes of Taps Played on a Bugle

The width of the black area is proportional to the loudness contributed by that particular bit of the organ of Corti. Source: Bell Telephone Laboratories, Inc.; courtesy, H. Fletcher.

Part II: APPLICATION

Chapter 6

Phonetics–The Linguistic Element of Interpretation

> Phonetics is the science of speech sounds [which are] considered [to be] elements of language; esp., the study of their formation by the speech organ and their apprehension by the ear, their attributes and their relation to other aspects of the language such as length, pitch, stress, sonority, their modification by neighboring sounds and their relation to orthoepy (pronunciation) and rhythm, also the practical application of this science to the understanding and speaking of a language.[1]

Phonetics provides visible symbols which express and unify the aural and phonatory elements of communication. These linguistic symbols serve all of humanity in consideration of dialectal differences which exist among the world's populations.

Phonetics is related to many disciplines. It is related to both morphology, which considers speech forms and words, and to etymology, which traces the origin and development of the word; to physiology and anatomy, which provide information regarding the structure and the functioning of the speech mechanism. It is related to psychology, which aids in the interpretation of the symbolic aspect of speech sounds, and to the study of semantics, the study of meanings, which will be discussed in Chapter Seven. The emphasis in this chapter is directed toward the development of a phonetic vocabulary to be used as an implement for the interpretation of speech sounds in singing.

The information within this volume rests upon the premise that textual intelligibility is obtained by a singer through the discipline of phonemic awareness. He can possess this awareness only by learning all of the sounds that are spoken within his language. Careful study of the International Phonetic Alphabet brings to the singer a discipline of the word. It teaches the singer to become aware of the great variation of mechanical adjustments of the articulators, for within this alphabet each symbol demands a particular articulatory position for most of the speech sounds that he will sing.

In song, the word is as important as the sound, for without speech symbols to interpret, a singer gives his song little meaning; it becomes merely an emotional outburst of sound. Singing, for public judgement, is a complex social act involving communication between the audience and the performer. The link which binds the two, audience and performer, and consummates understanding is the recognition of the word when it is united with the vocal sound. The achievement of communication demands textual intelligibility from the performer; without such intelligibility, concern for the artful song would cease, for the singing act would have lost the discipline of the word. This aspect of discipline is present within the art song, for all enduring art embodies discipline as its firm base.

Classic composers have conceived the art song as a perfect musical structure involving profound poetry as a vehicle of textual expression. Such composers have refined their talent and technical skill to attain an economy of utterance which lifts both text and music to a unified musical perfection. To attain the high emotional and intellectual level demanded by the music and the text, and thereby fill the dimensions of his musical creation, the singer must discipline himself to conform to a vocal system of order, refinement, and dedication.

Most audiences desire and hope to understand the text of the singer as he sings, and that in singing he will elevate the text in an artful manner so that the word will not be subservient to the beautiful sound. Attaining textual intelligibility is still possible while singing beautiful sound. The realization of such a goal is the mission of this book.

INTERNATIONAL PHONETIC ALPHABET

Spoken language has always preceded written language. In the development of any written alphabet, an attempt is made to symbolize in writing every sound that is spoken within the given environment. Written English developed from Latin symbols used by Christian missionaries in the sixth century. At that time, the written word was probably more closely related to the sound of the language than it is now. In a complex social order usage creates changes in the written symbols so that no modern language possesses a symbol for every sound. (Spanish is closest to such an ideal language, for the spelling in this language serves as a reliable guide to pronunciation.)

Because linguistic analysts needed an alphabet which would provide a symbol for every sound, the International Phonetic Alphabet was devised by the International Phonetic Association in 1886.[2] This alphabet was based upon the Broad Romic Alphabet of Henry Sweet, a British phonetician. The IPA, modified only slightly since that time, is employed by more people than any comparable alphabet because it supplies a consistency between the written symbol and the sound. One symbol must represent one sound, one sound must represent one symbol.

From one point of view phonetics is indispensable: Only through phonetics can one give even a rough classification and description of the sounds of any language. From another point of view, phonetic analysis is a hopeless task, for if one listens closely enough to any word that is uttered, the number of different features that one can find is endless.

In analyzing the speech sounds used in singing, one must constantly attempt to differentiate between those phonetic features of a language that are distinctive as cues of meaning and those that are nondistinctive. For this reason diacritical marks, placed upon or around each of the IPA symbols, are used to further interpret the speech characteristic of each vowel. They reveal the positions of the articulators at the time of utterance. A listing of the IPA is shown on pages 175-77. The analyses in this book will be based upon broad transcription techniques which employ the diacritical marks listed on page 174. These marks are only used when a refined analysis of the uttered sound is needed for dialectal classification.

The International Phonetic Alphabet is used throughout the world today in all serious works of pronunciation and in pronouncing dictionaries of all languages.[3]

The author has no intention of prescribing rules for correct pronunciation. However, in transcribing illustrative materials, one must decide which pronunciation to indicate. Therefore, all phonetic transcriptions in this work will be based upon the general American dialect found in *A Pronouncing Dictionary of American English* by John S. Kenyon and Thomas A. Knott.

The student should master the International Phonetic Alphabet by reading simple word forms and drills with nonsense syllables, words, and sentences. He should transcribe each exercise in the IPA symbols and transcribe peculiar pronunciation for duplication of the precise sound. Students should be encouraged to study in groups so that each student can be criticized by the others; self-criticism, a most valuable asset, can be developed through such a process.

The English language has forty-seven letters in the IPA but only twenty-six letters in the written alphabet. This difference occurs because each of the vowels in the English language is pronounced several different ways, necessitating the subdivision of vowel sounds.

The IPA is much better suited to the purpose of singing than a system of diacritical marks employed in some dictionaries, for in a diacritical system a greater number of symbols are used, and each sound is represented by a different symbol.

The following symbols of the IPA do not appear in English spelling:

[æ] as in *sat,* formed by combining the lower case letter *a* and *e*
[ɝ] General American *r,* a reversed Greek letter *epsilon* with a curl on the top
[ə] as in *above,* an inverted letter *e*
[ʌ] as in *up,* an inverted *v*
[ɔ] as in *all,* a reversed letter *c*
[θ] as in *bath,* the Greek letter *theta*
[ð] as in *bathe,* an old English form of *the*
[ʃ] *sh* as in *shock*
[ʒ] as in *vision,* elongated forms of *s* and *z*
[ŋ] a nasal, as in *hung,* a letter *n* with a tail.[4]

IPA symbols should be printed and bracketed rather than written so that they will be easily recognized and not confused with phonetic transcriptions. In all phonetic transcriptions, the phonetic symbols must represent all of the sounds heard when the word is pronounced. Do not include silent letters that appear in such words as *hour* [aur], *know* [no], *bone* [bon], and *eight* [et]. Doubled consonants are replaced with single consonants, as in *matter* [mætɚ]. Homonyms, two words spelled differently but pronounced the same—such as *know* and *no,* and *son* and *sun*—are transcribed the same: [no] and [sun]. If two words are spelled the same but are pronounced differently—such as *bow* (the verb) and *bow* (the noun)—the difference in sound must be represented in the transcription: [bau] and [bo].

Diacritical Marks Used in Broad Transcriptions

ʻ sign of aspiration
ʼ sign of inspiration
⊥ sign of raising the tongue
⊤ sign of lowering the tongue
⊣ sign of fronting the tongue
⊢ sign of retracting the tongue
ˌ beneath a consonant makes it a syllable
ˈ above and to the left of a syllable, primary stress
ˌ below and to the left of a syllable, secondary stress
ʔ glottal stop
ˇ trill
⊓ sign of dentality
˜ sign of nasalization
ː sign of lengthening
l̩ later as final in buckle [bʌkl̩]
n̩ nasal in final in button [butn̩]
t nasal in final in rotten [ratn]

TABLE I

Phonetic Symbols with Equivalent Sounds of English, French, German, and Italian

IPA Symbols	*English*		*French*		*German*		*Italian*	
			THE NEUTRAL VOWEL					
[ʌ]	up	[ʌp]	me	[mʌ]	—	—	—	—
			THE FRONT VOWELS					
[i]	eat	[it]	fils	[fis]	viel	[fil]	si	[si]
[ɪ]	it	[ɪt]	—	—	bis	[bɪs]	—	—
[e]	vacation	[vekeʃən]	chez	[ʃe]	leben	[lebən]	che	[ke]
[ɛ]	pet	[pɛt]	tete	[tɛ:t]	des	[des]	bello	[bɛl:o]
[æ]	pat	[pæt]	—	—	—	—	—	—
[a]	lamb	[lam]	glace	[glas]	—	—	—	—
			THE CENTRAL VOWELS					
[ɝ]	early	[ɝlɪ]	—	—	—	—	—	—
[ɜ]	early	[ɜlɪ]	—	—	—	—	—	—
[ɑ]	palm	[pɑm]	âme	[ɑ:m]	paar	[pɑ:r]	amare	[ɑmɑrɛ]
			THE BACK VOWELS					
[u]	food	[fud]	fou	[fu]	tun	[tu:n]	kura	[kura]
[ʊ]	foot	[fʊt]	—	—	mund	[mʊnt]	—	—
[o]	notation	[noteʃən]	—	—	so	[zo:]	otto	[ɔt:o]
[ɔ]	all	[ɔl]	coq	[kɔk]	morgen	[mɔrgən]	motto	[mɔt:o]
[ɒ]	sorry	[sɒrɪ]	—	—	—	—	—	—
			THE SCHWA VOWEL					
[ə]	above	[əbʌv]	le	[lə]	habe	[hɑbə]	—	—

TABLE I (*continued*)

IPA Symbols	*English*		*French*		*German*		*Italian*	
			THE SEMI-VOWELS					
[w]	witch	[wɪtʃ]	oui	[wi]	——	——	uomo	[wɔmo]
[ʍ]	which	[ʍɪtʃ]	——	——	——	——	——	——
[j]	you	[ju]	hier	[jɛːr]	ja	[ja]	ieri	[jɛri]
[l]	law	[lɔ]	les	[le]	legen	[legən]	la	[lɑ]
[r]	raw	[rɔ]	respect	[rɛspɛkt]	reiten	[rɑɪtn]	ricco	[rikːo]
			THE VOWEL GLIDES					
[ɑu]	now	[nɑu]	——	——	haus	[hɑus]	causa	[kɑuzɑ]
[ou]	no	[nou]	——	——	——	——	——	——
[eɪ]	day	[deɪ]	——	——	——	——	pei	[peɪ]
[ɔɪ]	boy	[bɔɪ]	——	——	feʊer	[fɔiər]	——	——
[ɑɪ]	lie	[lɑɪ]	——	——	zeit	[tsɑɪt]	mai	[mɑɪ]
			LARYNGEAL MIGRATIONS OF VOWELS					
[h]	hop	[hɑp]	——	——	hat	[hɑt]	——	——
[hj]	hue	[hju]	——	——	——	——	——	——
[ʔ]	oh! oh!	[ʔo! ʔo!]	——	——	——	——	——	——
			ORAL MIGRATIONS OF VOWELS					
[p]	pat	[pæt]	pas	[pas]	pressen	[prɛsən]	pei	[peɪ]
[b]	bat	[bæt]	bête	[bɛt]	bett	[bɛt]	barca	[bɑrkɑ]
[t]	two	[tu]	ta	[ta]	tal	[tɑl]	tempo	[tɛmpo]
[d]	do	[du]	du	[du]	des	[dɛs]	dente	[dɛnte]
[k]	class	[klæs]	que	[kə]	könig	[kønɪç]	che	[ke]
[g]	glass	[glæs]	guide	[gid]	gabe	[gɑbə]	golfo	[golfo]

TABLE I (*continued*)

IPA Symbols	*English*		*French*		*German*		*Italian*	
			THE CONTINUANT FRICATIVES					
[f]	fife	[faɪf]	femme	[fam]	fahren	[fɑːrɛn]	facile	[fɑtʃile]
[v]	five	[faɪv]	vous	[vu]	was	[vɑs]	verso	[vɛrso]
[θ]	bath	[baθ]	——	——	——	——	——	——
[ð]	bathe	[beɪð]	——	——	——	——	——	——
[s]	sue	[su]	ses	[se]	das	[dɑs]	si	[si]
[z]	zoo	[zu]	zele	[zeːl]	seele	[zeːlə]	casa	[kazɑ]
[ʃ]	mission	[mɪʃən]	creche	[krɛːʃ]	spass	[ʃpɑs]	fascisti	[fɑ′ʃisti]
[ʒ]	vision	[vɪʒən]	jamais	[ʒa′mɛ]	charge	[ʃɑrʒə]	——	——
			THE AFFRICATES					
[tʃ]	church	[tʃɝtʃ]	——	——	klatsch	[kl[ɑ]tʃ]	cera	[tʃerɑ]
[ʃt]	rushed	[rʌʃt]	——	——	——	——	——	——
[dʒ]	judge	[dʒʌdʒ]	——	——	——	——	gente	[dʒɛnti]
[ʒd]	rouged	[ruʒd]	——	——	——	——	——	——
			THE NASAL MIGRATIONS OF THE VOWELS					
[m]	mow	[mo]	mons	[mɔ̃]	memel	[meːməl]	prima	[primɑ]
[n]	no	[no]	non	[nɔ̃]	nun	[nuːn]	vano	[vɑno]
[ŋ]	sing	[sɪŋ]	——	——	finger	[fɪŋər]	vengo	[vɛŋgo]

EXERCISES AND DRILLS

1. Transcribe each of the following words that have the same central phoneme in the English language. Sing each word aloud and try to use exactly the same vowel sound for each word. Hold articulators in position for four beats—notice position of articulators in pronunciation of each word.

   [ɑ] father, psalm, alms, guardian, hearth, sergeant
   [a] lamb, ask, man, rapture, glad, hand
   [ʊ] put, cushion, boudoir, bosom, worsted, soot
   [i] beat, reef, believe, quay, machine, leave
   [ô] store, lord, memory, chore, snore, board
   [ɪ] rich, been, him, pity, crypt, since
   [e] dado, daisy, chaos, vacation, Danish, prayer
   [u] lose, blew, prove, whom, through, plume
   [o] mow, sew, boat, yeoman, though
   [ʌ] tub, come, brusque, blood, above
   [ə] above, unction, constable, firmament, lovable.

2. Memorize each of the following symbols and transcribe each of the following words using symbols that do not appear in the English language. Sing each word aloud and try to use exactly the same vowel sound for each word.

Vowels

[ɛ] said, lead, quest, leather, friend, leopard
[æ] back, sat, magic, shadow, dazzle, snatches
[ɔ] stalk, call, awe, dawn, fought, ultra, double
[ɜ] bird, church, earth, furry, burn, pert

Consonants

[ð] tithe, wither, southern, breathe, worthy, thither
[θ] path, theme, lengthen, method, mouth, thither
[ʒ] beige, Hoosier, vision, azure, garage, measure
[ʃ] anxious, sure, ocean, precious, tension, auction
[tʃ] church, righteous, butcher, champion, question
[dʒ] cage, judge, jam, soldier, engine, legion

[ɚ] never, sister, winter, shepherd, pleasure
[ŋ] hung, wringer, inkling, strangle, drinker
[j] champion, union, view, stupid, mayor
[ju] human, pneumonia, nuisance, knew, stupid
[ʍ] where, erstwhile, somewhat, who, whirl

Other Consonantal Sounds

[r] forlorn, for, warm, garden, morning
[m] hymn, diaphragm, mummer, camphor, symbol
[w] wear, twinkle, doing, quick, weather
[n] income, knife, ninny, nine, cotton
[v] halve, vivid, of, valve, have, very
[s] absurd, mass, fence, scent, discern, essence
[b] cab, table, raspberry, cabin, thimble
[k] chromium, concede, success, quick, acquire
[p] hiccough, pumpkin, happy, capture, empty
[g] ghost, rugby, guilty, trigger, brogue
[d] dawdle, bidder, handful, dreadful, traded
[t] little, pitfall, satisfy, postman, nut
[h] behind, anyhow, behead, pothole, human
[f] Stephen, phonate, prophet, soften, laugh

3. As a beginning drill, transcribe the following Biblical verses. Only the letters of the phonetic alphabet listed above have been used. Familiarity with the text, simplifies the task of matching the sound. However, this drill should be supplemented with the simple nonsense words in which the sounds are not familiar.

ðʌ twɛntɪ-θɜd sɑm

ðə lɔrd ɪz maɪ ʃɛpɚd; aɪ ʃæl nɑt wɑnt.
hi meɪkɪθ mi tu laɪ daʊn ɪn grin pæstʃɚz:
hi lidɪθ mi bɪsaɪd ðə stɪl wɑtɚz.
hi rɪstourɪθ maɪ soʊl:
hi lidɪθ mi ɪn ðə pæðz əv raɪtʃəsnɪs
fɔr hɪz neɪmz seɪk.
jeɪ, ðoʊ aɪ wɔk θru ðə vælɪ əv ðə ʃædoʊ əv dɛθ
aɪ wɪl fɪr noʊ ivəl: fɔr ðaʊ ɑrt wɪθ mi;
ðaɪ rɑd ænd ðaɪ stæf ðeɪ kʌmfɚt mi.

ðau prɪpɛrɪst ə teɪbəl bɪfor mi
ɪn ðə prɛzənts əv maɪn ɛnɪmiz:
ðau ənɔɪntɪst maɪ hɛd wiθ ɔɪl;
maɪ kʌp rʌnɪθ ouvɚ
ʃʊrlɪ gʊdnɪs ænd mɝsɪ ʃæl fɑlo mi ɔl ðə deɪz əv maɪ laɪf
ænd aɪ wɪl dwɛl ɪn ðə haʊs əv ðə lɔrd fɔr ɛvɚ.

From *The Bible*, King James Version

4. Practice reading these nonsense syllables aloud. Exaggerate lip-rounding, lip-spreading, voicing, and unvoicing of consonants.

I	II	III	IV
1. gə	1. deɪ	1. lʌnt	1. dugɪn
2. ʃæ	2. vɔɪ	2. hrɑp	2. ʃtɑlz
3. tu	3. nɛl	3. lɪkl	3. dʊdl
4. ɛŋ	4. wɝb	4. zɪks	4. geɪʃ
5. fi	5. nɛr	5. zrɪp	5. zoʊl
6. ʃɑ	6. aɪn	6. hwɪr	6. jaɪs
7. zʊ	7. taʊ	7. skoʊ	7. hrɛks
8. ɔɪ	8. saɪ	8. ðivə	8. ɪkəl
9. eθ	9. ðiz	9. ulbə	9. skum
10. aʊ	10. zɛt	10. bɝpɚ	10. mɑtu

V	VI	VII	VIII
1. skædʒ	1. pɑmpfɚ	1. pɔnrouz	1. əmæbəlɔɪ
2. kɔgɚn	2. ðɪŋgɔɪn	2. baʊnaɪk	2. æmbəlinə
3. snædʒ	3. ɪkʌtnɪk	3. hwɑpoʊk	3. nambɚdu
4. naɪgə	4. sælbun	4. meɪbɚli	4. feɪðənɔl
5. sɑgnɚ	5. bilaʊtʃ	5. hwaɪkən	5. munətʃɛp
6. zəθɪŋ	6. kæsɑnt	6. zɪmbɔɪŋ	6. lɪmɚnkɑt
7. ʃɪnəp	7. ʃtɑdɑn	7. hwaɪkən	7. skuŋpaʊl
8. tɔɪŋk	8. wɔɪsɛt	8. foʊbɪŋɑ	8. mægəlfrɑ
9. bɔkɪŋ	9. taɪkoʊ	9. kəmgæeɪ	9. diltɚʒæf
10. nɪmpɪ	10. woʊbɔd	10. zændɚzi	10. dæljəpaɪdə

5. Practice reading these nonsense sentences aloud. Exaggerate lip-rounding, lip-spreading, voicing and unvoicing of consonants. Strive for phonemic accuracy.

1. bɪt rɔɪ ʃtud ðə bɪtkən rɪ̇d əv ʍɪŋ.
2. hʌt jaɪv wɛnk dot tʃɔl mɪn wɑk taɪ tʃæp ɪn bæv.
3. ʍɔɪg ŋæp ʌp θrob ɪd ðə jʊk wɪp tʃɑr.
4. sɪv wət aʊd jaɪ tʃɪl sæb tæŋ wɪt so ruk ted.
5. sʌbɚ laɪt rudʒɪt wɪk θrit wɪb ðə tɛk sæz.
6. tʊd op ɔtɚ sæb ɔd ɪz ʌf dʒɛr haɪ sɑb.
7. tez ðə sɔk fæb ʌv saʊd iŋ dʒez θo hib aʊtgreb.
8. twəz bidɪb from ðæd wɪd ot dʒæd ɔm aɪt sæz wɪs.
9. wɑt kɔn saʊd əged ræd əv wæz bɔk don ɔn sɛb dʒæg.
10. ʍʌnt ɪn ðɑt dɛb dæg bæz rikə mɛm ʃɪg.
11. væt saʊt pod hɔt vɪz bɔk bæŋ sɪz bæb sɔŋ.
12. ðɔt aɪd sov ə sʌb tʃæk ɪp hɛt wɪʒ ɔr wæd.
13. waʊt səd zob aɪd seb tæf ʃʌg vɛt saɪg fæz.
14. twæk ɪn lot wʌb sov ɪg sɔɪk ɪn tæf gep.
15. saɪt jɚ ræŋət wæb ʃɑg su ɪd aʊrlɪ wɪtɜ ʃæb.
16. twɑk ju fɜdɚ sæʃiŋ aʊt ʌv tɛb so grod.
17. blɑt ðə brin sæz aʊtɚ saɪd əv taɪk bɪt aʊtɪŋ gɝ.
18. ʒɑt tɔk sɪŋ θrop sɔʃ pet jɪk dʒɑ tɔɪ sɛp.
19. təv jaʊ ʌt tʃæk mɔm tɪv sukɪ sɑkɪ taɪb tɪŋ.
20. ʃæv maɪm sɛd iŋ θrod jʌŋ ʃæk ɪn ðə bov.
21. tʃɛv ʃæz θæŋ sɑk bætɪk ɪn də nɛtæb tɚ go.
22. wɔɪ ʒɑg θraʊ ɔɪtɚ haɪ sɪv kud bɔkən tæz.
23. sɛpət ʍaip ɔlɚ nup tɑft tʃɔp uk aʊb dʒɛŋ.
24. ʒæt wʌk so mɛk wʌk ɪm ðə bɛz wɪb sæf.
25. suv ðæk hɔk fod mɛlət ʍaɪk wil kʌp sɑŋ tʃaɪk.

6. Transcribe into phonetic symbols.

HOW DO I LOVE THEE ?

How do I love thee? Let me count the ways.
I love thee to the depth and breadth and height
My soul can reach, when feeling out of sight
For the ends of Being and ideal Grace.
I love thee to the level of every day's
Most quiet need, by sun and candle-light.
I love thee freely, as men strive for Right;
I love thee purely, as men turn from Praise.
I love thee with the passion put to use
In my old griefs, and with my childhood's faith.

I love thee with a love I seemed to lose
With my lost saints,—I love thee with the breath,
Smiles, tears, of all my life!—and, if God choose,
I shall but love thee better after death.

ELIZABETH BARRETT BROWNING
From *Sonnets from the Portuguese**

7. Transcribe into phonetic symbols.

MIA CARLOTTA**

Giuseppe, da barber, ees greata for de "mash,"
Ee gotta da bigga, da blacka moustache,
Good clo'es an' good styla an' playnta good cash.

W'enevra Giuseppe ees walk on da street,
Da people dey talka, "how nobby! how neat!
How softa da handa, how smalla da feet."

Ee raisa hees hat an' ee shaka hees curls,
An' smila weeth teetha so shiny like pearls;
O! manny da heart of da seely young girls
He gotta.
Yes, playnta he gotta—
But notta
Carlotta!

Giuseppe, da barber, ee maka da eye,
An' lika da steam engine puffa an' sigh,
For catcha Carlotta w'en she ees go by.

Carlotta she walka weeth nose in da air,
An' look through Giuseppe weeth far-away stare,
As eef she no see dere ees som'body dere.

* Charles W. Woolbert and Servina E. Nelson, *The Art of Interpretive Speech* (New York: Appleton-Century-Crofts, Inc., 1945).

** From *Selected Poems of T. A. Daly*, copyright, 1936, by Harcourt, Brace & World, Inc., renewed, 1964, by Thomas A. Daly, Jr., and reprinted by permission of the publishers.

Giuseppe, da barber, ee gotta da cash,
Ee gotta da clo'es an' da bigga moustache,
Ee gotta da seely young girls for da "mash,"
But notta—
You bat my life, notta—
Carlotta.
I gotta!

T. A. DALY

SAMPLE PHONETIC TRANSCRIPTION

dʒuzɛp:i də bɑrbɛr iz gretə fər demaʃ.
i gatə də bigə də blakə mustaʃ,
gud kloz an gud stailə an plɛntə gud kaʃ.

wɛnɛvrə dʒuzɛp:i is wɔk ɔn də strit,
də piplə de tɔkə, aʊ nɑbi, aʊ nit;
aʊ sɔftə di andə, aʊ smɔlə də fit.

TO SIT IN SOLEMN SILENCE

To sit in solemn silence in a dull dark dock
In a pestilential prison with a life long lock
Awaiting the sensation of a short sharp shock
Of a cheap and chippy chopper on a big black block.

SIR WILLIAM GILBERT
From *The Mikado*

8. Transcribe into English.

ðə dʒæbɚwɔk

twəz brɪlɪg ænd ðə slaɪðɪ toʊvz
dɪd dʒaɪr ænd dʒɪmbəl ɪn ðə weɪb
ɔl mɪmzɪ wɝ ðə boʊrogoʊvz
ænd ðə moʊo ræðz aʊtgreɪb

bɪwɛr ðə dʒæbɚwɔk maɪ sʌn
ðə dʒɔz ðæt baɪt ðə klɔz ðæt skrætʃ
bɪwɛr ðə dʒʊb bɜd ænd ʃʌn
ðə frumiəs bændɚsnætʃ

hi tʊk hɪz vɔrpəl sɔrd ɪn hænd
lɔŋ taɪm ðə mæŋksəm foʊ hi sɔt
soʊ rɛstəd hi baɪ ðə tʌm tʌm tri
ænd stʊd əhwaɪl ɪn θɔt

ænd æz ɪn ʌfɪʃ θɔt hi stʊd
ðə dʒæbɚwɔk wɪð aɪz əv fleɪm
keɪm hwɪflɪŋ θru ðə tʌldʒɪ wʊd
ænd bɜbəld æz ɪt keɪm

wʌn tu wʌn tu ænd θru ænd θru
ðə vɔrpəl bleɪd wɛnt snɪkɚsnæk
hi lɛft ɪt dɛd ænd wɪð ɪts hɛd
hi wɛnt gəlʌmpfɪŋ bæk

ænd hæst ðaʊ sleɪn ðə dʒæbɚwɔk
kʌm tu maɪ ɑrmz maɪ bimɪʃ bɔɪ
oʊ fræbdʒəs deɪ kˈælu kˈæleɪ
hi tʃɔrtˌld ɪn hɪz dʒɔɪ

LEWIS CARROLL
From *Through the Looking Glass*

9. Transcribe this example* of General American dialect into English.

iɪf aɪ wɚ æskt ən əpɪnjən, aɪ wəd kɔl ðɪs ən ʌngrəmætɪkəl neɪʃən. ðɛr ɪz noʊ sʌtʃ θɪŋ əz ə pɝfɪkt græmɚ ənd aɪ doʊnt ɔlwɪz spik gʊd græmɚ məsɛlf, bʌt aɪ əv bɪn foʊrgæðɚɪŋ fɚ ðə pæst fju deɪz wɪð prəfɛsɚz əv əmɛrəkən junəvɝsətɪz ən aɪv hɜd ðəm ɔl seɪ θɪŋz laɪk ðɪs: "hi wʊd hæv laɪkt tə hæv dʌn ət." jul kætʃ səm ɛdʒəkeɪtəd əmɛrəkənz seɪɪŋ ðæt. ʍɛn ðɪz mɛn teɪk pɛn ɪn hænd, ðeɪ raɪt wɪð əz gʊd græmɚ əz ɛnɪ; bʌt ðə moʊmənt ðeɪ θroʊ ðə pɛn əsaɪd, ðeɪ θroʊ grəmætɪkəl mɔrəlz əsaɪd wɪð ət.

tʊ ɪləstreɪt ðə dɪsaɪrəbɪlətɪ əv kɑnsəntreɪʃən, aɪ məst:ɛl ju ə stoʊrɪ əv maɪ sɪks-jɪr-oʊld dɔtɚ. ðə gʌvɚnəs əd bɪn titʃɪŋ ɚəbaʊt ðə reɪndɪr, ænd, əz ðə kʌstəm wɑz, ʃi ritoʊld ət tə ðə fæməlɪ. ʃi rɪd(j)ust ðə hɪstərɪ əv ðæt reɪndɪr tə tu ɚ θri sɛntəntsəz, ʍɛn ðə gʌvɚnəs kud nɑṭ əv put ət ɪntu ə peɪdʒ. ʃi sɛd: "ðə reɪndɪr ɪz ə vɛrɪ swɪft ænəməl. ə reɪndɪr wʌnts

* Claude Merton Wise, *Applied Phonetics*, © 1957. Reprinted by permission of Prentice-Hall, Inc., Englewood Cliffs, N.J.

dru ə slɛd four hʌndrəd maɪlz ɪn tu aurz." ʃi əpɛndəd ðə kamɛnt, "ðɪs wəz rəgardəd æz ɪkstrɔrdnɛrɪ," ænd kənkludəd, "ʍɛn ðæt reɪndɪr wəz drɔɪŋ ðæt slɛd four hʌndrəd maɪlz ɪn tu aurz, ɪt daɪd."

əz ə faɪnəl ɪnstənts əv ðə fours əv lɪməteɪʃənz ɪn ðə dəvɛləpmənt əv kansəntreɪʃən, aɪ məst mɛntʃən ðæt bjutɪfəl krɪtʃɚ hɛlən kɛlɚ, hum aɪ hæv noun fɚ ðiz mɛnɪ jɪrz. aɪ æm fɪld wɪð:ə wʌndɚ əv ɚ nalɪdʒ əkwaɪrd bɪkɔz ʃʌt aut frəm ɔl dɪstrækʃən. ɪf aɪ kəd əv bɪn dɛf, dʌm ənd blaɪnd, aɪ ɔlso maɪt əv əraɪvd ət sʌmpθɪŋ.

MARK TWAIN

10. Transcribe this example of Southern dialect into English.

ðə marʃaz əv glɪn*

glumz əv ðə laɪv ouk bjutɪfəl breɪdɪd
ənd wouvən
wɪð ɪntrɪkɪt ʃeɪdz əv:aɪnz ðət mɪrɪəd-klouvən
klæmbə ðə fɔks əv ðə mʌltəfɔm bauz;
ɛmərəld twaɪlaɪts,
vɜdʒənəl ʃaɪ laɪts,
rɔt əv ðə livz tu əluə tə ðə
ʍɪspər əv:auz
ʍɛn lʌvəz peɪs tɪmɪdlɪ daun θru
ðə grin kaləneɪdz
əv ðə dɪm swit wudz, əv ðə
drɪə da:k wudz,
əv ðə hɛvənlɪ wudz ən gleɪdz
ðət rʌn tə ðə reɪdɪənt madʒənəl
sændbitʃ wɪðɪn
ðə waɪd si maʃɪs əv glɪn;
bjutɪfəl glumz, sɔft dʌsks ɪn ðə
nundeɪ faɪə,
waɪldwud praɪvəsɪz, klazɪts əv
loun dɪzaɪə,
tʃeɪmbə frəm tʃeɪmbə pa:tɪd
wɪð weɪvərɪŋ ærɪs əv livz,

* Claude Merton Wise, *Applied Phonetics*, © 1957. Reprinted by permission of Prentice-Hall, Inc., Englewood Cliffs, N.J.

sɛlz fə ðə pæʃənɪt plɛʒər əv
    præə tə ðə soul ðət grivz,
pjʊə wɪð ə sɛnts əv ðə pæsɪŋ əv
    seɪnts θru ðə wʊd,
kul fə ðə djutɪfəl weɪɪŋ əv ivəl wɪð gʊd;
oʊ breɪdɪd dʌsks əv ðɪ oʊk ənd.
    woʊvən ʃeɪdz əv ðə vaɪn
ʍaɪl ðə raɪətəs nundeɪ sʌn əv
    ðə dʒun deɪ lɔŋ dɪd ʃaɪn
ji hɛld mi fæst ɪn jʊə hɑ:t ənd aɪ
    hɛld ju fæst ɪn maɪn.

SIDNEY LANIER

11. Transcribe this example of British Stage dialect into English.

tə bi ɔ not tə bi*

tə bi ɔ not tə bi; ðæt ɪz ðə kwɛstʃən; wɛðə tɪz nɜʊblə ɪn ðə maɪnd tə sʌfə ðə slɪŋz ənd æɾɜuz əv aʊtreɪdʒəs fɔtʃən; ɔtə teɪk ɑmz əgeɪnst ə si əv trʌbl̩z,ɜ n̩ baɪ əpɜʊzɪŋ ɛnd ðəm? tə daɪ; tə slip; nɜʊ mɔ; æn baɪ ə slip tə seɪ wi ɛnd ðə hɑ:teɪk n̩ ðə θaʊzənd nætʃərəl ʃɒks ðət flɛʃ ɪz ɛə tu, tɪz ə kɒnsəmeɪʃən dɪvaʊtlɪ tə bi wɪʃt. tə daɪ; tə slip; pətʃɑns tə drim; aɪ, ðɛəz ðə rʌb; fɔ ɪn ðæt slip əv dɛθ wɒt drimz meɪ kʌm wɛn wi əv ʃʌfld ɔf ðɪs mɔtəl kɔɪl, məst gɪv əs pɔz; ðɛəz ðə rɪspɛkt ðət meɪks kəlæmɪtɪ əv sɜu lɔŋ laɪf; fɔ hu wəd bɛə ðə wɪps n̩ skɔnz əv taɪm, ðɪ əprɛsəz rɔŋ, ðə praʊd mænz kɒntjumlɪ, ðə pæŋz əv dɪspaɪzəd lʌv, ðə lɔz dɪleɪ, ðɪ ɪnsəln̩s əv ɒfis, ən ðə spɜnz ðət peɪʃənt mɛɾit əv ðɪ ʌnwɜðɪ teɪks, wɛn hi hɪmsɛlf maɪt ɪz kwaɪitəs meɪk wɪð ə 'bɛə bɒdkɪn? hu wəd fɑdl̩z bɛə, tə grʌnt n̩ swɛt ʌndə ə wɪəɾi laɪf, bət ðət ðə drɛd əv sʌmθɪŋ ɑftə dɛθ, ðɪ ʌndɪskʌvəd kʌntrɪ frəm huz bɔn nɛʊ trævələ rɪ' tɜnz pʌzl̩z ðə wɪl n̩ meɪks əs rɑðə bɛə ðɜuz ɪlz wi hæv ðən flaɪ tu ʌðəz ðət wi nɜu nɒt ɒv ðʌs kɒnʃəns dʌz meɪk kaʊədz əv əs ɔl n̩ ðʌs ðə neɪtɪv hju əv rɛzəljuʃən ɪz sɪklɪd ɔ wɪð:ə peɪl kɑst əv θɔt ənd ɛntəpraɪzɪz əv greɪt pɪtʃ n̩ mɜumənt wɪð:ɪs rɪgɑd ðɛə kʌɾənts tɜn əɾai n̩ luz ðə neɪm əv ækʃən sɒft ju naʊ ðə fɛəɾ ɜufiljə nɪmf ɪn ðaɪ ɔrɪzənz bi ɔl maɪ sɪnz rɪmɛmbəd.

* Claude Merton Wise, *Applied Phonetics*, © 1957. Reprinted by permission of Prentice-Hall, Inc., Englewood Cliffs, N.J.

12. Transcribe the following examples of Northern, Southern, and Eastern dialects.

Type I—*Northern**

'pæsɪdʒ frəm ˌrɪpvæn'wiŋkl̩

ðə gret 'ɛrɚ ɪn rɪps ˌkɑmpə'zɪʃən wəz ən ɪn'supərəbl̩ ə'vɝʒən tʊ ɔl kaɪndz əv 'prɑfɪtəbl̩ 'lebɚ. ɪt 'kʊdn̩t bi frəm ðə wɑnt əv ˌæsə'djuətɪ ɚ ˌpɜsə'vɪrəns, fɚ i wəd sɪt ɑn ə wɛt rɑk, wið ə rɑd əz lɔŋ ən 'hɛvɪ əz ə 'tɑrtɚz læns, ən fɪʃ ɔl de wɪð'aʊtə mɝmɚ, 'ivən ðo i 'ʃʊdn̩t bi ɪn'kɝɪdʒd baɪ ə 'sɪŋgl̩ 'nɪbl̩. hid 'kærɪ ə 'faʊlɪŋˌpis ɑn ɪz 'ʃoldɚ fɚ aʊrz tə'gɛðɚ, 'trʌdʒɪŋ θru wʊdz n̩ swɑmps, ənd ʌp hɪl ən daʊn del, tə ʃut ə fju 'skwɝəlz ɚ waɪld 'pɪdʒənz. hi wəd 'nɛvɚ rɪ'fɪuz tʊ ə'sɪst ə 'nebɚ, 'ivən ɪn ðə 'rʌfɪst tɔɪl, ənd wəz ə 'forˌmost mæn ət ɔl 'kʌntrɪ 'frɑlɪks fɚ 'hʌskɪŋ 'ɪndɪən kɔrn ɚ 'bɪldɪŋ ston 'fɛnsɪz; ðə 'wɪmɪn əv ðə 'vɪlɪdʒ, tu, jus tʊ ɪm'plɔɪ ɪm tə rʌn ðɛr 'ɛrəndz, ən tə du sʌtʃ 'litl̩ ɑd dʒɑbz əz ðɛr lɛs ə'blaɪdʒɪŋ 'hʌzbəndz 'wʊdn̩t du fɔr ðəm. ɪn ə wɝd, rɪp wəz 'rɛdɪ tʊ ə'tɛnd tʊ 'ɛnɪˌbɑdɪz 'bɪznɪs bət ɪz on; bət æz tə 'duɪŋ 'fæmlɪ ˌdjutɪ, ən 'kipɪŋ ɪz 'fɑrm ɪn 'ɔrdɚ, hi faʊnd ɪt ɪm'pɑsəbl̩.

ɪn fækt, hi dɪ'klɛrd ɪt wəz əv no 'jus tə wɝk ɑn ɪz fɑrm; ɪt wəz ðə most 'pɛstl̩ənt 'lɪtl̩ pis əv graʊnd ɪn ðə hol 'kʌntrɪ; 'ɛvrɪˌθɪŋ ə'baʊt ɪt wɛnt rɔŋ, ən 'wʊd go rɔŋ, ɪn spaɪt ɑv ɪm. hɪz 'fɛnsɪz wɚ kən'tɪnjʊəlɪ 'fɔlɪŋ tə 'pisɪz; hɪz kaʊz wəd 'iðɚ go ə'stre, ɚ gɛt ə'mʌŋ ðə 'kæbɪdʒɪz: hi 'kʊdn̩t 'kipm̩ ət hom; widz wɚ ʃʊr tə gro 'kwɪkɚ ɪn 'hɪz fildz ðən 'ɛniˌhwɛr'ɛls; ðə ren 'ɔlwɪz med ə pɔɪnt əv 'sɛtɪŋ 'ɪn dʒʌst əz i hæd səm 'aʊtəvˌdor 'wɜk tə du; so ðət ðo ɪz ˌpætrə'monɪəl ə'stet əd 'dwɪndl̩d ə'we 'ʌndɚ ɪz 'mænɪdʒmənt, 'ekɚ baɪ 'ekɚ, ən'tɪl ðɚ wəz 'lɪtl̩ mor lɛft ðən ə mɪr pætʃ əv 'ɪndɪən kɔrn ən pə'tetoz, jɛt ɪt wəz ðə 'wɝstkən'dɪʃənd fɑrm ɪn ðə 'nebɚˌhʊd.

Type II—*Southern**

'pæsidʒ frəm ˌripvæn'wiŋkl̩

ðə gret 'ɛrər ɪn rɪps ˌkɑmpə'zɪʃən wəz ən ɪn'supərəbl̩ ə'vɜʒən tʊ ɔl kaɪndz əv 'prɑfɪtəbl̩ 'lebə. ɪt 'kʊdn̩t bi frəm ðə wɔnt əv ˌæsə'djuətɪ ə ˌpɜsə'vɪrəns, fər i wəd sɪt ɔn ə wɛt rɑk, wið ə rɑd əz lɔŋ ən 'hɛvɪ əz ə 'tɑ:təz læns, ən fɪʃ

* By permission, from a transcription illustrating the use of the International Phonetic Alphabet, copyright by G. & C. Merriam Co., publishers of the Merriam-Webster Dictionaries.

ɔl de wɪð'aut ə 'mɜmə, 'ivən ðo i 'ʃudn̩t bi in'kɜrɪdʒd baɪ ə 'sɪŋgl̩ 'nɪbl̩. hid 'kærɪ ə 'faulɪŋˌpis ɔn ɪz 'ʃoldə fər auəz tə'gɛðə, 'trʌdʒɪŋ θru wudz n̩ swɔmps, ənd ʌp hɪl ən daun del, tə ʃut ə fju 'skwɜrəlz ə waɪld 'pɪdʒənz. hi wəd 'nɛvə rɪ'fjuz tu ə'sɪst ə 'nebə, 'ivən ɪn ðə 'rʌfɪst tɔɪl, ənd wəz ə 'foəˌmost mæn ət ɔl 'kʌntrɪ 'frɑlɪks fə 'hʌskɪŋ 'ɪndɪən kɔən ə 'bɪldɪŋ ston 'fɛnsɪz; ðə 'wɪmɪn əv ðə 'vɪlɪdʒ, tu, jus tu im'plɔɪ ɪm tə rʌn ðɛr 'ɛrəndz, ən tə du sʌtʃ 'lɪtl̩ ɑd dʒɑbz əz ðɛə lɛs ə'blaɪdʒɪŋ 'hʌzbəndz 'wudn̩t du fɔə ðəm. ɪn ə wɜd, rɪp wəz 'rɛdɪ tu ə'tɛnd tu 'ɛnɪˌbadɪz 'bɪznɪs bət ɪz on; bət æz tə 'duɪŋ 'fæmlɪ ˌdjutɪ, ən 'kipɪŋ ɪz 'fɑ:m ɪn 'ɔədə, hi faund ɪt ɪm'pɑsəbl̩.

ɪn fækt, hi dɪ'klæəd ɪt wəz əv no 'jus tə wɜk ɔn ɪz fɑ:m; ɪt wəz ðə most 'pɛstl̩ənt 'lɪtl̩ pis əv graund ɪn ðə hol 'kʌntrɪ; 'ɛvrɪˌθɪŋ ə'baut ɪt wɛnt rɔŋ, ən 'wud go rɔŋ, ɪn spaɪt ɑv ɪm. hɪz 'fɛnsɪz wə kən'tɪnjuəlɪ 'fɔlɪŋ tə 'pisɪz; hɪz kauz wəd 'iðə go ə'stre, ə gɛt ə'mʌŋ ðə 'kæbɪdʒɪz: hi 'kudn̩t 'kipm̩ ət hom; widz wə ʃuə tə gro 'kwɪkər ɪn 'hɪz fildz ðən 'ɛnɪˌhwær'ɛls; ðə ren 'ɔlwɪz med ə pɔɪnt əv 'sɛtɪŋ 'ɪn dʒʌst əz i hæd səm 'autəv-ˌdoə 'wɜk tə du; so ðət ðo ɪz ˌpætrə'monɪəl ə'stet əd 'dwɪndl̩d ə'we 'ʌndər ɪz 'mænɪdʒmənt, 'ekə baɪ 'ekə, ən'tɪl ðə wəz 'lɪtl̩ moə lɛft ðɔn ə miə pætʃ əv 'ɪndɪən kɔən ən pə'tetoz, jɛt ɪt wəz ðə 'wɜstkən'dɪʃənd fɑ:m ɪn ðə 'nebəˌhud.

Type III—*Eastern**

'pæsidʒ frəm ˌripvæn'wiŋkl̩

ðə gret 'ɛrər ɪn rɪps ˌkɒmpə'zɪʃən wəz ən ɪn'supərəbl̩ ə'vɜʒən tu ɔl kaɪndz əv 'prɒfɪtəbl̩ 'lebə. ɪt 'kudn̩t bi frəm ðə wɒnt əv ˌæə'djuətɪ ə ˌpɜsə'vɪrəns, fər i wəd sɪt ɒn ə wɛt rɒk, wɪð ə rɒd əz lɔŋ ən 'hɛvɪ əz ə 'tɑ:təz lans, ən fɪʃ ɔl de wɪð'aut ə 'mɜmə, 'ivən ðo i 'ʃudn̩t bi ɪn'kɜridʒd baɪ ə 'sɪŋgl̩ 'nɪbl̩. hid 'kærɪ ə 'faulɪŋˌpis ɒn iz 'ʃoldə fər auəz tə'gɛðə, 'trʌdʒiŋ θru wudz n̩ swɒmps, ənd ʌp hɪl ən daun del, tə ʃut ə fju 'skwɜrəlz ə waɪld 'pɪdʒənz, hi wəd 'nɛvə rɪ'fjuz tu ə'sɪst ə 'nebə, 'ivən ɪn ðə 'rʌfɪst tɔɪl, ənd wəz ə 'foəˌmost mæn ət ɔl 'kʌntrɪ 'frɒlɪks fə 'hʌskɪŋ 'ɪndɪən kɔən ə 'bɪldɪŋ ston 'fɛnsɪz; ðə 'wɪmɪn əv ðə 'vɪlɪdʒ, tu, jus tu ɪm'plɔɪ ɪm tə rʌn ðɛr 'ɛrəndz, ən tə du sʌtʃ 'lɪtl̩ ɒd dʒɒbz əz ðɛə lɛs ə'blaɪdʒɪŋ 'hʌzbəndz 'wudn̩t du fɔə ðəm. ɪn ə wɜd, rɪp wəz 'rɛdɪ tu ə'tɛnd tu 'ɛnɪˌbɒdɪz 'bɪznɪs bət ɪz

* By permission, from a transcription illustrating the use of the International Phonetic Alphabet, copyright by G. & C. Merriam Co., publishers of the Merriam-Webster Dictionaries.

on; bət æz tə 'duɪŋ 'fæmli ˌdjutɪ, ən 'kɪpɪŋ ɪz 'fɑ:m ɪn 'ɔədə, hi faundɪt ɪm'pɒsəbl̩.

ɪn fækt, hi dɪ'klɛəd ɪt wəz əv no 'jus tə wɜk ɒn ɪz fɑ:m; ɪt wəz ðə most 'pɛstl̩ənt 'litl̩ pis əv graund ɪn ðə hol 'kʌntrɪ; 'ɛvriˌθɪŋ ə'baut ɪt wɛnt rɔŋ, ən'wudgo rɔŋ, ɪn spaɪt ɒv ɪm. hɪz 'fɛnsɪz wə kən'tɪnjuəlɪ 'fɔlɪŋ tə 'pisɪz; hɪz kauz wəd'iðə go ə'stre, ə gɛt ə'mʌŋ ðə 'kæbɪdʒɪz: hi 'kudn̩t 'kipm̩ ət hom; widz wə ʃuə tə gro 'kwɪkər ɪn 'hɪz fildz ðən 'ɛnɪˌhwɛr'ɛls; ðə ren 'ɔlwɪz med ə pɔɪnt əv 'sɛtɪŋ 'ɪn dʒʌst əz i hæd səm 'autəvˌdoə 'wɜk tə du; so ðət ðo ɪz 'pætrə'monɪel ə'stet əd 'dwɪndl̩d ə'we 'ʌndər ɪz 'mænɪdʒmənt, 'ekə baɪ 'ekə, ən'tɪl ðə wəz 'lɪtl̩ moə lɛft ðən ə mɪə pætʃ əv 'ɪndɪən kɔən ən pə'tetoz, jɛt ɪt wəz ðə 'wɜstkən'diʃənd fɑ:m ɪn ðə 'nebəˌhud.

THE SOUNDS OF GERMAN

As a sound system, languages are either symmetrical or asymmetrical. Within the English language, the frontal vowels are formed by varying degrees of lip-spreading; the back vowels are formed by varying degrees of lip-rounding; the central vowels, being neutral, are neither spread nor rounded. Such a system is said to be symmetrical. Conversely, the vowel system that contains lip-rounded front vowels or lip-spread back vowels is said to be asymmetrical, depending upon their conformance to this system.[5]

The German language is asymmetrical in that the vowels that do not appear in the English Language are formed with rounded lips instead of spread lips. They are called rounded frontal vowels. (For kinesiologic analysis of these vowels, see p. 357-65 and Records 1-4 Bands 22 and 24.) The non-English sounds in German are the following:

Vowels

[y]	as in *fühlen*	[fylən]	made by lip-rounding the frontal	[i]
[ʏ]	as in *mütter*	[mytə]	made by lip-rounding the frontal	[ɪ]
[ø]	as in *Goethe*	[gøtə]	made by lip-rounding the frontal	[e]
[œ]	as in *öffnen*	[œfnən]	made by lip-rounding the frontal	[ɛ]

Consonants

[f]	as in *fahren*	[fɑrɛn]	teeth barely touching inside lower lip
[v]	as in *wo*	[vo]	teeth barely touching inside lower lip
[ç]	as in *ich*	[ɪç]	unvoiced as [h] in English *hue*

[x]	as in *ach*	[ɑx]	unvoiced velar scraped sound
[ř]	as in *rot*	[řot]	an uvular trilled[6]

THE SOUNDS OF FRENCH

The French language is asymmetrical. Three of the frontal vowels are formed by both lip-rounding and lip-spreading. Nasalizing of the frontal, central, and back vowels also determines asymmetry. (For kinesiologic analysis, see p. 357-73 and Records 1-4, Bands 25 and 28; French placement of [a] and [ɑ], Record 1, Band 29.) The non-English sounds in French are as follows:[7]

Vowels

[y]	as in *une*	[yn]	made by lip rounding the frontal [i]
[ø]	as in *boeufs*	[bø]	made by lip-rounding the frontal [e]
[œ]	as in *seul*	[sœl]	made by lip-rounding the frontal [ɛ]
[œ̃]	as in *un*	[œ̃]	made by lip-rounding the frontal [æ] a nasalized rounded [ɛ]
[ɛ̃]	as in *faim*	[fɛ̃]	made by nasalizing the frontal [æ]
[ɑ̃]	as in *camp*	[kɑ]	made by nasalizing [ɑ]
[õ]	as in *don*	[dõ]	made by nasalizing [o]

Consonants

[ɲ] as in *champagne* [ʃɑ̃paŋ] tongue is placed behind lower front teeth; similar to English word *onion*

[ɥ] as in *nuage* [nya:ʒ] a tense *w* made with tongue in position for [y]; lips-rounded for [y]

[ɾ] as in *sur* [sy:ɾ] the flipped *r* made with tongue tip

[r] as in *reste* [rɛst] the uvular trill

[ɥ] as in *lui* [ly] start with tight lips in position of glide to [i]

Chapter 7

Stress–The Emotional Element of Interpretation

THE SEMANTIC CHARACTER OF STRESS

Stress is the only semantic element which connects the singer's psychophysical sensation with the aesthetic meaning of the words he sings; through the use of stress, the singer transforms his concept of the meaning of a word to an audible declaration of its meaning.

Semantics, as a body of knowledge, is the study of meaning and is related to phonetics only through the acts of phonemic stress and pronunciation which convey meaning. However semantic awareness provides insight into the meaning of words that phonetics cannot give. "We think of *meaning* as the ideas, concepts, images and feelings which are associated in the mind with words."[1]

The interpretation of a vocal text requires that the singer organize, assemble, and transform a mass of raw information (ideas, images, concepts, feelings) into a persuasive, disciplined phonatory act which will convey aesthetic meaning, and unless the singer possesses a profound intellectual awareness of the words, much of the textual content of great poetry or prose within a song remains barren.

The singer's sensitivity to text lifts his singing from mediocrity to inspired song; the words must not only be understood, they must become beloved. This aspect of diction falls within that part of semantics that embodies images and feelings. With these tools of expression the singer emotionalizes and intensifies speech sounds, and he enables the listener to realize the meaning of the text.

This work cannot include the study of feeling and aesthetic emotion in their complex psychological structure, but it does provide within this chapter information that is directed toward the reconciliation of the physiological and the psychophysical elements of diction. It provides a means of interpretation that will enable the singer to present his aesthetic awareness of the word in a disciplined and musical manner.

THE LINGUISTIC CHARACTER OF STRESS

Stress is the distinguishing feature of the English language. Important syllables in English are more prominent; less important syllables are less prominent than in any other language. Stress, then, is the key to the pronunciation of an English word; if stress is misplaced, understanding the singer is difficult. Its absence leads to the plodding vocal line and unimaginative performance; its presence gives life and vigor to the words and points the way to eloquence in diction and prosody (Record 5, Bands 1-14).

Prosody as defined by Webster is "The science or art of versification." Such a definition embodies the systematic study of metrical structure of verse forms and stressed and unstressed syllables. Prosody in song is broadened to include the study of a preferred vowel sound (preferred for its aesthetic texture) upon a preferred pitch, for in song, melodic patterns or pitch variation substitute for intonation or inflection used in speech forms. Understandably, a rise in pitch will aid stressed points within the verbal syntax; at the same time, the pitch rise will create problems for unstressed points.

STRESSING AND UNSTRESSING IN SINGING

Stress is increased vocal force that emphasizes a phoneme* within a word to bring out its meaning and aesthetic qualities. Stress is often used interchangeably with accent, yet stress and accent are not identical in song. Stress has duration and is used to emphasize vowels, since it is controlled by pitch and note value. Accent carries with it an abruptness that is not complimentary to the vocal line and is used to emphasize consonants, particularly stop plosives, voiced and unvoiced. The phonetic symbol [ʔ] is used to indicate glottal stop accent in such words as *oh, oh* [ʔo,ʔo], *at* [ʔæt], and *each* [ʔitʃ].

The rhythm of the English language is formed by the alteration of stressed and unstressed syllables. "Unstressing" of the syllable is caused by a lethargy in respiration and articulation, which results in phonemic modifications. Singers of English attempt to pronounce stressed syllables with phonemic accuracy within the stable vowel position but do not feel that it is necessary to move the articulators, lips, and jaw into position for unstressed syllables. The result

* A phoneme is a sound family—that is, any letter or group of letters that sound the same although they may be spelled differently (*key, quay,* the same phoneme [i]; *boss, sauce,* the same phoneme [ɔ]). It is also the smallest unit of language which conveys meaning—Wet, Vet, Let (initial); Beet, Bit, Bate (medial); Beg, Bell, Beth (final).

is a migration of each unaccented phoneme into the neutral vowel [ʌ] or the central schwa [ə].

Unstressing, a very old peculiarity of the English language, has developed through the communication habits of mankind. Wise describes unstressing as a corollary to stressing as follows:

> *Unstressing* was a feature of Indo-European, the ancient parent language of most European tongues. From Indo-European it descended via primitive Germanic to West Germanic to old English to Middle-English to Modern English. By analogous paths it descended through West Germanic to old High German to Middle High German to Modern High German. From Indo-European, through Italic and Latin, it descended to French, and through old Slavic to Russian, in English and Russian and French usually only the sound of the vowel [e].[2]

Stressed and Unstressed Words

Words can be divided into two classes, content words and auxiliary words.

Content words—such as *president, remember,* and *yesterday*—have meaning in themselves and are usually stressed. Content words include nouns, verbs, adverbs, adjectives, and demonstratives (*this, that, these, those*).

If the singer stresses the subject, verb, direct object, adjective, and adverb within each sentence, he will be stressing the proper words most of the time.

Auxiliary words, usually unstressed, have little meaning in themselves and assist in expressing an idea. They include articles (*a, an, the*), prepositions (*to, of, in*), personal pronouns (*I, me, you, him*), possessive pronouns (*my, his, your*), relative pronouns (*who, that, which*), and conjunctions (*and, but, that, as*).

The group of unstressed words of one syllable includes most of the commonest words in the English language. The ten most frequently used words belong to this class: *the, of, and, to, a, in, that, it, is,* and *I*. These ten words make up twenty-five percent of all that is spoken or written in English, and one out of every four words used is chosen from this group.

Monosyllables have only a primary stress, but all polysyllables have both primary and secondary stress. Primary stress is identified by a single accent mark above and to the left of the stressed phoneme ['], and secondary stress by one accent mark below and to the left of the unstressed phoneme. Examples are *cat* [k'æt], *me* [m'i], and *up* ['ʌp]. Examples of polysyllables are *economical* [ˌɛkan'omikl] and Presbyterian [prˌɛzbɪt'ɪrɪan].

Rules for Singing Stressed and Unstressed Vowels

Stressed vowels sung within the stable vowel pitch range are ideally pronounced when sung as close to the basic vowel as possible without modification. For pitches higher than the stable vowel pitch range, rules for migration apply. (See Fig. 103, p. 234, Record 5, Bands 1-14.)

Unstressed vowels are almost always pronounced [ə] or [ɪ]. This rule is fundamental for English pronunciation.[3] The unstressed vowels are always sung toward the neutral vowel [ʌ] or schwa [ə] on all pitch levels. This alternated stressing-unstressing lends an eloquent lilt to the English language which must be preserved in song.[4]

EMPHATIC AND EMOTIONAL STRESS

Numerous varieties of stresses within languages relate to specific meaning within a particular sentence. Such subdivisions of subject area are used to teach drama and speech to persons who do not face the problems of phonemic duration within a preconceived musical rhythmic framework.

For the musician, two types of stress are sufficient, as an aid to textual intelligibility, to express the factual and emotional meaning within the art song, folk song, and opera. They are emphatic stress and emotional stress. Within each of these types are varying degrees of vocal force and emphasis, which enable the singer to use stress as an interpretive tool as well as a device to intensify a word.

Emphatic Stress

The primary objective of emphatic stress is to lift a word from the phrase for greater intelligibility. It is the assertion of key words within a sentence that reveal the thought content of the words in a compelling manner. These key words are always the subject, verb, direct object, adjectives, and adverbs.

Nouns and verbs are the principal vehicles for revealing thought content in the sentence, yet the singer must take great care to stress only those sounds that are important to the expression of an idea, since unnecessary emphasis will detract from stress already made.

Emphatic stress is used to describe in an unemotional manner matter-of-fact things, places, moods, conditions, and narrations. It is used mostly while singing a legato line, whether that line be fast or slow, piano or forte.

To attain good diction while using emphatic stress, the singer should stress each phoneme through increased vocal force so that it will emerge from other phonemes in the polysyllable or sentence. The singer should also lengthen the consonantal sound by imparting to each consonant firmness of both lip and tongue. It is impossible to sing a consonant (which is an interrupted vowel sound) with as much sonority as a vowel; therefore, duration, is substituted for sonority when singing all consonants.

In applying emphatic stress as an interpretive tool, the singer should consider the melodic line intervallically and rhythmically. Words will be stressed unconsciously if the pitch skip is upward and one word or a part of a word is sung on a higher pitch. This unconscious stressing also occurs when the word falls upon the primary or secondary accent points of duple, triple, or compound rhythms.

Drills for Emphatic Stress. Sing the following words upon the suggested note patterns, place the stress upon the proper syllable, apply the rules for stressing, (a) exaggerate the proper vowel sound at all stress points and (b) lighten the vocal force on all unstressed syllables.

Nouns		*Verbs*	
concert	[k'ɑnsərt]	concert	[kəns'ɜt]
conduct	[k'ɑndʌkt]	conduct	[kənd'ʌkt]
contest	[k'ɑntɛst]	contest	[kənt'ɛst]
contract	[k'ɑntrakt]	contract	[kəntr'akt]
desert	[d'ɛzɜt]	desert	[dɪʒ'ɜt]
digest	[d'ɑɪdʒɛst]	digest	[daɪdʒ'ɛst[
exploit	['ɛksplɔit]	exploit	[ɪkspl'ɔit]
incline	['ɪnklaɪn]	incline	[ɪnkl'ɑin]
increase	['ɪnkris]	increase	[ɪnkr'is]
insult	['ɪnsʌlt]	insult	[ɪns'ʌlt]
object	['ɑbdʒɛkt]	object	[ɑbdʒ'ɛkt]
project	['prɑdʒɛkt]	project	[prɑdʒ'ɛkt]
rebel	[r'ɛbəl]	rebel	[rɛb'ɛl]
record	[r'ɛkɔrd]	record	[rɛk'ɔrd]
survey	[s'ɜveɪ]	survey	[sɜv'eɪ]
suspect	[s'ʌspɛkt]	suspect	[səsp'ɛkt]

Miscellaneous Words
(with varying syllabic stress points)

(ˈ)		(ˈ)	
often	[ɔfən]	about	[abaut]
basement	[besmənt]	occur	[əkʌɾ]
collar	[kalɜ]	alive	[əlaɪv]
something	[sʌmθiŋ]	receive	[rɪsiv]
hundred	[hʌndrəd]	submit	[səbmit]
battle	[bætəl]	delight	[dɪlaɪt]

The following words have three, four, and five stressed syllables. Sing them, using the suggested melodic patterns. Apply emphatic stress rules *a* and *b* for stressing and unstressing of each word.

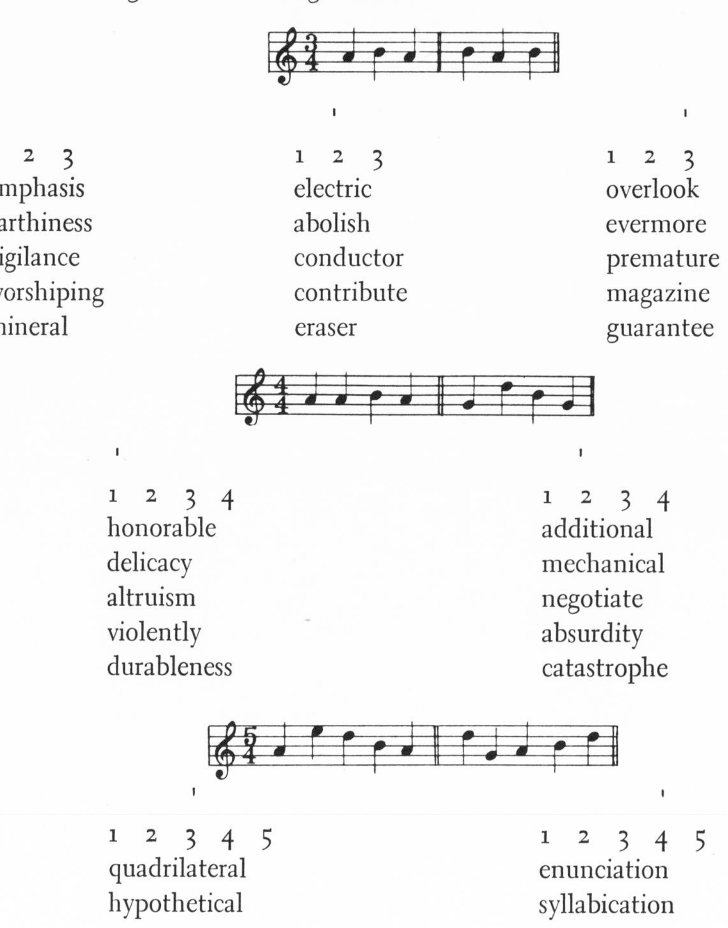

ˈ 1 2 3	ˈ 1 2 3	ˈ 1 2 3
emphasis	electric	overlook
earthiness	abolish	evermore
vigilance	conductor	premature
worshiping	contribute	magazine
mineral	eraser	guarantee

ˈ 1 2 3 4	ˈ 1 2 3 4
honorable	additional
delicacy	mechanical
altruism	negotiate
violently	absurdity
durableness	catastrophe

ˈ 1 2 3 4 5	ˈ 1 2 3 4 5
quadrilateral	enunciation
hypothetical	syllabication

indeterminate	pronunciation
immobility	antagonistic
inconsistency	appropriation

Emphatic Stress Within the Sentence. Flowing speech has a normal lilt that must be preserved. The sentence, "I h'ope to f'ind it," has two stressed words, *hope* and *find*. "Sh'e is a bea'utiful w'oman" has three stress points, *she*, *beautiful*, and *woman*.

Such stress points should be emphasized in song to preserve the natural rhythm of the language. In speech the stress points shift within the normal sentence. In song such changes in meaning are emphasized by using higher pitches, tenutos, or longer note values.

Note in the following examples how meaning shifts with stress:

Are you going to sing in the hall tonight? (No.)
Are *you* going to sing in the hall tonight? (Not I.)
Are you going to *sing* in the hall tonight? (No, play.)
Are you going to sing in the hall *tonight*? (Tomorrow.)

In song, the sentence stress is often lost because note values do not correspond to the natural rhythm of the language. In such cases, the sentence stress may be subtly stressed but never to such an extent that the strong melodic line is destroyed. The following song text is an excellent example of a composer's disregard for linguistic characteristics of his language.

Bois Epais, p.1. *Jean Baptiste Lully*

Lully wrote this aria in the Italian style and destroyed the rhythmic lilt of the French language by placing unstressed mutes (*bl,e, br,e, tr,e*) on accent points in the bar and by giving them long duration. Unless sentence stress and word stress are observed, the line has a tendency to plod. This tendency is partly caused by the strong irregular melodic line and partly by the matching chordal accompaniment.

In most songs the rhythm is compatible with the meter of the verse form. In such cases the natural rhythm of the phrase is easily maintained, as in the following example of emphatic stress (See Record 4, Band 29.):

Dover Beach, Baritone and String Quartet, p.3-4. *Samuel Barber*

Copyright by G. Schirmer, Inc., 1936, used by permission

The strong rhythmic accent upon the first beat of the bar assists in stressing the principal parts of speech. Logical rhythmic scansion is a composer's gift to the singer.

Emotional Stress

Emotional stress is used in varying degrees to intensify the word and heighten the drama of the situation.

The exclamations, "My God! My Father!" may be expressed with varying degrees of vocal force and still be classed as emotional stress. If the words were gasped in a hoarse whisper with each word "spaced with silence"[5] consonants would be stressed to the point of being plosives, "M,y G'od! M,y F'ath,er!" The effect would reveal more emotion than if it were shouted. Emotional stress does not always suggest loud singing. Where pitches and note values are written in the score, emotional stress should follow the wishes of the composer and should interpret the dynamic markings suggested, as in this example of emotional stress in which both stressing and unstressing must be observed:

Dover Beach, p.14-15. *Samuel Barber*

Copyright by G. Schirmer, Inc., 1936, used by permission

In this example the singer is able to use considerable vocal force at stress points and still stay within the musical boundaries of the text regarding note value, pitch, consonant, and vowel. Tone quality should be the first consideration of the singer in his attempt to fulfill the intensity (loudness) demands of the text, for to distort the vocalized sound for the sake of the text is to weaken the musical elements of the composition. In the following example of emotional stress every syllable must be stressed.

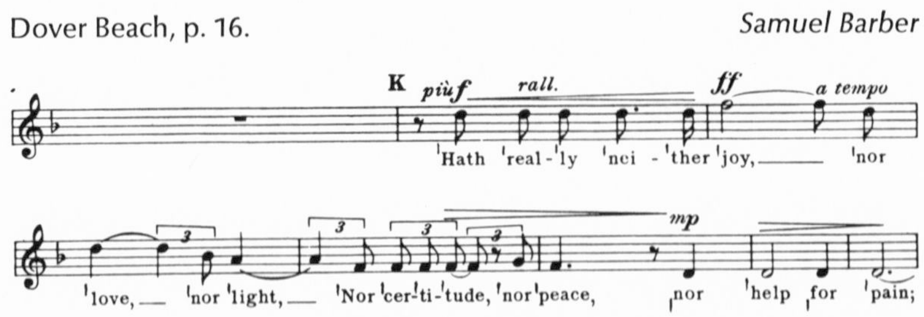

Copyright by G. Schirmer, Inc., 1936, used by permission

In this portion of the song the singer faces the task of sustaining intense emotion by gradually reducing vocal force, by increasing the stress of each phoneme and by giving each consonant more and more duration as the decrescendo is attained. This portion of the song is sheer drama. To be sung successfully, it must be staged, for the total body position must be controlled to make this passage persuasive.

Textual intelligibility within this line is realized only when the singer consciously controls emotional stress through the intelligent use of vocal force, phonemic emphasis, and consonantal duration. (See Record 4, Band 29.)

METHOD OF DETERMINING STRESS POINTS

In working out stress points within a new song, the student will find it helpful to proceed in the following manner:*

1. Underline the stress points, the subject, verb, and direct object. These parts of speech are basic words in determining meaning.
2. Underline those stress points within the adjectives that enrich the mood, idea, or drama.
3. Unimportant words that convey little meaning should not be underscored for stress (articles and prepositions).
4. Read the text aloud before singing and notice that emphasis of each word

* See song material, Chap. 11, p. 385, and Record 5, Bands 1-14.

will be matched by a stress within the rhythmic framework of the composition. Too many students rely upon this rhythmic emphasis to carry them through a rewarding singing experience. This procedure will never prove satisfactory. Stress must be conceived and applied beyond the music to bring about truly eloquent interpretation and successful diction in song.

Chapter 8

Styles and Dialects—The Social Element of Interpretation

Singing style is a mode or manner of vocal utterance which gives distinctive character and eloquence[1] to artistic expression. A tool of diction it involves the word (See p. 5.), which conveys the intimacy of meaning and personal intent. Styles of singing tend to be directed by the musical structure. Songs of the Baroque and Classical Periods demand a disciplined respect for the musical line that may confine the meaning and intent of the word within strict emotional boundaries, while romantic music removes these boundaries. Such disciplines are social restraints or freedoms that compel a singer to assume a style or manner when singing the songs of a particular form or period. However, a compelling social force which directs the establishment of style is the emulation of an ideal.

The reputable, cultured singer has a profound impact upon the diction of the vocal proletariat. When a singer becomes recognized nationally or even locally, his diction style of phonemic utterance is imitated in the area of his success.

Kantner and West describe the aspects of style thus, "There are two aspects of any style: the example set by the leader, and the emulation of that example by a significantly large body of followers. Until both of these aspects are manifest, no style has been created."[2]

Musical society, then, is divided into two distinct groups, leaders and followers. A vocal utterance, when first brought to the attention of the listening mass or follower group, will probably be accepted if the leader is popular enough, if he has the prestige of a national television show, or if the style is accepted by a prestige group and it uses the style with regularity. Examples of such musical styles are the singing of Bing Crosby, Frank Sinatra, Julie London, Barbra Streisand, Cab Calloway, and so on.

Each of these styles is in a state of change. Each is determined by the personality of the singer and by the receptivity of the follower group. Thus, one style may express the studied rustic colloquial speech of the country. Another may have the sophistication of the well-tailored nightclub entertainer who creates his own interpretation of any popular melody or show tune.

In the United States and Europe, acceptable styles of artful diction are those set by the cultured group of leaders in opera, concert stage, and oratorio. Yet even this group, when singing in English, tends to use aspects of the General American dialect, notably the General American [ɝ] [veɝɪ] or [maɝɪ] instead of the flipped [ɾ]. If members of this group continue to sing this vowelized [ɝ], it may in time be considered quite the proper vowel for singing. Style, then, is a transient characteristic, wholly susceptible to the impact of personality or culture, which is reflected in rhythm, stress, or vocalic sounds within the vocal art form.

Radio, television, and movies have stabilized linguistic change and have encouraged imitation of vocal diction and even vocal techniques for both teacher and student. For the curious, observant person, learning through such media has wrought wonders. However, social distinctions based on class, education, race, and wealth encourage the cǒntinuance of distinctive diction characteristics that are recognizably different from those of the cultured group.

Many teachers of formal singing rationalize their likes and dislikes on the basis of what they regard as the inherent beauty or ugliness of certain sounds and sound combinations. To such teachers, a sound is aesthetically attractive when it is employed in a word or combination that is inspiring to the intellect, comfortably produced, that is, free of vocal tensions, and pleasing to the ear —particularly if it is uttered by a class of people that is musically prominent, educated, traveled, and cultured.

Gray and Wise have discussed "beauty in American dialects" as follows:

> We sometimes see or hear discussions purporting to compare the relative beauty of the major American dialects. Such discussions are futile and reveal their futility through inconsistency. Any statement, for example, that the [æ] sound in the Southern and General American pronunciation of *grass* is unbeautiful falls down immediately before the fact that even in those dialects where grass is pronounced [gras], the [æ] sound nonetheless occurs in *lass* [læs], *package* [pækedƷ], *sadly* (sædlı], *attitude* [ætitud], and many other words, without arousing any criticism of its alleged unmusical quality. It is safe to say that any comparison of the various dialects intended to disparage one or more of them can be shown to be similarly inconsistent. It is reasonably certain, too, that such criticisms are usually made in an attempt to rationalize or justify adherence to a so-called "standard English," without real knowledge of any way, if indeed there is any, to compare the relative aesthetic values of dialects. Without venturing formally into the realm of aesthetics, the present

> authors are willing to risk the statement that beauty of utterance consists not so much in the selection of values to be assigned to vowels and consonants as in the manner of uttering these sound values (modifications). Of course our ideas of acceptability are conditioned, and rightly so, by the customary practice of educated people. For this reason, [sæs], however musically pronounced, could never be accepted as a well-sounding pronunciation of *sauce* so long as educated people pronounce it [sɔs]. But we reject [sæs] not because of any inherent lack of currency among educated people. It is safe to say that if all prejudice can be eliminated from an individual's judgement he will admit that any of our major dialects, when well spoken, is beautiful.[3]

THE DIALECT AREAS OF THE UNITED STATES

Style and dialect differ. "Styles are the emergence of set diction habits from speech forms of ancestor, parent, or community. They are constantly changing; a dialect is a survival of a successful style."[4]

Early in the history of America, communities were remote and isolated, and they developed various language patterns. The development of the railroad facilitated the mixing of speech cultures and brought to these communities a more standardized form of speech modeled after that of the British stage. Local and provincial dialects became widened and fused. As a result, today some seventeen distinct dialects exist in the United States.[5] Three of them, each including a number of subsidiary dialects, are major:

1. The Eastern dialect is spoken by about 19 million people in an area embracing New England, New York City, upstate New York, and northern Pennsylvania to the Ohio border.
2. The Southern dialect is spoken by 49 million people in an area including southern Delaware, southeastern Maryland, and southward through all the southeastern and southern coastal states, but embracing only a part of southeastern Texas. Exceptions within this area are the southern Appalachian highlands, the highlands of Arkansas and Louisiana, and the remainder of Texas.
3. The General American dialect is spoken by 112 million people throughout the rest of the nation.[6]

The rapid growth of the communication media has made the borders of these major speech areas less distinct and has given phoneticians cause to state: "There is in the making a common speech for America, not the 'standard speech' of phoneticians superimposed upon the people, but a standard speech arising spontaneously from the people."[7]

They are referring to the General American dialect, which is rapidly becoming the accepted standard of diction in both speech and song.

A DIALECT FOR SINGING

Vocal coaches and conductors tend to prefer the soft sounds of the Eastern dialect or the cultured phonemic substitutions inherent in British Stage speech. Such a preference is justified partly because the dialect has been stable for years, partly because it reeks with culture, and partly because phonemic refinement is needed when dealing with an art form in which cultured speech is the antithesis of colloquialism.

Phonemic variation among dialects is obvious when the spelling of the word is considered. Because of this variation, one must compare General American, British Stage dialect, and the Singers dialect, which is a suggested phonemic modification of General American and British Stage dialects for proper utterance in song.

The author's intention is not to become a reformer of pronunciation or to decide what phonemic utterance is "good" or "bad" within the singing experience. The decision to include the Singers dialect is based on a word recognition condition that can be observed in the singer-audience relationship: When excellent diction is part of a singer's established technique, the listener recognizes instantaneously the word that is directly related to its familiar pronunciation within speech forms. Therefore, it is the singer's duty, throughout all migration in pitch changes, to preserve the integrity of the authentic phoneme and not to select a migration that will cause the phoneme to migrate in a direction that is unnatural and will not enhance the vocalic sound.

If the Singers dialect has an identifying element, it is the tendency to approximate and modify the authentic General American sound toward an immediately adjacent phoneme at secondary accent points, rather than to depart from it as is often done in the British Stage dialect. For example:

	GENERAL AMERICAN	BRITISH STAGE	SINGERS
half	[h'æf]	[h'ɑf]	[h'af]
palace	[p'æla,s]	[p'æli,s]	[p'ala,s]

The Singers dialect demands both stress and phonemic substitution that is wholly compatible with good singing techniques and intelligibility. The prosody of the text within the melodic line and the duration of each phoneme within a variable pitch range demand an attention to migration problems that are easily solved by the alert student who has refined his vocalic utterances phonemically. The speech forms of the less dedicated will degenerate into colloquialism.

Within any society, the vowel is more unstable than the consonant. Styles in the production of the consonant change much more slowly, and trends are more difficult to discern. Therefore, the real emphasis here will be placed on the utterance of the vowel.*

DRILLS TO EMPHASIZE DIALECTAL VARIATION

These words may be used as ear-training drills which will enable the student to identify the phonemic differences between dialects. Each word should be first spoken then sung.

Unstressed Suffixes**

	GENERAL AMERICAN	BRITISH*** STAGE	SINGERS
palace	pælɪs	pælis	pælas, -is
plantain	plæntɪɴ	plæntin	plæntɪ·n
prelate	prelɪt	prelit	prɛlɪ·t
stinted	stintɪd	stintid	stintɪ·d
forfeit	fɔrfɪt	fɔ:fit	fɔrfɪ·t
chicken	tʃɪkɪn, -əɴ	tʃikin	tʃɪkɪ·n
pigeon	pɪdʒən, pɪdʒɪn	pidʒin	pidʒɪ·n
boxes	bɑksɪz	bɔksɪz	bɑksɪ·z
careless	kɛrlɪs, kær-	kɛəlis	kɛrlɪ·s
pocket	pɑkɪt	pɔkit	pɑkɪ·t
Alice	ælɪs	ælis	alɪs
stolid	stɑlid	stɔlid	stɑləd
coffin	kɔfin,	kɒfin	kɔfi·n

* Authentic source for the General American dialect is John S. Kenyon and Thomas A. Knott, *A Pronouncing Dictionary of American English* (Springfield, Mass.: G. & C. Merriam Co., 1953). For the Southern British Stage Dialect, it is Daniel Jones, *An English Pronouncing Dictionary* (London: J. M. Dent & Sons, 1926).* The Singers dialect was devised by the author. For a complete analysis of dialect differences in the United States, consult the bibliography on p. 409.

** A dot following a phonetic symbol indicates a slight migration toward the central schwa.

*** Daniel Jones alters the I.P.A. by using the following diacritical markings ɪ: = [i], i = [I], e = [ɛ], ɔ = [ɒ], ɔ: = [o], u: = [u], u = [ʊ], ə: = [ɜ].

crisis	krɑɪsɪs	krɑisis	krɑɪsɪ·s
tourist	turɪst	tuərɪst	turɪ·st
lettuce	lɛtɪs, -əs	lɛtis	lɛtɪ·s
minute	mɪnɪt, menjut	minit	minɪ·t
necklace	nɛklɪs	nɛklis	nɛklɪ·s
palate	pælɪt	pælit	palɪ·t
want	want, wɔnt, wɒnt	wɔnt	wɑnt
kitchen	kɪtʃɪn	kitʃin	kɪtʃɪ·n
ashes	æʃɪz	æʃɪz	aʃəs
ruthless	ruθlɪs, rɪuθ-	ru:θlis	ruθləs
bracket	brækɪt	brækit	brakɪ·t
chalis	tʃælɪs	tʃælis	tʃalɪ·s
pallid	pælɪd	pælid	palɪ·d
basis	besis	beisis	besɪ·s
limit	lɪmɪt	limit	lɪmɪ·t
infinite	ɪnfənɪt, -naɪt	infinit, infinait	ɪnfɪ·nɪ·t

Unstressed Endings

	GENERAL AMERICAN	BRITISH STAGE	SINGERS
sadden	sædn	sædn	sadən
sadness	sædnɪs	sadnɪs	sadnəs
passion	pæʃən	pæʃən	paʃən
sudden	sʌdn	sʌdn	sʌdən
table	tebl	teibl	teɪbəl
little	lɪtl	litl	litəl
petal	pɛtl	petl	pɛtəl
needed	nidɪd	ni:did	nidəd
hopeless	hoplɪs	houplis	hopləs
roses	rozɪz	rouziz	rozəs
woodland	wudlænd, -lənd (noun), -lənd (adj.)	wudlənd	wʊdlənd
idol	aɪdl	aidl	aɪdəl
patience	peʃəns	peɪʃəns	peʃəns
ocean	oʃən	ouʃən	oʃən
never	nɛvɚ	nevə	nɛvɜ
murmur	mɝmɚ	ma:ma	mɜmɜ
menace	mɛnɪs, əs	menəs	mɛnɪs, -as

riot	raɪət	raiet	raɪət
Christmas	krɪsməs	krisməs	krɪstməs
foreign	fɔrɪn, far-, fɒr-, -ən	fɔrin	fɔrɪ·n
prophecy	prafəsɪ	prɔfisi	prɑfəsɪ
nectar	nɛktɚ	nektə	nɛktər
shepherd	ʃɛpɚd	ʃepəd	ʃɛpɜd
quiet	kwaɪət	kwaiət	kwɑət
handsome	hænsəm	hænsəm	hansəm
enemy	ɛnəmɪ	enimi	ɛnəmɪ
traitor	tretɚ	treitə	tretɜ

Unstressed Medial Syllables

	GENERAL AMERICAN	BRITISH STAGE	SINGERS
celebrate	sɛləbret	selibreit	sɛləbreɪt
president	prɛzədənt	prezidənt	prɛzɪ·dənt
analysis	ənæləsɪs	anæləsis	analəsɪ·s
ability	əbɪlətɪ	əbiliti	əbɪlɪ·tɪ
felicity	fəlɪsətɪ	filisiti	fɛlisɪ·tɪ
Halifax	hæləfæks	hælifæks	halɪfaks
dandelion	dændlaɪən	dændilaiən	dandəlaɪ·n
handicap	hændɪkæp	handikæp	handɪ·kap
insanity	ɪnsænətɪ	insæniti	ɪnsanɪ·tɪ

Spelled with the Letter *A*

	GENERAL AMERICAN	BRITISH STAGE	SINGERS
air	ɛr, ær	ɛə	aɾ
are	ar, ˌar	aː	ɑɾ
ear	ɪr	iə	iɾ
pare	pɛr, pær	pɛə	paɾ
wear	wɛr	wɛə	waɾ
paralysis	parælәsɪs	pərælisis	paralɪsɪs
paradox	pærədɑks	pærədɔks	parədɑks
bear	ber	bɛə	baɾ

marry	mɛɾɪ	maeri	maɾɪ
fairy	fɛɾɪ	færi	faɾɪ

The Sound of [ɔ]

	GENERAL AMERICAN	BRITISH STAGE	SINGERS
ball	bɔl	bɔːl	bɔl
saw	sɔ	sɔː	sɔ
talk	tɔk	tɔːk	tɔk
caught	kɔt	kɔːt	kɔt
hawk	hɔk	hɔːk	hɔk
ought	ɔt	ɔːt	ɔt
draw	drɔ	drɔː	drɔ
cough	kɔf, kɒf	kɔːf	kɔf
dawn	dɔn	dɔːn	dɔn
slaughter	slɔtð	slɔːtə	slɔtɜ
nought	nɔt	nɔːt	nɔt
shawl	ʃɔl	ʃɔːl	ʃɔl
totter	tatð	tɔtə	tɑtɛ
pottage	patɪdz	pɔtidʒ	patadʒ
lot	lat	lɔt	lɑt
quantity	kwatətɪ	kwɔntiti	kwɑntətɪ
bob	bab	bɔb	bɑb
hod	hɔd	hɔd	hɑd
pop	pɔp	pɔp	pɑp
odd	ad, ɒd	ɔd	ɑd
squabble	skwəbl̩	skwɔbl	skwɑbəl
cot	kat	kɔt	kɑt
waddle	wɑdl	wɔdl	wɑ'dəl
hominy	hɑmənɪ	hɔmini	hɑmɪnɪ
squalid	skwɑlɪd	skwɔlid	skwɔlɪd
knob	nab	nɔb	nɑb
swallow	swalo, swɒlo	swɔlou	swɑlo
shop	ʃɑp	ʃɔp	ʃɑp
swan	swan, swɒn, swɔn	swɔn	swɑn
plod	plad	plɔd	plɑd

[ə] Instead of [r] after [ɪ, ɛ, ʊ, ai, au]

	GENERAL AMERICAN	BRITISH STAGE	SINGERS
clear	klɪr	kliə	klɪɾ
where	hwɛr	wɛə	hwɛɾ
sure	ʃur	ʃuə	ʃʊɾ
fire	faɪr	faɪə	faɪɾ
flour	fləʊr	flauə	flɑʊɾ
cheer	tʃɪr	tʃiə	tʃɪɾ
lear	lir	liə	lɪɾ
appear	əpir	əpiə	əpɪɾ
hour	aʊr	auə	ɑʊɾ
pyre	paɪr	paiə	paɾ
fear	fɪr	fiə	fɪɾ
dire	dəir	daiə	daɪɾ
veer	vɪr	vɪə	viɾ
everywhere	ɛvrɪhwɛr	evriwɛə	ɛvrɪhwɛɾ
therefore	ðɛrfor	ðɛəfɔ:	ðɛrfɔɾ
rear	rir	riə	riɾ
peer	pir	piə	piɾ
sour	saur	sauə	sɑʊɾ
nearly	nirlɪ	nɪəli	nirlɪ
acquire	əkwair	əkwaiə	əkwɑɪɾ

The Sound of [r] as a Final Phoneme

	GENERAL AMERICAN	BRITISH STAGE	SINGERS
luster	lʌstɚ	lʌstə:	lʌstɜ
reaper	ripɚ	ri:pə	ripɜ
Astor	æstɚ	æstə	astɜ
neighbor	nebɚ	neɪbə	neɪbɜ
upper	ʌpɚ	ʌpə	ʌpɜ
searcher	sɝtʃɚ	sə:tʃə	sɜtʃɜ
cooler	kulɚ	ku:lə	kulɜ
color	kʌlɚ	kʌlə	kʌlɜ
pallor	pælɚ	pælə	palɛ

plaster	plæstɚ	plæstə	plastɜ
pillar	pɪlɚ	pilə	pilɜ

The [t] as an Aspirate

	GENERAL AMERICAN	BRITISH STAGE	SINGERS
pretty	prɪtɪ, pɚtɪ	priti	prɪtɪ
city	sɪtɪ	siti	sɪtɪ
ditty	dɪtɪ	diti	dɪtɪ
jetty	dʒɛtɪ	dʒeti	dʒɛtɪ
battle	bætl	bætl	batəl
kitten	kɪtn	kitn	kɪtɛn
cotton	kɑtn	kɔtn	kɑtən
pattern	pætɚn	pætən	patɜn
flutter	flʌtɚ	flʌtə	flʌtɜ
rotten	rɑtn̩	rɔtn̩	rɑtən
witty	wɪtɪ	witi	wɪtɪ
Britain	brɪtn	britən	brɪtən
trotter	trɑtɚ	trɔtə	trɑtə
Saturday	sætɚdɪ	sætədi	satɜdaɪ
settle	sɛtl	setl	sɛtəl
kettle	kɛtl	ketl	kɛtəl
fatten	fætn	fætn	fatən

The [j] Sound Following Phonemes [d], [n], [l], [s], [t], [h]

	GENERAL AMERICAN	BRITISH STAGE	SINGERS
dew	dju, dɪu	dju	dju
tulip	tjuləp, tɪuləp	tju:lip	tjulɪp
neural	nj-, nɪ-, nurəl	njuərəl	njurəl
knew	nj, nɪ, nu	nju:	nju
nutrition	njutrɪʃən	nju:trɪʃən	njutrɪʃən
enthusiastic	ɪnθjuzɪæstɪk	inθju:ziæstik	ɛnθjuzɪastik
assume	asjum	asju:m	əsjum
resume	rɪzjum	rizju:m	rɪzjum
absolute	æbseljut	æbsəlu:t	absəljut
constitute	kənstətjut	kɔnstitju:t	kɑnstitjut

endue	ɪndju	indjuː	ɛndju
dutiful	djutifəl	djuːtiful	djutifəl
absolution	æbsəljuʃən	æbsəluːʃən	absəljuʃən
newsprint	njuzprɪnt	njuːzprint	njuzprɪnt
neutral	njutrəl	njuːtrəl	njutrəl
pursuant	pəsjuənt	pəsjuint	pɜsjuant
pneumonia	njumonja	njuːmonjə	njumonjɑ
suit	sut, sjut	sjut	sjut
presume	prɪzjum	prɪzjuːm	prɪzjum
enthusiasm	ɪnθjuzɪæzəm	inθjuːzɪæzm	ɛnθjuzɪazəm
neurosis	njurosɪs	njuərousis	njurosɪs
pursuit	pɚsjut	pəsjuːt	pɜsjut

The Stressed Sound of [ɜ]

	GENERAL AMERICAN	BRITISH STAGE	SINGERS
bird	bɝd	bəːd	bɜd
heard	hɝd	həːd	hɜd
fern	fɝn	fəːn	fɜn
kirk	kɝk	kəːk	kɜk
worst	wɝst	wəːst	wɜst
journal	dʒɝnl	dʒəːnl	dʒɜnəl
curl	kɝl	kəːl	kɜl
myrrh	mɝ	məː	mɜ
borough	bɝo	bʌrə	bʌɾo
worry	wɝɪ	wʌri	wʌɾɪ
courage	kɝɪdʒ	kʌridʒ	kʌɾɪdʒ
surrey	sɝɪ	sʌri	sʌɾɪ
furry	fɝɪ	fəːri	fʌɾɪ
first	fɝst	fəːst	fɜst
worm	wɝm	wəːm	wɜm
worth	wɝθ	wəːθ	wɜθ
her	hɝ	həː	hɜ
church	tʃɝtʃ	tʃəːtʃ	tʃɜtʃ
murkey	mɝkɪ	məːki	mɜkɪ
nervous	nɝvəs	nəːvəs	nɜvəs
tern	tɝn	təːn	tɜn
hearse	hɝs	həːs	hɜs

early	ɝlɪ	əːli	ɜli
furl	fɝl	fəːl	fɜl
burned	bɝnd	bəːnd	bɜnd
adjourn	adʒɝn	ədʒəːn	ədʒɜn
purse	pɝs	pəːs	pɜs

The [ʍ] Sounds

	GENERAL AMERICAN	BRITISH STAGE	SINGERS
which	hwɪtʃ	witʃ	hwɪtʃ
wheel	hwil	wil	hwil
when	hwɛn	wen	hwɛn
why	hwaɪ	wai	hwaɪ
whether	hwɛðɚ	weðə	hwɜðɜ
whisk	hwɪsk	wisk	hwɪsk
wheat	hwit	wiːt	hwit
white	hwaɪt	wait	hwaɪt
wharf	hwɔrf	wɔːf	hwɔrf
what	hwɑt	wɔt	hwɑt
wheeze	hwiz	wiːz	hwiz
whelp	hwɛlp	welp	hwɛlp
where	hwɛr	wɛa	hwaɾ
whey	hwe	weɪ	hweɪ
whiff	hwɪf	wif	hwɪf
Whig	hwɪg	wɪg	hwɪg
while	hwəɪl	wail	hwaɪl
whim	hwɪm	wim	hwɪm
whip	hwɪp	wip	hwɪp
whiskey	hwɪskɪ	wiski	hwɪskɪ
whisper	hwɪspɚ	wispə	hwɪspɜ
whistle	hwɪsl	wisl	hwɪsəl
whit	hwɪt	wit	hwɪt
whopper	hwɑpɚ	wɔpə	hwɑpɜ

The Sound of [ou]

In [ou] sounds where the tense [o] would normally be used in General American dialect, e.g., [o] in [bot] the present day practice within cultured British stage dialect is to substitute [ɜʊ] or [ɔ] for [o]. Only [oʊ] is found in

Jones, but [ɜʊ] is likely to be used much more often than [oʊ] in Southern British and on the British stage, for example, *boast* [bɜʊst], *grow* [grɜʊ], *oh* [ɜʊ].

	GENERAL AMERICAN	BRITISH STAGE	SINGERS
boast	bost	boust [ɜʊ]	bôst
grow	gro	grou [ɜʊ]	grô
oh	o	ou [ɜʊ]	ô
sole	sol	soul [ɜʊ]	sôl
doss	dos	dous [ɜʊ]	dôs
load	lod	loud [ɜʊ]	lôd
ghost	gost	goust [ɜʊ]	gôst
roam	rom	roum [ɜʊ]	rôm
no	no	nou [ɜʊ]	nô
smoke	smok	smouk [ɜʊ]	smôk
host	host	houst [ɜʊ]	hôst
whole	hwol	houl [ɜʊ]	hwôl
roll	rol	roul [ɜʊ]	rôll
cold	kold	kould [ɜʊ]	kôld
boat	bot	bout [ɜʊ]	bôt
bode	bod	boud [ɜʊ]	bôd
most	most	moust [ɜʊ]	môst
holy	holɪ	houli [ɜʊ]	hôlɪ
bestow	bɪstow	bistou [ɜʊ]	bɪstô
sew	so	sou [ɜʊ]	sô
dome	dom	doum [ɜʊ]	dôm
soldier	soldʒɚ	souldʒə [ɜʊ]	soldʒɛ

The [r] as a Medial Phoneme

(The flipped [ɾ] is used in intervocalic position or before another word beginning with a vowel.)

	GENERAL AMERICAN	BRITISH STAGE	SINGERS
merry	mɛɾɪ	meri	mɛɾɪ
fairy	fɛɾɪ	fɛari	fɛɾɪ
hurry	hɝɪ	hʌri	hʌɾɪ
furnish	fɝniʃ	fə:niʃ	fɜnɪʃ

glory	glori, glɔrɪ	glɔːri	glôɾɪ
curry	kɝɪ	kʌri	kʌɾɪ
sorry	sɔrɪ, sɑrɪ	sɔri	sɔɾɪ
near	nɪr	niə	nɪɾ
orate	oret, ɔret	ɔːreit	oɾet
starring	stɑrɪŋ	stɑːriŋ	stɑɾɪŋ
carry	kærɪ	kæri	kaɾɪ
very	vɛrɪ	veri	vaɾɪ
There are two.	ðɛr ar tu	ðeɾɑ tu	ðaɾ ɑɾ tu
Here it is.	hir it ɪz	hiet ɪz	hɪɾ ɪt ɪz
her intention	hɝ intɛnʃən	hɜ ɪntɛnʃən	hɾ ɪntɛnʃən
hearing	hɪrɪŋ	hɪəɪŋ	hɪɾɪŋ
forest	fɔrɪst	fɔrist	fɔɾast
pouring	poriŋ	pɔːriŋ	porɪŋ
tourist	turɪst	tuərist	tuɾɪst
tarry	tærɪ	tæri	taɾɪ
bury	bɛrɪ	beri	bɛɾɪ
fury	fjurɪ, fɝɪ	fjuɾɪ	fjuɾɪ
foray	fɔre	fɔrei	fɔɾe
coronation	kɔrəneʃən	kɔrəneiʃən	kɔɾəneʃən

[aɪl] as a Suffix

	GENERAL AMERICAN	BRITISH STAGE	SINGERS
reptile	rɛptl, ɾɜptɪl	reptail	reptaɪl
futile	fjutl, fjutɪl	fjutail	fjutəl
volatile	vɑlətil	vɔlətail	volətɪl
puerile	pjuarɪl	pjuərail	pjuərɪl
senile	sinail, -nɪl, -nl	sɪːnail	sɛnail
fertile	fɝtl	fəːtail	fɜtɪl
juvenile	dʒuvənɪl	dʒuːvinail	dʒuvənɪl

The Sound of [or]

	GENERAL AMERICAN	BRITISH STAGE	SINGERS
board	bɔrd	bɔːd	bôɾd

floor	flɔr	flɔ:	flɔɾ
sore	sɔr	sɔ:	sɔɾ
four	fɔr	fɔ:	fɔɾ
horse	hɔrs	hɔ:s	hɔɾs
shore	ʃɔr	ʃɔ:	ʃɔɾ
pour	pɔr	pɔ:	pɔɾ
coarse	kɔrs	kɔ:s	kɔ:s
mourn	mɔrn	mɔ:n	mɔɜn
fourteen	fɔrtin	fɔ:ti:n	fɔɜtin
adore	adɔr	adɔ:	ədɔɾ
explore	ɪksplɔr	iksplɔ:	ɛksplɔɾ
course	kɔrs	cɔ:s	kɔɾs
roar	rɔr	rɔ:	rɔɾ
deplore	dɪplɔr	diplɔ:	diplɔɾ
door	dɔr	dɔ:	dɔɾ

Miscellaneous Pronunciation

	GENERAL AMERICAN	BRITISH STAGE	SINGERS
ate	et	et	et
been	bɪn	bi:n	bɪn
either	iðɚ	ai:ðə	iðɜ
nephew	nɛfju	nevju	nɛfju
tomato	təmeto	təmɑ:tou	tameto
record	rɪkɔrd	rekɔ:d	rɪkɔrd
lieutenant	lutɛnənt	leftenant	ljutɛnant
schedule	skɛdʒul	ʃedju:l	skɛdʒul
pajamas	pədʒæmaz	pədʒɑ:məz	padzamas
against	əgɛnst	əgeinst	əganst

Chapter 9

Vowel Migration–The Intellectual Element of Interpretation

A PHONETIC APPROACH TO THE TEACHING OF SINGING

For years teachers of singing have been searching for a stable point of reference for teaching diction in all languages. The methods presently used are too diverse to be useful for the teacher or student of voice, and the international and dialectal variations of the spoken language prevent the model word method ([ɑ] as in *father*) from being an effective tool.

Three primary variations in teaching concepts used by the voice teacher today lead to a confused methodology. Each variation shall be discussed and a tool for teaching suggested, which, if used by both teacher and student, will help to reduce this confusion. It will help them to achieve a better understanding of the linguistic problems within a song. The teaching tool will also permit the student to make his own decisions regarding vowel modifications on all pitches, and will provide him with a new awareness of his vocal utterance.

Variation of pedagogical concept may be traced to the following:

1. Diversity of a teacher's preference of student vocal utterance.
2. Indiscriminate teaching of phonemic accuracy.
3. Misconceptions of vowel modification and of its usefulness in the middle and upper voice.

TEACHER PREFERENCE

The first consideration is the diversity of a teacher's preference of the student's vocal utterance as a cause of confusion in the teaching of vocal diction.

Throughout the Western world, wherever the art song has flourished, all phases of voice culture have been based upon teacher preference of sound. Teachers of voice have assembled their pedagogical skills by imitation from many different sources and by widely differing means. Most voice teachers today have acquired their pedagogical information through teacher direction; some have had direct contact with internationally famous teachers. Others have acquired their skill by reading and still others have had experience in concert and opera. Some who possess pianistic and musical ability have become voice teachers by observing vocal technique in action. Few teaching procedures, however, have been based on scientific investigation that has yielded stable, demonstrable techniques in the areas of phonation, respiration, and resonation.

Thus, the major cause of confusion for the student has been this wide variation of teacher background and the resulting variation in the teacher's control of the student's forces of respiration and phonation and his attempt to "place" each vowel sound and its migrations in the singer's vocal scale.

Understandably teachers of voice demand and get student loyalty and trust. With such compelling direction, the student is unable to determine by himself what vowel utterance is fitting or proper, for he must have the teacher's approval as he learns and perfects a song. No matter where a student may study voice, be it in Europe or the United States, he is plagued by the variation of opinion regarding the proper production of a vowel sound. Thus, possibly the goal of textual intelligibility in singing the vowel sounds of all languages may never be realized as long as the concepts of vowel sounds vary within each language and geographically with each nation. The teacher has the prerogative to decide which variation of [ɑ], [i], or [u] his student will sing. Seemingly the ultimate decision as to the choice of vowel to be sung by the student is tempered by the aesthetic judgment of the teacher and not by acoustical measurement.

PHONEMIC ACCURACY

The second consideration is the indiscriminate teaching of phonemic accuracy as a source of confusion in the teaching of vocal diction. Teachers of voice always have relied upon the auditory process for phonemic identification, and many students have developed fine techniques by imitating speech signals through auditory stimuli alone. Therefore, in learning to produce a sound they are not particularly aware of the fine manipulation of the articulators. Consider as an example the phoneme [ē], or the German *e*, as it is referred to in singing. This phoneme is difficult to teach by sound imitation. The student, if asked what he is doing with the articulators to make the sound, is at a loss to explain the action in detail. The palatogram and liguagram for this phoneme reveal a lateral movement of the tongue from the basic position. When the student becomes aware of this movement, he begins to conceive the vowel physiologically instead of tonally, and his ability to reproduce this phoneme correctly is greatly increased.

The importance of articulatory awareness as a factor in phonemic intelligibility is supported by a report prepared at the Haskins Laboratories, New York:

> There is evidence from perceptual studies that speech sounds are perceived by reference to the articulatory movements that produce them, and that this articulatory reference is important for the distinctiveness of speech as perceived. It is well known, at least in the case of simple stimuli, that man's ability to discriminate (i.e., to determine that two stimuli are the same or different) is very good, but that his ability to identify in absolute terms (i.e., to tell which stimulus it is) is poor. We can, for example, discriminate one to two hundred times as many pitches as we can identify absolutely. Now when a child hears a speech sound and undertakes, conceivably by trial and error, to mimic it, he is limited only by his differential sensitivity—that is, by his ability to determine whether the two sounds are the same or different—and that, as we know, is extremely acute. Given that the two acoustic stimuli are rather similar, but that the 'matching' responses are made with different muscles, as for example, in the case of /b/ and /d/, the feedback stimulation would be more distinctive than the acoustic signals themselves. Thus, one can, by mimicking, use his keen differential sensitivity as a basis for making absolute identification provided, of course, that the mimicking gestures themselves provide distinctive feedback stimulation.
>
> In general, however, the articulatory reference theory does not rest most directly on such considerations, but rather on the evidence which indicates that the relation between phoneme and articulation is more nearly one-to-one than is the relation between phoneme and acoustic signal. Thus, we have seen in this paper that perception of the phonemes is discontinuous (categorical) or continuous depending on the nature of the appropriate articulatory movements and not on the properties of acoustic signal. Elsewhere we have reviewed evidence bearing on the same general point. In that connection we pointed out that because of the characteristics of the articulators and the vocal tract, and because of the overlapping in time of the articulatory gestures, the relationship between articulation and the acoustic signal is often complex. For example, when stop consonants are articulated into different vowel cavities, as in the normal production of stop-vowel syllables, we find extreme cases in which large differences in articulation produce little or no difference in the "consonant" part of the acoustic signal; there is, also, the opposite case in which essentially the same consonant articulation produces (in different vowel contexts) very different acoustic results. We ask in these cases what happens to the perception and find always that it follows the articulation, not the sound.[1]

What are the cues for vowel recognition in flowing speech? Linguistic experiments[2] suggest that the movement of the articulators as they pass from consonant to vowel and back to consonant creates an acoustic signal which carries information to aid the listener in identifying both vowel and consonant. Since identification of vowels is very difficult when they are isolated from their consonantal environment, a reasonable assumption is that movement of the articulators provides a significant cue for vowel recognition in speech.

Singing demands that vowel postures be held firmly in place for many seconds upon many different pitch levels. Therefore, textual intelligibility in singing depends upon the firmness of consonantal articulation as well as the duration of the vowel produced within well-defined boundaries and sung within a specific acoustic area. (See Fig. 106, p. 245.)

In singing every word has its cue of recognition. Such cues depend upon the musical elements of frequency, intensity, and timbre within a particular linguistic environment; i.e., in one instance the cue may be the initial consonant, in another it may be the vowel. In still another, the cue may be the stressing of a nasal ending or sustaining a lateral. Whatever the cue may be, it may always be found in the prosodic elements of the song text, which have been united with the rhythmic and melodic elements of the music.

To identify these cues, the singer must first consider the pronunciation of the word, for pronunciation involves the choice of phoneme and the degree of stressing necessary to convey its meaning to the audience. Pronunciation should be considered before timbre because, when the singer concentrates upon the timbre of the sound, he frequently destroys the integrity of the vowel, and when he concentrates on the vowel he enhances the timbre.

Lack of textual intelligibility in song is not caused by singing the vowels [i], [e], [ɑ], [ô], and [u]; rather, vowel ambiguity stems from the promiscuous migration of these vowels from their true acoustic center to the vowels [ɪ], [ē], [ɔ], [o], and [ʊ].

The most intelligible sung word is one in which each consonant may be heard and in which each vowel is sung with a preconceived phonemic accuracy.

Model Word and Phonemic Accuracy

While teaching diction, the teacher often directs the student to sing models [ɛ] as in *get* or [ɑ] as in *father* because these are sounds with which to establish teacher concepts. This practice results in a preferred sound within the vocal pattern sung by the student. The student's task, then, is to remember the sensation and the sound of the teacher's preference word through the syntax and upon each pitch. However, the student tends to forget the sensation of the word described by the teacher and only retains the concept of the symbol;

this result does not assure phonemic accuracy. The student takes into the practice room the model words, which he is able to reproduce with numerous variations of sound. These sounds may be guttural, tense, and unsupported by adequate breath pressure; they may be sung with a tonal concept that depends upon voice quality rather than phonemic accuracy; they may be produced without regard to proper migration within specific pitch areas. In each case, these variations in vocalic utterance are caused by imbalances in the student's respiration, phonation, or resonance, and he becomes confused by what he hears and feels.

Spelling and Phonemic Accuracy

The students are not at fault in not remembering the teacher-preferred sound, for spelling is inconsistent in the English language. As noted by Daniel Jones:

> . . . many letters of the alphabet . . . have multiple sounds and are a source of confusion to the ear and eye. For example, the *a* in *part*, the *i* in *wind*, the *u* in *pun*. These sounds and symbols are easily learned, but there are many words in which these letters have a different sound, such as the *a* in *father, tall, candy, tap, watch;* the *i* in *blind, wind, machine, bird;* the *u* in *rule, but, put;* the *o* in *boat, lord, shove;* the *e* in *meat, break, bear.*[3]

Confusion also arises from the numerous ways in which an identical sound may be spelled as in *beat, piece, receive; pique, key, quay; boss, sauce; torn, warn; thought, caught, stalk.*

Thus, because of linguistic inconsistencies, the singer cannot depend upon the printed word to determine what sound he should use to match the teacher-preferred sound in song.

VOWEL MODIFICATION

The third aspect of the diversity of methodology in the teaching of vocal diction to be considered is that of vowel modification.

Pitch and Vowel Modification

Vowel modification, to the best of the knowledge available, was employed first by the Italian teachers of bel canto, and this concept seems to be the yard-stick for determining the technical excellence of singers today. The teachers of bel canto taught the development of a vocal scale without interruption or break throughout its length. The transition of registers, while singing up or down the scale, demanded a modification of the vowel in the upper notes to preserve the true vowel sound as well as to prevent such notes from becoming disagreeable or harsh. Thus, for many centuries, teachers have used the modification of vowels as a means of transition into the upper voice.

Acoustically, a sung phoneme is not the same as a spoken phoneme. Spectrography* has proven this point. Duration, pitch, and vocal force demand a larger opening of oral and pharyngeal cavities and prevent the sound from being the same. Therefore, all sung sounds are modifications of speech sounds. One recognizes the phonemes within a sentence that is sung, but one is aware of the vocalic change from speech to song. The singing of crescendos and the changing of pitch, diatonically or by skip, demand a controlled vowel modification of the word concept, or phoneme, that must be maintained if the word is to be understood.

If a singer is sustaining the word *lord* in the middle voice range, and wishes to crescendo the phoneme, open [ô] on the same pitch over four beats. He must choose between the phonemes [ɔ] as in *all* or [o] as in *oral* for his basic phoneme, or the word is misunderstood. Each of these phonemes has many variations of sound that could be understood in textual syntax. The listener is apt to hear these vocalized sounds as some kind of *aw*, and to depend upon the word order to give the meaning of the text. If the vowel is modified for reasons of sound preference, the word *lord* could end up sounding like [lard] or [lod]. If the word is properly sung on a pitch on the top of the staff, the word will be heard as [lʌd].

Intensity and Vowel Modification

The rule of crescendo or increased vocal force has been advanced by teachers of singing for many years; any increase in vocal force, whether gradual or sudden must be accompanied by an expansion or enlargement of the resonating system. Therefore, the greater the volume employed by the singer, the more the vowel will be modified from the basic word concept. However, good diction demands that the phoneme be recognized even though pitch and intensity factors change.

Vowel modification is employed by all voices in singing higher pitches. If the word *yearning* is sung upon the pitch, top line F, or a G above the staff with the General American [r] with the retroflexed tongue, the sound will be pinched and unmusical. If the Eastern [ɜ] is used to sing the lower pitches and is also employed to sing the top pitches, *yearning* will invariably change to

* The analysis of the tonal spectrum (See p. 132.) by means of the sonograph.

yawning unless the lips are protruded firmly and the retroflex *r* sound eliminated by keeping the tongue placed against the bottom front teeth, resulting in the Eastern *r* sound as in *urn* [ɜn]. Extreme rounding of the lips is required for the recognition of the vowel. The proper modification for the phoneme [ɜ] in singing the higher pitch is toward the [ʌ] as in *up*. Thus, the phonetic system suggests a satisfactory placement of the voice as well as good diction.

The reason each vowel is modified in singing with such an infinite variety of sounds, even to the extent of substituting a remotely related phoneme, is that teachers think aesthetically about a tonal placement and prefer one sound to another, disregarding the integrity of the vowel within the scale as related to intelligibility. Thus, the sound becomes more important than the word.

Vowel Color and Phonemic Migration

Vowel modification and *phonemic migration* are synonymous in usage but varied in concept. In singing both are controlled by auditory feedback.

Vowel modification is accomplished through psychological directives which suggest vowel coloring, i.e., a lighter or a darker sound for a particular vowel. Phonemic migration is also accomplished psychologically, but it is dependent upon physiological directives. These latter directives deliberately and consciously manipulate the articulators and resonating system. These manipulations effect the movement of one phoneme toward or away from another. By such movement any conceivable change in vowel quality may be realized. (See "Matching the Timbre of Recorded Sound," p. 232.)

What most teachers hear as a change in vowel color is actually a migration of the phoneme from its true acoustic center. Teachers and singers alike have been conditioned to think of sounds as "dark" or "bright" without regard to a basic phonemic position. The only reason such thinking persists as a teaching tool is that the singer has no point of reference for identifying a change in sound as a phonemic migration. Physiological changes of the articulators cause a shifting of energy within the sound spectrum; these shifts in energy are identifiable as phonemic changes (Fig. 76-78). These changes, the source of the diversity of teacher preference, have created a huge dilemma. Where is the starting point of vowel migration or modification? Modification or migration from what?

Does the teacher teach migration from the concepts of a speech sound, a sung sound, a sensation learned from another teacher, a variation of vowel color, or a psychological positioning of the sound outside the body?

Nothing is wrong with the psychological teaching technique that employs the foregoing concepts. Excellent singers have been developed using these concepts. However, such techniques tend to make students depend upon teacher opinion and teacher judgment, and they tend to be based more on personal aesthetics than facts.

Obviously one singer's pronunciation of the vowel sound in *father* is more closed or open, more pharyngeal or oral, more oral or nasal than another singer's. If the two singers are heard together the difference between the two types of pronunciation can be detected. Thus the student in the practice room forgets the teacher-preferred model and learns eventually to groove the sound through the laborious process of remembering the preferred vowel color through repetition.

Acoustically Stable Vowels

Another vowel sound, therefore, is needed to stabilize the teacher-student relationship in deciding which migration of the vowel is best. If a student can compare his vowel sound with a known, recorded, unchangeable vowel he will instantly know which sound is being uttered.

Therefore, one must have a series of acoustically stable sung vowels that will serve as a standard scale or measure by which the singer may compare all other sung vowels when they are produced at any pitch level or at any intensity and timbre. Such acoustically stable vowels have been designed by the author and are as follows:

1. *The Basic Vowel*—A standardized recorded vowel sound to be used as a point of phonemic reference for all singers.
2. *The Quality Alternate Vowel*—A modification of the basic vowel sung.
3. *The Pure Vowel*—An identifiable area, surrounding both the basic vowel and its quality alternate, which enables a singer to select the phoneme of his choice for any given pitch or intensity.

The Basic Vowel

The basic vowel is a sung vowel with controlled frequency and intensity that will serve as a standard scale or measure.* It results from a resonating

* The basic vowel is similar to the Daniel Jones cardinal vowel only in that it provides a specific acoustic point of reference from which vowel migration may be determined. The acoustic locations of the cardinal vowel and the basic vowel vary greatly because the extreme position of the articulator and the muscular tension present in the cardinal vowels [i], [a], and [u] are not used in forming the basic vowel. The basic vowel position was selected as a musically acceptable position that can be used by singers in all musical situations. (See p. 228.)

system coupled in a particular manner and reproducing a complex sound; when this sound is analyzed electronically, it has a standardized position on a two-dimensional formant chart (Fig. 101), determined by the frequency of the first and second formant. To identify one vowel sound from another, whether they are in sequence or in isolation, one needs only to determine the frequency of the two lowest resonance regions of the vocal spectrum (Fig. 76, p. 132).

The Formant Chart

In constructing the formant chart the migration characteristics of each vowel had to be evaluated. Considering only formant movement and disregarding formant band width and formant strength—the second formant moves twice the frequency interval for each vowel sound as does the first formant; e.g., in passing from [i] to [ɪ] the second formant moves 100 cycles while the first moves 40; from [ɪ] to [e]—the second formant, 100 cycles, the first, 45 cycles, etc. This characteristic formant movement may be observed in the back vowels as well as the frontal vowels.

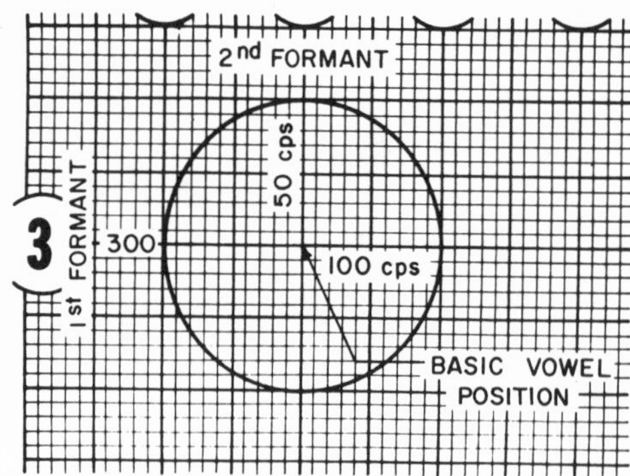

Fig. **99.** Basic Vowel Boundaries

The formant chart is, therefore, calibrated so that horizontal movement indicates twice the frequency interval as the vertical movement (Fig.99). In establishing the boundaries for the pure vowel a 100-cycle variation for the second formant and a 50-cycle variation for the first formant provided a logical area that could be displayed by means of a circle rather than an ellipse. The student finds it easier to conceive these pure vowel boundaries as a circle and to note the infringement of one phoneme upon another as sounds are sung.

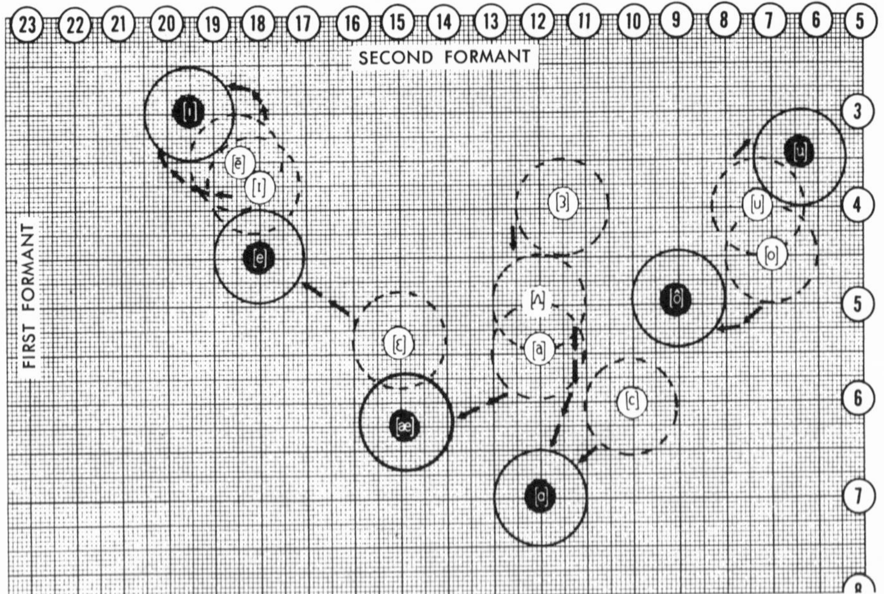

Fig. **100A.** The Basic and Quality Alternate Vowels, Male

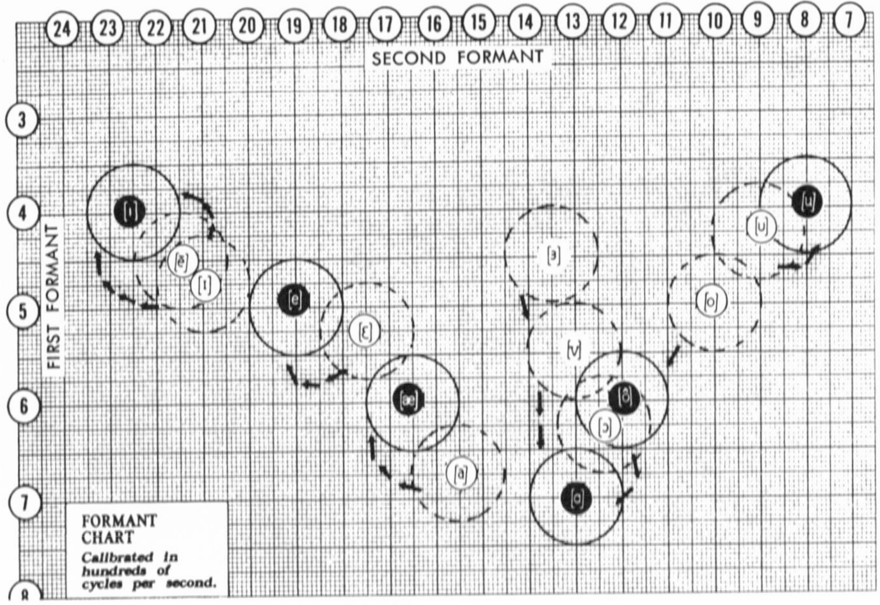

Fig. **100B.** The Basic and Quality Alternate Vowels, Female

Formant Frequencies of Basic and Quality Alternate Vowels for Males

PHONEME	FORMANT ONE	FORMANT TWO	FORMANT THREE
[i]	300	1950	2750
[ē]	350	1850	2650
[ɪ]	375	1810	2500
[e]	450	1800	2480
[ɛ]	530	1500	2500
[æ]	620	1490	2250
[a]	550	1200	2500
[ɑ]	700	1200	2600
[ɔ]	610	1000	2600
[ô]	490	900	2580
[o]	450	700	2500
[ʊ]	400	720	2500
[u]	350	640	2550
[ʌ]	500	1200	2675
[ɜ]	400	1150	2500

Formant Frequencies of Basic and Quality Alternate Vowels for Females

PHONEME	FORMANT ONE	FORMANT TWO	FORMANT THREE
[i]	400	2250	3300
[ē]	450	2125	3450
[ɪ]	475	2100	3450
[e]	500	1900	3250
[ɛ]	550	1750	3250
[æ]	600	1650	3000
[a]	675	1555	3300
[ɑ]	700	1300	3250
[ɔ]	625	1240	3250
[ô]	600	1200	3250
[o]	500	1000	3000
[ʊ]	425	900	3375
[u]	400	800	3250
[ʌ]	550	1300	3250
[ɜ]	450	1350	3050

The Quality Alternate Vowel

The quality alternate vowel is a sung phoneme in which frequency and intensity are not controlled. It requires a tongue, lip, and jaw position similar to that required by a basic vowel, and it can be easily substituted for its basic vowel in syntax.

The quality alternate vowel serves as a positive position for vowel migration, which enables a singer to preserve the integrity and meaning of the phoneme and still meet the demands of increased sonority and pitch change. For example, let us consider the migration of the basic vowel [i] to the quality alternate vowel [ɪ].

Vowel Migration. Very few teachers teach and very few singers sing the closed (tense) vowel [i] as it is phonetically recognized. The reason for this failure is that the singer is unaware that this phoneme is musically acceptable only at very low intensities (pianissimo and mezzo piano levels) and within a limited range—

Teacher and singer usually reject this phoneme on the grounds that such a vocal position develops tension of tongue and throat muscles and does not produce an aesthetically desirable sound. Most singing for performance is executed at intensities well above the mezzo piano level, where this phoneme loses its stability, and it is often sung above the pitch range in which it is recognizably stable. The necessity for the substitution, therefore, is normal and automatic.

One can readily agree that such a migration takes place. The question is how such a migration should be presented to the singer to enable him to develop a singing technique and to the prospective teacher as an implement for better teaching. Empirical evidence suggests that the singer should substitute conceptually the [ɪ] in the spelling of all words demanding the [i] phoneme, when intensity and pitch demand such a substitution. Such a migration automatically accomplishes three major physiological changes and one acoustical change:

1. A slightly lower jaw position.
2. A slightly lower tongue position.
3. A release of muscular tension in moving from a tense to a lax (closed to open) position.
4. Greater sonority for the sung phoneme.

The greatest advantage in phonemic substitution is that musical and intelligibility goals are accomplished without the student's having to imitate the teacher's sound.

When confronted with a word that demands a specific speech sound, such as *beat, sat, home,* and *soon,* the singer will be helped considerably if he will conceive a change in spelling to that of the proper quality alternate vowel. *Beat* will migrate toward [ɪ]; *sat* toward [a]; *home* toward [ʊ]; and *soon* toward [ʊ], depending upon the vocal force the singer is using or the pitch area of the sung sound.

Determining the Basic and Quality Alternate Vowels

Tests of phonemic identification in singing administered within major schools of music have provided evidence that not all vowel sounds are basic; that is, the sung sounds are not phonemically recognized for what they should be. A number of the vowels within a fifteen-phoneme series are mistaken for another vowel, while other vowels have a high frequency of recognition. The closed (tense) [ē] vowel as in *ewig,* used in German lieder, is persistently mistaken for [ɪ] and [e]. The low percentage of recognition reveals that such a phoneme is a quality alternate of [i], since it is made with a similar tongue and spread-lip position very much as the basic vowel [i] is made. The tongue remains in the same high frontal position but moves laterally. The jaw drops only slightly (See kinesiologic analysis, p. 265 and Records 1-4, Band 7).

The open (lax) vowel [e] is considered basic because of the high frequency of recognition—81 percent.* For the same reason, [æ] is considered a basic vowel. In addition [a] is considered a quality alternate of [æ] since it so frequently is mistaken for [æ] in the identification process. The percentage of error is 56.

Other phonemes having low percentages of recognition and considered to be quality alternates are [ɪ], [ɛ], [ɔ], [o], [ʊ]. Those six with high percentage of recognition and considered to be basic vowels are [i], [e], [æ], [ɑ], [ô], [u]. (For the basic vowels and their quality alternates, see Fig. 100A and 100B, p. 225.)

The singer's awareness of infringement upon a neighboring phoneme during phonation must be developed through ear-training. The student must develop an awareness of articulatory changes, particularly tongue-backing and lip-rounding.

To be useful for a singer, the position of any phoneme in relation to a basic vowel position must be judged conceptually. When the phoneme he is singing starts to migrate toward another, the singer should be aware of this occurrence and make the necessary physiological adjustments to bring the phoneme into the proper acoustical area.

The Pure Vowel

An Acoustic Definition. The pure vowel in song is determined by the pronunciation of any vowel within any linguistic environment when that vowel is sung within the stable vowel pitch range.

To determine the acoustic position of a pure vowel, one must first analyze it and place the position of its first and second formants upon a formant chart.

The pure vowel in song is a sung sound whose first and second formants are stabilized by a coupled mechanism for the duration of any note or series of notes whose second formant lies within an acoustical area 100 cycles from a basic vowel position or quality alternate position and whose first formant lies within 50 cycles from a basic vowel or quality alternate position (Fig. 101).

The theory of vowel migration is based upon the dominance of the "steady state formant structure characteristic"[4] of every sung vowel over the influence of environmental consonantal sounds as the primary cue to meaning and intelligibility. Speech sounds generally derive their cues of recognition and

* Descriptions of the test and test results are to be found in the Appendix.

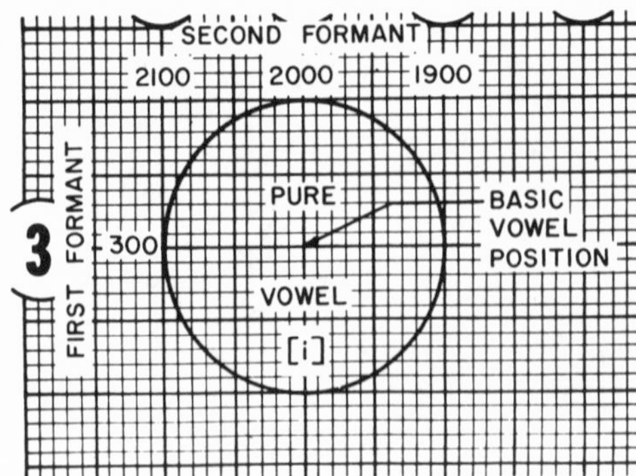

Fig. **101.** The Pure Vowel

meaning from transient, slow-moving environmental sounds which surround each vowel, where sung sounds do not. All drills and exercises are directed toward the acquisition of phonemic awareness by the singer to establish, for a brief moment, the steady state characteristics of a vowel with well-defined boundaries in its proper acoustic position.

This acoustical definition of the pure vowel, to be used only for analysis purposes, is the first of its kind for the sung vowel. Most phonetic texts accept any vowel to be a pure vowel "where the mechanism is held relatively stable in contrast to a vowel glide where movement is the essence of the sound."[5]

Thus, for phoneticians, the time or duration aspect of a vocal sound is the sole criterion of judgment in determining a pure vowel. Any variation of a phoneme could in this way be pure so long as it is relatively stable.

With the acoustic definition, the pure vowel sound need not possess duration as much as phonemic accuracy, for any deviation of more than 100 cps laterally or 50 cps vertically will be an infringement on the area of the adjacent pure vowel sound. Such infringement may be easily detected by the untrained ear.[6]

The Pure Vowel Area. The combined areas of the basic vowel and its quality alternate form the pure vowel area. Any sung phoneme which falls within this area during the production of rapidly moving speech forms will be recognized as the proper phoneme for a particular word provided the word is pronounced correctly.

A Psychological Definition of the Pure Vowel. A pure vowel sound is one which lies within the pure vowel area. It is a vowel in which the vocal mechanism is stable for the duration of any pitch and in itself is identified by the singer as the basic vowel or its quality alternate that provides the correct phoneme for the pronunciation of any word.

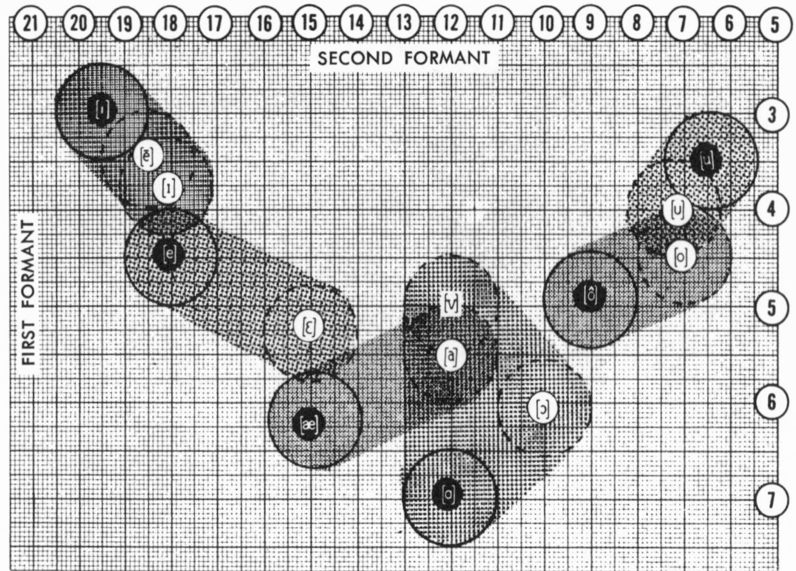

Fig. **102.** The Pure Vowel Area

When one is singing and needs to conceive a phoneme for a particular pitch or spelling of a word, the phoneme conceived should be a basic vowel that closely approximates the proper pronunciation of the word or its quality alternate. Either will be a pure vowel. In visualizing the vowel's position on a formant chart, such a pure vowel can be conceived of as a circular area with a radius of 100 cps laterally and 50 cps vertically measured from the basic vowel position, which is the center of the sung phoneme (Fig. 101).

When a sung sound has migrated away from the phoneme necessary for proper pronunciation to a position near the neutral vowel [ʌ] or an adjacent phoneme that is not the quality alternate, it is no longer a pure vowel. The integrity of the phoneme, which gives meaning, has been lost. For example, when he is singing within the stable vowel pitch range, the singer permits the word [kɔl] to migrate to [kʌl] or [kal], the integrity of the proper phoneme [ɔ] has been lost. The meaning has been changed and the vowel is no longer pure (Record 4, Band 30).

CRITERIA FOR REPRODUCING THE BASIC VOWEL

The foregoing basic acoustical phonemes help the student to become aware of the stability of each of his vowel utterances and permit him to control them at will, depending entirely upon the teacher's preference and efficient diction. These vowels have been chosen using the following criteria:

1. Each vowel must be an intelligible and a musically well-produced sound.*
2. Each vowel represents certain well-defined, physiological positions involving the tongue, labial orifice (lips), velum, mandible, and larynx, which have been determined by x-ray photographs and cinefluorography.

Tongue. To produce the basic vowel, the tip of the tongue must be placed against the bottom front teeth during production of all vowel sounds sung on pitches within the area of stability. (See "Pitch Range for All Vowel Sounds" presented below.)

Lips. In the high frontal, mid-frontal, and low frontal vowels, the lips are more spread than unrounded. In the lowback, mid-back, and highback vowels, the lips are rounded progressively more from lowback to highback positions.

Larynx. The laryngeal position is more lowered during phonation than the passive position assumed during normal breathing.

Vowel modification at various pitch levels is based on acoustical laws concerning cavity resonators and pitch. (Explanation of these laws and an application to vowel migration is found on p. 119.)

Pitch Range for All Vowel Sounds

All vowels are stable when they are sung within a very limited pitch range. When these pitches are exceeded or when the intensity increases, or when both occur together, a vowel migration occurs.

The basic vowel is stable in these pitch areas:

The top pitch range of each vowel has been determined through experimentation. For the female voice, the lower pitch range has been selected to include the chest register transition point. The transition into this area is taught as a change of mechanism, but rarely is it taught as a vowel migration. (For specific migration on these notes, see Fig. 49, p. 91.)

For the male voice, the vowel is stable on pitches lower than indicated. The lower pitches are selected as normal tessisturas for a mature male voice.

* Each vowel has been judged as to intelligibility by classes in phonetics at Indiana University and the University of Michigan, for results of testing see the Appendix, p. 401.

Obviously if these basic and quality alternate vowels are going to be used for singing, the student must know them so well that he can identify and sing each one with accuracy. The best way to do this is to imitate the vowel as it is reproduced from a record. Experiments have proven that this method of imitating physiological adjustment and vowel identification is highly reliable.[7] Once the basic vowels for singing have been learned, the work of comparing them can begin, and this procedure is invaluable for identifying and describing vowel sounds as they are sung in foreign languages. This method may also be used with equal success in the examination of variant pronunciations in English.

The teacher and the student must remember that these stable vowel points are in no way intended to be preferred centers of vocal utterance. They do provide an acoustical location which is the exact center of that phoneme for a sung tone. The teacher may prefer a warmer, darker sound for that particular phoneme than the basic vowel sound and may demonstrate it for the student to follow. For example, as the student sings *father* with a very frontal [ɑ], the teacher preferring a darker sound would suggest that the student sing the next low, back phoneme [ɔ] as in *all,* and the result would be *fawther*. If the central phoneme [ʌ] as in *up* is suggested, the resulting word would be *futher*. The trick is to modify the vowel without migrating too far from the basic vowel position. To fulfill the teacher's directive, the student need only lower the jaw and thus increase the vertical dimension of the oral cavity. The lip position must be unrounded and the laryngeal position firmly stabilized. Such acute vowel recognition requires a well-trained ear.

Matching the Timbre of Recorded Sound

To set an arbitrary acoustic standard for a specific phoneme is not difficult; however, it is very difficult, but not impossible, to suggest a standard for timbre.

One must remember that what a singer hears as a change in vowel color is actually a migration of the phoneme.

Phoneme and timbre (vowel sound and voice quality) are not synonymous, yet, in the singing process, the direction of the singer's thought toward one will affect the other. If the singer concentrates upon timbre he impairs the integrity of the vowel. If he concentrates upon the phoneme he enhances the timbre.

In reproducing the vowel sounds recorded here, matching the timbre should not be considered the major vocal objective for the following reasons:
1. When singers of any voice classification imitate the recorded examples of

the basic vowels or their quality alternates, it is possible for each voice to reproduce phonemes within the same acoustic area but with different timbre.

2. Timbre may be imitated by the employment of several combinations of breath pressure and laryngeal controls within a similar resonating system; i.e., two voices of the same classification, sonority, and tessitura can match timbre by using different techniques. (See "Vocal Pedagogy and Laryngeal Controls," p. 102.)

However, primary positions of resonation and articulation directly affect the migration of each phoneme, and if the positions of the resonators and articulators are duplicated when matching the recorded sound, the timbre will be more similar than if such controls are disregarded.

In the production of the basic vowels and their quality alternates, preserving the integrity of the phoneme involves only the controlled positioning of the articulators (tongue, lips, mandible, and the resonators, oral and pharyngeal cavities). To increase the intensity of the sound (vocal force), thought is always directed toward the control of the resonators and articulators and not toward the control of the timbre. Variations of the breath pressure will affect both vowel and timbre, but in this volume, the author can only assume that proper breathing techniques are employed that will result in a balanced effort in effecting each sound. ("Laryngeal Action and Pitch Change," p. 101.)

To summarize, in imitating the basic vowel and quality alternates from recorded sound, matching the timbre is accomplished by concentrating upon the phoneme and disregarding the timbre. If the recorded phoneme is matched, the quality or timbre of the vowel will be more nearly similar within each pitch range and intensity variation. In this instance phonemic aspects of the word are conceived before quality. Quality thus becomes a result of and not the cause of the vocalic utterance.

Vowel Migration Above the Stable Pitch Range

When singing a pitch that skips into the area above the stable vowel pitch range (Fig. 103, p. 234) or in singing a sustained sound that stays above the stable vowel pitch range, vowel migration is necessary to preserve an even scale and phonemic identity.

The frontal vowels will migrate downward to the phoneme directly below them (Fig. 103) with the exception of the quality alternate [I]. This vowel is stable in all voices to top space E, treble staff, except for the bass voice in which [ē] is stable to D and [ɪ] is stable to F above the bass staff.

For the central and back vowels [ɑ] and [ɔ] the migration is always toward the neutral vowel [ʌ]; the [ô] and [o] will migrate toward the quality alternate [ʊ], which remains stable throughout the vocal range; only at extreme levels of intensity does [ʊ] migrate to [ʌ].

The Migration Chart (Fig. 103) serves as a guide for teaching transitions into the upper voice and brings to the student greater intelligibility and ease

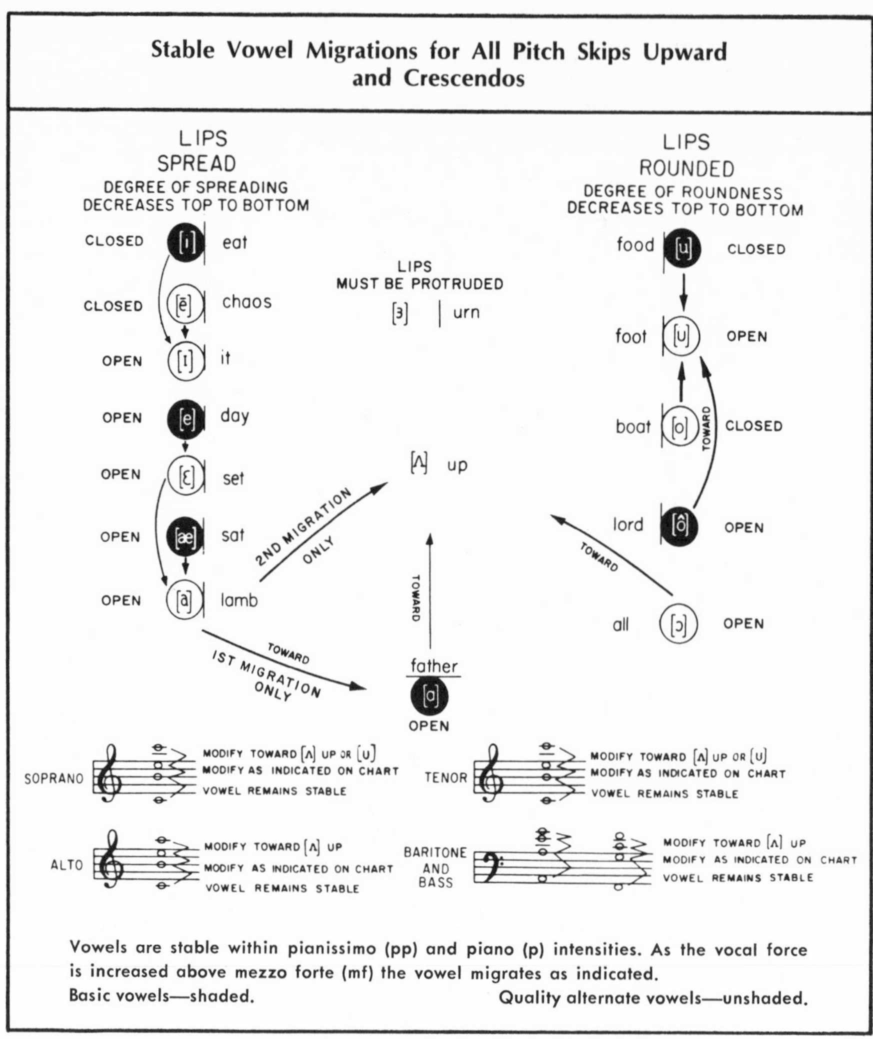

Fig. **103.** Vowel Migration Chart

of production, provided breath support is constant. Specific information for each vowel and its migration within the entire singing range is given in Chapter Ten.

Extreme Lip Positions

In speech, unstressing is an outstanding phenomenon of Germanic languages, and especially of English. In English the vowel of any unaccented syllable tends to be reduced to either [ɪ] or [ə], i.e., *city* [sɪtɪ] and *reject* [rɪdʒɛkt], or *open* [opən] and *Cuba* [kjubə].

In singing, most vowels and consonants are formed with much more vitalized muscular tonus in lips, mouth, and tongue than in speech. This vitality must be present in passages sung piano as well as in those sung forte. Relaxation of the articulatory musculature causes vowels to migrate toward either [ɪ] or [ə] and the integrity of the phoneme suffers. For example, sing *was* [wɑz] instead of [wʌz], *don't* [dont] instead of [dʌnt], also *event* [ivɛnt] instead of [ɪvɛnt].

Fig. 104 illustrates the ever present tendency of vowels to migrate toward schwa when lip tension is lost.

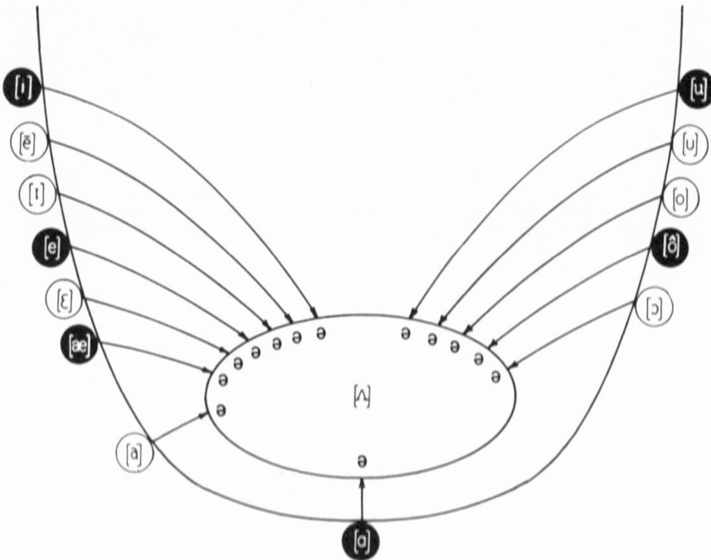

Fig. **104.** If the Vowel Posture is Lethargic or if Lip Tension Is Not Maintained, the Vowel Tends to Migrate Toward Schwa

In singing pitches above the staff, the schwa is approached, yet never completely embraced. The characteristic lip position of the phoneme being uttered must be maintained to preserve the phonemic qualities of the vowel.

A pedagogy which advocates immobility or relaxation of the articulators for reasons aesthetic or musical thrwarts textual intelligibility and presents the singer with problems of both range and flexibility of vocal utterance.

Proper pronunciation, which involves the choice of phoneme and stress, will preserve linguistic characteristics.

Point, Projection, and Focus

In singing, point, projection, and focus are related directly to the approximation of the vocal utterance to the basic vowel or quality alternate position. Any sung sound that migrates too far toward the neutral vowel when sung within the stable vowel pitch range will lose all three of these qualities. In this regard, the proper lip-spreading and lip-rounding, mandibular position, and tongue position must be observed to maintain maximum point, projection, and focus within this pitch range. This rule also applies to the first migration pitch range. The singer must permit the frontal phonemes to migrate toward the suggested phoneme below, but he must avoid phonemic migration to the neutral vowel. For the central and back vowels, where the normal migration is toward the neutral vowel [ʌ] or [ʊ], the singer should attempt to move toward but not to the [ʌ] or [ʊ] and to preserve the integrity of the phonemes as much as possible. In the upper range when the neutral vowel is embraced, slight lip-rounding will, in most cases, bring the sung sound into focus and increase the projection or carrying power of the phoneme.

Sung sounds that tend to migrate toward the schwa or neutral vowel may seem to possess more depth or to be more unctious to the singer or listener when sung within a small hall or room. In a large hall, the sung sound loses its depth, sonority, and volume, and intelligibility suffers.

RULES OF DICTION AND THE BASIC VOWEL THEORY

Diction is a complex word. It embodies the following:

1. Pronunciation considers the task of utterance with regard to the phoneme and stress; meaning depends upon pronunciation.
2. Enunciation considers the utterance of each word with regard to fullness, clearness, and sonority. This concept involves the vocal force that energizes speech in song.

3. Articulation considers the action of the speech organs in forming the vowels and consonants. Without articulation, pronunciation and enunciation cannot be realized.

Spatial Problems

With textual intelligibility as the major objective, this basic vowel theory rests upon the premise that good diction imposes two rules on singers; both involve phonemic accuracy, audience proximity, instrumental masking, and the size of the auditorium.

The First Rule. If the auditorium is large and the distance from the stage to the total audience is great, the singer's first consideration must be to sing in the exact center of the basic vowel or within the pure vowel area, and to give the vowel its greatest possible duration in note value. His second consideration must be to overstress his consonants by giving them longer duration.

When instrumental accompaniment masks the vocal sound as in opera or oratorio, the singer uses greater vocal force in all pitch ranges, thus making the previously described articulatory exaggeration mandatory; for as the vocal force increases, the dimensions of the vocal resonators also increase, forcing the singer to seek phonemic accuracy for greater intelligibility.

The Second Rule. The singer's primary concern, if the auditorium is not large or if a microphone is to be used, is to sing near the basic vowel or within the pure vowel area, and to give the vowel its proper duration in note value—just as he would do in a large auditorium. In the small auditorium, however, the consonants must be normal and not overstressed.

The Consonant and Legato Singing

Clear enunciation of the consonant is essential to the intelligibility of the sung word, and great care must be taken so that the formation of the consonants does not interfere with the proper resonation of each phoneme in a manner that would destroy the vocal line.

Psychological imagery has often been used in the teaching of consonants to assure a definitive action of the articulators. One such illustration by the teacher is that the interruption of the vocalized sound by the articulators while forming the consonants should be similar to the act of quickly passing a knife through a column of water extending from faucet to sink. The water column, representing the vocal line, has not lost its cylindrical contour by the interruption of the knife blade, but consonants formed in this manner are much too brief. Rapid articulation of the consonants is not the goal of good diction and such an illustration is very misleading. The maintenance of a legato line depends upon a rapid movement from one vowel position, through the consonant to the following vowel in such a manner that neither vowel is affected by the consonantal articulation. The consonant must have enough duration to possess undeniable entity in the vocal line. It must complement the vowel, but although it is of shorter duration, it must never be of lesser importance than the sustained sound. To move rapidly and accurately from vowel to consonant to vowel, always within the rhythmic framework, demands flexibility of jaw, lips, mouth, and tongue. This positive action must occur slightly before each beat point to permit the vowel to sound on the beat; therefore, every consonant must be slightly anticipated by a proper preparation of the articulators. The major mistake in forming consonants is that the mouth, lips, and tongue are not sufficiently supple to provide timing of mouth, tongue, and jaw movements for each successive sound. The total effort often is not synchronized and coordinated muscularly.

In viewing the x-ray studies of the consonants the reader will notice the dramatic change that occurs in the total resonating system particularly within the laryngeal area. The larynx is thrust violently forward and upward in producing the voiced continuants and must recover its stability for any vowel which follows. Such interruption and recovery of the phonatory mechanism is a most constant and complicated process. However, in artistic singing this articulatory act has been molded into an artistic unity through vocal discipline.

To instruct a singer to articulate his consonants rapidly may discourage the singer from placing sufficient emphasis on the consonants to make them audible and may prevent the singer from using them intelligently for dramatic effect.

The vowel provides the emotional warmth to the sung sound but the consonant provides the eloquence of singing style. This fact is particularly important in a consideration of stress within a word or phrase. For when consonant and vowel are properly stressed and unified, a word becomes alive and persuasive.

The Use of Consonants in Opera

All consonants may be used to intensify the words in dramatic situations, but some are more difficult to control than others. Exaggeration of voicing in the voiced continuants and increasing the duration of the friction sounds of those that are unvoiced becomes one of the most important factors in the dramatic use of consonants where instrumental masking is employed. The voiced sounds are more dominant than the unvoiced, and the dramatic nature of the plosives is expressed in their plosive release. The voiced plosives are extremely useful in creating dramatic effects.

Complete understanding of the function of each consonant and the pressures and tensions of the lips, tongue, and mouth necessary to produce them are most essential to the singer if he is to successfully master articulation.

COMMUNICATION PROBLEMS

Fig. 105A and 105B indicates the area of variation of each of the basic vowels and their quality alternates with the exception of open basic [ô] as they are used during normal communication in speech.

> In conversational speech, each vowel may vary 250 to 500 cycles from its normally used center and will be understood. The child's voice and the extremely high-pitched voice will have higher first and second formants, which will cause the vowel to appear to the left of the dot that indicates normal clustering of that particular phoneme. The female voice, also having high formants, will appear more often to the left of the dot than to the right. The male voice and lower-pitched female voices will appear around the clustering dot.[8]

Despite the extreme variation of phonemic utterance in speech as indicated by Fig. 105A, textual intelligibility is achieved. This is largely due to the speaker's tendency to repeat each phoneme occurring within the same "linguistic environment"* with the same articulatory positions.

"As a rule, the more consistently a phoneme is pronounced within a particular linguistic environment the greater the intelligibility."[9] Such intelligibility also has social causes and when the lax phonemic demands of speech are compared with the specific phonemic demands of song, the reasons for discipline within singing become self-evident (See Fig. 105A and 105B.)

In ordinary conversation phonemic accuracy is not demanded because:

1. Each speaker speaks the same dialect.
2. The speaker is close to his listener and does not have a spatial problem; vocal force is kept at a low level.
3. Both persons have an awareness of and an interest in the subject being communicated.

* Linguistic environment is a term used to identify similarity of phonemic usage in pronunciation, i.e., if *e*, preceded by *b* and followed by *t* is always pronounced [bit] (beet); the environment is considered to be similar. This rule applies to all phonemes.

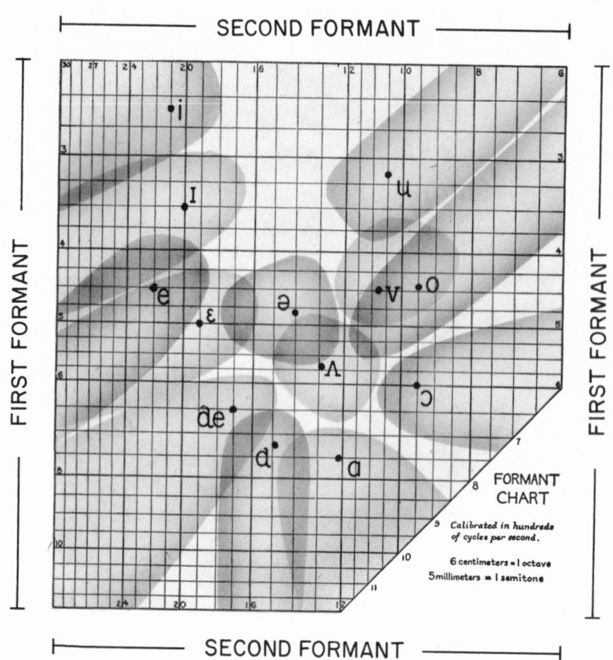

Fig. **105A.** Formant Averages for Vowels in Speech

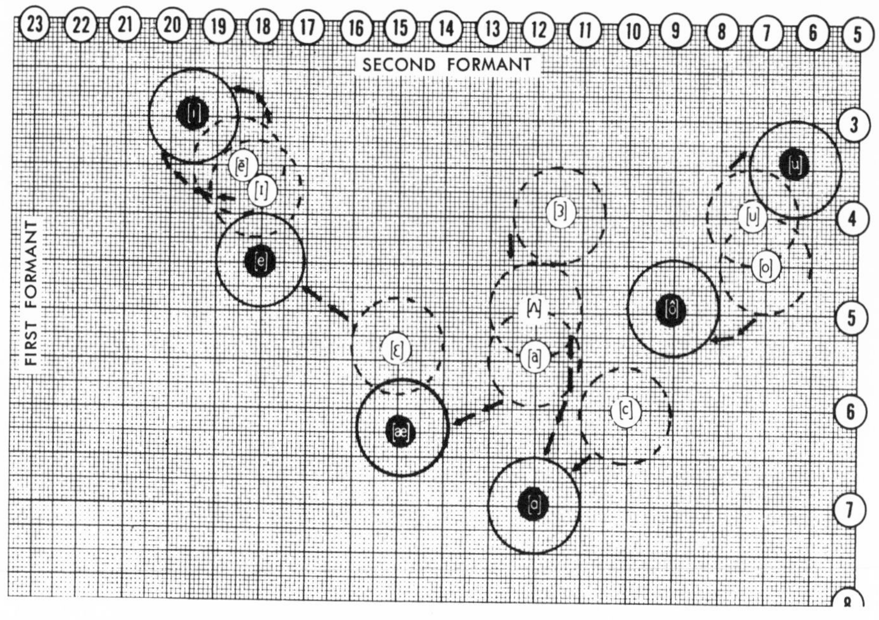

Fig. **105B.** Basic and Quality Alternate Vowels in Singing

4. The attention of each person is focused upon content and not upon the quality of the spoken word.

In singing, phonemic accuracy is demanded because:

1. The amount of space between audience and performer varies; in addition, instrumental masking may also be used.
2. The singer conveys unfamiliar textual material to the listener; often it is poetry with strange vocabulary and word order.
3. The singer encounters articulation problems while singing flowing, connected sounds. In these instances he is most likely to place the sound ahead of the word in vocal importance. Singers strive to sound well at all times, and intelligibility tends to be forgotten. In such instances he should sing the phoneme within the pure vowel area and stress consonants. Such stress will not disrupt the legato line. This fact is difficult to teach to one who has not had stage experience.
4. The singer faces problems pertaining to the duration of the vowel sound, pitch, rhythm, and stress.
5. The singer must shape the oral and pharyngeal cavities into larger molds and hold them in position much longer in song than in speech.
6. The singer must exaggerate the textual lines through physical deportment. His face and body must reveal interest that can be seen by the audience in order to avoid an impression of lethargy and to provide the text with animation and buoyancy. These personality factors are singers' tools that greatly aid intelligibility in song.

Phonetic Instability. A singer cannot possibly repeat any vowel sound exactly as he first stated it; no matter how hard he tries, infinitesimal variation will occur. Thus, as in cases of dialectical differences, hearing plays a major part in the development of dialect, for the speaker will always follow the line of least resistance and control his phonatory muscles to conform to his environmental pressures. He will tend to speak and sing what he hears.

The influence of neighboring sounds upon both vowel and consonant causes a variation in a singer's diction. The sound may be of long or of short duration. As an example, consider the phoneme [t]. When one pronounces the words *but, bit, bent,* or *best,* everyone recognizes the final letter *t,* but few singers realize that each one is produced with a slightly different tongue position.

When one pronounces the phoneme [ɑ] as in *bar* [bɑr], *father* [fɑðə], *nat* or *fine* [fɑɪn], the variation in tongue position causes an alteration in the spectrum although the phoneme may seem to be the same.

Once the singer confronts a vocal pattern involving pitch changes and duration, alterations of the mechanism are made that affect this consonant or vowel, alterations too numerous to mention here. However, a fundamental movement for the [t] or the [ɑ] always remains the same and permits the observer to recognize the meaning of the word.

Because of this tendency for phonemic variation in singing the student should think of each sung sound as some specific phonetic symbol. In doing so, he will soon become skilled in forming the lip, tongue, and jaw positions that are necessary to produce such specific phonemes. In developing this awareness, he will also create concepts of the acoustic qualities of the sung sound and the manner in which it differs from the speech sound as he sees it upon the printed page.

This conceptual transition from printed symbol to the sung sound is a task from which the singer will never free himself. No vocal technique becomes so perfect that the performer no longer needs to plan or predesign his vocal utterance through thoughtful observance of and respect for that physiological adjustment which will yield the most accurate phoneme possible for any particular word within the vocal text.

The word is not more important than the sound, nor is the sound more important than the word. However, a vast difference exists between speech techniques for communication and speech techniques for singing. Problems of vowel production encountered by singers are not encountered in communicative speech.

DICTION PROBLEMS IN SINGING FLOWING TEXT

While diction involves the analysis of the physiological position of single speech sounds, one cannot overlook the fact that speech in song is continuous and generally flows smoothly. The muscular process is coordinated in such a manner that, despite problems of duration and pitch, one sound is linked to another. This act is consummated by the expert singer with an economy of articulatory movement and vocal force; however, an overwhelming majority of singers do not fulfill this ideal. The problem is obvious when one considers the difference between the tasks of speech and of song.

The average speech rate is about 250 words a minute with a continuous vocal flow blended into numerous vowels and consonants. Speech in song is much slower, sometimes 50 words a minute. Time signature, tempo, and, most of all, duration of the notes compel the singer to sustain a muscular position for the phoneme for several beats before he can consider the next phoneme. Theoretically, this process should make the singer's text intelligible, but usually this is not the case. He often is instructed to link all words in continuous sound and to smooth out pitch skips into a rounded line, but, until he can see each phoneme separately in his thinking, he will be faced with diction problems.

In all artistic utterances articulatory lethargy tends to encumber speech. E. L. Stevens describes the problem as follows:

> In general, the actualization of a given phoneme as an acoustic signal is achieved through a given set of instructions to the speech mechanism, including the larynx and the various structures above the larynx. When instructions for a particular phoneme are given, the mechanical response of the muscles and the structures to which they are attached is not immediate and a certain time elapses before the structures are displaced to positions appropriate to the phoneme. If instruction for a sequence of phonemes are given in rapid succession, the structures spend most of the time in transit from one position to another and frequently do not achieve configurations corresponding to one phoneme before they begin to maneuver toward positions appropriate to the next phoneme. Superimposed upon the rapidly changing instructions to the articulatory structures are somewhat slower commands to the musculature that controls the breath stream and supplies the steady air pressure that is modulated by the perypheral structures. . . . As a consequence of the smooth and continuous motion of the articulatory mechanism, sharp boundaries marking changes from one phoneme to another are not observable in the speech wave.[10]

This statement by Stevens emphasizes the tendency toward phonemic lethargy in song. A basic rule of diction is that the integrity of the phoneme must be considered constantly throughout the vocal scale. Analyzing the movements of continuous speech is impossible, but one can examine the sung phoneme in isolation, for the basic concept of this book is that each phoneme must be conceived separately.

In flowing speech singers tend to approach the phonemes promiscuously and to neglect to approximate them—

However, each phoneme should be conceived separately and lifted out of its contextual environment—

A list of problems encountered in singing flowing speech follows:

1. The singer's attention is directed more to the sound than to the words.
2. Unless the singer has mastered respiration and phonation problems related to the support of the tone through various pitch skips upward, he is constantly plagued with the question, "Am I singing correctly?" It is an inherent trait among all singers to want to "above all, sound well."
3. The singer's attention is directed to pressures and tension throughout his body during the changes of pitch. He is often told that these changes of pitch must be sung without tensions and pressures, and he will often sing a phoneme remotely related to that demanded by the text because it feels easier. The singer must learn that the words *pressure* and *tension* are not synonymous; that many vowels on high pitches demand pressures to sustain both pitch and vowel form; that tensions in the production of vowels, although often present with pressure, will disappear to a degree (but never altogether) when forces of respiration and phonation and articulation are properly balanced.

When rhythmic problems are added to the flowing speech, phonemes tend to be only approximated—

Mausfellen Sprüchlein
Hugo Wolf
MEINE AL–TE KA–TZE
TANZT WAHRSCHEINLICH MIT, HÖRST DU?

When singing such songs as *Mausfallen Sprüchlein*, each singer must give duration, be it ever so slight, to the home base position of each vowel. Such action may be conceived as overarticulation by many teachers, but the rewards to the singer in intelligibility are great. The articulatory organs cannot be held in an absolutely fixed or rigid position during phonation. Numerous imperceptible movements always occur in the speech mechanism; they are uncontrollable and cause slight but discernible changes in the vocalic sound.

Even so, singing is at its best when the singer conceives of the vowel sound in flowing speech as a series of rectangular sections linked together by consonantal break points. This concept is a most important one in achieving good diction in song.

The singer gives maximum sound to the pure vowel utterance by locking the mandible, tongue, and pharyngeal area into place for the duration of the pitch. Such a system assists him in reaching his goal of maximum sound for every word that he sings.

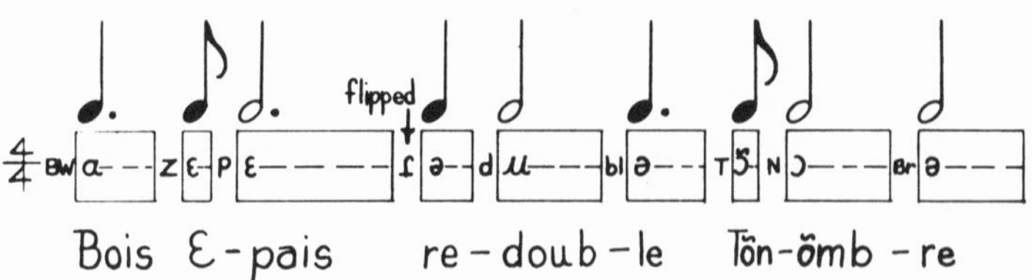

Fig. **106.** The Singer Should Conceive Each Vowel in the Vocal Line as a Rectangular Area

Since vowels are parts of words, each vowel sound is approached and followed by a different sound. The inexperienced singer tends to conceive of his vowels as a series of elliptical sections instead of rectangular sections.

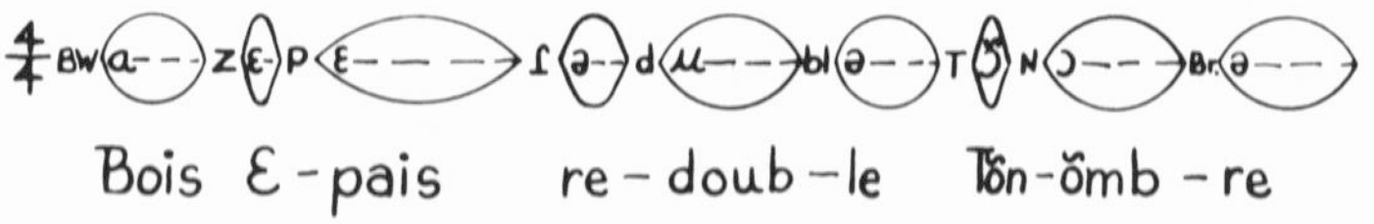

Bois Ɛ-pais re-doub-le Tõn-õmb-re

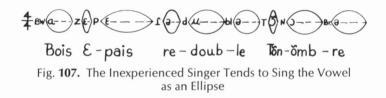

Fig. **107.** The Inexperienced Singer Tends to Sing the Vowel as an Ellipse

In such undisciplined singing, the pure vowel area is approximated and has an extremely short duration at the point of maximum sound. It is always coming from one sound and going to another.

The environment (or consonants that surround a vowel) previously described, is the cause for the vocal fault. The elliptical shape is indicative of the intervowel glides or dipthongs, *ai, oi, iu.*

Vowel Size and Auditory Feed Back

The concept of "vowel size" as described by Rose[11] brings to the student a recognizable sensation which he must learn to associate with a proper breath pressure ratio. The term suggests an enfoldment of an imagined specific area by the oral cavity. The resulting lowered jaw position gives the singer a new sensation of vowel recognition as it is instantaneously fused with tonal sonority through his ability to hear the sound and feel the stretched position of the articulators as he applies the pressure of breath.

Every singer must eventually create for himself a sensation table of "vowel size" involving vowel recognition, articulatory position, and breath pressure for every type of sound he wishes to sing. This sensation table is usually acquired through the singer's experience in singing specific passages within song literature, for every mood that the singer interprets demands an open or a closed vowel, sung piano or forte, and these choices change as each pitch is raised and each intensity varied.

In the very early stages of training, the singer is reluctant to accept a large vowel size because his enlarged resonating system and his inability to control the breath pressure create a sound which sounds extremely loud to him and since he is only aware of the sensation of producing such a vowel at the speech level of normal communication he fails to fuse the auditory-articulatory sensation and does not open his mouth.

At this point the teacher should reinforce the preferred concept by using the term *vowel size* rather than the directives: lower the jaw, sing louder; sing more darkly, etc.

Physical Problems and Diction

The physical problems of respiration, phonation, resonance, and articulation are usually presented in that order by most voice teachers. Logically, diction problems would be the final consideration of the teacher in teaching a song to a student. In singing a phoneme, however, all singers ultimately synthesize the resonance and diction aspects into a unity. The twofold aspect of singing—as a unity and also as a sum of parts—requires that one learn the phonemes first. For example, one can learn to write fluently by first learning letters; one can learn to dance rhythmically and harmoniously, as though the body were in constant unified flux, although one learns single steps one at a time. Instead of thinking of lowering the larynx, opening the mouth, rounding the lips, and placing the tongue forward, the experienced singer would unify these separate acts into a composite pattern; the resulting sound will become his hallmark, and he will always be judged by this particular vocalic quality.

This chapter can not serve as a directive in how to unify and coordinate the sensations respiration, phonation, resonation, and articulation, it provides only a point of departure for the phoneme in the basic vowels; therefore, it shall not linger on the problems of presenting the numerous parts which form the gestalt or whole pattern of each of the above mentioned forces in singing. It is sufficient to point out the impossibility of avoiding positions and movements of the lips, tongue, mandible and size of oral and pharyngeal opening (vowel size) when one attempts to imitate the basic vowel. The best procedure is for students to synthesize the movements of these parts as they listen.

The basic vowel will find its greatest acceptance in the teacher training institutions, which need to teach young singers how to impart their singing skill to another potential singer, or to teach young singers how to teach others to teach. Psychological teaching is tolerated where learning how to sing is terminal and where there is little concern for the manner in which a teacher may direct a student to produce a tone. The student may be told to place a tone at the forehead, the top of the head, or the front teeth. Any of these positions provides a point of reference by which the student focuses his attention and remembers his sensation during the production of the sound so that he reproduces it to the teacher's satisfaction. This student may develop into a fine singer with such a method, but to impart such information to a potential teacher is to thwart his development into an educator who knows the proven physiological and acoustical reasons for the sound's existence and who can produce any of the sounds repeatedly.

Good diction is forever bound to singing style and personality. These last two qualities are often endowed characteristics and cannot be taught convincingly. However, the mechanism of diction and phonation can always be analyzed and directives can be given to the student which will enable him to produce a tone that may be evaluated and reproduced by all teachers. This is as far as science dares to go, for style and personality are aesthetic elements that give song its wings. From this point on the teacher's directives are at their very best.

Chapter 10

Kinesiologic Analysis of Speech Sounds in Singing

THE CARDINAL VOWELS

In 1918 Daniel Jones published his significant work, *An Outline of English Phonetics,* in which he devised a standard set of vowels to be used as points of reference for all phonetic transcription. These vowels are unlike the vowels of any language and are somewhat evenly spaced acoustically (Fig. 108). They have as their physiological basis specific tongue positions. Only the vowels at each corner of the diagram can rightly be called cardinal, however, for only these have specific tongue positions that assure accurate reproduction.[1]

The [i] is made with the tongue as high and as far front as possible without interrupting the sound, the [a] is made with the tongue as low and as far front as possible, the [ɑ] is made with the tongue as low and as far back as possible, and the [u] is made with the tongue as high and as far back as possible.

The remaining four vowels termed cardinal—[e], [ɛ], [ɔ], and [o]—are made by accurately moving the tongue. For the frontal vowels, the tongue is moved downward one third of the vertical distance from the frontal [i] position toward [a] to obtain the vowel [e], two thirds of the vertical distance from [i] to [a] to obtain the vowel [ɛ]. For the back vowels, the tongue is moved downward one third of the vertical distance from the high back [u] to [ɑ] to produce [o], two thirds of the vertical distance downward toward [ɑ] to produce [ɔ]. To reproduce these vowels requires practice in imitating each vowel sound from a record as they are recorded by Jones.[2] Anyone using these vowels must depend upon the ear for careful discrimination of [e], [ɛ], [ɔ], and [o], in which the tongue positions guide the speaker to the cardinal [i], [a], [ɑ], and [u].

The cardinal vowels are theoretic vowels, and the concept of specific tongue positions as well as specific acoustical points have long proved valuable as teaching tools since the mental image of the tongue position has to be corrected in practice by the ear. They are also indispensable as reference points in examining dialects and in organizing unwritten tribal sounds into a written

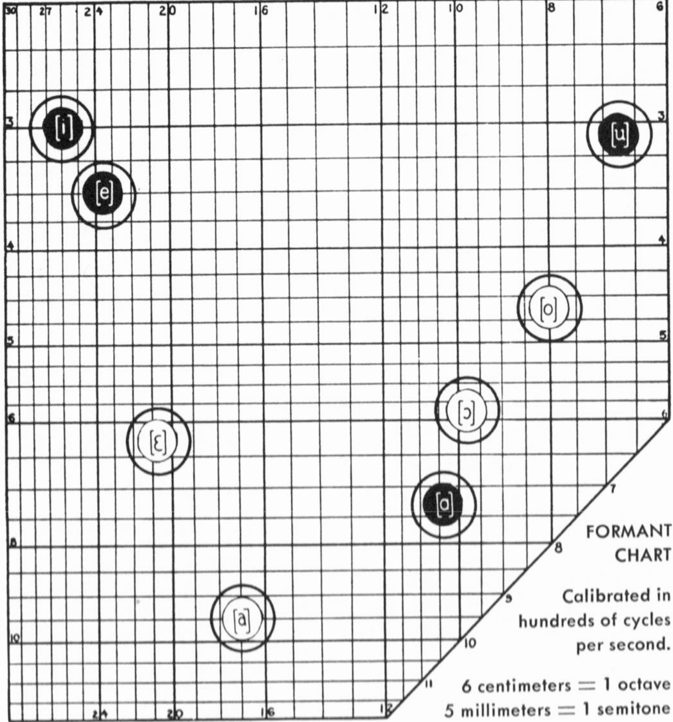

Fig. **108.** The Cardinal Vowels

Spectrograms of the cardinal vowels as recorded by Daniel Jones reveal their acoustical positions as shown in the above chart. Although Dr. Jones suggests that they are equidistant acoustically, analysis does not prove this to be true.

language. Fig. 109 is a vowel diagram used by Jones[3] in showing the acoustic position of English vowels in relation to the Jones cardinal vowels.

The cardinal vowels could be used as a basis for the sung vowel but for two reasons:

1. They are not musically acceptable as a model for imitation by students as a properly produced vocalic sound.
2. They are based upon tongue and jaw positions designed for speech sounds and do not have the cavity adjustment necessary for an acceptable sung sound.

The basic vowels and their quality alternate vowels are conceptually similar to the Jones cardinal vowels. It is hoped that the basic vowels will prove to be as useful a teaching tool for singing as the Jones vowels have proved to be for speech.

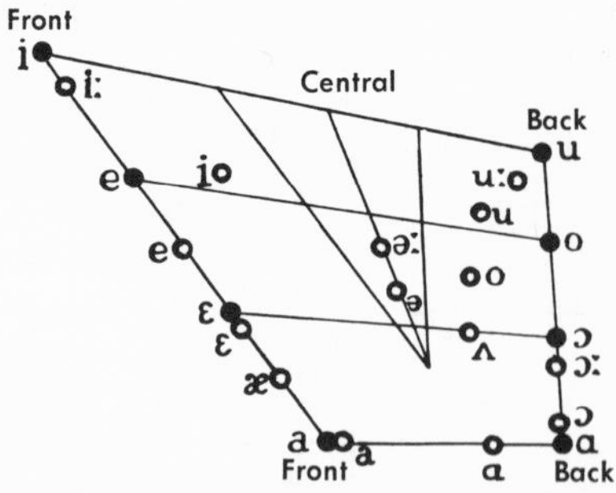

Fig. **109.** Diagram Illustrating English Vowels

The tongue position of the English Vowels compared with those of the cardinal vowels. (The circles indicate the position of the highest point of the tongue; cardinal vowels are black, English vowels, an open circle.) Source: Daniel Jones, *An English Pronouncing Dictionary* (New York: E. P. Dutton Co., 1926).

METHODS FOR EXAMINING THE WORD IN SONG

Vowels and consonants may be identified in the singing tone by three methods—acoustic, position, and movement.

Acoustic Method

The acoustic method of identifying words considers the manner in which the speech sound is heard and describes the vowel in such auditory terms as high pitch, low pitch; stressed, unstressed; long, short; weak or strong.

Speech sounds possess a quality interpreted as tones or noises. Vowels are considered tonal because their spectra consist of regular vibrations; consonants are considered noises because their spectra consist of irregular vibrations. Vowels also possess a degree of sonority that enables us to identify them and use them in a musical situation. The most sonorous vowel is the vowel [ɑ], which has an uninterrupted flow of sound through the resonating system. As lip-rounding is used to produce the back vowels [ɔ], [o], and [u], and lip-spreading is used to produce the frontal vowels [æ], [e], and [i], thereby, the sonority is decreased.

Some consonants—such as the nasals [m], [n], and [ŋ]; the glides [w] and [r]; and the liquid [l]—possess a degree of sonority. The degree of interruption of the sound is obvious. Other consonants are considered to be noise; they are voiced and unvoiced. Their names imply the degree of friction employed in their production by lips, tongue, or velum. They are fricatives such as [f], [θ], and [ʃ]; affricates such as [ts] and [dʒ]; plosives such as [p], [t], and [k]; and nasals such as [n], [l], and [ŋ].

In singing, the noises and tones of speech sounds are super-imposed upon a pitch pattern that affects not only the efficient musical production of the sound and its meaning, but also its sonority and its intelligibility.

Analysis by Position

This method considers all speech sounds in song by position of the articulatory mechanism at the time of phonation. Such a study involves a knowledge of anatomy to determine the structure of the speech mechanism and its function in making a particular sound.

For many years phonetics has been based upon the position of the tongue during phonation. Such terms as frontal, back, and central apply to both the tongue position and to the group of vowels (Fig. 110).

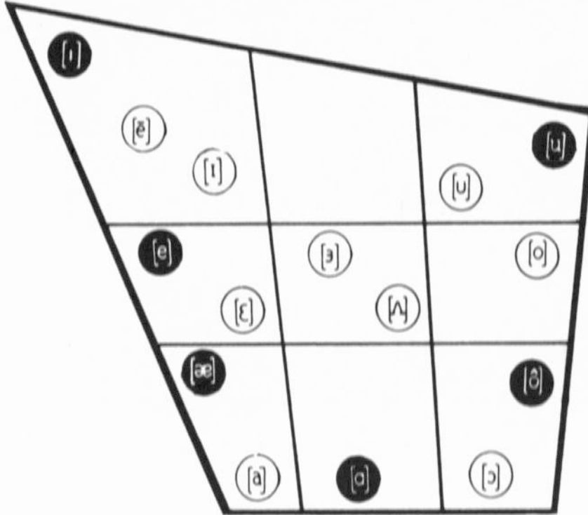

Fig. **110.** Vowel Diagram

For consonants, the terms bilabial, labial-dental, dental, alveolar, retroflex, uvular, pharyngeal, glottal, and so forth are used to indicate positions of the tongue and lips during articulation.

Analysis by Movement

This method considers the movements that are necessary to arrive at a particular speech sound. Continuant, stop, and glide are typical terms. The analysis of intervowel glides and sounds in combination within communicative speech where duration of each sound is slight is a useful approach.

SYNTHESIS OF TWO METHODS OF ANALYSIS

In this volume the acoustic, the position, and the movement methods are combined in analyzing and describing illustrative materials. Physiological terminology is used as indicated in Fig. 111 and in the listings of terms beginning on page 253. The meaning of acoustic terms used is self-evident. For example, if the phoneme [k] is identified as voiceless, lingua-velar, and stop plosive, the identification has simply described the manner in which the consonant is made:

1. Voiceless—in that there is no laryngeal vibration, only frictional sound (acoustic approach).
2. Lingua-velar—because the dorsum of the tongue makes contact at the velar ridge (position approach).
3. Stop plosive—because escaping air, suddenly released, causes a plosive sound (acoustic approach).

If the phoneme [ʒ] is identified as a voiced, linguapalatal, fricative, continuant, the manner in which the sound is made has been described:

1. Voiced—because the vocal folds are vibrating.
2. Linguapalatal—because the tip of the togue makes contact with the prepalatal area at the alveolar ridge.
3. Fricative—because identification of the sound depends upon its friction characteristics.
4. Continuant—because the sound is not interrupted but maintains its identity for the duration of the utterance.

In the following kinesiologic analysis each phoneme will be identified by type. This term indicates the positions of the articulators. Vowels will be identified by the positions of the tongue, the degree of jaw opening, and the position of the lips; e.g., the basic vowel [i] would be listed as high front, close, spread, and the rounded frontal vowel [œ] as mid-front, half-open, rounded.

Consonants

Since consonants are interruptions of the vowels at points of stricture in the phonatory tract, they are identified by absence or presence of laryngeal vibration, by point of stricture, and by duration. For example, the consonant [x] (German, in *Bach*) would be voiceless, linguaposterior, palatal, continuant, fricative, and the consonant [g] would be voiced, lingua-velar, stop plosive.

The use of such terminology by both students and teachers provides a means of reaching understanding with the greatest economy. These terms also tend to make directives more physiological than psychological, which is the aim of this book. (See Table II, p. 254.)

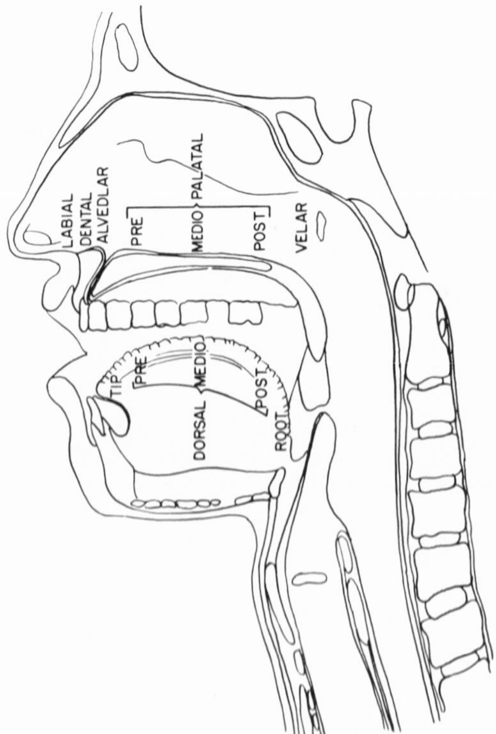

Fig. **111.** Physical Geography of the Speech Mechanism

TERMS PERTAINING TO THE PARTS OF THE SPEECH MECHANISM

alveolar ridge—The upper or lower gum ridge.

dental—Pertaining to the teeth.

glottis—Space between the vocal folds.

glottal stroke—When the vocal folds are firmly approximated and a sudden expulsion of air causes them to burst open, the resulting sound tends to be rough and metallic. The action is called *coup de glotte* or the stroke of the glottis. The phonemic symbol for the glottal stroke is [ʔ].

labial—Pertaining to the two lips.

TABLE II. *Speech Sounds Used in Song*

Points of Stricture		Bilabial Upper-Lower Lips		Labiodental Upper Teeth and Lower Lip		Dental Upper Teeth and Tongue		Alveolar Alveolar Ridge & Tongue Tip	
Classification of Sounds		Voiced	Voice-less	Voiced	Voice-less	Voiced	Voice-less	Voiced	Voice-less
Consonants	Plosives	b	p					d	t
	Nasals	m						n	
	Laterals							l	
	One Tap Trill								
	Retroflex								
	Fricatives		ʍ	v	f	ð	θ	z	s
	Glides	w							
Vowels		y	u						
	High		ʊ						
		ʏ							
	Mid		o						
		œ	ô					n̩ l̩	
			ɔ						
	Low								
Dipthongs									
	High								
	Mid								
	Low								

Palatal-Alveolar		Palatal-Alveolar		Palatal		Velar		Nasal		Glottal	
Front Palate and Tongue Tip		Front Palate & Tongue Blade		Hard Palate and Tongue Blade		Velum and Dorsum		Velum Dropped			
Voiced	Voiceless	Voiced	Voiceless	Voiced	Voiceless	Voiced	Voiceless	Voiced	Voiceless	Voiced	Voiceless
						g	k			ʔ	
						ŋ		m n ŋ			
		ʒ	ʃ								h

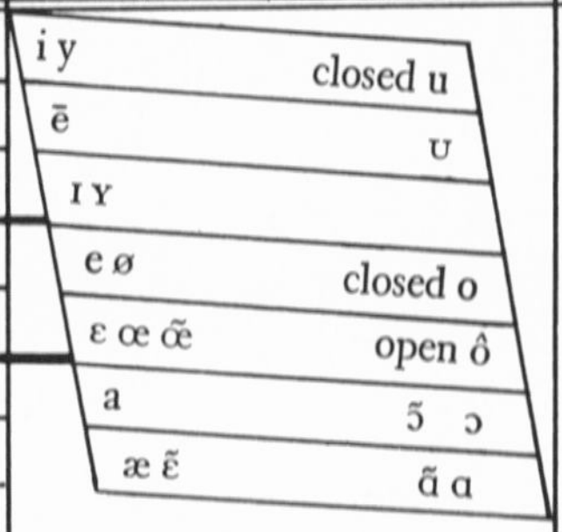

i y — closed u
ē — ʊ
ɪ ʏ
e ø — closed o
ɛ œ œ̃ — open ô
a — ɔ̃ ɔ
æ ɛ̃ — ɑ̃ ɑ

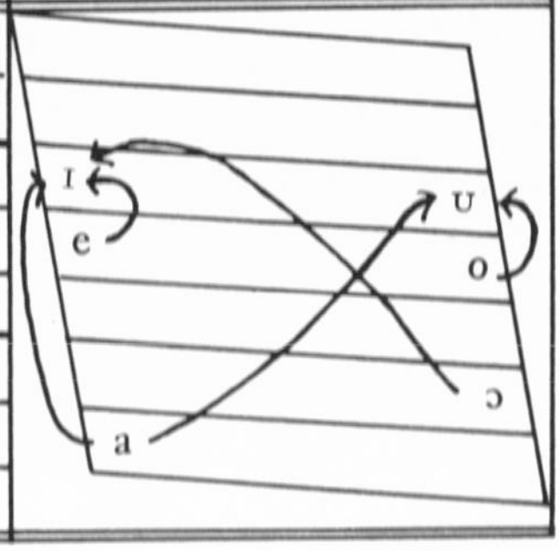

ɪ e — ʊ o
a — ɔ

lateral—The sound of [l]; sounds in which the air stream is emitted through a lateral orifice formed along one or both sides of the tongue.

lingual—Pertaining to the tongue.

mandible—Lower jaw.

maxilla—Upper jaw.

nasal—The sound of [m] and [n], created by closing the labial orifice and permitting the uvula to be suspended away from the pharyngeal wall in the neutral position. This position permits the passage of air into both the oral and nasal cavities. The nares of the nose then become the outer orifices. The [m] is the most easily produced speech sound in the English language. It is the [ŋ] sound emitted as a continuant. The port into the nasopharynx is open. The oral cavity does not serve as a resonator during the production of this phoneme.

nasal port—The open space created between the oropharynx and nasopharynx when the uvula is removed from the pharyngeal wall during the production of nasal sounds.

oral or buccal—Pertaining to the mouth cavity.

palate—Roof of the oral cavity. (See also soft palate.)

prepalatal—Pertaining to the anterior part of the hard palate.

mediopalatal—Pertaining to the middle part of the hard palate.

postpalatal—Pertaining to the posterior part of the hard palate.

pharynx—Extends vertically (eleven centimeters in the male) from the base of the skull to the upper border of the sixth cervical vertebra; the pharynx is subdivided into the following:

nasopharynx—Extends from the base of the skull to the velum.

oropharynx—Extends from the velum to the tip of the epiglottis.

laryngopharynx—Extends from the tip of the epiglottis to the superior surface of the vocal folds.

pharyngeal wall—Posterior surface of the pharynx.

raphe—A line of union between two contiguous and similar structures.

sibilant—The sound of [s]; a friction sound emitted through a very narrow orifice.

tongue—A movable fleshy projection of the floor of the mouth that includes the following parts:

tip—The extreme forward edge of the tongue.

blade—The forepart of the tongue.

dorsum—That portion of the upper tongue between blade and root.

predorsum—The portion of the upper tongue surface that lies immediately posterior to the blade.

mediodorsum—The mid-point of the dorsum.

postdorsum—The portion of the upper tongue surface that lies immediately anterior to the root.

radix—The point at which the tongue root joins the epiglottis. (See Fig. 22B.)

root—The portion of the upper surface of the tongue that lies within the pharynx.

uvula—The pendulous projection on the middle lower border of the velum; it is functional during the production of nasal sounds, and it separates the oro-pharynx and nasopharynx during the production of vowels and consonants.

vallecula—Space between the epiglottis and the radix of the tongue. (See Fig. 21A.)

velum—The soft palate.

prevelar—Pertaining to the anterior part of the soft palate.

postvelar—Pertaining to the posterior part of the soft palate.

TERMS PERTAINING TO THE PRODUCTION OF VOWELS

closed, open, half-closed, half-open—The size of the aperture between the maxilla and mandible.

closed vowels—Singer's term for a tense vowel in phonetics, refers to the amount of tension in the articulatory musculature; tense vowels are [i], closed [ē], [o], [u], [ʌ] above the staff.

front, mid, central, back, high, low—These terms refer to that area of the upper tongue surface showing the highest point of arching during the production of a given vowel; [i], high front; [ɛ], mid-front; [a], low front; [ɑ], low central; [ʌ], mid-central [ɔ], low back; [u], high back.

lip protrusion—Trumpet shape used in the production of the vowels [ɔ], [ʊ], and [ɜ].

lip-rounding—A circular closure of the labial orifice used for production of most of the back vowels.

lip-spreading—Achieved by raising the corners of the lips, it is used for the production of the frontal vowels.

open vowels—Singer's term for lax vowels in phonetics; it refers to the absence of tension in the articulatory musculature; lax vowels are [ɪ], open [e], [ɛ], [æ], [a], [ɑ], [ɔ], [ô], [ʊ], [ʌ] within the staff.

pure vowel—Defined acoustically, a sound that is sustained by a stabilized mechanism for the duration of the pitch within an acoustical area of two semitones from the center of the basic vowel or its quality alternate. Defined psychologically, the pure vowel sound is one which lies within the pure vowel area. It is a vowel in which the vocal mechanism is stable for the duration of any pitch and in itself is identified by the singer as the basic vowel or its quality alternate that provides the correct phoneme for the pronunciation of any word.

tongue-backing—The movement of the dorsum of the tongue backward to an arched position, high and extremely backed for the vowel [u], low and less backed for [ɔ].

TERMS PERTAINING TO THE PRODUCTION OF CONSONANTS

A consonant is an interruption of a vowel sound by the movement of the lips, teeth, tongue, or velum which results in an obstruction within the oral cavity. This obstruction interrupts the phonated sound altogether or confines it to a hum or a friction noise. In terms of movement, phoneticians consider consonants to be either continuant or stops. An explanation and classification of these consonantal sounds follows:

affricates—A stop plosive followed by a continuant fricative with both sounds originating in the same organic position, such as [ts] and [dz].

aspiration—A stop plosive followed by a puff of unvoiced air (explosion), such as [p] as in *pot,* [t] as in *talk.*

continuant fricative—A consonant sound that results from frictional noise caused by the breath passing through a small oral opening between the teeth or lips, such as voiced fricatives [v], [ð], [ʒ], [z]; unvoiced [f], [θ], [ʃ], [s].

long consonant—A consonant that is held long enough in its production to give the effect of doubling the sound without actually repeating the movements necessary to make it. Examples are *this city* [ðɪːsɪtɪ], *come Mary* [kʌmːerɪ], *cat tail* [katːeɪl]. The modifier [ː] indicates lengthening.

retroflex—Describes sounds for which the tongue tip is curled upward and backward, as in the General American [ɝ].

stop plosive—A consonant sound produced by stopping the air stream at some point in the oral cavity to build up pressure and then releasing it suddenly. Voiced stop are [b], [d], [g]; unvoiced are [p], [t], [k].

unaspiration—A stop plosive made without an outward explosion of air (implosion) such as [h] in *hot,* [d] as in *doll.* In singing, implosion occurs in the use of plosives that are normally exploded when they are followed by a voiced consonant. Examples are listed below:

What do—[t] is normally aspirated.
Help me—[p] is normally aspirated.
Walk down—[k] is normally aspirated.

unvoiced—Vocal folds are not approximated and phonation does not occur during the production of unvoiced consonants [p], [t], [k], [f], [θ], [ʃ], [s].

voiced—Vocal folds are approximated and phonation occurs during the production of voiced consonants [b], [d], [g], [v], [ð], [z], [ʒ].

THE NECESSITY FOR PHONEMIC ACCURACY

The establishment of a correct phonemic placement in the vocalic utterance of a student depends upon a fundamental law of teaching: the teacher must know how to attain such a placement either by psychological or physiological method. Physiological systems have an advantage here, for recordings and diagrams are not necessary to implement teaching if the teacher really knows the physiological positions of the articulators for a specific phoneme. Such a teacher demonstrates, using himself as an audio-visual tool, and by such a method attains his objectives in pronunciation, enunciation, and articulation.

The confusion in teaching procedures may be understood when one realizes that all of the fifteen phonemes may be established within a singer's technique through either lip-rounding or lip-spreading and either sound may be accepted by some teachers as good diction and suitable for communication in song. However, in teaching vowels for singing the singer and the teacher must accept the fact that, to achieve a standard pronunciation of a word which is free from the dialectal tendencies of a national minority, the singer must master the ideal and proper vocal placement of the vowel sounds within every word, monosyllable, or polysyllable, regardless of the linguistic environment in which they may appear.

As an example, a rounded frontal [y] is not [i] nor is it used in the English language. Likewise [ø] is not [ē]; nor [œ], [ɛ]. These rounded frontals are used in both the French and German languages and should be recognized by the performer as proper for that language. Other abuses more frequently heard include [nɔt] for [nɑt], [ʌgɪnst] for [ʌganst], [kɑf] for [kɔf], etc. The vowel migration drills which follow are devices which must be understood and then imitated by comparison with the recorded examples. This will establish an ear-training program for phonemic accuracy which will lead to better intelligibility of the word and a greater consideration of its prosodic significance within a specific linguistic environment.

VISUAL ANALYSIS OF ARTICULATORY MOVEMENT

In the following kinesiologic analysis, the radiographs, which reveal the movements of the articulators, are the result of six years of research in phonemic identity in song by the author at the Indiana University Medical Center in Indianapolis, Indiana.

The teacher or singer viewing these radiographs, lip positions, and palatograms will realize that the positions of the articulators as well as the cavity contours will be identical for men, women, and children if an identical phoneme is to be reproduced. Greater or lesser cavity dimension will alter the acoustic position of each phoneme, but the sound will not lose its phonemic integrity; i.e., if a female singer, viewing the page for the phoneme [i] places the tongue in the suggested position, with the points of tongue contact at the palate suggested by the palatogram and the suggested degree of lip-spreading, an identical phoneme will be assured. These visuals are designed to implement the recorded sound of these phonemes, and with some practicing and ear-training they may be reproduced accurately. Gradually the physiological sensation will dominate, and the student will remember how such a phoneme feels when sung within specific tonal areas. Every attempt must be made to use these vowels in context for this is the goal of phonemic accuracy in song.

VOWEL MIGRATION DRILLS AND RECORDED EXAMPLES

The following exercises and recorded examples are disciplinary drills which employ the same concepts of support as the basic drills introduced in Chapter Two on page 11, namely, "Sustain the sound with the breath pressure." To use these drills efficiently the teacher and the student must memorize the Vowel Migration Chart (Fig. 103, p. 234). Both teacher and student must also determine the pitch boundaries of the stable vowel pitch range in which all vowels are pure and of the first and second migration pitch areas in which all vowels are modified to a varying degree dependent upon the vocal force and the sung pitch. The objectives of the drills and these exercises are as follows:

1. To unify and coordinate the forces of respiration and phonation through action in song.
2. To provide an awareness of the physical sensation and action of the abdominal and back musculature, consciously controlled.
3. To refine to a point of perfection this basic action of pulsated tones throughout the vocal range.

4. To bring to the student the awareness that the total body is the vocal instrument.

Three goals must be attained in each exercise:

1. The breath must precede the sound. To create such a physiological condition a state of suspended muscular tension must be present at the start of phonation. Such a condition is identified by the absence of glottic shock; the absence of a metallic sound. The presence of a very slight aspirate which is coordinated instantaneously with the phonated sound.
2. The breath pressure must sustain the sound. The sensation of effort must be felt at the belt line. The concept of sustaining the breath pressure is one of constantly and firmly closing a circle around the middle part of the body.
3. The integrity of the vowel must be preserved in diatonic and intervallic pattern. The movement of each vowel from its position within the stable vowel pitch range to that of the first and second migration pitch ranges must be conceived and employed. To assure the student that he is properly employing abdominal control of breathing for singing, he may be permitted to overpulsate each line to assure the achievement of the concept of sustaining the sound with the breath.

All Concone exercises or similar scale studies first should be conceived as pulsated tones sung in the same rhythmic pattern as the exercise. The physical sensation of the level rhythmic pattern should then be applied to the melodic pattern. Such practice provides the student with a physical awareness of support that he may miss if he sings only the melodic study. The student will usually be able to sing the level pulsated pattern properly, but when he sings the melodic pattern, inconsistencies of pitch and breath support will be discovered. The student should drill persistently upon such points until the smoothness of the pulsated level pattern has been transferred to the melodic pattern.

The ideal condition is a fast scale without noticeable pulsations. This condition is realized when the singer achieves economy of effort and impeccable bodily control of the intonation and flexibility (Records 1-4, Bands 2 and 4).

CONCONE EXERCISES

The numbers which appear to the left of the drills on pages 298 to 340 correspond with the numbers of the recorded examples. The soprano voice appears on Record 1, Bands 1-30; mezzo soprano on Record 2, Bands 1-21; tenor on Record 3, Bands 1-21; and bass, Record 4, Bands 1-30.

ANALYSIS OF THE BASIC VOWEL [i]

(See pp. 298 and 299 for migration drills and illustrations.)

Stable Vowel Pitch Range

The vowel [i] is seldom sung in its stable position by the untrained singer; the sound of this phoneme must be taught by the teacher. With practice, however, this high frontal vowel can become an acceptable sound within the singer's repertoire of phonemes. Most singers tend to sing this vowel too loudly, with the tongue too high and too close to the front, and without increasing the size of the pharynx. As a result, the sound of this phoneme is constricted and unmusical. As an alternate, the singer invariably substitutes the quality alternate vowel [ɪ].

To use this phoneme properly two rules must be observed:

1. Within the stable vowel pitch range (Records 1-4, Band 7)—the basic vowel [i], must be sung only at double piano and piano levels of intensity. At mezzo forte levels, this phoneme migrates normally toward the quality alternate vowel [ɪ] (Fig. 103).

2. The singer must hold the larynx at a slightly higher position in soft passages to preserve the phoneme [i] and to prevent its migration toward the rounded frontal [y]. This phoneme is acceptable in singing soft passages that lie within the stable vowel pitch range. Its use increases textual intelligibility and enhances the singer's style through increased effort for articulation.

Type. High front, close, spread, loosely coupled.

Labial Orifice. The lips are spread by slightly extending the corners of the mouth to form an orifice elongated transversely and quite narrow vertically. The spreading should be accentuated for sound sung within double piano and piano intensities. As the intensity increases from a mezzo forte to a forte, the labial orifice is slightly increased vertically by lowering the mandible. This increase in the size of the orifice permits the phoneme to migrate toward the quality alternate [ɪ].

Tongue. The tip of the tongue is held firmly against the bottom front teeth. The blade and the dorsum touch the palatal area at each lateral tooth line. The tongue is grooved along the medial raphe from the blade to the root. The groove becomes more pronounced from the postdorsal area, and it increases in depth from the tongue root to the anterior-posterior dimension of the pharyngeal cavity during the utterance of this vowel. The radix of the tongue moves anteriorly a distance of approximately twenty-four millimeters from its position in a passive state; the hyoid bone and the tip of the epiglottis move with it. This movement enlarges the opening of the vestibule and increases the total dimension of that resonator, thereby altering its resonance characteristics. The back orifice is located at the point of greatest constriction. It is short, extending from the prepalatal to the mediopalatal position. However, the tongue groove is shallow from the blade to the dorsum. This long, constricted channel gives the vowel [i] its individual characteristic. The front cavity is smaller than the back cavity. With an increase in vocal force, the muscular tension of the tongue decreases laterally and is accompanied by the lowering of the mandible. These actions increase the vertical dimension of the oral cavity at the dorsal area, thus causing the vowel to migrate toward the quality alternate [ɪ].

Mandible. The mandible is closed, permitting a vertical opening of one-half inch between the teeth at the center. With an increase in vocal force from mezzo piano to forte, the mandible is lowered slightly; this lowering increases both front and back orifices and enlarges the front cavity, thus causing a migration of the phoneme toward the quality alternate [ɪ].

Laryngeal Position. The larynx is lowered to a position slightly below that of the passive state but slightly higher than that used in singing the neutral vowel [ʌ]. As the intensity increases, a lower laryngeal position is assumed to impart stability to the phonatory system. The lower position is accompanied by a slight tilt of the thyroid cartilage, which increases the tension of the vocal folds (Fig. 27B, p. 58).

Velum. The superior-posterior heel of the velum rests firmly against the pharyngeal wall to prevent the sound from leaking into the nasal cavities. The uvula is suspended downward away from the pharyngeal wall into the oropharynx.

First Migration Pitch Range

Labial Orifice. In comparison with their position for the stable vowel, the lips are less spread at the corners. The vertical dimension of the labial orifice changes little at low intensity levels. This condition persists if pitches within this modification area are approached from below or if a sung sound originates upon such a pitch. As the vocal force exceeds mezzo forte, the lips are less spread and the vertical dimension of the labial orifice increases. The phoneme then migrates toward the quality alternate [ɪ].

Tongue. The tip of the tongue is held firmly against the bottom front teeth. The tongue is lowered slightly from the blade to the mediodorsal area, increasing the vertical dimension of the oral cavity. The blade and dorsum touch the palate at each lateral tooth line. The tongue is grooved from the mediodorsum to the root. The radix of the tongue is more relaxed and permits the epiglottis to move closer to the pharyngeal wall. Although the opening of the vestibule is unrestricted, this movement changes its conformation and resonance characteristics. The back orifice is short, the point of maximum constriction is in the mediodorsum and the mediopalatal area. The oral cavity is smaller than the pharyngeal cavity. As the vocal force increases, the muscular tension of the tongue decreases laterally; this movement is accompanied by a lowering of the mandible. These actions increase the vertical dimension of the oral cavity from the blade to the dorsum, and the vowel migrates toward the quality alternate [ɪ].

Mandible. In comparison with its basic vowel position, the position of the mandible is slightly lower during the production of low intensity sounds. As the intensity increases above mezzo forte, the mandible is lowered as in the production of the phoneme [ɪ].

Laryngeal Position. The laryngeal position is lowered approximately one centimeter from that assumed when producing the basic vowel [i]. As vocal force increases above mezzo forte, the larynx is lowered slightly to increase the vertical dimension of the pharynx. The tilt of the thyroid cartilage is increased.

Velum. The velum is pressed firmly against the pharyngeal wall.

Second Migration Pitch Range

Labial Orifice. When compared with the sound produced within the first modification pitch range, the labial orifice is elongated vertically by lowering the mandible. Lip-spreading is eliminated.

Tongue. The tongue is lowered from the blade to the dorsum, but the tongue arch retains its stable vowel conformation. The tongue has a shallow groove from the tip of the dorsum, and it is deeply grooved from the dorsum to the root. The blade and the dorsum touch the palatal area at each lateral tooth line. The radix of the tongue is more relaxed and permits the epiglottis to move closer to the pharyngeal wall. Although the opening of the vestibule is unrestricted, this movement changes its conformation and resonance characteristics. The back orifice is located at the point of greatest constriction at the mediodorsum-mediopalatal position. This tongue-fronting tends to preserve the integrity of the phoneme [ɪ] even though the pitch is high. As the vocal force is increased, these movements are accentuated. The vowel produced is the quality alternate phoneme [ɪ].

Mandible. The mandible is lowered slightly. The lowering increases as the vocal force increases.

Laryngeal Position. The laryngeal position is approximately one centimeter lower than that assumed during the production of the phoneme [ʌ] in the first modification pitch range. This laryngeal distension produces a similar increase in the vertical dimension of the pharynx, which permits the pharyngeal resonator to be compatible with the increase in intensity. The thyroid tilt is approximately the same as it is when the sound is produced in the first modification pitch range.

Velum. The velum is pressed firmly against the pharyngeal wall.

ANALYSIS OF THE QUALITY ALTERNATE CLOSED VOWEL [ē]

(See pp. 300 and 301 for migration drills and illustrations.)

Stable Vowel Pitch Range

The closed vowel [ē] seldom occurs in stressed syllables in American speech. The phoneme [ē] in the words *name, tame,* and *game* become diphthongs and are pronounced [nēɪm], [tēɪm], and [gēɪm]. The expert singer will tend to minimize such a result and sing the pure phoneme open [e], which is the proper phoneme to use when singing English songs.

The phoneme closed [ē] is indispensable when singing German lieder or the French art song. Such German words as *ewig* [ēvɪg], *rede* [rēdə], *gewesen* [gavēzan], and *edel* [ēdəl] and the French words *passer* [pɑsiē], *dēs* [de], *pieds* [pjē], and *efforts* [ēfɔr] demand the closed vowel [ē] position in song.

An illustration of the usage of this phoneme in English, German, and French is on Record 5, Bands 1-14.

Type. High front, close, spread, loosely coupled.

Labial Orifice. The lips are spread by extending the corners of the mouth; the resulting orifice is elongated transversely and quite narrow vertically, a position similar to that used for [i]. When the vowel is sung within double piano and piano intensities, the spreading should be accentuated. As the vocal force increases, the muscular tension of the tongue increases laterally to preserve the integrity of the phoneme. Unless the vocal force is extreme, this phoneme is stable to top line F. The normal migration in fortissimo passages is toward the quality alternate vowel [ɪ].

Tongue. The tip of the tongue is held firmly against the bottom front teeth. The blade and dorsum touch the palatal area at each lateral tooth line, but the lateral spreading from the tip to the dorsum is much more pronounced than it is in producing the vowel [i]. This lateral spreading—the significant characteristic of this phoneme—slightly increases the vertical dimension of the oral cavity from the tip of the tongue to the mediodorsal area. This slight movement of the tongue blade is the only difference between the [i] and the closed [ē] phonemes. The tongue is grooved along the median raphe from the blade to the root. The groove becomes more pronounced from the postdorsal area; it increases in depth at the tongue root and adds to the anterior-posterior dimension of the pharyngeal cavity. The back orifice is located at the point of greatest constriction, the mediopalatal-mediodorsal position. The front cavity is smaller than the back cavity. The radix of the tongue has moved anteriorly approximately nineteen millimeters from its passive position; the hyoid bone and the tip of the epiglottis move with it. This movement enlarges the opening of the vestibule and increases the total dimension of that resonator, thereby altering its resonance characteristics. An increase in vocal force increases the muscular tension of the tongue laterally to preserve the integrity of the phoneme. When the vocal force is extreme, the normal migration is toward the [ɪ]. However, if the tongue stricture is firm this phoneme does not migrate.

Laryngeal Position. The larynx is lowered to a position slightly lower than that assumed during the passive state and approximately the same as that used to produce the vowel [i]. As the vocal force increases, a lower laryngeal position is assumed to impart stability to the phonatory system. The pharyngeal position is lowered by a slight tilt of the thyroid cartilage, which increases the tension of the vocal folds.

Velum. The superior-posterior heel of the velum rests firmly against the pharyngeal wall and prevents the sound from leaking into the nasal cavities. The uvula is suspended downward away from the pharyngeal wall into the oropharynx, which suggests a relaxed muscular state.

First Migration Pitch Range

Labial Orifice. When sounds are sung at low intensity within this pitch range, the lips retain their spread characteristic. The labial orifice is elongated transversely and slightly more open vertically. If tongue stricture is maintained, this phoneme does not migrate.

Tongue. When singing the phoneme closed [ē] at low intensities within the first migration pitch range, the tongue position does not change from that assumed during the production of closed [ē] within the stable vowel pitch range. The tip of the tongue is held firmly against the bottom front teeth. The blade and dorsum are in firm contact with the palate at the lateral tooth line. The tongue root retains its deep groove. The back orifice is located at the point of greatest constriction at the mediopalatal-mediodorsal position. The pharyngeal cavity is long and wide in comparison with the oral cavity. The position of the epiglottis remains unchanged. As the vocal force increases, the muscular tension of the tongue is increased to preserve the integrity of the phoneme. When vocal force is extreme, the vowel will migrate to the quality alternate vowel [ɪ].

Mandible. The mandible is no lower than it is for singing within the basic vowel pitch range.

Laryngeal Position. The larynx is approximately one centimeter lower than it is for singing within the basic vowel pitch range. This lowering increases the vertical dimension of the pharynx. The tilt of the thyroid cartilage remains unchanged.

Velum. The velum is pressed firmly against the pharyngeal wall and is shortened from its pendulus position.

Second Migration Pitch Range

Labial Orifice. In comparison to its position for the sound produced in the first migration pitch range, the labial orifice is elongated vertically by lowering the mandible. Lip-spreading is eliminated.

Tongue. The tip of the tongue is held firmly against the bottom front teeth. The blade and dorsum are in firm contact with the palate at each lateral tooth line. The tongue is grooved from the tip to the root, and the groove is deepened from the dorsum to the base of the root. Tongue-backing is less accentuated in this second migration pitch range; therefore, the tongue hump is lower at the dorsal-velar position. The frontal area from tip to predorsum is also lower because of the lateral spreading and a relaxation of the muscular tension of the tongue. This lateral tension identifies this phoneme as [e] rather than [i]; otherwise, the tongue positions of each vowel are similar. The deepened tongue groove increases the anterior-posterior dimension of the pharynx from the postdorsal position to the tongue root. The back orifice is located at the mediopalatal-mediodorsal position. The position of the epiglottis is unchanged.

The front cavity is smaller than the back cavity. The radix of the tongue has moved anteriorly a distance of approximately five millimeters from its position in a passive state, and the hyoid bone and the tip of the epiglottis move with it. This movement enlarges the opening of the vestibule and increases the total dimension of that resonator, thereby altering its resonance characteristics. As vocal force increases these movements of the tongue become more accentuated. When vocal force is extreme within the pitch range, the integrity of the [e] phoneme must be preserved by extreme lateral spreading and muscular tension of the frontal part of the tongue from tip to mediodorsum; otherwise, the sound will migrate to the phoneme [ɪ].

Mandible. The mandible is lowered slightly in comparison with the mandibular position of the first migration pitch range of the phoneme [e].

Laryngeal Position. The larynx is lowered approximately five millimeters from its position for the phoneme [ē] closed when it is sung within the first modification pitch range. The vertical dimension of the pharynx increases as the larynx is lowered. The tilt of the thyroid cartilage is the same as when the phoneme is produced within the first modification pitch range.

Velum. The velum rests firmly against the pharyngeal wall.

ANALYSIS OF THE QUALITY ALTERNATE VOWEL [ɪ]

(See pp. 302 and 303 for migration drills and illustrations.)

Stable Vowel Pitch Range

Type. High front, close, spread, loosely coupled.

Labial Orifice. The lips are less tense than they are in producing the vowel [i]. Tension is decreased. The corners of the lips are not extended. The labial orifice is elongated transversely and is quite narrow vertically. The vertical opening is slightly increased from that of the vowel [i]. For sounds sung within double piano and piano intensities, the spreading should be accentuated. As the intensity increases from mezzo forte to forte the lowering of the mandible slightly increases the labial orifice vertically. This increase in the vertical dimension of the orifice is needed to maintain good vocalic sound. When it is sung within the basic vowel pitch range, the vowel [ɪ] does not migrate to another phoneme.

Tongue. The tip of the tongue is held firmly against the bottom front teeth. The blade and dorsum touch the palatal area at each lateral tooth line. The tongue is grooved along the median raphe from the blade to the root. The groove becomes more pronounced from the postdorsal area and deepens at the tongue root, thus adding to the anterior-posterior dimension of the pharyngeal cavity during the utterance of this vowel. The radix of the tongue moves anteriorly approximately two centimeters; it moves with it the hyoid bone and the lip of the epiglottis. This movement enlarges the opening of the vestibule and increases the total dimension of that resonator, thereby altering its resonance characteristics. The back orifice is located at the point of greatest constriction at the prepalatal area where the tongue groove starts and where the medial raphe is closest to the palate. The front cavity is small compared to the back cavity. An increase in vocal force requires an increase in lateral muscular tension of the tongue to preserve the integrity of the phoneme.

Mandible. The mandible is lowered approximately one quarter of an inch, to permit a vertical opening three quarters of an inch wide between the teeth at the center. With the increase in vocal force from mezzo piano to forte, the mandible is lowered, slightly increasing the vertical dimension of both front and back orifices and enlarging the front cavity. If the tongue stricture is preserved, this vowel will not migrate. The singer must apply maximum vocal force to dislodge this phoneme, for it is the most stable of the frontal vowels. This stability is understandable when one realizes that all unstressed syllables are either [ə] or [ɪ].

Laryngeal Position. The larynx is lowered to a position slightly lower than that assumed during the passive state and approximately the same as that used for singing the vowel [i]. As the vocal force increases, a lower laryngeal position is assumed to impart stability to the phonatory system. The lower position is accompanied by a slight tilt of the thyroid cartilage, which increases the tension of the vocal folds.

Velum. The superior-posterior heel of the velum rests firmly against the pharyngeal wall and prevents the sound from leaking into the nasal cavities. The uvula is suspended downward away from the pharyngeal wall into the oropharynx.

First Migration Pitch Range

Labial Orifice. When this phoneme is sung within the first migration pitch range, the labial orifice assumes the same position required for the quality alternate vowel when it is sung within the basic pitch range. As vocal force increases, the labial orifice is enlarged vertically by lowering the mandible to increase the sonority of the sounds.

Tongue. In comparison with the vowel [ɪ] sung within the stable vowel pitch range the point of constriction is greatest at the mediopalatal position. A deepening of the tongue groove from the postdorsum to the tongue root increases the anterior-posterior dimension of the pharynx. The cavity system is still loosely coupled. As vocal force increases, the tension of the tongue is decreased laterally and the mandible is slightly lowered. The point of constriction is maintained at the mediopalatal position preserving the integrity of the phoneme [ɪ]. The radix of the tongue moves anteriorly a distance of approximately one centimeter and moves the hyoid bone and the lip of the epiglottis with it. This movement enlarges the opening of the vestibule and increases the total dimension of that resonator, thereby altering its resonance characteristics.

Laryngeal Position. The laryngeal position is approximately one centimeter lower than that assumed during the production of this phoneme within the stable vowel pitch range. The tilt of the thyroid cartilage is accentuated. The lower laryngeal position increases the pharyngeal cavity vertically. As vocal force increases, the movement is accentuated.

Velum. The velum is pressed firmly against the pharyngeal wall.

Second Migration Pitch Range

Labial Orifice. In comparison with their position when the vowel [ɪ] is sung in the first modification pitch range, the lips are less tense as the pitch is raised. The labial orifice increases vertically. As the intensity increases, lip tension is increased to preserve the integrity of the phoneme. The enlargement permits the phoneme to increase in sonority.

Tongue. The tip of the tongue is held firmly against the bottom front teeth. The blade and dorsum are in firm contact with the palate at each lateral tooth line. The tongue is grooved from the tip to the root, this groove deepens from the dorsum to the base of the root. Tongue-backing is less accentuated in the second migration pitch range; therefore, the tongue hump is lower at the dorsal-velar position. This action permits a longer and wider pharyngeal resonating area by extending the back resonator to the back orifice, which is maintained at the mediopalatal-mediodorsal position. The front cavity is smaller than the back cavity. The position of the epiglottis remains unchanged. As vocal force increases, these tongue movements become more accentuated. If tongue stricture is maintained this phoneme remains stable when vocal force is increased.

Mandible. The mandible is lowered slightly from the position for vowel [ɪ] sung within the first modification pitch range.

Laryngeal Position. The larynx is lowered one centimeter from the position for the phoneme [ɪ] sung within the first migration pitch range. The pharynx increases vertically as the larynx is lowered. The tilt of the thyroid cartilage is the same as for the first migration pitch range.

Velum. The velum is pressed firmly against the pharyngeal wall.

ANALYSIS OF THE BASIC VOWEL OPEN [e]

(See pp. 304 and 305 for migration drills and illustrations.)

Stable Vowel Pitch Range

Type. Mid-front, half-open, spread, loosely coupled.

Labial Orifice. The lips are spread less than they are for producing the closed vowel [ē]. The labial orifice is wider transversely than vertically, and the musclar tension of the lips is relaxed. As vocal force increases, the vertical dimension of the orifice is increased by lowering the mandible, but some characteristic spreading is maintained. As the cavity enlarges, this phoneme migrates toward the quality alternate [ɛ].

Tongue. The tip of the tongue is held firmly against the bottom front teeth. The blade and dorsum do not touch the palatal area at the lateral tooth line because the mandible has been lowered; the position of the tongue and its conformation is the same as that assumed while producing the closed [ē] with two exceptions: (a) the tongue groove is not as deep from the tip to the mediodorsal area, and (b) the lateral spreading of the dorsum is more relaxed, thus causing an increase in the vertical dimension of the oral cavity from tip to mediodorsal position. The tongue is grooved along the median raphe from the tip of the mediodorsal area, where the superior surface is rounded. The groove is deepened from the postdorsal area to the tongue root, adding to the anterior-posterior dimension of the pharyngeal cavity. The back orifice is located at the point of greatest constriction at the mediodorsal-mediopalatal position. The radix of the tongue moves anteriorly approximately fifteen millimeters from its position in a passive state, and moves the hyoid bone and the tip of the epiglottis with it. This movement enlarges the opening of the vestibule and increases the total dimension of that resonator, thereby altering its resonance characteristics. The front cavity is small in comparison with the back cavity. An increase of vocal force requires an increase laterally in the muscular tension of the tongue to preserve the integrity of the phoneme. When vocal force is extreme, the normal migration is toward the quality alternate [ɛ].

Mandible. The mandible is lowered one-quarter of an inch from the mandibular position of closed [ē], creating a vertical opening of one and one-quarter inches between the teeth at the center. As vocal force increases, the mandible is lowered farther. As a fortissimo is reached, the vertical increase in oral cavity causes the vowel to migrate toward the quality alternate [ɛ].

Laryngeal Position. The larynx is held slightly lower than its passive position and approximately three quarters of an inch lower than that assumed in producing the closed vowel [ē]. As the vocal force is increased, the lowered position is accentuated, and the thyroid cartilage tilts forward to increase the tension of the vocal folds.

Velum. The superior-posterior heel of the velum rests firmly against the pharyngeal wall to prevent sound from leaking into the nasal cavities. The uvula is suspended downward away from the pharyngeal wall into the oropharynx.

First Migration Pitch Range

Labial Orifice. The lips are spread less than they are for producing the phoneme within the basic pitch range. The muscular tension of the lips is relaxed. The labial orifice is as wide vertically as transversely. As vocal force is increased, the vertical dimension of the orifice is increased by lowering the mandible.

Tongue. The tip of the tongue is held firmly against the bottom front teeth. The blade and dorsum do not touch with the palatal area at the lateral tooth line. The tongue is humped in a symmetrical arc from tip to blade. The tongue has a shallow groove from the tip to the dorsum, but it is deeply grooved from the dorsum to the root. The vertical dimension of the oral cavity is increased slightly by lowering the mandible. The pharyngeal cavity is larger transversely in comparison to its size when the phoneme closed [ē] is sung within the first migration pitch range. The back orifice is located at the point of greatest constriction at the mediodorsal-mediopalatal position. The front cavity is small compared to the back cavity. The position of the epiglottis remains unchanged. An increase in vocal force necessitates an increase in the muscular tension of the tongue to preserve the integrity of the phoneme. When vocal force is extreme, the normal migration is toward the open [e].

Mandible. The mandible is lower than it is for the basic vowel position. As vocal force increases, the mandible is lowered further to permit the phoneme to migrate to the quality alternate [ɛ].

Laryngeal Position. The larynx is lowered slightly from the basic vowel position, causing a slight increase in the vertical dimension of the pharynx. As vocal force is increased, the laryngeal lowering is accentuated.

Velum. The velum rests firmly against the pharyngeal wall.

Second Migration Pitch Range

Labial Orifice. When compared with the position for the same sound produced in the first migration pitch range, the labial orifice is elongated very slightly vertically. Lip-reading is eliminated.

Tongue. The tip of the tongue is held firmly against the bottom front teeth. The frontal part of the tongue from tip to dorsum does not change its conformation from that required by the vowel [e] produced in the first migration pitch range. The tongue is more deeply grooved from the blade to the postdorsum, thus increasing the dimension of both oral and pharyngeal cavities. The oral cavity is smaller than the pharyngeal cavity. The back orifice is formed at the point of greatest constriction at the mediodorsal-mediopalatal position. The position of the epiglottis remains unchanged. As vocal force increases, the tongue movements are accentuated, and the vowel migrates toward the phoneme [ɛ].

Mandible. The posterior of the mandible is unchanged from that of the vowel [e] sung within the first migration pitch range. As the vocal force is increased, the mandible is lowered to permit greater sonority. The vowel then migrates toward the phoneme [ɛ].

Laryngeal Position. The larynx is lowered approximately seven centimeters when compared with the phoneme [e] open sung in the first migration pitch range. The vertical dimension of the pharynx is increased as the larynx is lowered. The tilt of the thyroid cartilage is the same as when the phoneme is produced within the first migration pitch range.

Velum. The velum rests firmly against the pharyngeal wall.

ANALYSIS OF THE QUALITY ALTERNATE VOWEL [ɛ]

(See pp. 306 and 307 for migration drills and illustrations.)

Stable Vowel Pitch Range

Type. Mid-front, half-open, spread, loosely to tightly coupled.

Labial Orifice. The lips are in the same position as they are for producing the vowel [e] open—wider transversely than vertically. Muscular tension of the lips is slightly relaxed. As vocal force is increased, the vertical dimension of the orifice is increased by lowering the mandible, but the characteristic spreading demanded of the phoneme is maintained. As the cavity enlarges, the phoneme migrates toward the quality alternate vowel [a].

Tongue. The tip of the tongue is held firmly against the bottom front teeth. The tip, blade, and dorsum of the tongue are not grooved. The tongue is grooved from the post-dorsal area to the tongue root, increasing the anterior-posterior dimension of the pharynx. The oral cavity is enlarged vertically. The conformation of the tongue is identical to that for producing the vowel [e] open, except that the mediodorsal-mediopalatal area is flattened. The back orifice is formed at this point. The front cavity is smaller than the back cavity. The radix of the tongue moves anteriorly approximately fourteen millimeters from its passive position, and the hyoid bone and the tip of the epiglottis move with it. This movement enlarges the opening of the vestibule and enlarges the total dimension of that resonator, thereby altering its resonance characteristics. As vocal force is increased, the oral cavity is enlarged vertically by lowering the mandible, thus causing the vowel to migrate toward the quality alternate vowel [a].

Mandible. The position of the mandible is identical to that assumed when producing the vowel [e] open. The vertical opening is approximately one and one-quarter inches between the teeth at the center. As vocal force is increased, the mandible is slightly lowered, increasing the vertical dimension of the oral cavity. The phoneme [ɛ] then migrates toward the quality alternate phoneme [a].

Laryngeal Position. The larynx is lowered to a position slightly lower than that assumed in a passive state, approximately the same as that assumed in producing the vowel [e] open. As vocal force is increased, the lower pharyngeal position is accentuated to stabilize the phonatory tube, and the thyroid cartilage tilts forward slightly to increase the tension of the vocal folds.

Velum. The superior-posterior heel of the velum rests firmly against the pharyngeal wall and prevents sound from leaking into the nasal cavities. The uvula is suspended downward away from the pharyngeal wall into the oropharynx.

First Migration Pitch Range

Labial Orifice. The lips are relaxed and in the same position as they are to produce the vowel [e] in its basic pitch range. The labial orifice is wider transversely than vertically. As vocal force is increased, the mandible is lowered to increase the vertical dimension of the orifice. As the oral cavity is enlarged, the phoneme migrates toward the quality alternate vowel [a].

Tongue. The tip of the tongue is held firmly against the bottom front teeth. The tip, blade, and mediodorsum are not grooved. The postdorsum and root are deeply grooved, increasing the anterior-posterior dimension of the pharynx. The tongue hump is more rounded and lower at the dorsum than it is when the phoneme is sung in the basic vowel pitch range, and thereby, the vertical dimension of the oral cavity is increased. This enlargement is caused by slightly increasing the muscular tension of the tongue laterally to preserve the integrity of the phoneme. The back orifice is formed at the point of greatest constriction at the mediodorsal-mediopalatal area. The radix of the tongue has moved anteriorly approximately three millimeters from its position in the stable vowel pitch range. This movement enlarges the opening of the vestibule and increases the total dimension of that resonator, thereby altering its resonance characteristics. As vocal force is increased, the oral cavity is enlarged vertically by lowering the mandible, and the vowel migrates toward the quality alternate vowel [a].

Mandible. The mandible is lower than it is when this phoneme is sung in the stable vowel pitch range. As vocal force increases, the oral cavity is increased vertically, thus causing the phoneme [ε] to migrate toward the quality alternate vowel [a].

Laryngeal Position. The larynx is lowered approximately one and one-half centimeters from the position used for singing this phoneme in the basic vowel pitch range. This lower position increases the vertical dimension of the pharynx. As vocal force is increased, the laryngeal lowering is accentuated to stabilize the phonatory tube. The tilt of the thyroid cartilage remains approximately the same as it was when the phoneme was sung in the stable vowel pitch range.

Velum. The posterior heel of the velum is pressed firmly against the pharyngeal wall to prevent sound from passing into the nasal cavities.

Second Migration Pitch Range

Labial Orifice. The lips are more relaxed than they were for singing the vowel [e] in its first migration pitch range. The labial orifice has the same vertical and transverse dimensions. As vocal force increases, the orifice is enlarged vertically by lowering the mandible. This enlargement of the orifice permits the sound to become more sonorous.

Tongue. The tip of the tongue is held firmly against the bottom front teeth. The predorsum is highly arched. The tongue groove is deepened at the postdorsum and the root area is deeply grooved. The enlargement of the pharyngeal cavity extending from mediodorsum to the tongue root is extreme. The inner orifice is located at the predorsum, prepalatal position. The radix of the tongue is more relaxed, and it thus permits the epiglottis to move three millimeters closer to the pharyngeal wall than in the first modification pitch range. Although the opening of the vestibule is unrestricted, this movement changes its conformation and resonance characteristics.

Mandible. When compared with the phoneme [ɛ] sung in the first migration pitch range, the mandible is in approximately the same position. As vocal force increases, the mandible is lowered, causing the phoneme to migrate to the quality alternate vowel [a].

Laryngeal Position. The larynx is lowered approximately seven millimeters from the position of the first migration pitch range. The pharynx is increased in its vertical dimension. The tilt of the thyroid cartilage is unchanged.

Velum. The posterior heel of the velum is pressed firmly against the pharyngeal wall.

ANALYSIS OF THE BASIC VOWEL [æ]

(See pp. 308 and 309 for migration drills and illustrations.)

Stable Vowel Pitch Range

Type. Low front, half-open, spread, tightly coupled.

Labial Orifice. The lips are spread. Tension is increased at the corners as it is in producing the high frontal [ɪ]. The orifice is wider transversely than vertically; as vocal force is increased, the vertical dimension of the orifice is increased by lowering the mandible. As the cavity enlarges, this phoneme migrates directly to the quality alternate [a]. If the position and tension of the narrowed orifice are maintained and if the mandible is not lowered as vocal force is increased, this vowel becomes quite blatant and unmusical. The phoneme [æ] in its basic position can be used in song only at pianissimo and piano intensity levels. Even at these intensities singers should modify this vowel toward the quality alternate [a].

Tongue. The tip of the tongue is held firmly against the bottom front teeth. The tongue is not grooved from the tip to the predorsal area, but it is deeply grooved from the postdorsum to the root, thus increasing the anterior-posterior dimensions of the pharynx. The conformation of the tongue hump is identical to that used to produce the vowel [ɛ] except that the dorsum is lowered and flattened, causing the vertical dimension of the frontal oral cavity to increase. The back orifice is located at the point of greatest constriction at the mediodorsal area. The front cavity is smaller than the back cavity. The radix of the tongue moves anteriorly approximately eight millimeters from its passive position, and it moves the hyoid bone and the tip of the epiglottis with it. This movement enlarges the opening of the vestibule and increases the total dimension of that resonator, thereby altering its resonance characteristics. As vocal force increases, the oral cavity is increased vertically by lowering the mandible, thus causing the vowel to migrate toward the quality alternate vowel [a].

Mandible. The mandible is lowered to permit a vertical opening approximately one and three-quarters inches between the teeth at the center. As vocal force is increased, the mandible is lowered slightly. The increase vertically in the cavity dimension causes the phoneme to migrate toward the quality alternate vowel [a].

Laryngeal Position. The larynx is not lower than the position assumed while producing the vowel [ɛ]. The thyroid tilts considerably less than for [ɛ].

Velum. The superior-posterior heel of the velum rests firmly against the pharyngeal wall to prevent sound from leaking into the nasal cavities. The uvula is suspended into the oropharynx away from the pharyngeal wall.

First Migration Pitch Range

Labial Orifice. The lips are spread less laterally than they are for singing the phoneme [æ]. Tension at the corners of the lips is reduced. The labial orifice does not change vertically until the vocal force is increased above mezzo forte. The enlarged orifice permits the vowel to become more sonorous.

Tongue. The tip of the tongue is held firmly against the bottom front teeth. The tongue hump is lower from the blade to the postdorsum, increasing the oral cavity vertically. The lateral tension of the tongue is increased to preserve the integrity of the phoneme. The transverse dimension of the pharyngeal cavity does not change. The tongue is grooved from the mediopalatal position. The front cavity is smaller than the back cavity. The position of the epiglottis remains unchanged. As vocal force is increased, the movement of the oral and pharyngeal cavities is accentuated causing the phoneme to migrate toward the quality alternate vowel [a].

Mandible. The mandible is lower than it is for singing this phoneme in the basic vowel pitch range. This lowering increases the oral cavity vertically. As the vocal force increases, the mandible is lowered. The enlarged vertical dimension of the oral cavity permits the phoneme [æ] to migrate to the quality alternate vowel [a].

Laryngeal Position. The laryngeal position is lower than it is for singing in the basic vowel pitch area. The laryngeal lowering of approximately one centimeter causes the increase in the vertical dimension of the pharynx. The tilt of the thyroid cartilage is unchanged.

Velum. The superior-posterior heel of the velum is pressed firmly against the pharyngeal wall.

Second Migration Pitch Range

Labial Orifice. In comparison with their position for the phoneme [æ] sung within the first migration pitch range, the lips are without lateral tension. Lowering the mandible enlarges the labial orifice vertically. As the vocal force increases, the orifice is elongated to permit the phoneme to attain greater sonority.

Tongue. The tip of the tongue is held firmly against the bottom front teeth. The tongue is lowered and deeply grooved from the predorsum to the tongue root. The tongue is fronted and humped from the tip to the blade. The increase in the transverse dimension of the pharynx is greatest at the mediodorsal-velar position. The back orifice is formed at the predorsal-prepalatal position. The front cavity is smaller than the back cavity. The position of the epiglottis remains unchanged. The open throat so often described by vocal pedagogues is necessary to produce this phoneme accurately within this pitch area. The phoneme produced is that of the quality alternate vowel [a]. At extreme forte intensity, the neutral vowel [ʌ] is substituted for [a].

Mandible. The mandible is no lower than it is when this phoneme is sung in the first migration pitch range. As intensity is increased, the mandible is lowered, and the phoneme attains greater sonority.

Laryngeal Position. The larynx is lowered approximately one centimeter from its position for the first migration. The laryngeal position is approximately one centimeter lower than it is when the phoneme [a] is sung in the first modification pitch area. The vertical dimension of the pharynx is increased. The tilt of the thyroid cartilage is unchanged. As vocal force increases, the laryngeal lowering is accentuated.

Velum. The velum is firmly pressed against the pharyngeal wall.

ANALYSIS OF THE QUALITY ALTERNATE VOWEL [a]

(See pp. 310 and 311 for migration drills and illustrations and Record 1, Band 29 for French placement of this vowel.)

Stable Vowel Pitch Range

The quality alternate vowel [a], known phonetically as the medial [a], is the most useful point of migration of any of the low or mid-frontal vowels. The quality alternate vowel [a] is always substituted for [æ] at all pitch levels and when the vocal force is above mezzo forte.

When it is sung in the first migration pitch area, the quality alternate vowel [a] is the normal migration point of all words spelled with *e* and those that demand the use of the phoneme [ε]. Such words are *quest* [kwεst], *any* [εnɪ], *friend* [frεnd], *said* [sed], and *weather* [wεðə].

Type. Low frontal, half-open, neutral, tightly coupled.

Labial Orifice. The lips are not as tense as they are for production of the vowel [æ]. They are neither raised at the corners nor spread, but a very slight tension at the corners of the lips must be maintained to prevent the phoneme [a] from migrating to the low central vowel [ɑ]. The vertical dimension of the orifice is increased by lowering the mandible from the position used for [æ]. As intensity increases, the cavity is enlarged vertically and the phoneme migrates toward the basic vowel [ɑ].

Tongue. The tip of the tongue is held firmly against the bottom front teeth. The root of the tongue is backed slightly toward the pharyngeal wall, and the dorsum is lower than it is for producing [æ]. The postdorsal area is slightly grooved and the root is deeply grooved, thus increasing the anterior-posterior dimension of the pharyngeal cavity. The cavity system has no definite point of constriction. The points indicated by arrows are of equal constriction. The front cavity is slightly larger than the back cavity. The radix of the tongue moves anteriorly approximately six millimeters from its passive position, and the hyoid bone and the tip of the epiglottis move with it. This movement enlarges the opening of the vestibule and increases the total dimension of that resonator, thereby altering its resonance characteristics. As the vocal force increases, the oral cavity is enlarged vertically by lowering the mandible, and the vowel migrates toward the basic vowel [ɑ]. This cavity system is singly resonant and is a good example of a tightly coupled system.

Mandible. The mandible is approximately one-quarter of an inch lower than it is for producing [æ] to permit an opening of one inch between the teeth at the center. As the vocal force is increased, the mandible is lowered slightly. The increase in the vertical cavity dimension causes a migration of this phoneme toward the basic vowel [ɑ].

Laryngeal Position. The larynx is held slightly lower than it is for producing [æ], and the tilt of the thyroid cartilage is much more pronounced. As the vocal force increases, the thyroid tilt is accentuated to increase the tension of the vocal folds.

Velum. The superior-posterior heel of the velum is slightly arched and does not approximate the pharyngeal wall; therefore, some of the sound passes into the nasal cavity. The resulting slight nasality is noticeable in this phoneme when it is compared with [æ].

First Migration Pitch Range

Labial Orifice. When compared with their position for singing the vowel [a] in the basic vowel pitch range, the lips are less tense at the corners but not as completely relaxed as they are for the low central phoneme [ɑ]. The labial orifice is approximately the same in its vertical and transverse dimensions. As vocal force is increased, the labial orifice is increased vertically by lowering the mandible.

Tongue. The tip of the tongue is held firmly against the bottom front teeth. The arching and backing of the tongue is approximately the same as it is when this phoneme is sung in the basic vowel pitch range. The root of the tongue is grooved. The unstable back orifice is located at the point of greatest constriction at the root–pharyngeal wall position. The front cavity is smaller than the back cavity. The radix of the tongue moves anteriorly approximately two millimeters from its position in the stable vowel migration pitch range. This movement enlarges the opening of the vestibule and increases the total dimension of that resonator, thereby altering its resonance characteristics. The vertical dimension of the oral cavity is approximately the same as it is when this phoneme is sung in the basic vowel pitch range. As vocal force is increased, the vertical dimension of the oral cavity is increased by lowering the mandible, this increase gives the phoneme greater sonority and causes it to migrate toward the basic low central vowel [ɑ].

Mandible. When compared with the phoneme [a] sung within the basic vowel pitch range, the mandible is lowered very slightly. As the vocal force is increased, the phoneme is lowered but not as far as it is to produce the low central phoneme [ɑ]. The integrity of the phoneme can be preserved within the first migration pitch range. Intelligibility is lost when the low central phoneme [ɑ] is substituted for [a] at intensity levels below forte.

Laryngeal Position. The larynx is lowered approximately one centimeter from the laryngeal position assumed within the basic vowel pitch range. The vertical dimension of the pharynx is increased. The tilt of the thyroid cartilage is unchanged.

Velum. The superior-posterior heel of the velum is firmly pressed against the pharyngeal wall.

Second Migration Pitch Range

Labial Orifice. When compared with their position when the phoneme [a] is sung in the first migration pitch range, the lips are flexibly tense but very slightly protruded or rounded. This lip position prevents the phoneme from becoming blatant; it is also a stable vocal position for the singer. The labial orifice is elongated vertically. As vocal force increases, the position of the lips and the labial orifice is accentuated.

Tongue. The tip of the tongue is held firmly against the bottom front teeth. When this phoneme is sung within the second migration pitch range, the tip and blade assume a higher position than when it is sung within the first migration pitch range. The dorsum and root are very deeply grooved, thus increasing the vertical dimension of the pharynx from the mediodorsum to the root. The weak inner orifice is formed at the point of greatest constriction at the predorsum–alveolar ridge position. The frontal position of this orifice preserves the integrity of the phoneme [a]. The system is tightly coupled. As the intensity is increased, the tongue position is accentuated, and the phoneme migrates to the neutral vowel [ʌ]. The radix of the tongue has moved anteriorly approximately three millimeters from its position in the first migration pitch range. This movement enlarges the opening of the vestibule and increases the total dimension of that resonator, thereby altering its resonance characteristics.

Laryngeal Position. The laryngeal position is approximately six millimeters lower than its position when the phoneme [a] is sung within the first migration pitch range. The vertical dimension of the pharynx is increased. The tilt of the thyroid cartilage remains unchanged.

Velum. The superior-posterior heel of the velum is pressed firmly against the pharyngeal wall.

ANALYSIS OF THE BASIC VOWEL [ɑ]

(See pp. 312 and 313 for migration drills and illustrations and Record 1, Band 29 for French Placement of this vowel.)

Stable Vowel Pitch Range

Type. Low central, open, neutral, loosely coupled.

Teachers of voice often reach agreement when considering the placement of the frontal or the back vowels, however, they are often most critical of the production of the low central vowel [ɑ]. In consideration of this professional difference of opinion, this phoneme has been recorded to make the musical sound acceptable to both teacher and singer.

The tongue is the most important articulator in the production of this most controversial vowel. The tongue position is more important than the mandibular position or labial opening as a control implement for the production of the vast number of acceptable sounds within this phoneme. The tongue position of the basic vowel [ɑ] is more rounded from the tip to the blade and the tongue-backing is less extreme than in the cardinal [ɑ] of Daniel Jones. Acoustically, this phoneme is positioned more toward the cardinal [ʌ]. The cardinal [ɑ] of Daniel Jones is an acceptable sound to the Latin ear.

Labial Orifice. A slight tension is maintained at the lateral borders of the lips when this vowel is produced in the stable vowel position. Unless this tension is present, the vowel [ɑ] will migrate to the neutral vowel [ʌ]. The vertically elongated shape of the labial orifice is created by the extreme lowering of the mandible. The vowel [ɑ] is made with the lowest mandibular position of all of the vowels. Slight lip-rounding will cause the vowel to migrate to the quality alternate [ɔ]. As force is applied, the lateral tension is removed from the lips, the labial orifice is elongated vertically and the vowel migrates toward the neutral vowel [ʌ].

Tongue. The tip of the tongue is held firmly against the bottom front teeth. The postdorsal area is backed and flattened, forming the back orifice where the postdorsum is closest to the pharyngeal wall at the level of the second cervical vertebra. The tongue is flattened from the tip to the dorsal area. The postdorsum is slightly grooved. The oral cavity is large when compared with the back cavity.

The radix of the tongue moves anteriorly approximately four millimeters from its passive position and moves with it the hyoid bone and the tip of the epiglottis. This movement enlarges the opening of the vestibule and increases the total dimension of that resonator, thereby altering its resonance characteristics. As vocal force is increased, the tongue is raised slightly from the tip to the dorsum. The backing and flattening is less accentuated. This action with the relaxed labial orifice causes the vowel [ɑ] to migrate toward the neutral phoneme [ʌ].

Mandible. The mandible is lowered to permit an opening of approximately one and one-half inches between the teeth at the center. As vocal force is increased, the mandible is slightly lowered, causing a vertical increase in the size of the oral cavity. Care should be taken by the singer to eliminate tension in the labial orifice as the cavity dimension increases vertically. This action will eliminate the blatancy of this phoneme and will permit the migration of the vowel toward the neutral vowel [ʌ].

Laryngeal Position. Both the laryngeal position and tilt of the thyroid cartilage are the same as those assumed for the production of [a].

Velum. The superior-posterior heel of the velum is slightly arched and loosely approximates the pharyngeal wall. A slight leakage of sound into the nasal cavity is permitted. The uvula remains pendulous in the oropharynx away from the pharyngeal wall.

First Migration Pitch Range

Labial Orifice. To preserve the integrity of the [ɑ], the lips should retain the flexible tension required in singing the vowel [ɑ] within the basic vowel pitch range. Singers have a strong tendency to relax the lips and permit them to assume the neutral, flaccid condition. A slightly modified [ɑ] can be preserved in the first migration pitch range.

The labial orifice is elongated vertically by lowering the mandible. The singer must be careful not to protrude or round the lips while singing at low intensity levels in this first migration pitch area. Lip-rounding will cause an immediate substitution of the phoneme [ɔ]. As vocal force is increased, the labial orifice is elongated by lowering the mandible, and the phoneme migrates toward the neutral vowel [ʌ].

Tongue. The tip of the tongue is held firmly against the bottom front teeth. The tongue is slightly rounded from the tip to the mediodorsum. It is slightly grooved from blade to postdorsum. Tongue-backing is accentuated at the root position. The back orifice is formed where the root is close to the pharyngeal wall at the level of the second cervical vertebra. The oral cavity is larger than the pharyngeal cavity. The position of the epiglottis remains unchanged. As vocal force is increased, the tongue is arched slightly at the dorsum. Tongue-backing is less accentuated and the anterior-posterior dimension of the back orifice increases. This action causes the phoneme to migrate toward the neutral vowel [ʌ].

Mandible. The mandible is lower than when this phoneme is sung within the basic vowel pitch range. As the vocal force is increased, the lowering is accentuated.

Laryngeal Position. The laryngeal position is two centimeters lower than it is when this phoneme is sung within the basic vowel pitch range. The vertical dimension of the pharynx is increased. The tilt of the thyroid cartilage is unchanged.

Velum. The superior-posterior heel of the velum is firmly pressed against the pharyngeal wall. The phoneme [ɑ] has no nasality in it when it is sung within the first migration pitch range.

Second Migration Pitch Range

Labial Orifice. When compared with the vowel [ɑ] sung within the first migration pitch range, the lips are more relaxed at the corners. The labial orifice is elongated vertically. It is flexibly tense and very slightly protruded. This protrusion adds stability to the vocalic sound. It should not be confused with lip-rounding. In the second migration pitch range, the labial orifice assumes the shape of the neutral vowel [ʌ].

Tongue. The tip of the tongue is held firmly against the bottom front teeth. In comparison with its position when the phoneme [ɑ] sung is within the first migration pitch range, the tongue is raised from the tip to the predorsum. The mediodorsum and postdorsum are extremely flattened, and this flattening vertically enlarges the oral cavity at the dorsal-velar position. The dorsum is shallowly grooved, and the root is deeply grooved. The back orifice is formed at the point of greatest constriction where the upper tongue root is close to the pharyngeal wall at the level of the second cervical vertebra. The oral cavity is larger than the pharyngeal cavity.

The radix of the tongue moves anteriorly approximately ten millimeters from its position in the first migration pitch range. This movement enlarges the opening of the vestibule and increases the total dimension of that resonator, thereby altering its resonance characteristics. As vocal force is increased, the tongue position described above is accentuated. The phoneme sung in this position is the neutral vowel [ʌ].

Mandible. The mandible is lower than it is when this phoneme is sung within the basic vowel pitch range. When the vocal force is increased, the lowering is accentuated.

Laryngeal Position. The laryngeal position is approximately one centimeter lower than it is when this phoneme is sung within the first migration pitch range. The pharynx is enlarged vertically, but the tilt of the thyroid cartilage remains unchanged. As vocal force is increased, the lower laryngeal position is accentuated.

Velum. The superior-posterior heel of the velum is pressed firmly against the pharyngeal wall. The sung phoneme [ʌ] lacks nasality within the second migration pitch range.

ANALYSIS OF THE QUALITY ALTERNATE VOWEL [ɔ]

(See pp. 314 and 315 for migration drills and illustrations.)

Stable Vowel Pitch Range

Type. Low back, slightly rounded, open, loosely coupled.

Labial Orifice. The lips are firmly tense in a slightly rounded and protruded position. The labial orifice has the same vertical dimension as that assumed during the production of [ɑ]. As vocal force is increased, the lip-rounding is slightly relaxed, causing a slight migration of this phoneme toward the neutral vowel [ʌ].

Tongue. The tip of the tongue is held firmly against the bottom of the front teeth. The postdorsal area is backed and flattened more than when producing [ɑ]. The radix of the tongue moves anteriorly approximately two millimeters from its passive position. This movement only slightly enlarges the opening of the vestibule and slightly increases the total dimension of that resonator, thereby altering its resonance characteristics. The back orifice is formed at the point of greatest construction where the postdorsal area is close to the pharyngeal wall at the level of the third cervical vertebra. The tongue is flattened from the tip of the mediodorsal area. The dorsum is slightly grooved. The oral cavity is large when compared with the pharyngeal cavity. As vocal force is increased, the postdorsum of the tongue is less backed, the back orifice disintegrates and the vowel migrates toward the neutral vowel [ʌ].

Mandible. The mandible is slightly higher than the position assumed while producing the vowel [ɑ]. As intensity is increased, the mandible is lowered very slightly, increasing the vertical dimension of the oral cavity. This action, with the alteration of tongue-backing, causes the phoneme to migrate toward the neutral vowel [ʌ].

Laryngeal Position. The laryngeal position is lower than during the production of the vowel [ɑ]. The tilt of the thyroid cartilage is less than that in producing any other vowel with the exception of the closed [e], which is similar to a position of the passive state. As intensity is increased, tension of the vocal folds is realized by a lowered laryngeal position and a very slight tilt; in other phonemes, the laryngeal position is stabilized and the thyroid tilt is exaggerated.

Velum. The superior-posterior heel of the velum loosely approximates the pharyngeal wall. Some of the sound may pass into the nasal cavities. The uvula is not as pendulous but extends into the oropharynx away from the pharyngeal wall.

First Migration Pitch Range

Labial Orifice. When compared with the phoneme [ɔ] sung within the basic vowel pitch range, the lips are more rounded and slightly protruded. The labial orifice is increased in vertical dimension by lowering the mandible. The lip protrusion must be accentuated as the orifice opens to preserve the integrity of the phoneme. As the vocal force is increased, the labial orifice is further elongated vertically by lowering the mandible. The phoneme will then migrate toward the neutral vowel [ʌ].

Tongue. The tip of the tongue is held firmly against the bottom front teeth. When compared with the phoneme [ɔ] sung within the basic pitch range, the tongue is slightly more rounded from the tip to the dorsum. The dorsum is backed and slightly grooved. The tongue root is more deeply grooved than when the phoneme is sung in the basic pitch range. The back orifice is formed at the upper tongue-root position at the level of the second cervical vertebra. The oral cavity is larger than the pharyngeal cavity. As vocal force is increased, the vertical dimension of the oral cavity is increased by lowering the mandible. The tongue-backing at the dorsum is less accentuated, and the phoneme [ɔ] migrates toward the neutral phoneme [ʌ]. The radix of the tongue moves anteriorly a distance of approximately seven millimeters from its position in the stable vowel pitch range. This movement enlarges the opening of the vestibule and increases the total dimension of that resonator, thereby altering its resonance characteristics.

Mandible. The mandible is lower than it is during the production of the phoneme [ɔ] in the basic vowel pitch range; as the vocal force is increased, the lowering is accentuated.

Laryngeal Position. The laryngeal position is two centimeters lower than it is when this phoneme [ɔ] is sung in the basic vowel pitch range. The vertical dimension of the pharyngeal cavity is increased. The tilt of the thyroid cartilage is unchanged.

Velum. The superior-posterior heel of the velum is firmly pressed against the pharyngeal wall. The phoneme [ɔ] has no nasality when it is sung within the first migration pitch range.

Second Migration Pitch Range

Labial Orifice. In comparison with their position for singing the phoneme [ɔ] within the first migration pitch range, the lips are flexibly tense and protruded. Protrusion must not be confused with lip-rounding, which is the characteristic of the following phoneme, the basic vowel [ô]. Lip protrusion involves thrusting the lips forward to increase the length of the neck of the labial orifice. This neck provides stability to the phoneme when it is sung within this high pitch range. Lip protrusion occurs only in the production of the low back phoneme [ɔ], the high back phoneme [ʊ], and the high central phoneme [ɜ] in the basic vowel pitch range and first and second migration pitch ranges. It is used in the second migration pitch range of the phonemes [ɑ], [ʌ], [ô], [o], [ʊ], and [u] when the vocal force is increased above mezzo forte intensity.

The labial orifice is elongated vertically from the position assumed during the production of [ɔ] in the first migration. The elongation is made by lowering the mandible. As vocal force is increased, the elongation is accentuated.

Tongue. When compared with its position for singing the phoneme [ɔ] within the first migration pitch range, the tongue retains a similar conformation from the tip to the predorsum. It is lower at the mediodorsum and postdorsum. The backing is more accentuated than it was for the first migration pitch range. The tongue is shallowly grooved from the dorsum to the base of the root. The radix of the tongue moves anteriorly approximately four millimeters from its position in the first migration pitch range. This movement enlarges the opening of the vestibule and increases the total dimension of that resonator, thereby altering its resonance characteristics. The back orifice is formed at the postdorsal position at the level of the second cervical vertebra. The front cavity is larger than the back cavity. As vocal force is increased, this position is accentuated. The phoneme sung is that of the neutral vowel [ʌ].

Mandible. The mandible is lower than the position assumed in producing the phoneme [ɔ] in the first migration pitch range. As vocal force is increased, the lowering is accentuated.

Laryngeal Position. The larynx is only slightly lower than it is when the phoneme [ɔ] is produced in the first migration pitch range. The tilt of the thyroid remains unchanged. As vocal force is increased, the larynx is lowered approximately four millimeters. The conformation of the pharynx is approximately the same.

Velum. The superior-posterior heel of the velum is firmly pressed against the pharyngeal wall.

ANALYSIS OF THE BASIC VOWEL OPEN [ô]

(See pp. 318 and 319 for migration drills and illustrations.)

Stable Vowel Pitch Range

Phoneticians do not include this phoneme as a sound of the English language. It is the sound of the open Italian [ô]. However, for a singer or for a teacher of voice the sound is indispensable as a teaching tool for the proper pronunciation of English sounds. It is also an efficient phonemic choice for maximum sonority in song.

This phoneme is used in all [ou] sounds where the [o] is a stressed syllable, and where an open sound is preferred to the closed tense [o]; the off glide (diphthong) to the [u] must be reduced to a minimum. The usual substitution for this phoneme is the open [ɔ], which is used within the British Stage dialect (See p. 236.) Singers of English cannot use the [ɔ] phoneme when singing such words as *roll, cold, smoke, dose, boast, roam, sew,* and *holy.* In many instances the closed tense [o] may be substituted for [ô] particularly in piano and pianissimo passages (Record 5, Bands 7, 9, 11, 13) in the art song and German lieder.

Type. Mid-back, half-closed, slightly rounded, loosely coupled.

Labial Orifice. The lips are tensely rounded, but the labial orifice is slightly smaller and rounder than it is for singing the phoneme [ɔ] in both vertical and transverse dimensions. The singer should conceive of this phoneme as a rounded open [ô], not as a member of the [ɔ] phoneme. To produce the phoneme [ô], lip protrusion is to be avoided; rather, the outer edges of the lips are drawn together in a circular formation without disturbing the volume of the oral cavity or the openness of the labial orifice. As vocal force is increased, the lip-rounding must be maintained to preserve the integrity of the phoneme. However, as the intensity of the sound reaches the level of mezzo forte to forte, the labial orifice tends to be more open as the singer attempts to gain greater sonority. The phoneme then migrates toward the quality alternate vowel [ʊ].

Tongue. The tip of the tongue is held firmly against the bottom front teeth. The tongue arch is higher at the postdorsal, prevelar area than during the production of the vowel [ɔ]. The back orifice is formed at the point of greatest constriction where the upper root area is close to the pharyngeal wall at the level of the second cervical vertebra. The radix of the tongue moves anteriorly approximately nine millimeters from its passive position and moves with it the hyoid bone and the tip of the epiglottis. This movement enlarges the opening of the vestibule and increases the total dimension of that resonator, thereby altering its resonance characteristics. The small back orifice forms a loosely coupled system, and it, with the small front orifice, gives to the vowel its characteristic [ô] quality. As vocal force is increased, tongue-backing is slightly decreased, thus disintegrating the back orifice and causing the vowel to migrate toward the quality alternate vowel [ʊ].

Mandible. The mandible is held at a slightly higher position than it is for producing the vowel [ɔ]. The vertical opening is approximately one inch between the front teeth. As the vocal force is increased, the mandible is lowered slightly, increasing the vertical dimension of the oral cavity. This action, combined with slight relaxation of the front orifice and the alteration of the back orifice, causes the phoneme to migrate toward the quality alternate vowel [ʊ].

Laryngeal Position. The laryngeal lowering is approximately the same as it is for producing the low back and central vowels, but the tilt of the thyroid cartilage is extreme in order to stabilize and add tension to the vocal folds.

Velum. The velum is held firmly against the pharyngeal wall to prevent sound from passing into the nasal cavity. The uvula is tense and away from the pharyngeal wall.

First Migration Pitch Range

Labial Orifice. Lip-rounding and tension of the lips are the same as they are for the phoneme [o] sung within the stable vowel pitch range. A low mandibular position keeps the labial orifice open to preserve the open characteristic of this phoneme. Retaining the open [ô] in sung sounds throughout the first migration pitch range is possible only when the vocal force demanded ranges from mezzo forte to forte. When pianissimo sounds are required, the closed [o] is substituted because the damped-out high partials have a soft effect and because this phoneme provides a greater resistance for vocal control.

Tongue. The tip of the tongue is held firmly against the bottom front teeth. The tongue is arched slightly more from tip to predorsum than it is when this phoneme is sung within the basic vowel pitch range. The tongue is grooved and lowered at the dorsum and root. It is not grooved at the point of greatest constriction where the back orifice is formed and where the post-dorsum is close to the pharyngeal wall at the second cervical vertebra.

The tongue-backing is extreme. The oral cavity is larger than the pharyngeal cavity. The position of the epiglottis remains unchanged. As vocal force increases, tongue-backing slightly decreases, disintegrating the back orifice and causing the vowel to migrate toward the quality alternate vowel [ʊ].

Mandible. The mandible is slightly lower than it is for the phoneme [ô] sung within the basic vowel pitch range. As vocal force is increased, the mandible is lowered, increasing the vertical dimension of the labial orifice and oral cavity at the blade-dorsal position. This action, combined with the relaxing of the front orifice and the widening of the back orifice, causes the phoneme to migrate toward the quality alternate vowel [ʊ].

Laryngeal Position. The laryngeal position is approximately one centimeter lower than it is when this phoneme [ô] is sung within the basic vowel pitch range. The vertical dimension of the pharynx is increased. The tilt of the cartilage is not changed.

Velum. The superior-posterior heel of the velum remains pressed against the pharyngeal wall. The sound is free of nasality.

Second Migration Pitch Range

Labial Orifice. In comparison with their position when the phoneme is sung within the first modification pitch range, the lips are flexibly tense and rounded rather than protruded. While learning to sing this phoneme within the second migration pitch range, the neutral vowel [ʌ] should be sung without attempts to achieve proper lip-rounding. The phoneme should be sung with the lips loose and flaccid. When the vocalic sound is stabilized with proper breath support, the lip-rounding should be accentuated by changing the labial orifice to a slightly rounded rather than elongated position. The slight lip-rounding and the large labial orifice causes this phoneme to migrate toward the quality alternate vowel [ʊ]. Such a migration or substitution is vocally permissible. However, the singer who is seeking vocal refinement will learn to control this phoneme in the upper pitch ranges for greater intelligibility.

Tongue. The tip of the tongue is held firmly against the bottom front teeth. The tongue conformation from tip to the blade is the same as it is when the phoneme [ô] is produced within the first migration pitch range. The dorsum of the tongue is lowered. Tongue-backing is accentuated. The orifice is formed at the point of greatest constriction where the postdorsum is close to the pharyngeal wall between the second and the third cervical vertebra. The oral cavity is larger than the pharyngeal cavity. The radix of the tongue moves anteriorly approximately three millimeters from its position in the first migration pitch range. This movement enlarges the opening of the vestibule and increases the total dimension of that resonator, thereby altering its resonance characteristics. As the vocal force is increased, the labial orifice becomes less tense, the tongue-backing is less accentuated and the phoneme migrates to [u].

Mandible. The mandible is held at a lower position than it is for producing the phoneme within the first migration pitch range. As vocal force is increased, the mandibular lowering is accentuated, increasing the anterior-posterior dimension of the labial orifice and the oral cavity at the blade-dorsal position. As the labial orifice becomes elongated and less rounded, the phoneme migrates to the quality alternate vowel [ʊ].

Laryngeal Position. The laryngeal position is one centimeter lower than it is when the phoneme [ô] is sung within the first migration pitch range. The vertical dimension of the pharynx is increased. The tilt of the thyroid cartilage remains unchanged.

Velum. The superior-posterior heel of the velum remains firmly pressed against the pharyngeal wall.

ANALYSIS OF THE QUALITY ALTERNATE VOWEL CLOSED [o]

(See pp. 318 and 319 for migration drills and illustrations.)

Stable Vowel Pitch Range

The secret of singing this mid-back, closed vowel correctly is to respect its production within the intensity levels of piano and double piano. In some instances in lieder the phoneme open [ô] will sound open and harsh; such passages are invariably marked *p* or *pp*. Within these passages the vowel [o] is most beautiful (Records 1-4, Band 17).

Type. Mid-back, closed, rounded, loosely coupled.

Labial Orifice. The lips are tense and the rounding is quite extreme. The labial orifice is approximately one inch in its vertical and transverse dimensions. When vocal force is increased, the labial orifice tends to become more relaxed as the singer attempts to attain maximum sonority. The phoneme then migrates to the basic vowel [ô].

Tongue. The tip of the tongue is held firmly against the bottom front teeth. The tongue is flattened and with a shallow groove from the tip to the predorsum. The tongue arch is considerably lower and flattened from the blade to the mediodorsal area, but from the postdorsal area to the root the arch is the same as that assumed during the production of the open [ô]. The back orifice is formed at the point of greatest constriction where the postdorsum is close to the pharyngeal wall at the level of the second cervical vertebra. The small back orifice forms a loosely coupled system with the small front orifice, and gives the vowel its characteristic [o] quality. The front cavity is larger than the back cavity. The radix of the tongue moves anteriorly approximately eight millimeters from its position in a passive state and moves with it the hyoid bone and the tip of the epiglottis. This movement enlarges the opening of the vestibule and increases the total dimension of that resonator, thereby altering its resonance characteristics. As vocal force is increased, the tongue-backing is slightly decreased, disintegrating the back orifice and relaxing the labial orifice causing the vowel to migrate toward the quality alternate vowel [ʊ].

Mandible. The mandible is held slightly lower than it is for producing the basic vowel [ô]. The vertical opening between the front teeth is approximately one and one-quarter inches. As the vocal force is increased, the mandible remains fixed while the front and back orifices are relaxed to permit the singer to attain maximum sonority. The vowel then migrates to the quality alternate vowel [ʊ].

Laryngeal Position. The laryngeal position is six centimeters lower than it is during the production of the open basic vowel [ô]. The extreme forward tilt of the thyroid cartilage is approximately the same as that assumed during the production of [o].

Velum. The velum is held firmly against the pharyngeal wall and prevents any sound from passing into the nasal cavity. The uvula is tensed and held away from the pharyngeal wall.

First Migration Pitch Range

Labial Orifice. The lips retain the rounded tension required for singing this phoneme within the basic vowel pitch range. The labial orifice is opened by lowering the mandible; as the vocal force is increased, the orbicular tension of the lips is relaxed and the mandibular lowering is accented, thus causing the phoneme to migrate toward the basic vowel [ô].

Tongue. The tip of the tongue is held firmly against the bottom front teeth. The blade and predorsum form a concave, shallowly grooved depression. The dorsum is extremely arched and backed and is not grooved. The tongue root has a shallow groove. The back orifice is formed at the point of greatest constriction where the postdorsum is close to the pharyngeal wall at the level of the space between the second and third vertebra. The oral cavity is larger than the pharyngeal cavity. The position of the epiglottis remains unchanged.

As the vocal force increases, the labial orifice relaxes somewhat, the tongue is less backed, and the phoneme migrates to the quality alternate vowel open [ʊ] as the sonority of the phoneme is increased.

Mandible. The mandible is held slightly lower than it is when the phoneme [o] is sung within the basic vowel pitch range. As the vocal force is increased, the mandible is lowered, increasing the vertical dimension of the oral cavity at the blade-palatal position.

Laryngeal Position. The laryngeal position is approximately one centimeter lower than it is when this phoneme is sung within the basic vowel pitch range. The vertical dimension of the pharynx is increased slightly. The tilt of the thyroid cartilage is not as accentuated.

Velum. The posterior-superior heel of the velum is pressed firmly against the pharyngeal wall.

Second Migration Pitch Range

Labial Orifice. When compared with their position for the phoneme [o] sung within the first migration pitch range, the lips are flexibly tense and rounded rather than protruded, very similar to the position assumed during the production of open [ô] within the second migration pitch range. The basic phonemic position sung is that of the quality alternate vowel [ʊ] but with slight lip protrusion; as vocal force is increased, the lips are less rounded and the labial orifice is opened slightly by lowering the mandible. The sonority of the phoneme is increased as the vowel [o] migrates toward the quality alternate vowel [ʊ].

Tongue. The tip of the tongue is held firmly against the bottom front teeth. The tongue is less depressed at the blade, predorsal position than it is when the phoneme is sung within the first migration pitch range. The tongue-backing and arching of the dorsum are unchanged. The back orifice is formed at the point of greatest constriction at the postdorsum–pharyngeal wall position at the level of the second cervical vertebra. The oral cavity is larger than the pharyngeal cavity. The radix of the tongue moves anteriorly approximately five millimeters from its position in the first migration pitch range. This movement enlarges the opening of the vestibule and increases the total dimension of that resonator, thereby altering its resonance characteristics. As the vocal force is increased, the labial orifice becomes less tense, the tongue-backing is less accentuated and the phoneme migrates to the quality alternate vowel [ʊ].

Mandible. The mandible is held at a lower position than it is for producing the phoneme [o] within the first migration pitch range. As vocal force is increased, the mandibular lowering is accentuated, increasing the vertical dimension of the oral cavity. Lowering the mandible is the basic movement affecting the labial orifice, oral cavity, and tongue position. The combined movements of these three anatomical parts cause the phoneme [o] to migrate to the quality alternate vowel [ʊ].

Laryngeal Position. The larynx is lowered approximately one centimeter from the position assumed while producing the phoneme [o] in the first migration pitch range. The vertical dimension of the pharynx is increased. The thyroid tilt does not change.

Velum. The superior-posterior heel of the velum is pressed firmly against the pharyngeal wall.

ANALYSIS OF THE QUALITY ALTERNATE VOWEL (ʊ)

(See pp. 320 and 321 for migration drills and illustrations.)

Stable Vowel Pitch Range

Type. High back, closed, rounded, loosely coupled.

Labial Orifice. The lips are tensely protruded with the labial orifice open slightly more than it is during the production of the closed vowel [o] but not as open as it is for the basic vowel [ô]. The labial orifice is elongated vertically. As vocal force is increased, the lip protrusion is held firmly tense to preserve the integrity of the phoneme. The labial orifice is increased in its vertical dimension. This phoneme does not migrate to another vowel when sung within the basic vowel pitch range if lip protrusion is held firmly tense.

Tongue. The tip of the tongue is held firmly against the bottom front teeth. The tongue arch is considerably depressed from the blade to the medio-dorsal area as it is during the production of the vowel [o]. The oral cavity is nearly symmetrical in shape from the tongue blade to the medio-dorsal area. The tongue is slightly grooved from the blade to the root. The tongue is backed as extremely as it was during the production of the vowel [o]; therefore, the back orifice creates a loosely coupled system.

The pharyngeal cavity is equal in area to the back cavity. The back orifice is located at the point of greatest constriction where the postdorsum is closest to the pharyngeal wall at the level of the second cervical vertebra. The radix of the tongue moves anteriorly a distance of approximately ten millimeters from its position in a passive state and moves with it the hyoid bone and the tip of the epiglottis. This movement enlarges the opening of the vestibule and increases the total dimension of that resonator, thereby altering its resonance characteristics. As the vocal force is increased, the vertical dimension of the oral cavity is increased by lowering the mandible to permit the singer to attain greater sonority. If the lip protrusion is preserved, the vowel does not migrate when it is sung within the basic vowel pitch range.

Mandible. The mandible is raised slightly higher than it is for producing the vowel [o]. The vertical opening between the front teeth is approximately one inch. As the vocal force is increased, the mandible is lowered slightly to permit the singer to attain greater sonority. If lip protrusion is preserved, this phoneme does not migrate to another phoneme when it is sung within the basic vowel pitch range.

Laryngeal Position. The laryngeal position is not as low as it is for producing the vowel closed [o] but its lowered position is identical to its position for other back vowels. The tilt of the thyroid cartilage is extreme and identical to that assumed during the production of [o].

Velum. The velum is held firmly against the pharyngeal wall to prevent sound from passing into the nasal cavities. The uvula is tense and held away from the pharyngeal wall.

First Migration Pitch Range

Labial Orifice. The lips are tensely protruded more than they were in singing the phoneme [ʊ] sung within the basic vowel pitch range. Without lip protrusion the phoneme [ʊ] migrates immediately to the neutral vowel [ʌ]. The labial orifice is elongated in its vertical dimension by lowering the mandible. As vocal force is increased, the elongation of the labial orifice is accentuated if lip protrusion is preserved.

Tongue. The tip of the tongue is held firmly against the bottom front teeth. The tongue height and arching are the same from the tip to the predorsum as they were for the phoneme [ʊ] sung in its basic vowel position. The dorsum is less backed but more deeply grooved. The tongue root is also grooved. The vertical dimension of the oral cavity is increased by lowering the mandible. The back orifice is formed at the point of greatest constriction at the postdorsum–pharyngeal wall position at the level of the third cervical vertebra. The radix of the tongue moves anteriorly approximately five millimeters from its position in the stable vowel pitch range. This movement enlarges the opening of the vestibule and increases the total dimension of that resonator, thereby altering its resonance characteristics. The oral cavity is larger than the pharyngeal cavity.

As vocal force is increased, the tongue position is accentuated. Provided the lip protrusion is increased, the phoneme does not migrate when it is sung within the first migration pitch range.

Mandible. The mandible is lower than it is when the phoneme [ʊ] is sung in the first migration pitch range. As vocal force is increased, the mandibular lowering is accentuated.

Laryngeal Position. The laryngeal position is approximately one centimeter lower than it is when the phoneme [ʊ] is sung within the basic vowel pitch range. The vertical dimension of the pharynx is increased; the tilt of the thyroid cartilage remains unchanged. As vocal force increases, the laryngeal lowering is accentuated.

Velum. The superior-posterior heel of the velum is firmly pressed against the pharyngeal wall.

Second Migration Pitch Range

Labial Orifice. The lips remain tensely protruded when singing within the second modification pitch range. The labial orifice is elongated vertically. As vocal force is increased, lips and orifice are stabilized. The phoneme does not migrate.

Tongue. The tip of the tongue is firmly pressed against the bottom front teeth. The tongue arch at the tip and blade is the same as it is when the phoneme [ʊ] is sung within the first migration pitch range. The dorsum is lowered and more deeply grooved. The tongue-backing is the same. The back orifice is formed at the point of greatest constriction at the postdorsum–pharyngeal wall position at the level of the third cervical vertebra. The base of the root is drawn anteriorly, increasing the anterior-posterior dimension of the pharynx and the valecula. This position of the epiglottis is the same as that assumed in the first migration pitch range. The oral cavity is larger than the pharyngeal cavity. As vocal force increases, the position of the tongue is stabilized. The phoneme [ʊ] does not migrate provided the lip protrusion is not reduced.

Mandible. The mandible is slightly lower than it is when this phoneme is sung in the first migration pitch range. As vocal force increases, extreme tension in the protruded lip position stabilizes the mandible.

Laryngeal Position. The larynx is lowered approximately one and one-half centimeters from the laryngeal position assumed during the production of [ʊ] within the first migration pitch range. The vertical dimension of the pharynx is increased a similar distance. The tilt of the thyroid cartilage increases as the vocal force increases; the laryngeal position is stabilized.

Velum. The superior-posterior heel of the velum is firmly pressed against the pharyngeal wall.

(Text continued on page 349)

DRILLS AND VISUAL ANALYSIS

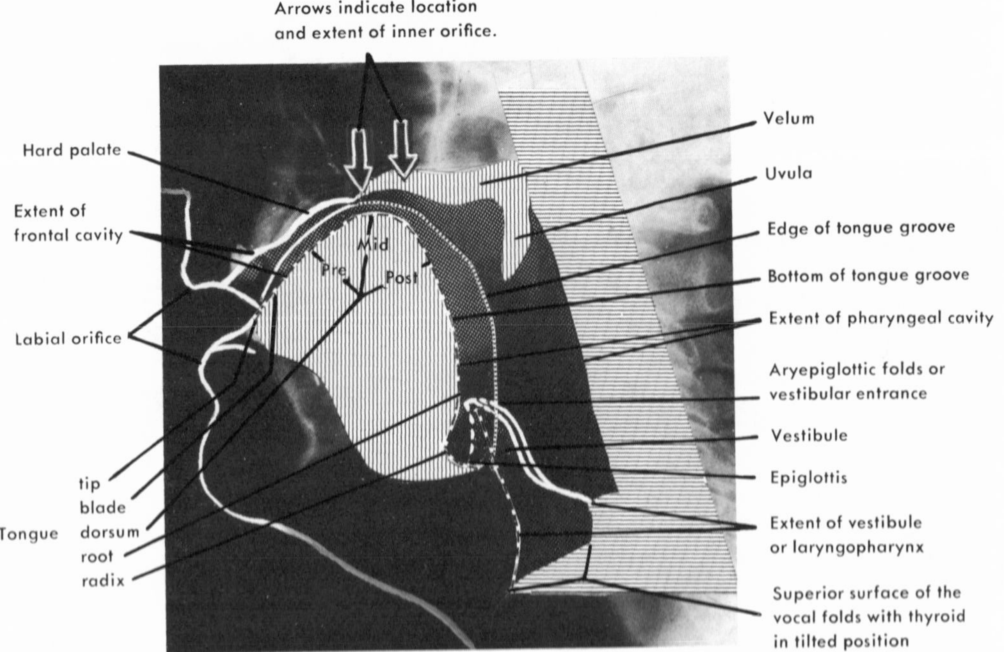

Movement of these anatomical parts may be observed in the radiographs which follow.

MIGRATION DRILLS FOR THE BASIC VOWEL [i]

Transpose these drills into a key suitable for the student.

Stable Vowel Pitch Range

Within this pitch range, this phoneme should be conceived in its purest form and sung at intensities ranging from pianissimo to piano. When singing forte or making a crescendo, the singer should think of the phoneme migrating only slightly toward the phoneme [ɪ].

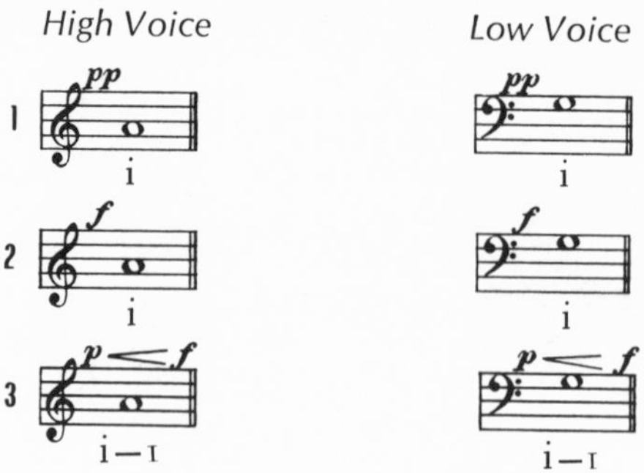

First Migration Pitch Range

When singing within this pitch range, the singer should think of the phoneme [i] migrating more completely toward the phoneme [ɪ].

Second Migration Pitch Range

When singing within this pitch range, the singer should think of substituting the phoneme [ɪ] for the phoneme [i].

Stable Vowel
Pitch Range

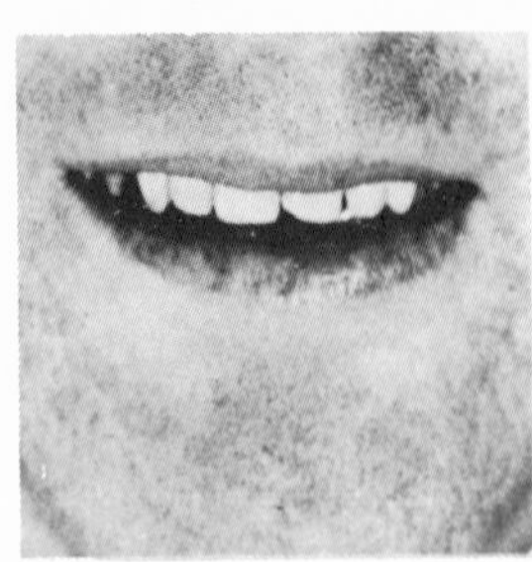

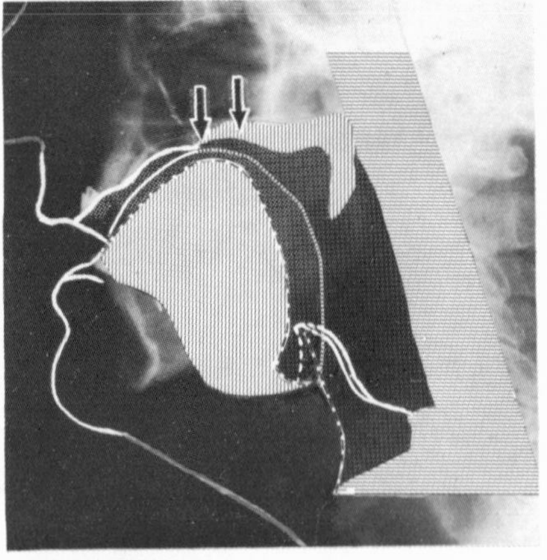

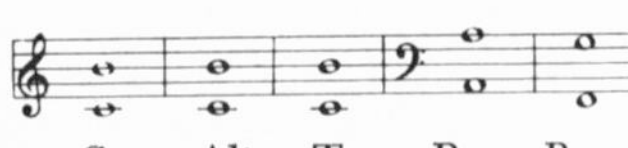

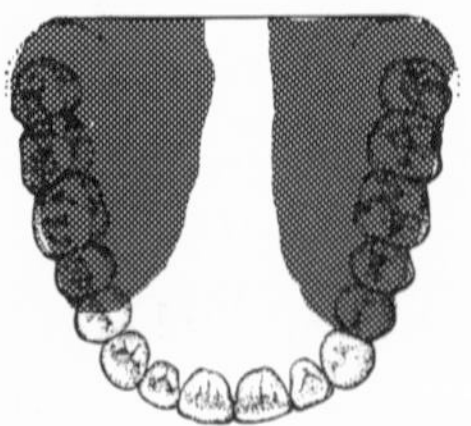

First Migration
Pitch Range

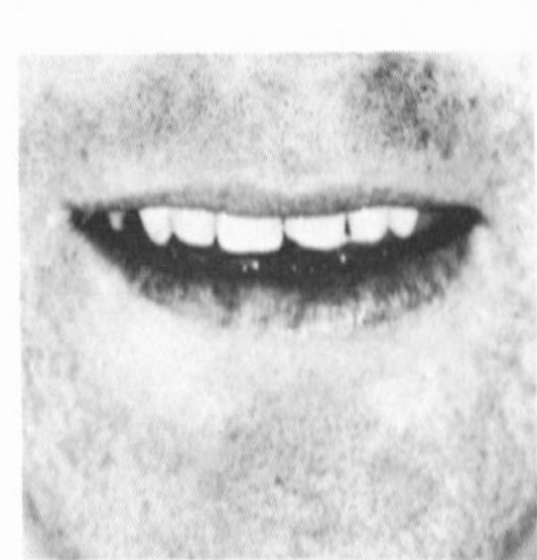

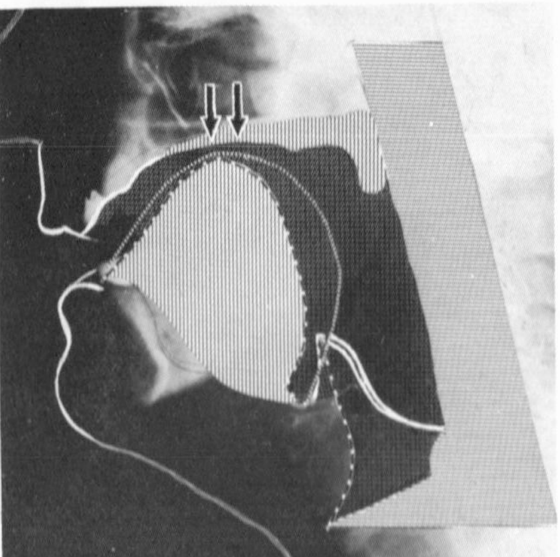

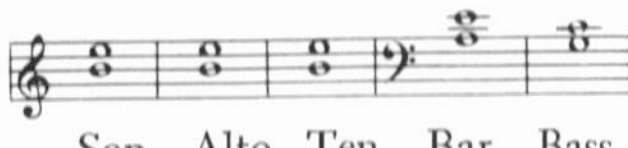

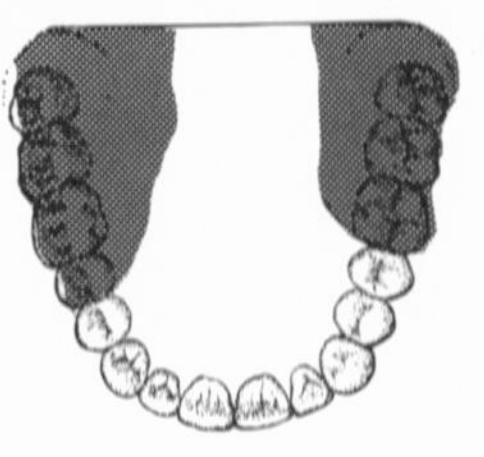

Second Migration
Pitch Range

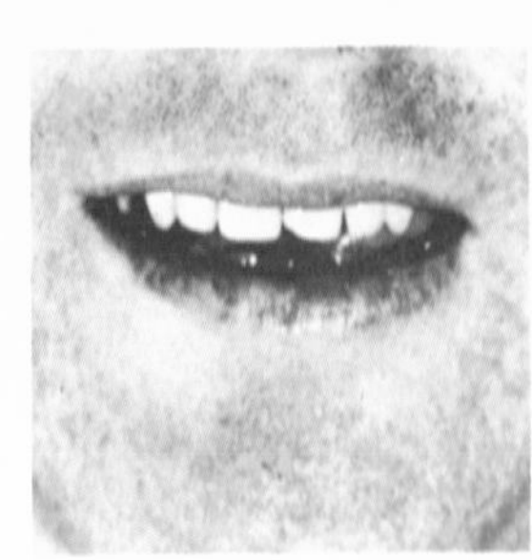

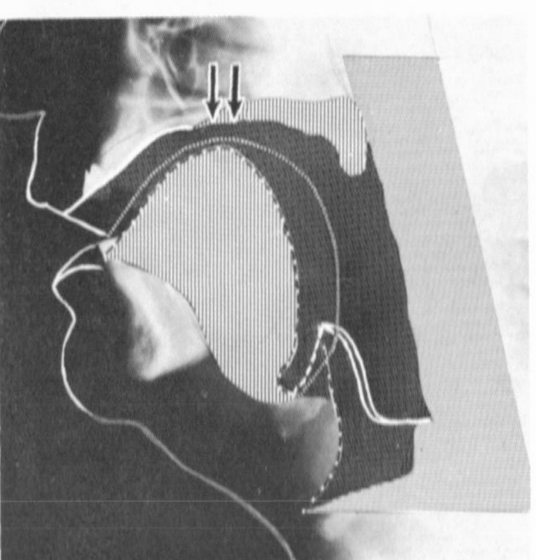

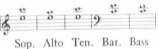

Sop. Alto Ten. Bar. Bass

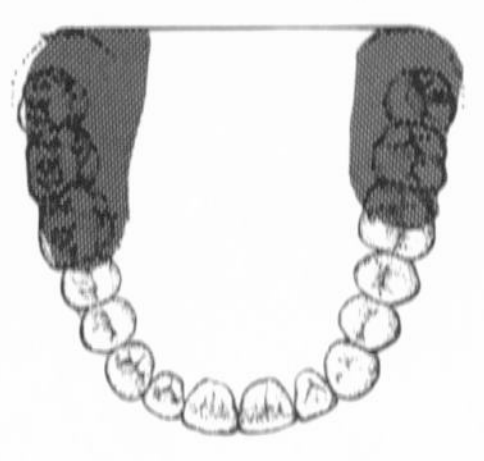

Fig. **112.** The Basic Vowel [i]

	F1	F2	F3
Male	300	1950	2750
Female	400	2250	3300

MIGRATION DRILLS FOR THE QUALITY ALTERNATE CLOSED VOWEL [ē]

Transpose these drills into a key suitable for the student.

Stable Vowel Pitch Range

Within this pitch range, this phoneme should be conceived in its purest form and sung at intensities ranging from pianissimo to piano. When singing forte or making a crescendo, this phoneme [ē] is stable and does not migrate.

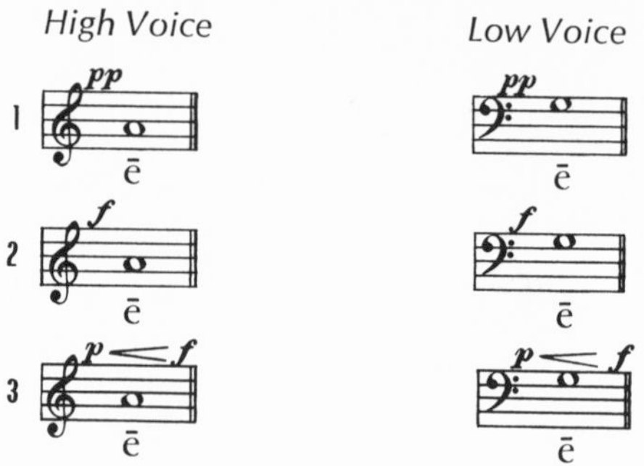

First Migration Pitch Range

Within this pitch range this phoneme [ē] is stable and does not migrate.

Second Migration Pitch Range

When singing within this pitch range, singing forte, or making a crescendo, the singer should attempt to maintain the tongue position for the phoneme [ē], but he should use a lower jaw position for the topmost note.

Stable Vowel
Pitch Range

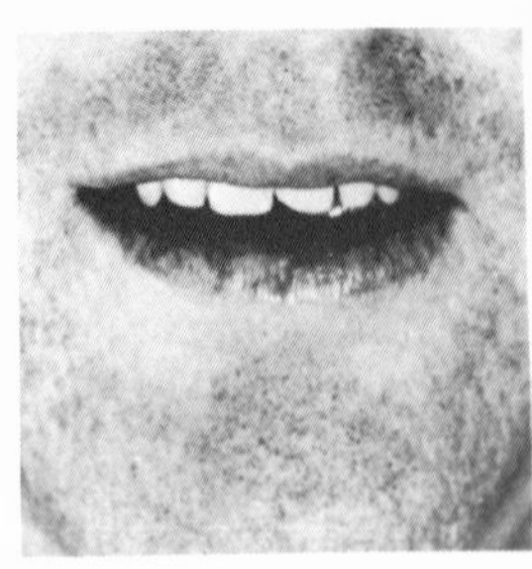

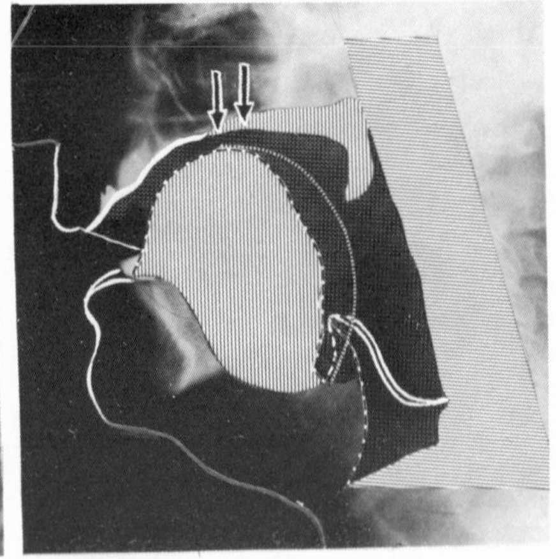

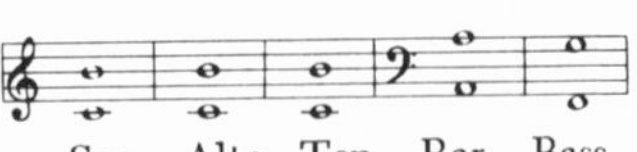

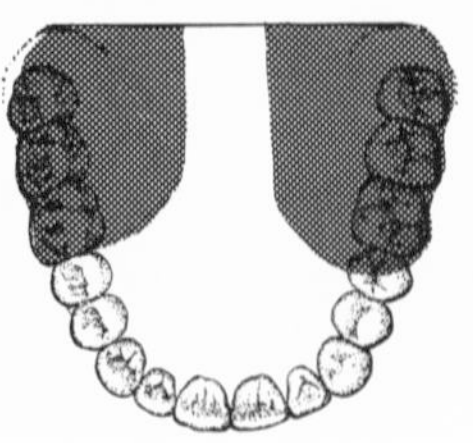

First Migration
Pitch Range

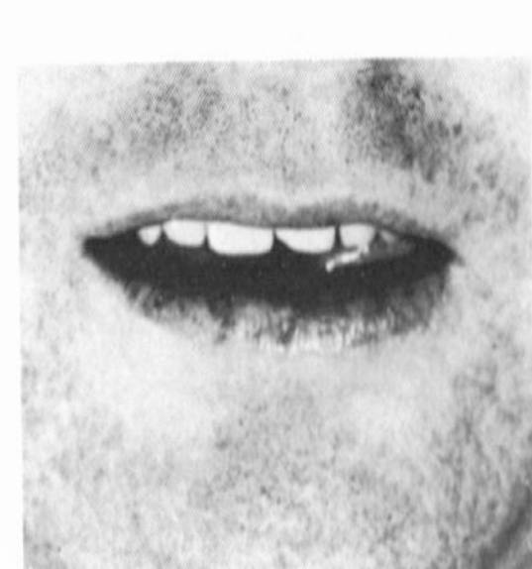

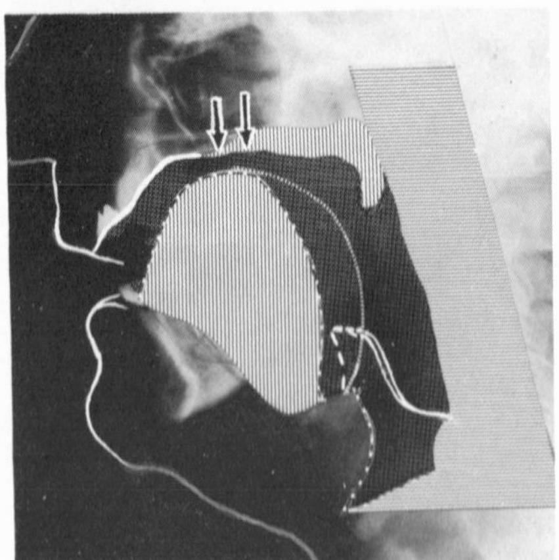

Sop. Alto Ten. Bar. Bass

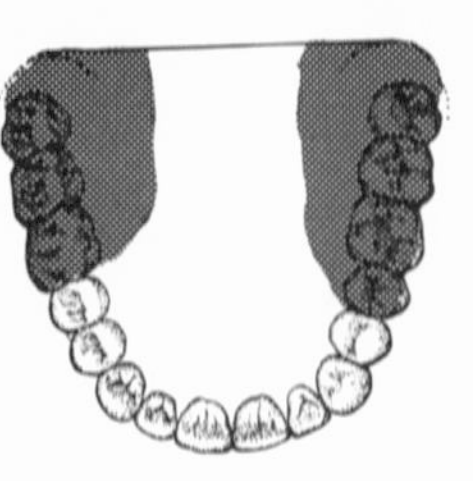

Second Migration
Pitch Range

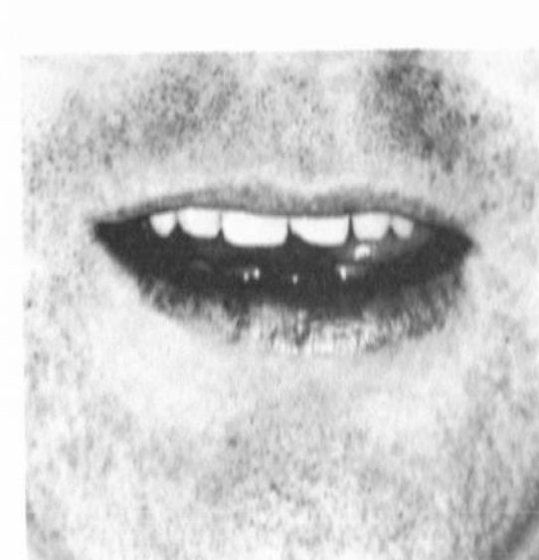

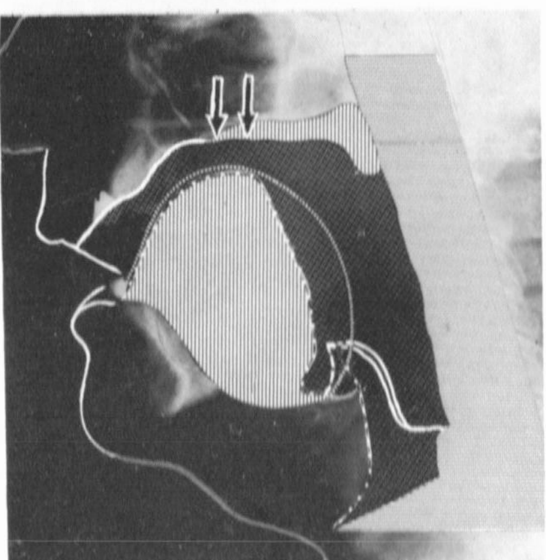

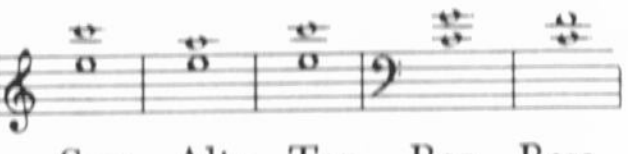

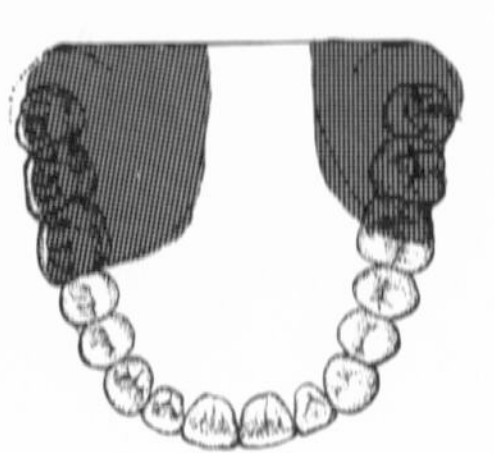

Fig. **113.** The Quality Alternate Vowel Closed [ē]

	F^1	F^2	F^3
Male	350	1850	2650
Female	450	2125	3450

MIGRATION DRILLS FOR THE QUALITY ALTERNATE VOWEL [ɪ]

Transpose these drills into a key suitable for the student.

Stable Vowel Pitch Range

When singing within this pitch range, this phoneme should be conceived in its purest form and sung at intensities ranging from pianissimo to piano. When singing forte or making a crescendo, this phoneme [ɪ] is stable and does not migrate.

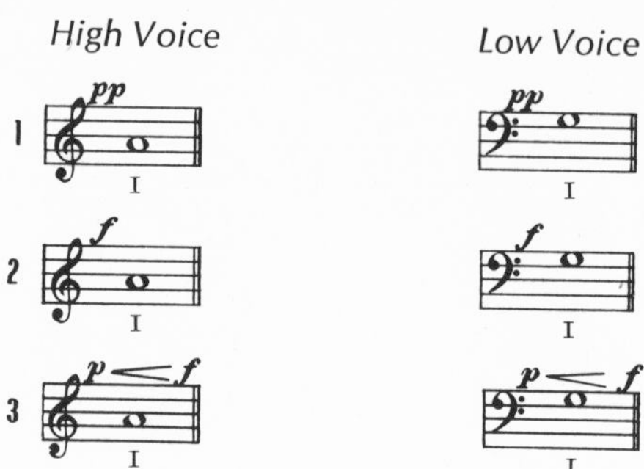

First Migration Pitch Range

Within this pitch range, this phoneme [ɪ] is stable and does not migrate.

Second Migration Pitch Range

When singing within this pitch range, singing forte, or making a crescendo, the singer should attempt to maintain the tongue position for the phoneme [ɪ], but he should use a lower jaw position for the topmost note.

Stable Vowel
Pitch Range

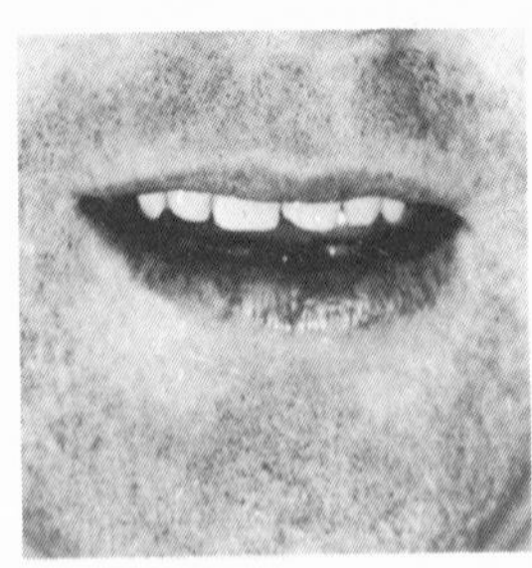

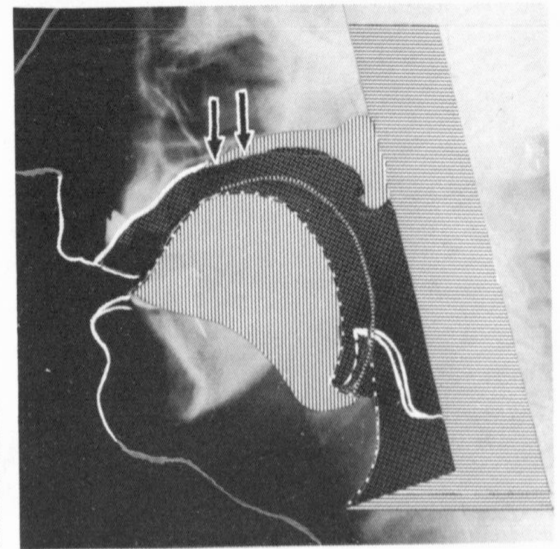

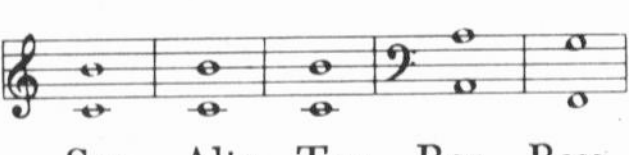

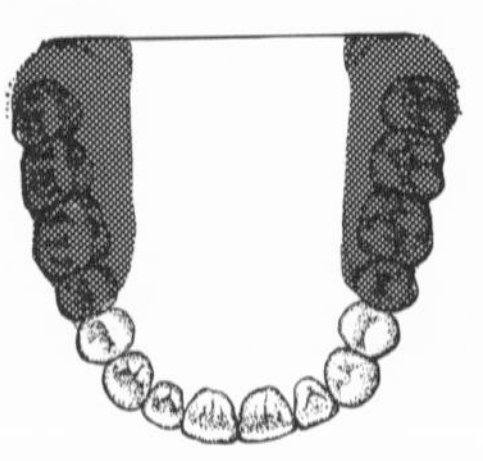

First Migration
Pitch Range

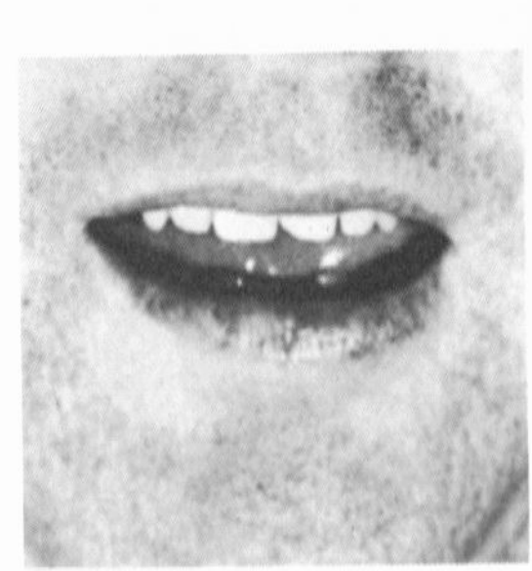

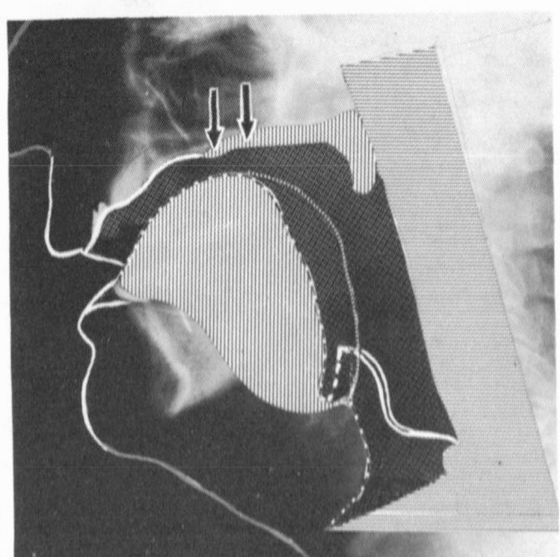

Sop. Alto Ten. Bar. Bass

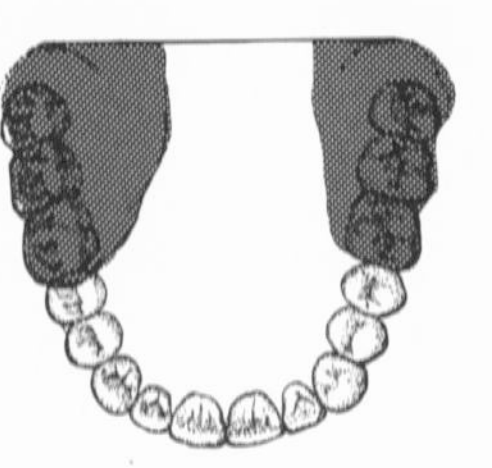

Second Migration
Pitch Range

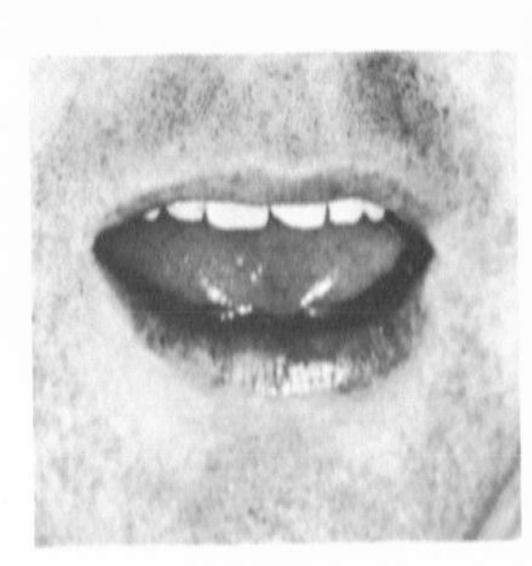

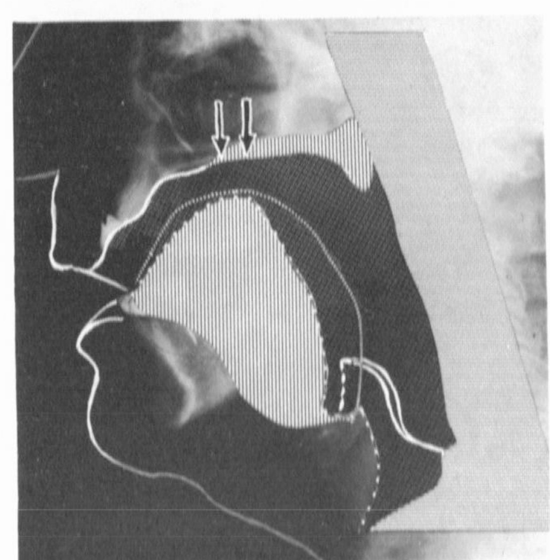

Sop. Alto Ten. Bar. Bass

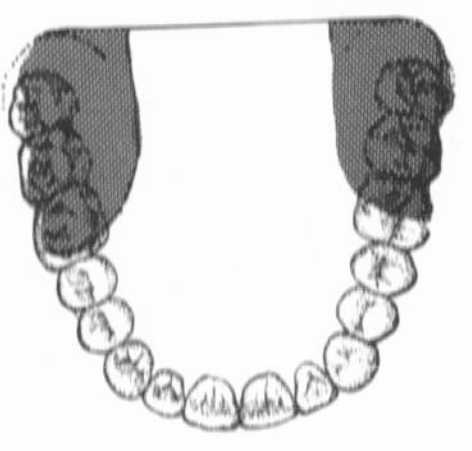

Fig. **114.** The Quality Alternate Vowel [ɪ]

	F^1	F^2	F^3
Male	375	1810	2500
Female	475	2100	3450

MIGRATION DRILLS FOR THE BASIC VOWEL OPEN [e]

Transpose these drills into a key suitable for the student.

Stable Vowel Pitch Range

Within this pitch range, this phoneme should be conceived in its purest form and sung at intensities ranging from pianissimo to piano. When singing forte or making a crescendo, the singer should think of the phoneme migrating only slightly toward the phoneme [ε].

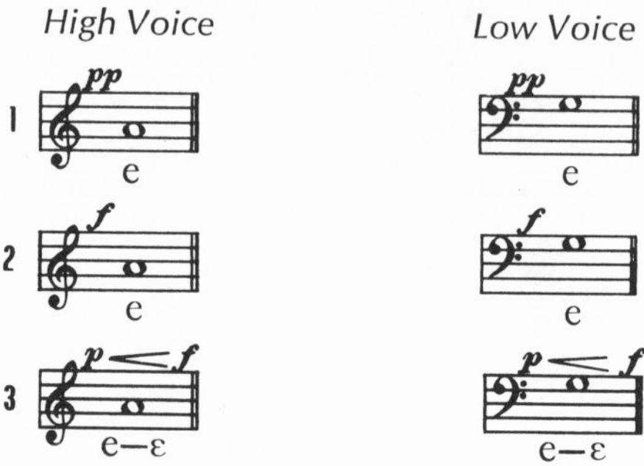

First Migration Pitch Range

When singing within this pitch range, the singer should think of the phoneme [e] migrating more completely toward the phoneme [ε].

Second Migration Pitch Range

When singing within this pitch range, the singer should think of substituting the phoneme [ε] for the phoneme [e].

Stable Vowel
Pitch Range

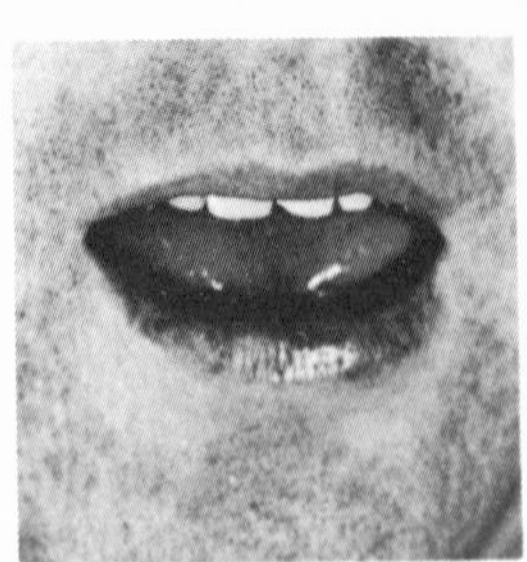

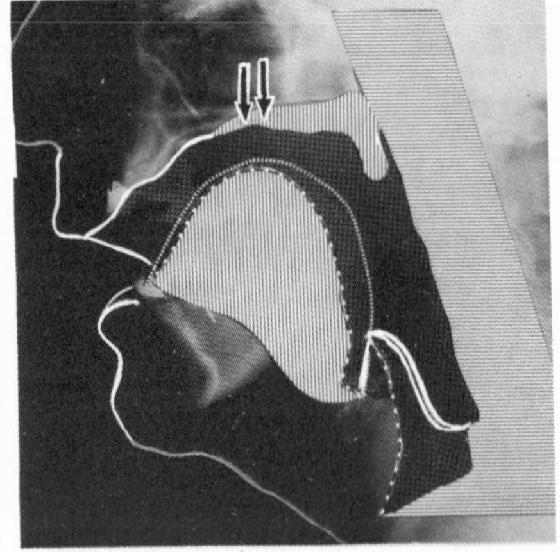

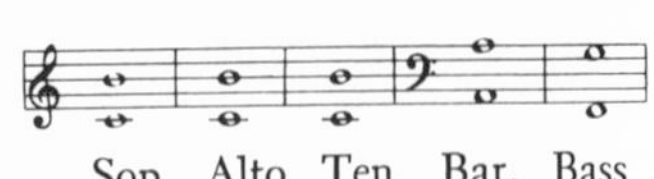

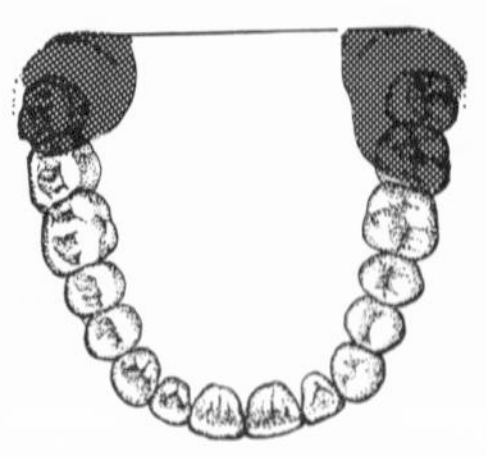

First Migration
Pitch Range

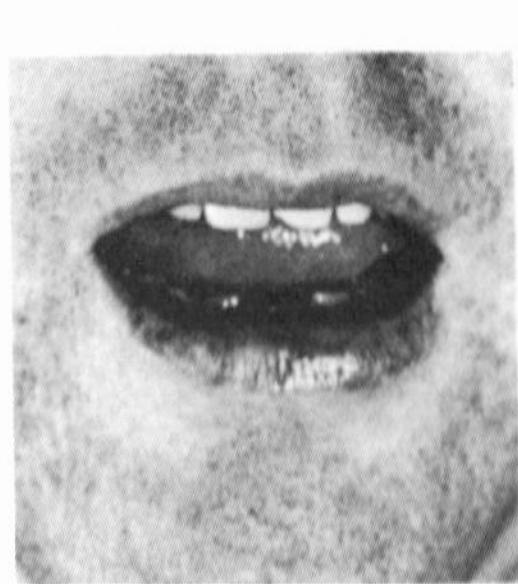

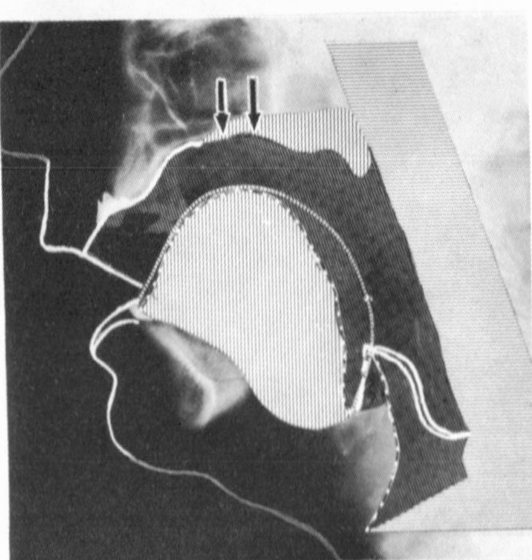

Sop. Alto Ten. Bar. Bass

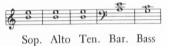

Second Migration
Pitch Range

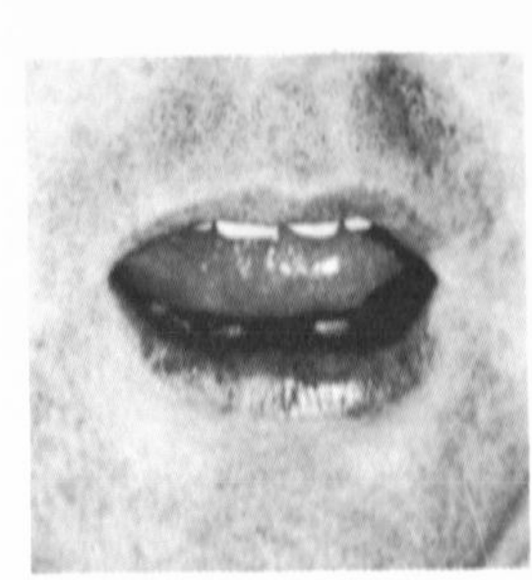

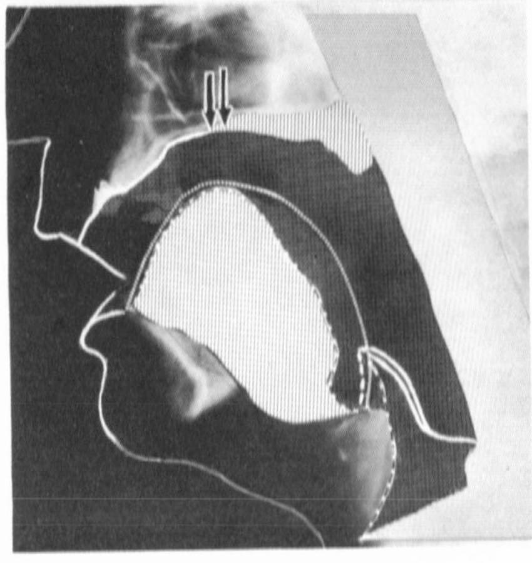

Sop. Alto Ten. Bar. Bass

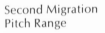

Fig. **115.** The Basic Vowel Open [e]

	F1	F2	F3
Male	450	1800	2480
Female	500	1900	3250

MIGRATION DRILLS FOR THE QUALITY ALTERNATE VOWEL [ɛ]

Transpose these drills into a key suitable for the student.

Stable Vowel Pitch Range

Within this pitch range, this phoneme should be conceived in its purest form and sung at intensities ranging from pianissimo to piano. When singing forte or making a crescendo, the singer should think of the phoneme migrating only slightly toward the phoneme [a].

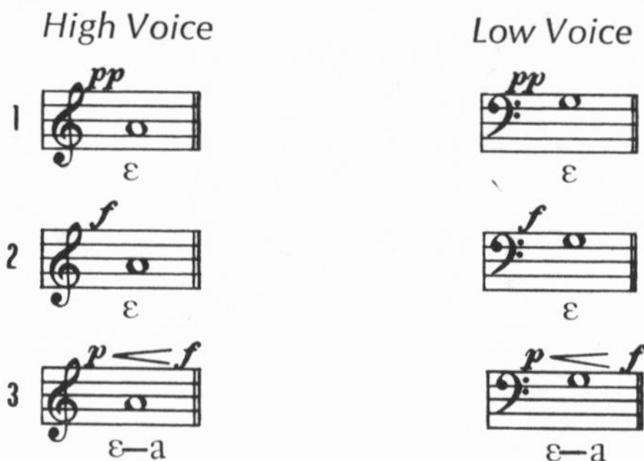

First Migration Pitch Range

When singing within this pitch range, the singer should think of the phoneme [ɛ] migrating more completely toward the phoneme [a].

Second Migration Pitch Range

When singing within this pitch range, the singer should think of substituting the phoneme [a] for the phoneme [ɛ].

Stable Vowel
Pitch Range

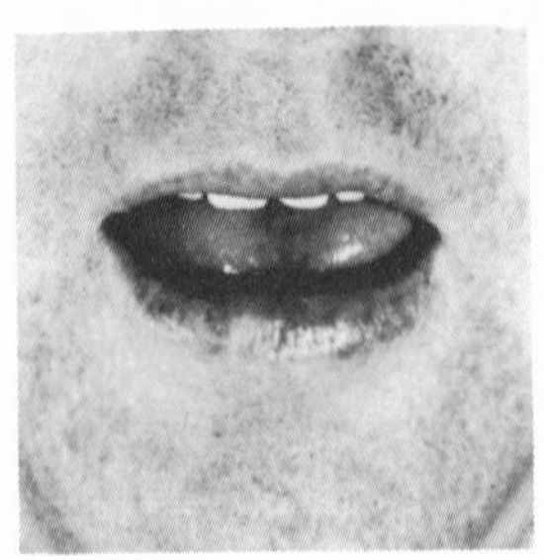

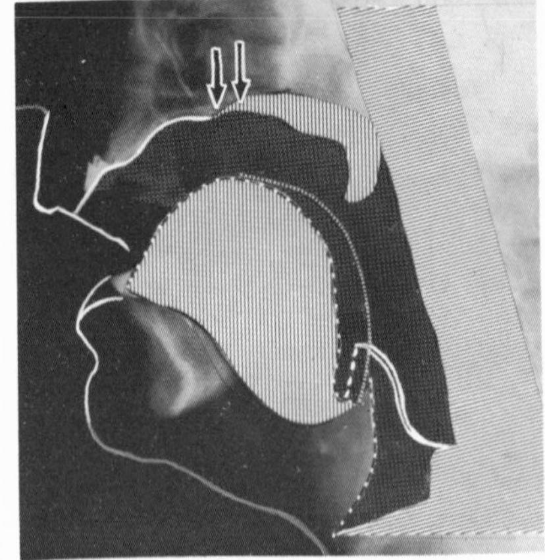

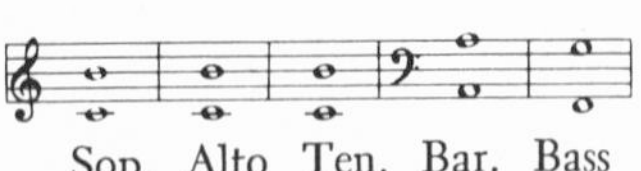

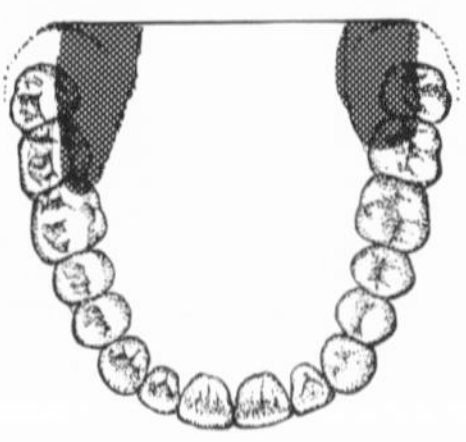

First Migration
Pitch Range

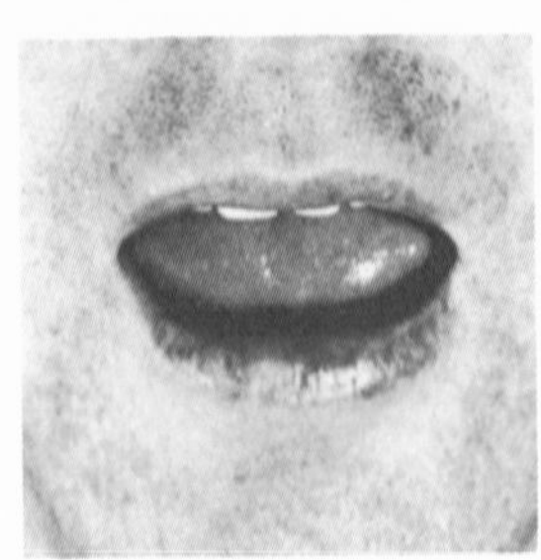

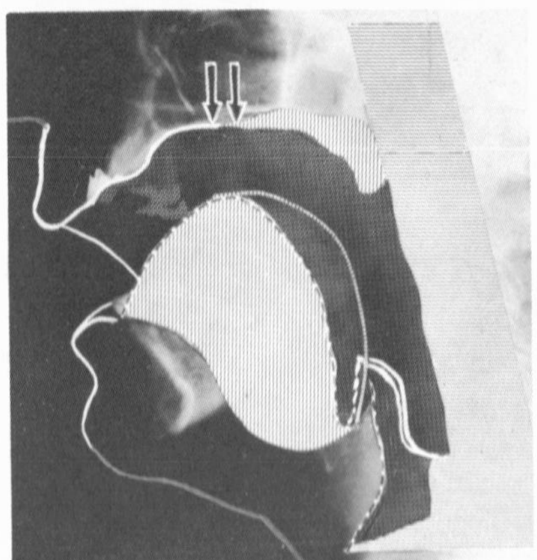

Sop. Alto Ten. Bar. Bass

Second Migration
Pitch Range

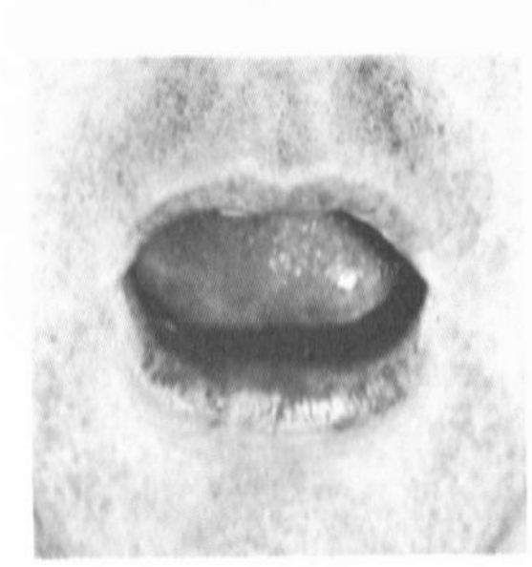

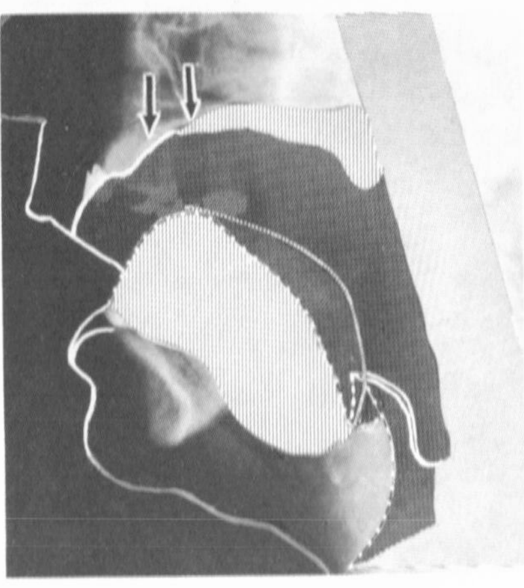

Sop. Alto Ten. Bar. Bass

Fig. **116.** The Quality Alternate Vowel [ɛ]

	F1	F2	F3
Male	530	1500	2500
Female	550	1750	3250

MIGRATION DRILLS FOR THE BASIC VOWEL [æ]

Transpose these drills into a key suitable for the student.

Stable Vowel Pitch Range

This phoneme [æ] is seldom used in song because of its open blatancy. When it is used within this pitch range, it should be sung at intensities ranging from pianissimo to piano. When singing forte or making a crescendo, the singer should always substitute the phoneme [a] for the phoneme [æ].

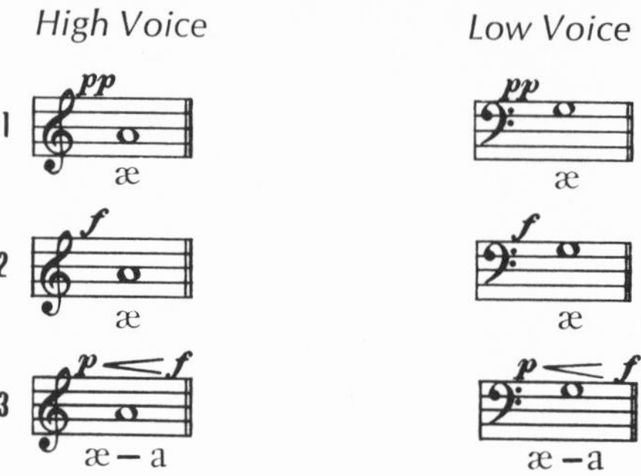

First Migration Pitch Range

When singing within this pitch range, the singer should think of substituting the phoneme [a] for the phoneme [æ].

Second Migration Pitch Range

When singing within this pitch range, the singer should substitute the phoneme [a] for the phoneme [æ].

Stable Vowel
Pitch Range

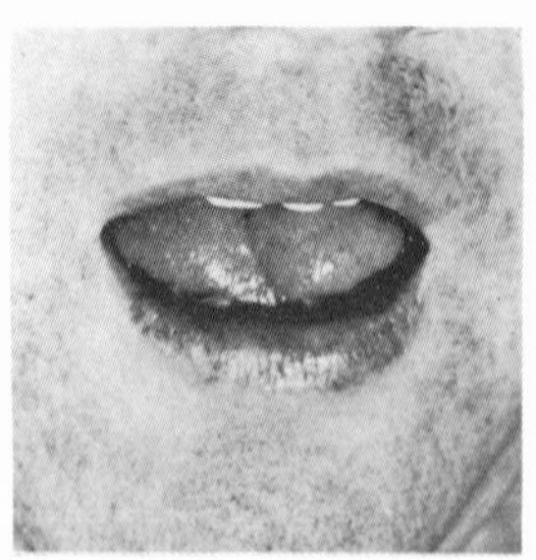

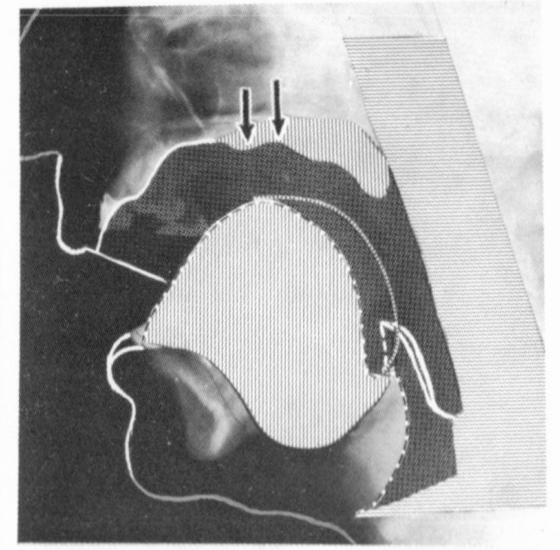

First Migration
Pitch Range

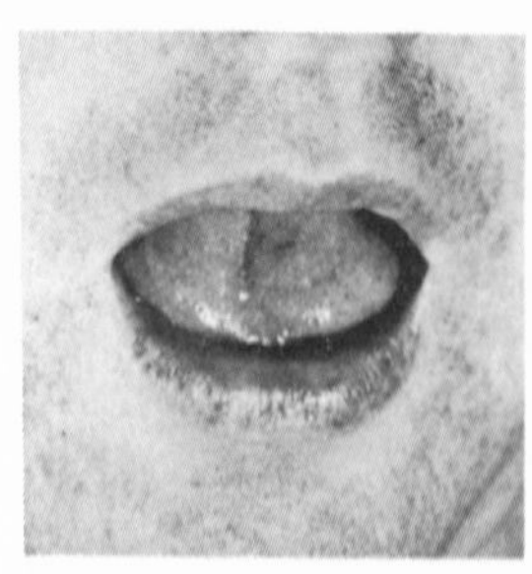

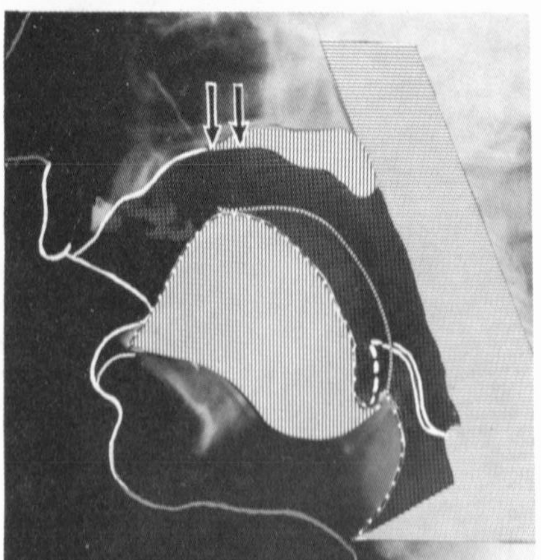

Sop. Alto Ten. Bar. Bass

Second Migration
Pitch Range

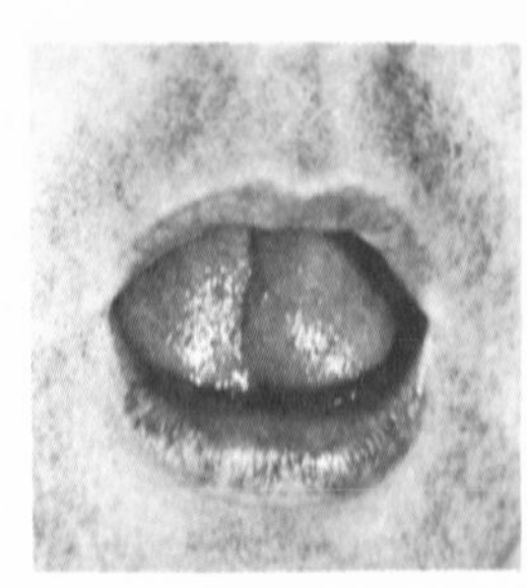

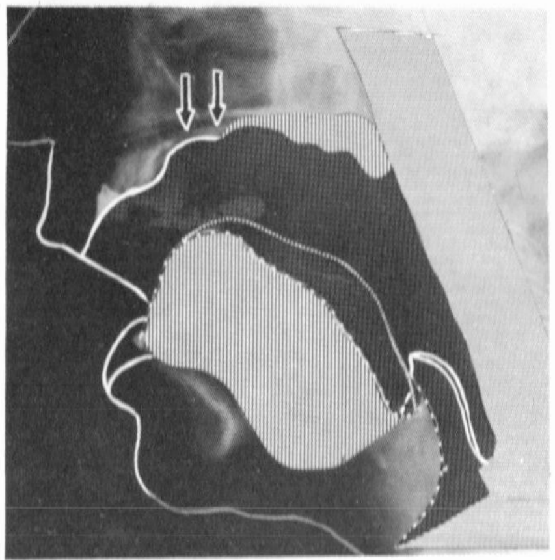

Sop. Alto Ten. Bar. Bass

Fig. **117.** The Basic Vowel [æ]

	F^1	F^2	F^3
Male	620	1490	2250
Female	600	1650	3000

MIGRATION DRILLS FOR THE QUALITY ALTERNATE VOWEL [a]

Transpose these drills into a key suitable for the student.

Stable Vowel Pitch Range

Within this pitch range, this phoneme should be conceived in its purest form and sung at intensities ranging from pianissimo to piano. When singing forte or making a crescendo, the singer should think of the phoneme [a] migrating only slightly toward the phoneme [ɑ].

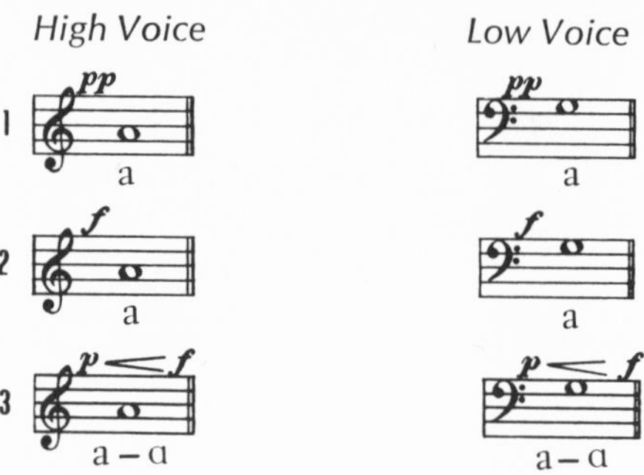

First Migration Pitch Range

When singing within this pitch range, the singer should think of the phoneme [a] migrating more completely toward the phoneme [ɑ].

Second Migration Pitch Range

When singing within this pitch range, the singer should think of substituting the phoneme [ʌ] for the phoneme [ɑ].

Stable Vowel
Pitch Range

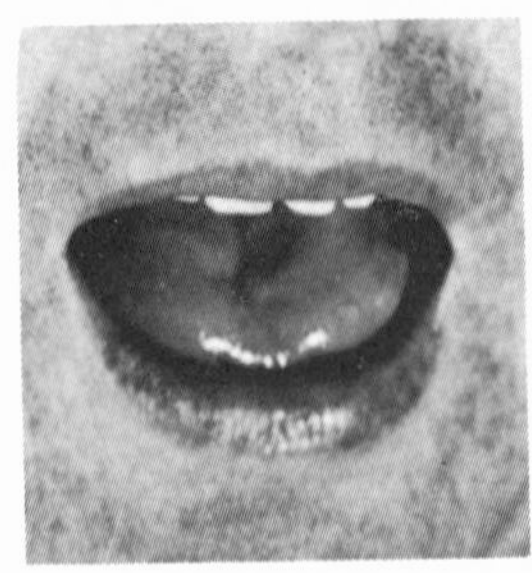

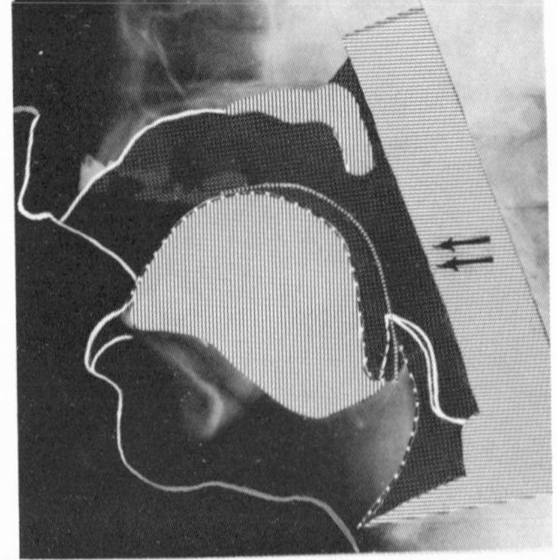

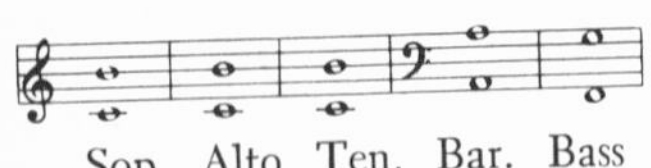

First Migration
Pitch Range

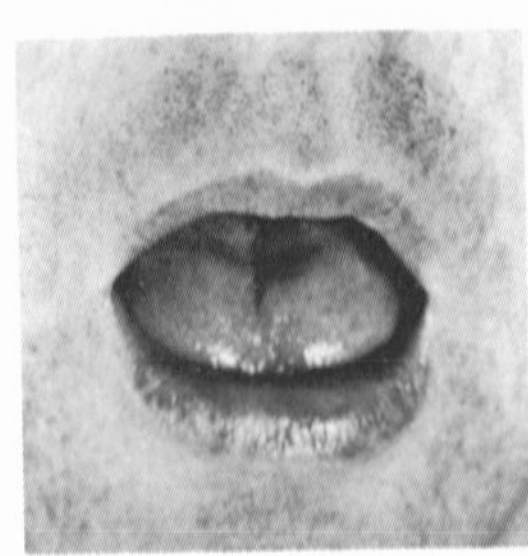

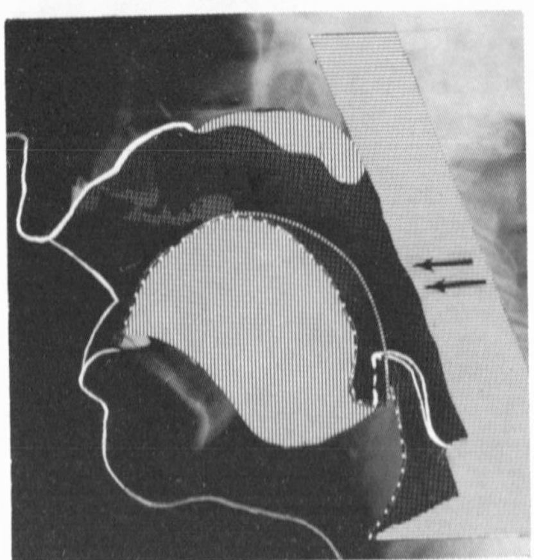

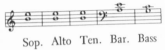

Sop. Alto Ten. Bar. Bass

Second Migration
Pitch Range

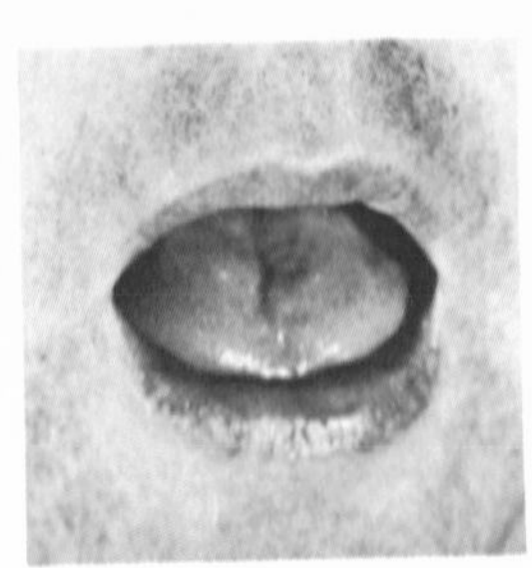

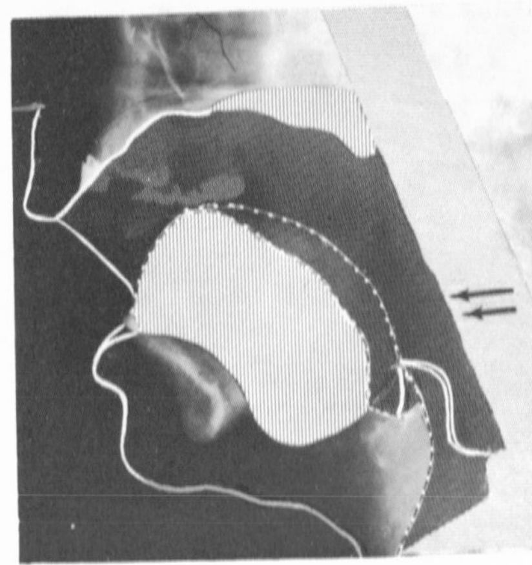

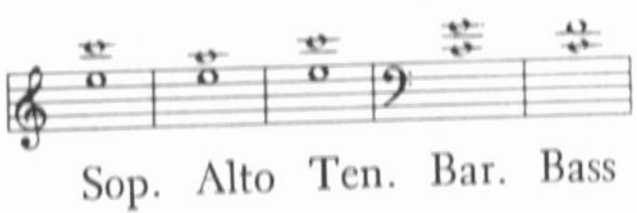

Fig. **118.** The Quality Alternate Vowel [a]

	F1	F2	F3
Male	550	1200	2500
Female	675	1555	3300

MIGRATION DRILLS FOR THE BASIC VOWEL [ɑ]

Transpose these drills into a key suitable for the student.

Stable Vowel Pitch Range

Within this pitch range this phoneme should be conceived in its purest form and sung at intensities ranging from pianissimo to piano. When singing forte or making a crescendo, the singer should think of the phoneme migrating only slightly toward the phoneme [ʌ].

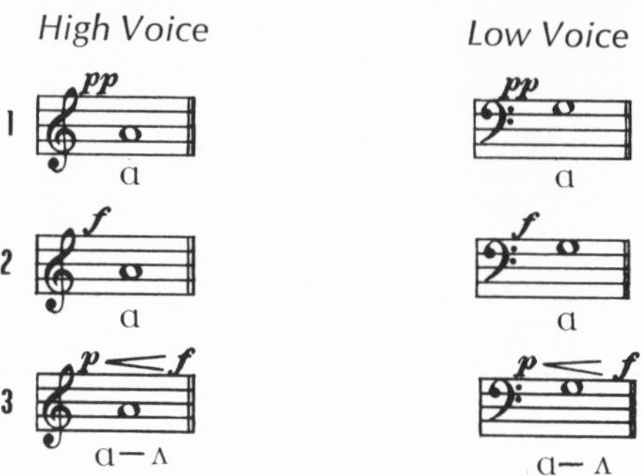

First Migration Pitch Range

When singing within this pitch range, the singer should think of the phoneme [ɑ] migrating more completely toward the phoneme [ʌ].

Second Migration Pitch Range

When singing within this pitch range, the singer should think of substituting the phoneme [ʌ] for the phoneme [ɑ].

Stable Vowel
Pitch Range

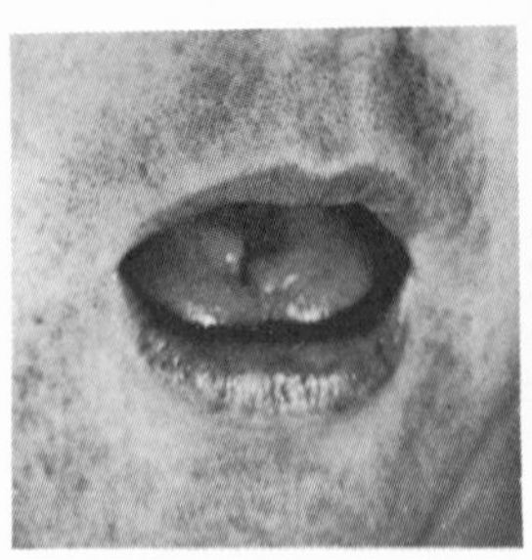

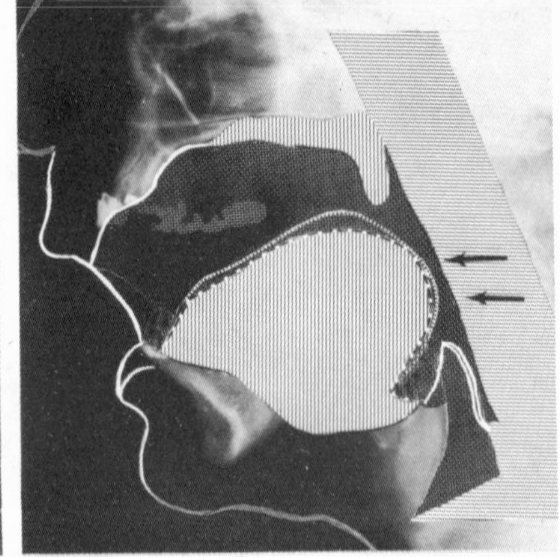

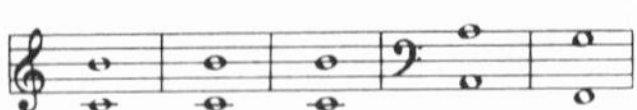

First Migration
Pitch Range

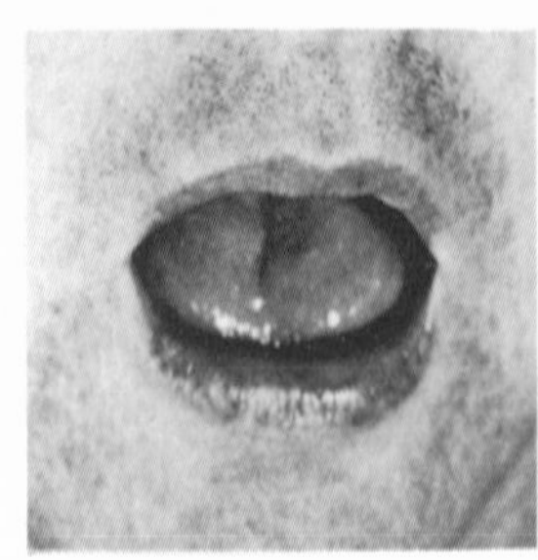

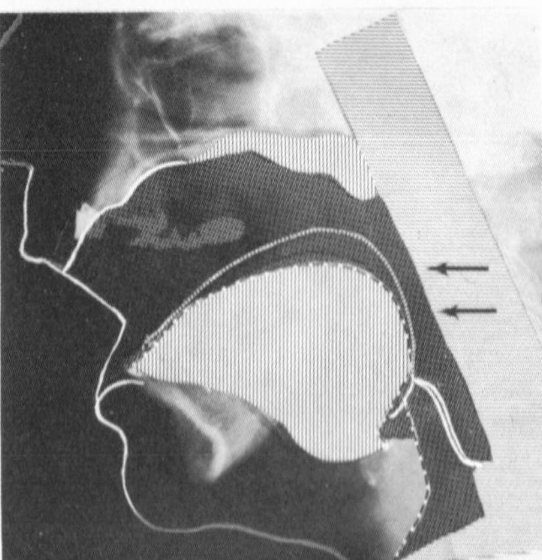

Sop. Alto Ten. Bar. Bass

Second Migration
Pitch Range

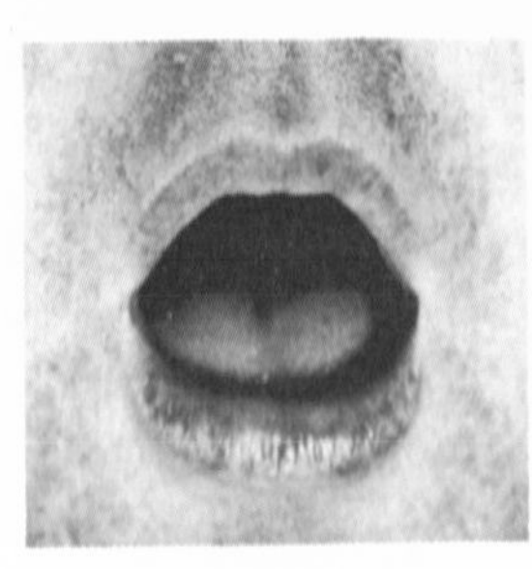

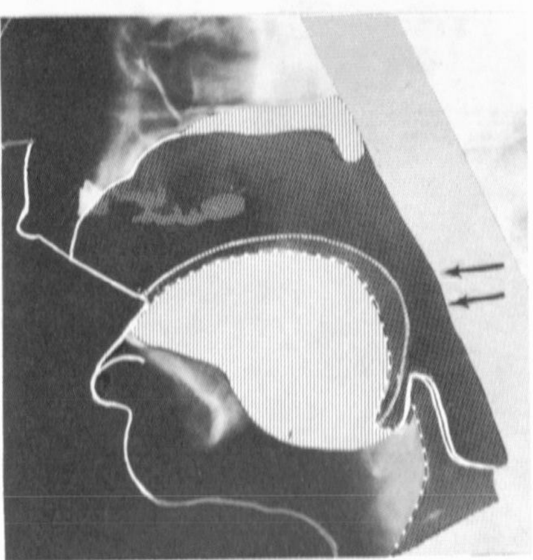

Sop. Alto Ten. Bar. Bass

Fig. **119.** The Basic Vowel [ɑ]

	F1	F2	F3
Male	700	1200	2600
Female	700	1300	3250

MIGRATION DRILLS FOR THE QUALITY ALTERNATE VOWEL [ɔ]

Transpose these drills into a key suitable for the student.

Stable Vowel Pitch Range

When singing within this pitch range, the singer should attempt to preserve the integrity of the vowel at all intensity levels. Lip-rounding should be maintained in crescendo and forte passages.

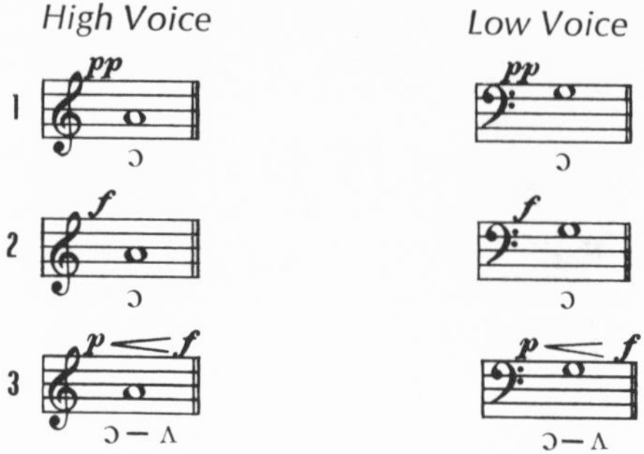

First Migration Pitch Range

When singing within this pitch range, the singer should think of the phoneme [ɔ] migrating more completely toward the phoneme [ʌ].

Second Migration Pitch Range

When singing within this pitch range, the singer should think of substituting the phoneme [ʌ] for the phoneme [ɔ].

Stable Vowel
Pitch Range

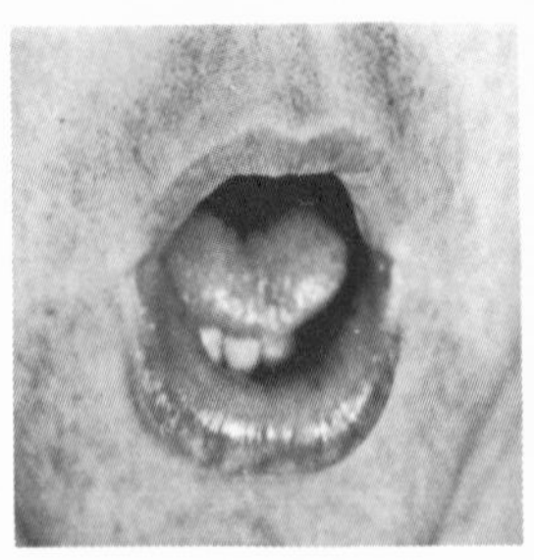

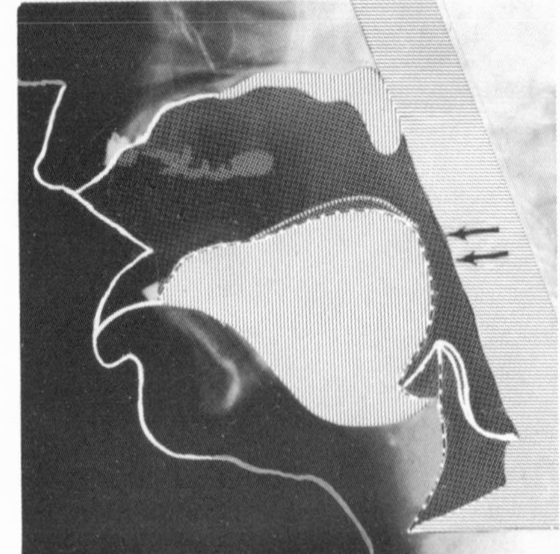

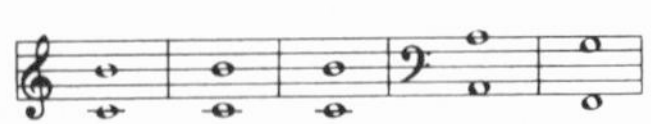

First Migration
Pitch Range

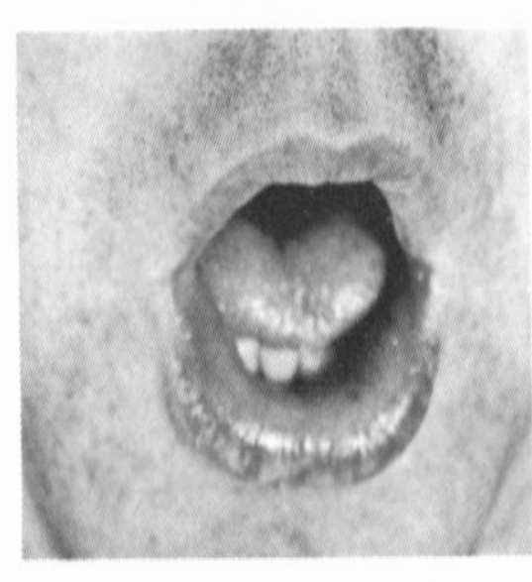

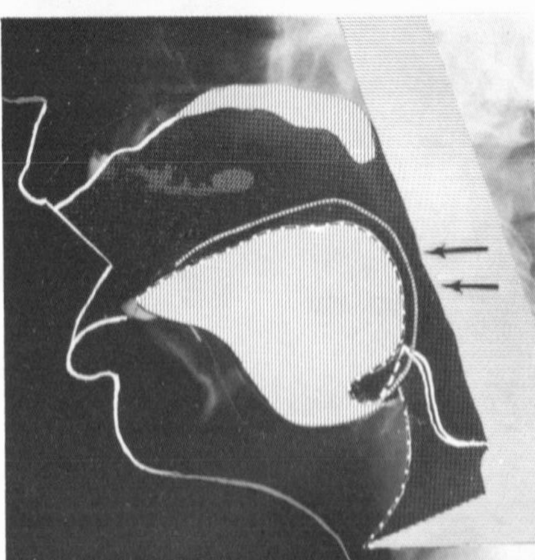

Sop. Alto Ten. Bar. Bass

Second Migration
Pitch Range

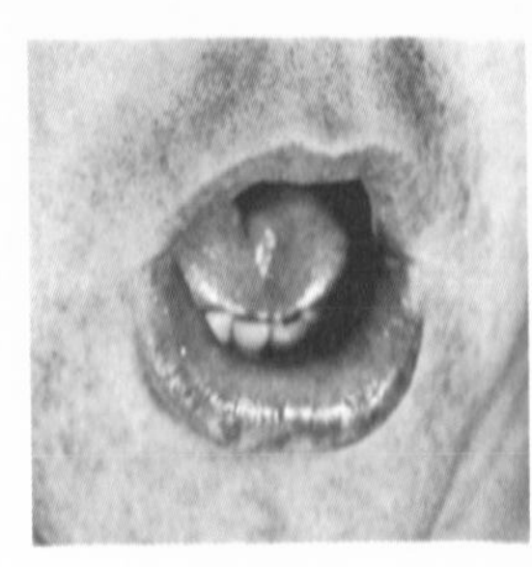

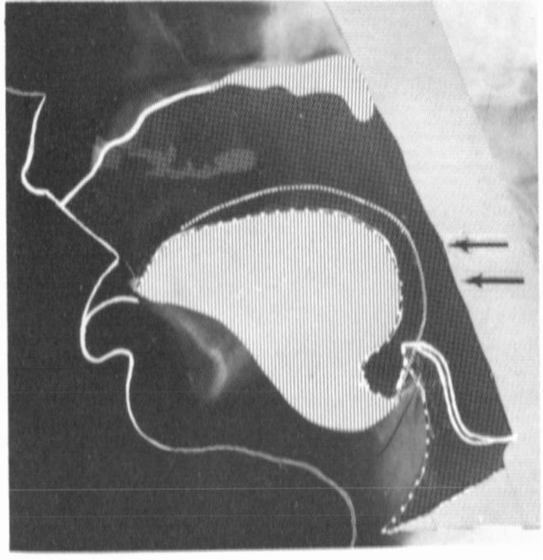

Sop. Alto Ten. Bar. Bass

Fig. **120.** The Quality Alternate Vowel [ɔ]

	F^1	F^2	F^3
Male	610	1000	2600
Female	625	1245	3250

MIGRATION DRILLS FOR THE BASIC VOWEL OPEN [ô]

Transpose these drills into a key suitable for the student.

Stable Vowel Pitch Range

When singing within this pitch range, the singer should attempt to preserve the integrity of the vowel at all intensity levels. Lip-rounding should be maintained in crescendo and forte passages.

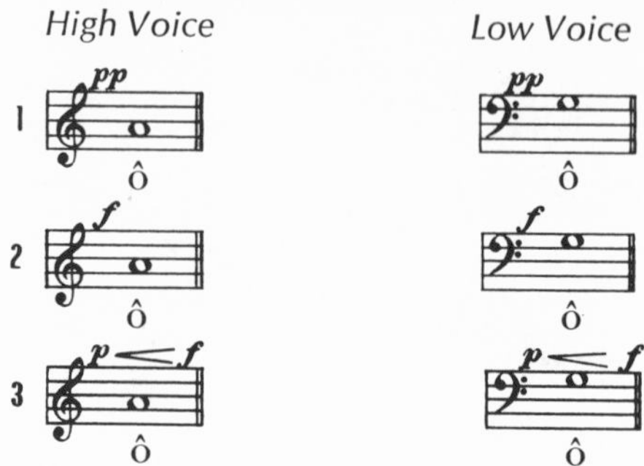

First Migration Pitch Range

When singing within this pitch range, the singer should think of the phoneme [ô] migrating more completely toward the phoneme [ʊ].

Second Migration Pitch Range

When singing within this pitch range, the singer should think of substituting the phoneme [ʊ] for the phoneme [ô].

Stable Vowel
Pitch Range

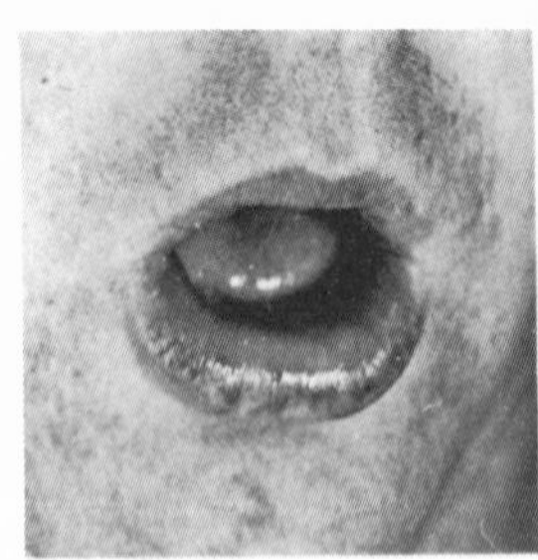

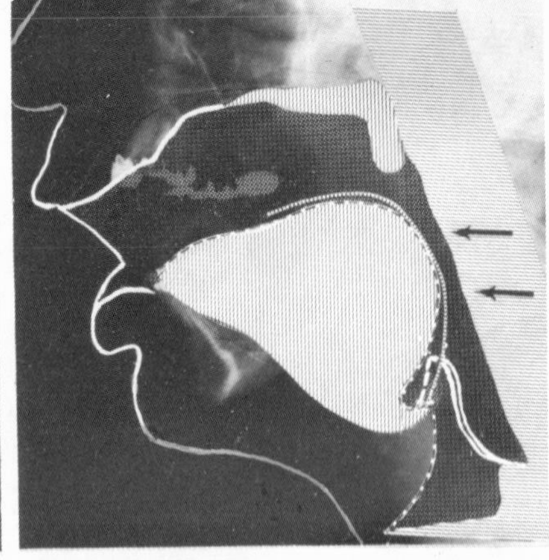

Sop. Alto Ten. Bar. Bass

First Migration
Pitch Range

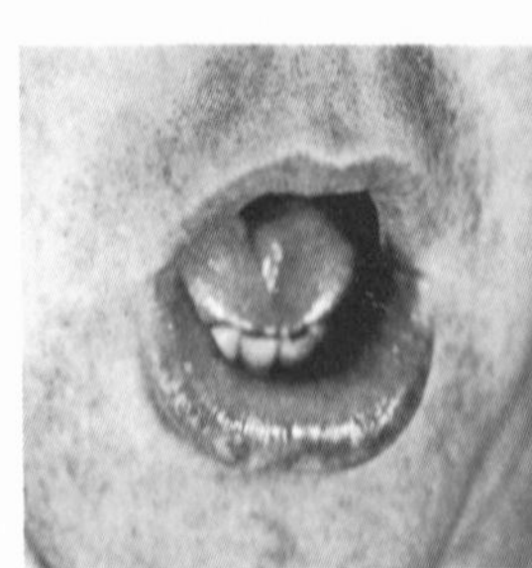

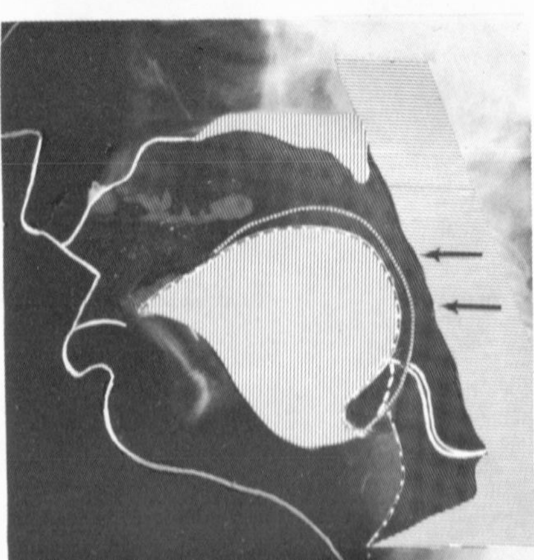

Sop. Alto Ten. Bar. Bass

Second Migration
Pitch Range

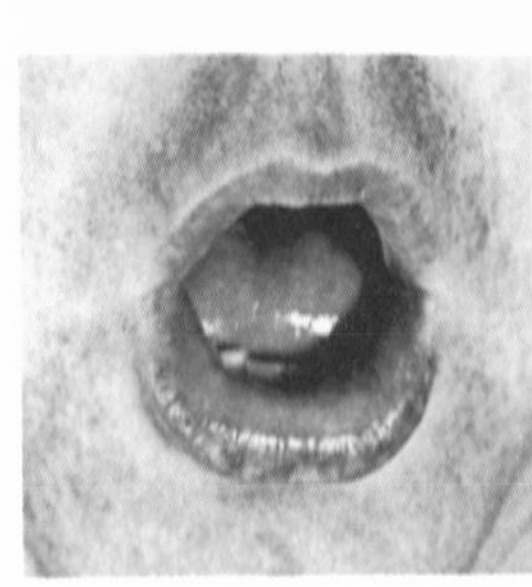

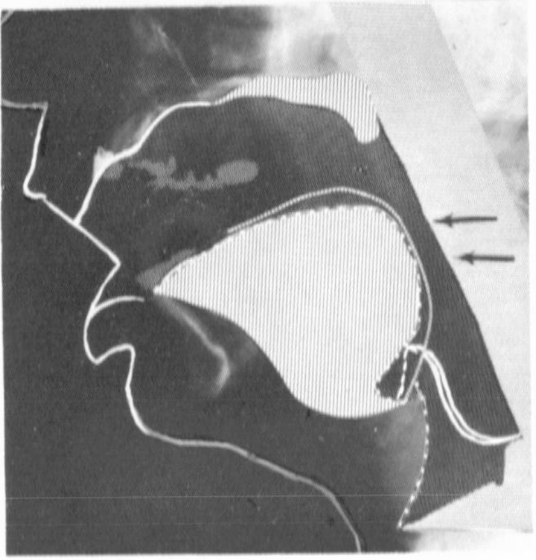

Sop. Alto Ten. Bar. Bass

Fig. **121.** The Basic Vowel Open [ô]

	F¹	F²	F³
Male	490	900	2580
Female	600	1200	3250

MIGRATION DRILLS FOR THE QUALITY ALTERNATE VOWEL CLOSED [o]

Transpose these drills into a key suitable for the student.

Stable Vowel Pitch Range

Within this pitch range, this phoneme should be conceived in its purest form and sung at intensities ranging from pianissimo to piano. When singing forte or making a crescendo, the singer should think of the phoneme migrating only slightly toward the phoneme [ʊ].

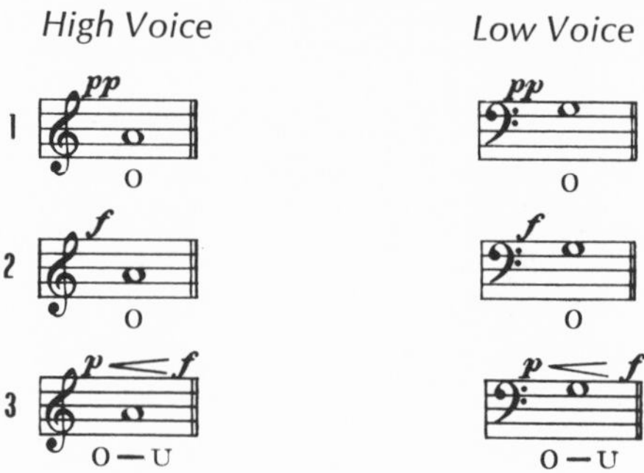

First Migration Pitch Range

When singing within this pitch range, the singer should think of the phoneme [o] migrating more completely toward the phoneme open [ʊ].

Second Migration Pitch Range

When singing within this pitch range, the singer should think of substituting the phoneme [ʊ] for [ô].

Stable Vowel
Pitch Range

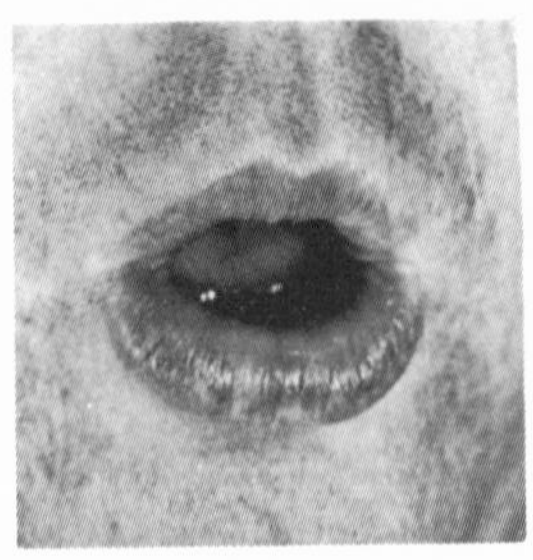

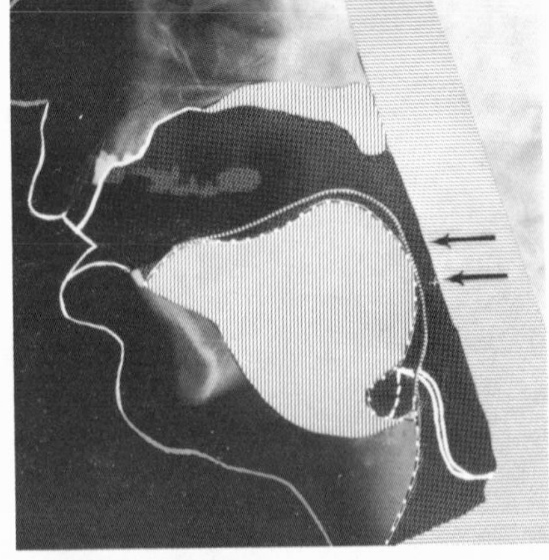

First Migration
Pitch Range

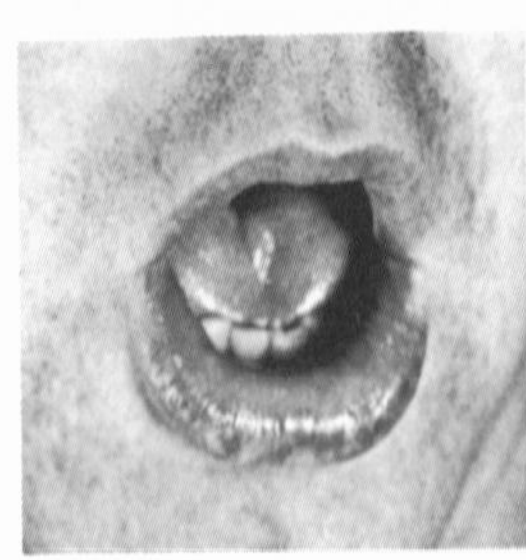

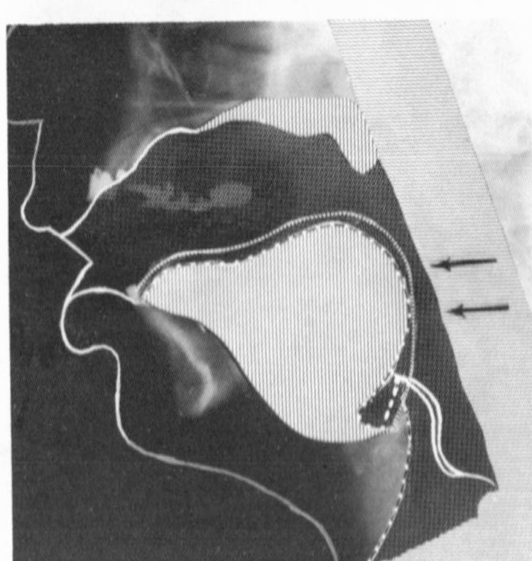

Sop. Alto Ten. Bar. Bass

Second Migration
Pitch Range

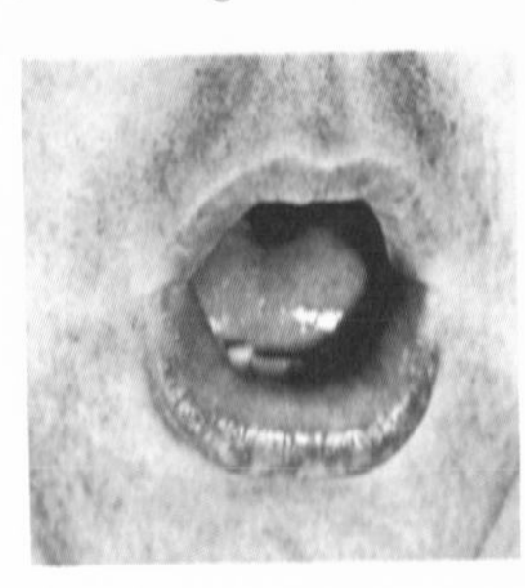

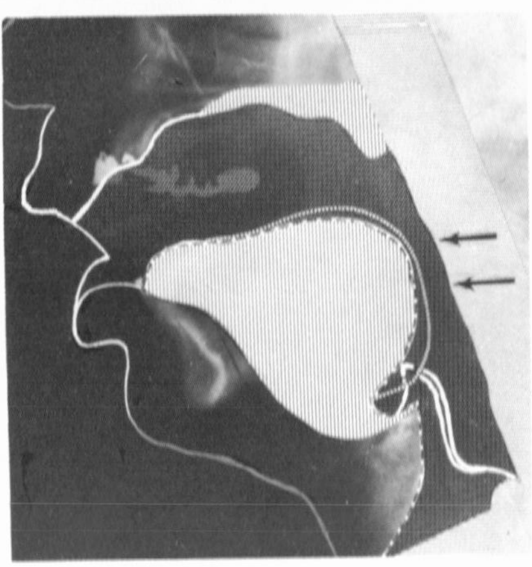

Sop. Alto Ten. Bar. Bass

Fig. **122.** The Quality Alternate Vowel Closed [o]

	F1	F2	F3
Male	450	700	2500
Female	500	1000	3000

MIGRATION DRILLS FOR THE QUALITY ALTERNATE VOWEL [ʊ]

Transpose these drills into a key suitable for the student.

Stable Vowel Pitch Range

Within this pitch range, this phoneme should be conceived in its purest form and sung at intensities ranging from pianissimo to piano. When singing forte or making a crescendo, this phoneme [ʊ] is stable and does not migrate.

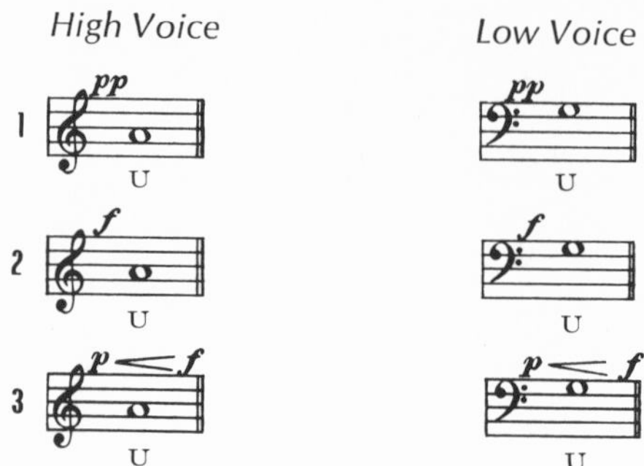

First Migration Pitch Range

Within this pitch range this phoneme [ʊ] is stable and does not migrate.

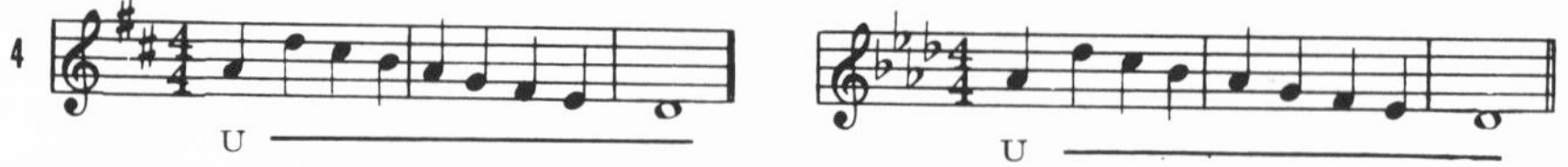

Second Migration Pitch Range

When singing within this pitch range, the singer should accentuate lip protrusion, maintain tongue position, but use a lower jaw position for the topmost note.

Stable Vowel
Pitch Range

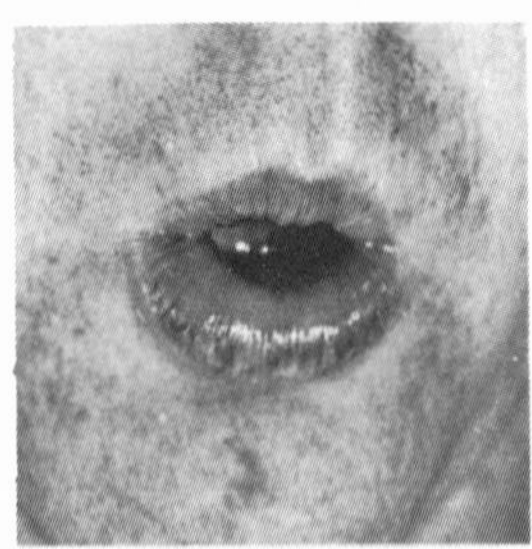

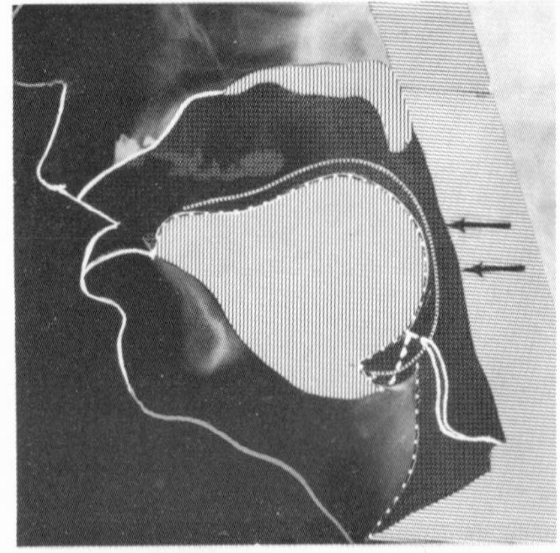

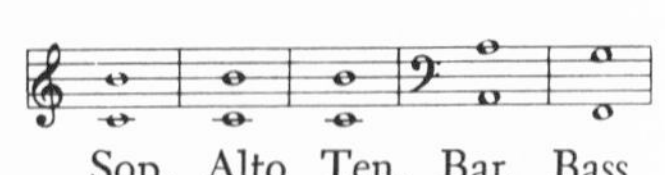

First Migration
Pitch Range

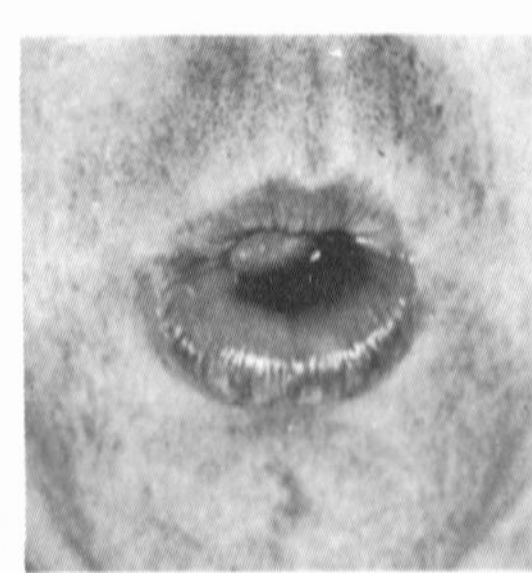

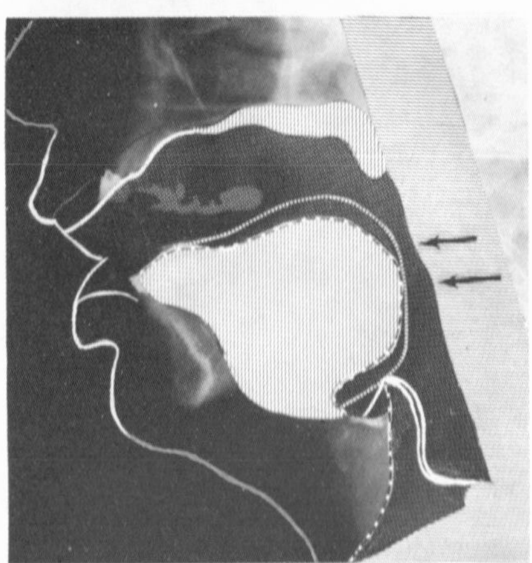

Sop. Alto Ten. Bar. Bass

Second Migration
Pitch Range

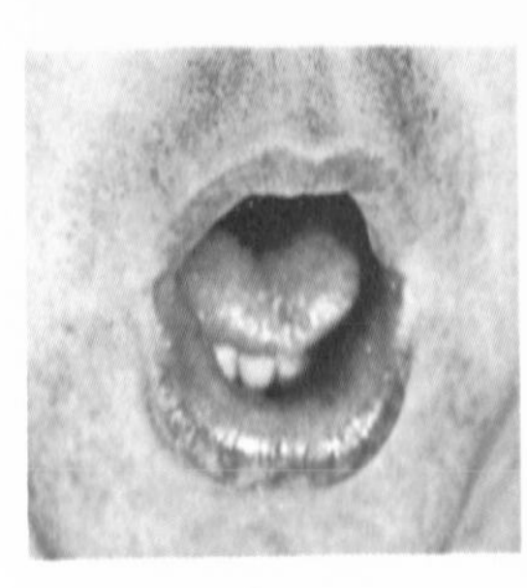

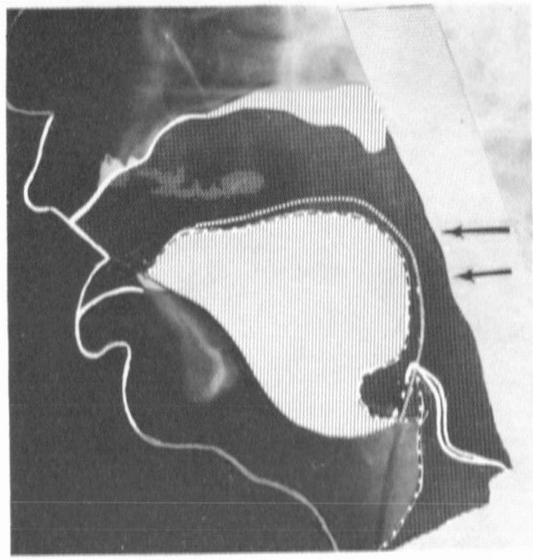

Sop. Alto Ten. Bar. Bass

Fig. **123.** The Quality Alternate Vowel [ʊ]

	F1	F2	F3
Male	400	720	2500
Female	425	900	3000

MIGRATION DRILLS FOR THE BASIC VOWEL [u]

Transpose these drills into a key suitable for the student.

Stable Vowel Pitch Range

Within this pitch range this phoneme should be conceived in its purest form and sung at intensities ranging from pianissimo to piano. When singing forte or making a crescendo, the singer should think of the phoneme [u] migrating toward the phoneme [ʊ].

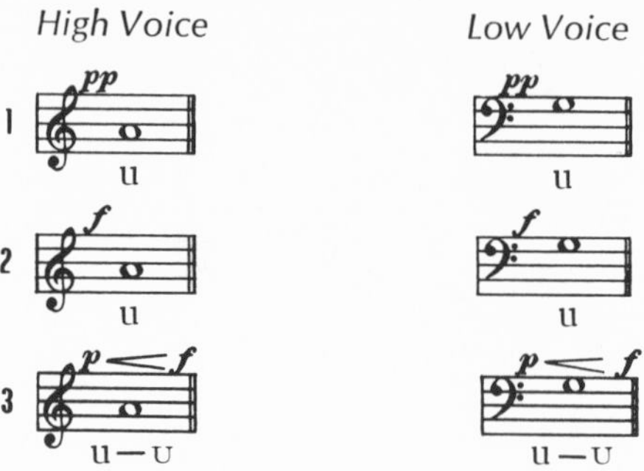

First Migration Pitch Range

When singing within this pitch range, the singer should think of the phoneme [u] migrating more completely toward the phoneme [ʊ].

Second Migration Pitch Range

When singing within this pitch range, singing forte, or making a crescendo, the singer should attempt to maintain lip and tongue positions for the phoneme [ʊ], but he should use a lower jaw position for the topmost note.

Stable Vowel
Pitch Range

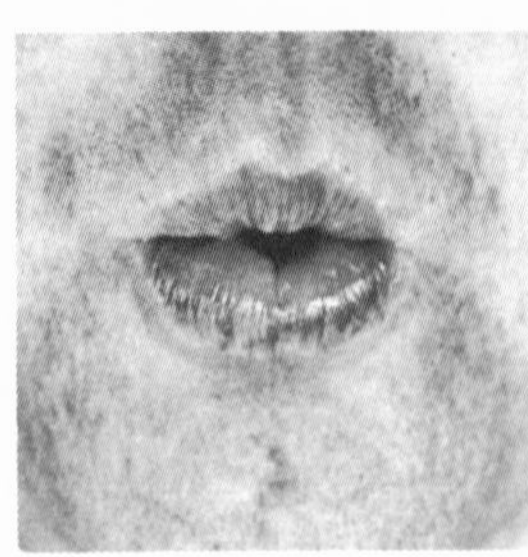

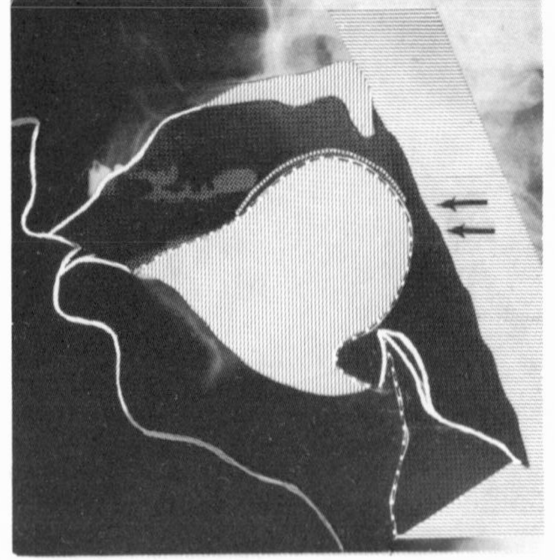

Sop. Alto Ten. Bar. Bass

First Migration
Pitch Range

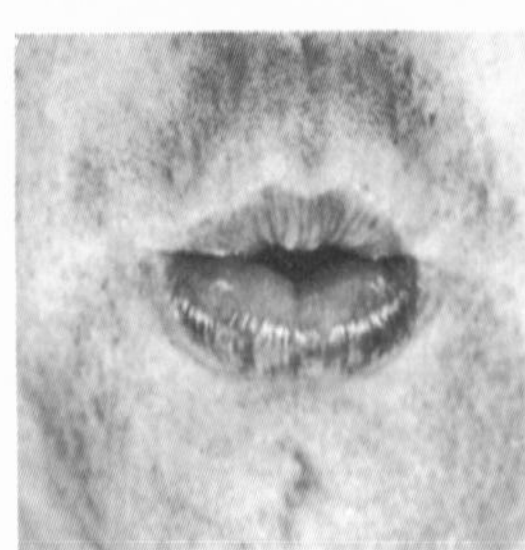

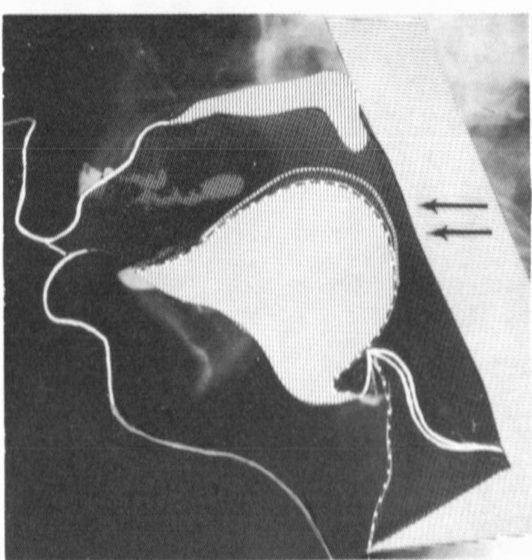

Sop. Alto Ten. Bar. Bass

Second Migration
Pitch Range

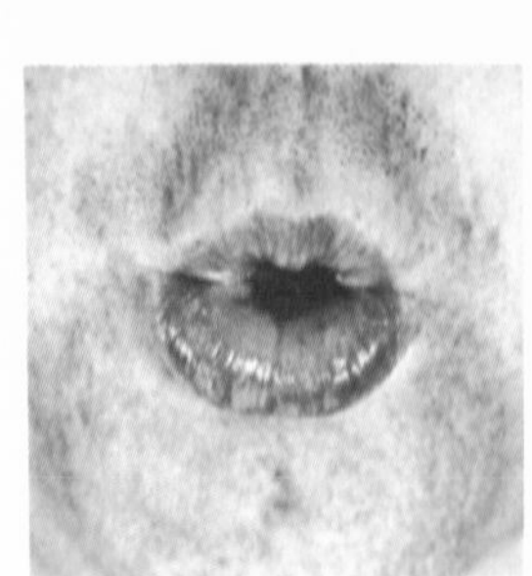

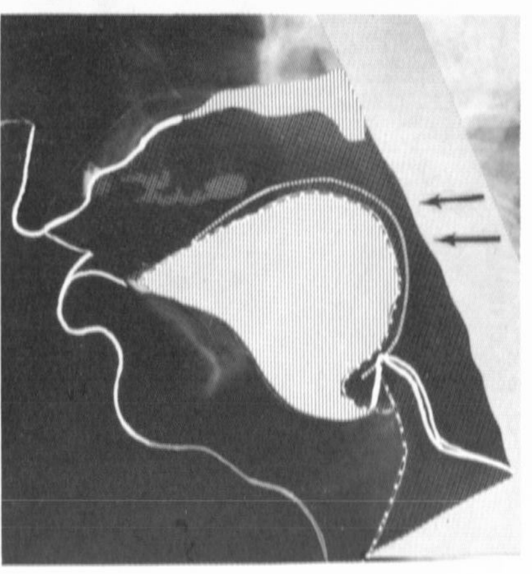

Sop. Alto Ten. Bar. Bass

Fig. **124.** The Basic Vowel [u]

	F1	F2	F3
Male	350	640	2550
Female	400	800	3250

MIGRATION DRILLS FOR THE NEUTRAL VOWEL [ʌ]

Transpose these drills into a key suitable for the student.

Stable Vowel Pitch Range

Within this pitch range, this phoneme should be conceived in its purest form and sung at intensities ranging from pianissimo to piano. When singing forte or making a crescendo, this phoneme [ʌ] is stable and does not migrate.

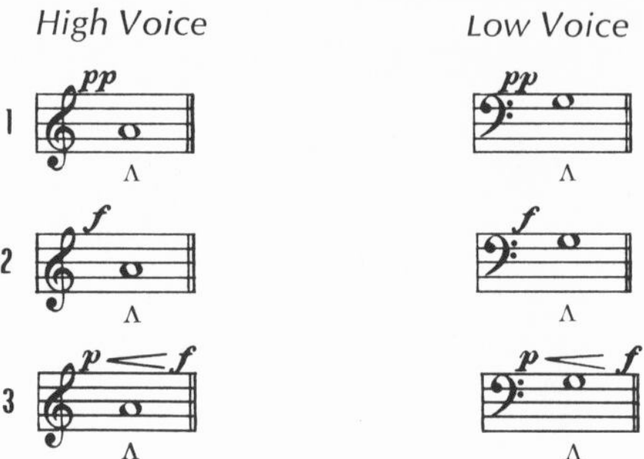

First Migration Pitch Range

Within this pitch range this phoneme [ʌ] is stable and does not migrate.

Second Migration Pitch Range

When singing within this pitch range, singing forte, or making a crescendo, the singer should attempt to maintain the tongue position for the phoneme [ʌ], but he should use a lower jaw position for the topmost note.

Stable Vowel
Pitch Range

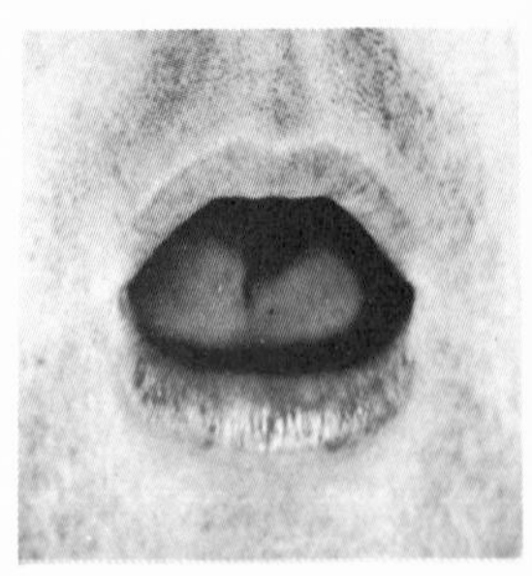

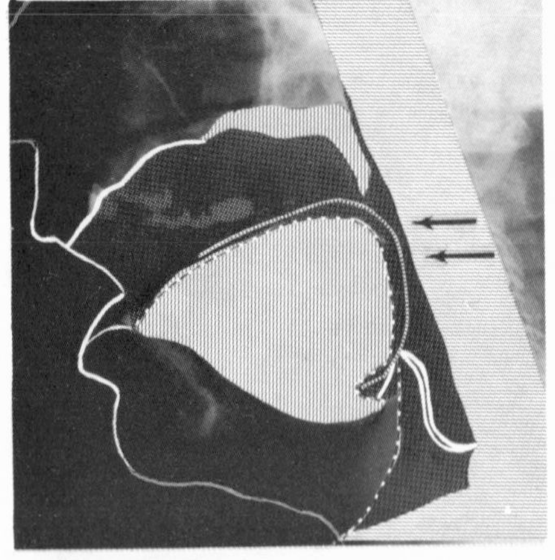

Sop. Alto Ten. Bar. Bass

First Migration
Pitch Range

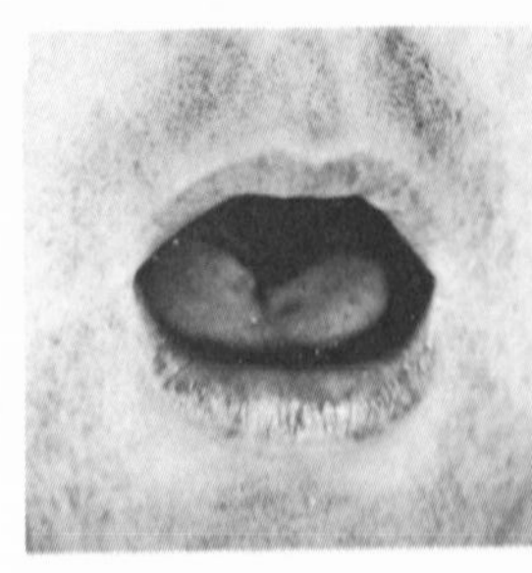

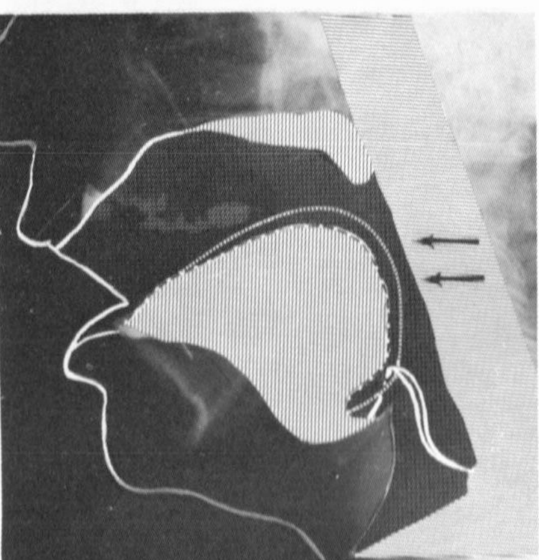

Sop. Alto Ten. Bar. Bass

Second Migration
Pitch Range

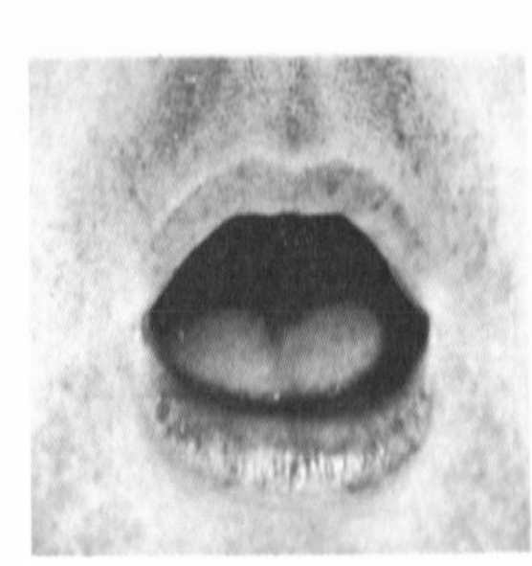

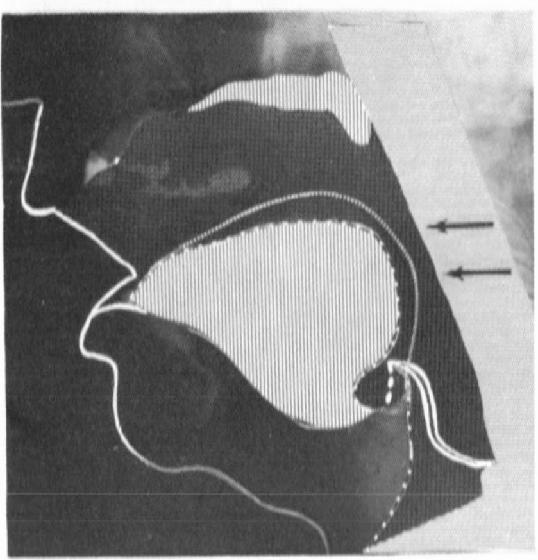

Sop. Alto Ten. Bar. Bass

Fig. **125.** The Neutral Vowel [ʌ]

	F^1	F^2	F^3
Male	500	1200	2675
Female	550	1300	3250

MIGRATION DRILLS FOR THE HIGH CENTRAL, ROUNDED VOWEL [ɜ]

Transpose these drills into a key suitable for the student.

Stable Vowel Pitch Range

Within this pitch range, this phoneme should be conceived in its purest form and sung at intensities ranging from pianissimo to piano. When singing forte, or when making a crescendo, this phoneme [ɜ] is stable and does not migrate.

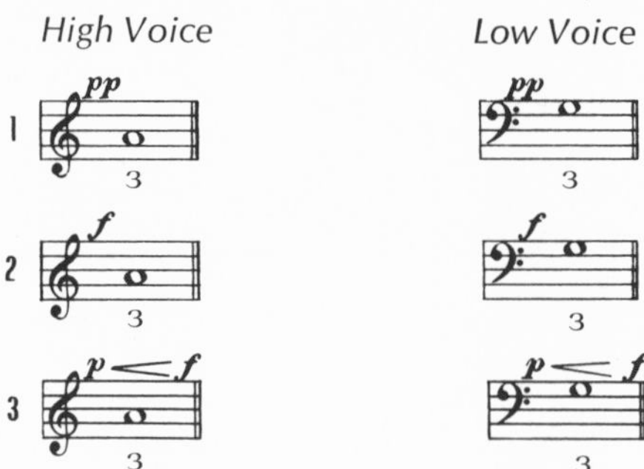

First Migration Pitch Range

Within this pitch range, this phoneme [ɜ] is stable and does not migrate.

Second Migration Pitch Range

When singing within this pitch range, or singing forte, or making a crescendo, the singer should attempt to maintain lip and tongue positions for the phoneme [ɜ], but he should use a lower jaw position for the topmost note.

Stable Vowel
Pitch Range

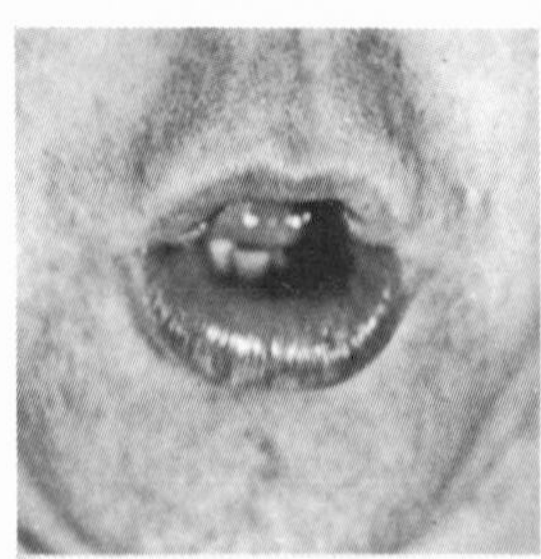

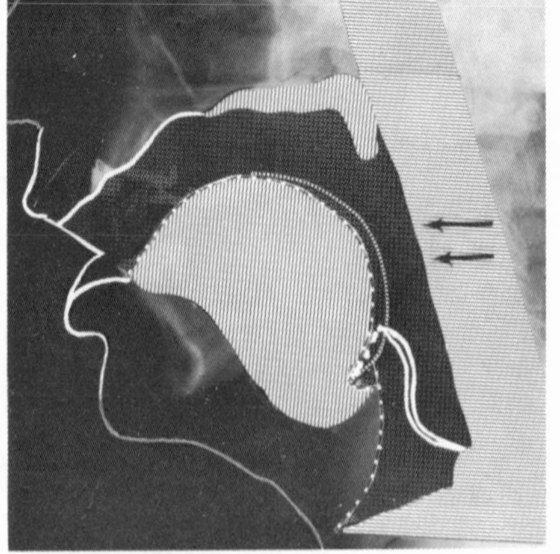

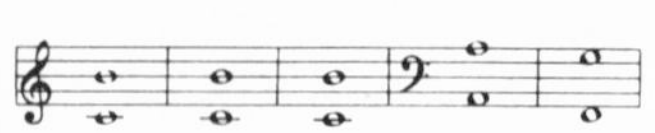

First Migration
Pitch Range

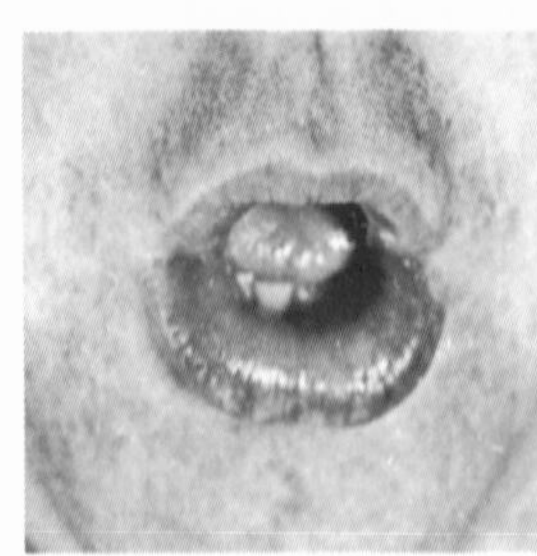

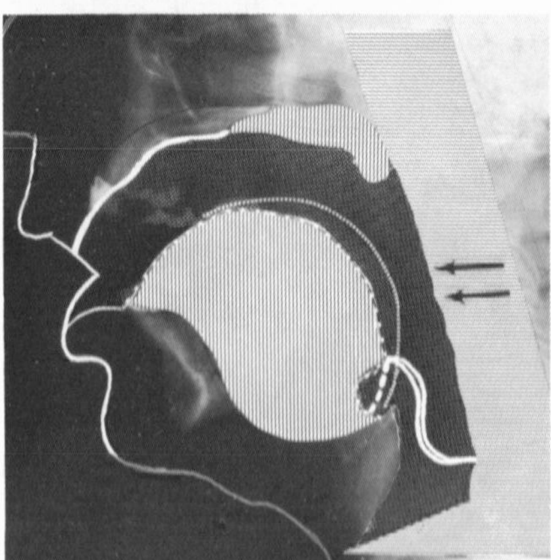

Sop. Alto Ten. Bar. Bass

Second Migration
Pitch Range

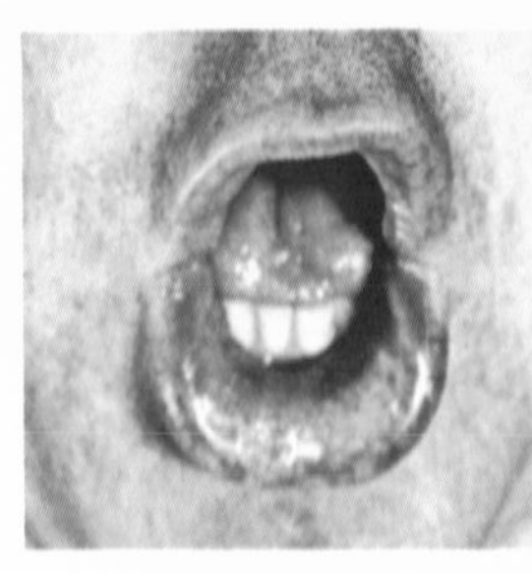

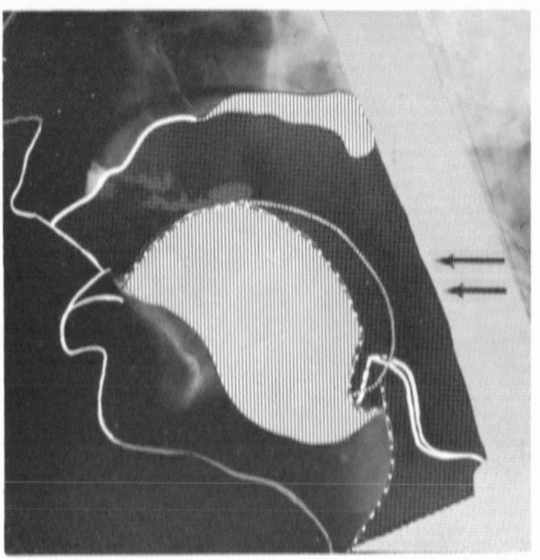

Sop. Alto Ten. Bar. Bass

Fig. **126.** The High Central Rounded Vowel [ɜ]

	F^1	F^2	F^3
Male	400	1150	2500
Female	450	1350	3050

MIGRATION DRILLS FOR THE ROUNDED FRONTAL VOWEL [y] LONG UMLAUT Ü AND [Y] SHORT UMLAUT Ü

Transpose these drills into a key suitable for the student.

Stable Vowel Pitch Range

Within this pitch range, this phoneme should be conceived in its purest form and sung at intensities ranging from pianissimo to piano. When singing forte, or when making a crescendo, the singer should think of the phoneme migrating only slightly toward the phoneme [Y].

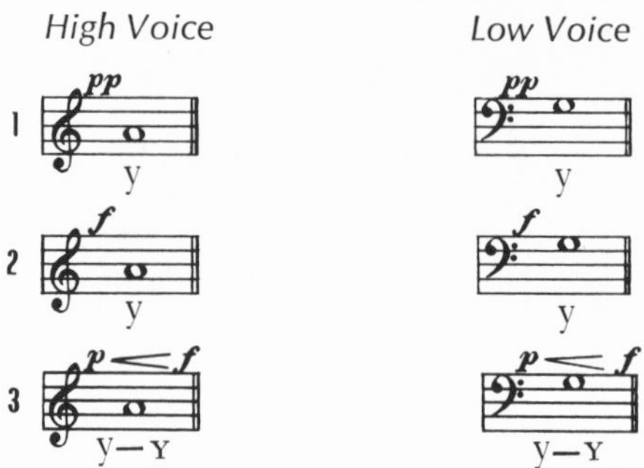

First Migration Pitch Range

When singing within this pitch range, the singer should think of the phoneme [y] migrating more completely toward the phoneme [Y].

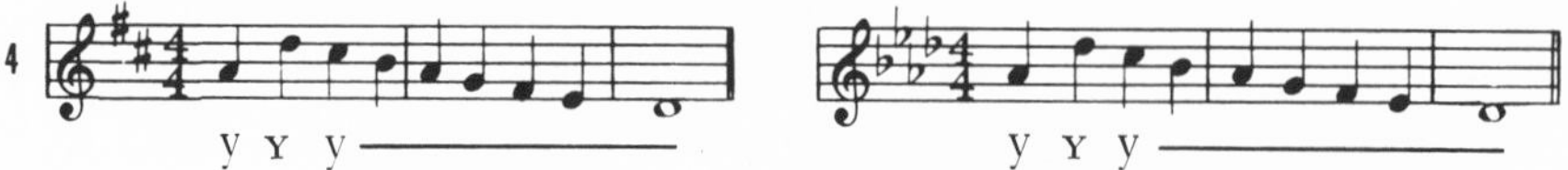

Second Migration Pitch Range

When singing within this pitch range, the singer should think of substituting the phoneme [Y] for the phoneme [y].

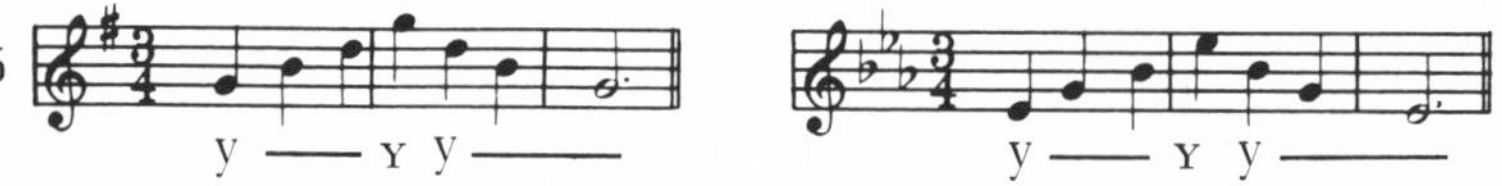

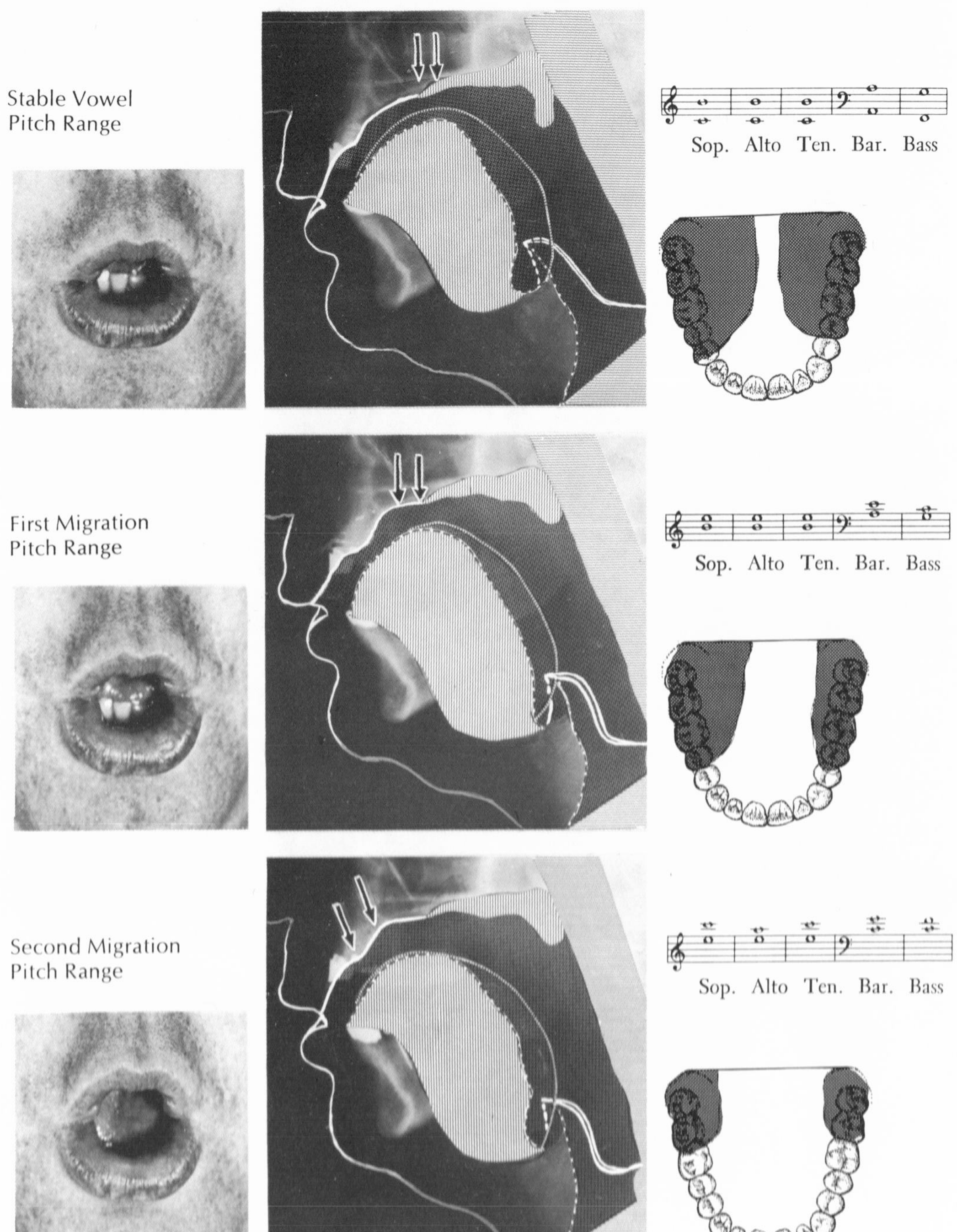

Fig. **127.** The Rounded Frontal Vowel [y] Long Umlaut *Ü* and [Y] Short Umlaut *Ü*

MIGRATION DRILLS FOR THE ROUNDED FRONTAL VOWEL [ø]

Transpose these drills into a key suitable for the student.

Stable Vowel Pitch Range

When singing within this pitch range this phoneme [ø] is stable and does not migrate.

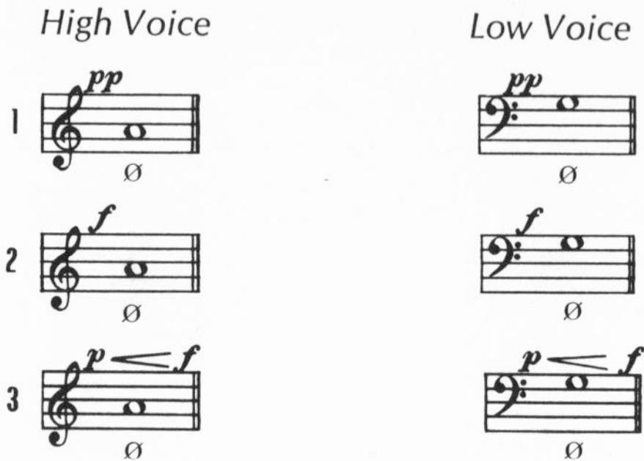

First Migration Pitch Range

Within this pitch range this phoneme [ø] is stable and does not migrate.

Second Migration Pitch Range

When singing within this pitch range, singing forte, or making a crescendo, the singer should attempt to maintain the tongue position for the phoneme [ø], but he should use a lower jaw position for the topmost note.

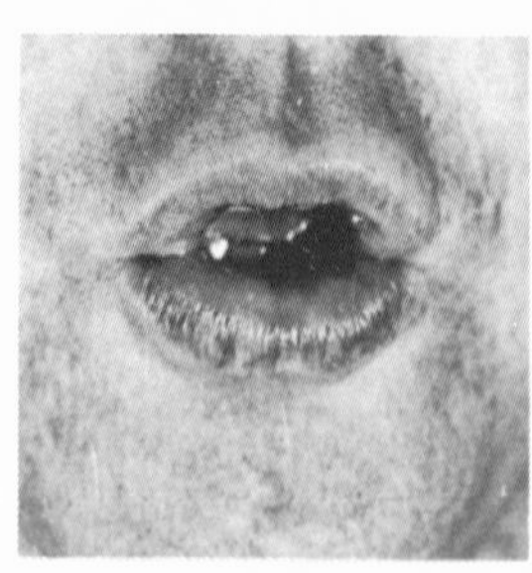

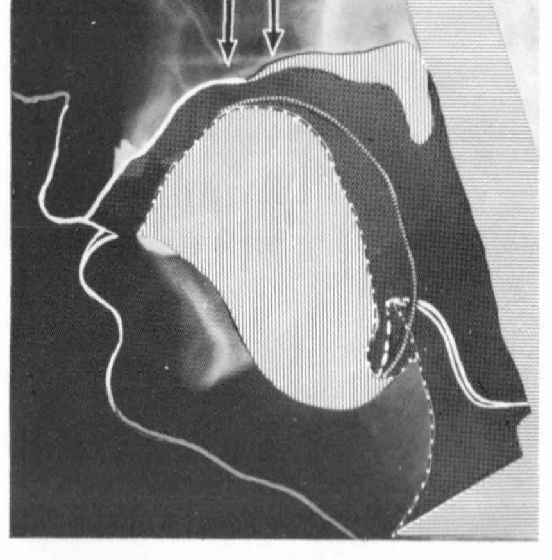

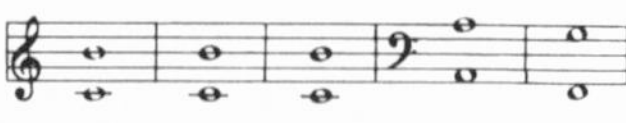

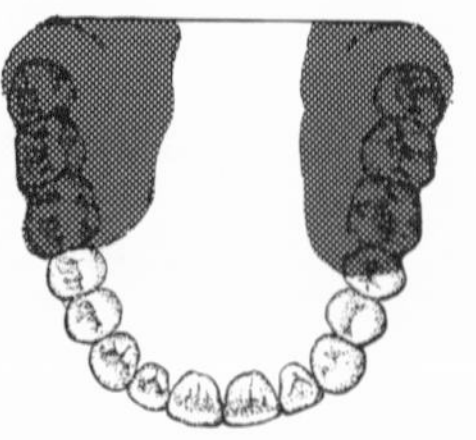

First Migration
Pitch Range

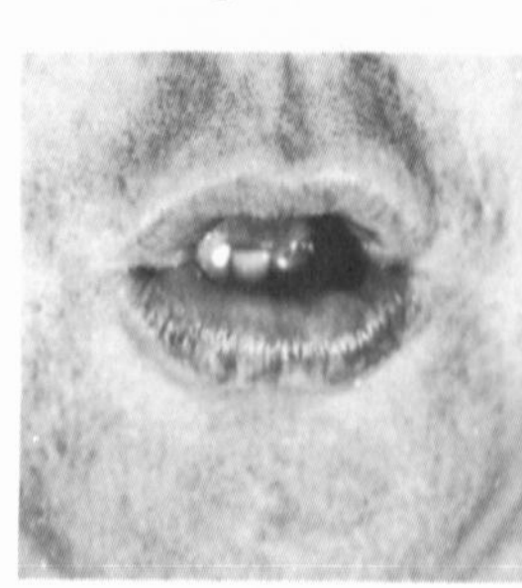

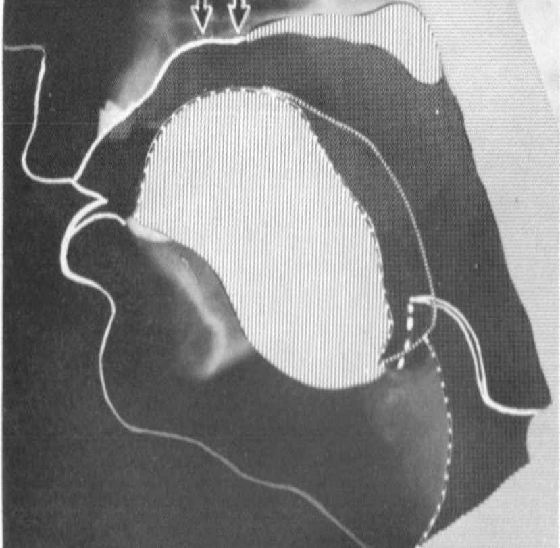

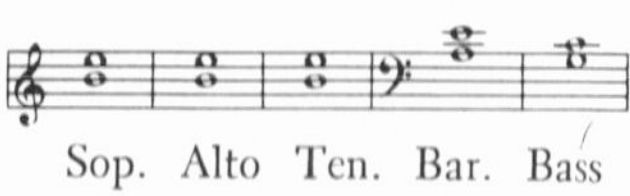

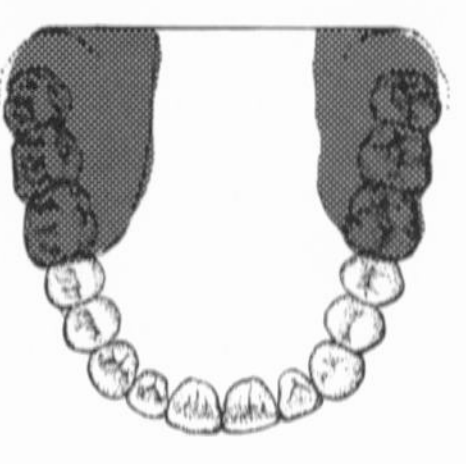

Second Migration
Pitch Range

Sop. Alto Ten. Bar. Bass

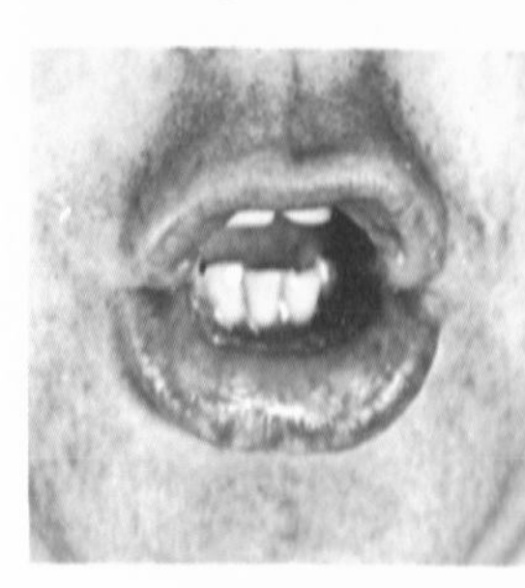

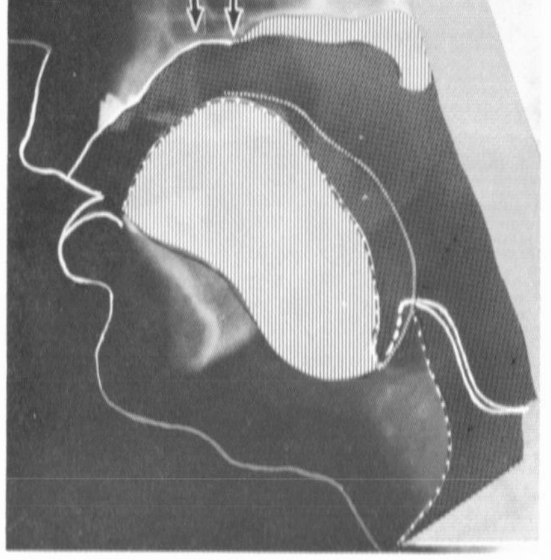

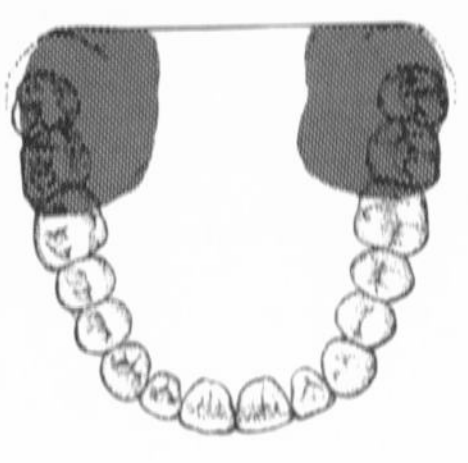

Fig. **128.** The Rounded Frontal Vowel [ø]

MIGRATION DRILLS FOR THE ROUNDED FRONTAL VOWEL [œ]

Transpose these drills into a key suitable for the student.

Stable Vowel Pitch Range

Within this pitch range, this phoneme should be conceived in its purest form and sung at intensities ranging from pianissimo to piano. When singing forte or making a crescendo, the singer should think of the phoneme migrating only slightly toward the phoneme [a].

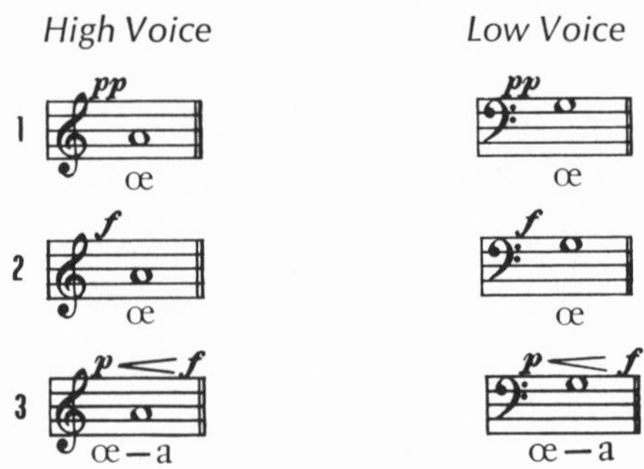

First Migration Pitch Range

When singing within this pitch range, the singer should think of the phoneme [œ] migrating more completely toward the phoneme [a].

Second Migration Pitch Range

When singing within this pitch range, the singer should think of substituting the phoneme [a] for the phoneme [œ].

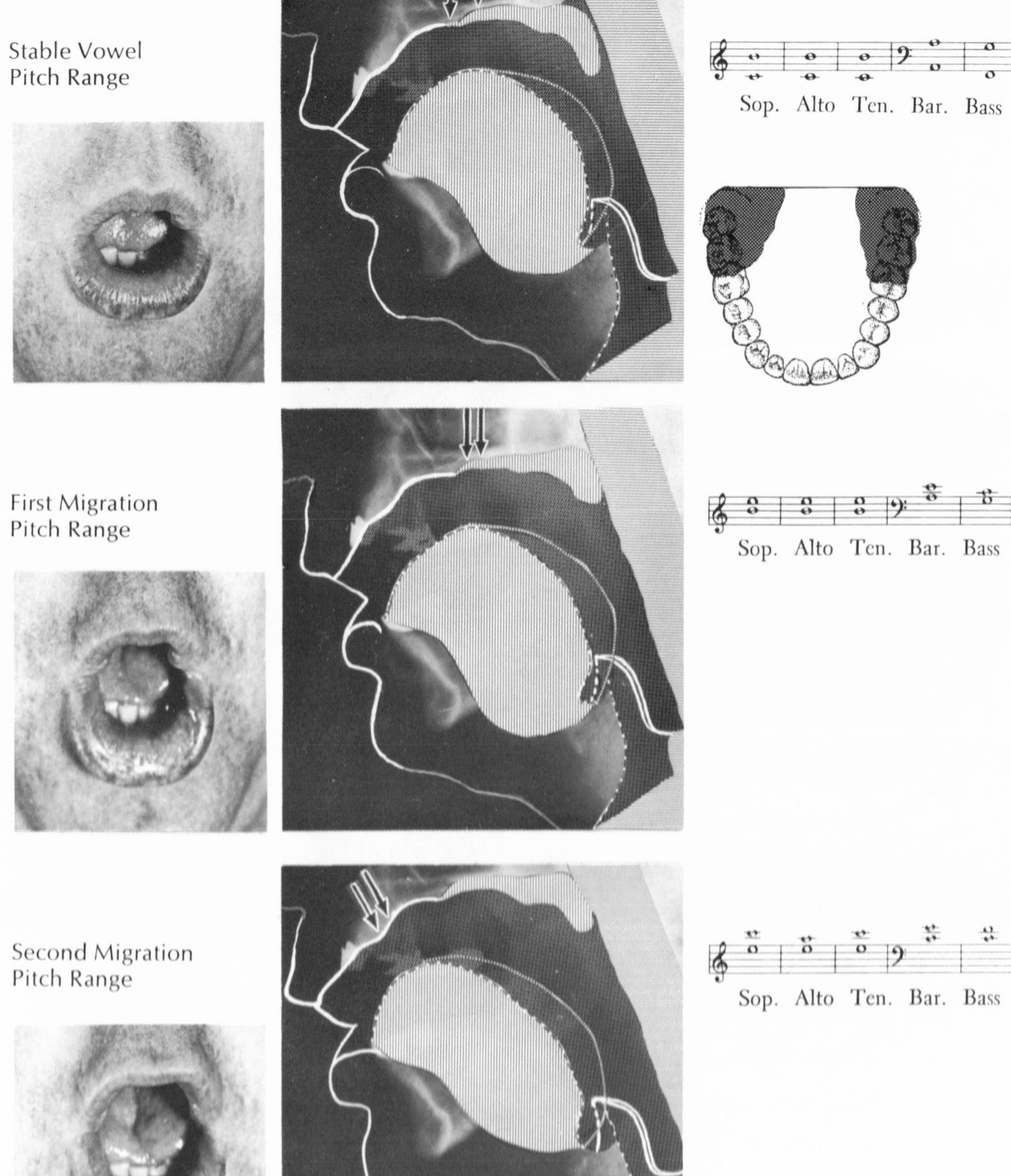

Fig. **129.** The Rounded Frontal Vowel [œ]

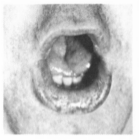

MIGRATION DRILLS FOR THE FRENCH NASAL VOWEL [ɛ̃]

Transpose these drills into a key suitable for the student.

Stable Vowel Pitch Range

Within this pitch range this phoneme should be conceived in its purest form and sung at intensities ranging from pianissimo to piano. When singing forte or making a crescendo, the singer should think of the phoneme migrating only slightly toward the phoneme [ã].

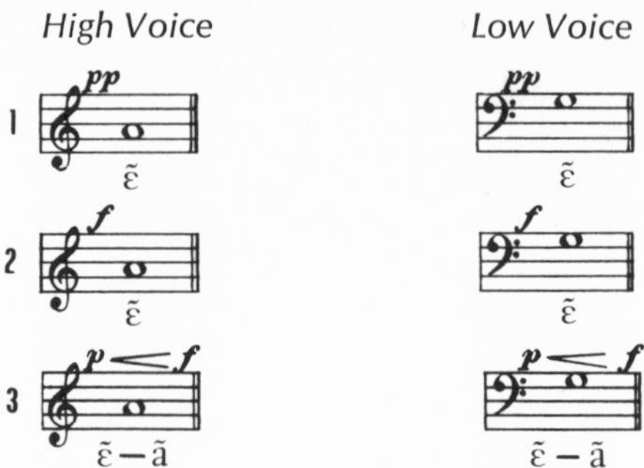

First Migration Pitch Range

When singing within this pitch range, the singer should think of the phoneme [ɛ̃] migrating more completely toward the phoneme [ã].

Second Migration Pitch Range

When singing within this pitch range, singing forte, or making a crescendo, the singer should attempt to maintain lip-rounding and the tongue position for the phoneme [ɛ̃], but he should use a lower jaw position for the topmost note.

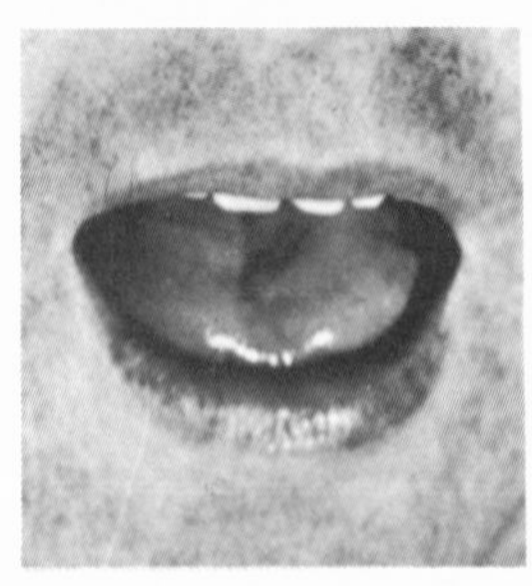

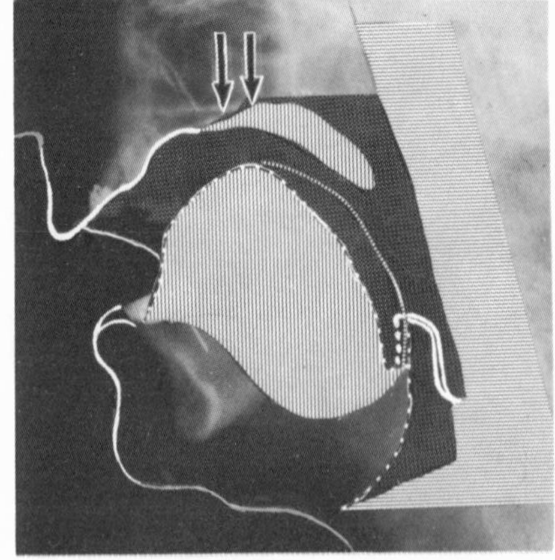

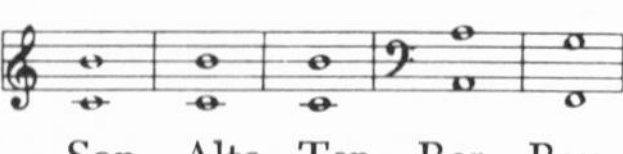

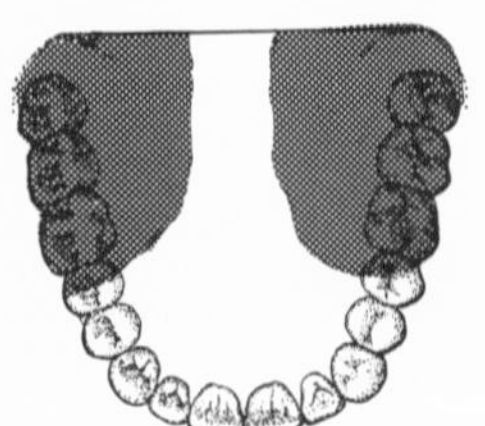

First Migration
Pitch Range

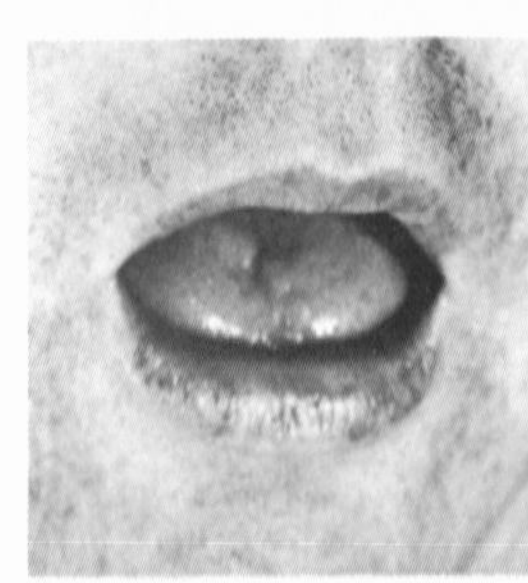

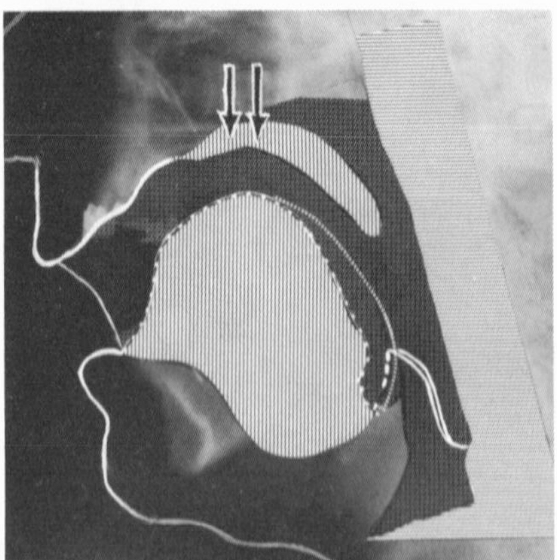

Sop. Alto Ten. Bar. Bass

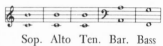

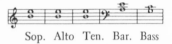

Second Migration
Pitch Range

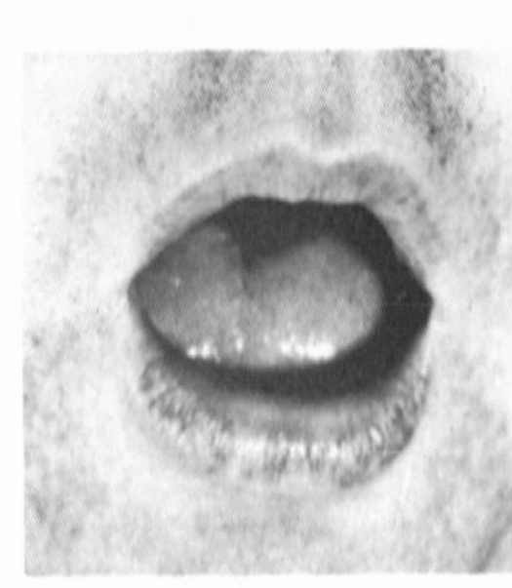

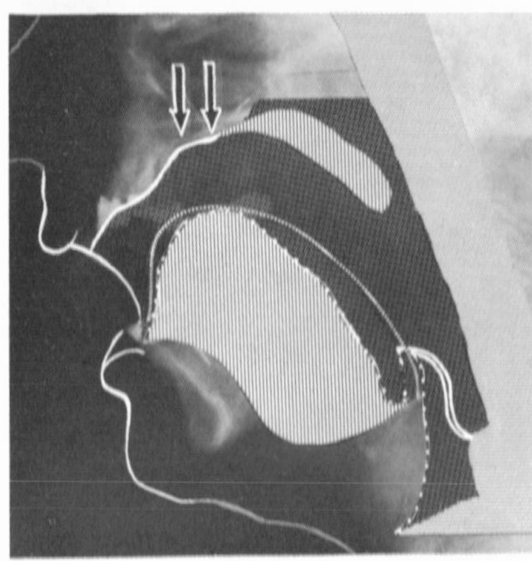

Sop. Alto Ten. Bar. Bass

Fig. **130.** The French Nasal Vowel [ɛ̃]—*Bien*

MIGRATION DRILLS FOR THE FRENCH NASAL VOWEL [œ̃]

Transpose these drills into a key suitable for the student.

Stable Vowel Pitch Range

Within this pitch range this phoneme should be conceived in its purest form and sung at intensities ranging from pianissimo to piano. When singing forte or making a crescendo, the singer should think of the phoneme migrating only slightly toward the phoneme [a].

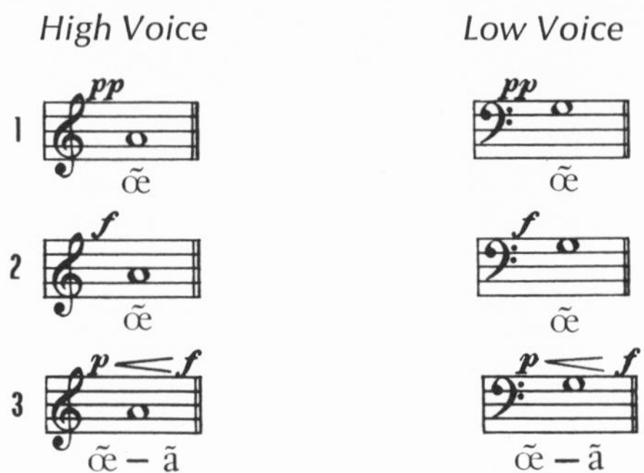

First Migration Pitch Range

When singing within this pitch range the singer should think of the phoneme [œ] migrating more completely toward the phoneme [a].

Second Migration Pitch Range

When singing within this pitch range, or singing forte, or making a crescendo, the singer should attempt to maintain lip-rounding and the tongue position for the phoneme [a], but he should use a lower jaw position for the topmost note.

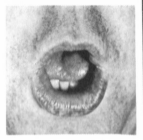

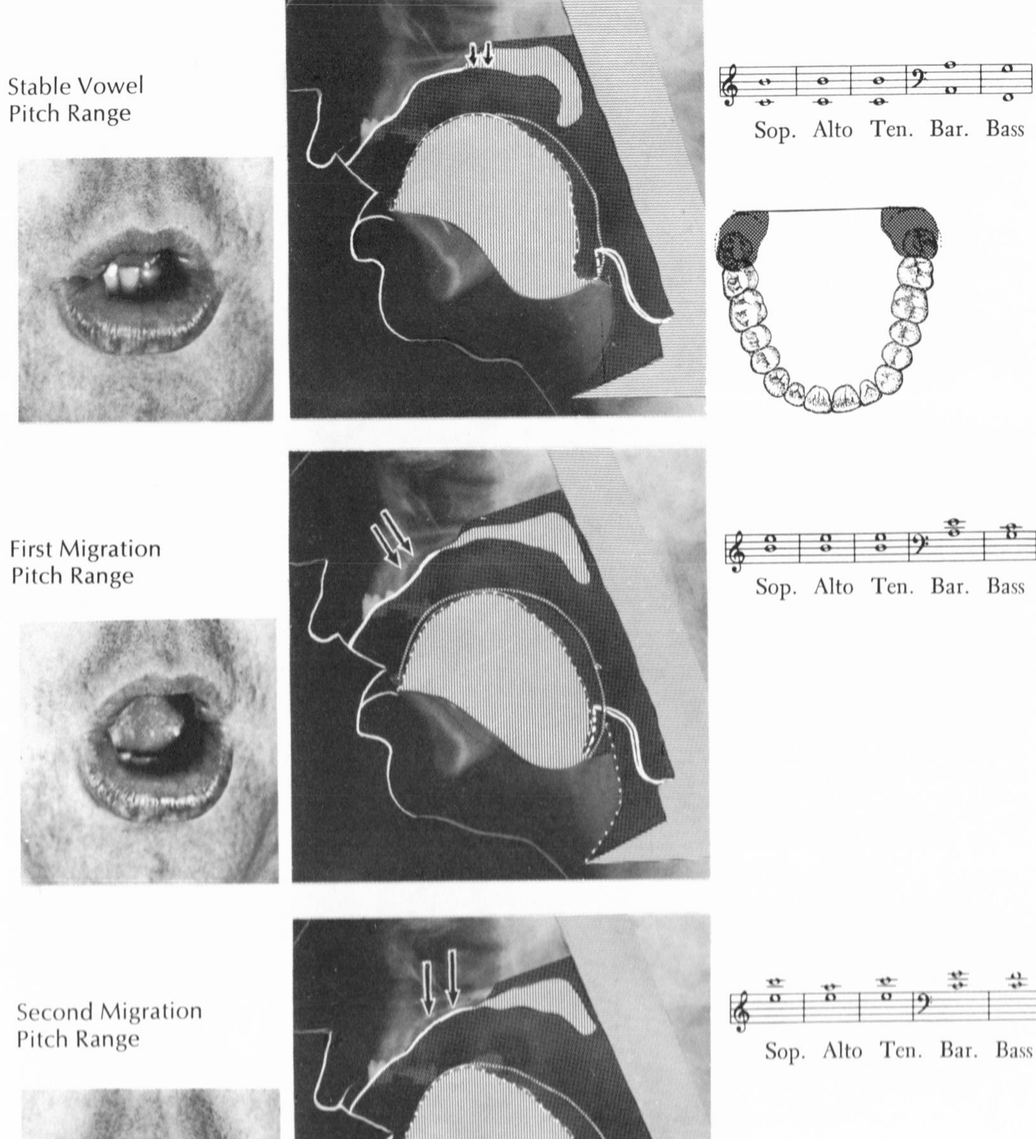

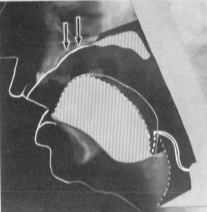

Fig. **131.** The French Nasal Vowel [œ̃]—*Chacun*

MIGRATION DRILLS FOR THE FRENCH NASAL VOWEL [ɑ̃]

Transpose these drills into a key suitable for the student.

Stable Vowel Pitch Range

Within this pitch range, this phoneme should be conceived in its purest form and sung at intensities ranging from pianissimo to piano. When singing forte or making a crescendo, the singer should think of the phoneme migrating only slightly toward the phoneme [ʌ].

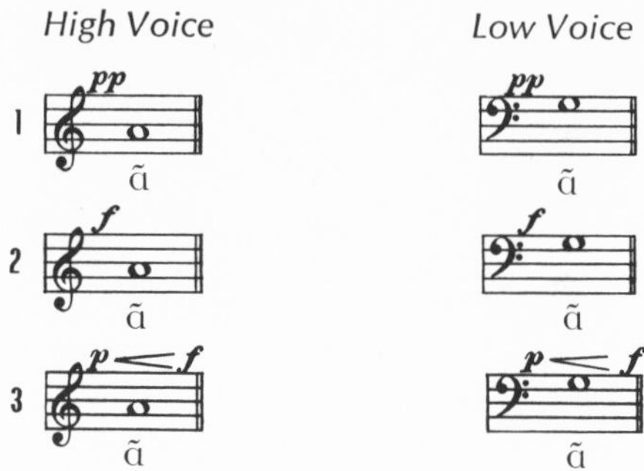

First Migration Pitch Range

When singing within this pitch range, the singer should think of the phoneme [ɑ̃] migrating more completely toward the phoneme [ʌ].

Second Migration Pitch Range

When singing within this pitch range, singing forte, or making a crescendo, the singer should attempt to maintain the tongue position for the phoneme [ʌ], but he should use a lower jaw position for the topmost note.

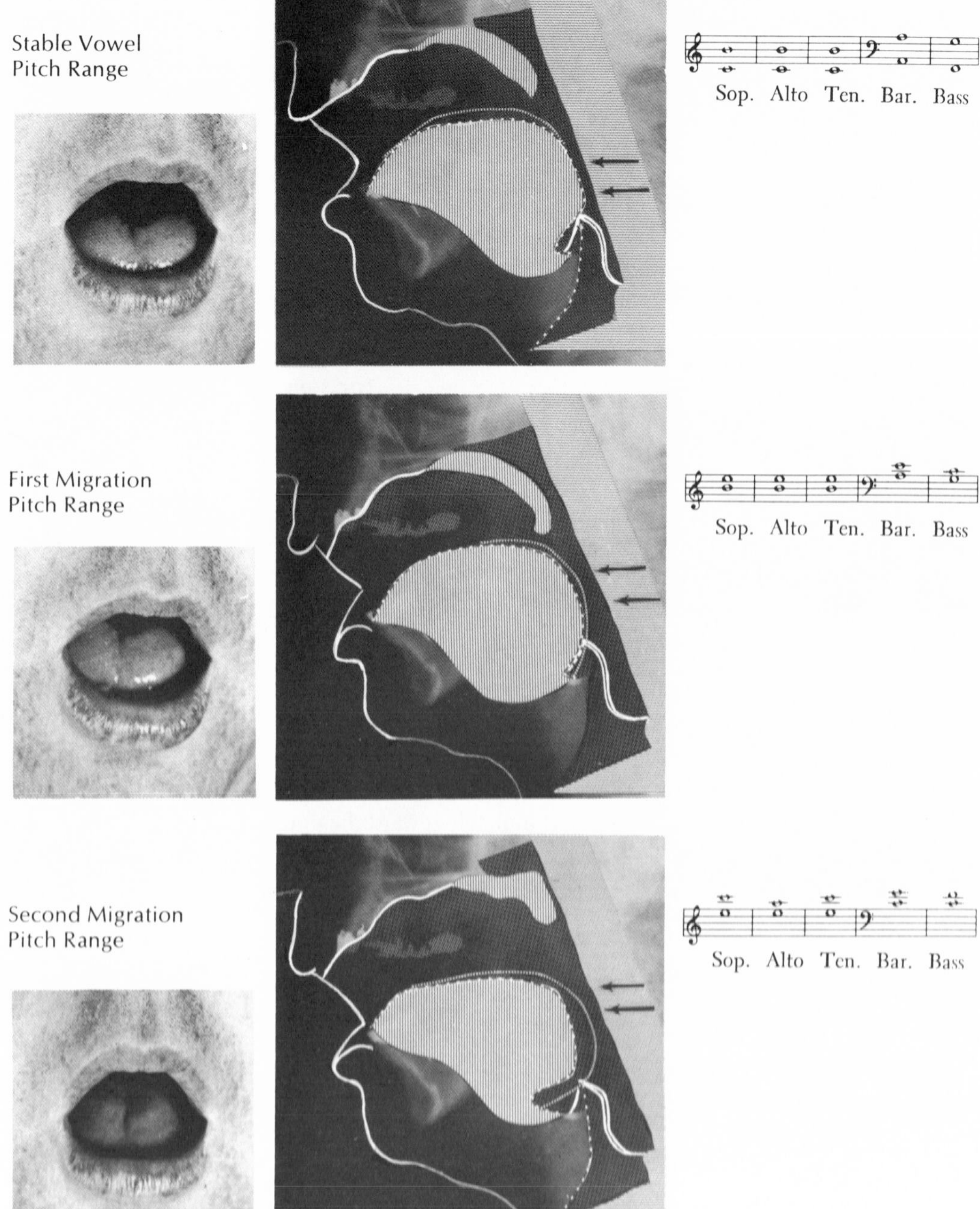

Fig. **132.** The French Nasal Vowel [ɑ̃]—*Quand*

MIGRATION DRILLS FOR THE FRENCH NASAL VOWEL [õ]

Transpose these drills into a key suitable for the student.

Stable Vowel Pitch Range

When singing within this pitch range, this phoneme should be conceived in its purest form and sung at intensities ranging from pianissimo to piano. When singing forte or making a crescendo, the singer should think of the phoneme migrating only slightly toward the phoneme closed [o].

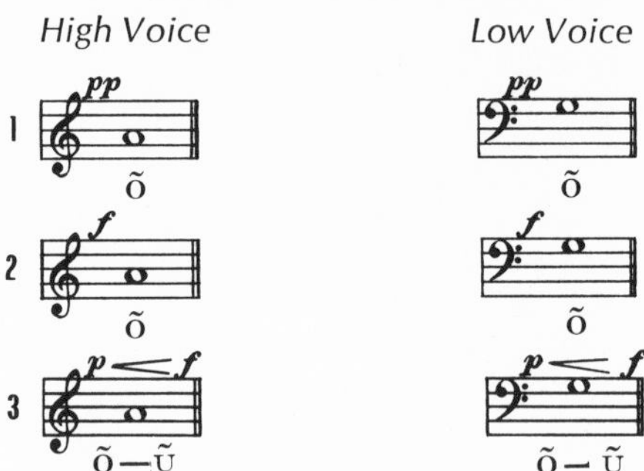

First Migration Pitch Range

When singing within this pitch range, the singer should think of the phoneme [õ] migrating more completely toward the phoneme [ʊ].

Second Migration Pitch Range

When singing within this pitch range, when singing forte, or when making a crescendo, the singer should attempt to maintain lip-rounding and the tongue position for the phoneme [ʊ], but he should use a lower jaw position for the topmost note.

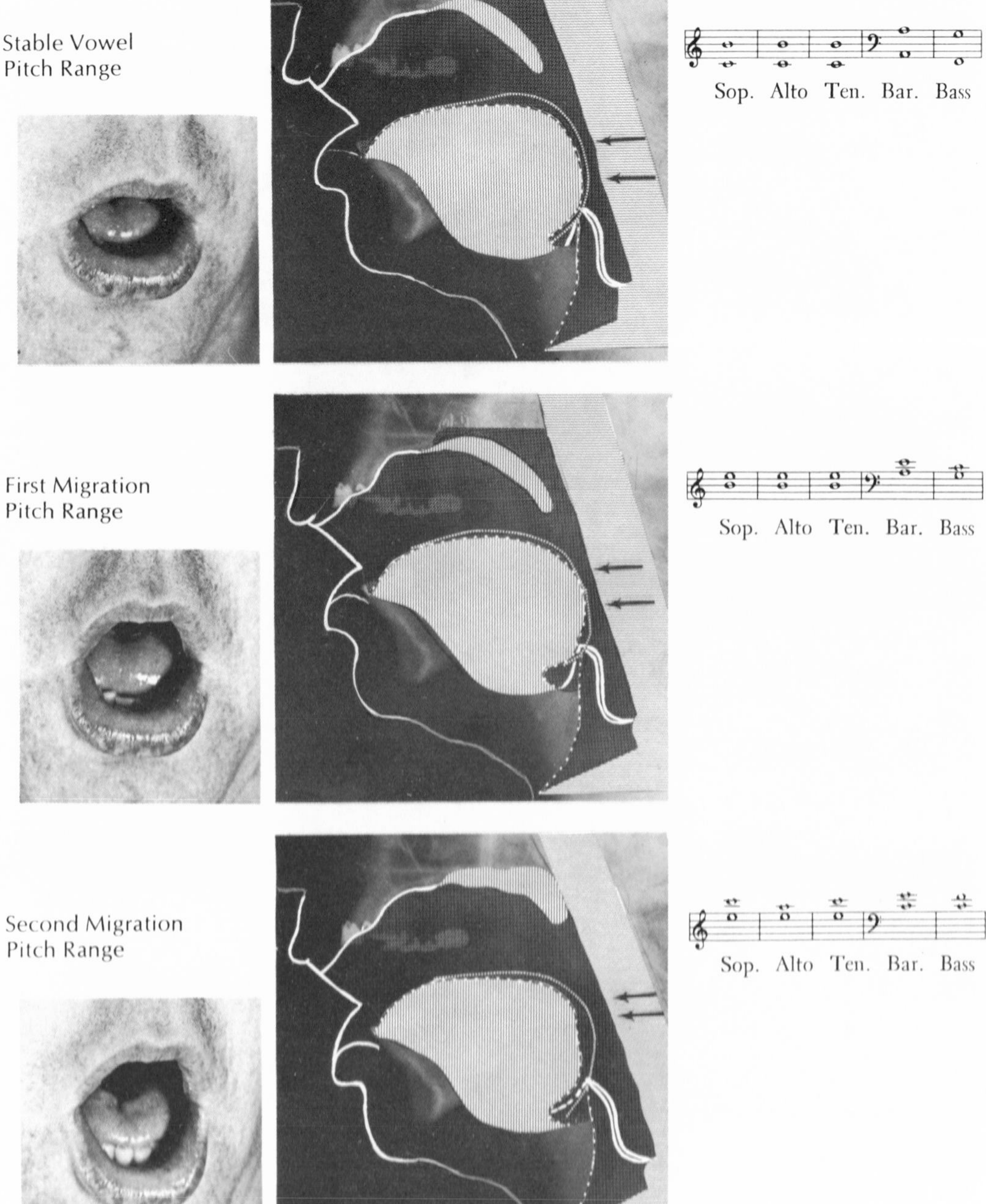

Fig. **133.** The French Nasal Vowel [õ]—*Garçon*

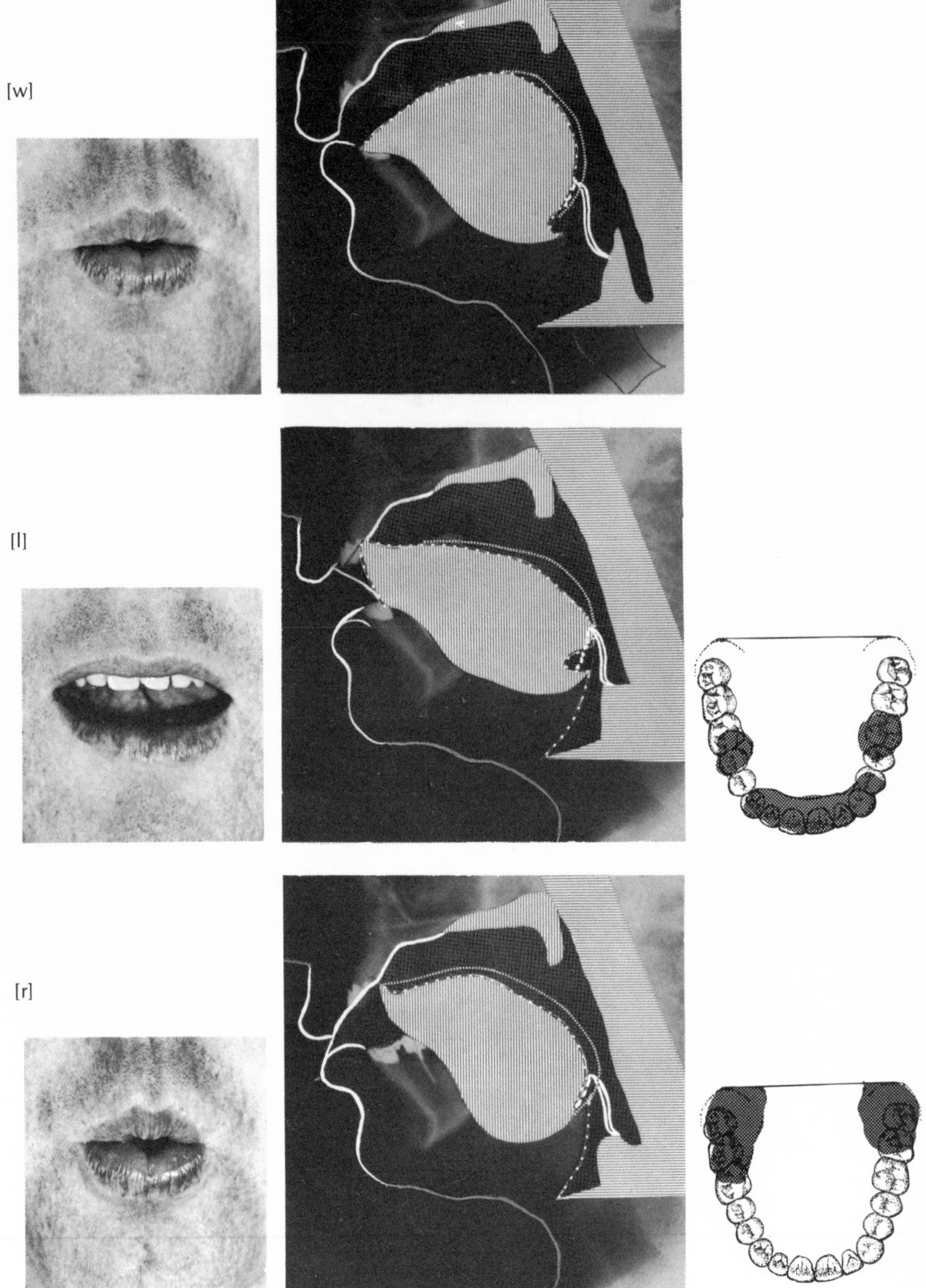

Fig. **134.** The Semivowels [w], [l], and [r]

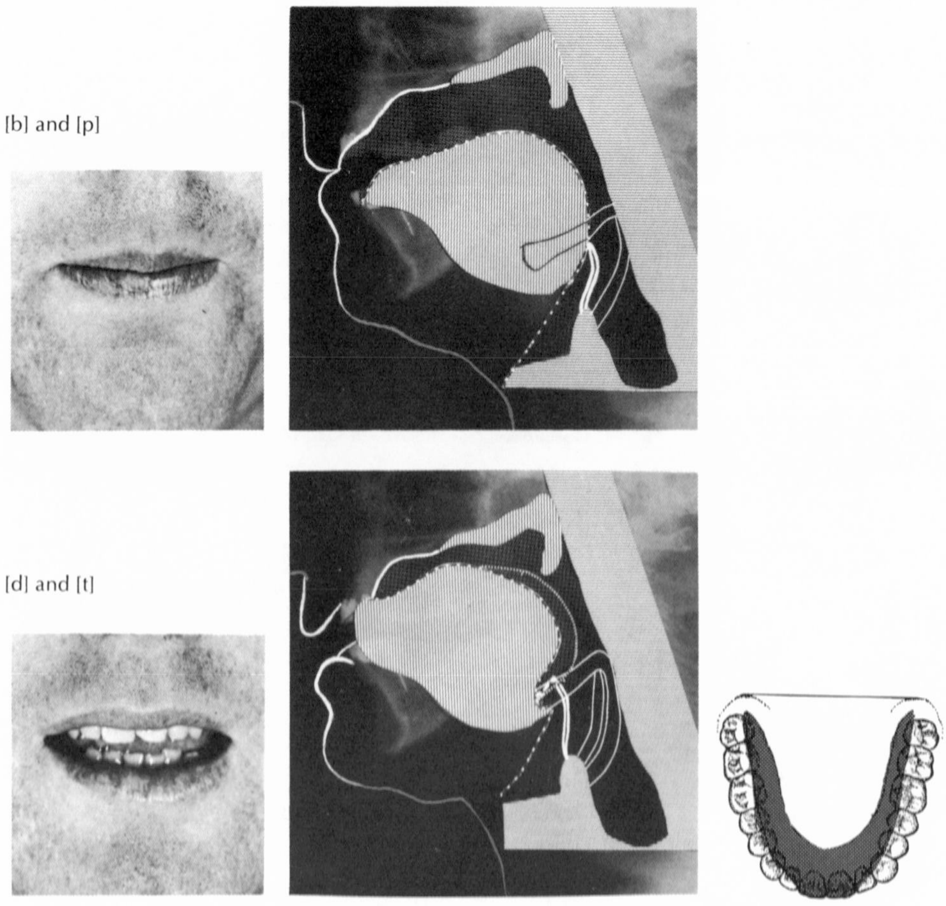

Fig. **135.** The Stop Plosives [b], [p], [d], and [t]

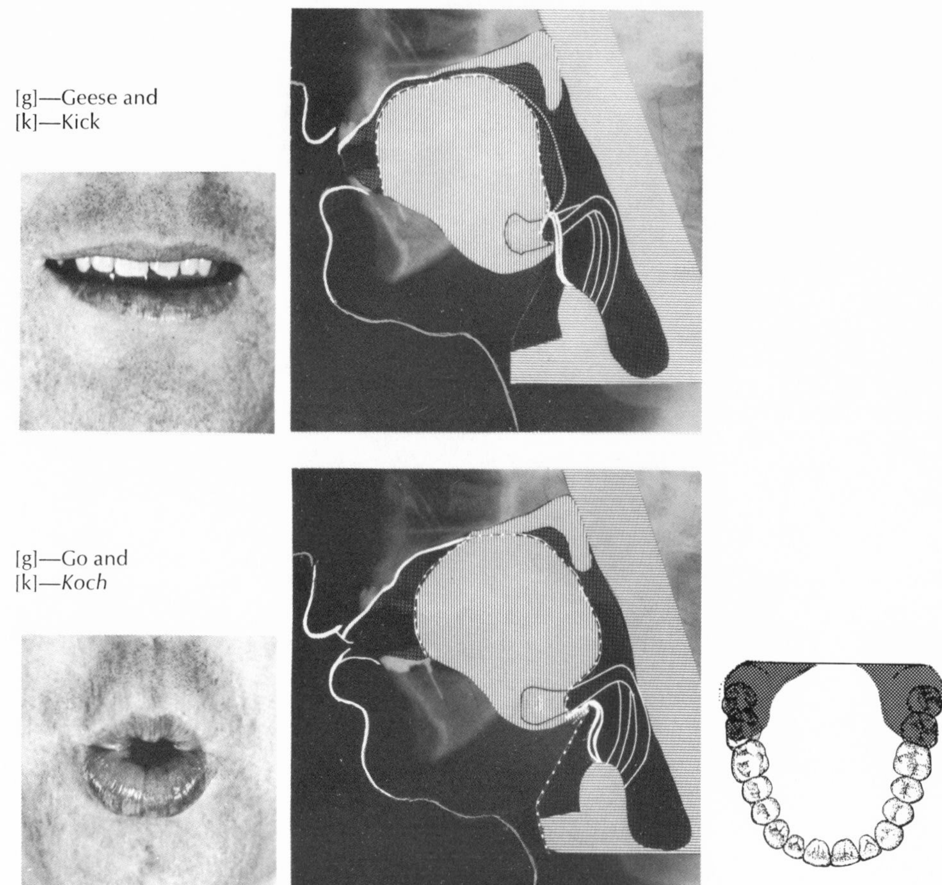

Fig. **136.** The Stop Plosives [g] and [k]

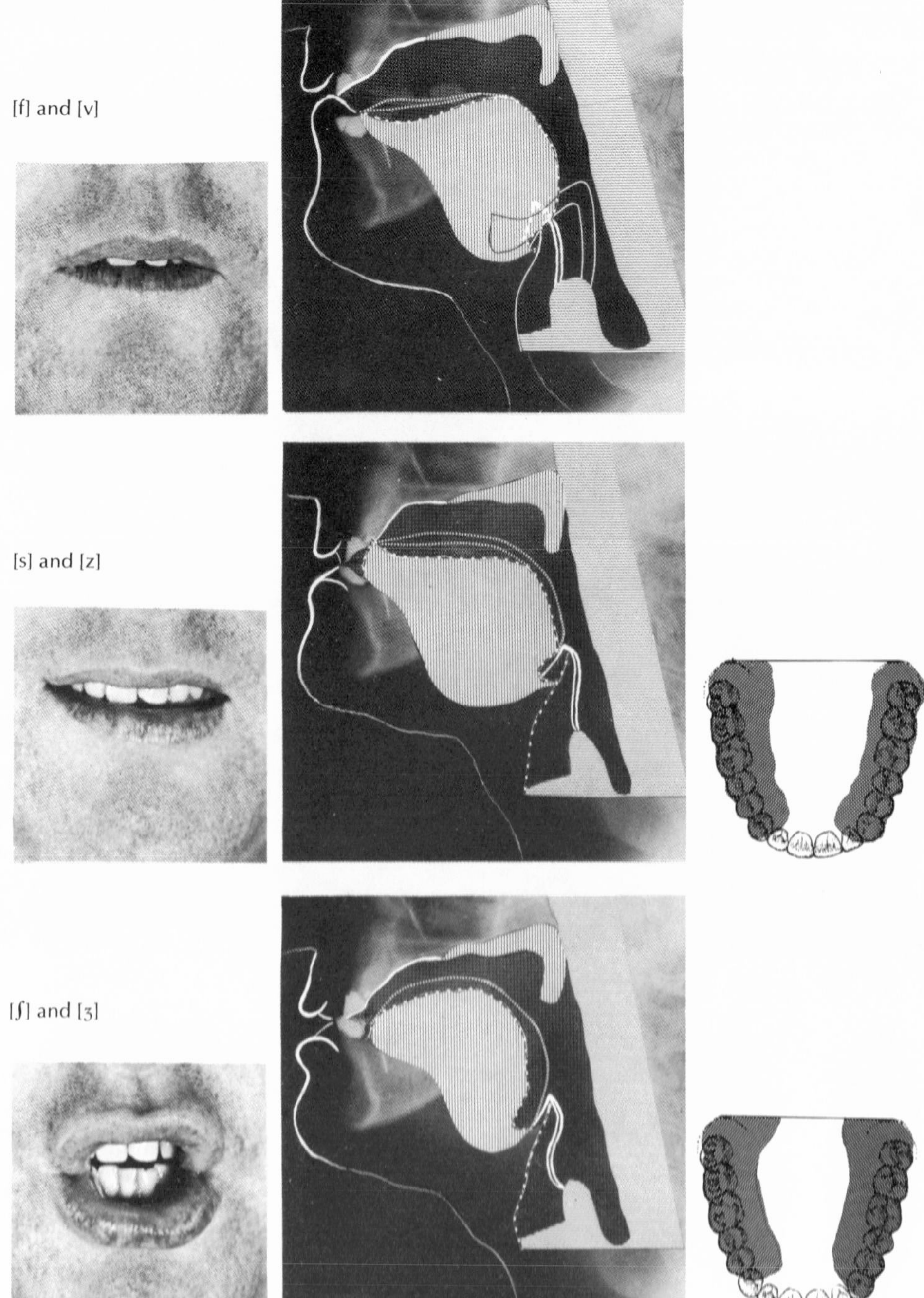

Fig. **137.** The Continuant Fricatives [f], [v], [s], [z], [ʃ], and [ʒ]

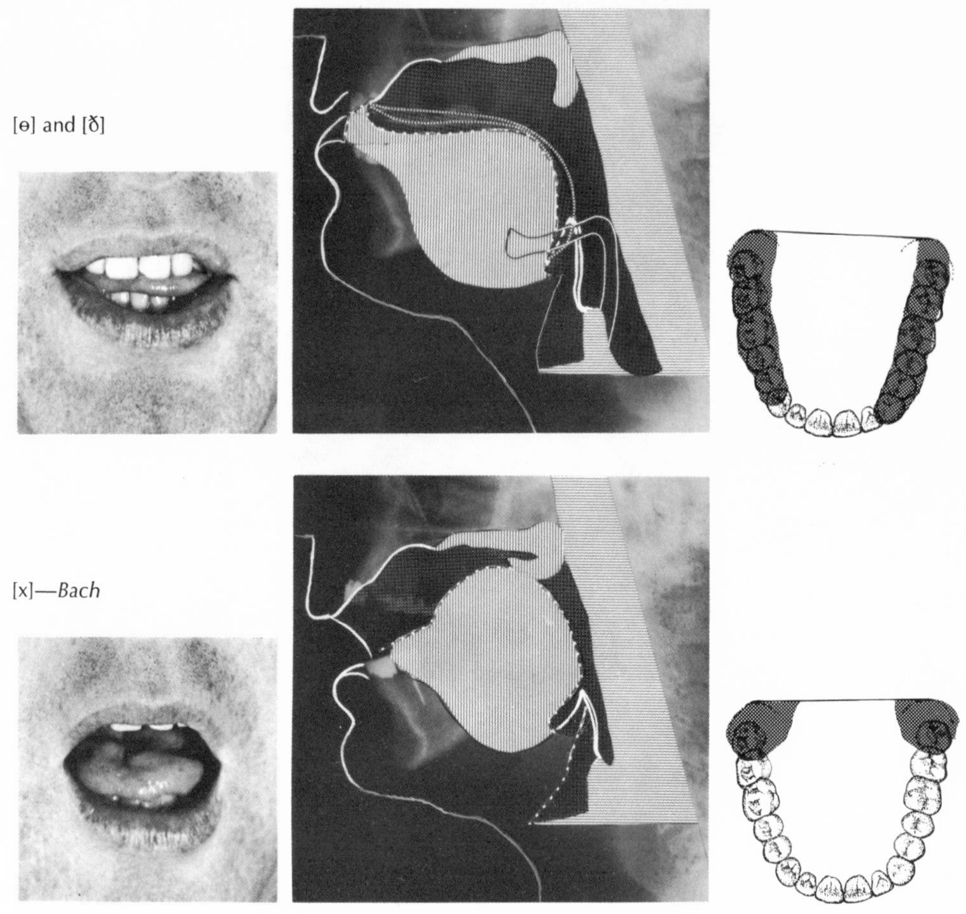

Fig. **138.** The Continuant Fricatives [θ], [ð], and [x]

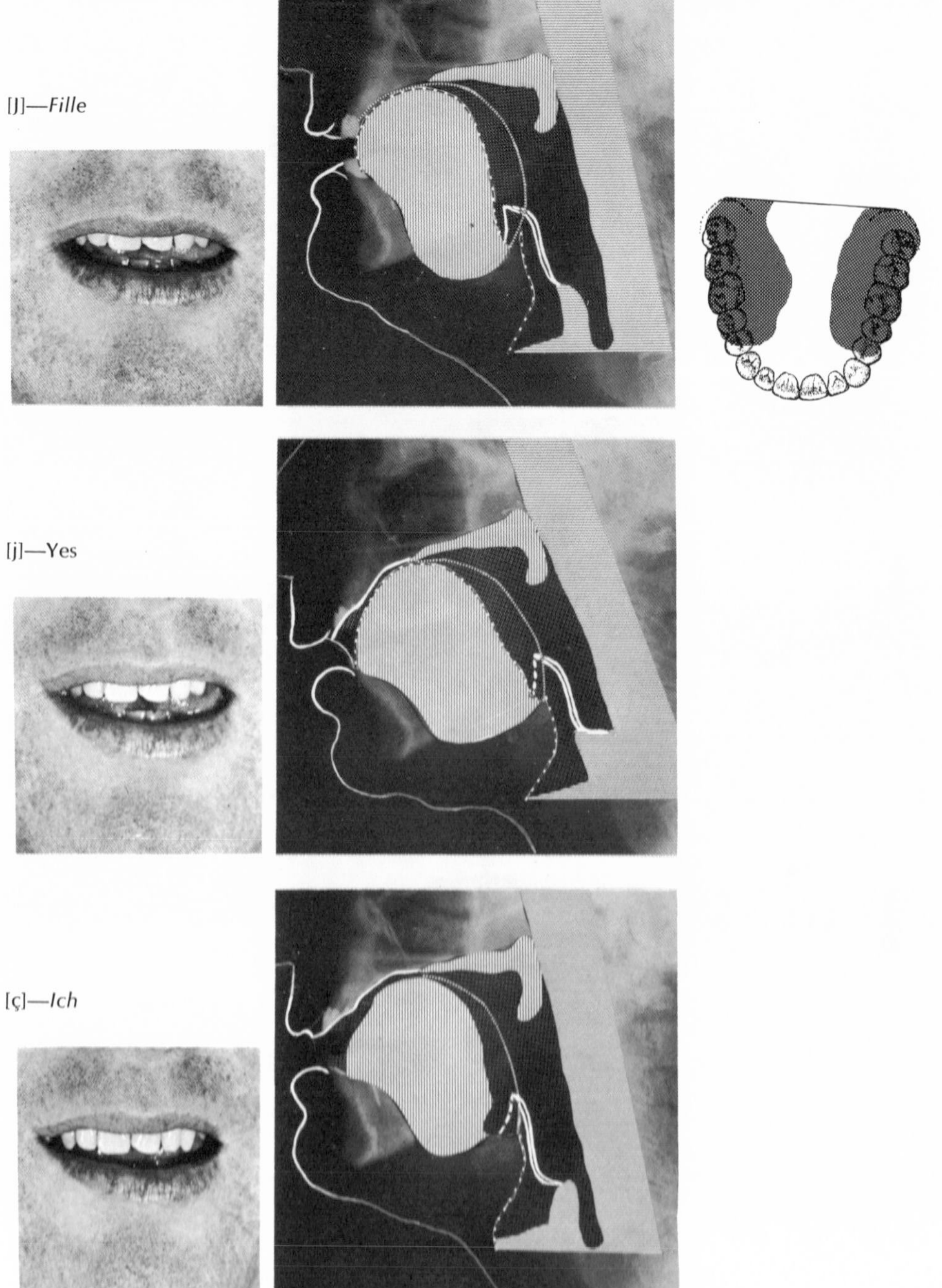

Fig. **139.** The Continuant Fricatives [J], [j], and [ç]*

* The palatograms for [j] and [ç] are the same as for [J].

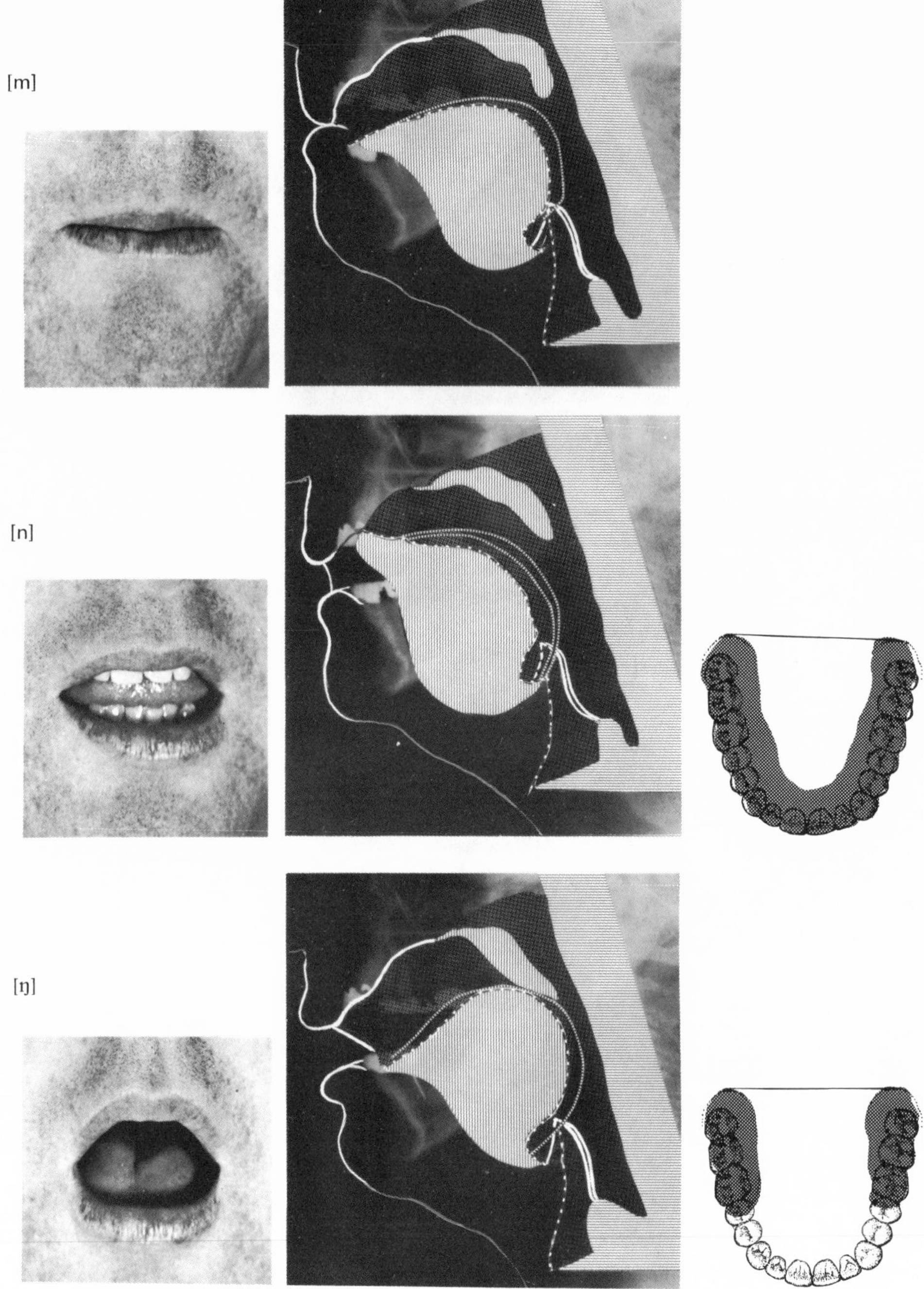

Fig. **140.** The Nasal Consonants [m], [n], and [ŋ]

ANALYSIS OF THE BASIC VOWEL [u]

(See pp. 322 and 323 for migration drills and illustrations.)

Stable Vowel Pitch Range

The tense closed vowel [u] is not accepted as a good vocalic sound by many voice teachers because of the small tense labial orifice created by extreme lip-rounding and the small back orifice which is caused by the high tongue-backing characteristic of this phoneme. The small front and back orifices create considerable back pressure or resistance against the vocal folds, imparting to the singer the sensation of tension and expenditure of effort. This sensation is present only when the vocal force exceeds the mezzo forte intensity level. Therefore this phoneme is used most successfully at low intensity levels. It is highly acceptable for both singer and listener when sung at pianissimo, piano, or mezzo forte intensities within any pitch area.

The closed [u] is indispensable as an interpretive tool in singing the art song in the English language. Its use is imperative in all German lieder, for the closed [u] phoneme is a highly regarded tool of prosody used by all German composers to enhance the musical text with a colorful, dark sound. For greater sonority, the phoneme will migrate naturally to the phoneme [ʊ].

Type. High back, closed, rounded, loosely coupled.

Labial Orifice. The lips are rounded. The labial orifice is tense, circular, and the smallest required for production of any of the vowels. As vocal force is increased to the mezzo forte intensity level, lip-rounding is held firmly tense to preserve the integrity of the phoneme. When singing sounds of intensities greater than mezzo forte, the tension of the lips is relaxed, the lip-rounding is accentuated and the phoneme migrates to the vowel [u], adding sonority to the vocalic sound.

Tongue. The tip of the tongue is held firmly against the bottom front teeth. The tip and blade are low and flattened. The tongue arch begins at the predorsal area and reaches its greatest height at the postdorsal-velar area. The base of the tongue root is drawn anteriorly, causing an increase in the anterior-posterior dimension of the valeculus and the laryngopharynx. The back orifice is located at the point of greatest constriction where the postdorsum is closest to the pharyngeal wall at the level of the second vertebra. The pharyngeal cavity is large when compared with the oral cavity. The radix of the tongue moves anteriorly a distance of approximately eighteen millimeters from its passive position and moves the hyoid bone and the tip of the epiglottis with it. This movement enlarges the opening of the vestibule and increases the total dimension of that resonator, thereby altering its resonance characteristics. As vocal force is increased to piano or mezzo forte intensities, lip-rounding is maintained to preserve the integrity of the phoneme. When intensities above the level of mezzo forte are sung, the tension of the labial orifice is relaxed slightly and the tongue-backing is less accentuated, causing the vowel to migrate to the quality alternate vowel [ʊ].

Mandible. The mandible is higher than it is for production of the vowel [ʊ]. The vertical opening is approximately three-quarters of an inch between the front teeth. As the vocal force is increased above mezzo forte, the mandible is lowered slightly to permit the singer to attain greater sonority. The phoneme then migrates to the quality alternate vowel [ʊ].

Laryngeal Position. The low laryngeal position and the forward tilt of the thyroid cartilage are identical to that used for production of the vowel [ʊ].

Velum. The velum is held firmly against the pharyngeal wall to prevent sound from passing into the nasal cavities. The uvula is tense and held away from the pharyngeal wall.

First Migration Pitch Range

Labial Orifice. The lips are more rounded than they are in singing this phoneme within the basic vowel pitch range. The labial orifice remains tensely circular. This position is assumed at intensity levels of piano and pianissimo only within this pitch range. As the vocal force is increased, the labial orifice becomes less tense and less rounded. The tongue-backing is less accentuated, and the phoneme migrates toward the vowel [ʊ], thereby adding sonority to the vocalic sound.

Tongue. The tip of the tongue is held firmly against the bottom front teeth. The blade is depressed but the dorsum is arched and extremely backed at the velar–pharyngeal wall position. The base of the tongue root is drawn anteriorly, causing an increase in the anterior-posterior dimension of the valeculus and the laryngopharynx. The back orifice is located at the point of greatest constriction at the postdorsum–pharyngeal wall position at the level of the second cervical vertebra. The oral and pharyngeal cavities are approximately equal in cavity dimension. The position of the epiglottis remains unchanged. As vocal force is increased from a mezzo piano to a forte, the labial orifice is less tense and less rounded; the dorsum is less arched and less backed, causing an increase in the anterior-posterior dimension of the back orifice. The phoneme then migrates toward the vowel [ʊ].

Mandible. The mandible is lower than it is when the phoneme [u] is sung within the basic vowel pitch range. As vocal force is increased, the low mandibular position is accentuated, thus causing an increase in the vertical dimension of the oral cavity.

Laryngeal Position. The larynx is lowered approximately one centimeter from the position assumed during the production of the vowel [u] in the basic vowel position. The vertical dimension of the pharynx is increased by lowering the larynx. The tilt of the thyroid cartilage is not changed. As vocal force increases, the laryngeal lowering is exaggerated, and this lowering combined with the alterations of other articulators, the phoneme migrates to the phoneme [ʊ].

Velum. The superior-posterior heel of the velum is firmly pressed against the pharyngeal wall.

Second Migration Pitch Range

Labial Orifice. When compared with their position in producing the phoneme [u] in the first migration pitch range, the lips have lost their rounded tension and are protruded to assume the position of [ʊ]. The labial orifice is elongated vertically. As vocal force is increased, the vertical dimension of the labial orifice is increased by lowering the mandible. Lip protrusion must be maintained to preserve the integrity of the phoneme.

Tongue. The tip of the tongue is held firmly against the bottom front teeth. The blade is slightly depressed. The dorsum is less arched and less backed than during the production of the vowel [u] in the first migration. The back orifice is wider at the point of greatest constriction at postdorsum–pharyngeal wall position. The base of the tongue root is drawn anteriorly, causing an increase in the anterior-posterior dimension of the lower pharynx and the valeculus. The oral cavity is larger than the pharyngeal cavity. The position of the epiglottis remains unchanged. As vocal force increases, the tongue position is stabilized. Lip protrusion causes the phoneme to migrate to the vowel [ʌ].

Mandible. The mandible is lowered from the position assumed during the production of [u] in the first migration pitch range. As vocal force is increased, the mandibular lowering is accentuated.

Laryngeal Position. The larynx is raised approximately one centimeter from its position during the production of the phoneme [u] within the first migration pitch range. The vertical dimension of the pharynx is decreased by raising the larynx. The tilt of the thyroid cartilage is not changed. As vocal force is increased, the laryngeal position is stabilized and the phoneme sung is that of the vowel [ʊ].

Velum. The velum is firmly pressed against the pharyngeal wall.

ANALYSIS OF THE NEUTRAL VOWEL [ʌ]

(See pp. 324 and 325 for migration drills and illustrations.)

Stable Vowel Pitch Range

The neutral vowel [ʌ] is a stressed vowel; its unstressed counterpart is known as the central schwa [ə]. Musical notation demands definite periods of duration to be observed for all unstressed vowels. Some periods are as short as a sixteenth note, others as long as a quarter note. In either event, the tongue, lip, and jaw positions of the sung sound [ə] or [ʌ] are identical. Schwa is of shorter duration as a speech sound, but as a sung sound it may be of long duration although it is always unstressed. The neutral vowel [ʌ] is a stressed sound and will substitute for other vowels as the pitch is raised or as the intensity is increased. It is an open vowel when it is sung within the stable vowel and first migration pitch ranges, but it is always a closed vowel when it is sung within the second migration pitch range. The function of the neutral vowel as a point of vowel migration has been explained in Chapter Nine under vowel migration (Fig. 103, p. 234). A thorough knowledge of these migrations will provide the teacher with an awareness of the function of this phoneme in its stressed form that will aid in solving problems of range and intelligibility.

Type. Low central, half-open, neutral, loosely coupled.

Labial Orifice. The lips are unrounded and not spread. The dimensions of the orifice are approximately one inch vertically and one and one-half inches laterally. The singer has a feeling of flaccidity and looseness in both face and lips while singing within the basic vowel pitch range. As the intensity is increased, the mandible is lowered, causing a vertical increase in the dimension of the labial orifice and also in the oral cavity. This phoneme does not migrate with an increase in intensity when it is sung within the basic vowel pitch range, and provided the lips retain their neutral flaccidity, the vowel becomes more sonorous.

Tongue. When this phoneme is sung within the basic vowel pitch range, the tongue must be firmly pressed against the bottom front teeth. The dorsum of the tongue is flattened to assume a low back position, creating a frontal cavity of even dimension extending from the labial orifice to the point where the upper tongue root forms a constriction near the pharyngeal wall at the base of the second cervical vertebra. At this point, the back orifice is formed and couples the oral and pharyngeal cavities. The pharyngeal cavity is smaller than the oral cavity. The radix of the tongue moves anteriorly approximately four millimeters from its position in a passive state and moves with it the hyoid bone and the tip of the epiglottis. This movement enlarges the opening of the vestibule and increases the total dimension of that resonator, thereby altering its resonance characteristics. As vocal force increases, the tongue retains its flat conformation from the tip to the postdorsal area. The back orifice is slightly widened as the tongue-backing becomes less accentuated. This action together with the increase in the vertical dimension of the oral cavity, adds sonority to this neutral phoneme. The vowel does not migrate provided the labial orifice remains loose and flaccid.

Mandible. The mandible is stable at a half-open position with a vertical opening approximately one and one-half inches between the teeth at the center. As vocal force is increased, the mandible is lowered. The phoneme does not migrate.

Laryngeal Position. The larynx is lowered to a position slightly lower than that assumed during the passive state (approximately six millimeters). As the intensity is increased, the laryngeal position is stabilized, but the thyroid cartilage is tilted forward by the contraction of the cricothyroid muscle to impart stability to the phonatory system and to increase the tension of the vocal folds.

Velum. The superior-posterior heel of the velum is extended in a lax arch to the pharyngeal wall but does not make firm contact with it. This light occlusion permits a leakage of some of the sound into the nasal cavities, adding to the vowel a color characteristic which distinguishes it from the frontal [a].

First Migration Pitch Range

When compared with the neutral vowel [ʌ] sung within the stable vowel pitch range, the lips, labial orifice, tongue, mandible, laryngeal position, and velum do not change.

Second Migration Pitch Range

Labial Orifice. When compared with its position in singing the neutral vowel within the first migration pitch range, the labial orifice is somewhat rounded as a result of lip protrusion. When the neutral vowel is sung on pitches that lie above the staff, the lips must be protruded lest the phoneme acquire a blatant sound resembling that of the open [ɑ].

Tongue. The tip of the tongue is held firmly against the bottom front teeth. The blade is depressed. The dorsum is much lower than this phoneme when it is produced within the stable and first migration pitch range. The tongue is backed and grooved at the tongue root. The tongue-backing is not so extreme as it is during the first migration pitch range. Therefore, the point of constriction that forms the inner orifice is more open. The orifice is formed at the position of the tongue root and the pharyngeal wall at the level of the first cervical vertebra.

The pharyngeal cavity is increased in its vertical and anterior-posterior dimension by lowering the larynx. The radix of the tongue has moved anteriorly approximately twelve millimeters from its position in the first migration pitch range. This movement enlarges the opening of the vestibule and increases the total dimension of that resonator, thereby altering its resonance characteristics. The vowel does not migrate, provided the labial orifice remains protruded and open.

Mandible. The mandible is lowered from the position assumed during the first migration, causing an increase in the vertical dimension of the oral cavity. As vocal force is increased, the vowel does not migrate.

Laryngeal Position. The larynx is lowered approximately eight millimeters from the position used for the production of this phoneme within the first migration pitch range. As vocal force is increased, the thyroid cartilage is tilted forward by the action of the cricothyroid muscle to impart stability to the phonatory system and to increase the tension of the thyroarytenoid muscle.

Velum. The nasal part is closed by the velum, which is pressed firmly against the pharyngeal wall.

ANALYSIS OF THE HIGH, CENTRAL, ROUNDED VOWEL [ɜ]

(See pp. 326 and 327 for migration drills and illustrations.)

Stable Vowel Pitch Range

Type. High, central, closed, rounded, loosely coupled.

Labial Orifice. The lips are tensely protruded. The labial orifice is as open as it is during the production of the vowel [ʊ]. The orifice is slightly wider in its vertical than in its transverse dimension. As vocal force is increased, the lip protrusion is held firmly tense to preserve the integrity of the phoneme. Lip protrusion must be exaggerated when the intensity is increased above mezzo forte, because this phoneme has a tendency to migrate to the neutral vowel when lip tension is slightly relaxed, and the orifice is elongated by lowering the mandible.

Tongue. The tip of the tongue is held firmly against the bottom front teeth. The tongue arch is symmetrically rounded from the tip to the root. The base of the tongue root is drawn anteriorly, an action that increases the anterior-posterior dimension of the valeculus and the laryngopharynx. The tongue is slightly grooved at the dorsum. The root is deeply grooved. Within the oral cavity, the superior surface of the tongue is equidistant from the palate from tip to dorsum. The point of constriction where the tongue is nearest the pharyngeal wall is at the level of the first cervical vertebra. The tight coupling of the oral and pharyngeal cavities makes this phoneme singly resonant. The radix of the tongue moves anteriorly ten millimeters from its position in a passive state and moves with it the hyoid bone and the tip of the epiglottis. This movement enlarges the opening of the vestibule and increases the total dimension of that resonator, thereby altering its resonance characteristics.

The singer should not produce this phoneme with the tongue in retroflex position. When the tip of the tongue is stabilized at the bottom front teeth and the lip-rounding is extreme, this phoneme is a satisfying substitute for the retroflex General American [ɝ].

Mandible. The mandible is lowered to create a vertical aperture approximately three-quarters of an inch between the front teeth. As the vocal force is increased, the mandible is lowered, increasing the vertical dimension of the oral cavity. As the dimension of the oral cavity and labial orifice is increased, greater sonority is achieved.

Laryngeal Position. The laryngeal position is the same as it is for producing the back vowels. The forward tilt of the thyroid cartilage is decreased considerably from the position used to sing the back vowels at low intensities. The position is similar to that of the front vowels. As the vocal force increases, the tilt of the thyroid cartilage also increases.

Velum. The superior-posterior heel of the velum is pressed firmly against the pharyngeal wall to prevent sound from passing into the nasal cavities. The uvula is tense and away from the pharyngeal wall.

First Migration Pitch Range

Labial Orifice. The lips are tensely protruded. The labial orifice is elongated slightly more than it is during the production of the vowel [ɜ] in the stable vowel pitch range. The elongation is caused by the lowering of the mandible. As vocal force is increased, the lip protrusion must be held firmly tense to prevent a migration of this phoneme to the neutral vowel [ʌ].

Tongue. The tip of the tongue is held firmly against the bottom front teeth. The tongue arch is symmetrically rounded from the tip to the dorsum.

For this phoneme, the tongue positions of the stable vowel pitch area and first migration pitch area are identical. The rounded arch gives the phoneme [ɜ] its particular quality, and when this tongue position is coupled with the firmness of the protruded lips, the phoneme assumes great stability even when extreme vocal force is exerted.

Mandible. The mandible is lowered only slightly from the position assumed during the production of [ɜ] in the stable vowel pitch range.

Laryngeal Position. The laryngeal position is the same as it is when the phoneme [ɜ] is produced in the stable vowel pitch range.

Velum. The velum is shortened and firmly pressed against the pharyngeal wall to prevent sound from passing into the nasal cavities.

Second Migration Pitch Range

Labial Orifice. The lips remain tensely protruded. The labial orifice is open slightly more than it is in the first migration pitch range. To acquire greater sonority at the higher pitch level, the singer must lower the mandible and retain the excessive lip protrusion so the lips are also less rounded. As vocal force is increased, the phoneme will migrate toward the neutral vowel position, an effect caused by relaxing the labial orifice and lowering the mandible.

Tongue. The tip of the tongue is held firmly against the bottom front teeth. The tongue arch is lower at the postdorsal area than it is when the vowel is produced in the first migration. This movement causes an increase in the anterior-posterior dimension of the pharynx and causes the cavity to become more singly resonant. The back orifice is arched to provide the [ɜ] characteristic to the phoneme. The radix of the tongue moves anteriorly approximately six millimeters from its position in the first migration pitch range. This movement enlarges the opening of the vestibule and increases the total dimension of that resonator, thereby altering its resonance characteristics. When vocal force is extreme, the tongue is flattened and the phoneme migrates to the neutral vowel [ʌ].

Mandible. The position of the mandible is changed little when this phoneme is sung within the first migration pitch range.

Laryngeal Position. The larynx is lowered one centimeter from its phonatory position within the first migration pitch range. This movement causes an increase in the vertical dimension of the pharynx. As vocal force is increased, this position is accentuated.

Velum. The superior-posterior heel of the velum is pressed firmly against the pharyngeal wall to prevent sound from passing into the nasal cavities.

ANALYSIS OF THE ROUNDED FRONTAL VOWEL [y] LONG UMLAUT Ü AND [ʏ] SHORT UMLAUT Ü

(See pp. 328 and 329 for migration drills and illustrations.)

Stable Vowel Pitch Range

The rounded frontal vowel [y] is not used in the English language, but is used extensively in German and French. When singing the German lieder and the French art song it is imperative that the student have mastered this sound within the stable vowel pitch range and its migration positions, for many beautiful tonal effects are possible when this phoneme is produced correctly.

The home base of this phoneme is the phoneme [i], and the [i] sound must be heard even though the lips are rounded to form [u]. Such lip tension builds up impedance or back pressure that should be preserved to retain the integrity of the phoneme; should the lip-rounding and the frontal tongue position be relaxed, the phoneme wili be lost, and meaning within the text will suffer. The rounded frontal [ʏ] demands a similar lip and tongue position, but it is built on [ɪ] and is of shorter duration in singing. The variation between these two phonemes will only be noted in the stable vowel pitch range.

Type. High front, closed, rounded.

Labial Orifice. The lips are tensely rounded much the same as when producing [u]. The lips must be held in this position even when vocal force is increased to preserve the integrity of the phoneme. When the vocal force is above a mezzo forte, the phoneme migrates to the vowel [ʏ], which has the phoneme [ɪ] as its home base.

Tongue. The tip of the tongue is held firmly against the bottom front teeth. The tongue blade and dorsum are in contact with the palate at each lateral tooth line. The tongue is grooved along the medial raphe from the blade to the root. The tongue groove becomes progressively pronounced from the postdorsal area to the tongue root, increasing the anterior-posterior dimension of the pharyngeal space during the utterance of this vowel. The inner orifice is at the point of greatest constriction at the predorsal-palatal position.

The front cavity is smaller than the back cavity. As the vocal force increases to forte or louder, the muscular tension of the tongue is decreased laterally by a lowering of the mandible. This combined action increases the vertical dimension of the oral cavity at the dorsal area. If the labial orifice remains tensely rounded, the vowel will migrate to the umlaut [ʏ], whose home base sound is [ɪ].

Mandible. The mandible is closed to permit a vertical opening of one-half inch between the teeth at the center. As vocal force is increased above forte the mandible is lowered slightly to increase both the front and back orifices and to enlarge the front cavity. This action causes a migration of the phoneme toward the umlaut sound [ʏ].

Laryngeal Position. The larynx is lowered to a position slightly lower than that assumed during the passive state but slightly higher than it is for singing the neutral vowel [ʌ]. As the intensity increases, a lower laryngeal position is assumed to impart stability to the phonating system. The lower position is accompanied by a slight tilt of the thyroid cartilage, which increases the tension of the vocal folds.

Velum. The superior-posterior heel of the velum rests firmly against the pharyngeal wall to prevent sound from leaking into the nasal cavities. The uvula is suspended downward away from the pharyngeal wall suggesting a lax condition.

First Migration Pitch Range

Labial Orifice. The lips retain the tensely rounded position used in the stable vowel pitch range. The vertical dimension of the labial orifice does not change at low intensity levels. As the vocal force is increased above a mezzo forte, the lips are less rounded and the labial orifice is increased in its vertical dimension. The phoneme then migrates to the umlaut [ʏ].

Tongue. The tip of the tongue is held firmly against the bottom front teeth. The tongue is lowered slightly from the blade to the postdorsal area, increasing the vertical dimension of the oral cavity. The blade and dorsum are in contact with the palate at each lateral tooth line. The tongue groove extends from the blade to the root, and it becomes deeper at the root. The back orifice extends from the blade to the mediodorsum at the palatal area. The oral cavity is smaller than the pharyngeal cavity. As vocal force increases, the muscular tension of the tongue is decreased laterally by lowering the mandible. This combined action increases the vertical dimension of the oral cavity from the blade to the dorsum, and the vowel migrates to the umlaut [ʏ].

Mandible. During the production of low intensity sounds, the mandible is lowered from its basic vowel position. As the intensity increases above mezzo forte, the mandible is lowered as it is in the production of the phoneme [ɪ].

Laryngeal Position. The laryngeal position is lowered approximately one centimeter from the laryngeal position used to produce the umlaut vowel [y] in the stable vowel position. As vocal force is increased above mezzo forte, the larynx is lowered slightly to increase the vertical dimension of the pharynx. The forward tilt of the thyroid cartilage is increased.

Velum. The velum is pressed firmly against the pharyngeal wall, and the uvula is shortened. These positions suggest a more tense condition than in the stable vowel pitch area.

Second Migration Pitch Range

Labial Orifice. When compared with the position used for the first migration pitch range, the lips are protruded to preserve the integrity of the phoneme [y]. The labial orifice is much more open and less tense; the opening is increased by lowering the mandible.

Tongue Position. The tip of the tongue is pressed firmly against the bottom front teeth. The tongue is lowered from the blade to the dorsum, the result of lowering the mandible. The tongue has a shallow groove from the tip to the dorsum, and it is deeply grooved from the dorsum to the root. The blade and dorsum are in contact with the palatal area at each lateral tooth line. The back orifice is located at the point of greatest constriction at the blade–alveolar ridge position. Tongue-fronting tends to preserve the integrity of the phoneme [y] even though the pitch is high. As vocal force is increased, the combined action of the described movements are accentuated. The vowel produced is the umlaut [ʏ].

Mandible. The mandible is lowered slightly, an action that becomes more pronounced as the vocal force is intensified.

Laryngeal Position. When this phoneme [y] is produced in the second migration pitch range, the laryngeal position is about the same as that assumed in the first migration pitch range. The laryngeal distention is accomplished at lower pitch ranges and is sustained into the second migration ranges without appreciable change. The vowel sung within the second migration pitch range is the umlaut [ʏ]. The migration is identical to that of [i] to [ɪ]. The thyroid tilt is approximately the same as that assumed during the production of the umlaut [ʏ] within the first migration pitch range.

Velum. The velum is pressed firmly against the pharyngeal wall.

ANALYSIS OF ROUNDED FRONTAL VOWEL [ø]

(See pp. 330 and 331 for migration drills and illustrations.)

Stable Vowel Pitch Range

Type. High front, closed, rounded.

Labial Orifice. The lips are tensely rounded and protruded. The labial orifice is less open than it is for producing the vowel [ē] in the stable vowel area.

When vocal force is increased, the extreme rounded position of the lips must be held firmly to preserve the integrity of the umlaut sound. The sound of the phoneme [ē] must be heard as the basic phoneme upon which this vowel is formed.

Tongue. The tip of the tongue is held firmly against the bottom front teeth. The blade and dorsum are in contact with the palatal area at each lateral tooth line. The spreading of the dorsum laterally is identical to that tongue position assumed when producing the vowel [e]. This lateral spreading is the significant characteristic of this phoneme. The tongue is grooved along the median raphe from the blade to the root; the groove is more pronounced from the postdorsal area to the base of the root in the stable vowel pitch range than it is when the anterior-posterior dimension of the pharynx is increased.

The back orifice is located at the point of greatest constriction at the prepalatal-predorsum position. The pharyngeal cavity is long and wide when compared with the oral cavity. As vocal force is increased to preserve the integrity of the phoneme.

When vocal force is increased, the lip-rounding becomes less tense. The high frontal position of the tongue is less accentuated, and the vowel migrates toward the rounded frontal vowel [œ].

Mandible. The mandible is closed, permitting a vertical opening of one-half inch between the teeth at the center. As vocal force is increased above forte, the mandible is lowered slightly, increasing both front and back orifices and enlarging the front cavity, causing a migration of the phoneme toward the umlaut sound [œ].

Laryngeal Position. The larynx is lowered to a position slightly lower than the passive position and approximately the same as that used in producing the vowel [e]. As the vocal force increases, a lower laryngeal position is assumed to impart stability to the phonatory system. The lower laryngeal position is accompanied by a slight tilt of the thyroid cartilage, which increases the tension of the vocal folds.

Velum. The superior-posterior heel of the velum rests firmly against the pharyngeal wall to prevent sound from leaking into the nasal cavities. The uvula is suspended downward away from the pharyngeal wall into the oropharynx, thus suggesting a relaxed muscular state.

First Migration Pitch Range

Labial Orifice. The lips remain tensely rounded and protruded; the labial orifice is as rounded as it is for producing the vowel [o]. As the vocal force is increased, the lips retain their state of tension, but the labial orifice is slightly opened by lowering the mandible.

Tongue. Because the lips are extremely rounded, holding the tongue firm in a high frontal position is difficult, but it is necessary for the proper production of this umlaut sound. The singer must constantly listen for the sound of [e] to emerge within the sung word; for listening will help him to achieve proper tongue position for the phoneme [ø].

The tip of the tongue is held firmly against the bottom front teeth. The blade and dorsum are in firm contact with the palate at the lateral tooth line. The tongue groove is accentuated at the postdorsal-root position, causing an increase in the anterior-posterior dimension of the pharynx at this point. The high arch of the medio-dorsal position is reduced, but the tongue-fronting is sustained, to form the back orifice at the prepalatal–alveolar ridge position. As vocal force is increased, the tongue-fronting is lost because of lowering the mandible, which increases the vertical dimension of the oral cavity. The phoneme then migrates to the umlaut [œ].

Mandible. The mandible is lowered approximately one centimeter from the position assumed within the stable vowel pitch range. This act assists in increasing the vertical dimension of the oral cavity.

Laryngeal Position. The laryngeal position remains the same as when the phoneme [ø] is reproduced within the stable vowel pitch range.

Velum. The velum is pressed firmly against the pharyngeal wall, and the uvular portion is drawn and shortened, thus suggesting an increase in muscular tension.

Second Migration Pitch Range

Labial Orifice. The lips remain tensely rounded and protruded; the labial orifice retains its orbicular opening without change in dimension.

Tongue. The tip of the tongue is held firmly against the bottom front teeth; the blades and dorsum are in contact with the palatal area at each lateral tooth line. The tongue is less arched from the blade to the dorsum than it is when this phoneme is produced in the first migration pitch range. This lowering increases the vertical dimension of the oral cavity. The tongue groove is deeper and more accentuated at the postdorsal-root position, and thus increases the anterior-posterior dimension of the pharynx at that position.

The tongue-fronting is maintained to preserve the integrity of the phoneme but not so acutely as when the phoneme is produced within the first migration pitch range. The back orifice is formed at the point of greatest constriction at the tongue blade–alveolar ridge position. As vocal force is increased, the vertical dimension of the oral cavity is increased to attain greater sonority. The phoneme [ø] then migrates toward the umlaut [œ], which has the phoneme [ɛ] as its home base.

Mandible. The position of the mandible is unchanged when it is compared with the production of the phoneme [ø] within the first migration pitch range. The increase in oral cavity dimension is entirely caused by tongue movement.

Laryngeal Position. The larynx is lowered eight millimeters from the position assumed for the production of the phoneme [ø] in the first migration position. This movement increases the vertical length of the pharynx and stabilizes the vocal mechanism. The thyroid cartilage tilts forward very slightly, and increases the tension of the vocal folds during the production of the higher pitched sounds.

Velum. The velum is firmly pressed against the pharyngeal wall. The uvular portion is shortened and suggests a condition of muscular tension.

ANALYSIS OF THE ROUNDED FRONTAL VOWEL [œ]

(See pp. 332 and 333 for migration drills and illustrations.)

Stable Vowel Pitch Range

Type. Mid-front, half-open, rounded.

Labial Orifice. The lips are rounded and slightly protruded. The labial orifice increases vertically compared to its size in producing the phoneme [ø] within the stable vowel pitch range. As vocal force is increased, the phoneme tends to migrate toward the quality alternate vowel [ɛ] as the mandible is lowered. If lip-rounding is maintained, the integrity of this phoneme [œ] may be preserved in a sonorous, forte sound.

Tongue. The tip of the tongue is held firmly against the bottom front teeth. The postdorsal edges of the tongue are in contact with the palatal area at the lateral tooth line. The tongue is not grooved from its tip to the mediodorsal position. It is deeply grooved from the postdorsum to the base of the tongue root, to increase the anterior-posterior dimension of the pharynx. The back orifice is formed at the point of greatest constriction at the predorsal-mediopalatal position. As vocal force increases, the oral cavity is increased vertically by lowering the mandible, thus causing the vowel [œ] to migrate toward the quality alternate vowel [a]. If lip-rounding is sustained, the integrity of the phoneme [œ] may be maintained in a sonorous, forte sound.

Mandible. The mandible is held at a position one-half inch lower than it is when the vowel [ø] is produced within the stable vowel pitch range. The vertical opening between the teeth at the center is approximately one and one-quarter inches. As vocal force increases, the mandible is slightly lowered, to increase the vertical dimension of the oral cavity. The phoneme [œ] then migrates toward the quality alternate vowel [a]. If lip-rounding is sustained, the integrity of the phoneme may be preserved through a sonorous forte.

Laryngeal Position. The laryngeal position is one-eighth inch lower than it is for production of the phoneme [ø] within the stable vowel pitch range. The thyroid cartilage is tilted forward from its passive position to increase the tension upon the vocal folds.

Velum. The velum is pressed firmly against the posterior pharyngeal wall. The uvula is, suspended downward into the oropharynx, suggesting a state of relaxed musculature.

First Migration Pitch Range

Labial Orifice. The lips are rounded and slightly protruded. The labial orifice is increased vertically approximately one-half inch from the position used for the production of phoneme [ø] in the stable vowel pitch range. As the vocal force is increased above mezzo forte, lip-rounding must be accentuated to preserve the integrity of the phoneme.

Tongue. The tip of the tongue is held firmly against the bottom front teeth. The tip and blade are symmetrically rounded and ungrooved. The dorsum and the root are deeply grooved. The point of greatest constriction is long; it extends from the blade–alveolar ridge position to the predorsum-prepalatal position. The cavity system is tightly coupled, suggesting a singly resonant system. As vocal force is increased, the characteristic umlaut sound may be preserved by lip-rounding. If the lip-rounding disintegrates with the increased vocal force, the phoneme will migrate to the quality alternate vowel [a].

Mandible. The position of the mandible does not change when the phoneme [œ] is sung in the stable and first migration pitch ranges.

Laryngeal Position. The larynx is lowered approximately one-quarter of an inch from the position assumed during the production of the phoneme [œ] within the stable vowel pitch range. This movement increases the vertical dimension of the pharynx and aids in stabilizing the phonatory tube. The slight forward tilt of the thyroid cartilage increases the tension of the vocal folds.

Velum. The velum is firmly pressed against the posterior pharyngeal wall. The uvula is drawn upward to increase the thickness of the velum through muscular tension.

Second Migration Pitch Range

Labial Orifice. The lips are rounded and slightly protruded. The vertical dimension of the labial orifice does not change when the phoneme is sung in the first or second migration pitch ranges. When vocal force is increased, lip-rounding must be sustained. When it is not sustained, the phoneme will migrate to the neutral vowel [ʌ]. High notes require less lip-rounding.

Tongue. The tip of the tongue is held firmly against the bottom front teeth. The tip and blade are symmetrically rounded and ungrooved. The dorsum and root are deeply grooved, creating an increase in the anterior-posterior dimension of the pharynx at the root position and an increase in the vertical dimension of the oral cavity at the dorsal-velar position. The point of greatest constriction is located at the blade-alveolar ridge position. When this phoneme is sung in the second migration pitch range, the back orifice is more clearly defined than it is when the phoneme is sung in the first migration pitch range. The cavity system is tightly coupled, suggesting a singly resonant system. The lip-rounding and tongue-fronting are prime factors in determining the sound of this phoneme. Sonority is attained by the large pharyngeal space. As vocal force is increased, the integrity of the phoneme may be preserved by lip-rounding. If the labial orifice distintegrates with increased vocal force, the phoneme will migrate to the neutral vowel [ʌ].

Mandible. The mandibular position used for singing the phoneme [œ] remains the same within both the first and second migration pitch ranges. The major change is in the tongue position. As vocal force is increased, the mandible may be lowered slightly to attain greater sonority. If tongue-fronting and lip-rounding are not sustained, the phoneme will migrate toward the neutral vowel [ʌ].

Laryngeal Position. The larynx is lowered one-quarter of an inch from the position assumed for the production of this phoneme within the first migration pitch range. This extreme lowering increases the vertical dimension of the pharynx and serves to stabilize the phonatory tube. The thyroid cartilage is tilted farther forward than it is for the production of this phoneme within the first migration pitch range. As vocal force is increased, the above movements are accentuated, and the phoneme migrates toward the neutral vowel [ʌ].

Velum. The velum is pressed firmly against the pharyngeal wall. The velum is short and thickened, thus suggesting muscular tension.

ANALYSIS OF THE FRENCH NASAL VOWEL [ɛ̃]

(See pp. 334 and 335 for migration drills and illustrations.)

Stable Vowel Pitch Range

Type. Mid-front, half-open, spread, nasal.

Any vowel sound can be nasalized by lowering the soft palate and allowing a part of the air stream to exit through the nose. In French, four vowel sounds are regularly nasalized when they occur in certain situations. These vowels are [ɛ̃], [œ̃], [ɑ̃], and [õ].

Except for the velar position, the French nasals [ɛ̃], [œ̃], [ɑ̃], and [õ] require the same tongue, lip, mandibular, and laryngeal position as the basic or quality alternate vowels upon which they they are formed. Therefore, they will migrate as those vowels do (Fig. 103, p. 234). The nasal [ɛ̃] is a rounded frontal vowel formed on [æ]. The migration of this phoneme in different pitch areas will conform to the phoneme [a].

Labial Orifice. The lips are in the same position as that used in producing the vowel [æ]. They are wider transversely than vertically. The muscular tension of the lips is maintained. As vocal force is increased, the vertical dimension of the orifice is increased by lowering the mandible, but the characteristic spreading demanded of the phoneme is maintained. As the cavity is enlarged, the phoneme migrates toward the quality alternate vowel [a].

Tongue. The tip of the tongue is held firmly against the bottom front teeth. The tip blade and predorsum are not grooved. The groove extends from the mediodorsal area to the tongue root.

The radix of the tongue is relaxed, permitting the epiglottis to be closer to the pharyngeal wall than when this phoneme [ɛ̃] is produced as an unnasal sound. This position of the epiglottis closes the opening to the vestibule and alters the characteristic of that resonator. The tongue is extremely arched at the mediodorsal-mediopalatal position where the back of the orifice is formed.

The front cavity is smaller than the back cavity. As vocal force is increased, the oral cavity is increased vertically by lowering the mandible, causing the vowel to migrate toward the quality alternate vowel [a].

Mandible. The position of the mandible is identical to that assumed in producing the quality alternate vowel [ɛ̃]. The vertical opening is approximately one and one-quarter inches between the teeth at the center. As vocal force is increased, the mandible is slightly lowered, increasing the vertical dimension. The phoneme [ɛ̃] then migrates toward the quality alternate phoneme [ã].

Laryngeal Position. The larynx is raised to a position six millimeters above the position used to produce the vowel [ɛ]. As vocal force is increased, the lower laryngeal position is accentuated to stabilize the phonatory tube and the thyroid cartilage tilts forward slightly to increase the tension of the vocal folds.

Velum. The velum is extended posteriorly in a slight arc into the oropharynx, permitting direct access of the phonated sound through the open nasal port into the nasal cavity.

First Migration Pitch Range

Labial Orifice. The lips are relaxed and in the same position as they are for producing the vowel [ɛ] in its first migration pitch range. The labial orifice is wider transversely than vertically. As vocal force increases, the vertical dimension of the orifice is increased by lowering the mandible. As the oral cavity is enlarged, the phoneme migrates toward the quality alternate vowel [ã].

Tongue. The tip of the tongue is held firmly against the bottom front teeth. The tip, blade, and predorsum are not grooved. A deep groove extends from the mediodorsum to the tongue root, increasing the anterior-posterior dimension of the pharynx.

The radix of the tongue has moved anteriorly approximately five millimeters, and moves the hyoid bone and the tip of the epiglottis with it. This movement enlarges the opening of the vestibule and increases the total dimension of that resonator, thereby altering its resonance characteristics. The tongue arch is the same as it is in the production of the phoneme [ɛ̃] in the stable vowel pitch range. The point of greatest constriction is at the mediodorsum-mediopalatal position, but this orifice is more open than it is when [ɛ̃] is sung in the stable vowel pitch range. The lower position of the mandible causes an increase in the vertical dimension of the oral cavity. As vocal force is increased, the oral cavity is increased in its vertical dimension by lowering the mandible, thereby causing the vowel to migrate toward the quality alternate vowel [a].

Mandible. The mandible is lower than it is for singing this phoneme in the basic vowel pitch range. As vocal force is increased, the oral cavity is increased in its vertical dimension, causing the phoneme [ɛ̃] to migrate toward the quality alternate vowel [ã].

Laryngeal Position. The larynx is approximately one and one-half centimeters lower than it is when [ɛ̃] is sung in the basic vowel pitch range. This lower position increases the vertical dimension of the pharynx. As vocal force is increased, the laryngeal lowering is accentuated to stabilize the phonatory tube. The tilt of the thyroid cartilage remains approximately the same as it is for the phoneme [ɛ̃] sung in the stable vowel pitch range.

Velum. The velum and uvular appendage is extended downward into the oropharynx in a slightly arched position, thus permitting the phonated sound to pass into the nasal cavities.

Second Migration Pitch Range

Labial Orifice. The lips are more relaxed than they are when the vowel is sung in its first migration pitch range. The labial orifice is the same vertically and transversely. As vocal force is increased, the orifice is increased vertically by lowering the mandible. This enlargement of the orifice permits the phoneme to become more sonorous.

Tongue. The high arched conformation, the degree of tongue-fronting, and the depth of the groove at the root are approximately the same as they are when this phoneme is produced in the first migration pitch range. The tongue is deeply grooved from the mediodorsum to the root, causing an increase in the anterior-posterior dimension of the pharyngeal cavity at that point. The radix of the tongue moves anteriorly and moves with it the hyoid bone and the tip of the epiglottis. This movement enlarges the opening of the vestibule and increases the total dimension of that resonator. As vocal force increases, the vertical dimension of the oral and pharyngeal cavities is increased to permit the phoneme to become more sonorous. The vowel will then migrate toward the quality alternate vowel [ã].

Mandible. The mandible is in approximately the same position as it is when the phoneme [ɛ̃] sung is in the first migration pitch range. As vocal force is increased, the mandible is lowered, causing the phoneme to migrate to the quality alternate vowel]ã[.

Laryngeal Position. The larynx is lowered approximately seven millimeters from the position of the first migration pitch range. The pharynx is increased in its vertical dimension. The tilt of the thyroid cartilage is unchanged.

Velum. The velum and its uvular appendage is arched downward into the oropharynx. The nasal port is open, permitting passage of the phonated sound into the nasal cavities.

ANALYSIS OF THE FRENCH NASAL VOWEL [œ̃]

(See pp. 336 and 337 for migration drills and illustrations.)

Stable Vowel Pitch Range

Type. High front, half-open, rounded nasal.

Labial Orifice. To produce the nasalized, rounded frontal vowel [œ̃], built on [ɛ], the lips are rounded and slightly protruded. The labial orifice assumes the same vertical dimension as the phoneme [œ̃] when it is sung in the stable vowel pitch range. If lip-rounding is maintained vocal force is increased to a forte, the integrity of the phoneme [œ] may be preserved, and it will not migrate. If lip-rounding is lessened, the phoneme tends to migrate toward the quality alternate vowel [ɛ].

Tongue Position. The tip of the tongue is held firmly against the bottom front teeth. The postdorsal edges of the tongue are in contact with the palatal area at the lateral tooth line. The tongue is not grooved from the tip to the mediodorsal position. It is deeply grooved from the postdorsum to the base of the tongue root, increasing the anterior-posterior dimension of the pharynx. The radix of the tongue is relaxed to permit the epiglottis to closely approximate the pharyngeal wall. This position of the epiglottis tends to close the opening to the vestibule and alters the characteristics of that resonator. The back orifice is formed at the point of greatest constriction at the predorsal-prepalatal position. As the vocal force increases, the size of the oral cavity is increased vertically by lowering the mandible, thus causing the vowel [œ̃] to migrate toward the quality alternate vowel [ɛ]. If lip-rounding is accentuated, the integrity of the phoneme may be maintained.

Mandible. The mandible is held at a position one-half inch lower than it is for producing the vowel [ɛ] in the stable vowel pitch range. The vertical opening between the teeth at the center is approximately one and one-quarter inches. As vocal force is increased, the mandible is slightly lowered, thus increasing the vertical dimension of the oral cavity. The phoneme [œ̃] may be preserved if lip-rounding is accentuated.

Laryngeal Position. The laryngeal position is one-eighth inch lower than it is for production of the phoneme [œ] within the stable vowel pitch range. The thyroid cartilage is tilted forward from its passive position to increase the tension upon the vocal folds.

Velum. The velum is withdrawn from the pharyngeal wall. The uvula is curved and pendulous within the oropharynx, thus permitting the phonated sound to pass into the nasal cavity.

First Migration Pitch Range

Labial Orifice. The lips are rounded and slightly protruded. The position of the labial orifice is identical to the position used to produce the phoneme [œ] within the stable vowel pitch range. As vocal force increases above a mezzo forte, lip-rounding must be extremely accentuated to preserve the integrity of the phoneme.

Tongue. The tip of the tongue is held firmly against the bottom front teeth. The tongue is grooved from the predorsum to the root. The radix of the tongue moves anteriorly approximately five millimeters and moves the hyoid bone and the tip of the epiglottis with it. This movement enlarges the opening of the vestibule and increases the total dimension of that resonator, thereby altering its resonance characteristics. The point of greatest constriction is located at the predorsal-prepalatal position. The cavity system is tightly coupled, suggesting a singly resonant system. As vocal force is increased, the integrity of the nasal [œ̃] may be preserved if the velum is firm in its position away from the pharyngeal wall. If the lip-rounding disintegrates with the increased vocal force, the phoneme will migrate to the quality alternate vowel [ɛ].

Mandible. The mandibular position is the same for singing the phoneme [œ] in both the stable and first migration pitch ranges.

Laryngeal Position. The larynx is lowered approximately one-quarter of an inch from the position assumed during the production of the phoneme [œ̃] within the stable vowel pitch range. This movement increases the vertical dimension of the pharynx and helps to stabilize the phonatory tube. The slight forward tilt of the thyroid cartilage increases the tension of the vocal folds.

Velum. The velum is separated from the pharyngeal wall but is held firmly tense. It does not assume the relaxed arched position used in the stable vowel pitch range.

Second Migration Pitch Range

Labial Orifice. The lips are rounded and slightly protruded. The vertical dimension of the labial orifice remains the same for the first or second migration pitch ranges. When vocal force is increased, the lip-rounding must be sustained, or the phoneme will migrate to the neutral vowel [ʌ].

Tongue. The tip of the tongue is held firmly against the bottom front teeth. The tip and blade are symmetrically rounded and ungrooved. The tongue is grooved from the predorsal position to the root. The deepened groove at the root causes an increase in the anterior-posterior dimension of the pharynx. The radix of the tongue root moves anteriorly a distance of approximately five millimeters and moves the hyoid bone and the tip of the epiglottis with it. This movement enlarges the opening of the vestibule and increases the total dimension of that resonator, thereby altering its resonance characteristics. The point of greatest constriction is located at the predorsal-prepalatal position. The cavity system tends to be tightly coupled, suggesting a singly resonated system. The lip-rounding and tongue-fronting are prime factors in determining the sound of this phoneme. Sonority is attained by the large pharyngeal and nasal space. As vocal force is increased, the integrity of the phoneme may be preserved by lip-rounding. If the labial orifice disintegrates with the increased vocal force, the phoneme will migrate to the neutral vowel [ʌ].

Mandible. The position of the mandible is the same whether this phoneme [œ̃] is sung within the first or second migration pitch ranges. The major change is in the tongue position. As vocal force increases, the mandible is lowered slightly to attain greater sonority. If tongue-fronting and lip-rounding are not sustained, the phoneme will migrate toward the neutral vowel [ʌ].

Velum. The velum is separated from the pharyngeal wall, but it is firm throughout its length and shortened to permit the phonated sound to pass into the nasal cavities.

ANALYSIS OF THE FRENCH NASAL VOWEL [ɑ̃]

(See pp. 338 and 339 for migration drills and illustrations.)

Stable Vowel Pitch Range

Type. Low frontal, half-open, neutral, nasal.

The lips are less tense than they are to produce the vowel [æ]. They are neither raised at the corners nor spread. This phoneme is pronounced as though it was built upon the vowel [ɔ] and not [ɑ], which is too open for this sound. As vocal force is increased the vertical dimension of the orifice is increased by lowering the mandible, and the vowel migrates toward [ɔ].

Tongue. The tip of the tongue is held firmly against the bottom front teeth. The tongue is arched and rounded evenly from the tip to the root. It is grooved from the predorsum to the postdorsum but without a groove to the tongue root. The radix of the tongue is relaxed to permit the epiglottis to be close to the pharyngeal wall. This position of the epiglottis tends to close the opening to the vestibule and alters the characteristics of that resonator. The oral cavity is larger than the pharyngeal cavity. The back orifice is formed at the point of greatest constriction at the postdorsal–pharyngeal wall position. As vocal force is increased, the pharyngeal cavity is enlarged and causes the vowel to migrate toward the neutral vowel [ʌ].

Mandible. The mandible is lowered to a position permitting an opening of approximately one and one-half inches between the teeth at the center. As vocal force is increased, the mandible is lowered slightly and causes an increase in the vertical dimension of the oral cavity. Care should be taken by the singer to eliminate tension in the labial orifice as the cavity dimension increases vertically. This action will eliminate the open blatancy of this phoneme and will permit the migration of this nasal vowel [ɑ̃] toward the neutral vowel [ʌ].

First Migration Pitch Range

Labial Orifice. To preserve the integrity of the nasalized [ɑ̃] the lips must maintain the same state of flexible tension required in singing the quality alternate vowel [ɔ]. Singers have a strong tendency to relax the lips and to permit them to assume the neutral, flaccid condition. This nasalized vowel can be sung mixed or more open than closed within the first migration pitch range.

The labial orifice is elongated vertically by lowering the mandible. Care must be taken not to protrude or round the lips while singing at low intensity levels in this first migration pitch area.

Lip-rounding will cause an immediate migration to the phoneme [õ]. As vocal force is increased, the labial orifice is elongated by lowering the mandible, and the phoneme migrates toward the neutral vowel [ʌ].

Tongue. The tip of the tongue is held firmly against the bottom front teeth. The tongue is rounded from tip to root. It is slightly grooved from post-dorsum to root. The radix of the tongue moves anteriorly approximately five millimeters, and moves the hyoid bone and the tip of the epiglottis with it. This movement enlarges the opening of the vestibule and increases the total dimension of that resonator, thereby altering its resonance characteristics. The oral cavity is larger than the pharyngeal cavity. The back orifice is formed at the point of greatest constriction at the postdorsum–pharyngeal wall position. As vocal force increases, tongue-backing is maintained; the pharyngeal cavity is increased in its lower dimension and thus the phoneme [ɑ̃] migrates toward the neutral vowel [ʌ].

Mandible. The mandible is lower than it is when this phoneme is sung within the basic vowel pitch range. As the vocal force is increased, the lowering is accentuated.

Laryngeal Position. The laryngeal position is five millimeters lower than it is when this phoneme is sung within the basic vowel pitch range. The vertical dimension of the pharynx is increased. The tilt of the thyroid cartilage is unchanged.

Velum. The velum is loosely arched downward into the oropharynx away from the pharyngeal wall, permitting the passage of the phonated sound into the nasal cavities.

Second Migration Pitch Range

Labial Orifice. The lips are more relaxed at the corners than they are when the nasal vowel [ɑ̃] is sung within the first migration pitch range. They are flexibly tense and slightly protruded. The labial orifice is elongated vertically. This protrusion adds stability to the vocalic sound and tends to preserve the phoneme. It should not be confused with lip-rounding. In the second migration pitch range, the labial orifice assumes the shape of the neutral vowel [ʌ].

Tongue. The tip of the tongue is held firmly against the bottom front teeth. When compared with the phoneme nasal [ɑ̃] sung within the first migration pitch range, the tongue is raised from the tip to the predorsum. The mediodorsum and postdorsum are extremely flattened, thus increasing the vertical dimension of the oral cavity at the dorsal-velar position. The dorsum has a shallow groove and the root is deeply grooved. The back orifice is formed at the point of greatest constriction where the upper tongue root is close to the pharyngeal wall at the level of the second cervical vertebra. The oral cavity is larger than the pharyngeal cavity. As vocal force increases, the described position of the tongue is accentuated. The phoneme sung in this position is the neutral vowel [ʌ].

Mandible. The mandible is lower than it is when this phoneme is sung within the basic vowel pitch range. When vocal force increases, the lowering is accentuated.

Laryngeal Position. The laryngeal position is approximately one centimeter lower than it is when this phoneme is sung within the first migration pitch range. The vertical dimension of the pharynx is increased. The tilt of the thyroid cartilage is unchanged. As vocal force is increased, the lower laryngeal position is accentuated.

Velum. The velum is withdrawn from the pharyngeal wall. It is thicker and shorter than it is for its position in the stable vowel and first migration pitch ranges. The nasal port is opened to permit the phonated sound to pass into the nasal cavities.

ANALYSIS OF THE FRENCH NASAL VOWEL [õ]

(See pp. 340 and 341 for migration drills and illustrations.)

Basic Vowel Pitch Range

Type. Mid-back, half-closed, slightly rounded, nasal.

Labial Orifice. The lips are tensely rounded, but the labial orifice is slightly smaller and rounder in both vertical and transverse dimensions than when singing the phoneme [ɔ]. The singer should conceive of this phoneme as a rounded closed [o], not as a member of the [ɔ] phoneme. To produce the phoneme [õ], lip protrusion is to be avoided; rather, the outer edges of the lips are drawn together in a circular formation without disturbing the volumes of the oral cavity or the openness of the labial orifice. As vocal force increases, the lip-rounding must be maintained to preserve the integrity of the phoneme. However, if the intensity of the sound increases above a mezzo forte, the labial orifice tends to be more open as the singer attempts to gain greater sonority. The phoneme then migrates toward the quality alternate vowel [ʊ].

Tongue. The tip of the tongue is held firmly against the bottom front teeth. The tongue is low and flattened from the blade to the postdorsum. It is slightly grooved from the predorsum to the root. The tongue-backing is extreme. The radix of the tongue is relaxed to permit the epiglottis to be close to the pharyngeal wall. The position of the epiglottis tends to close the opening to the vestibule and alters the characteristics of that resonator. The oral cavity is larger than the pharyngeal cavity. The point of greatest constriction is located at the postdorsum–root position and the pharyngeal wall at the level of the second and third vertebrae.

Mandible. The mandible is held at the same position as that assumed in the production of the quality alternate vowel open [ô]. The vertical opening is approximately one inch between the front teeth. As the vocal force is increased, the mandible is lowered slightly, increasing the vertical dimension of the oral cavity. This action combined with the slight relaxing of the front orifice and an increase in the anterior-posterior dimension of the back orifice causes the phoneme to migrate toward the quality alternate vowel [ʊ].

Laryngeal Position. The laryngeal lowering is the same as that used to produce the low back vowels, but the tilt of the thyroid cartilage is extreme in order to stabilize and add tension to the vocal folds.

Velum. The velum is loosely arched downward into the oropharynx away from the pharyngeal wall to permit the phonated sound to pass into the nasal cavities.

First Migration Pitch Range

Labial Orifice. Lip-rounding and tension of the lips are unchanged from the position used in singing the phoneme [õ] within the stable vowel pitch range. The labial orifice must be kept round by sustaining a low mandibular position to preserve the closed characteristics of this phoneme. The closed quality of this vowel can be retained into the first migration pitch range only when the vocal force demanded ranges from mezzo forte to forte. When pianissimo and piano sounds are required, this vowel must then be damped by approaching the basic vowel closed [o] but with a relaxed velum and uvula. In such a case the mandible must be extremely lowered.

Tongue. The tongue position does not alter from that assumed in producing the nasal vowel [õ] in the stable vowel pitch range.

Mandible. The position of the mandible does not change from that assumed in singing the nasal vowel [õ] in the stable vowel pitch range.

Laryngeal Position. The laryngeal position is the same as that assumed in producing the nasal vowel [õ] in the stable vowel pitch range.

Second Migration Pitch Range

Vocal maturation and articulatory skill are necessary to sing this phoneme properly within the second migration pitch range. While learning to sing this phoneme within the second migration pitch range, the neutral vowel [ʌ] should be sung without attempts to achieve proper lip-rounding or relaxation of the velum. The neutral vowel should be sung with the lips loose and flaccid. When the vocalic sound is stabilized with proper breath support, the lip-rounding should be accentuated by changing the labial orifice to a slightly rounded rather than an elongated position. The slight lip-rounding and the large labial orifice causes this phoneme to migrate toward the neutral vowel [ʌ]. Such a migration or substitution is vocally permissible for this nasal vowel [õ], but the singer who is seeking vocal refinement will learn to lip-round and drop the velum in the upper pitch ranges for greater intelligibility.

Tongue. The tip of the tongue is held firmly against the bottom front teeth. The tongue conformation from tip to blade is the same as when the phoneme [õ] is produced within the first migration pitch range. The dorsum of the tongue is lowered. The tongue-backing is accentuated. The back orifice is formed at the point of greatest constriction where the postdorsum is close to the pharyngeal wall between the second and third cervical vertebra. The radix of the tongue moves anteriorly eight millimeters and moves with it the hyoid bone and the tip of the epiglottis. This movement enlarges the opening of the vestibule and increases the total dimension of that resonator, thereby altering its resonance characteristics. The oral cavity is larger than the pharyngeal cavity. As the vocal force is increased, the labial orifice becomes less tense, the tongue-backing is less accentuated, and the phoneme migrates to the quality alternate vowel [ʊ].

Mandible. The mandible is held at a lower position than it is to produce the phoneme within the first migration pitch range. As vocal force is increased, the mandibular lowering is accentuated, increasing the anterior-posterior dimension of the labial orifice and the oral cavity at the blade-dorsal position. As the labial orifice is less rounded and more elongated, the phoneme migrates to the neutral vowel [ʌ].

Laryngeal Position. The laryngeal position is one centimeter lower than it is when the phoneme [ô] is sung within the first migration pitch range. The vertical dimension of the pharynx is increased. The tilt of the thyroid cartilage remains unchanged.

Velum. The velum is short, thick, and tense as it loosely approximates the pharyngeal wall and permits some of the phonated sound to pass into the nasal cavities. The singer may remove the velum completely from the pharyngeal wall by conscious muscular controls to attain greater nasality. The degree of nasality for this phoneme is a studio problem. In solving it the student should be guided by the teacher's judgment.

ANALYSIS OF THE SEMIVOWELS [w], [l], AND [r]

(See p. 342 for illustrations.)

The Semivowel Glide [w]

Type. Voiced, bilabial glide.

The sound which characterizes this phoneme is the rapid movement of the lips permitting the voiced sound to change from a phoneme [u] to a following vowel. If there is no lip movement the sound remains a continuant [u]. Therefore, the acoustic effect of [w] is given only when the mechanism begins moving toward the position of the following vowel.

Labial Orifice. The lips are tensely rounded and protruded as in the production of the vowel [u]. For the singer the labial orifice at the start of the glide must be very small. The positioning of the orifice is always directed to the lip position of the vowel which follows.

Tongue. The tip of the tongue is held firmly against the bottom front teeth. The conformation of the tongue resembles that of the neutral vowel [ʌ] not [u].

Mandible. The mandible is held in close position during the introductory or [u] stage. It is then rapidly dropped to assume the position required of the following vowel.

Larynx. The larynx assumes the position of the neutral vowel [ʌ].

Velum. The velum is firmly pressed against the pharyngeal wall.

The Semivowel [r]

The phoneme [r] may be produced as a sung sound in numerous ways. Only four varieties will be considered here: the central vowel [ɜ], the semivowel [r], the rolled or trilled [ř], and the semirolled or one tap [ɾ].

The phoneme [r] is greatly influenced by its neighboring sounds which tend to weaken rather than strengthen it. Therefore, when it is sung this phoneme must possess resonance qualities that will permit it to be musically acceptable on all pitches and aesthetically acceptable within texts. The central vowel [ɜ] is a phoneme which meets these requirements for words with *r* as a final consonant, such as *luster, color, pillar,* and also in words with the stressed sound of *r*, such as *earth, worry, bird, nervous.* (See "A Dialect for Singing," p. 204.)

The use of this phoneme [ɜ] in these words is logical because it is sonorous, it complements the vocal line, suggests culture, and the method by which it is reproduced is simple and stable.

In singing the flipped [ɾ] is used wherever it is found between two vowels, such as *merry, glory, pouring, bury;* often words with *r* as a final consonant are preceded by [ɪ], [ɛ], [ʊ], [ɑ], [i], such as *rear, fire, sure.*

The semivowel glide [r] may be used in words which begin with the phoneme [r], such as *run, rove, rather,* and in words in which it is preceded by a consonant, *crush, grieve, growl.* To eliminate the common sound of the general American phoneme [ɝ], which may also be used in a similar environment, the semivowel [r] should be formed from the closed [u] position with the lips extremely rounded, the tongue slightly in retroflex and preceding through the glide to the neutral vowel position (Fig. 126). Such a lip movement provides the singer with a phoneme of greater sonority and lends it an articulatory deftness that increases its intelligibility.

The general American retroflexed [ɝ] creates some aesthethic difficulties when it is used within poetic texts, partly because it sounds clumsy in the vocal line and partly because the sound is too common for poetry of great refinement and sensitivity.

The articulatory mechanism for the production of the semivowel [r] is positioned in the following manner.

Labial Orifice. The lips are tensely rounded as they are in the production of the vowel closed [u]. The labial orifice is extremely small.

Tongue. The tip of the tongue is raised and lightly touches the alveolar ridge immediately behind the upper teeth. The tongue is slightly backed and lowered at the dorsum during the first stage of forming the [u]. In the final stage the tongue assumes the position of the vowel which follows.

Mandible. The mandible is held in a close position.

Larynx. The larynx is held in the neutral vowel position without being constricted nor distorted.

Velum. The velum loosely approximates the pharyngeal wall.

The flipped [ɾ] sound is made with a single tap of the tongue against the alveolar ridge. The singer must keep the tongue in a retroflexed position while reproducing the phoneme.

The rolled or trilled [ř] is produced by firmly pressing the tongue tip against the alveolar ridge while it is in retroflex and permitting the voiced breath stream to rapidly vibrate the tip and blade. It is important that the mandible be held very firm during the trill.

ANALYSIS OF THE STOP PLOSIVES [b], [p], [d], [t], [g], AND [k]

(See pp. 343 and 344 for illustrations.)

The Consonants [b] and [p]

Type. Voiced and unvoiced, bilabial, stop plosives.

The plosive sound which identifies this consonant is caused by the sudden release of impounded air effected by lowering the mandible and a simultaneous protrusion and relaxing of the lips, or by dropping the velum to allow the air to be emitted through the nasal cavities as in the word *cabman*.

The articulatory mechanism is positioned in the following manner.

Labial Orifice. The lips are firmly closed and tensed against the oral air pressure. In singing this act must be exaggerated beyond the neutral position of lax utterance in speech.

Tongue. The tip of the tongue is held firmly against the bottom front teeth. The tongue is flattened and backed in a manner comparable to the position of the neutral vowel [ʌ].

Mandible. The mandible is held in a half-closed position and it is suddenly lowered as the lips part to release the impounded pressure through the mouth. In singing the amount of depression of the mandible and eversion of the lips varies and depends largely upon the environment of the phoneme within the context. When the velum is raised and the nasal emission of the air is used the mandible is held firmly tense during the implosion period.

Larynx. In forming the voiced consonant [b] the larynx is drawn forward and upward causing a distortion of the trachea and a constriction of the vestibular entrance. The lower pharyngeal area is greatly enlarged.

Velum. The velum is firmly pressed against the pharyngeal wall except when it is dropped to permit the passage of air into the nasal cavities.

The Consonants [d] and [t]

Type. Voiced and voiceless, lingua-alveolar, stop plosives.

The plosive sound which identifies the consonant [d] is caused by the sudden release of impounded air through the mouth effected by the lowering of the mandible and a simultaneous lowering of the tongue, or by dropping the velum to allow the air to be emitted through the nasal cavities as in the word *sadden* [sædn̩].

Labial Orifice. The lips are slightly parted and protruded. The more the lips are everted in the production of this vowel the greater the intelligibility of the consonant [d].

Tongue. The tip of the tongue is elevated and broadened to make firm contact with the alveolar ridge immediately posterior to the upper front teeth. The entire tongue is raised to a point of contact with the teeth forming a firm seal against the rising air pressure. The sudden removal of the tip of the tongue from the alveolar ridge causes the escape of the dammed up air stream.

In such words as *saddle* [sædl̩] the air is emitted laterally by keeping the tip of the tongue firmly pressed against the alveolar ridge and relaxing the lateral borders of the tongue. In such words as *sádden* [sædn̩] the velum is lowered and permits the sound to be emitted through the nasal cavities.

The dental [d] used in Spanish, French, and Italian is formed by placing the upper surface of the tongue tip against the upper teeth instead of the alveolar ridge.

The Mandible. The mandible is held firmly at the half-closed position. It is lowered as the tongue is lowered and releases the impounded air.

Larynx. The larynx is drawn forward and upward during the production of the voiced [d], and it causes a distortion of the trachea and a constriction of the vestibule. The lower pharyngeal cavity is greatly enlarged.

Velum. The velum is firmly pressed against the pharyngeal wall except when it is lowered to permit the passage of air into the nasal cavities.

The Consonants [g] and [k]

Type. Voiced and unvoiced, lingua-velar, stop plosives.

The plosive sound which identifies this voiced consonant [g] is caused by the sudden release of the impounded air pressure through the mouth effected by the dropping of the postdorsum of the tongue and closing the nasal port.

Labial Orifice. The lips are slightly parted and protruded. The degree of opening may vary with phonemic environment.

Tongue. The tip of the tongue is held firmly against the bottom front teeth. The postdorsum of the tongue is elevated to form an airtight contact with the velum and the posterior hard palate. The sides and back of the tongue are in contact with the molar teeth. This velar-postdorsal position is used only when the [g] is followed by a low central or back vowel as in *going* or *good.* When [g] is followed by a frontal vowel as in *geese* or *gear* the point of occlusion is at the mediodorsal-mediopalatal position. However for the purposes of singing, the symbol [g] will be used to represent all of the sounds in the series. The explosion of the impounded air may occur laterally by releasing the tension on the sides of the tongue as in the word *wiggle* [wɪgl] or through the nasal cavities by lowering the velum as in the word *signal* [sɪgnl].

The points of occlusion for the voiceless [k] follow the same rules of phonemic environment as does the voiced [g]. In such words as *car, cough, cold,* where [k] is followed by a low central or back vowel the point of occlusion is at the postdorsal and velar positions. Where [k] is followed by a frontal vowel in words such as *key, kin,* the occlusion is at the mediodorsal-mediopalatal position.

Mandible. The mandible is held firmly at the half-open position.

Larynx. In producing the voiced consonant [g] the larynx is drawn forward and upward causing a distortion of the trachea and an extreme constriction of the vestibule. The lower pharynx is enlarged at the entrance to the esophagus.

Velum. The velum is firmly pressed against the pharyngeal wall and it is only dropped to permit the passage of the impounded air through the nasal cavities during the production of words demanding a nasal explosion, such as *signal.*

ANALYSIS OF THE CONTINUANT FRICATIVES [f], [v], [s], [z], [ʃ], AND [ʒ]

(See p. 345 for illustrations.)

The Consonants [f] and [v]

Type. Voiced and unvoiced, labiodental, fricative, continuants.

The friction sound which identifies these consonants is caused by the articulatory mechanism.

Labial Orifice. The lower lip is raised to make a loose contact with the lower incisors.

Tongue. The tip of the tongue is held firmly against the lower front teeth. The dorsum is ungrooved, low, and slightly backed.

Mandible. The mandible is raised to closed position.

Laryngeal Position. The larynx is drawn forward and upward only in the production of the voiced phoneme causing a distortion of the trachea and a constriction of the vestibular entrance.

Velum. The velum is firmly pressed against the pharyngeal wall.

The Consonants [z] and [s]

Type. Voiced and unvoiced, lingua-alveolar, fricative continuant.

The friction sound which identifies this consonant is created by the passage of a small jet of air through an opening formed along the median raphe of the tongue. The jet of air passes over the cutting edge of the lower incisors producing the high frequency buzz that, with the laryngeal sound is characteristic of this phoneme [z].

Labial Orifice. The lips are slightly spread and the corners are raised. The bilabial orifice must be open in the shape of an elongated oval. The degree of opening varies with the individual.

Tongue. The tongue is flattened and elevated so that its lateral borders are in contact with the upper teeth and the alveolar ridge. The dorsum of the tongue is grooved. The tip of the tongue is firmly pressed against the alveolar ridge; it is shallowly grooved, to permit the air to be directed downward, directly over the lower incisors creating the friction sound.

The tongue position varies considerably from one individual to another. The formation of the teeth being the most variable factor affecting the production of the consonant [z]. In a common variable position the tongue is placed against the inner borders of the lower teeth, causing the blade to be rolled against the alveolar ridge; although the tongue is grooved, the air jet produces less buzz.

Mandible. The mandible is held in a nearly closed position, but the movement may be varied without a noticeable change in the sound of this phoneme.

Laryngeal Position. The vocal folds are approximated and the larynx is drawn forward and upward during the production of the voiced phoneme causing a distortion of the trachea and a constriction of the vestibular entrance. An enlargement of the lower pharynx and piriform sinus extends to the entrance of the esophagus.

Velum. The velum is firmly pressed against the pharyngeal wall.

The Consonants [ʃ] and [ʒ]

Type. Voiced and unvoiced, linguapalatal, fricative, continuants.

The friction sound which identifies this consonant is produced by the passage of air through a wide but shallow orifice between the top of the tongue and the palate. The voiced air stream passes through this orifice out between the lips and teeth. The articulatory mechanism is positioned in the following manner.

Labial Orifice. The labial orifice is oval shaped and slightly protruded. The lips are more rounded than they are to produce the phoneme [z]. This rounding creates a small cavity between the lips and the teeth which adds a characteristic resonance to the phoneme.

Tongue Position. The tip of the tongue is flattened, raised, and drawn forward contacting the hard palate just posterior to the alveolar ridge. The lateral borders of the tongue are in contact with the inner borders of the teeth forming a wide but shallow orifice between the tip of the tongue and the hard palate.

This linguapalatal orifice is wider and formed farther back on the palate than it is for the phoneme [z], and the labial orifice is also more rounded and protruded.

Mandible. The mandible remains at the half-closed position.

Laryngeal Positions. The vocal folds are approximated. The larynx is drawn forward and upward only in the production of the voiced phoneme causing a distortion of the trachea and a constriction of the vestibular entrance. The lower pharyngeal area is enlarged.

Velum. The velum is firmly pressed against the pharyngeal wall.

ANALYSIS OF THE CONTINUANT FRICATIVES [θ], [ð], [x], [J], [j], AND [ç]

(See pp. 346 and 347 for illustrations.)

The Consonants [θ] and [ð]

Type. Voiced and unvoiced, linguadental, fricatives, continuants.

The sounds of these two phonemes do not appear in German, French, and Italian. Foreigners trying to learn the English language find these sounds very difficult to learn. A usual substitution is the dental [t] or [d] or in some cases the sibilant [s].

The friction sound which identifies these consonants results from the passage of the voiced air stream through an orifice formed by the grooved tip of the tongue and the edges of the upper front teeth.

Labial Orifice. The lips are spread and slightly raised at the corners.

Tongue. The tip of the tongue is in light contact with the upper incisors and slightly protruded so that the inferior surface rests upon the lower teeth. The tongue is silghtly grooved from blade to dorsum. The dorsum is raised and lies in contact with the inner borders of the upper teeth and with the alveolar ridge leaving a wide central cavity for the passage of the air stream.

Mandible. The mandible is raised to a half-closed position.

Laryngeal Position. The vocal folds are approximated. The larynx is drawn forward and upward only in the production of the voiced phoneme causing a distortion of the trachea and a constriction of the vestibular entrance. The lower pharyngeal area is enlarged to the esophageal entrance.

Velum. The velum is firmly pressed against the pharyngeal wall.

The Consonant [x] (German Bach)

Type. Voiceless, lingua, posteriorpalatal, fricative, continuant.

This consonant is used only when it is preceded by low frontal, low central, and back vowels.

The friction sound which identifies this consonant results from the passage of air through a narrow channel at the postdorsum-velar position which is partially blocked by the uvula. The articulatory mechanism is positioned in the following manner.

Labial Orifice. The lips are relaxed and the labial orifice is open as in the production of the phoneme [ɑ].

Tongue. The tip of the tongue is held firmly against the bottom front teeth. The blade and predorsum are flattened. The postdorsum is backed and raised at the velar position.

Mandible. The mandible is lowered to the position assumed in the production of the vowel [ɑ].

Larynx. The larynx is held in the same position as it is to produce the vowel [ɑ].

Velum. The velum is relaxed to permit the uvula to be in contact with the tongue at the postdorsal position. The uvula is doubled up, lying upon the postdorsum of the tongue with its tip pointing anteriorly. The position is probably caused by the breath pressure behind the velar closure.

The Continuant Fricatives [J], [j] and [ç]

Type. Voiced and voiceless, lingua anteriorpalatal, fricative, continuants.

The articulatory positions of these three phonemes are identical in the sung sound.

The friction sound which identifies these consonants, [J], [j], and [ç], results from the passage of air through a very narrow slit along the median raphe of the tongue as the dorsum is held firmly against the roof of the mouth at the palatal position. The voiced phoneme [J] is used in pronouncing the French word *fille*. The voiced phoneme [j] is used in pronouncing the English word *yes*. The unvoiced phoneme [ç] is used in pronouncing the German word *ich*.

Labial Orifice. The lips are spread and raised slightly at the corners. The labial orifice is narrow and oval shaped.

Tongue. The tip of the tongue is held firmly against the bottom front teeth. The lateral edges of the blade and predorsum are firmly pressed against the upper back teeth and roof of the mouth at the prepalatal position. The tongue has a shallow groove along the median raphe.

Laryngeal Position. The larynx is stable as in the production of the neutral vowel [ʌ].

Mandible. The mandible is held in closed position.

Velum. The velum is firmly pressed against the pharyngeal wall.

ANALYSIS OF THE NASAL CONSONANTS [m], [n], AND [ŋ]

(See p. 348 for illustrations.)

The Nasal [m]

Type. Voiced, bilabial stop, nasal continuant.

The nasal sound which identifies this phoneme is caused by permitting the voiced sound to pass into the nasal cavities by closing the labial orifice and lowering the velum.

Labial Orifice. The lips are firmly pressed together closing the labial orifice.

Tongue. The tip of the tongue is held firmly against the bottom front teeth. The tongue conformation is exactly the same as that for the neutral vowel [ʌ] in all modification positions.

Mandible. The position is the same as that used to produce the neutral vowel [ʌ] in all migration positions.

Velum. The velum is relaxed and withdrawn from the pharyngeal wall.

The Nasal [n]

Type. Voiced, lingua-alveolar stop, nasal continuant.

The nasal sound which identifies this phoneme is caused by permitting the voiced sound to pass into the nasal cavities by pressing the blade of the tongue firmly against the alveolar ridge and lowering the velum.

Labial Orifice. The lips are relaxed and slightly everted.

Tongue. The tip of the tongue is held firmly against the alveolar ridge. The dorsum and edges of the tongue are raised so as to touch the teeth and palate. The postdorsum and root are deeply grooved to form a large pharyngeal cavity.

Mandible. The mandible is held at the half-open position.

Larynx. The larynx is stable and a phonated sound is produced as in the neutral vowel [ʌ].

Velum. The velum is relaxed and removed from the pharyngeal wall.

The Nasal [ŋ]

Type. Voiced, linguavelar stop, nasal continuant.

The nasal sound which identifies this phoneme is caused by permitting the voiced sound to pass into the nasal cavities by pressing the velum against the dorsum of the tongue. The articulatory mechanism is positioned in the following manner.

Labial Orifice. The lips are neutral and relaxed. The labial orifice is oval shaped.

Tongue. The tip of the tongue is pressed firmly against the bottom front teeth. The dorsum of the tongue is raised so as to form a firm contact with the velum at the postdorsal position. The tongue root is backed close to the pharyngeal wall creating a large lower pharynx.

Mandible. The mandible is held at the half-open position.

Larynx. The larynx is held stable. A phonated sound is produced as in the phoneme [ʌ].

Velum. The velum is lowered to contact the postdorsum of the tongue.

Chapter 11

Record 5, Prosodic Elements in Song

The singing of two songs, one in French and English, and the other in German and English by four singers provides the listener with an opportunity to study all of the musical and aesthetic elements of each song which are here displayed in a controlled musical mold.

The recording displays three personal dimensions of each singer:

1. His vocal endowment, i.e., the beauty of his vocal sound, the vibrato rate, his range and tessitura.
2. His vocal technique, i.e., his breathing and control of intensity.
3. His sensitivity to text, i.e., what he does with the word to enhance its meaning by using stress and intensity through refined techniques of articulation, how he chooses the proper phoneme to assure the correct pronunciation of the word and the manner in which he controls this phoneme within various frequencies and intensities, how he makes the word come to life so that the listener may understand instantly the emotional content and meaning of the word.

It must be remembered that these singers are professionals and that each possesses the technical mastery which would have enabled him to fulfill any variation of tempo or intensity if he chose to do so. Nevertheless, the interpretation of each song varies with each of the four singers.

Of the three areas of analysis, endowment, technique, and sensitivity to text, the most rewarding area for analysis is sensitivity to text. Within this personal dimension the song becomes a success or a failure, for here the singer is creating or destroying the values of intimacy and personal intent, or the meaning of the word. See the word, an implement of interpretation, p. 5.

To prove this point employ the following analytical procedure:
Choose the singing of either song that you like the best. Write down the reasons why you prefer this particular rendition—

1. Beauty of voice.
2. Refinement of vocal technique.

3. The degree to which the singer is successful in his attempt to make each word light up, that is, in his attempt to make each word beloved.

Now, using the criteria of judgment that you have devised, try to make your singing of the same song more meaningful and thereby beautiful.

SUGGESTED PROCEDURE FOR USING THE SONG EVALUATION GUIDE

The student will record in English the songs, "Au Clair de la Lune" by Jean Baptiste Lulli and "Widmung" by Robert Schumann. After the student has been oriented in the process of analysis and after he has thoroughly mastered his songs, they should be recorded in the original language and the analytical process repeated.

Analysis of these recordings is made with the assistance of the following voice-technique inventory. Such recording and analysis may be made at any time during the student's experience with formal voice training within studio or diction classes. In both instances the inventory is most successful after the student has memorized the text and music. No singer is able to concentrate upon himself until he has mastered the textual and the musical elements of his song.

The disciplines of phonemic identification and stress as well as the principles of vowel migration are presented to the student by dramatic comparison as he listens to the recorded examples of the same song.

The instructor will thoroughly analyze the student recording and by means of the inventory refer to sections of the text to which the errors of the song are directly related.

EVALUATION GUIDE FOR DRILLS AND SONGS

Breathing

Breath Intake (adequate—inadequate)
Chest (is—is not) held high
Breathing is (clavicular—thoracic—abdominal)

Expiration

The sound (is—is not) sustained by the breath
The singer needs (more—less) breath pressure
Drills are needed in:

Phonation

Vocal force (too little—too great—adequate)
Tensions in the neck and the throat result from:
Pitch problems result from:
Range problems result from:

Diction

Check pronunciation of: ______, ______, ______, ______.
Tongue lacks firmness on:
Tongue in retroflex on:
Lip rounding (excessive—insufficient—adequate)
Lip spreading (excessive—insufficient—adequate)
Jaw is (too open—too closed—adequate)
Consonants need (voicing—lip movement—firmness at the palate—accentuation of initial and the final consonants.)
Vowel migration (effective—indifferent—careless)

Musical

Emphatic stress (more—less)
Emotional stress for dramatic fulfillment
Hold vowels for the duration of the note value
Rhythmic insecurity at:

The Songs

Lulli's "Au Clair de la Lune," arranged by Bainbridge Crist has been chosen as a study piece for the development of proper diction and interpretive habits in a spatial environment for four reasons:

1. The tonal compass of the song does not exceed an octave and all pitches lie within the stable vowel pitch range, (C to C for all voices).
2. There are no excessive intensity problems within the song. A mezzo-forte level should be maintained in all verses where vowel variety and tonal contrasts should be attained by employing more piano tones than forte. The singer should attempt to hear his voice in the hall even though he is singing mezzo forte. This song should be a fine discipline for the loud singer.
3. The text provides a sophisticated situation that demands a stylistic interpre-

tation from the student. He must employ all of the subtleties of stress, phonemic accuracy, and body discipline to sing this song successfully. The same song, sung by soprano, alto, tenor, and bass (Record 5), reveal slight alterations of dynamic levels but all radiate enthusiasm for the meaning of the word and its position within the textual syntax.

4. The musical accompaniment, when played expertly, provides a musical background that entices the singer to become a part of an ensemble. As the unity of ensemble is perfected the elements of diction, i.e., pronunciation, enunciation, and articulation become disciplined tools of utterance.

Phonetic transcriptions of the song texts in English, French and German are provided and should be used as criteria for phonemic accuracy and vowel coloring. Compare the recorded songs with these transcriptions.

Only the soprano and bass sing the French text. Soprano, alto, tenor, and bass sing the song in English. The phonemic positions of the French vowels within this song and within the basic drills have been recorded by Flora Wend—the eminent French soprano.

"Au Clair de la Lune" in French and English is found on Record 5 as follows:

Soprano	French	Band 1
	English	Band 2
Mezzo Soprano	English	Band 3
Tenor	English	Band 4
Bass	French	Band 5
	English	Band 6

"Widmung" by Robert Schumann is an excellent study piece because the intervallic skips provide an opportunity for the singer to observe and apply the principles of phonemic migration at intensity levels of mezzo forte to forte as well as mezzo piano to mezzo forte.

The teacher should determine the intensity dimension of the student voice in this song by demanding that the singer extend himself vocally to attain the impassioned fervor and jubilation concealed within this song text. Such emotional levels are never reached unless the singer effects a total unification of mind, body, and voice, in that order.

The proper phonemic position for each note is indicated above the song text for both English and German and the proper interpretation of these positions may be observed in the recordings of these songs by soprano, alto, tenor, and bass.

"Widmung" in German and English are found on Record 5 as follows:

Soprano	German	Band 7
	English	Band 8

Mezzo Soprano	German	Band 9
	English	Band 10
Tenor	German	Band 11
	English	Band 12
Bass	German	Band 13
	English	Band 14

AU CLAIR DE LA LUNE
(French)

o klɛr də la lynə mon ami pjɛro
prɛtə mwa ta plymə pur ə krir œ̃ mo
ma ʃɑ̃dɛl ə mortə ʒə nɛ ply də fœ
uvrə mwa ta portə pur lamur də djœ
o klɛr də la lynə pjɛro repõdi
ʒə nə pa də plymə ʒə swi dɑ̃ mo li
va ʃe la vwazinə ʒə krwa kɛl-y-e
kar dɑ̃ sə kwizinə õ balə brɪke
o klɛr də la lynə lə mabl, lybɛ̃
frap ʃe lə brynə ɛl repõ sudɛ̃
ki frap də la sɔrtə rl di a sõ tur
uvrə mwa ta pɔrtə pur də djœ damur
o klɛr de la lynə õ ny vwa kə pœ
õ ʃɛrʃə la plymə õ ʃɛrʃə dy fœ
ɑ̃ ʃɛʃə də lə sortə ʒə n'sə kɔ̃ truva
mə ʒ'sə kə lə pɔrtə syr œ sə fɛrma

(English)

ɪn ðə palɪd munlaɪt, pjɛro, frɛnd ʌv maɪn,
lɛt mi hav ə gus kwɪl dzʌst tu raɪt ə laɪn
bɜnt aut ɪz maɪ kandəl, nat ə spark ɪz gɪvn,
opɛn kwɪk jɔr dɔr pliz, fɔr ðə lʌv əv hɛvn,
ɪn ðə palɪd munlaɪt pjɛro kɔld and sɛd
bʌt aɪ hav no gus kwɪl, aɪ hav gɔn tu bɛd
go and ask aur nebɔr ʃi me hav ə kwɪl
aɪ kan hir hɜ wɔkɪŋ ɪn hɜ kɪtʃən stɪl
ɪn ðə palɪd munlaɪt at hɜ dɔr hi kraɪd
and ðə dark aɪd medən ansɜd frʌm ɪnsaɪd
hu kʌmz laudlɪ nakɪŋ? aɪ sɛd hi maɪ dʌv
opɛn nau jɔr dɔr pliz fɔr ðə gɔd ʌv lʌv.
hwɛr ðə palɪd munbimz darklɪ lɪt ðə naɪt
ðe lʊkt fɔr ə gus kwɪl ðe lʊkt fɔr ə laɪt
hwat ðe faund ðɛ sɜtʃɪŋ, ðat aɪ nɛvɜ nju
bʌt aɪ no ðə dɔr klozd fast ʌpɔn ðə tu.

Au Clair de la Lune

In the Moonlight

LULLI

English words by
A.M von BLOMBERG

Harmonized by
BAINBRIDGE CRIST

Andante
(rit.)
a tempo
Au clair de la lu - ne, Mon a - mi Pier - rot,
In the pal - lid moon - light, Pier - rot, friend of mine,
p
rit.
sempre una corda
Pêd.
Prê - te - moi ta plu - me, Pour é - crire un mot;
Let me have your goose quill, Just to write a line;
Ma chan - delle est mor - te, Je n'ai plus de
Burnt out is my can - dle, Not a spark is
poco rit.

a tempo
feu. Ou - vre - moi ta - por - te
giv'n; O - pen, quick, your door, please,
a tempo
riten.
a tempo
Pour l'a - mour de Dieu. Au clair de la lu - ne,
For the love — of heav'n. In the pal - lid moon - light,
riten.
colla voce
a tempo
Pier - rot ré - pon - dit: Je n'ai pas de
Pier - rot called and said: But I have no
plu - me Je suis dans mon lit,
goose - quill, I have gone to bed;
poco rit.
Va chez la voi - si - ne, Je crois qu'elle y
Go and ask our neigh - bor, She may have a
poco rit.

a tempo
est; Car dans sa cui - si - ne
quill, I can hear her walk - ing
a tempo
Ped.
riten. a tempo
(poco rit.)
On bat le bri - quet.
In her kitch - en still.
a tempo
riten.
poco rit.
a tempo
Au clair de la lu - ne, L'ai - ma - ble Lu - bin,
In the pal - lid moon - light, At her door he cried,
a tempo
I due pedale
Frap - pe chez la bru - ne. Ell' ré - pond sou - dain:
And the dark - eyed maid - en An - swered from in - side:
poco rit.
Qui frapp' de la sor - te? Il dit à son tour:
Who comes loud - ly knock - ing? I, said he, my dove;
poco rit.

a tempo
riten.
a tempo
(rit.)
Ou-vre moi ta por - te Pour le Dieu d'a-mour.
O-pen now your door, please, For the god_ of love.
a tempo
riten.
a tempo
rit.
Ped.
a tempo
Au clair de la lu - ne, On n'y voit qu'un peu
Where the pal-lid moon - beams Dark-ly lit the night,
a tempo
Ped.
On cher-che la plu - me, On cher-che du feu.
They looked for the goose quill, They looked for a light.
poco rit.
En cher-chant d'la sor - te Je n'sais c'qu'on trou - va:
What they found there search - ing, That I nev-er knew:
poco rit.
riten.
Mais j'sais que la por - te Sur eux se_ fer - ma.
But I know the door clos'd Fast up-on_ the two.
riten.
colla voce
pp
Ped.

WIDMUNG
(English)

ðau art maɪ laɪf maɪ sol and hart
ðau boθ maɪ dʒɔɪ and sadnɛ s art
ðau art maɪ hɛʌn maɪ matʃlɛs lʌvɜ
maɪ wɜld ʌv blɪs hwɛrɪn aɪ hʌvɜ
ðau art ðə grev hwɛrɪn ar kast fɔrɛvɜ
 ɔl maɪ sɔro past
ðau brɪŋɛst rɛst and pis əbaɪdɪŋ
hɛvn ɪz θru ði mi kaɪndlɪ gaɪdɪŋ
so hast ðaɪ lʌv θru mi ʌpilɛd,
aɪ si maɪ ɪnmost sɛlf rivilɛd
ðau lɪftɛst mi bijɔnd maɪ sɛlf
gud dʒinjʌs ðau maɪ bɛtɜ sɛlf
ðau art maɪ laif maɪ sol and hart
ðau boθ maɪ dʒɔ i and sadnɛs art
ðau art maɪ hɛvn maɪ matʃlɛs lʌvɜ
ðə wɜld ʌv blɪs hwɛrɪn aɪ hʌvɜ
gud dzinjʌs ðau maɪ bɛ tɛɜ sɛlf.

(German)

du maɪnə zēlə du maɪn harts
du maɪnə vôn o du maɪn ʃmarts
du maɪnə vɛlt in der ɪç lēbə
maɪn hɪməl du darʌɪn ɪç ʃvēbə o du maɪn grab
In das hɪnab ɪç ēvɪg maɪnɛm kumɜ gab
du bɪst di ru du bɪst dēr fridan
du bɪst fom hɪməl mir bəʃidʌn
das du mɪç libst maç mɪç mir vērt
daɪn blik hat mɪç for mir fɛr klœrt
du hēbst mɪç libɛn ybɜ mɪç
maɪn gutɜ gaɪst maɪn bɛsrɛs ɪç
du maɪnə zēlə du maɪn harts
du maɪnə vôn o du maɪn ʃmarts
du maɪnə vɛlt in dēr ɪç lēbə
maɪn hɪməl du darʌɪn ɪç ʃvēbə
mʌɪn gutɜ gaɪst maɪn basras ɪç

DEDICATION
(WIDMUNG)

(Composed in 1840)

hov - er, Thou art the grave where-in I cast For ev - er
schwe - be, o du mein Grab, in das hin - ab ich e - wig
con Pedale
all my sor - row past.
mei - nen Kum - mer gab!
rit.
(𝅗𝅥 = 69)
p
Thou bring-est
Du bist die
p a tempo
rest and peace a - bid - ing;
Ruh', du bist der Frie - den,
Heav'n is through thee me kind - ly
du bist vom Him - mel mir be -
guid - ing; So has thy love to me ap - peal'd, I see my
schie - den: Dass du mich liebst, macht mich mir werth, dein Blick hat

rit.
in - most self re - veal'd; Thou lift - est
mich vor mir ver - klärt, du hebst mich
rit.
a tempo
rit.
me be-yond my-self; good gen-ius thou, my bet-ter
lie - bend ü - ber mich, mein gu - ter Geist, mein bess'-res
a tempo
p
rit.
a tempo
self. Thou art my life, my soul and heart, Thou both my
Ich! Du mei-ne See - le, du mein Herz, du mei-ne
a tempo
f
joy and sad-ness art, Thou art my heav'n, my match-less
Wonn', o du mein Schmerz, du mei-ne Welt, in der ich
rit.
lov - er, The world of bliss where-in I hov - er, Good gen-ius
le - be, mein Him - mel du, da-rein ich schwe - be, mein gu - ter
cresc. (steigend e und accel. eilend.)
rit.

thou, my bet - ter self!
Geist, mein bess' - res Ich!
a tempo
p
rit.
a tempo
rit.

APPENDIX

BIBLIOGRAPHY

NOTES

INDEX

Appendix

Test Results

As a speech sound, each of the fifteen phonemes [i], [e], [ɪ], [ē], [ɛ], [æ], [a], [ɑ], [ɔ], [ɒ], [o], [ʊ], [u], [ʌ], and [ɜ] may be considered basic because each is a phoneme. Dialectal tendencies in speech permit a leniency of departure from each phonemic entity, but communication is always consummated. (See Fig. 105A.)

As sung sounds, phonemes required in the proper pronunciation of a word are most frequently altered from their phonemic centers and substituted by the singer as he selects a certain timbre, color, or articulatory position. This faulty process tends to place voice quality, timbre, and color ahead of phonemic integrity. In such a process of substitution the meaning of the word is often impaired. (See the first objective on p. o.)

Accurate phonemic selection is achieved by the singer in his production of isolated vowel sounds only when his selection of a phoneme is disciplined by his aural awareness of that phoneme. The phoneme cannot remain a concept; it must become a sound. All singers need much more specific training to develop this aural awareness.

Accurate phonemic identification is attained by the listener when the sung phoneme is nearest to that acoustic position in which the phoneme is properly pronounced. Cues for its identification are glides, caused by consonantal movement to and from the phoneme; however, a proper singing technique reduces glides to a minimum. (See steady state formant structure characteristics, p. 228.)

The singing of any vowel sound is a conceptual process involving the selection of some phonemic entity within a tonal environment suggested by the proper pronunciation of a word. A testing procedure must seek answers to the following question: Which of the numerous phonemic choices available to the singer should be considered the proper "home base" position that will serve as a point of reference from which all sung phonemes may be instantly determined by the singer to preserve the meaning of the word.

The recognition tests I (male) and II (female) were designed by the author to determine which of fifteen sung phonemes were the most frequently identified correctly under controlled conditions.

To construct Tests I and II the author, a bass, and a professional soprano, sang each of the vowel sounds [i], [e], [æ], [ɑ], [ô], and [u] and made them conform to a musical standard of vocal utterance that was acceptable to a selected group of faculty members at Indiana University. To control uniformity of each vowel, well-defined physiological positions of the tongue, labial orifice, velum, mandible, and larynx were used. (See p. 231.) The positions of these physiological parts were determined by means of cinefluoroscopy and X-ray photographs. The intensity of each vowel was subjectively judged by the faculty members to be mezzo forte but not forte. Although the integrity of the vowels [i], [ɑ], [ô], and [u] are affected by the intensity level at which they are produced, it was reasoned that to assure a uniformity of identification all phonemes should be sung at the same level. Each vowel was analyzed acoustically and positioned upon a formant chart. The frequency of formants one and two determined each position.

To arrange a random sampling of the six phonemes, each phoneme was written upon six cards and shuffled ten times. The random sampling for males differed from that for females. Each card was then numbered and a master tape was made by a dubbing process, repeating each vowel in its numerical random order upon the tape. Each sung vowel on the test was identified by speaking the number assigned to each vowel one second before the sung sound was heard.

This process provided the necessary contrast to the sung sound and enabled those judging the sounds to keep accurate track of each vowel and record their judgments in the proper numbered squares upon the intelligibility sheets.

These tests were presented to 224 students enrolled in classes in phonetics at the University of Michigan or in classes in vocal pedagogy at Indiana University. All students participating in the tests had been drilled in phonetic transcription.

The high percentage of recognition of these six vowels when sung in random order are displayed in Tests I and II.

Tests III (male) and IV (female) were designed in the same manner as Tests I and II by the same singers to determine the extent of phonemic recognition when nine additional phonemes were sung with the six predetermined basic vowels. These nine phonemes were [ē], [ɪ], [ɛ], [a], [ɔ], [o], [ʊ], [ʌ], [ɜ]. The tests were presented to the same classes at the University of Michigan and Indiana University.

The results of the tests, displayed in Charts II and III, have determined the acoustic position of each of the fifteen phonemes used in the phonetic system within this work. Vowels with the highest frequency of recognition proved to be the predetermined basic vowels [i], [e], [æ], [ɑ], [ô], [u]. The

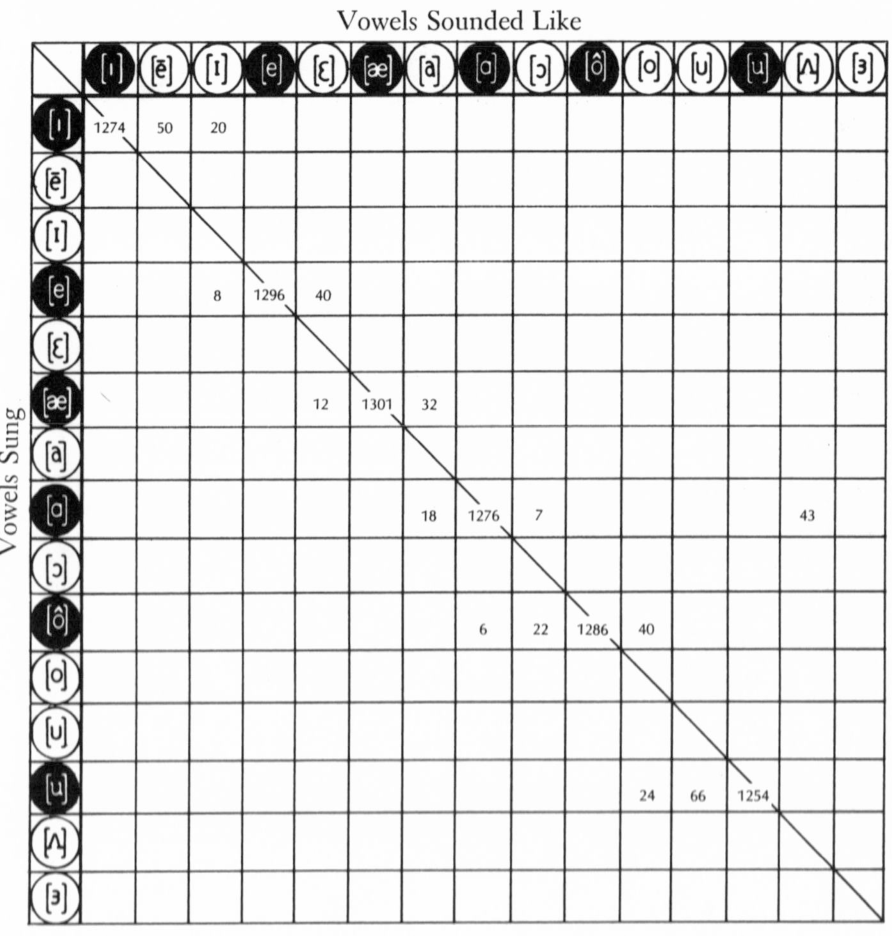

Vowels Sounded Like (columns); Vowels Sung (rows)

	[i]	[ē]	[ɪ]	[e]	[ɛ]	[æ]	[a]	[ɑ]	[ɔ]	[ô]	[o]	[ʊ]	[u]	[ʌ]	[ɜ]
[i]	1274	50	20												
[ē]															
[ɪ]															
[e]			8	1296	40										
[ɛ]															
[æ]					12	1301	32								
[a]															
[ɑ]							18	1276	7					43	
[ɔ]															
[ô]								6	22	1286	40				
[o]															
[ʊ]															
[u]											24	66	1254		
[ʌ]															
[ɜ]															

Test I. Frequency of Recognition of Basic Vowels, Male Voices

The figures on the diagonal line indicate the frequency of correct recognition of the basic vowels [i], [e], [æ], [ɑ], [ô], and [u] in 1,344 responses by 224 persons. The numbers on either side of the central line indicate the frequency of error and the vowels mistaken for the basic vowels.

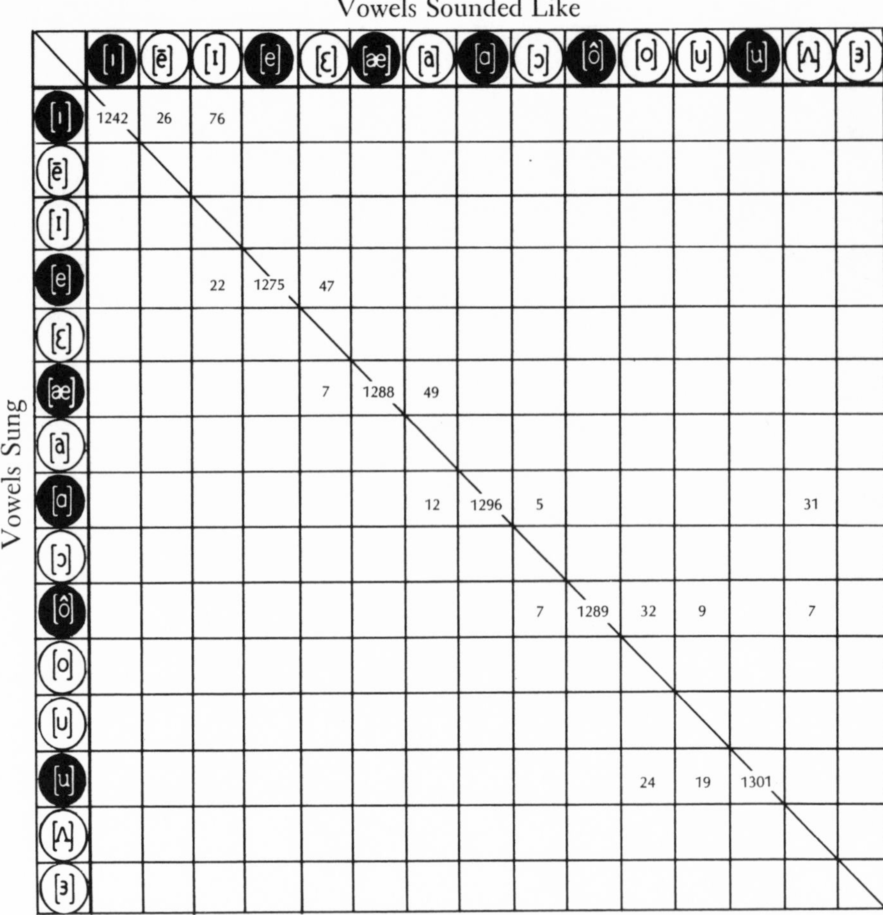

Vowels Sounded Like

Vowels Sung	[i]	[ē]	[ɪ]	[e]	[ɛ]	[æ]	[a]	[ɑ]	[ɔ]	[ô]	[o]	[ʊ]	[u]	[ʌ]	[ɜ]
[i]	1242	26	76												
[ē]															
[ɪ]															
[e]			22	1275	47										
[ɛ]															
[æ]					7	1288	49								
[a]															
[ɑ]							12	1296	5					31	
[ɔ]															
[ô]									7	1289	32	9		7	
[o]															
[ʊ]															
[u]											24	19	1301		
[ʌ]															
[ɜ]															

Test II. Frequency of Recognition of Basic Vowels, Female Voices

The larger figures on the central line indicate the frequency of correct recognition of the basic vowels [i], [e], [æ], [ɑ], [ô], and [u] in 1,344 responses by 224 persons. The numbers on either side of the central line indicate the frequency of error and the vowels mistaken for the basic vowels.

Vowels Sounded Like

Vowels Sung	[i]	[ē]	[ɪ]	[e]	[ɛ]	[æ]	[ā]	[ɑ]	[ɔ]	[ô]	[o]	[ʊ]	[u]	[ʌ]	[ɜ]
[i]	438	570	321	1	2	2	2	1						4	3
[ē]	26	354	282	426	123	16	12	4	2	1	2	1	2	2	91
[ɪ]	25	364	908	14	5	3	2	7							16
[e]		64	75	1049	124		30	2							
[ɛ]		49	58	88	634	50	288	5			2	6		3	161
[æ]		14	11	44	126	919	164	18	8			1		4	35
[ā]			2	3	104	297	754	53	13	3		4		72	39
[ɑ]		9	11	7	5	18	56	479	122		3	3	8	616	7
[ɔ]					2		7	76	752	101	5	3		396	2
[ô]								24	112	1001	103	75	7	20	2
[o]								1	29	480	630	183	12	2	8
[ʊ]					2		1	16	1	23	35	1095	105	14	52
[u]						1		4			37	178	1201	3	20
[ʌ]				1	4	2	39	72	74	17	12	31		1061	31
[ɜ]				2	10	5	64	3	2	1	1	45	7	1	1203

Test III. Frequency of Recognition of All Phonemes, Male Voices

The figure on the diagonal line indicates the frequency of correct recognition of that sung phoneme in 1,344 responses by 224 persons. The numbers on either side of the central line indicate the frequency of error and the vowel mistaken as the sung vowel.

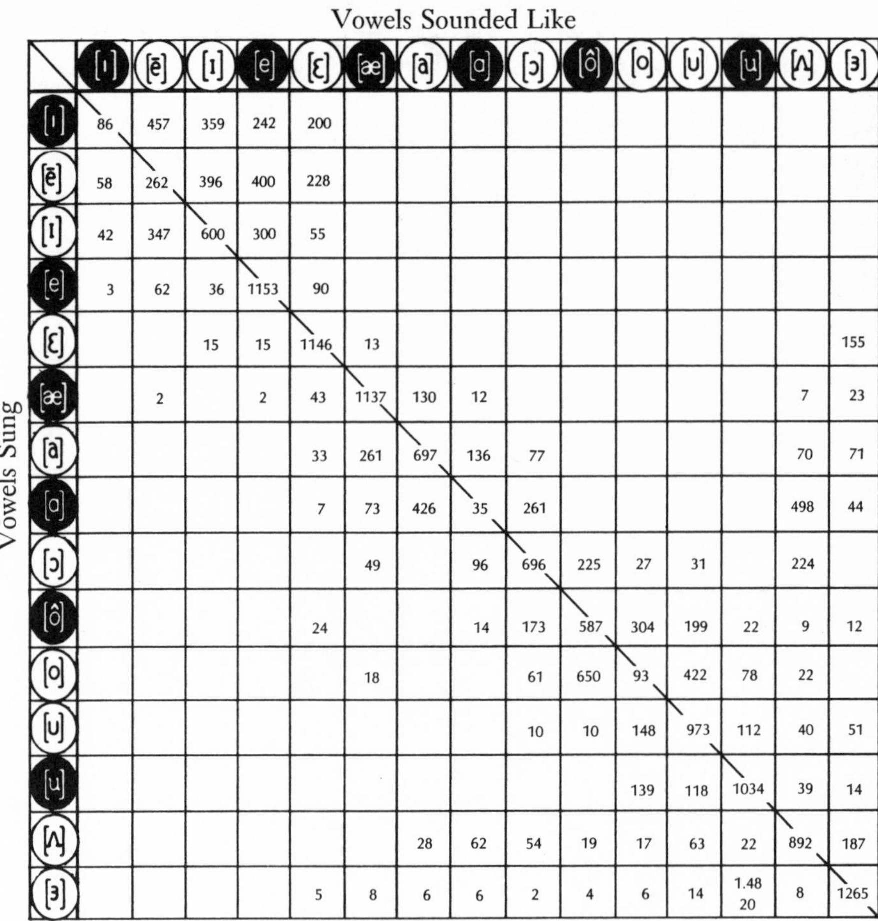

Vowels Sounded Like (columns); Vowels Sung (rows)

	[i]	[ē]	[ɪ]	[e]	[ɛ]	[æ]	[a]	[ɑ]	[ɔ]	[ô]	[o]	[ʊ]	[u]	[ʌ]	[ɜ]
[i]	86	457	359	242	200										
[ē]	58	262	396	400	228										
[ɪ]	42	347	600	300	55										
[e]	3	62	36	1153	90										
[ɛ]			15	15	1146	13									155
[æ]		2		2	43	1137	130	12						7	23
[a]					33	261	697	136	77					70	71
[ɑ]					7	73	426	35	261					498	44
[ɔ]						49		96	696	225	27	31		224	
[ô]					24			14	173	587	304	199	22	9	12
[o]						18			61	650	93	422	78	22	
[ʊ]									10	10	148	973	112	40	51
[u]											139	118	1034	39	14
[ʌ]							28	62	54	19	17	63	22	892	187
[ɜ]					5	8	6	6	2	4	6	14	1.48 20	8	1265

Test IV. Frequency of Recognition of All Phonemes, Female Voices

The figure on the diagonal line indicates the frequency of correct recognition of that sung phoneme in 1,344 responses by 224 persons. The numbers on either side of the central line indicate the frequency of error in judgment and the vowel mistaken for the sung vowel.

vowels of lower frequency of recognition [ē], [ɪ], [ɛ], [a], [ɔ], [o], [ʊ], [ʌ], [ɜ], were considered to be the quality alternate of a particular basic vowel.

Since all sung vowels are altered by variations in intensity and frequency the name "quality alternate" means that it is a color substitute for that vowel, which must be pronounced in a specific manner to preserve the meaning within the word. The quality alternate vowel is not controlled by frequency or intensity as is the basic vowel. (The application of these vowels in the singing process may be found on p. 226.)

Two vowels, [i] and [ɑ] are considered to be basic vowels although they were not most frequently recognized as the intended phoneme. The vowel [i] which can only be sung properly at intensity levels of pianissimo or piano was sung mezzo forte and had migrated to its quality alternate position of [ɪ] or [e] and was so identified. (See Tests III and IV.) The vowel [ɑ] at mezzo forte intensity had migrated into the neutral vowel position of [ʌ] and was properly recognized.

Percent of Recognition			*Greatest Conflict of Recognition*			
MALE		FEMALE	MALE		FEMALE	
[i]	94.73	92.41	[ɪ] 1.49	[e] 50.00	[ɪ] 5.65	[e] 1.93
[ē]						
[ɪ]						
[e]	96.42	94.86	[ɛ] 2.97	[ē] .59	[ɛ] 3.49	[ē] 1.64
[ɛ]						
[æ]	96.80	95.83	[ə] 2.38	[ɛ] .89	[a] 3.64	[ɛ] .52
[a]						
[ɑ]	94.64	96.43	[ʌ] 3.20	[a] 1.52	[a] .89	[ɔ] .37
[ɔ]						
[ô]	95.68	95.90	[o] 2.97	[ɑ] 1.63	[o] 2.38	[ɔ] .52
[o]						
[ʊ]						
[u]		93.30	[ʊ] 4.91	[o] 1.78	[o] 1.78	[u] 1.71
[ʌ]						
[ɜ]						

TABLE III. *Percent of Recognition of Basic Vowels*

The percent of recognition of each vowel sung in Tests I and II is indicated above. The vowels most often mistaken as the sung vowel are indicated under greatest conflict of identification for each vowel.

Percent of Recognition			*Greatest Conflict of Recognition*					
MALE		FEMALE	MALE			FEMALE		
[i]	32.58	6.40	[ɪ] 42	[e] 23		[ɪ] 26	[e] 35	[ɜ] 14
[ē]	26.30	19.49	[e] 31	[ɪ] 20		[ē] 29	[i] 29	[ɛ] 16
[ɪ]	67.55	44.64	[ē] 27			[ē] 25	[e] 22	
[e]	78.05	85.58	[ɛ] 9	[ē] 5	[ɪ] 4	[ɛ] 7	[e] 4	[ɪ] 2
[ɛ]	47.17	87.60	[a] 21	[ɜ] 11	[e] 6	[ɜ] 10	[e] 1.5	[ʌ] 1.5
[æ]	68.37	84.03	[a] 12	[ɛ] 9		[a] 9	[ɛ] 10	
[a]	56.10	50.52	[æ] 22	[ɑ] 15		[ɑ] 10	[ɔ] 5	[ʌ] 5
[ɑ]	35.63	2.60	[ʌ] 46	[ɔ] 9		[ʌ] 38	[a] 31	[ɔ] 19
[ɔ]	55.90	51.79	[ʌ] 29	[o] 8	[ɑ] 5	[o] 16	[ʌ] 16	[ɑ] 7
[ô]	74.47	43.67	[ɔ] 8	[o] 8	[u] 5	[o] 22	[ʊ] 15	[ɔ] 12
[o]	46.87	6.91	[o] 35	[ʊ] 13		[ô] 48	[ʊ] 31	[u] 6
[ʊ]	81.47	72.35	[u] 8	[ɜ] 4	[o] 2	[u] 8	[o] 11	
[u]	89.36	77.16	[ʊ] 13	[o] 3		[o] 10	[u] 9	
[ʌ]	78.94	66.37	[ɑ] 5	[ɔ] 5	[ɜ] 2	[ɜ] 14	[u] 4	[ɑ] 6
[ɜ]	89.50	94.12	[a] 5	[u] 3		[u] 1	[ʊ] 1	

TABLE IV. *Percent of Recognition of Basic Vowels*

The percent of recognition of each vowel sung in Tests III and IV is indicated above. The vowels most often mistaken as the sung vowel are indicated under greatest conflict of identification for each vowel.

Bibliography

CHAPTER 2

Respiration

Books and Dissertations

Campbell, E. J. Moran. *The Respiratory Muscles and the Mechanics of Breathing.* London: Lloyd-Luke, Ltd., 1958.

———. "The Muscular Control of Breathing in Man." Unpublished Ph.D. dissertation, University of London, 1954.

Fenn, W. O. "Introduction to the Mechanics of Breathing," *Respiration*, Vol. III of Sec. III, *Handbook of Physiology*. Washington, D.C.: American Physiological Society, 1964, pp.357-60.

Grant, John Charles Boileau. *A Method of Anatomy*, 5th ed. Baltimore: Williams & Wilkins Co., 1952.

Gray, Giles Wilkeson, and Claude Merton Wise. *The Bases of Speech*. New York: Harper & Brothers, 1959.

Gray, Henry. *Anatomy of the Human Body*, ed. Charles M. Goss. 25th ed. Philadelphia: Lea & Febiger, 1950.

Hoff, H. E., and C. G. Breckenridge. "Regulation of Respiration," *A Textbook of Physiology*, ed. J. F. A. Fulton. Philadelphia: W. B. Saunders Co., 1955, pp. 867-86.

Hashiko, Michael S. "Electromyographic Study of Respiratory Muscles in Relation to Syllabication." Unpublished Ph.D. dissertation, Purdue University, 1957.

Idol, Harriet R. "A Statistical Study of Respiration in Relation to Speech Characteristics," *Studies in Experimental Phonetics*, ed. Giles Wilkeson Gray. Louisiana State University Studies, No. 27. Baton Rouge: Louisiana State University Press, 1936, pp.79-98.

Meader, Clarence L. and John H. Muyskens. "General Semantics," Pts. I & II of *Handbook of Biolinguistics*, ed. Herbert C. Weller. Toledo, Ohio: Toledo Speech Clinic,* 1950.

* 630 West Woodruf at Scott Wood, Toledo 2, Ohio.

Myer, Edmund J. *Vocal Reinforcement.* Boston: Boston Music Co., 1913.

———. *Position and Action in Singing.* Boston: Boston Music Co., 1911.

Respiration, Sec. III, Vols. 1-3, of *Handbook of Physiology.* Washington, D.C.: American Physiological Society, 1964. The most valuable source of information on respiration, forty monographs, extensive bibliography on respiration.

Seashore, Carl E. *The Vibrato.* University of Iowa Studies in the Psychology of Music, Vol. I. Iowa City: University of Iowa Press, 1932.

Sheil, Richard F. "A Study of Respiration with Relation to Somatype." Unpublished Ph.D. dissertation, University of Michigan, 1962.

Periodical Monographs

Best, R. R. "The Function of the Diaphragm and Intercostal Muscles and Their Clinical Significance," *Nebraska State Medical Journal,* Vol. 13 (1928), 143-45.

Briscoe, G. "The Muscular Mechanism of the Diaphragm," *Journal of Physiology* (London), Vol. 14 (1920), 46-53.

Campbell, E. J. Moran. "The Variations in Intra-Abdominal Pressure and the Activity of the Abdominal Muscle During Breathing: A Study in Man," ibid., Vol. 12 (1955), 282-90.

——— and J. H. Green. "The Expiratory Function of the Abdominal Muscles in Man: An Electromyographic Study." ibid., Vol. 70 (1953) 409-18.

——— and ———. "The Effects of Increased Resistance to Expiration on the Respiratory Behavior of the Abdominal Muscles and Intra-Abdominal Pressure," ibid., Vol. 86 (1957), 556-62.

Draper, M. A., Peter Ladefoged, and D. Whitridge. "Respiratory Muscles in Speech," *Journal of Speech and Hearing Research,* Vol. 2 (1959), 16-27. Electromyography of external and internal intercostal, latissimus dorsi, rectus abdominus, obliques, and diaphragm.

Freud, E. D. "Voice Physiology and the Emergence of a New Vocal Style," *Archives of Otolaryngology,* Vol. 62 (1955), 50-58.

Hashiko, Michael S. "Sequence of Action of Breathing Muscles During Speech," *Journal of Speech and Hearing Research,* Vol. 3 (1960), 291-97.

Lemon, W. S. "The Function of the Diaphragm," *Archives of Surgery* (Chicago), Vol. 17 (1928c), 840-53.

Lindsley, Charles F. "The Psychological Determinants of Voice Quality," *Speech Monographs,* Vol. 1 (1934), 79-116.

Murtaugh, J. A. and C. J. Campbell. "The Respiratory Function of the Larynx," *Laryngoscope,* Vol. 61 (1961), 581-90.

Otis, A. B., W. O. Feen, and H. Rahn. "Mechanics of Breathing in Man," *Journal of Applied Psychology,* Vol. 2 (1950), 562-607.

Polgar, F. "Studies on Respiratory Mechanics," *Journal of American Roetgenology,* Vol. 51 (1949), 637-57.

Tarneau, Jean. "Psychological and Clinical Study of the Pneumophonic Synergy," *NATS Bulletin,* February 1958, 12-15.

CHAPTER 3

Phonation: The Larynx as a Biological-Biosocial Organ

Books and Dissertations

Cates, H. A. and J. V. Basmajian. *Primary Anatomy*. Baltimore: Williams & Wilkins Co., 1955.

Curry, Robert. *The Mechanism of the Human Voice*. New York: Longmans Green & Co., 1940.

Davis, Kenneth L., Jr. "A Study of the Function of the Primary Resonating Areas and Their Relation to the Third Formant in the Singing Tone." Unpublished Mus. D. dissertation, School of Music, Indiana University, 1964.

Dickson, D. R. "An Acoustic and Radiographic Study of Nasality." Unpublished Ph.D. dissertation, Northwestern University, 1961.

Harrington, D. C. "An Experimental Study of the Subjective and Objective Characteristics of Sustained Vowels at High Pitches." Unpublished Ph.D. dissertation, Louisiana State University, 1950.

Holmes, Gordon. *History of the Progress of Laryngology from the Earliest Time to the Present*. London: Medical Press, 1885.

Husler, Frederick, and Yvonne Rodd-Marling. *Singing: The Physical Nature of the Vocal Organ*. London: Faber & Faber, 1965.

Moses, Paul J. *The Voice of Neurosis*. New York: Grune & Stratton, 1954.

Negus, V. E. *The Mechanism of the Larynx*. St. Louis: C. V. Mosby Co., 1949.

Sobotta, Johannes. *Atlas of Human Anatomy*. 3d ed. Vol. I & II. New York: G. E. Steichert & Co., 1933.

Stanley, Douglas. *Your Voice*. New York: Pitman Publishing Corp., 1929.

———. *The Science of Voice*. New York: Carl Fisher, Inc., 1929.

Vennard, William. *Singing, the Mechanism and the Technique*. Los Angeles: University of California, 1964.

Westerman, Kenneth N. *Emergent Voice*. Ann Arbor, Mich.: Edwards Bros., 1955.

Whitworth, James R. "A Cinefluorographic Investigation of the Superlaryngeal Adjustments in the Male Voice Accompanying the Singing of Low Tones and High Tones." Unpublished Ph.D. dissertation, State University of Iowa, 1961.

Wright, Johnathan. *A History of Laryngology and Rhinology*. London: Lea & Febiger, 1914.

Periodical Monographs

Anderson, Faaborg K. "Action Potentials from Internal Laryngeal Muscles During Phonation," *Nature*, Vol. 178 (1956), 340-41.

———. "Electromyographic Investigation of the Intrinsic Laryngeal Muscles in Humans," *Acta-Physiology Scandinavia*, suppl., Vol. 140, (1957), 1-150.

Brewer, D. W., F. B. Briess, and Faaborg K. Anderson. "Phonation," *Annals of Otolaryngology, Rhinology, and Laryngology*, Vol. 49 (1940), 203.

Fink, B. R., M. Basek, and V. Epanchin. "Respiratory Movements of the Vocal Cords," *Federation Proceedings Symposium*, Vol. 15 (1950), 63-64, experimental biology.

Flanagan, J. L. "Some Properties of the Glottal Sound Source," *Journal of Speech and Hearing Research*, Vol. 1 (1958), 99-116.

Green, J. H. and E. Neil. "The Respiratory Function of the Laryngeal Muscles," *Journal of Physiology* (London), Vol. 129 (1955), 134-41.

Harrington, R. "A Study of the Mechanism of Velo Pharyngeal Closure," *Journal of Speech and Hearing Disorders*, Vol. 9 (1941), 325-45.

Hartog, C. M. "The Function of the Ventricle of Morgagni," *Acta-Otolaryngologica*, Vol. 10 (1926), 253-56.

Hollien, Harry. "Vocal Pitch Variation Related to Changes in Vocal Fold Length," *Journal of Speech and Hearing Research*, Vol. 3 (1960), 150-56.

——— and James Curtis. "A Laminagraphic Study of Vocal Pitch," ibid., 361-71.

——— and Paul Moore. "The Measurements of the Vocal Folds During Changes in Pitch," ibid., 157-65.

Kenyon, E. E. "Relocation of Oral Articulative Mats to Speech and Intrinsic Laryngeal Musculature in General to the Function of the Vocal Cords," *Archives of Otolaryngology*, Vol. 5 (1927), 481-501.

Landeau, Michel. "Voice Classification," *NATS Bulletin*, October 1963, 4-8.

——— and H. Zuili. "Vocal Emission and Tomograms of the Larynx," ibid., February 1963, 6-11.

Lloyd, W. F., F. E. Negus, and E. Neil. "Observation on the Mechanics of Phonation," *Acta-Otolaryngologica*, Vol. 48 (1958), 205-38.

Moore, Paul, and Hans Von Leden. "Dynamic Variations on the Vibratory Pattern in the Normal Larynx," *Phoniatrica*, 10, 4 (1958), 205-38.

Perkins, William, Granville Sawyer, and Peggy Harrison. "Research on Vocal Efficiency," *NATS Bulletin*, December 1958, 4-7.

Pressman, Joel J. "Physiology of the Vocal Folds in Phonation and Respiration," *Archives of Otolaryngology*, Vol. 35 (1942), 355.

———. "Sphincter Action of the Larynx," ibid., Vol. 33 (1941), 351.

Sonesson, B. "On the Anatomy and Vibrating Pattern of the Human Vocal Folds," *Acta-Otolaryngologica*, suppl., Vol. 1 (1956), 940.

Sonnonin, Aatto A. "Is the Length of Adjustment of the Vocal Fold the Same at All Different Levels of Singing," *Acta-Otolaryngologica*, Vol. 163 (1954), 219-31.

———. "The Role of the External Laryngeal Muscles in Length Adjustment of the Vocal Cords in Singing," *Acta-Otolaryngologica*, Vol. 48 (1947), 16-25.

Strong, Leon. "Mechanism of Laryngeal Pitches," *Anatomical Record*, Vol. 63 (August 25, 1935), 13-28.

Technical Aspects of Visible Speech, Bell Telephone System Monograph, B-1415. New York: Bell Telephone Laboratories, 1946, pp.1-89.

Van Den Berg, Janwillem. "On the Air Resistance and the Bernoulli Effect of the Human Larynx," *Journal of the Acoustical Society of America*, Vol. 29 (1957), 626-31.

———. "Physiology and Physics of Voice Production," *Acta-Physiologica et Pharmacologia Neerlander*, Vol. 5 (1956), 40-55.

———. "Direct and Indirect Determination of Mean Subglottic Pressure," *Folio Phoniatrica*, Vol. 7 (1956), 1-24.

———. "On the Role of the Laryngeal Ventricle in Voice Production," ibid., Vol. 7 (1955), 57-69.

———. "Subglottic Pressure and Vibration of the Vocal Folds," ibid., Vol. 9 (1957), 65-71.

Vennard, William. "The Coupe de Glotte," *NATS Bulletin*, February 1964, 14-17.

REGISTRATION

Books and Dissertations

Appelman, D. Ralph. "A Study by Means of Planigraph, Radiograph, and Spectrograph of the Physical Changes Which Occur During the Transition from the Middle to the Upper Register in the Male Voice." Unpublished Ph.D. dissertation, School of Music, Indiana University, 1953.

Harris, Ronald, "Chronaxy," *Electrodiagnosis and Electromyography*, ed. Sidney Licht. New Haven, Conn.: E. Licht, Pubs., 1956, pp.126-45.

Harrison, F. "An Experimental Analysis by X-Ray." Unpublished Ph.D. dissertation, University of Southern California, 1956. Includes photographs of some resonator adjustments in efficient and inefficient voice production in low-pitched male voices.

Siegel, L. W. "An Investigation of Possible Correlation Between the Chronaxy of a Branch of the Accessory Nerve and Voice Classification." Unpublished Master's thesis, School of Music, Indiana University, 1963.

Taff, Merle E. "A Study of Vowel Modification in Register Transition in the Male Singing Voice." Unpublished Ph.D. dissertation, School of Music, Indiana University, 1964.

Periodical Monographs

Davis, Hallowell. "Relationship of Chronaxy of Muscle to the Size of the Stimulating Electrode," *Physiology*, Vol. 57 (July 1923), lxxxi.

French, T. R. A. "A Photographic Study of the Laryngeal Image During the Formation of Registers in the Singing Voice," *New York State Journal of Medicine*, Vol. 49 (1899), 95-98.

Husson, Raoul. "The Classification of Human Voices," *NATS Bulletin*, 13, 4 (May 1957), 6-11.

———. "Excitabilité recurrentielle et entudues vocales masculines et feminines des voix aduites cultivées, semi cultivées et incultées," *Review of Laryngology, Otolaryngology, and Rhinology*, suppl., Vol. 40 (1954), 260.

———. "A New Look at Phonation," ibid., 12, 2 (December 1956), 12-14.

Luchsinger, R. "Falsett und Vollton der Kopfstinme," *archiv fur obren, Nasin, und Kehlkopfheilkunde*, Band 155, 505-19.

Rubin, Henry J., and Charles C. Hirt. "The Falsetto," *Laryngoscope,* 70, 9 (September 1960), 1,309-10.

Ruth, Wilhelm. "The Registers of the Singing Voice," *NATS Bulletin,* May 1963, 2-5.

Van Den Berg, Janwillem. "Vocal Ligaments Versus Registers," *NATS Bulletin,* December 1963, 16-19.

CHAPTER 4

Laws That Govern Vocal Sound

ACOUSTICS

Books

American Standard Acoustical Terminology. Sponsored by the Acoustical Society of America. New York: American Standards Association, 1960. Includes mechanical shock and vibration.

Bartholomew, Wilmer T. *Acoustics of Music.* New York: Prentice-Hall, Inc., 1942.

Culver, Charles A. *Musical Acoustics.* New York: McGraw-Hill Book Co., Inc., New York, 1956.

Denes, Peter B., and Elliot N. Pinson. *The Speech Chain.* Bell Telephone Laboratories Science Series. Baltimore: Williams & Wilkins Co., 1964.

Fant, Gunnar M. C. *Acoustic Theory of Speech Production.* The Hague, Netherlands: Mouton & Co., 1960.

Flanagan, J. L. *A Speech Analyser for a Formant-Coding Compression System.* Scientific Report, No. 4 (AFCRC-TN-55-793). Cambridge, Mass.: Acoustics Laboratory, Massachusetts Institute of Technology, 1955.

Hall, Jody, and Earle L. Kent. *The Language of Musical Acoustics.* Elkhart, Ind.: C. G. Conn, Ltd., 1957.

Helmholtz, Herman L. F. *On the Sensations of Tone.* Translated by Alexander J. Ellis, 4th ed. New York: Dover Publications, 1954 (paperback).

Jeans, Sir James. *Science and Music.* London: Cambridge University Press, 1961.

Miller, G. A. *Language and Communication.* New York: McGraw-Hill Book Co., Inc., 1951.

Paget, Sir Richard. *Human Speech.* New York: Harcourt, Brace & Co., 1930.

Taylor, Robert M. *Acoustics for the Singer.* Emporia: Kansas State Teachers College, 1958.

Periodical Monographs

Bartholomew, Wilmer T. "A Physical Definition of Good Voice Quality in the Male Voice," *Journal of the Acoustical Society of America,* Vol. 9 (July 1934), 25-33.

DeLattre, Pierre. "Vowel Color and Voice Quality: An Acoustic Articulatory Comparison," *NATS Bulletin,* October 1958, 4-7.

Flanagan, J. L. "Some Properties of the Glottal Sound Source," *Journal of Speech and Hearing Research*, Vol. 1 (1958), 99-116.

Fry, D. B. and L. Manon. "The Basis for the Acoustical Study of Singing," *Journal of the Acoustic Society of America*, Vol. 29 (1957), 690-92.

Lewis D. and Charles E. Tuthill. "Vocal Resonance." *Journal of Acoustical Society of America*, Vol. 14 (1942), 32-35.

Truby, J. M. "Acoustico-Cineradiographic Analyses Consideration," *Acta-Radiologica*, suppl., Vol. 182 (1959), 1-227.

Van Den Berg, Janwillem. "Transmission of the Vocal Cavities," *Journal of the Acoustical Society of America*, 27, 1 (1955), 161-68.

———, J. T. Zantima, and P. Durenbal. "On the Air Resistance and the Bernoulli Effect of the Human Larynx," *Journal of the Acoustical Society of America*, 29, 5 (May 1957), 626-31.

Vennard, William. "The Bernoulli Effect in Singing." *NATS Bulletin*, February 1961, 8-12.

VOWEL ANALYSIS

Books and Dissertations

Arment, Hollace Elbert. "A Study by Means of Spectrographic Analysis of the Brightness and Darkness Qualities of Vowel Tones in Women's Voices." Unpublished D.M.A. dissertation, School of Music, Indiana University, 1960.

Helmholtz, Herman L. F. *On the Sensations of Tone*. Translated by Alexander J. Ellis. 4th ed. New York: Dover Publications, Inc., 1954.

Ostwald, Peter F. *Soundmaking: The Acoustic Communication of Emotion*. American Lecture Series. Springfield, Ill.: Charles C Thomas, Pub., 1963.

Potter, Ralph L., George A. Kopp, and Harriet Green. *Visible Speech*. New York: D. Van Nostrand Co., Inc., 1947.

Pulgram, Ernst. *Introduction to the Spectography of Speech*. The Hague, Netherlands: Mouton & Co., 1959.

Scott, David. "A Study of the Effect of Changes in Vocal Intensity upon the Harmonic Structure of Selected Singing Tones Produced by Female Singers." Unpublished D.M.A. dissertation, School of Music, Indiana University, 1960.

Tuthill, Curtis E. "Timbre and Sonance Aspects of the Sustained Vowel." Unpublished Master's thesis, State University of Iowa, 1936.

Wendall, Ronald W. "Vowel Formant Frequencies and Vocal Cavity Dimensions." Unpublished Ph.D. dissertation, University of Iowa, 1957.

Periodical Monographs

Black, J. W. "The Effects of the Consonant on the Vowel." *Journal of the Acoustical Society of America*, Vol. 19 (1939), 203-5.

Cooper, F. S. "Spectrum Analysis," *Journal of the Acoustical Society of America*, Vol. 22 (1950), 761-62.

———, Alvin M. Lieberman, and J. M. Borst. "The Interconversion of Audible and Visible Patterns as a Basis for Research in the Perception of Speech." *Proceedings of the National Academy of Sciences,* Vol. 37 (1951), 318-25.

———, et al. "Some Experiments on the Perception of Synthetic Speech Sounds," *Journal of the Acoustical Society of America,* Vol. 24 (1952), 597-606.

Crandel, Irving B. "The Sounds of Speech," *Bell System Technical Journal,* Vol. 4 (October 1925), 586-626.

DeLattre, Pierre. "The Physiological Interpretation of Sound Spectrograms," *Publication of the Modern Language Association,* Vol. 66 (September 1951), 864-75.

———. "Vowel Color and Voice Quality," *NATS Bulletin,* Vol. 15 (October 1958), 4-8.

——— and John Howie. "Of the Effect of Pitch on the Intelligibility of Vowels," ibid., May 1962, 6-8.

———, et al. "An Experimental Study of the Acoustical Determinants of Vowel Color," *Word,* 13, 3 (December 1952), 195-210. Observations on one and two formant vowels synthesized from spectrographic patterns.

Dunn, H. K. "Methods of Measuring Vowel Formant Band Widths," *Journal of the Acoustical Society of America,* 33, 12 (December 1961), 1,737-46.

Hall, Robert A., Jr. *French.* Language Monograph, No. 24. *Language,* suppl., July-September 1948.

House, A., and E. L. Stevens. "Estimation of Formant Band Widths from Measurements of Transient Response of the Vocal Tract," *Journal of Speech and Hearing,* Vol. 1 (1958), 309-15.

Koenig, W., H. K. Dunn, and L. Y. Lacey. "The Sound Spectrograph," *Journal of the Acoustical Society of America,* Vol. 18 (July 1946), 1-89.

Kelley, J. P., and L. B. Higley. "A Contribution to the X-Ray Study of Tongue Position on Certain Vowels," *Archives of Speech,* Vol. 1 (January 1934), 84-95.

Ladefoged, Peter, and D. C. Broadbent. "Information Conveyed by Vowels," *Journal of the Acoustical Society of America,* Vol. 29 (1958), 98-104.

Lewis, D., and Charles E. Tuthill. "Resonant Frequencies and Damping Consonants of Resonators Involved in the Production of Sustained Vowels" ([o] and [a]), *Journal of the Acoustical Society of America,* Vol. 9 (April 1940), 451-56.

Locke, W. N., and R. M. S. Heffner. "Notes on the Length of Vowels," *American Speech,* Vol. 2 (October 1936).

McGinnis, C. S., M. Elnich, and M. Kraichman. "A Study of the Vowel Formants of Well-Known Male Operatic Singers," *Journal of the Acoustical Society of America,* Vol. 23 (July 1951), 440-46.

Moll, K. L. "Cinefluorographic Techniques in Speech Research," *Journal of Speech and Hearing Research,* Vol. 3 (1960), 227-41.

Oncley, Paul. "Higher Formants in the Human Voice," *Journal of the Acoustical Society of America,* Vol. 24 (March 1952), 175.

Parementer, C. E. and S. N. Traveno. "Vowel Positions as Shown by X-Ray," *Quarterly Journal of Speech,* Vol. 18 (June 1932), 351-69.

Peterson, Gordon E. "The Evaluation of Speech Signals," *Journal of Speech and Hearing Research,* 19, 2 (June 1954), 158-68.

———. "Parameters of Vowel Quality," *Journal of Speech and Hearing Research,* 4, 1 (March 1961), 10-29.

———. "The Phonetic Value of Vowels," *Language*, October-December 1951, 541-53.
———. "Vocal Gestures," *Record* (Bell Telephone Laboratories), Vol. 29 (1951), 500-510.
———. "Vowel Formant Measurements," *Journal of Speech and Hearing Research*, 2, 2 (June 1959), 173-84.
——— and Harold L. Barny. "Control Methods Used in a Study of the Vowels," *Journal of the Acoustical Society of America*, Vol. 26 (March 1952), 175-78.
——— and M. S. Coxe. "The Information Bearing Elements of Speech," *Journal of the Acoustical Society of America*, Vol. 24 (1952), 629-37.
——— and ———. "The Vowels [e] and [o] in American Speech," *Quarterly Journal of Speech*, 39, 1 (February 1953), 33-41.
Potter, Ralph K., and Gordon E. Peterson. "The Representation of Vowels and Their Movements," *Journal of the Acoustical Society of America*, Vol. 20 (July 1948), 228-35.
Siegenthaler, B. M. "A Study of the Intelligibility of Sustained Vowels," *Quarterly Journal of Speech*, April 1960, 36-208.
Stevens, Kenneth N., and Arthur S. Hours. "An Acoustical Theory of Vowel Production and Some of Its Implications," *Journal of Speech and Hearing Research*, 4, 4 (December 1961), 303-20.
Stewart, J. Q. "An Electrical Analogue of Vocal Organs," *Nature*, Vol. 110 (September 1922), 311-12.
Taylor, H. C. "The Fundamental Pitch of English Vowels," *Journal of Experimental Psychology*, Vol. 16 (1933), 565-82.
Wolf, S. K., D. Stanley, and W. J. Sette. "Quantitative Studies in the Singing Voice," *Journal of the Acoustical Society of America*, Vol. 6 (April 1935), 255-66.

VOCAL PEDAGOGY

Books

Christy, Van Ambrose. *Expressive Singing*. Dubuque, Iowa: W. C. Brown Co., 1961.
Duey, Phillip A. *Bel Canto in Its Golden Age*. New York: King's Crown Press, 1951.
Fields, V. A. *Training the Singing Voice*. New York: King's Crown Press, 1947.
Judson, L. S., and A. T. Weaver. *Voice Science*. New York: Appleton-Century-Crofts, Inc., 1942.
Luchsinger, Richard, and Godfrey E. Arnold. *Voice-Speech-Language*, trans. Godfrey E. Arnold and Evelyn Robe Finkbeiner. Belmont, Calif.: Wadsworth Publishing Co., Inc., 1965.)
Moses, Paul. *The Voice of Neurosis*. New York: Grune & Stratton, 1954.
Ostwald, Peter. *Soundmaking Acoustic Communication of Emotion*. Springfield, Ill.: Charles C Thomas, 1963.
Proschowsky, Franz. *The Way to Sing*. Boston: C. C. Birchard & Co., 1923.
Reid, Cornelius L. *Bel Canto*. New York: Coleman-Ross, 1950.

Rose, Arnold. *The Singer and the Voice*. London: Faber & Faber, 1962.

Russell, G. Oscar. *The Vowel*. Columbus: Ohio State University Press, 1928.

———. *Speech and Voice*. New York: Macmillan Co., 1931.

Witherspoon, Herbert. *Singing; a Treatise for Teachers and Students*. New York: G. Schirmer, Inc., 1925.

———. *Thirty-Six Lessons in Singing for Teachers and Students*. Chicago: Miessner Institute of Music, 1930.

Periodical Monograph

Van Den Berg, Janwillem, and William Vennard. "Toward an Objective Vocabulary for Voice Pedagogy," *NATS Bulletin*, Feb. 15, 1959, 10-15.

CHAPTER 5

Hearing

Books

Ades, Harlow W. "Central Auditory Receptors," *Neurophysiology*, Vol. 1, of Sec. 1, *Handbook of Physiology*. Washington, D.C.: American Physiology Society, 1959, pp.565-84.

Davis, Hallowell. *Hearing and Deafness*. 4th ed. New York: Rinehart Books, Inc., 1951.

Denes, Peter B., and Elliot N. Pinson. *The Speech Chain*. New York: Bell Telephone Laboratories, 1964.

Fletcher, Harvey. *Speech and Hearing*. 2nd. ed. New York: D. Van Nostrand Co., Inc., 1929.

Neff, William D. (ed.). *Contributions to Sensory Physiology*. Vol. 1. New York: Academic Press, Inc., 1965.

Stevens, S. S., and Hallowell Davis. *Hearing*. New York: John Wiley & Sons, 1938.

——— and ———. *Hearing, Its Psychology and Philosophy*. New York: John Wiley & Sons, 1938.

——— and George Warhofsky. *Sound and Hearing*. New York: Time, Inc., 1965.

Von Békésy, Georg. *Experiments in Hearing*. New York: McGraw-Hill Book Co., Inc., 1960.

Periodical Monographs

Ekstrom, E. Ross. "Control of Singing Intensity as Related to Singer Experience." Unpublished Mus.D. dissertation, School of Music, Indiana University, 1959.

Fairbanks, Grant, Arthur S. House, and Eugene L. Stevens. "An Experimental Study of Vowel Intensities," *Journal of the Acoustical Society of America*, Vol. 20 (July 1950), 457-59.

Fletcher, Harvey. "Loudness, Pitch, and Timbre of Musical Tones and Their Relation to the Intensity, the Frequency, and the Overtone Structure," *Journal of the Acoustical Society of America*, Vol. 6 (October 1934), 59-69.

——— and W. A. Munsen. "Loudness, Its Definition, Measurement, and Calculations," ibid., Vol. 5 (1933), 82.

Hollien, Harry. "Some Laryngeal Correlates of Vocal Pitch," *Journal of Speech and Hearing Research*, 3, 1 (1960), 52-58. X-rays of men and women of different ranges—higher voices have smaller larynxes, tenor larger than alto but same pitch range.

Husson, Raoul. "How the Acoustics of a Hall Affect the Singer and Speaker," *NATS Bulletin*, February 1962, 8-13.

Lasse, LeRoy T. "The Effect of Pitch and Intensity on the Vowel Quality in Speech," *Archives of Speech*, Vol. 2 (July 1937), 41-60.

Stout, Barrett. "The Harmonic Structure of Vowels in Singing in Relation to Pitch and Intensity," *Journal of the Acoustical Society of America*, Vol. 10 (April 1930), 137-48.

Von Békésy, Georg. "Description of Some Mechanical Processes of the Organ of Corti," *Journal of the Acoustical Society of America*, 25, 4 (July 1953), 786-90.

CHAPTER 6

Phonetics

Broussard, J. F. *Elements of French Pronunciation*. New York: Charles Scribners & Sons, 1918.

Gillieron, J. *Table de Atlas Linguistique de la France*. Paris: H. Champion, 1912.

Herman, Lewis and Marguerite. *American Dialects*. New York: Theatre Arts Books, 1947.

Hockett, C. T. A *Manual of Phonology*. Bloomington: Departments of Anthropology and Linguistics, Indiana University, 1955.

———. A *Course in Modern Liguistics*. New York: Macmillan Co., 1958.

Jesperson, Otto. *Lehrbuch der Phonetik*. Leipsig and Berlin: B. G. Teuhner, 1926.

Jones, Daniel. *An Outline of English Phonetics*. 8th ed. New York: E. P. Dutton & Co., 1956.

———. *The Phoneme, Its Nature and Use*. Cambridge, Eng.: W. Heffer & Sons, 1956.

———. *An English Pronouncing Dictionary*. New York: E. P. Dutton & Co., 1926.

Kantner, Claude, and Robert West. *Phonetics*. New York: Harper Bros., 1960.

Kenyon, John Samuel, and Thomas Knott. A *Pronouncing Dictionary of American English*. Springfield, Mass.: G. & C. Merriam Co., 1944.

Kurath, Hans. *The Linguistic Atlas of New England*. Providence, R.I.: Brown University Press, 1939.

———. *Handbook of the Linguistic Geography of New England*. Providence, R.I.: Brown University Press, 1939.

Ladefoged, Peter. *Elements of Acoustic Phonetics*. Chicago: University of Chicago Press, 1962.

Nitze, W. A., Ernest H. Wilkins, and Clarence E. Parmenter. A *Handbook of French Phonetics*. New York: Henry Holt & Co., 1929.

Osgood, Charles E. and Thomas A. Sebeok, ed. *Psycholinguistics*. Bloomington: Indiana University Press, 1965.

Peterson, Gordon E. *Systematic Research in Experimental Phonetics*. No. 4. New York: Bell Telephone Laboratories, 1954.

Pike, Kenneth L. *Phonetics*. Ann Arbor: University of Michigan Press, 1943.

———. *Phonemics*. Ann Arbor: University of Michigan Press, 1947.

Prator, Clifford H., Jr. *Manual of American English Pronunciation*. Rev. ed. New York: Holt, Rinehart & Winston, 1960.

Siebs, Theodore. *Deutsche Buhnenasprache Hochsprache*. Koln, Ger.: Albert Ahn, 1961.

Scripture, E. W. *Researches in Experimental Phonetics*, Washington, D.C.: Carnegie Institute, 1906.

Wangler, Hans Heinrich. *Atlas Deutsche Sprachlaute*. Berlin: Akademie-Verlag, 1961.

Ward, Ida C. *The Phonetics of English*. New York: D. Appleton Century Co., 1929.

Wise, Claude Merton. *Applied Phonetics*. Englewood Cliffs, N.J.: Prentice-Hall, Inc., 1957.

Periodical Monographs

Caffee, Nathaniel M. "The Phonemic Structure of Unstressed Vowels in English," *American Speech*, May 1951, 103-9.

Dunn, H. K., and H. L. Barney, "Artificial Speech in Phonetics and Communications," *Journal of Speech and Hearing Research*, 1, 1 (March 1958), 23-29.

Joos, Martin. Acoustic Phonetics, *Language* suppl., Monograph No. 23, Linguistic Society of America, 24, 2 (April-June 1948).

Lieberman, A. M., Pierre DeLattre, and F. S. Cooper. "The Role of Selected Stimulus Variables in the Perception of the Unvoiced Stopped Consonants," *American Journal of Psychology*, Vol. 65 (1952), 491-516.

Read, Allen Walker. "An Account of the Word 'Semantics,'" *Word*, Vol. 4 (1948), 78-79.

Notes

CHAPTER 2

Respiration

1. E. J. Moran Campbell, *The Respiratory Muscles and the Mechanics of Breathing*. (London: Lloyd Luke, Ltd., 1958), p.xi.

2. Ibid., p.100.

3. Emilio Agostoni, "Action of the Respiratory Muscles," *Respiration*, Vol. I of Sec. III, *Handbook of Physiology* (Washington, D.C.: American Physiological Society, 1964), p.378.

4. Campbell, loc. cit.

5. Edmund J. Myer, *Vocal Reinforcement* (Boston: Boston Music Co., 1913), p.37.

6. J. J. Pressman, "Physiology of the Vocal Cords in Phonation and Respiration," *Archives of Otolaryngology*, Vol. 35 (1942), p.355.

7. Arnold Rose, *The Singer and the Voice* (London: Faber & Faber, 1962), p.92.

8. Campbell, p.100. W. O. Fenn, "Introduction to Mechanics of Breathing," *Respiration*, Sec. III of *Handbook of Physiology* (Washington, D.C.: American Physiology Society, 1964), pp.357-60; B. R. Fink, M. Basek, and V. Epanchin, "Respiratory Movements of the Vocal Folds," *Federation Proceedings Symposium*, Vol. 15 (1965), 63-64.

9. Charles F. Lindsley, "The Psychophysical Determinants of Voice Quality," *Speech Monographs*, Vol. 1 (1934), 79-116; Harriet R. Idol, "A Statistical Study of Respiration in Relation to Speech Characteristics," in *Studies in Experimental Phonetics*, ed. Giles Wilkeson Gray, Louisiana State University Studies, No. 27 (Baton Rouge: Louisiana State University Press, 1936), pp.79-98.

10. Giles Wilkeson Gray and Claude Merton Wise, *The Bases of Speech* (3rd ed.: New York: Harper & Brothers, 1959), p.139.

11. Harlan Bloomer and Hide H. Shohara, "The Study of Respiratory Movements by Roentgen Kymography," *Speech Monographs*, Vol. 8 (1941), 91-101.

12. H. A. Cates and J. V. Basmajian, *Primary Anatomy* (3rd ed.; Baltimore: Williams & Wilkins Co., 1955), p.132.

13. Campbell, p.8.

14. O. L. Wade, "Movements of the Thoracic Cage and Diaphragm in Respiration," *Journal of Physiology,* Vol. 124 (1954), 193-212.

CHAPTER 3

Phonation: The Larynx as a Biological-Biosocial Organ

1. V. E. Negus, *The Mechanism of the Larynx* (St. Louis: C. V. Mosby Co., 1931), p.230.

2. L. S. Judson and A. T. Weaver, *Voice Science* (New York: Appleton-Century-Croft, Inc., 1942), p.xv.

3. Negus, p.5.

4. Johannes Sobotta, *Atlas of Human Anatomy* (3rd ed., Vols. I and II; New York: G. E. Steichert & Co., 1933).

5. G. A. Piersol (ed.), *Human Anatomy* (New York: J. B. Lippincott Co., 1930), pp.1,825-26, as cited in Joel J. Pressman, "Physiology of the Vocal Cords in Phonation and Respiration," *Archives of Otolaryngology,* Vol. 35 (1942), 378.

6. Piersol, loc. cit.

7. R. Husson, "Excitabilité Recurrentielle et Entendues Masculines et Feminines Des Voix Adultes Cultivées, Semi Cultivées et Incultées," *Review of Laryngology, Otolaryngology, and Rhinology,* suppl., Vol. 110 (1954), 260.

8. W. F. Floyd, V. E. Negus, and E. Neil, "Observations on the Mechanisms of Phonation," *Acta-Otolaryngologica,* Vol. 48 (1944), 17-25; L. W. Siegel, "An Investigation of the Possible Correlation Between the Chronaxy of a Branch of the Accessory Nerve and Voice Classification (Master's thesis, School of Music, Indiana University, 1963), p.69.

9. Chevalier Jackson, "Myasthenia Laryngis," *Archives of Otolaryngology* (Chicago), 32 (1940), 434-63; H. A. Schatz, "The Art of Good Tone Production," *Laryngoscope,* Vol. 48 (September 1938), 656.

10. Jackson, p.450.

11. Paul Moore and Hans Von Leden, "Dynamic Variations in the Vibratory Pattern of the Normal Larynx, *Folia Phoniatrica,* 10, 4 (1958), 205-38; William Vennard, *Singing, the Mechanism and the Technic* (Los Angeles: University of Southern California, 1964), pp.39-40: Gunnar Fant, *Acoustic Theory of Speech Production* (The Hague, Netherlands: Mouton & Co., 1961), p.266; Judson and Weaver, p.65.

12. Svend Smith, "Remarks on the Physiology of the Vibration of the Vocal Cords," *Folio Phoniatrica,* Vol. 6 (1954), 166-79.

13. Ibid.

14. Figures on volumes from Judson and Weaver, p.95.

15. Albert Musehold, *Allgemeine Akustik und Mechanik des Menschlichen Stimmorgans* (Berlin: Julius Springer, 1913), p.113.

16. D. Ralph Appelman, "Study by Means of Planigraph Radiograph, and Spectrograph of Physiological Changes During Register Transition in the Vocal Tones (Ph.D. dissertation, School of Music, Indiana University, 1953), pp.108, 113, 118.

17. Giuseppe Bellussi and Allesio Visendaz, "Il Problema Dei Registri Vocali Alla Luce della Tecnica Roentgenstratigrafica," *Archivo Italiano di Otologia Rinologia e Laringologia,* March-April 1949, 130.

18. M. Nadoleczeny, Milliaud and R. Zimmerman, "Categories et Registres de la Voice," *Revue Francaise de Phoniatrie,* January 1937, 21-31; Bellussi and Visendaz, p.130-51.

19. Nadoleczeny and Zimmerman, p.24.

20. Manuel Garcia, *Hints on Singing* (New York: Schuberth & Co., 1894), p.7.

21. Richard Luchsinger and Arnold Godfrey, Voice, Speech, Language 1965 (Belmont, Calif.: Wadsworth Publishing Co., 1965), p.103.

22. Diday and Petrequin, "Memoires sur une Nouvelle Espèce de Voix Chantee," *Gazette Medícal Paris,* 8 (1840), 305.

23. Gordon E. Peterson, "Production and Classification of Sounds," in Claude Merton Wise, *Applied Phonetics* (Englewood Cliffs, N.J.: Prentice Hall, Inc., 1957), p.54.

24. Appelman, p.189.

25. Edmund J. Meyer, *Vocal Reinforcement,* (Boston: Boston Music Co., 1913), p.37.

26. Joel J. Pressman, "Physiology of the Vocal Cords in Phonation and Respiration," *Archives of Otolaryngology,* Vol. 35 (1942), 378; Aatto A. Sonnonin, "The Role of the External Laryngeal Muscles in Length Adjustment of the Vocal Cords in Singing," *Acta-Otolaryngology,* Vol. 48 (1957), 16-25: Arnold Rose, *The Singer and the Voice* (London: Faber & Faber, 1961), p.114; Janwillem Van Den Berg, "Subglottic Pressure and the Vibration of the Vocal Folds," *Folio Phoniatrica,* Vol. 9 (1957), 65-71.

27. Cornelius Reid, *Bel Canto, Principles and Practices,* (New York: Coleman Ross Co., 1950), pp.84-107.

28. Ibid., p.86.

29. Ibid., p.98.

30. Ibid.

CHAPTER 4

Laws That Govern the Vocal Sound

1. Charles A. Culver, *Musical Acoustics* (New York: McGraw-Hill Book Co., Inc., 1956), p.18.

2. Sir James Jeans, *Science and Music* (Cambridge, Eng.: Cambridge University Press, 1961), p.36.

3. *American Standard Acoustic Terminology* (New York: American Standards Association, 1960), def. 3.21 and 13.7.

4. Ibid., def. 12.9.

5. Ibid., def. 13.7.

6. Ibid., def. 1.18.

7. Martin, Joos, *Acoustic Phonetics*, Monograph No. 23, *Language* suppl., 24, 2 (April-June 1948), p.17.

8. Ibid., p.18.

9. Gunnar Fant, *Acoustic Theory of Speech Production* (The Hague, Netherlands: Mouton & Co., 1961).

10. *American Standard Acoustical Terminology*, (New York: Acoustical Society of America, 1942), p.18.

11. Gordon E. Peterson, "Production and Classification of Sounds," *Applied Phonetics*, ed. Claude M. Wise. (New York: Prentice Hall, 1957), p.52.

12. Hallowell Davis, *Hearing and Deafness* (New York: Rinehart Books, Inc., 1951), p.63.

13. Fant, p.265.

14. Kenneth L. Davis, Jr., "A Study of the Function of the Primary Resonating Areas and Their Relation to the Third Formant in the Singing Tone" (Mus.D. dissertation, School of Music, Indiana University, 1964).

15. L. S. Judson and A. T. Weaver, *Voice Science* (New York: Appleton-Century Croft Co., 1942), p.92.

16. Sir Richard Paget, *Human Speech* (New York: Harcourt, Brace & Co., 1930), pp.1-21: G. Oscar Russell, *Speech and Voice* (New York: Macmillan Co., 1931), pp.36-45.

17. Herman Helmholtz, *On the Sensations of Tone* (4th ed.; New York: Dover Publications, 1954), p.117.

18. Paget, loc. cit.

19. D. C. Miller, *The Science of Musical Sounds* (New York: Macmillan Co., 1922), p.232.

20. G. Oscar Russell, *The Vowel* (Columbus: Ohio State University Press, 1928), p.95.

21. H. K. Dunn, "The Calculations of Vowel Resonances and an Electrical Vocal Tract," *Journal of the Acoustical Society of America*, Vol. 22 (1951), 752.

22. Irving B. Crandall, "Dynamic Study of the Vowel Sounds," *Bell System Technical Journal*, Vol. 6 (January 1927), 110-116.

23. Fant, pp.113-14.

24. Dunn, loc. cit.

25. Fant, p.15.

26. Ralph K. Potter, George A. Kopp, and Harriet Green, *Visible Speech* (New York: D. Van Nostrand Co., 1947), p.8.

27. Pierre DeLattre, *The Physiological Interpretation of Sound Spectrograms* (New York: Modern Language Association of America, 1951), pp.864-75.

28. Peterson, p.53.

CHAPTER 5

Sound as Sensation

1. L. S. Judson and A. T. Weaver, *Voice Science* (New York: Appleton-Century Croft Co., 1942) p.321.
2. Hallowell Davis, *Hearing and Deafness* (New York: Rinehart Books, Inc., 1951), p.29.
3. Stanley Smith Stevens and Hallowell Davis, *Hearing* (New York: John Wiley & Sons, Inc., 1963), p.451.
4. *American Standards Acoustic Terminology* (New York: American Standards Association, 1960), def. 13.17.
5. Davis, p.37.
6. Ibid., p.39.
7. Stevens and Davis, p.70.
8. W. R. Miles, "Accuracy of the Voice in Simple Pitch Singing," *Psychological Review Monographs*, 16, 69 (1914), 13-66, as quoted in Stevens and Davis, loc. cit.
9. Stevens and Davis, p.70.
10. Stanley Smith Stevens and Fred Warhofsky, *Sound and Hearing*, a volume in the Life Science Library, p. 78. Reprinted by permission of Time-Life Books, © 1965 by Time, Inc.
11. Ibid.
12. Ibid.
13. Stevens and Davis, p.25.
14. *American Standard Acoustic Terminology*, def. 1.58.
15. Stevens and Davis, loc. cit.
16. Ibid., p.451.
17. Peter B. Denes and Elliot N. Pinson, *The Speech Chain* (New York: The Bell Telephone Laboratories, Inc., 1964), p.33.
18. *American Standard Acoustical Terminology*, def. 12.3.
19. Stevens and Warhofsky, p.81.
20. Georg Von Békésy, *Experiments in Hearing* (New York: McGraw-Hill Book Co., Inc., 1960), pp.238-57.
21. Stevens and Warhofsky, p.82.
22. Harvey Fletcher and W. A. Munson, "Loudness: Its Definition, Measurement, and Calculation," *Journal of the Acoustical Society of America*, Vol. 5 (1933), 82-108; S. S. Stevens, "A Scale for the Measurement of the Psychological Magnitude: Loudness," *Psychological Review*, Vol. 43, (1936), 405-16.
23. S. S. Stevens and F. Warhofsky, p.83.
24. Denes and Pinson, p.83.
25. Ibid., p.68.
26. Stevens and Davis, pp.268-79; Denes and Pinson, p.70.
27. Davis, p.60.
28. Von Békésy, pp.439-531, patterns of vibration and wave motion within the cochlea.

29. Ibid., pp.635-710, electrophysiology of the cochlea.

30. Ibid., pp.535-39, frequency analysis within the cochlea as quoted in Denes and Pinson, p.112.

CHAPTER 6

Phonetics—The Linguistic Element of Interpretation

1. *Webster's New International Dictionary* (2nd ed., unabr.; Springfield, Mass.: G. & C. Merriam Co., Pub., 1960), p.1,884.

2. Claude M. Wise, *Applied Phonetics* (Englewood Cliffs, N.J.: Prentice-Hall, Inc., 1957), p.8.

3. *American College Dictionary* (New York: Random House, 1962); *Cassell's New French Dictionary* (New York: Funk & Wagnalls Co., 1951); *Cassell's New German Dictionary* (New York: Funk & Wagnalls Co., 1939); *Heath's Standard French and English Dictionary* (Boston: D. C. Heath & Co., 1961); Daniel Jones, *An English Pronouncing Dictionary* (New York: E. P. Dutton Co., 1926); John S. Kenyon and Thomas A. Knott, A *Pronouncing Dictionary of American English* (2nd ed.; Springfield, Mass.: G. & C. Merriam Co., 1953).

4. Claude Kantner and Robert West, *Phonetics* (New York: Harper & Bros., 1960), p.10.

5. Ibid., p.106.

6. Hans-Heinrich Wängler, *Atlas Deutscher Sprachlaute* (Berlin: Akadamic Verlag, 1961), p.26.

7. Wise, p.349.

CHAPTER 7

Stress—The Emotional Element of Interpretation

1. Allen Walker Read, "An Account of the Word 'Semantics,' " *Word*, Vol. 4 (1948), 78-79.

2. Claude M. Wise, *Applied Phonetics* (Englewood Cliffs, N.J.: Prentice-Hall, Inc., 1957), p.12.

3. Clifford H. Prator, Jr., *Manual of English Pronunciation* (New York: Holt, Rinehart, & Winston, 1960), p.16.

4. Ibid.

5. Margaret Schlauch, *The Gift of Tongues* (New York: Modern Ages Books, 1942), p.176.

CHAPTER 8

Styles and Dialects—The Social Element of Interpretation

1. *Webster's New Collegiate Dictionary* (5th ed., Springfield, Mass.: G. & C. Merriam Co., Pub., 1960), p.283.

2. Claude Kantner and Robert West. *Phonetics* (New York: Harper & Bros., 1960), p.283.

3. G. W. Gray and C. M. Wise, *The Bases of Speech* (New York: Harper & Bros., 1959), p.262.

4. Kantner and West, p.290.

5. Lewis and Marguerite Herman, *American Dialects* (New York: Theater Arts Books, 1947), p.x.

6. Hans Kurath, A *Word Geography of Eastern United States* (Ann Arbor: University of Michigan Press, 1949), pp.3-8.

7. Kantner and West, loc. cit.

CHAPTER 9

Vowel Migration—The Intellectual Element of Interpretation

1. A. M. Lieberman, et al., "A Motor Theory of Speech Perception," (Haskins Laboratory Report), *Proceedings of Speech Communications Seminar* (Stockholm: The Seminar, 1962), pp.6-7.

2. J. W. Black, "The Effect of the Consonant upon the Vowel," *Journal of the Acoustic Society of America*, Vol. 1 (1938), 203-5; A. S. House and G. Fairbanks, "Influence of Consonantal Environment upon Secondary Acoustical Characteristics of Vowels," *Journal of the Acoustical Society of America*, Vol. 25 (1953), 110; I. J. Hirsh and E. G. Reynolds, "The Recognition of Synthetic and Natural Vowels," *Journal of the Acoustical Society of America*, Vol. 25 (1953), 832; and M. C. Schultz, "A Preliminary Investigation of the Acoustical Characteristics of Interphonemic Transitions" (Ph.D. dissertation, State University of Iowa, 1955), p.109.

3. Daniel Jones, *An Outline of English Phonetics* (8th ed.; New York: E. P. Dutton & Co., Inc., 1956), p.6.

4. Black, loc. cit.

5. Claude Kantner and Robert West, *Phonetics* (New York: (Harper & Bros., 1960), p.60.

6. Lieberman, p.4.

7. See Pierre DeLattre, et al., "An Experimental Study of the Acoustic Determinants of Vowel Color: Observations on One- and Two-Formant Vowels Synthesized from Spectrographic Patterns," (Haskins Laboratory Report), *Word*, Vol. 8 (December 1952), 195-210.

8. Fred W. Householder, Department of Linguistics, Indiana University.

9. Ibid.

10. E. L. Stevens, "The Acoustical Aspect of Speech Production," *Respiration*, Vol. I of Sec. III, *Handbook of Physiology*, (Washington, D.C.: American Physiology Society, 1964), p.353.

11. Arnold Rose, *The Singer and the Voice* (London: Faber & Faber, Inc., 1962), p.214.

Index

(Illustrations are identified by italic numbers.)